Time Out

Copenhagen

Penguin Books

PENGUIN BOOKS

Published by the Penguin Group
Penguin Books Ltd, 27 Wrights Lane, London W8 5TZ, England
Penguin Books USA Inc., 375 Hudson Street, New York, New York 10014, USA
Penguin Books Australia Ltd, Ringwood, Victoria, Australia
Penguin Books Canada Ltd, 10 Alcorn Avenue, Toronto, Ontario, Canada M4V 3B2
Penguin Books (NZ) Ltd, 182-190 Wairau Road, Auckland 10, New Zealand

Penguin Books Ltd, Registered Offices: Harmondsworth, Middlesex, England

First published 2001
10 9 8 7 6 5 4 3 2 1

Copyright © Time Out Group Ltd, 2001
All rights reserved

Colour reprographics by Westside Digital Media, 9 Bridle Lane, London W1
and Precise Litho, 34-35 Great Sutton Street, London EC1
Printed and bound by Cayfosa-Quebecor, Ctra. de Caldes, Km 3 08 130 Sta, Perpètua de Mogoda, Barcelona, Spain

Edited and designed by
Time Out Guides Limited
Universal House
251 Tottenham Court Road
London W1T 7AB
Tel + 44 (0)20 7813 3000
Fax+ 44 (0)20 7813 6001
Email guides@timeout.com
www.timeout.com

Editorial
Editor Jonathan Cox
Consultant Editor Michael Booth
Deputy Editors Richard Lines, Andrew White, Lily Dunn
Listings Editor Camilla Berner
Proofreader Gill Harvey
Indexer Selena Cox

Editorial Director Peter Fiennes
Series Editor Ruth Jarvis
Deputy Series Editor Jonathan Cox
Editorial Assistant Jenny Noden

Design
Art Director John Oakey
Art Editor Mandy Martin
Senior Designer Scott Moore
Designers Benjamin de Lotz, Lucy Grant
Scanning/Imaging Dan Conway
Picture Editor Kerri Miles
Deputy Picture Editor Olivia Duncan-Jones
Picture Admin Kit Burnet
Ad Make-up Glen Impey

Advertising
Group Advertisement Director Lesley Gill
Sales Director Mark Phillips
Advertisement Sales (Copenhagen) Politikens
Lokalaviser Grafisk
Advertising Assistant Catherine Shepherd

Administration
Publisher Tony Elliott
Managing Director Mike Hardwick
Financial Director Kevin Ellis
Marketing Director Christine Cort
General Manager Nichola Coulthard
Production Manager Mark Lamond
Production Controller Samantha Furniss
Accountant Sarah Bostock

This guide was written by Michael Booth, with the exception of:
Architecture Jonathan Cox, Thomas Dalvang-Fleurquin. **Copenhagen Today** Michael Booth (*Denmark & the EU* David Duchin). **Danish Design** David Sandhu, David Duchin (*Great Danes: Arne Jacobsen* Michael Booth). **Accommodation** Thomas Dalvang-Fleurquin. **Sightseeing** Michael Booth (*This is hardcore* David Sandhu). **Restaurants** Michael Booth (*All the best ingredients* David Sandhu, Michael Booth). **Shops & Services** Michael Booth, Ellen Servinis. **Children** Trine Beckett. **Galleries** David Duchin. **Gay & Lesbian** Bernardo 'Ynad' Javier. **Nightlife** Trudy Follwell, Birthe Hansen, Julia Tierney. **Performing Arts** Lea Strömgren, David Duchin. **Sport** Marcus Hoy (*Danish football & The Laudrup dynasty* Peterjon Cresswell, Nikolaj Steen Møller). **Directory** Trine Beckett. **Further Reference** Jonathan Cox, Richard Lines (*20th-century Danish writers* David Duchin).

The Editor would like to thank:
Camilla Berner, Trine Beckett, Sophie Blacksell, Selena Cox, Thomas Dalvang-Fleurquin, David Duchin, Trudy Follwell, Will Fulford-Jones, Lesley McCave, but most of all Michael Booth for a truly superhuman effort.

With thanks to Go, the low cost airline from British Airways, which flies to Copenhagen from London Stansted up to four times a day. To book call 0845 60 54321 or visit the website at go-fly.com

Maps by JS Graphics, 17 Beadles Lane, Old Oxted, Surrey RH8 9JG.
Street map data based on material supplied by Lovell Johns Ltd.

Photography by Paul Avis except: page 6, 17 Art Archive; page 7 National Museum; page 11, 16, 91, 255, 258, 271 AKG; page 20, 93 Hulton Getty; page 37, 40 Danish Design Centre; page 23 All Over Press, Denmark; page 5, 25, 27, 31, 34, 35, 41, 45, 57, 63, 75, 76, 77, 80, 86, 87, 100, 102, 112, 192, 241, 243, 244, 246, 248, 273, 279 Jonathan Cox; page 95 Hans Peterson; page 99 DOWIC; page 203 Planet Foto; page 226 Finn Heidelberg; page 231 Jacob Mydskov; page 239 Empics; page 256 Odense Turist Bureau; page 259, 261, 268, 277 The Danish Tourist Board Copenhagen V, Denmark.
The following photographs were supplied by the featured establishments pages 38, 197, 1.

Contents

Introduction

Every once in a while a poll is published that ranks the world's cities by the quality of life they offer their inhabitants. Copenhagen always does very well, and in the last one it came joint second (way ahead of London, Paris, San Francisco and Barcelona, incidentally). But this kind of accolade can sometimes appear a mixed blessing. With the likes of Zurich and Berne at number one, and Auckland and Helsinki sharing the second spot, it seems that a city's ability to render its inhabitants inert with boredom is the main criterion for a high ranking.

But Copenhagen isn't an Auckland or a Berne. It's far more apt to compare it to its other co-second placers, Sydney and Amsterdam – cities that pulse with imagination and style, and have the verve to go against the grain once in a while. Copenhagen isn't just a great place to lay your hat because everything works, no one's going to rob you and its shops are full of really cool stuff to buy; it also entices visitors in the same way that Sydney and Amsterdam do – all are cities that open their arms to you, cities with a seemingly endless capacity to surprise and amuse.

Here's an everyday story to illustrate the point. A Copenhagen artist recently felt the urge to strip naked, paint herself yellow and walk the length of the city's main shopping street, Strøget, pushing a line-painting machine of the type used to mark out football pitches. This in itself is an uncommon occurrence in most cities. What gives it a particularly Danish resonance was that, before setting off for the centre of town, she contacted the appropriate authorities to ask for permission. And they gave it! In Copenhagen no one allowed themselves to bat an eyelid, and the artist realised her vision to the unquestionable benefit of mankind.

But does the freedom for people to do improbable things in public necessarily mean a city is going to be a fun place to visit? In some cases, no, but in Copenhagen's case, yes it does. Though this is very much a city run on rules and regulations (to a sometimes stifling extent for its inhabitants), schizophrenic Copenhagen is still about as liberal as they come in terms of tolerance towards the unconventional and openness to the new.

The benefits for visitors hungry for fresh experiences are everywhere, from the brave new architecture of the Royal Library extension to the ramshackle corrugation of Christiania. In Copenhagen, you'll be amazed at how many of the people you pass on the street will have the potential to fascinate, stimulate, flummox or charm. Whether you become embroiled in a conversation about existentialism (founded by the archetypal Copenhagener, Søren Kierkegaard) with a goatee in a bar in Pisserenden, or have a heated debate about Peter Schmiechel's decline over a Carlsberg down on Nyhavn, you'll find Copenhageners to be enthusiastic conversationalists (in your language, of course), with a sharp sense of humour.

Why else should you go? Well, this is one of the most design-literate cities in the world, (furniture a speciality), home to countless supermodels and impossibly cool, cutting-edge creatives. It boasts a quartet of the very finest art museums; the variety and quality of its shopping remains undiluted by international chains or too many department stores; it is eminently accessible on foot; and at its medieval heart lies an exceptionally pretty mix of stucco-fronted townhouses, busy canals and grand squares. Thanks to a loathing of skyscrapers and an avoidance of conflict with Germany during two wars, Copenhagen's skyline is still dominated by the 16th and 17th centuries, and the monuments of their megalomaniac kings. Copenhagen is not a city to blow its own trumpet, but that can often give you the satisfying sensation that you are unearthing its secrets for the first time.

And it can do cosy like nowhere else. When the clouds descend like a dense, wet duvet, and the temperature goes Arctic, the siren voice of Copenhagen's candlelit cafés beckons you in a way that the Little Mermaid could only dream of. They even have a special word for this enticing cosiness, 'hygge', which, though frustratingly untranslatable, to the Danes conjures images of roaring fires, red wine, great food and a mellow, warm conviviality.

There is an online version of this guide, as well as weekly events listings for over 30 international cities, at www.timeout.com.

ABOUT TIME OUT GUIDES

The first edition of the *Time Out Copenhagen Guide* is one of an expanding series of *Time Out* City Guides, now numbering over 30, produced by the people behind London and New York's successful listings magazines. Our guides are all written and updated by resident experts who have striven to provide you with all the most up-to-date information you'll need to explore the city or read up on its background, whether you're a local or a first-time visitor.

THE LOWDOWN ON THE LISTINGS

Above all, we've tried to make this book as useful as possible. Addresses, telephone numbers, websites, transport information, opening times, admission prices and credit card details are all included in our listings. And, as far as possible, we've given details of facilities, services and events, all checked and correct as we went to press. However, owners and managers can change their arrangements at any time. Before you go out of your way, we'd advise you to telephone and check opening times, ticket prices and other particulars. While every effort has been made to ensure the accuracy of the information contained in this guide, the publishers cannot accept responsibility for any errors it may contain.

PRICES AND PAYMENT

We have noted where venues such as shops, hotels and restaurants accept the following credit cards: American Express (**AmEx**), Diners Club (**DC**), MasterCard (**MC**) and Visa (**V**). Many businesses will also accept other cards, including Switch or Delta and JCB. Many shops, restaurants and attractions will also accept travellers' cheques issued by a major financial institution (such as American Express).

THE LIE OF THE LAND

The centre of Copenhagen is blessedly small, and easy to traverse by foot. No one takes a bus or train to get from one side to the other (Copenhageners cycle everywhere), and few sights are more than 15 minutes' walk apart. Therefore, public transport details are only included for destinations outside the city centre. We've included postal codes only for organisations or venues to which you might want to write. Map references indicate the page and square on the street maps at the back of the book, and within the Sightseeing chapter.

TELEPHONE NUMBERS

All phone numbers in Copenhagen have eight digits. There are no area codes. The international dialling code for Denmark is 45.

ESSENTIAL INFORMATION

For all the practical information you might need for visiting the city, including visa and customs information, advice on disabled facilities and access, emergency telephone numbers and local transport, turn to the **Directory** chapter at the back of the guide. It starts on page 280.

MAPS

The map section at the back of this book includes useful orientation and overview maps of the country and city (starting on page 306; the street index begins on page 314). Within each Sightseeing chapter there is also a close-up map of the relevant area. On page 242 you'll find a large-scale locality map for planning trips out of town.

LET US KNOW WHAT YOU THINK

We hope you enjoy the *Time Out Copenhagen Guide*, and we'd like to know what you think of it. We welcome tips for places that you consider we should include in future editions and take note of your criticism of our choices. There's a reader's reply card at the back of this book for your feedback – or you can email us on copenhagenguide@timeout.com.

Sponsors & advertisers

We would like to stress that no establishment has been included in this guide because it has advertised in any of our publications and no payment of any kind has influenced any review. The opinions given in this book are those of *Time Out* writers and entirely independent.

In Context

The British under the Duke of Wellington bombard Copenhagen in 1807.

History

Founded by a power-crazed bishop and gilded by a king's untrammelled vanity, Copenhagen has braved fire, plague and war, but many of its finest buildings still stand as a testament to nearly 1,000 years as Scandinavia's pre-eminent city.

Glance at a modern-day map of Denmark and you'll immediately notice that its capital seems to lie carelessly placed well out of the action on the island of Sjælland (Zealand), to the far eastern edge of the country. You can't help but think that either the more central island of Fyn (Funen), or the mainland peninsula of Jylland (Jutland), would have made more sensible locations for the country's economic and political hub. In truth, this natural harbour with its two neighbouring islets on the coast of the Øresund (Sound) was little more than a remote inhospitable salt marsh for the early part of Denmark's bloody, feudal history, which did indeed play out its major scenes elsewhere.

Evidence of human life in Denmark exists from 80,000 years ago in the form of discarded animal bones. But while the rest of Denmark busied itself with reindeer hunting, flint mining, the Bronze Age, the Viking Age, and the repelling of Charlemagne's advances on the southern border of Jylland (c800), Havn (Harbour), as Copenhagen was known, was little more than an insignificant

trading centre for the copious quantities of herring that inhabited the Øresund. It was said that this pungent, oily fish (still a staple of the Danish diet) was so common in these waters, which connect the Baltic with the North Sea, that fishermen could scoop them up into their boats with their bare hands. No wonder they had little interest or involvement in the royal power struggles that divided Denmark from as early as 700, and saw Ribe, on Jylland, emerge as the country's first international trading centre.

The Vikings

The Vikings, who originally swept across northern Europe from southern Sweden around 800, established the first Danish state and rapidly augmented it with three of the four Anglo-Saxon kingdoms, as well as Norway. The Vikings (meaning 'sea robbers') even took Seville in 844 and stormed Paris in the 880s. The subsequent retaking by the nascent Danes of Skåne (or Scania, now southern Sweden, directly opposite Copenhagen) was to be the

catalyst for the voracious expansion of
Copenhagen 300 years hence, but at the time the
villagers probably remained oblivious to their
strategic potential. It is likely, too, that they
remained unruffled by the conversion of the
unifying Viking king **Harald I Bluetooth** (and
eventually the entire country) to Christianity
by a German missionary named Poppo around
965; and played no part in the growing fad for
regicide. Harald was mysteriously killed while
relieving himself in the woods in 987, and many
of his successors over the next 170 years met
with similarly murky fates, culminating in 1157
with **Valdemar I the Great** as the only royal
left standing.

Despite its anonymity in the grand scheme
of Danish prehistory, archaeological finds and
burial mounds have yielded evidence that
Copenhagen has been a site of settlement for
around 6,000 years. Some of those burial mounds
can still be seen in the districts of Bellahøj and
Vigerslev, while later names given to the
settlements that clustered around the harbour
during the early Middle Ages are still used for
some of the city's suburbs. The first written
mention of Havn came in 1043, by which time
it had started to grow as a busy midway point
between Roskilde (the Episcopal seat and a centre
of royal power) and the trading centres on the
south coast of Sweden (now under Danish rule),
where a spectacular autumn trade fair was held
for two months each year, attracting merchants
and fishermen from the surrounding Baltic
countries. Those passing through – Germans,
Norwegians, Dutch and English – may also have
taken advantage of the easy crossing from Havn
to Sweden to make their pilgrimage to the other
major religious centre of the time, in Lund. In all,
the village was already beginning to consolidate
its position as an important hub for the region.

In those days this settlement of wattle and
daub houses lay between the present-day town
hall square (Rådhuspladsen) and the sea. The
remains of its church, Sankt Clemens, can still
be seen in the basement toilets of a bar, Club
Absalon, on Frederiksbergade.

The Middle Ages

The gold mine of Denmark's medieval history,
despite its preponderance to myth and legend,
is the late 12th-century chronicle of Saxo
Grammaticus, *Gesta Danorum* (Deeds of the
Danes), in which, incidentally, the Hamlet
legend arises. Grammaticus refers to Havn as
Mercatorum Portus, meaning 'the Traders' Port'
('København' in Danish), and the prosaic name
stuck. He records how control over Copenhagen
was granted by Valdemar to his blood brother
Bishop Absalon (who commissioned Saxo's
history) around 1160, a pivotal point in the
city's ascendancy. (*See page 8* **Great Danes:
Bishop Absalon**.)

Over the next century numerous churches
blossomed on what was still an unappealing,
boggy piece of coast, among them **Vor Frue
Kirke** (later the site of Copenhagen's current
cathedral; *see page 73*), and **Sankt Petri
Kirke** (also still a site of worship; *see page 73*),
and, in 1238, an abbey of greyfriars was
founded, whose church (**Helligåndskirken**;
see page 71) still sits in the middle of Strøget,
modern-day Copenhagen's main shopping
street. Meanwhile, the town's ramparts were
improved and expanded, enclosing a space
seven times larger than before.

'The town's income from the herring trade at that time was comparable to that of modern-day oil-rich states.'

Aside from its fortuitous location there was a
further impetus behind Copenhagen's tenfold
growth over the next decades. It's no
exaggeration to say that the town's income from
the herring trade at that time was comparable to
that of modern-day oil-rich states. Once
preserved in salt, the fish provided a widely
exported and lucrative commodity, particularly
popular in Catholic countries during Lent, when
the faithful would fast for up to 180 days.

That magnitude of wealth, and the strategic
location of Copenhagen on the most important
approach to the Baltic Sea, was bound to attract
unwanted suitors. First in line were the powerful

Viking helmets at **Nationalmuseet** (*p62*).

Great Danes Bishop Absalon

By all accounts (many of them his own) **Bishop Absalon** was a wily, well-educated administrator, admiral, general and religious leader. He was born around 1128 into the powerful Sjælland family of Hvide and brought up together with the king's son, later to become King Valdemar I the Great. Absalon returned from studying at the Sorbonne in 1157 to be granted the bishopric of Roskilde by his childhood companion. Upon Valdemar's death in 1182, Absalon consolidated his power by taking charge of the king's son, Knud IV, through whom he essentially ruled Denmark.

It was out of these close ties between Church and Crown that Copenhagen was founded. For many years the east coast had been pestered by heathen Wendish pirates, a Slavic race from the southern Baltic coast. But in 1167 Absalon, who had fought beside Valdemar against the Wends, began work on a fort from which to repel them, and then serve as a base for their ultimate annihilation. The fort of Havn was built on a piece of ground, the present-day Slotsholmen, which had been used for drying fishing nets, and some of its ruins are still visible in the cellars of Christiansborg Slot (see page 84), the current Danish parliament building. Over the next few years this boggy wasteland and its simple stone fort would assume great strategic importance in the defence of Sjælland, and as a jumping-off point for Denmark's Baltic empire.

Absalon's defeat of the Wends and capture of their stronghold on the island of Rügen (where he symbolically used a sacred wooden effigy of their god Svantevit for firewood), lit the touch paper for rapid expansion by Denmark into the Baltics, a region whose history would be inextricably linked with Copenhagen's over the coming centuries. Though this ersatz king was probably more concerned with grasping as much power as possible, time would show Absalon to be the founding father of Scandinavia's greatest city. He died in 1201 and was buried in the church of the family monastery of Sorø.

North German trading cities, united under the **Hanseatic League**. A Hanseatic fleet, based in Lübeck, sailed on Copenhagen in 1249 and was repelled before attacking again, this time with stonemasons who were better equipped to flatten Absalon's fort. The Lübeckers, riled by Copenhagen's increasing dominance of the Baltic region, attempted to block the town's access to the sea by scuttling ships in the main channel, but as with many conflicts to come, the Copenhageners simply picked themselves up and rebuilt to fight another day.

In the late 12th and early 13th centuries King Valdemar and his sons **Knud (Canute) VI** and **Valdemar II the Victorious** reigned over a triumphant and expansionist Denmark, which not only conquered the Baltic Wends, but devoured Estonia and Holstein, and lorded it over Lübeck. This ended ignominiously with loss of control of these Baltic territories in 1227. Another bout of regicide saw off **Erik IV Ploughpenny** in 1250, by the hand of his brother **Abel**; **Christoffer I**, meanwhile, fell foul of the classic poisoned chalice ruse in 1259; while the murder of **Erik V Klipping** when hunting in 1286 is unexplained to this day. Near bankruptcy threatened the country under the spendthrift **Erik VI Menved**'s rule (1286-1319). The lowest point came between 1332 and 1340 when Denmark found itself rulerless and at times near to anarchy, controlled in turn by the old enemies of Holstein and Sweden.

Prior to this black period, Copenhagen's first charter had been written in 1254. In it, the wily Bishop Jakob Erlandsen gave the town's merchants special privileges in order to win their support against the king. Copenhagen's first land survey was produced 80 years later and clearly shows the genesis of the present-day city centre with Gammeltorv as its hub and Vestergade and Nørregade radiating from it. By now the population had spiralled to 5,000, making it probably the most populous Nordic town of the time, but, tellingly, 20 per cent of landowners appear to have been of German origin, with the leading guild of the time being the Tyske Kompagni (the German Company). It seems the perpetual, and often uncourted, influence of its dominant southern neighbour had already begun to make its mark on Copenhagen. The seeds had been sown for a hate-hate relationship that many Danes studiously maintain with Germany to this day.

The Kalmar Union

Calm was restored to Denmark when **Margrethe I**, daughter of yet another Valdemar, came to power in 1375 (ruling under the snappy title of 'Sovereign Lady and Master,

the Protector of the Kingdom of Denmark').
An efficacious networker, she married the
Norwegian king and added sovereignty of
Sweden to her list of honours before formalising
a Nordic alliance, the **Kalmar Union** in 1397,
and then ensuring her adopted grandnephew
Erik VII of Pomerania, inherited the lot. By
the start of the 15th century the Kalmar Union
encompassed Norway, Sweden, Finland, Iceland
and the immensity of Greenland, and was the
largest kingdom in Europe. Erik was crowned
at Kalmar in 1397, aged 14.

The second spurt of Copenhagen's growth
came when Erik VII finally and conclusively
seized control of the town from the Church in
1417. Not only was the king now in control, but
he was so fond of Copenhagen that he made it
his permanent home, ending the perambulatory
tradition of Denmark's monarchy that up until
then had functioned on the basis that wherever
they laid their crown was their home. Perhaps
here, with the advent of this first royal
endorsement, we can see the burgeoning of
the town's self-importance as a Paris of the
north, whose inhabitants typically consider
themselves separate from, and above, the rest
of the country to this day. Ask a Copenhagener
his opinion of someone from Jylland, for
example, and the response will usually be a
put-down. (Jyllanders, meanwhile, tend to
express the typical bemused disdain of the
country dweller for city folk.)

In 1438, the disaffected Swedes withdrew
from the Kalmar Union, prompting the Danish
nobility to depose the king. Bizarrely, Erik VII
lived out the rest of his life with his mistress
as a (by all accounts successful) pirate on the
Baltic island of Gotland. In 1448, a distant
relative, **Christian I**, the first of the Oldenburg
dynasty, was crowned king of Denmark,
Sweden and Norway in the first royal coronation
to be held in Copenhagen. Inevitably the city
now became the economic, political and cultural
focus for the nation.

København Slot (Copenhagen Castle; on the
site of the present-day Christiansborg Slot)
expanded, while noblemen's houses
mushroomed around it in as close proximity
as possible to the king. The remnants of one
of these houses can still be seen in the
vaulted cellar of Kong Han's Restaurant at
6 Vingårdsstræde, while the University Senate
building (or Konsistorium) behind Frue
Plads is all that remains of Denmark's first
university, founded in 1479 by the king.
If you want to see something of the town's
medieval fortifications, the only remnant is
Jarmers Tårn, which sits ignominiously on
a roundabout at the junction of HC Andersens
Boulevard and Nørre Voldgade.

By 1500, between 10,000 and 12,000 people
lived within Copenhagen's ramparts. All who
caught a glimpse of the town, either from sea or
land, would have been left in no doubt of its pre-
eminence and wealth, symbolised by the vast
palace and spectacular landmarks, like the
vertiginous, four-pronged (as it was then) copper
spire of Vor Frue Kirke. The town revelled in
unprecedented riches as its guilds dominated
those of the Hanseatic League (whose influence
was slowly waning), while the king, too, grew
wealthy from the new tolls demanded of all who
sailed from the North Sea through the narrow
strait between Helsingør and southern Sweden
on their way to the Baltic. There was no doubt
that this was now Denmark's capital, and its
leading citizens ruled the land via the Rigsråd
(National Assembly), made up of clergy,
prominent estate owners and the king.

'If the hat on my head knew what I was thinking, I would pull it off and throw it away.' (Christian II)

A more apt seat of power the Machiavellian
Christian II could not have hoped to inherit.
Though politically astute enough to marry a
sister of Holy Roman Emperor Charles V,
Christian had a tendency to recklessness that
saw him keep his Dutch mistress, Dyveke, close
at hand in a house around the corner from the
palace. She died suddenly in 1517, and, believing
her to have been poisoned by the governor of
Copenhagen Castle, Christian vented his grief on
his courtiers with an indiscriminate purge. This
merely enhanced his reputation as a schemer
not to be crossed. He was later reported to have
said, 'If the hat on my head knew what I was
thinking, I would pull it off and throw it away.'

In 1520 he murdered 100 leading members
of the Swedish nobility (he detested the
aristocracy) during a reconciliation celebration,
later known as the 'Stockholm Bloodbath',
and earned himself the nickname in Sweden
of Christian the Tyrant. That did little for
Christian's reputation abroad or at home, where
his stringent taxation added to his unpopularity,
eventually forcing him to flee Denmark for
poverty in Holland. He was replaced, in 1522, by
his uncle, who reigned as **Frederik I**. On his
uppers, Christian took up an offer from allies
in Norway to assume their country's crown
but as he attempted to lay siege to Oslo he was
captured by the Danish fleet. Meanwhile, ever-
awkward Copenhagen remained loyal to the old
king, prompting Frederik to lay siege to the
town for a month, with eventual success.

The Danish Reformation

Meanwhile, the birth of the 16th century was a tense, troubled time throughout Europe as the Catholic Church's increasingly poor public relations began to turn large sections of the continent against it. Out of this discontent in 1517, in the German town of Wittemburg, had emerged the Lutheran Church. Martin Luther's church door antics were to have an almost immediate domino effect on Denmark.

In 1526 a council of nobles elected to split the Danish Church from the Holy See in Rome. This sent out anti-Catholic signals to the populace, some of whom took it upon themselves to express their disillusionment with the Catholic Church by ransacking its buildings.

During Frederik's rule, several popular uprisings – with Copenhagen as a particular hotbed – had unsuccessfully tried to unseat the monarch and replace him with the exiled, pro-Lutheran Christian II. But when Christian finally returned as a prisoner to a Denmark now ruled entirely by Frederik I in 1532, it was to spend the rest of his life imprisoned in Sønderborg Castle. Christian may have had the last, hollow laugh, however, as he outlived his next two successors.

Upon Frederik's death in 1533 the Catholic prelates intervened to postpone the accession of his son **Christian III**, whose Lutheran tendencies they were having none of. Unforeseen by the prelates, the Danish people were as sick of the arrogance of the Catholic Church as much of Europe was by that time, but they wanted Christian II back. His supporters in Copenhagen, both peasants and more prosperous townspeople, continued their belligerent stance by seizing control of the town. The mercantile character of Copenhagen and its people had determined that they'd rather take their chances by joining the Hanseatic League, and the mayor of Lübeck, always happy to help stir up trouble in Copenhagen, weighed in on Christian II's side with an army of German mercenaries under commander Count Christopher of Oldenburg.

The involvement of the Lübeckers was to provoke one of the most damaging tiffs in Copenhagen's history: the '**Grevens Fejde**' (Counts' Feud) of 1534-6, Denmark's last civil war. The Germans' meddling and its accompanying peasant revolt so concerned the bishops that they finally relented and allowed Christian III to take the throne and suppress Copenhagen. He was crowned in Vor Frue Kirke in 1534. His coronation charter did, however, include the handing over of ultimate power to the aristocracy of the Rigsråd from the Crown.

Christian III finally recaptured Copenhagen in July 1536, having heaped yet more suffering, starvation and slaughter upon the city with another lengthy siege during which the population were said to have been reduced to eating rats to survive. By this stage, the return of his capital, and a surprisingly lenient reconciliation with the traders who had led the revolt, was the icing on the cake of an empire that engulfed much of southern Sweden, Norway, the Faroes, Iceland and Greenland, as well as the troublesome Holstein and Schleswig regions on the southern border with Germany.

(Holstein and Schleswig, slightly less relevant to a history of distant Copenhagen than they are to Denmark as a whole, were a constant source of tension between Denmark, Germany and the inhabitants of the two regions – all of whom were pulling in different directions towards different sovereignties. Lord Palmerston once famously commented that there had only ever been three men who fully understand the Holstein and Schleswig issue: 'The first was Prince Albert, who is now dead. The second is a German professor, who has since gone mad. The third is myself, and I have forgotten the details.')

As things turned out, the bishops were to lose power anyway as, in order to pay his own German mercenaries (without whom he would never have retaken Copenhagen), Christian III was forced to liquidate many of the Church's assets. As the final stroke of a brilliant coup that heralded the **Danish Reformation** of 1536, Christian III imprisoned the bishops. In a display of the consensual diplomacy that still typifies Denmark's political machinations, Christian III offered the bishops the 'get-out' of conversion to Lutheranism, with the added sweetener that under the new doctrine they could now marry and have children. Nearly all accepted, with two consequences: most of Denmark's priests remained with their flock; and those flocks increased substantially. (In fact, in several churches from that era you can find epitaphs to their wives who died young, often during childbirth, attesting to the priests' new-found reproductive zeal.) Lutheranism was now the official religion of Denmark, whose capital celebrated with extravagant festivities. The nobility benefited hugely from the transfer of money from the Church, not to mention exemption from taxes. Across Denmark, and especially in Copenhagen, this wealth was made manifest in grand Renaissance mansions. In fact, most of Danish society basked in unprecedented economic prosperity.

This growth of the capital and the resultant expansion of the population to over 20,000 was often tempered by an increase in the frequency of epidemics that raged through the town. To improve sanitation, in 1581 a conduit was built from Emdrup sø, a few kilometres to the north, to feed fresh water to a new well on Gammeltorv. Further development of the town in the latter part of the century was overseen by a thrusting governor, **Christoffer Valkendorf**, who revitalised the harbour and adorned numerous churches with towers, many paid for out of his own pocket. The well on Gammeltorv, now the site of the Caritas Fountain, was named after him.

Christian IV

Into this brave new world of wealth, expansion and optimism was born one of the great figures of Danish history. To this day, he is a man with whom Danes enjoy a paradoxical relationship that blends scorn with admiration, gratitude and sympathy. Copenhagen was to be his grandest epitaph, and into its modern-day skyline is still written his vision, bravura and conceit. Denmark's 'Sun King', **Christian IV**, was a man possessed of heroic appetites, who never let the tedious demands of reality get in the way of a heroic scheme. He ruled for 60 years, and is probably Denmark's best-remembered monarch.

Christian IV: the 'architect-king'.

> **'Christian IV was a man possessed of heroic appetites, who never let the tedious demands of reality get in the way of a heroic scheme.'**

It is hard to know where to begin in detailing the transformation that Copenhagen underwent during Christian IV's reign. You could perhaps equate it to London under Elizabeth I, or the arrival of the Mafia in Vegas. The city grew in all directions (literally, thanks to reclaimed land) in the grandest of styles, with new buildings; a remodelling of its coastal access; improved defences and housing; the construction of entire new districts, bridges, churches, palaces, towers, observatories and theatres; and all the glittering hallmarks of the Renaissance. Upon his death, however, Copenhagen and all of Denmark would be a spent force, bankrupt, defeated, humiliated and seemingly doomed to an existence of debt and suppression by its enemies. But many enjoyed the ride.

If the celebrations of the earlier part of the century had been worthy of note, the thousands of guests from all over Europe who revelled in the banquets, jousting, pageants, concerts and fireworks that marked Christian IV's coronation in 1596, ensured their eclipse. The feasting lasted for days – 25,000 drinking vessels were specially made for the celebration, which had been on hold

since the death of Christian III in 1588, because his son was at that time still only 11.

Christian IV was a complex, highly educated man with widespread interests in music, architecture and foreign affairs. He married Anna Catherine of Brandenburg; after she died in 1612 he went on to father 24 children, half of them out of wedlock by a variety of mistresses. In 1617 Christian married one of them, Kirsten Munk, morganatically (she was considered to be far below him socially so had no right to his possessions or title). Much to the king's fury she gave birth to a child that clearly wasn't his (he'd been away at war while the child had been conceived) and was banished in 1630. Christian, in his misery, turned to her chambermaid for comfort. (This episode in Christian's life is enjoyably romanticised in Rose Tremain's 2000 Whitbread Prize-nominated novel *Music And Silence*.)

The problem was that the many ambitious construction projects undertaken during his rule, not to mention Christian's long simmering rivalry with his close contemporary King Gustavus Adolphus of Sweden during the Thirty Years War (1618-48), were a constant burden on the country's finances. When Christian came to the throne Copenhagen had little industry to speak of, and most of his subjects made their livings through agriculture. But though he tried his best to establish industry in the capital, its wheeler-dealer trading heritage always somehow seemed to undermine a fruitful work ethic. Copenhagen's products could never match the quality of those

Dannebrog

The Danes' love of myth is put to good use in explaining the origin of the **Dannebrog**, Denmark's national flag. The red banner with a white cross is said to have fallen from the sky on 15 June 1219, as a holy inspiration to the Danish troops, led by King Valdemar II the Victorious against the pagan Estonians at Lyndanise, with an accompanying celestial voice to explain its importance. But the flag is more likely to have been given to the nation by the Pope to mark the crusade. It was first used on the seal of the Kalmar Union in 1397, but appeared long before that in the coat of arms of the Estonian city of Talinn.

Ask any Dane and he or she will tell you that the Dannebrog, a white cross on a red background, is the oldest national flag in the world, and most will be well versed in its protocol: flags must be taken down at dusk and raised only during daylight (although a pennant version can be left up by the lazy overnight); a Dannebrog must never be allowed to touch the ground, and so on. These days the Dannebrog is the standard rectangle of most national flags, but the royal family, the State and the navy are permitted to fly a swallow-tailed version.

Few nations respect and use their flag as much as Denmark, and Dannebrogs are hauled up to mark everything from coronations to the cat's birthday. If a Dane has a garden (or even a window box), a flagpole will feature prominently in it. During buffets no piece of cheese or cake will remain unadorned by a small paper version for too long.

made by the best European craftsmen, which was a source of constant frustration and embarrassment to the king.

Christian's first priority was to cement Copenhagen's position as the major harbour of the region, and, with this in mind, the channel between Sjælland and the small nearby island of Slotsholmen was straightened, narrowed and reinforced with wharfs. Slotsholmen was extended and, as the century closed, a new armoury (Tøjhuset) and supply depot (Proviardhuset) were constructed to maintain the fighting readiness of the navy. These buildings still stand, and several of the huge iron mooring rings where the King's fleet were tethered can also still be seen on the walls of the old Royal Library's garden (*see page 86*).

Holland, not Germany, was now the dominant cultural influence on Denmark, and Dutch styles and town planning practices were often in Christian's mind when fermenting the grand schemes for his capital. The town hall was rebuilt magnificently in the Dutch style (sadly, this building is long gone), and an elaborate fountain dedicated to the goddess Caritas (meaning Charity) was erected in the centre of Gammeltorv where Valkendorf's well once stood. The fountain and its statuary were rebuilt in the 1890s, but it still stands in the square and is one of Copenhagen's most charming sights.

In 1617, following the Kalmar War in which Denmark had failed to curb Sweden's expansionism, it was decided that Slotsholmen's military buildings were vulnerable to attack and work began on a new district, **Christianshavn**, built to the west of Amager as a defence system and to provide desperately needed housing. Christianshavn was modelled as a kind of mini Amsterdam, and is still perfectly preserved with a grid of streets, a central square and a canal. To fuel the growth of his pet project, the King granted Christianshavn independent trading centre status and gave away land in the new quarter, with tax breaks for those who built promptly. A remnant of this boom can be seen at No.30 Strandgade, where a large merchant's mansion with sandstone façade stands today. If you want to see how the other half lived, check out No.14 Sankt Annægade, more typical of a hoi poilloi's dwelling of the period.

Further symbols of Christian's reign are found in the much expanded palaces, prime among them the richly decorated **Rosenborg Slot** (Rosenborg Castle; home today to the crown jewels; *see page 100*). But the most extraordinary of his creations is the **Rundtårn** (Round Tower; *see page 69*), an ambitious observatory graced by a radical, stepless spiral ramp, completed in 1642. Amazingly, this Renaissance beacon is another of the period's architectural treasures that has survived to enrich the Copenhagen skyline.

Another entirely new district, **Nyboder** (Navy Booths; next to Kastellet, on the north side of the centre) grew up to house Christian's naval personnel. The sailors were billeted in very low, single-storey, ochre-painted terraced cottages.

Copenhagen-based international trading companies attempted to establish colonies in Africa and Asia, but they were as fleas on the shoulders of comparable Dutch and British enterprises. Instead, to try and raise money, Christian attempted to turn Copenhagen into the financial capital of Europe by ordering the construction of **Børsen** (the Stock Exchange; *see page 82*), but despite the building's unquestionable architectural and decorative splendour (this wedding cake of a building can hold its own against any of the more startling modernist works of the city today, the highlight being a fabulous spire of three intertwined dragon tails), that, too, was a damp squib. Increasingly desperate for cash, a fateful attempt to establish a silver mining venture in Norway followed, and failed.

In 1523, Sweden had split from Queen Margrethe I's Kalmar Union, and during Christian's reign the growing strength and confidence of Denmark's northerly neighbour was to threaten the very existence of the Danish State. At stake was control of access to the Baltic, which usually meant control of the region itself. In 1611, in a bid to protect his vital income from the Sound tolls (extorted at Helsingør castle, the model for Shakespeare's Elsinore, north of Copenhagen), and to restore the Kalmar Union, Christian declared war on Sweden. The **Kalmar War** raged, with Denmark generally dominant until 1613, when a peace accord brokered by the British concluded with a large ransom being paid by the Swedes to Denmark.

Danish triumphalism was short lived, however, as Christian and his forces soon became embroiled in the **Thirty Years War** (1618-48), in an effort to protect Danish interests on the north coast of Germany from Swedish expansion. The Danes' involvement in the war ended with a devastating defeat by the Swedes at the battle of **Lutter-am-Barenburg** in 1626. The Danes got off more lightly than they deserved in the final peace settlement at Lübeck in 1629, in which Christian had to promise to take no further part in the war.

Christian's reign was to be marked by a third fateful conflict, **Torstensson's War** (1643-5), named after the Swedish general Lennart Torstensson who marched on Jylland after Christian had raised the Sound tolls to try to recover the costs of past military failures. It was during this war, while in the thick of the action on his flagship *Trefoldigheden* during the **Battle of Kolberger Heide** in July 1644, that the 67-year-old Christian lost his right eye and received 23 shrapnel wounds. A much heftier defeat by united Dutch and Swedish forces in October ended the war, and a peace treaty, signed in 1645, saw Denmark cede large areas of territory (chiefly central parts of Norway, Halland and the islands of Gotland and Osel) to Sweden, and waive future Sound tolls. This was a dramatic and humiliating moment in Danish history, for which you sometimes suspect the Danes have yet to fully forgive their northern neighbours. Thirty years followed in which Denmark barely survived as an independent state.

Christian didn't live to see his nation's darkest moment, however. He'd already been dead ten years when his successor **Frederik III**, Prince Bishop of Bremen (who'd taken the throne after his elder brother drank himself to death, doubtless at the prospect of having to inherit such a shambles), started another Swedish-Danish war in 1658. The Swedish king Karl X Gustav and his army crossed the ice from Jylland to Fyn but then found the ice breaking up as they got to Sjælland. Nevertheless, the Swedes still forced the Danes to accept the humiliating **Treaty of Roskilde** by which Denmark ceded Scania (the southern tip of Sweden). Not content, Karl Gustav decided he wanted to take the whole of Denmark and besieged Copenhagen in the winter of 1658-9. He led his German troops (camouflaged in white hooded cloaks) across the frozen sea surrounding Slotsholmen, but, in a last gasp of defiance, Frederik himself is said to have led the fight against Karl Gustav's army. As the enemy propped their ladders against the castle walls, all able-bodied citizens of Copenhagen assembled above them to rain down anything that wasn't nailed to the ground. This spirited defence with cannon shot, bullets, pistols, logs and boiling tar and water to melt the ice, gave time for a Dutch army to arrive and save the capital (not to mention Holland's interests in a free-access Baltic).

> ## 'Europe would never again allow Denmark, now a third of its former size, to hold power in the region.'

The sudden death of Karl Gustav at the start of 1660 ended Sweden's ambitions to conquer Denmark, but the price of Denmark's salvation was steep, and Frederik was forced to capitulate control of the Sound (and its tolls), as well as all of Denmark's provinces to the east (though the island of Bornholm pluckily fought back to Danish rule). Two attempts to win back southern Sweden in 1675 and 1709 resulted in no permanent gains for the Danes, despite several victories in battle. Europe would never again allow Denmark, now a third of its former size, to hold power in the region.

Absolute monarchy

The support given by the people of Copenhagen to the king left him with little choice but to concede more trading and tax advantages to the town. But, unhappy with the growing power of Copenhagen's nobility, in an impressive and bloodless coup against the still powerful nobility, Frederik made himself 'king by God's grace'; in other words, the absolute monarch. The ceremony to create Denmark's first absolute monarchy took place on 8 October 1660, in the square in front of København Slot (Copenhagen Palace; on the site of today's Christiansborg Slot). The new regime was formalised in the 1665 Kongeloven (The Royal Act). Though this document conferred total power over all of Denmark upon the king, making him and his male heirs the highest authority on earth and above all laws, no one was allowed to see it for 50 years and no copies were made. (This most absolute of Acts was to cause problems later on when, firstly, Frederik's successor **Christian V** had to crown himself in 1670 because no one else was thought to have appropriate authority, and then, more seriously, when **Christian VII** turned out to be mad as a balloon, and no one was in a position to judge him unfit to rule.)

'In an impressive and bloodless coup... Frederik made himself "king by God's grace"; in other words, the absolute monarch.'

Once again Copenhagen picked itself up to rebuild and refortify, with the construction of a new rampart to protect Slotsholmen. Out of this came the new quarter of **Frederiksholm**, which sprang up on reclaimed land between the Frederiksholm Canal and modern-day Vester Volgade. The western defences were further strengthened by shallow man-made lakes around which were built low-rise, half-timbered houses (which could be easily demolished if the town were attacked), while new roads, Store Kongensgade, Borgergade and Adelgade, were built. The impressive Kongens Nytorv square was laid out in 1670 and was soon surrounded with imposing baroque houses and abutted by Nyhavn canal – today one of the city's major tourist draws. An improved water supply, a company of watchmen and new street lighting complimented a fast growing, modern capital whose population had doubled within 100 years to 60,000 by the early 18th century. Many would have gained employment in the forerunner of the civil service, established by Frederik to run the foreign service, the military and commercial affairs. To pay for all of this, the king sold off countless properties and estates, including much of the booty gained from the ransacking of the Church during the Reformation.

The next few decades saw a limited return to prosperity and a restrengthening of the navy, which was all the encouragement several

successive, though largely ineffective, Danish kings needed to try to recapture their lost empire. Frederik III's son Christian V was the first to attempt to avenge defeat by their neighbours in the **Skåne Conquest** (which took place in the south of Sweden from 1675-9). He gained little from the war other than the restoration of national pride, as the rest of Europe preferred that no one country dominate access to the Baltic. In fact, the next few decades were essentially one long wound-licking exercise on the part of the Danes, with the Swedes constantly under attack, until things were finally patched up with the marriage of one of the Danish princesses to the Swedish king Gustav III.

A final, conclusive peace treaty with Sweden, signed in 1720, at last gave everyone breathing space to concentrate on domestic affairs, while the following pan-European boom increased demand for agricultural produce, which Denmark was happy to meet. As a now determinedly neutral state, it was even happier to exploit the wars that raged elsewhere by profiting from the largely indiscriminate sale of supplies to all sides. Meanwhile, when he wasn't Swede-bashing, Christian V (who reigned until 1699) had busied himself in his administrative centre at Christiansborg Slot, refining the laws of the land in the **Danske Lov** (Danish Law) of 1683.

Fire & renewal

In 1711, during the reign of Christian's successor, **Frederik IV**, Copenhagen was ravaged by a plague in which 23,000 people died. It was also razed to the ground by fire twice during the century (in 1728 and 1795). The first fire broke out in a candle-maker's in Nørreport, and strong winds, negligible water supplies and general chaos ensured it travelled swiftly across town, destroying 1,700 houses, the town hall and the university, and leaving 12,000 people homeless. The situation was made worse by the fact that the firemen happened to be drunk that night (they had spent the money they'd earned for fire drills on booze) and that a local brewer, in a rush to help, left a lamp burning in his stable, igniting another, separate blaze. Similar slapstickery helped the 1795 fire along when firemen couldn't find the keys to the pump house beside Sankt Nicokaj Kirke, and its burning spire collapsed into the surrounding neighbourhood.

Happily, the building of the new five- and six-storey town houses, taller than any before them, and the grand public buildings that replaced the combustible wooden, low-rise constructions of the 17th century, were strictly monitored by the building codes of the time, with the result that the capital was reborn more splendid than before. The castle, too, was completely demolished (even though Frederik IV had rebuilt it at great expense a few years earlier) and vast amounts of money were spent replacing it with the baroque **Christiansborg Slot** (*see page 84*), only for the second fire to return it to the ground.

To celebrate the 300th anniversary of the House of Oldenburg, headed since 1746 by **Frederik V**, work began in 1749 on a grand new quarter, **Frederiksstaden** (*see page 88*). It was designed by the architect Nicolai Eigtved (*see page 91* **Great Danes: Niels 'Nicolai' Eigtved**) with wide, straight streets fronted by elegant, light rococo palaces. At the heart of the new area was Amalienborg Plads, circled by four palaces, financed by the leading noblemen of the town. The most spectacular of these was the palace of Moltke; its neo-classical dining room these days often plays host to state banquets. To the north of the quarter **Frederiks Hospital** was built; it is now home to Kunstindustrimuseet (the Museum of Decorative Arts; *see page 92*). The same year saw the founding of what is still one of Denmark's leading newspapers, *Berlingske Tidende*.

When another fire at Christiansborg levelled a large part of the palace, the royal family found themselves homeless. They commandeered the four Amalienborg palaces, employing the CF Harsdorff to connect them with an elegant colonnade, and have lived there ever since.

The second, larger fire of the century broke out on Gammelholm in 1795 and was as destructive as the first, but again this only gave the city's architects and builders the chance to keep up with the fashion for the neo-classical. For the very highest echelon of Danish society in the Age of Prosperity nothing less than columns would do, and if you go to No.14 Ved Stranden or the headquarters of Handelsbanksen on Kongens Nytorv (built as the private home for leading ship owner Erikh Erikhsen) you can see for yourself the excesses of the age. The fire also destroyed buildings in the centre of town, making Nytorv and Gammeltorv into one large square.

Perhaps the ultimate expression of Copenhagen's new-found grandeur was the unveiling of a huge statue by the French artist Jacques Saly of Frederik V astride a horse, which has stood since that day in the centre of Amalienborg Plads. The extraordinary cost of this gilded monument, erected in 1770, was borne by the Asiatic Company, from monies earned from the spice trade. More colonial wealth came from the West Indian Company, who ran the three Danish West Indian islands: St Thomas, St John and St Croix, producing sugar and rum, as well as from small colonies in Africa

Janteloven

If you ever find yourself wanting to open a can of worms in the company of Danes ask them about Janteloven, the Law of Jante. Jantelov is a uniquely Danish phenomenon created by the misanthropic writer, Aksel Sandemose. His 1933 novel *En flygtning krydser sit spor* (*A Fugitive Crosses His Tracks*) is set in a fictional Danish town called Jante. Based on his experiences of small-town Danish life, Sandemose depicted Jante as a suffocatingly law-ridden town for oppressively small-minded people (and the writer eventually upped and left for Sweden).

Jantelov essentially distils Denmark's collectivist, conformist, homogenous nature and blends it with Sandemose's unique outlook. Its basic tenets include: 'Thou shalt not presume that thou art any wiser than us' (No.3); and 'Thou shalt not presume that thou art going to amount to anything' (No.8). Generally 'getting above oneself' is frowned upon; instead, modesty and understatement is the accepted norm.

Though it is a fictional creation, many Danes still genuinely believe Jantelov to be a Medieval creed. You should never underestimate the influence of Janteloven – it pervades all of Danish society, much to the irritation of the current queen who has spoken out against its self-defeating influence. It is why, for example, everyone drives egalitarian Peugeots as opposed to exclusive Mercedes (the preserve of taxi drivers). If a Dane does buy a Mercedes, he should be prepared to put up with friends asking 'How much is the fare to the airport?', by way of a joke. As hard as it might be for foreigners to understand, Danes genuinely find it embarrassing if one of their friends exhibits their greater wealth in such a way.

In other words, Danes are masters of the tall poppy syndrome, though they prefer to describe it using an old Danish proverb: 'The higher up a monkey climbs, the more you see of its bottom.' (Though exceptions are made for the Danish football team, Victor Borge, and other popular heroes.)

Though Jantelov is more closely adhered to in the provinces, do not be fooled by thrusting, cosmopolitan Copenhageners who claim it has no place in their modern lives. Scratch the surface of the city, and Jantelov isn't far beneath.

The cunning count and the crazy king

King Christian VII's madness gave the opportunity for one of the most fascinating figures of Danish history to emerge and, for a brief time, seize power. **Johan Friedrich von Struensee**, a German, was appointed the king's physician in 1768 and so enamoured was the king by his new doctor that Struensee was granted notable powers of state. The rights to the king's wife weren't officially sanctioned, but the doctor took those too, and promptly began an affair with Christian's 18-year-old queen, Caroline Matilda, the sister of King George III of England.

Struensee proceeded to dismiss the prime minister, and for 16 months essentially ruled Denmark, issuing 2,000 decrees, many of which were designed to give the aristocracy as hard a time as possible. These days the doctor would be seen as a social pioneer and awarded a Nobel Prize for his work in restricting exploitation of the poor and overhauling the prisons. He caused a sensation in Europe by banning censorship in 1770, and his hatred of the upper classes and his redistribution of the king's treasury would have seen him lauded in Paris 20 years later. However, the law-abiding Danes were not yet ready for such upheaval, and Struensee's German background, coupled with false rumours that he was ill-treating the king, made him unpopular with the people, prompting a coup in January 1772.

Led by the queen mother, the coup took place at a palace ball, while the doctor was being arrested at the theatre in Christiansborg Slot. The king was forced into signing a statement against Struensee, which given his past malleability can't have been difficult. But with no evidence that the king's hand had been forced by Struensee, or indeed proof of

any wrongdoing at all, the queen mother had a problem justifying her actions in constitutional terms. Instead, Struensee had his right hand cut off and was then beheaded and his quartered remains publicly displayed for the crime of dallying with the queen, despite having tried to cover himself by ruling that adultery was no longer illegal. Caroline Matilda, meanwhile, was bundled off to live on one of her brother's estates, where she died aged 24. Her daughter by Struensee remained in Copenhagen because, although no blood relation to Christian, she was considered to be the king's heir.

Thereafter, the new, fervently nationalistic rulers passed a law that precluded foreigners from holding a government post.

and the North Atlantic. Copenhagen was the base for both companies, and as such conducted a busy trade in slaves from the Gold Coast.

Huge warehouses to contain sugar, tea and porcelain grew up in Christianshavn, and such trading goods would later serve the needs of the American War of Independence, among other conflicts. Boom time had returned to the city. Vast profits gave the impetus for Denmark's first banking system and saw everyone from the stone masons to the portrait painters revelling in full employment. Coffee shop society, newspapers and cultural and scientific associations flourished.

Less successful was Eigtved's massive domed church, to be called **Frederikskirken**, and planned as the centre piece of Frederikstaden. Frederik V had envisioned the Vatican in Rome when he approved the new quarter's plan, with this church as Copenhagen's St Peter's. Huge quantities of marble were shipped from Norway and some of Europe's finest masons and bricklayers began to erect the walls. Sadly, funds ran out during the reign of Christian VII and the project stood stillborn at a height of ten metres (33 feet) until the industrialist CF Tietgen funded its completion in 1894. Today the church is better known as **Marmorkirken** (the Marble

Church; *see page 88*), despite the substitution
of Danish limestone for the rest of the walls.
It might have been interpreted as an ominous
omen of Copenhagen's immediate future, had
the populace not been too busy making hay
while the sun, of what became known as 'the
Palmy Days', was shining.

In 1771 Kongens Have (the King's Gardens)
opened. This new attraction was a huge success
with the flourishing bourgeoisie, whose
voracious appetite for the pursuit of nature was
a symptom of the new Age of Enlightenment.
One of those less likely to fully participate in
the educational revolution was the new king
Christian VII (1766-1808) who managed to
rule for 42 years despite frequent and prolonged
bouts of insanity.

In 1784 the 16-year-old crown prince Frederik
(later **Frederik VI**) took power and acted as
regent until his father's death in 1808. By 1801,
he probably wished he hadn't.

The English bombardment of 1807.

Napoleonic Wars

During the 18th century Denmark's neutrality
had proved increasingly irksome to the English,
who had frequently made her merchant fleet
(which was an enthusiastic supplier to the
enemies of the English, as it was to anyone
with gold enough to pay for their services) the
target of the Royal Navy. To protect itself from
increased interference by the English, Denmark
had entered into an armed neutrality pact with
Russia and the old foe Sweden, but this only
irritated the English more, and, in April 1801, a
fleet under Admirals Nelson and Parker sailed
into the Sound and commenced bombardment
of the Danish navy. The Danes only survived
thanks to a change in the direction of the wind
which left some of the English fleet at risk of
being driven ashore. Nelson was instructed by
his commanders to withdraw, but, though he
had been impressed by the Danes' courage, he
merely put his telescope up to his blind eye,
and ignored them. Instead, he sent an envoy to
threaten Frederik with the destruction of his
entire fleet, including the burning alive of its
crews, unless he surrendered and withdrew
from the pact. This Frederik did, but not before
the clash had cost the Danes a thousand men.
However, Denmark continued to profit from the
trade that had so angered the British, and Anti-
British fervour swept Copenhagen. That anger
would be fuelled six years later when the
British, under the Duke of Wellington, returned
with a show of force that made the 1801 battle
seem a mere firework display.

Napoleon was on the move across Europe,
and, with his fleet already destroyed by Nelson
at Trafalgar, there were strong rumours in 1807

that the French were about to commandeer the
Danish navy as a replacement. In fact, Frederik
was preparing to defend his country from attack
by the French in the south when he was visited
by an English envoy who offered him this
ultimatum: surrender the Danish fleet to
Britain, or the British would come and take it
for themselves. The Danes refused and, despite
heavy criticism from the British parliament,
the British navy sailed again on still neutral
Copenhagen and bombarded it for three days.
30,000 British soldiers landed north of the city,
the university quarter was set alight and more
than 300 houses were destroyed. The spire of
Vor Frue Kirke toppled symbolically to the
ground. The naval yard was demolished, much
of the city centre was set on fire, another 1,000
people were killed and, in the end, the British
sailed off with 170 ships, despite the efforts of
plucky gunboats which the Danish navy would
row out to becalmed British warships and attack
with muskets. The only ship left standing in
Copenhagen harbour was a yacht previously
given by the King of England to Frederik, his
nephew. Copenhagen was the first European
city ever to suffer such a bombardment.

Understandably, the Danes now baulked at
an alliance with the British, siding instead with
Napoleon. This was a decision they were to rue
in the painful years hence when Denmark and
Norway were blockaded by the British. Much
of Norway starved while Denmark fared little
better, enduring great hardship until the death of
Napoleon. This saw Sweden (now in alliance with
Britain) take control of Norway, which had been
as much a part of Denmark for 450 years as

Sjælland. The loss of the consistently problematic duchies of Schleswig and Holstein to Germany in 1864, following a brief attack by Otto von Bismarck, would further diminish a Danish Empire that had once dominated the Baltic.

A period of introspection, from which many might say Denmark has never really emerged, followed, typified by the slogan: 'We will gain internally what was lost externally'. In fact, despite a nationwide drive to grow new oak trees with which to rebuild the navy (many of which still flourish in the countryside), Denmark would not officially go to war again until its troops took part in a UN peacekeeping exercise in Bosnia in April 1994.

The Golden Age

Fortunately, this was to be a period of cultural growth for a country struggling to come to terms with a new identity based on little more than a shared language. With all hope of playing a role on the international stage gone, and with little financial power to wield either (Denmark as a state was declared bankrupt in 1813 and sold its colonies in Africa and India), the country instead began to extend itself in the arts and sciences. The storyteller Hans Christian Andersen (born in Odense, but a Copenhagen dweller for most of his life; *see page 255* **Great Danes: Hans Christian Andersen**), leading light of the existentialism movement Søren Kierkegaard (the archetypal Copenhagener; *see page 112* **Great Danes: Søren Kierkegaard**) and the theologian Nikolai Frederik Severin Grundtvig (*see page 124* **Great Danes: NFS Grundtvig**) each contributed to the emergence of a defined Danish identity during the 19th century. More than the king, the aristocracy or the church, these world-renowned figures were to save Denmark from being subsumed by its neighbours.

> **'This flexing of its artistic and intellectual muscles was symptomatic of an age of broader social change in Denmark.'**

This was also to be a golden age for Danish art. Many painters learned their craft elsewhere in Europe before returning to Denmark to depict the unique ethereal light and colours of the Danish landscape. Among the most notable were Christen Købke, his mentor and founder of the Danish School of Art Christoffer Wilhelm Eckersberg, JT Lundbye and Wilhelm Marstrand. Denmark's greatest sculptor, the neo-classicist Bertel Thorvaldsen (*see page 81* **Great Danes: Bertel Thorvaldsen**), also returned to a hero's welcome after 40 years in Rome, while August Bournonville revitalised the Danish ballet at Det Kongelige Teater (the Royal Theatre; *see page 77*). Denmark also looked to its past to restore its sense of national pride, with the romantic poet Adam Oehlenschläger's mythologising of the country's history in his epic poems, and the historical novels of BS Ingemann. As a counterbalance, the Dagmar Theatre (1883) and Det Ny Teater (1908) became known for their adventurous, modern programming.

This flexing of its artistic and intellectual muscles was symptomatic of an age of broader social change in Denmark, which has culminated today in the social equality that so typifies the nation. The major impetus for this came from the Education Act of 1814 which introduced compulsory schooling and eradicated illiteracy. This in turn gave a new generation the confidence and wherewithal to expand its horizons; in Denmark's case with the widespread forming of co-operative societies. The seeds had been sown for a Danish social system defined by its ruthless equality in which modern-day Danes will proudly tell you that, 'Few have too much and even fewer have too little.'

Unlike the aftermath of past wars, Copenhagen rebuilt only modestly following the British attack. The town hall was eventually reconstructed on the eastern side of Nytorv, while Christiansborg and Vor Frue Kirke were also repaired (Thorvaldsen's sculptures gracing the latter's interior). The 'corn boom' of the 1830s further revitalised growth and the industrial revolution consolidated the city's revival, with a prosperous shipyard, Burmeister & Wain, starting up on Christianshavn in 1843. Tivoli gardens opened in the same year, using part of the old city moat as its lake, but the less well off would have preferred Bakken's beergarden in Dyrehaven. Frederiksberg also became an entertainment mecca with its numerous skittle alleys, variety halls and dance venues. To help keep the revellers well oiled the Carlsberg brewery expanded, moving to the suburb of Valby. Carlsberg's owner, Carl Jacobsen, would later use his profits to create a marvellous art collection which he opened to the public at what is now the **Ny Carlsberg Glyptotek** in 1897 (and whose Etruscan exhibits and collection of paintings by Paul Gauguin are one of the highlights of Copenhagen's art treasures today; *see page 64*). Visitors would doubtless have used Denmark's first railway line to travel to the capital's many new attractions; it was built from Copenhagen to Roskilde by English navvies, and opened in 1847.

Democracy & growth

With such potent augurs of the coming modern age, Frederik VII knew that the days of absolute power were waning, and when in March 1848 a demonstration culminated with a loud (but relatively peaceful) protest outside his palace, the king capitulated immediately saying: 'I am happy to be able to tell you that I have already complied with what you are demanding.' Denmark's first written constitution followed in 1849, without a drop of blood being spilt, establishing two elected chambers, **Folketinget** and **Landstinget** (the latter abolished in the 1950s), as well as an independent judiciary. In fact, the peaceful nature of this instant progression from dictatorship to democracy set the tone for all future political life in Denmark, with one exception: on 21 October 1885 a printer named Julius Rasmussen attempted to shoot the prime minister. The bullet was deflected by the PM's coat button and he survived unscathed.

Copenhagen's political and artistic life may have been moving with the times during the mid 1800s, but the standard of living for most of its 130,000 inhabitants, crowded tightly in cellars and ever higher tenements, had not. In 1853 a cholera outbreak killed 5,000 people, finally prompting the new City Council (founded in 1840) to do something about the water supply and hospital provision.

Housing remained a dire problem, despite the progressive new terraces in Østerbro, and, in 1852, the ban on construction outside the city's defences was lifted. In the latter part of the century a huge building boom saw swathes of land filled with inhospitable blocks of small so-called 'corridor' flats (one-room properties arranged like the rooms of a hotel along one long corridor). Blågårdsgade, Nørrebro and Vesterbro became notorious for the prevalence of such slum housing. Similar squalor festered behind the majestic façades of Kongens Nytorv. Yet as soon as new housing popped up, the population expanded to fill it. By 1900, more than 400,000 people had moved to Copenhagen to escape the grinding poverty of rural areas. (To give some idea of the capital's disproportionate growth, the next largest towns in Denmark had around 20,000 inhabitants.) Immigration from Norway, Germany and Sweden swelled the numbers further, as Copenhagen's growing banking industry, chemical plants and light industries attracted a huge work force, and its new toll-free harbour, Frihavn, opened to the south of the city to counter competition from Hamburg.

More happily, the council granted permission for the creation of a new open space, Ørsteds Parken, where the city's levelled ramparts once stood, together with the building of the Botanisk Have (Botanical Gardens), Statens Museum For Kunst (the National Gallery) and a new observatory. In 1888, Denmark held its version of London's Great Exhibition on Rådhuspladsen. The agricultural, industrial and art displays attracted over 1.3 million people from Denmark and the surrounding countries. Strøget, the city's main shopping street, flourished with the arrival of the major department stores Illum and Magasin du Nord and their radical new window displays, as well as the new gas lighting. Electricity came to the capital in 1892 (electric trams followed in 1897), as did flushing toilets and a vastly improved sewerage system that made full use of the Øresund. The prostitutes who operated in the slums behind Kongens Nytorv were forced to move to Vesterbro when the area was redeveloped, but they may have found some consolation in the founding of the Rudolph Berg Hospital, which specialised in sexually transmitted diseases.

By the 1900s attention turned again to the city's defences, which had been rendered obsolete by the new generation of long-range guns. Coastal forts were built along the Øresund and, in 1910, Middelgrunden and Flakfortet were constructed on artificial islands off the coast to the east. To repel inland invaders a 15-kilometre (9-mile) series of lakes and canals were dug to be flooded in an emergency. Some are now used for water sports.

In 1913 Copenhagen gained its international emblem, HC Andersen's **Den Lille Havfrue** (the Little Mermaid), a diminutive statue planted on some rocks in Langelinie, south of Frihavn. Ever since, visitors to the statue have been united in their sense of anticlimax (occasionally someone vents their disappointment by cutting her head off).

Denmark had undergone a complete political transformation during the 19th century, with the emergence of trade unions and a socialist labour movement, which later became the Social Democratic Party. Despite a slight hiccup, when all of its leaders were induced by bribes to emigrate to the US, the party had its first members elected to the Folketing in 1884. The 1899 September Agreement laid down the rules for all future trade disputes, and by the beginning of the 20th century the four main parties that would dominate Danish politics had emerged. None would ever hold an absolute majority, so it is hardly surprising that compromise remains the defining characteristic of Danish political and social debate.

This unity through consensus undoubtedly helped the nation survive the tribulations of the coming century, as, once again, Denmark's existence as an independent state was gravely threatened.

Two World Wars

Despite its neutrality, Denmark was very much in Germany's pocket during World War I. It still, however, made provision for an outright attack by Germany, calling up 60,000 men to form a defence force, most of whom were stationed on the fortifications of Copenhagen. Fortunately they weren't needed, and Denmark survived the Great War intact. Though the majority suffered rationing and shortages, the higher echelons of Copenhagen society did rather well out of the war, selling goods to both sides of the conflict. These opportunists were nicknamed the 'Goulash barons' on account of the cans of meat they sold to the German and British armies, and their much flaunted wealth was to be a focus for social discontent over the next few years.

Taking their cue from the Russian Revolution, Denmark's Communist Party sought to highlight the growing chasm between Copenhagen's rich and the rest of the country. In typical Danish style, their protest only degenerated into violence on one occasion (with a riot at the Vegetable Market), but **Christian X** was rattled enough to dismiss his government in 1920 amid allegations of a coup d'état by the press. The subsequent 'Easter Crisis' saw Denmark veer towards a national

Great Danes Thorvald Stauning

Thorvald Stauning was the great figure of Danish politics in the early part of the 20th century, transforming his party from near-revolutionaries to true social democrats representative of a broad demographic. In 1924 this hard drinking, hard working, womanising cigar sorter became prime minister, with the continued unity of Denmark his greatest aim. A champion of inclusive politics and a tactical magician, Stauning appointed the first woman government minister (Nina Bang, who became minister for education in 1924) and helped revive the shaky Danish economy with the famous Kanslergade Agreement (named after the street on which the PM lived) between his government and the Liberals. The

Kanslergade Agreement was a response to an economic crisis that saw unemployment rise to 40 per cent and large-scale labour disputes. It allowed for the devaluing of the krone against the English pound, which in turn resuscitated Denmark's agricultural industry. Perhaps equally important, it was a significant retort to the growing right wing movement. The agreement was signed on 30 January 1933, the same day that Hitler became chancellor of Germany. Danes are fond of making a comparison between the nationalist policies of their socialist leader and those of the Germans' own (supposedly) socialist leader, and the radically different methods with which both were implemented.

Jewish exodus

There was one section of the Danish population for whom the supposed co-operative nature of the German occupation meant little: Denmark's Jews. For the first few years of the war they escaped persecution, but with the end of the official co-operation policy in 1943, and the subsequent power struggle between the German plenipotentiary in Denmark, Werner Best, and the German commander-in-chief, General von Hanneken, their fate was sealed. To curry favour with Berlin, Best sent a telegram asking what was to be done with Denmark's Jews, though he claims to have regretted this and tried to stop the telegram. The news was leaked to the Danish resistance who in turn told the leaders of the Jewish community. Denmark's Jews (most of them Copenhagen residents) immediately went into hiding; around 200 were arrested on 1 October (mainly the elderly who didn't want to leave their homes) by a special unit brought in from Norway.

Under the cover of darkness, and in all manner of makeshift craft, nearly 7,000 Jews, the vast majority of the population, were then spirited away across the Øresund to Sweden and safety by their fellow Danes.

Probably the two best-known Danes of Jewish extraction had already left Denmark, however. Borge Rosenbaum left in 1940 to forge a career in comedy as **Victor Borge**, famously returning in secret a few months later to visit his dying mother. 'Mama, I'm going to Hollywood to get into the movies, and when I do, I'll send for you, and we'll live in California in a big house with a swimming pool,' he said. 'Borge, don't let it go to your head,' she replied; while atomic physicist Niels Bohr (see page 74 **Great Danes: Niels Bohr**), who left one month before the mass evacuation, would later play a significant role in the ending of the war through his work on the development of the atomic bomb.

strike, only for that reliable Danish spirit of compromise and discussion – led by Social Democrat leader Thorvald Stauning (*see page 20* **Great Danes: Thorvald Stauning**) – to save the day.

Between the wars Copenhagen's infrastructure continued to expand with a new railway, the S-tog, linking the suburbs with the city centre, and the building of Kastrup (now Copenhagen) airport on Amager in 1925.

> **'Denmark's Aryan genes ensured it was… spared much of the brutality and suppression endured by neighbouring occupied states.'**

When World War II broke out on 1 September 1939, Denmark braced itself to hold tight and sit out the conflict in peaceable neutrality, just as it had 25 years earlier. It was soon disavowed of that notion, when on 9 April 1940 Hitler's troops landed at Kastellet, fired a few shots on Amalienborg Slot (killing 16 Danes) and issued an ultimatum: allow Germany to take control of Denmark's defences or watch Copenhagen be bombed from the sky. After an hour-and-a-half of deliberation the

Danish government and king agreed and entered into a unique deal whereby the country remained a sovereign state but Germany gained access to Norway, the Atlantic and Sweden. Denmark's Aryan genes ensured it was welcomed into the bosom of the Third Reich and, as a rich agricultural provider, it was spared much of the brutality and suppression endured by neighbouring occupied states.

Most Danes took a while to recover from the shock of this supposedly friendly occupation by 200,000 soldiers, and its resistance movement was slow in forming. It wasn't really galvanised into action until the banning of the Danish Communist Party in 1941. Indeed, many in the government, including foreign minister Erik Scavenius, openly opposed resistance, endorsing instead full co-operation with the Germans.

During these dark days of occupation Christian X became an important point of stability for the Danish people, for whom his daily horseback ride through the streets of Copenhagen was a comforting symbol of continuity. In 1940, the people received another royal morale boost with the birth of Princess Margrethe, named after the last Danish queen to have taken on the Germans and won. (Through a revision of the law of accession Margrethe became the current, much loved queen in 1972; *see page 93* **Great Danes: Queen Margrethe II**.)

Luckily, some Danes chose to ignore Scavenius's recommendations, most notably those who helped 7,000 Jews to escape certain death (*see page 21* **Jewish exodus**), and, by 1943, when the Germans began a brutal suppression of young Danish dissenters, hostility towards the occupiers had been well fueled. The 'August Uprising' of that year saw industrial action and sabotage increase to the extent that Hitler personally demanded that the Danish government declare a state of emergency and punish saboteurs by death. They refused and resigned, prompting the Germans to begin disarming the Danish army. Before they could commandeer the navy, it sank itself. The official policy of collaboration had ended, and from June 1944 the state secretly financed the resistance movement.

By the end of the war the Danish Resistance numbered around 60,000. They were never called upon to fight, however, and documents unearthed after the war revealed that the German army had expected them to be far more troublesome than they were. But, perhaps as a result, compared to most of Europe's capitals Copenhagen survived the war with little damage. Liberation was anxiously awaited, but would it be the Russians or the British who arrived first? In the end it was Field Marshall Montgomery who accepted the surrender of occupying forces on 4 May 1945, a close shave for Denmark. It was marked by huge celebrations as across the country black-out curtains were torn down and replaced by candles, a symbol to this day of Danish freedom. The Royal Dragoons reached Copenhagen on 8 May where they were, again, greeted by vast, jubilant crowds.

Post-war Denmark

In 1945 Denmark was recognised as an allied power, and as such was a founding member of the United Nations. But already a new world power, once again too close for Denmark's comfort, was making expansionist rumblings. With the advent of the Cold War and the Soviet Union (only 35 kilometres/22 miles away) breathing down its neck, Denmark realised that its neutrality policy was no longer viable and, together with Norway, it became a founding member of NATO.

Post-war Denmark, governed by an endless series of coalitions dominated by the Social Democrats, faced several other immediate domestic problems which the founding of its welfare state would address. Culminating in the Social Security Act of 1976, the provision by the government of a safety blanket for the sick, the unemployed and the elderly has been one of Denmark's most widely admired achievements.

Critics, however, will point out that it was initially largely funded by foreign loans, and has seen modern Denmark burdened by a vast public sector work force and the crippling income tax levied to pay for it.

Post-war Copenhagen, meanwhile, still had some surprises in store. In 1968, its students, like the rest of the Western world's, grew restless, but, this being Copenhagen, their protest was hardly cataclysmic. Aside from storming the office of Copenhagen University's vice-chancellor and smoking all his cigars, the students caused little trouble. Nevertheless, the University was sufficiently chastened to abolish professorial powers.

'Eventually the government gave in and allowed Christiania to continue as a "social experiment".'

Copenhagen's youth unrest lasted well into the 1970s and its ultimate trophy still draws tourists from around the world. In 1971 a group of squatters occupied Bådsmandsstræde Barracks, 41 hectares (17 acres) of former military accommodation, on the eastern side of Christianshavn. In protest against what they saw as oppressive social norms (and others saw as an attempt to side-step the law and avoid taxes), the squatters announced the founding of the Free State of Christiania (*see page 105*). The police moved in, but underestimated the commune, whose numbers had been swollen by many like-minded hippies from across the country. Eventually the government gave in and allowed Christiania to continue as a 'social experiment' and its thousand or so inhabitants quickly began creating their own schools, housing, businesses and recycling programmes. The commune has probably become best known for its tolerance of drugs. Though still technically illegal in Denmark, the sale and consumption of soft drugs on its main drag, Pusher Street, is tolerated by the police, though hard drugs are supposedly outlawed.

With its capital more densely crowded than ever, Denmark sought to decentralise industry and intensify urban planning. A somewhat idealised 'Finger Plan' in which the city's expansion would incorporate open spaces was drawn up in 1947, but was soon discarded to make way for more suburbs. Copenhagen's first tower blocks were built in 1950 at Bellahøj, but a public outcry curbed the extent to which they could be used to solve the perennial housing shortage. Instead, an urban renewal programme saw Adelgade and Borgergade, among other

The Danish football team celebrate their 1992 European Championships victory.

areas, refurbished. Much of Nørrebro and Vesterbro were also developed during the 1960s, and the latter would benefit from a second renewal programme at the end of the century.

The use of cars increased exponentially in Copenhagen during this time, and as a result Strøget, for centuries the city's main shopping street, was pedestrianised in 1962. Though initially wary, its shop owners soon enjoyed booming trade, enhanced by the de-restriction of pornography which enlivened one or two window displays. In 1967, the street played host to a great party when the city celebrated its 700th anniversary; a table laden with food and drink stretched along the full length of Strøget.

Though Copenhagen's pre-eminence as a port came to an end with the advent of the superships (too big for the Øresund, they were made instead for Gothenburg and Hamburg), in the 1970s the city nevertheless enjoyed full employment. That, in turn, led to a shortage of workers and efforts were made to attract foreigners from southern Europe, Turkey and Pakistan, who tended to settle in Nørrebro and Vesterbro. Like London's docks, Copenhagen's water side was to be redeveloped with expensive housing, exclusive restaurants and new businesses.

In June 1992 Europe would twice more turn its attention to Denmark, which emerged from the margins of the European Union to stick a spanner in the works of the progression towards federality, and from the margins of European football to defeat an old foe.

Never a wholehearted member of the EU, 51 per cent of Danish voters went a step further in June '92, rejecting the pivotal Maastricht Treaty and causing a mighty kerfuffle in the process. There were protests, some violent, on the streets of Copenhagen. In the end the Danes finally ratified the Treaty, but only after they had been promised exemptions from common defence and currency commitments.

Meanwhile, the Danish national football team, brought in to replace the war-torn Yugoslavians in the European Championships, promptly won the trophy, beating Germany in the final. The team returned to an unprecedented heroes' welcome in Copenhagen, its players destined to be fêted in perpetuity. Even its term as Cultural Capital of Europe in 1996, and the 25th anniversary of Queen Margrethe's reign in 1997, were eclipsed by the football celebrations.

▶ For more on the **Vikings**, see page 262.
▶ For more on the **Hamlet** legend, see page 265.
▶ For more on **Christian IV**'s architectural projects, see page 31.
▶ For more on **Danish artists**, see page 202.
▶ For more on the **liberalisation of pornography**, see page 114.
▶ For more on Danish attitudes to the **EU**, see page 27.

Key events

c800 Vikings establish first Danish state.
c965 The Viking state converts to Christianity.
1043 First written mention of 'Havn'; the village develops as a regional commercial hub.
1157-82 Reign of Valdemar I the Great and unification of country after civil war.
1160 Control over Copenhagen given by King Valdemar I the Great to Bishop Absalon.
1238 Founding of Helligåndskirken and abbey of greyfriars on modern-day Strøget.
1249 Attack of Lübeck on Copenhagen.
1254 Copenhagen's first charter written.
c1334 First land survey of Copenhagen; population around 5,000, making it the largest town in Scandinavia.
1375 Margrethe I comes to power.
1397 Establishment of the Kalmar Union, uniting Denmark, Sweden, Norway, Finland, Iceland and Greenland.
1417 Erik VII seizes control of Copenhagen from the Church.
1438 Swedes withdraw from the Kalmar Union and Danish nobility depose Erik.
1520 Christian II has 100 leading Swedish nobles murdered in the 'Stockholm Bloodbath'.
1526 Council of Danish nobles elects to split the Danish Church from Rome.
1534-6 'Grevens Fejde' (Counts' Feud), between supporters of Christians II and III.
1536 Christian III takes Copenhagen, imprisons the bishops and completes the Danish Reformation.
1611-13 Kalmar War with Sweden; ends with Swedes paying a large ransom to the Danes.
1618 Denmark enters the Thirty Years War.
1626 Defeat of Danes by Swedes at Lutter-am-Barenburg ends their involvement in the war, formalised in the 1629 Treaty of Lübeck.
1643-5 Torstensson's War ends with Danish defeat and territorial losses to the Swedes.
1648 End of the Thirty Years War; death of Christian IV.
1658 Danish-Swedish War ends with defeat for Danes and humiliating Treaty of Roskilde, whereby Scania is ceded to the Swedes.
1659 Swedish king Karl X Gustav crosses the ice to attack Copenhagen; citizens hold off the Swedes until a relieving Dutch army arrives.
1660 Frederik III establishes absolute monarchy.
1675-9, 1699-1700, 1709-20 Unsuccessful wars against the Swedes.
1683 Christian V refines the law, Danske Lov.
1711 Plague in Copenhagen kills 23,000.

1728 Major fire in the capital.
1795 Another great fire in Copenhagen.
1801 Bombardment of the city by the British.
1807 Second British bombardment and requisition of the Danish fleet.
1814 Education Act introduces compulsory schooling and combats illiteracy.
1848 Frederik VII convenes a national assembly which abolishes absolute monarchy.
1848-51 Revolt of duchies of Schleswig and Holstein ends with return to the status quo.
1849 A new democratic constitution is enacted and a parliament and independent judiciary established; rights of free speech, assembly and religion are guaranteed.
1852 Ban on building outside Copenhagen's defences lifted, sparking a construction boom.
1853 Cholera kills 5,000 in Copenhagen.
1864 Prussians declare war on Denmark and take Schleswig.
1888 Copenhagen hosts a major world trade fair and exhibition.
1892 Electricity introduced in Copenhagen.
1899 September Agreement lays down the rules for all future trade disputes.
1914-18 Denmark remains neutral and unscathed during World War I.
1920 'Easter Crisis' following Christian X's dismissal of his government veers towards a general strike until Stauning's compromise restores the country's equilibrium.
1940 Denmark allows the Germans into the country, while remaining a sovereign state.
1943 'August Uprising' leads to the end of official policy of collaboration.
1945 The British liberate Denmark.
1949 Denmark joins NATO.
1971 Occupation of former barracks by squatters leads to founding of Christiania.
1973 Denmark joins European Community.
1976 Social Security Act provides a safety net for the sick, elderly and unemployed.
1992 Danes reject the Maastricht Treaty by a narrow margin; Denmark beats Germany in the final of the European Championships.
1993 Denmark, excepted from the common defence and single currency provisions, accepts the Maastricht Treaty.
1996 Copenhagen is European City of Culture.
1998 Danes ratify Amsterdam Treaty, moving the country closer to European integration.
2000 Øresund Fixed Link from Copenhagen to Malmö opens; Danes vote against the adoption of the euro.

Copenhagen Today

Evelyn Waugh called the Danes 'the most exhilarating people in Europe'. He wasn't wrong.

Something extraordinary is happening to Copenhagen right now. This ancient and beautiful harbour town, home of the oldest monarchy in the world and previously best known for its pastries and fairy tales, is transforming itself into the most modern, vibrant, yet habitable metropolis in Europe. A process that began around the mid '90s has, in the 21st century, seen the city emerge from its unassuming Scandinavian chrysalis to take flight upon a wave of ambition and confidence totally alien to the rest of Denmark's inward-looking populace. But then, Copenhagen always has been more than a little different from the rest of the country.

The metamorphosis began with the city's hugely successful stint as European City of Culture in 1996; it built up momentum with the opening of the new Terminal 3 at Kastrup (now Copenhagen) Airport, which over the coming years will help transform the city into the region's travel hub, serving 32 million passengers a year; and reached critical mass with the opening of the Øresund Fixed Link to Sweden on 1 July 2000. Along the way the city's restaurant scene was totally transformed, commerce boomed, its museums enjoyed major overhauls and Copenhagen woke up one morning to discover that it had become the design capital of the world.

Copenhagen is located on the east side of the largest of the Danish islands, Sjælland (Zealand), and the smaller adjoining island of Amager. The city is made up of two communes: Copenhagen (88 square kilometres/34 square miles) and Frederiksberg (9 square kilometres/3.5 square miles), as well as, beyond them, 26 further communes in the area known as Greater Copenhagen. Within the two central communes live a total of 580,000 people, but if you add on the rest of Greater Copenhagen the city's population jumps to 1.5 million, and if you include the catchment area of the so-called Øresund Region, now accessed by the bridge, the population reaches almost three million.

Although that's cooking the books a little, the fact that this is one of the world's smallest capitals is very much integral to its charm for visitors. Small is beautiful, as they say, and you can walk it, too.

For several decades Copenhagen's population was actually declining by around 10,000 a year, but that trend has been reversed and the figure is once again steadily increasing by a couple of thousand per annum, thanks in part to immigration. That, however, has brought the city one of its greatest challenges: how to integrate immigrants from southern and eastern Europe, Asia and Africa. Since the 1960s these new arrivals have tended to live in two main areas in the centre of the city: Vesterbro and

Nørrebro, leading to worries that Copenhagen is becoming ghettoised. That is largely nonsense (as any visitor to either quarter will realise), but there have occasionally been violent clashes between second-generation immigrants and the police, particularly in Nørrebro. Racism is on the increase throughout Denmark, incited by, among others, the far-right nationalist Dansk Folkeparti, a deeply unattractive bunch of extremists, many of whom are simply career politicians who see the emotive issue of race as a convenient stepping stone to power. The party, led by Pia Kjærsgaard (a woman so charmless she was snubbed even by dodgy Austrian politicians on a recent visit), has increased its support from seven per cent to 15 per cent since 1998.

'Copenhagen is still one of the safest cities in the world.'

And despite the Folkeparti's claims to the contrary, figures show that Copenhagen is still one of the safest cities in the world. In the late 18th century, visiting Englishman Nathaniel Wraxhall wrote of Copenhagen: 'One can walk through the city at midnight in complete safety. One hears no word of robbery or murder, nor is it necessary to go helmeted or with a dagger concealed beneath one's cloak as in southern European lands,' and not much has changed

The world's most nearly perfect city?

In Context

Copenhagen tomorrow

If it were possible to buy shares in a city, Copenhagen would be the hottest tip around. The next few years should see the Danish capital cement its position as Scandinavia's premier city. Not since the early years of Christian IV's reign, 400 years ago, has it been on such a roll, and once again its fortuitous geography looks set to transform the city from a small capital to a major northern European centre for trade, industry, finance and commerce.

On 1 July 2000 the **Øresund Fixed Link** opened – an engineering triumph as significant to Scandinavia as the Channel Tunnel was to Britain and France. Connecting Copenhagen with its Swedish neighbour Malmö, the 16-kilometre (10-mile) bridge and tunnel across (and under) the Øresund – the water between Sjælland and southern Sweden – is the final link in a chain of bridges connecting the Jylland peninsular (and mainland Europe) with the island of Fyn (whose own spectacular road and rail bridge to Sjælland opened in 1998), and then Sjælland to Sweden. With the inauguration of the road and rail Fixed Link the populations of Copenhagen and Malmö face a future that many predict will see the two effectively merge over the coming decades (some even say that a new language could evolve, blending Danish and Swedish into 'Swanish'). Both cities should reap the rewards of the multi-billion dollar investment in the newly-named 'Øresund Region' that is predicted for the next few decades.

Designing the Fixed Link to incorporate one of the world's finest airports (on Amager), hasn't done any harm either. Passenger numbers are expected to increase from 17 million in 1997 to an estimated 25-30 million in 2005, many of whom will be accommodated in the stunning new **Terminal 3**, designed by Danish architect Henning Larsen. Thanks to a state-of-the-art fast-link railway, passengers can now travel from right inside the new terminal to Central Station in just 12 minutes, the fastest airport to city centre journey of any capital in Europe. (And the bargain 18kr fare is a great way to assuage visitors' fears about the myth of Copenhagen as an expensive city). The final jigsaw pieces in the city's transport infrastructure are a ten-kilometre (six-mile), round-the-clock **metro** link through the city from the airport to Frederiksberg (with

driverless trains designed by renowned Italian car stylist Giorgio Guigaro), due to open in 2002, and, in the next few years, the extension of the trans-Øresund train service north of Copenhagen to Helsingør.

Meanwhile, Copenhagen's harbour front continues its rejuvenation with sophisticated apartments, restaurants and shops, and there are plans to develop a further four million square metres (almost five million square yards) of land (some of it reclaimed). The harbour itself still flourishes; the number of ships calling at Copenhagen each year has risen to over 23,000, up 20 per cent on late '80s figures.

The arts are also in line for investment. Det Kongelige Theater (the Royal Theatre) has been awarded funding for a full-scale renovation, a new opera house has been given the go-ahead, and, even more ambitiously, the Danish Broadcasting Corporation are to build a state-of-the-art (there's that phrase again) complex in an entirely new town, **Ørestad**, which will emerge on marshlands adjacent to the airport on the island of Amager over the next decade. Already attracting the interest of various multinationals, and with an extension of Copenhagen University planned here, Ørestad is set to become the third biggest city development project in Europe after London's Docklands and La Défense in Paris.

Copenhagen's budgetary surplus, coupled with an unprecedented wave of optimism and self-confidence, has ensured that only Berlin rivals it for the number of building projects currently on the go.

since. Of course crime does exist, but violent crime is on a downward trend, as are offences against property (while in the rest of Denmark the figures are static), although, worryingly, sexual offences are rising. In Denmark a mere two per cent of the national budget goes to the police, prisons and judicial system.

Copenhagen also remains one of the richest cities in the world, with a budget surplus expected to grow into billions of kroner over the next few years. In fact, it hasn't been this prosperous since the Middle Ages, when the herring used to virtually jump into the fishing boats from the surrounding waters. You need only look at the impressive building projects – both public and private – that have reinvigorated the skyline (and in the case of the current mini-metro project, the subsoil, too), to realise that the city is awash with money. The new bridge is, of course, the most significant of these, but structures like the striking new

extensions to Det Kongelige Bibliotek (the Royal Library; *see page 86*) and Statens Museum For Kunst (the National Gallery; *see page 98*) and or the new headquarters of the Danish building society Nykredit, are all unmistakable symbols of an upwardly mobile city. And there's more to come (*see page 27* **Copenhagen tomorrow**) with the massive planned harbour developments and the various ambitious projects on Amager, which include a new town and beach complex.

Though Copenhageners display their wealth more brazenly than their compatriots (most Jyllanders consider Copenhageners irredeemably flash), they still shun ostentatious profligacy. In Germany, every middle class family strives to place a Mercedes on their driveway; the Danes make do with the latest Bang & Olufsen stereo in their living room.

Future economic indicators are optimistic, too. Denmark looks set to enjoy a period of

Denmark and the EU

The Danish relationship with the European Union has always been a strained one. Denmark has been a member since 1972, but even then it was only because the Danes didn't want to lose their agricultural export of bacon and butter to the UK.

It's not so much a love-hate relationship, as no one here seems to really, truly love the EU; it's more of a realist versus nationalist situation. Denmark has always received more in agricultural subsidies from the EU than they've paid into it. For decades, regions of Denmark have been receiving development aid earmarked for mountain farmers because of a loophole in subsidy laws pertaining to the farming of near-barren land. There are no mountains in Denmark.

The 1993 re-vote on the overturned Maastricht Treaty only just achieved a 'yes' vote (51.05%), even though all four of the Danish points of contention with the original treaty had been amended. The resulting proposal, known as the Edinburgh Treaty, gave Denmark the right to abstain from military co-operation with the EU, the common currency, European citizenship, and being subject to EU jurisdiction in international affairs.

The primary Danish worry regarding the EU is the feeling that saying 'yes' to the European Union is saying 'yes' to political integration with the rest of Europe. Danes are afraid that areas like taxation and social services will be harmonised, which would mean the

eradication of the welfare state that defines Denmark. Danish politicians frequently use southern European countries like Greece as examples of how 'bad' it could get.

The right wing in Denmark, characterised by the Dansk Folkeparti, believe that saying yes to the EU is saying yes to foreigners in Denmark. There are, however, concerns at the DF that a referendum defeat of any opposition stance to EU proposals would make right-wing politics in Denmark appear synonymous with a losing battle.

Saying yes to the EU could also be bad for the Danish stock market, because it would no longer be independent of the European central market, and, so there would no longer be any reason to invest in a Danish business as opposed to, say, a Greek one.

Danes are inherently sceptical of foreign ideas. They'd rather do things on their own. But why? There are four theories currently being bounced around. The first is the fact that Denmark hasn't been directly involved in fighting a European war since 1864 (when Denmark lost a huge piece of border territory to Germany). The Danes haven't had to dig their dead out of ruins, or have their roads turned into highways for German tanks. The Benelux countries have, which makes it easier to understand their desire to tie Germany into economic, military and political co-operation.

A second reason is that the Danish state is very decentralised, with the local counties industrial peace, following a number of major labour agreements; it exports more than it imports; unemployment is down to below ten per cent; and dozens of international conglomerates, including Daimler-Chrysler, Dell and Nokia have flocked to the newly developed industrial areas of the city, lured by an ultra-efficient, highly educated, multi-lingual workforce, and the city's slick infrastructure and peerless airport. Copenhagen is now a world centre for biotechnology and a favoured city for IT and communications giants, while Denmark as a whole is invariably placed at, or near, the top of the various indices that rate such apparent intangibles as 'Future Readiness' (No.1, World Economic Forum 1999), 'Quality of Human Resources' (No.2 behind Finland, World Competitiveness Yearbook 1999), 'Satisfaction with Life' (No.1, Eurobarometer 1997), 'Best Place to Live' (No.1, University of Pennsylvania 1998),

and 'Most Attractive Country in which to Live and Work' (No.1, Oxford Research 1998). It's hardly surprising that the city is referred to as the 'Singapore of Europe' by international business analysts.

That doesn't mean that there aren't any dark clouds above Christiansborg. Denmark as a whole has the highest suicide rate in the world, and Copenhagen has recently topped a survey of European cities' rates of premature death (residents are more likely to die before they reach 65 than those of any other European city, particularly from lung cancer). Copenhageners are also uneasy about the suffocating intrusion of the State into their everyday lives, and the massive taxes levied upon them (25 per cent sales tax and, on average, 52 per cent income tax). Especially as, despite the tax burden, the state health system is showing signs of weakness, house prices and the cost of living are rising, and there's still nowhere to park that car you paid through the nose for.

'Garrison Keillor called Denmark the World's Most Nearly Perfect Nation.'

But as for actually changing things in any significant way, well, no one seriously wants to do that, and for good reason: Copenhagen works. It is a tolerant, well-ordered, clean, efficient, reliable, beautiful, law-abiding, highly educated and prosperous city, though you will never hear a Dane boast about it (even in bullish Copenhagen they usually prefer a language infused with self-mockery and modesty). No wonder American author Garrison Keillor, who lived here for a while and was married to a Dane, called Denmark the World's Most Nearly Perfect Nation.

As far as the next ten years go, the big question is: can an advanced, prosperous capital city that is expanding exponentially and competing for a slice of global industry still retain its character and culture, and offer its inhabitants a pleasant environment in which to live? It's what every European capital, be it London, Rome, Madrid or Paris, has been striving for, and largely failing to achieve. If anywhere can, Copenhagen can.

wielding a large proportion of decision-making power. Both the right and left wings of parliament are against over-centralised control, and it isn't hard to see how a parliament in Brussels could resemble that.

The third theory is that in Denmark there is a long tradition of public hearings to decide the direction of the country's political agenda. The centralisation of a second, decision-making parliament in Brussels would rob people of such grass roots democracy.

The fourth theory is that the mandate system, whereby Danish politicians in Brussels are obliged to fight for those who gave them their mandate in the first place, will be threatened by any increase in EU parliament power.

The debate rages on, with the pro-Europeans squaring off against the nationalists, and the battle looks to be a long one. There are indications, too, that this fight won't be confined simply to the halls of parliament, far from the Danish people. The rest of Europe can expect highly vocal opposition from Denmark to every step along the European road (as the 'No' vote against the adoption of the euro in autumn 2000 made abundantly clear). History, however, suggests that in the end it'll be the health of the Danish economy that takes precedence.

▶ For more on the **Øresund Fixed Link**, see page 246.
▶ For more on **contemporary architecture**, see page 36.
▶ For more on the **Danes attitude to other Scandinavians**, see page 252.

Thorvaldsens Museum. *See p33.*

Architecture

The charm of the old and the shock of the new.

Copenhagen is a city of surprises – and its architecture is no exception. From the colourful 18th-century houses of Nyhavn and Gråbrødretorv to monumental 19th-century neo-classical constructions and ground-breaking modernist buildings, the city displays a remarkable diversity and yet somehow manages to present a coherent whole.

Although almost nothing survives of pre-17th-century Copenhagen (a series of major fires saw to that), a closer look reveals a city of considerable architectural substance and distinctiveness. King Christian IV's marvellous 17th-century monuments, the Danish rococo expressed at its finest in the stately district of Frederiksstaden, Golden Age classicism's geometric, grandiose constructions, and 20th-century functionalism's sleek lines all marry an international sensibility with a characteristic Danish lightness of touch and inventiveness. Danish architecture is especially fascinating in its detail. The best way to enjoy it is to simply stroll the city, to get close to the works, and, where possible, get inside. (For further details of the buildings mentioned below, consult the index.)

ORIGINS 1167-1588

Slotsholmen, the small island in the centre of the city, is where Copenhagen was born. There is evidence of a small fishing village (called Havn, meaning 'harbour') on the site for several hundred years before King Valdemar I the Great gave the district to his blood brother Bishop Absalon, but it was Absalon's construction of a fortress on the island that is traditionally regarded as the foundation of the city. Remarkably, the ruins of Absalon's castle were uncovered underneath the current Christiansborg Slot and can be visited (together with remnants from subsequent palaces on the site) in the **Ruinere Under Christiansborg**.

During the Middle Ages, the town spread out from Slotsholmen towards present-day Rådhuspladsen. The oldest standing building in Copenhagen is **Helligåndskirken** (Church of the Holy Spirit) on Strøget. The church complex includes the remains of a late 13th-century convent and the late Gothic **Helligåndhus**, dating from the 15th century. This was once a hospital and is now the only surviving medieval building in the city. (Most of the current church is 19th-century.) A fragment of medieval Copenhagen's church, Sankt Clemens, can still be seen within the basement toilets of a bar, Club Absalon, on Frederiksberggade (Strøget).

CHRISTIAN IV 1588-1648

When Christian IV succeeded to the throne in 1588, Copenhagen had just become the capital of the kingdom. Christian was the first king to play a decisive role in the planning of the city, helping to shape Copenhagen into what it is today. Most of the buildings from this time are fine examples of Dutch Renaissance architecture, but the king was directly involved with a great many projects, and his personal tastes and whims had a distinctive influence on many of the buildings.

Before the reign of the architect-king, the borders of the city were Vester Voldgade, Nørdre Voldgade and Gothersgade, three roads that still encircle the old centre today. Christian's big idea was the expansion of the city to almost twice its previous size. Rosenborg Slot, built at the northern corner of the old city, and Kastellet citadel (1662-4), along the coast further to the north, would be the two main edifices of this new area. New Copenhagen's fortification line can still be discerned today, in the shape of the lakes that run through Tivoli, Ørsteds Parken, Botanisk Have and Østre Anlæg park, ending at Kastellet.

Christian's New Copenhagen included the building of the **Nyboder** district (between Sølvgade and Østerport), a residential area of 616 cottages for the military; it was ground-breaking both in terms of aesthetics and housing efficiency (distribution of light, air and traffic). Many of these picturesque, ochre-painted rows have been altered and restored over the years; the only original houses are at Sankt Poulsgade 20-40.

The earliest major work of his reign (1599-1605) was the transformation of Slotsholmen; he built a naval yard, supply depot (**Provianthuset**), brewery (**Kongens Bryghus**, supplying the navy's beer) and arsenal (**Tøjhus**; now Tøjhusmuseet). The 160-metre (520-feet) long arsenal and distinctive eight-storey hip-roofed brewery still stand.

To house the new naval yard workers, Christian embarked on another major construction project: **Christianshavn**. Begun in 1617, the king employed Dutch engineers to lay out the new quarter, partially on reclaimed land, across the water to the east of Slotsholmen. A number of well-preserved residences in this Amsterdam-like district survive, notably on Sankt Annæ Gade (Nos.28, 30 and 32, dating from around 1640). Today, like Nyboder, Christianshavn is a sought-after residential area.

The tireless king was also responsible for a number of Copenhagen's most distinctive individual buildings. The long, low **Børsen**

Clockwise (from top left): **Kongens Bryghus**, **Børsen**, the **Rundetårn** and **Rosenborg Slot**.

Amalienborg Slot. *See p33.*

(the Old Stock Exchange; 1619-24) is one of Copenhagen's most beautiful buildings, and is topped by the four intertwining tails of the famous Dragon Spire (1625), which was unexpectedly ordered from a famous fireworks maker of the time – a typically creative touch from Christian. The king indulged himself most fully and personally in the building of the delightful Dutch Renaissance **Rosenborg Slot** (1606-34), then outside the city walls. **Holmens Kirke** (1619; *see page 83*) and the grand gabled house at Amagertorv 6 (1616) are also both impressive Dutch Renaissance pieces (although the façade of the latter was rebuilt 100 years ago). Christian's last project was the extraordinary brick **Rundetårn** (Round Tower; 1637-42), Europe's oldest functioning observatory, distinguished by its inner spiral ramp, which was wide enough to allow a coach and horses to climb to the top.

The disastrous fires of the 18th century meant that very little domestic architecture survives from Christian's reign. The modest houses at Magstræde 17-19 are almost the only remaining examples.

BAROQUE & ROCOCO 1648-1759

Christian IV's successor completed the fortifications at **Kastellet**, but Denmark's disastrous 17th-century wars against the Swedes, and her bankrupt treasury, meant that it wasn't until towards the end of the century that any money could be found for public building.

Christian V laid out the grand square of **Kongens Nytorv** in the 1680s. **Charlottenborg** palace (1672-83) faces the square on the corner of Nyhavn. This huge, sober baroque building marks a decisive break with the previously popular decorated-gable style.

Probably a finer example of Danish baroque architecture, however, is **Vor Frelsers Kirke** (1682-96) in Christianshavn. Built by **Lambert van Haven**, who had a first-hand knowledge of cutting-edge European baroque. Its distinctive, playful spire, with its external spiral staircase, wasn't added until 1749-50 (by **Laurids de Thurah**; the design was based on the spire of Borromini's Sant'Ivo alla Sapienza in Rome).

Other examples of Italian-influenced baroque architecture include the **Røde Kancellibygning** (Red Chancellery; 1715-20) at Slotsholmgade 4 and Nicolai Eigtved's **Prinsens Palæ** (Prince's Palace; 1742-45; now home to Nationalmuseet). French rococo ornamentation became popular in the mid 18th century, and was used in what was Copenhagen's most ambitious building project of the time: **Christiansborg Slot** (1733-45; burned down in 1794). This combination of massive, square, pompous Italian baroque buildings with French rococo decoration came to be characteristic of Danish rococo style, and is seen at its best around Frederiksstaden, north of Kongens Nytorv.

Named after King Frederik V (reigned 1746-66), **Frederiksstaden** was the first large-scale urban building project since the reign of Christian IV. Court architect **Nicolai Eigtved** masterminded an ambitious grid-plan quarter, the centrepiece of which were the four palaces that today make up **Amalienborg Slot** (1750-60), home of the Danish Royal family. Set around the grand octagonal space of Amalienborg Slotplads, the palaces are linked by Frederiksgade to the striking, circular **Frederikskirken** (better known as **Marmorkirken**, the Marble Church; 1749-70), which was not completed until 1874. The **Odd Fellow Palæ** (1755) and **St Frederiks Hospital** (now Kunstindustrimuseet; 1752-4), both on Bredgade, are further fine examples of Danish rococo; the latter is an early instance of modular planning (with identical rooms repeated around its sides).

While the aristocracy were populating Frederiksstaden, Copenhagen's merchants and townsfolk were living in Dutch-influenced houses, like those on Gråbrødretorv and Nyhavn. Few survived the great fire of 1795 intact (although most were restored); the modest house at Nyhavn 9 is a rare exception.

CLASSICISM & NEO-CLASSICISM 1759-1848

There was little major building in Copenhagen in the second half of the 18th century, although **Caspar Frederik Harsdorff** did introduce the restrained elegance of classicism in **Harsdorffs Hus** (1779-80) at Kongens Nytorv 3-5 and **Erichsens Palæ** (1797-9) at Holmens Kanal 2-4.

Harsdorff's pupil, **Christian Frederik Hansen** was the central figure in Danish architecture during Denmark's so-called Golden Age (1800-50). The destruction caused by the fire of 1795 and the 1807 bombardment by the English provided a blank canvas for Hansen's ascetic, disciplined romantic classicism. Fine examples include **Domhuset** (1805-15) on Nytorv, the severe radicalism of **Vor Frue Kirke** (Church of Our Lady; 1811-29) and the box-like **Christiansborg Slotskirke** (1811-28), with its modest Ionic portico and coffered dome.

In contrast, **MGB Bindesbøll**'s riotously colourful decorative scheme for **Thorvaldsens Museum** (1839-48) is an important late example of neo-classicism, with its frescoes along the exterior walls, and lavish use of colour both within and without.

ECLECTICISM 1848-1914

Following the year of Europe-wide revolutions, 1848, the new Danish king Frederik VII accepted the end of absolute monarchy,

ushering in a period of major civic building. Among the largest projects were **Vilhelm Dahlerup** and **Ove Petersen**'s magnificent Italian Renaissance-style **Det Kongelige Theater** (the Royal Theatre; 1872-4). Dahlerup was also responsible (with Georg EV Møller) for the stodgy, graceless **Statens Museum For Kunst** (the National Gallery; 1889-96) and more impressive, richly decorated **Ny Carlsberg Glyptotek** (the New Carlsberg Sculpture Museum; 1892-7 – the more severe extension at the back was added by Hack Kampmann in 1901-6). Other significant public works built in the stately red-brick National Romantic style were **Martin Nyrop**'s **Rådhuset** (the Town Hall; 1892-1905), with its eclectic Dutch- and Italian-influenced detail, and **Heinrich Wenck**'s **Hovedbanegården** (Central Station; 1904-11). When CF Hansen's **Christiansborg Slot** burned down in 1884 (except for the Slotskirke), **Thorvald Jørgensen** designed its undistinguished replacement, with its neo-rococo façade, clad with 750 different types of granite from all over Denmark.

Towards the end of the 19th century, the dramatic industrialisation-fuelled increase in the city's population and the growth of the middle classes led to property development outside the city ramparts, which were taken down in 1852 and replaced by parks (from **Tivoli** to **Østre Anlæg** park).

The first efforts to improve the housing of the poor were **MGB Bindesbøll**'s simple, small terraced cottages (Østerbrogade 57/Øster Allé 34; 1853), which followed the pattern of Nyboder and provided an influential model for future social housing. These were followed by the **Kartoffelrækkerne** ('Potato Rows') housing in Østerbro (between the lakes and Øster Farimagsgade, and further north around Kildevældsgade), built in 1873-89 and 1892-1903 by **Frederik Bøttger**. The charming, two-storey, yellow-brick gabled houses are now highly desirable residences.

The early 20th century witnessed the construction of the few major works of **Anton Rosen**, the city's sole representative of art nouveau (though he worked in a wide range of styles). His office building at Frederiksberggade 16 (part of Strøget; 1907) is closer to Roman art nouveau than Belgian; the glass and steel façade of the **Savoy Hotel** on Vesterbrogade 34 (1906) is influenced by the contemporary Chicago style; while his masterpiece, the **Palace Hotel** (1907-10) on Rådhuspladsen, is brick-heavy National Romantic in structure, although the decoration is art nouveau-influenced.

NORDIC CLASSICISM 1914-28

It wasn't until the 20th century that Danish architects and designers truly stepped out from behind the influences of the dominant European and American styles. Neutral Denmark emerged from World War I in relative prosperity and, with the rest of Scandinavia, turned its back on the romantic, nationalistic, ornate themes of the previous 60 or so years to develop an almost brutally ascetic version of classicism that was entirely its own.

Public housing projects, such as the massive **Hornebækhus** housing block (Ågade/Skotterupsgade/Borups Allé/ Hornebækgade 5; 1922-3) by Kay Fisker, show Nordic Classicism at its most uncompromising. Belonging to the same period is the sinister-looking **Politigården** (Police Headquarters; 1918-24). Quite why a modern social democratic state like Denmark would choose to build such a huge, classically severe four-storey edifice – a chilling precursor of later fascist architecture – is a mystery.

Another notable building of the time is **Grundtvigs Kirke** in Bispebjerg (1921-40), built by PV Jensen Klint and his son Kaare (who was to have a significant role to play in the development of 20th-century Danish design). Based on a hugely enlarged version of a Danish country church, this stark, striking building can be seen as a bridge between National Romanticism and modernism.

FUNCTIONALISM/INTERNATIONAL MODERNISM 1928-60

Functionalism was first conceptualised by the Swedish architect Gunnar Asplund in an exhibition in Stockholm in 1930, inspiring architects across Scandinavia to adopt and adapt the tenets international modernism.

Denmark's continuing government programme of social housing provided plenty of opportunities for Danish architects to put their ideas into practice. The first project to create a major impact was **Arne Jacobsen's Bellavista** housing development (1934) and **Bellevue Theatre** (1937), near fashionable Bellevue beach in Klampenborg. Taking much inspiration from the German modernists, Bellavista is uncompromisingly modern, with white surfaces and large windows everywhere. Among the most striking examples of the movement are the works of **Vilhelm Lauritzen**, whose particular triumphs include **Radiohuset** (Danish Radio Headquarters; 1937-41) and **Kastrup Airport** (now Copenhagen Airport; 1936-9). Functionalism was also characterised by its preoccupation with design, and many prominent architects, most notably Jacobsen, also made names for

Detail: **Ny Carlsberg Glyptotek**. *See p33.*

themselves in interior and furniture design. Jacobsen's most comprehensive work was the **Radisson SAS Royal Hotel** (1956-61), Copenhagen's first skyscraper, which he designed down to the last detail, from doorknobs to curtain rods. Recent renovations were roundly criticised by architectural historians, as only room 606 was left entirely intact. Another interesting example of 'total design' is the **Langelinie Pavillion** (1944), which is a few steps from the Little Mermaid, and makes the trip up there worthwhile.

Modernist buffs might like to also seek out some of the lesser-known gems of the period, such as Kai Gottlob's **Svagebørnsskolen/ Friluftskole** at Sumatravej/Samøsvej on Amager (1937) and Jacobsen's **Munkegårds Skolen** (1956-7) at Vangedevej 178, Gentofte, just north of Copenhagen.

SOCIAL DEMOCRATIC PLURALISM 1960-95

An influential current in the 1960s and 1970s was dense low-rise housing, which sometimes reflected the era's hippy ideals, with shared facilities including gardens, balconies and sometimes even living rooms. This 'social' housing was a counter-current to the cold, systematic elements of modernism, and was largely initiated by the **Vandkunsten** architecture practice, which remains true to the 'social' style today – its **Dianas Have** housing scheme in Hørsholm (1994) is seen as a landmark piece, worth the trip up north for its harmonious integration with nature and social aspect.

But 1960s Copenhagen also saw the construction of the type of pre-fabricated high-rise blocks that were to blight much of Europe – much of Nørrebro remains brutalised by '60s Eastern Bloc-like 'panel buildings' today. A notable example, however, of how such housing can work is the five 16-storey **Høje Gladsaxe** blocks (Gladsaxevej, Søborg; 1963-8), which now gleam in silver and blue following a restoration and remodelling in the early '90s.

Arne Jacobsen's last architectural project was the transatlantic-style 'slab on a podium' **Nationalbanken** (1965-78); it was finished after his death in 1971 by the currently ultra-hip firm of **Dissing + Weitling**.

New public buildings were scarce between the 1960s and the 1990s, and most building efforts were devoted to suburban developments. The biggest change in the city centre was the creation of pedestrianised Strøget (1962). Other interesting features here include the charming renovation of the Pistolstræde passage (1971) and the Amagertorv tiled public square (1995).

The state Lutheran Church funded a large and lavish post-World War II programme of ecclesiastical building. Notable products of this include **Jørn Utzon**'s (of Sydney Opera House fame) rectilinear-without, curvy-within

Bagsværd Kirke (1974-6) on Taxvej in Bagsværd, and the courtyard-centred, pitched-roofed **Egedal Kirke** (Egedalsvej 3, Kokkedal; 1990) by the **Fogh & Følner** practice.

Architects have also been given free rein in the **Egebjerggård** experimental housing quarter of Ballerup (1985-98). It consists of a huge variety of different types of experimental houses by a number of architectural firms, ranging from the endearingly organic to the fiercesomely neo-brutalist.

THE DANISH WAVE 1995-

Contemporary Danish architecture might very well be called the Danish Wave in the future, since this was the name given to a huge international exhibition of contemporary Danish culture – with a prominent place given to architecture – presented in Australia, Japan and New York between 1997 and 2000.

By the mid '90s Danish-designed buildings had been turning heads internationally for some time, but major modern works were scarce in Denmark. The designation of Copenhagen as the European City of Culture in 1996 prompted a period of intense renovation and development, which has continued over the past five years. Two major architectural works to come out of the event were **Henning Larsen**'s ultra-cool new Impressionists gallery in the **Ny Carlsberg Glyptotek** (1996) and **Søren Robert Lund**'s ship-like **Arken Museum For**

The '**Black Diamond**'. See p36.

Into the future…

The highest-profile building project in Copenhagen at the beginning of the millennium is an entire new town: **Ørestad**. A three square-kilometre (one square-mile) area south of the city has been set aside to accommodate many of those who are expected to be drawn into the region following the opening of the **Øresund Fixed Link** to Malmö. Preparations started even before the bridge opened in July 2000, and even though both the regional trains and the Metro (under construction) already have stops at Ørestad, the area's future remains uncertain. The high cost of development fixed by the Ørestad Development Corporation has considerably dampened the original enthusiasm over the new town, and only the national broadcasting network, DR, and Denmark's leading performance theatre troupe, Hotel Pro Forma, have definite contracts for spaces in central Ørestad. Furthermore, other than a large pharmaceutical laboratory headquarters, only one significant private project is planned – a huge shopping centre with a state-of-the-art cinema complex. A question mark remains over whether Ørestad will be able to sell enough of its units to be economically viable.

Most of the other major building plans in Copenhagen are on the waterfront. One of the most ambitious and visionary schemes is a residential development in Copenhagen's southern harbour, **Sydhavn**. The original twist here is that it won't take place by the water, but on the water – fund-raising has started for the building of a new network of canals and artificial islands. South Copenhagen may soon resemble a futuristic Nordic Venice. Fittingly, the layout of this new water-bound district is to be the work of two Dutch architects, just as Christianshavn was (for the same purpose, and also on reclaimed land) 300 years ago.

Another major project is the new **opera house**, also to be built by the waterfront on Holmen's Dokø, facing Amalienborg Slot. The design has been assigned to prominent architect **Henning Larsen** and the funds are to come from Denmark's biggest company Mærsk/AP Møller, which has already offered around 1.3 billion kroner (Mærsk own half of the property on Holmen). It is also likely that a tunnel will be built between Holmen and Langelinie, so that a road would go straight from the airport to northern Copenhagen, thereby avoiding the city centre.

Moderne Kunst (Arken Museum of Modern Art; 1994-6), located on the coast just south of Copenhagen. **Anna Maria Indrio**'s slick annex to **Statens Museum For Kunst** (the National Gallery) followed soon after (1998).

Langelinie in Østerbro was the first area to benefit from the current round of waterfront renovations, but none of Langelinie's achievements are as spectacular as the two most stylish examples of contemporary Danish architecture: Schmidt, Hammer and Lassen's **'Black Diamond'** (1995-9), the new extension to Det Kongelige Bibliotek (the Royal Library) by the waterfront of Slotsholmen, and the new **Terminal 3** (1999) at Copenhagen Airport. Both combine sharp, clean lines with sober tones, and use modern materials to create slick-looking, spacious structures with dark glass façades. The importance of glass walls is also clear in the massive, ultra-modern buildings (2000) on Christianshavn, next to Knippelsbro, which are impressive examples of crisp new architecture, though somewhat lacking in charm.

Such projects, crowned by the completion of the **Øresund Fixed Link** tunnel and bridge between Copenhagen and Malmö in Sweden in 2000, represent Danish architecture at the start of the new millennium. Danish architetects today wrestle with two opposing approaches. On one side is the desire to continue to develop a fundamentally Nordic tradition (simple lines, functional designs, local materials); on the other is the influence of prevailing international fashions. It is likely that if a distinctive Danish architectural style is to emerge in the future, it will spring from a compromise between these two contradictory tendencies.

▶ For more on **Christian IV**, see page 11.
▶ For more on **Christianshavn**, see page 102.
▶ For more on **Rosenborg Slot**, see page 100.
▶ For more on **Nicolai Eigtved**, see page 91.
▶ For more on **Frederiksstaden**, see page 88.
▶ For more on Denmark's **Golden Age**, see page 18.
▶ For more on **Arne Jacobsen**, see page 38.
▶ For more on the **Øresund Fixed Link**, see page 246.

The **Dansk Design Center**.
See p40.

Danish Design

Sleek, chic and timelessly modern, Denmark's designers are still world leaders.

In no field have the Danes had a greater global impact than in the world of contemporary interiors. Inspired by the iconoclastic wave of modernism at the beginning of the 20th century, and particularly by the radicalism of the Bauhaus movement, Danish designers began to look at the way objects are designed anew.

'The form of an object follows its function.' (Kaare Klint)

The most succinct expression of the new philosophy was architect **Kaare Klint**'s assertion that 'The form of an object follows its function.' In the 1930s, Klint (influenced by his father PV Jensen Klint) wrote again and again in his notes that architecture and interior should be unified in what he called 'the living life'. Design should be intrinsic to function, styling should exist only to enhance practicality. Allying this idea with the

traditional hallmarks of good Danish design – industrial quality, outstanding craftsmanship and artistic flair – Klint produced a series of ground-breaking designs, and passed on his theories as a teacher of furniture design at Copenhagen's Royal Academy of Architecture.

Klint's students were advised that if, for example, they were making a chair, then its function (ie comfort) should be the starting point – studying human proportions and posture and applying this scientific rationale to the furniture was the primary objective. Børge Mogensen, Mogens Koch and Hans J Wegner were among his students, and their production of simple, practical furniture swept across the country in the 1950s; their designs remain classics today.

TRAILBLAZERS

Even before the 1950s, there were a number of Danish pioneers who influenced concepts of modern functionalism. The silverware created by **Georg Jensen** (*see page 165*), for example, was particularly revolutionary. Trained as a sculptor

Great Danes Arne Jacobsen

The architect **Arne Jacobsen** was one of a group of Danish designers – including Poul Henningsen, Hans J Wegner, Finn Juhl, Verner Panton, Kaare Klint, Poul Kjærholm and Jørn Utzon – who together helped create a design legacy from which Denmark still profits. In a country where good design is a topic of everyday conversation, like sport or politics, it is hardly surprising that Jacobsen is something of an icon.

Born in 1902, he graduated from the Copenhagen Academy of Arts in 1928, and ran a private practice from 1930 until his death in 1971. His first major work was the **Bellavista Housing Estate**, overlooking the sea at Klampenborg, a few kilometres north of the city. This simple, white, some might say austere complex, built in 1934, included apartments (every one with a sea view), a pool and a theatre, and crystallised his principle of 'economy plus function equals style'. Today Bellavista houses an excellent restaurant dedicated to Jacobsen design and named after him (see page 273 **Jacobsen**).

Jacobsen helped to introduce Functionalism to Denmark. Embracing new materials, as well as the most up-to-date manufacturing techniques, he maintained high standards of craftsmanship, even in his mass-produced works. Jacobsen embraced the principle of 'total design' wholeheartedly, often designing not only buildings, but their gardens, lighting, furnishings and interiors, right down to the door handles and, in the case of the **Radisson SAS Royal Hotel** (see page 61; Copenhagen's first skyscraper, erected on Vesterbrogade near Tivoli in 1960), even the cutlery used in the restaurant. Everything in room 606 – lamps, fabrics, cutlery, glasses and door handles – is Jacobsen-designed and has been left untouched as a tribute to the master.

He went on to design buildings in Denmark, England and Germany, including Århus town hall (1939), St Catherine's College, Oxford (1966), the Danish Embassy in London (1969) and the city hall in Mainz (1970). What was to be one of his greatest achievements, **Nationalbanken** (the National Bank) on Holmens Kanal in Copenhagen, turned out to be his last. (He died before it was completed, and the job was finished by two of the architects from his studio, Dissing & Weitling, in 1971. This duo now run the hottest architecture firm in the country.)

But even if you have never seen any of his buildings, chances are you will recognise several of Jacobsen's chair designs, including the 'Egg' (1958), the 'Swan' (1958) and the 'Ant' (1952). The latter proved an instant classic. It was the first in a series of lightweight chairs with seats and back in one piece of moulded wood, and revolutionised ideas of what a chair should look like. The 'Ant' became particularly famous following its use in the David Bailey portrait of a naked Christine Keeler.

In recent years, examples of Jacobsen's furniture, and those of his Danish contemporaries, have become highly collectible with values rising accordingly. You should, however, be able to pick up a worn example of one of his simpler, mass produced chairs for under 1,000kr in the second-hand furniture shops of Copenhagen. See page 159.

and silversmith, Jensen opened his first silverworks in Copenhagen in 1904 and, from then until his death in 1935, he challenged conventions of design. The cutlery, bowls and jewellery he created with the painter Johan Rohde were at the vanguard of modern design.

'My aim is to beautify the home and those who live there. I am searching for harmony.' (Poul Henningsen)

At the same time that Jensen was challenging cutlery conventions, fellow Copenhagener **Poul Henningsen**, horrified by what he saw on his journey home from his design studio, was innovating in home lighting. 'From the top of a tram car, you look into all the homes and you shudder at how dismal people's homes are,' he wrote. 'It doesn't cost money to light a room correctly, but it does require culture. My aim is to beautify the home and those who live there. I am searching for harmony.' So, in 1924, Henningsen designed a multi-shade lamp based on scientific analysis of its function. The size, shape, and position of the shade determines the distribution of the light and the amount of glare. The 'PH' lamp, which featured several shades to help correct the colour and shadow effect of the light, won a competition at the Paris World Fair, and Poul Henningsen became a star. His lamps are still available, and you will find PH lamps in many Danish households, particularly the classic PH-Contrast (1962).

Other design trailblazers included silversmith **Kay Bojesen**, whose 'Grand Prix' silver service (1938) was the template for aspiring cutlery designers, and the artist **Ebbe Sadolin** with his plain white tableware which was considered quite radical at the time.

BIG NAMES OF THE '50S AND '60S
Two of the biggest names of 1950s' Danish furniture design were **Nanna Ditzel** (who is still working and winning prizes for her revolutionary designs today) and the legendary **Arne Jacobsen** (*see page 38* **Great Danes: Arne Jacobsen**). Jacobsen and his contemporary **Poul Kjaerholm** (whose PK22 chair was based on Mies van der Rohe's Barcelona design) were criticised, though, for creating designs only the elite could afford.

In the 1960s, **Verner Panton**, one of Jacobsen's former colleagues, addressed that problem, and took on the challenge of pushing the boundaries of design aesthetics even further. Panton trained at the Royal Danish Academy of Fine Arts in Copenhagen, and initially worked in Arne Jacobsen's

Poul Henningsen's 'artichoke' lightshade.

architectural practice (helping with the 'Ant' chair project). He established his own design office in 1955, and is credited with the design of the first single-form injection-moulded plastic chair – the 'Stacking' chair, designed in 1960. International attention soon centred on Panton's designs, based on geometric forms, and constructed from cheap, tough plastics that had previously only been used for industrial purposes. Combined with a use of vivid colours and outlandish shapes, Panton's inspirational style helped define the 'pop' aesthetic of the 1960s, with design icons like the 'Flowerpot' lamp, the 'Cone' chair and the Panton chair. Although Panton's work was dismissed by some contemporary critics as a fashion fad, before his death in 1998 it had been reassessed and was regarded by a new generation of designers as way ahead of its time.

WHERE TO SEE IT AND BUY IT

Panton is not the only Danish designer to have enjoyed a recent renaissance. Style and fashion magazines have embraced the Danish look as contemporary, and walking around Copenhagen, it looks as modish as ever.

Stereo Bar (*see page 215*) illustrates the point perfectly. This hip DJ bar is kitted out with streamlined Danish Modern furnishings, though few of its trendy habituées ever think twice about the Panton motif painted on the walls, the Søren Østergaard and Arne Jacobsen chairs, or the PH lamps; they simply see this popular bar's interior as modern, despite the fact that its design is, essentially, 50 years old.

The prize-winning architecture studio of **Jørn Utzon** (of Sydney Opera House fame) has designed the **Paustian** furniture showroom and warehouse (*see page 164*) and **Interstudio**, nearby on Amerika Quay. Then there's the streamlined modernism of **Gubi** (*see page 166*), not to mention the hip second-hand shops on Ravnsborggade in Nørrebro and Bredgade,

north of Kongens Nytorv. Don't miss **Moving Furniture** at Silkegade 5 (*see page 160*), which specialises in limited edition, ground-breaking, one-of-a-kind classics (all at least 25 years old).

A good one-stop shop for Danish design is the elegant **Illums Bolighus** on Amagertorv (*see page 165*). Even if you can't afford a major purchase, it's well worth wandering through the gallery/museum-style halls containing the pure genius of a Jensen stainless steel watch, the perfect porcelain of **Bing & Grøndhal**, or the crystal creations of contemporary Danish craftsman like Michael Bang, Torben Jørgensen and Allan Scharf. Even the outside of the store has designer pedigree: the geometric patterns of the marble-paved fountain square were designed by Bjørn Nørgaard in 1996.

Further up Strøget is the five-storey glass-fronted **Bodum** shop (*see page 165*) and opposite is a **Bang & Olufsen** hi-fi showroom (*see page 164*), themselves both excellent examples of modern Danish product designers who have penetrated worldwide markets.

For those interested in learning more about Danish design, **Kunstindustrimuseet** (the Museum of Decorative and Applied Art; *see page 92*) houses a collection of Danish design through the ages. At Holmen, the **Royal Academy School of Architecture** hosts exhibitions as does **Arkitekturcentret** at Gammel Dok (*see page 105*), which also houses a bookshop and café.

However, since January 2000, Danish design has had the showcase it deserves: the five-storey **Dansk Design Center** (built by the prolific architect Henning Larsen). Behind the smoked-glass exterior there are interactive installations, interesting exhibitions (although, disappointingly, no permanent collection), conferences, a design shop and a café. (*See also page 62.*)

The centre promises to act as a 'window to the world' for Danish design, and a meeting place for designers, industry figures and innovators from all over the world. A spokeswoman for the centre defines Danish design as 'work with a human touch. The Swedes and Finns all believe in clean lines and using natural materials,' she explains, 'but the Danish designers have managed to use these Scandinavian principles in a less clinical way – they have a great feeling for beauty.'

► For more on **contemporary Danish architecture**, see page 36.
► For more on **classic and contemporary design shops**, see pages 159-64.

Accommodation

Accommodation   42

Accommodation

Prices are high and imagination low in most of Copenhagen's hotels.

Over the last few years Copenhagen has seen an unprecedented number of major construction projects (*see page 27*), and the hotel industry has provided its fair share – no fewer than five luxury hotels (First Hotel Copenhagen, DGI-Byens Hotel, the Copenhagen Strand Hotel, the Marriott and the Hilton Copenhagen Airport) have been built in the last couple of years.

The city now boasts upwards of 10,000 hotel beds, yet the building boom has failed to keep pace with the growing number of visitors (both holiday-makers and business folk) to the city, which has pushed accommodation prices skywards. Room rates are very expensive – particularly during the high tourist season from May to September – and budget alternatives are hard to find. Still, the city harbours a few secrets and surprises for cost-conscious travellers.

Given the Danes' long history of design excellence, those visitors expecting top-range Danish hotels to be havens of slick contemporary style will be disappointed. The modern 'boutique' hotel has yet to reach Copenhagen and most of the high-end places are of the nondescript international chain variety or the quaintly twee 'English country house' type. At the other end of the scale, there's no widespread Danish tradition of bed and breakfast establishments, so budget travellers often have to make do with sterile, basic, small hotels. Probably the classiest and best value accommodation in town are the centrally located short-stay serviced apartments offered by **Citilet Apartments** (*see page 50*).

RESERVATIONS, RATINGS & RATES

Booking in advance is always a good idea, but if you arrive without a reservation, the **Wonderful Copenhagen Tourist Information Bureau** (*see page 292*) can make same-night reservations for hotels throughout Copenhagen at reduced rates. The service is also available from the tourist information desk in Copenhagen Airport's arrivals hall. The system also caters for advance bookings at standard rates.

Another trick to save pennies is to haggle directly with the hotel staff, who will often give reductions if they're not fully booked, especially outside the tourist season. Some hotels offer special weekend rates.

Denmark has a one- to five-star ranking system for hotels, comparable to those of most other European countries (this is explained at www.danishhotels.dk/engelsk/stjerner.html). As a rough guide, a double room in a one-star hotel should be around 525kr per night; 800kr in a two-star; 1,220kr in a three-star; 1,530kr in a four-star and 2,400kr in a five-star. We categorise the hotels below in terms of their cheapest double room. Breakfast is normally included in the price.

Most low- and mid-range Copenhagen hotels are in the Vesterbro neighbourhood, just west of Central Station (be aware that this is also the red light district, although it does have its share of trendy cafés, bars and restaurants), while the more prestigious hotels (except the Radisson SAS Royal), tend to be on the other side of the city centre, near Kongens Nytorv and Amalienborg Slot. For accommodation catering primarily for a gay clientele, *see page 211*.

Deluxe (1,900kr and above)

Tivoli & around

First Hotel Vesterbro
Vesterbrogade 23-29, 1620 Copenhagen K (33 78 80 00/fax 33 78 80 80/www.firsthotels.com). **Rates** 1,448kr-1,648kr single; 2,098kr-2,548kr double. **Credit** AmEx, DC, MC, V. **Map** p310 P10. This very modern four-star hotel (opened in early 2000) was the first new hotel to be built in Copenhagen in 15 years. Most of its 403 rooms are small but equipped to a high standard; ten rooms are even (rather patronisingly, one can't but feel) geared to female guests, with cosmetics and fashion magazines. Well located at the beginning of busy Vesterbrogade, First Hotel also boasts a marble and glass lobby, a stylish atrium, an IT centre and the excellent Alex Vinbar & Kokken (*see p129*). **Hotel services** *Air-conditioning. Bar. Business services. Disabled: adapted rooms. Laundry. Limousine service. No-smoking floors. Parking. Restaurant.* **Room services** *Dataport. Iron. Minibar. Room service (6.30-11am; 6-10pm). Telephone. Turndown. TV: cable/pay movies/web TV.*

Plaza
Bernstorffsgade 4, 1577 Copenhagen V (33 14 92 62/fax 33 93 93 62/www.accorhotel.dk). **Rates** 1,695kr single; 1,895kr-2,095kr double; 3,295kr-6,495kr suite. **Credit** AmEx, DC, MC, V. **Map** p310 P11.

The Arne Jacobsen-designed **Radisson SAS Royal Hotel**.

King Frederik VIII commissioned the building of the Plaza in 1913 and it retains a distinctive early 20th-century atmosphere, fitted out with leather and wood, and with a very cool glass elevator. The Library Bar (*see p147*) boasts the accolade of being dubbed 'one of the five best bars in the world' by *Forbes Magazine*, and a central pillar in the lounge carries plaques naming the hundreds of famous personalities who have stayed here over the years. Even though the Plaza's no longer so popular among the glitzy and glamorous, it still enjoys the best view over Tivoli of any hotel, and is very centrally located, next to Central Station. Each room is individually decorated in old-fashioned classical style.
Hotel services *Air-conditioning. Bars. Business services. Concierge. Garden. Laundry. Limousine service. No-smoking floor. Parking. Restaurants (2).*
Room services *Iron. Minibar. Room service (7am-midnight). Telephone. TV: cable/pay movies.*

Radisson SAS Royal Hotel

Hammerischsgade 1, 1611 Copenhagen V
(33 42 60 00/fax 33 42 61 00/www.radissonsas.com).
Rates 2,050kr-2,450kr single; 2,350kr-3,350kr double; 2,995kr-11,000kr suite. **Credit** AmEx, DC, MC,V.
Map p310 O11.
Vying for five-star prestige with the d'Angleterre (*see below*), the Radisson SAS Royal couldn't be more different in style. From the outside, the hotel is no more than an unadorned tower block, but the interior – designed from top to bottom in 1960 by legendary Danish designer and architect Arne Jacobsen (*see p38*) – is quite exceptional. The lounge and café are filled with rounded minimalist shapes that have gone full circle, so to speak, from cutting-

edge stylish to hopelessly dated to trendy once again. Room 606 has legendary status: the original 1960 design has been strictly preserved, and the hotel prints a special postcard of the room, available only to those who stay in the room. The hotel's central location is another boon – Tivoli, Central Station and Rådhuspladsen are a short stroll away. Recent prominent guests include Luciano Pavarotti, Tina Turner and the Dalai Lama.
Hotel services *Air-conditioning. Babysitting. Bar. Beauty salon. Business services. Concierge. Disabled: adapted rooms. Garden. Gym. Laundry. Limousine service. No-smoking floors. Parking. Restaurant.*
Room services *Dataport. Iron. Minibar. Room service (24hrs). Telephone. Turndown. TV: cable/pay movies.*

Nyhavn & around

Hotel d'Angleterre

Kongens Nytorv 34, 1050 Copenhagen K
(33 12 00 95/fax 33 12 11 18/www.remmen.dk).
Rates 1,995kr-2,995kr single; 2,295kr-3,595kr double. **Credit** AmEx, DC, MC, V.
Map p311 M15.
Unique in its class, Copenhagen's most prestigious hotel offers a level of service that no other hotel in the capital can match. The massive 18th-century building with its 124 bedrooms is located at the upmarket end of Strøget on Kongens Nytorv, facing café-lined Nyhavn. From the Spice Girls and Metallica to guests of the royal family (Amalienborg Slot, the Queen's residence, is round the corner), anybody who's made it stays here. Traditional to its

Flying high: the **Hotel d'Angleterre**. *See p43.*

core, Hotel d'Angleterre has been selected as one of the top ten hotels in Europe and is frequently voted best hotel in Denmark. The fitness centre, swimming pool and sauna are open to non-residents for 200kr and the morning buffet (until 10.30am) doesn't cost much more than brunch in a trendy café.
Hotel services *Air-conditioning. Babysitting. Bar. Beauty salon. Concierge. Gym. Laundry. Limousine service. No-smoking rooms. Parking. Restaurant. Swimming pool (indoor).* **Room services** *Dataport. Iron. Minibar. Room service (24hrs). Telephone. Turndown. TV: satellite.*

Further afield

Radisson SAS Scandinavia Hotel

Amager Boulevard 70, 2300 Copenhagen S (33 11 23 24/fax 33 96 55 55/www.radissonsas.com). **Rates** 1,670kr single; 1,970kr double; 2,970kr suite. **Credit** AmEx, DC, MC, V.
The biggest hotel in Copenhagen houses the Copenhagen Casino, four restaurants, a large lounge bar, a conference centre for 1,200 people and a total of 542 bedrooms. Although it's only a 15-minute walk from Rådhuspladsen, the SAS Scandinavia is not as centrally located as most other Copenhagen hotels. There are eight non-smoking floors and 'theme floors' featuring different design styles, such as 'oriental', 'hi-tech' and 'Scandinavian'. The simple fact that there are over 200 busy employees gives it a buzz. Both the Top of the Town Wine Bar (*see*

p154) on the 25th floor and the Blue Elephant Thai restaurant in the basement are flashy and exclusive, but extravagantly overpriced. It attracts a largely business clientele.
Hotel services *Air-conditioning. Babysitting. Bars (2). Beauty salon. Business services. Concierge. Disabled: adapted rooms. Gym. Laundry. Limousine service. No-smoking floors. Parking (free). Restaurants (4). Swimming pool (indoor).* **Room services** *Dataport. Minibar. Room service (6.30am-11.30pm). Telephone. Turndown. TV: cable/pay movies.*

Expensive (1,300kr-1,900kr)

Tivoli & around

DGI-Byens Hotel

Tietgensgade 65, 1704 Copenhagen V (33 29 80 50/ fax 33 29 80 59/www.dgi-byen.dk). **Rates** 1,195kr single; 1,395kr double; 1,995kr suite. **Credit** AmEx, DC, MC, V. **Map** p310 Q11.
One of the newest hotels in the city (opened at the turn of the millennium), this is just one part of the new DGI sports and cultural centre, located on the site of a former meat market. The spacious rooms are distinguished by the sort of modern, minimalist Scandinavian design that is remarkably hard to find in the capital's hotels. Vandkulturhuset ('the Water Culture House'), Copenhagen's state-of-the-art swimming pool and spa, is in the same building as the hotel and offers one free visit per guest per day. Bowling, volleyball, badminton, climbing, fencing and many other sporting activities can also be enjoyed within the DGI building.
Hotel services *Disabled: adapted rooms. Gym. Laundry. No-smoking rooms. Parking. Swimming pool (indoor).* **Room services** *Dataport. Iron. Minibar. Telephone. Turndown. TV: cable/ pay movies.*

Hotel Savoy

Vesterbrogade 34, 1620 Copenhagen K (33 26 75 00/fax 33 26 75 01). **Rates** 945kr single; 995kr twin; 1,500kr-1,800kr double. **Credit** AmEx, DC, MC, V. **Map** p310 P10.
The Savoy is a friendly family hotel located close to Central Station in an area that combines red light district seediness with trendy café life. The hotel has recently been renovated, so the old-fashioned rooms and the splendid façade are now complemented with a brand new lobby and reception area.
Hotel services *Bar. Concierge. Limousine service.* **Room services** *Iron. Minibar. Room service (5.30-10pm). Telephone. TV: cable.*

Imperial Hotel

Vester Farimagsgade 9, 1606 Copenhagen V (33 12 80 00/fax 33 93 80 31/www.imperialhotel.dk). **Rates** 1,395kr-2,230kr single; 1,795kr-2,795kr double. **Credit** AmEx, DC, MC, V. **Map** p310 N11.
A reliable and well-run hotel, centrally located in the cinema/theatre area, near the lakes and the planetarium, and a short stroll from Tivoli. The

Accommodation

71 Nyhavn – a winning harbourside location.

lounge is spacious and comfortable and the Imperial Garden Restaurant, in the indoor garden, is decent (if overpriced). There are 163 bedrooms, decorated in a clean, fresh, unfussy style, within the 1958 building.

Hotel services *Babysitting. Bar. Business services. Concierge. Disabled: adapted rooms. Garden. Laundry. Limousine service. No-smoking floors. Parking. Restaurant.*
Room services *Dataport. Iron. Minibar. Room service (6.30am-10pm). Telephone. TV: cable/ pay movies.*

Kong Frederik

Vester Voldgade 25, 1552 Copenhagen V (33 12 59 02/fax 33 93 59 01/www.remmen.dk). **Rates** 1,270kr-1,670kr single; 1,370kr-1,770kr double; 2,270kr-6,570kr suite. **Credit** AmEx, DC, MC, V. **Map** p310 O12.

This elegant, old-fashioned hotel, located a few metres from Rådhuspladsen and Strøget, goes full tilt for trad English style, with dark wood panelling, Chesterfields and a fireplace. The layout of the bedrooms varies from room to room, but all are elegant and have en suite bathrooms. In the lobby hang portraits of all Denmark's (many) King Frederiks, and the new restaurant, Frederiks, is accessible straight from the street – it's worth visiting both for its decor (until mid 2000 it was a well-known pub, imported piece by piece from London, called Queen's) and its haute cuisine. The site has been used as an inn since the 14th century, although the present building was rebuilt and given its current name in 1898.

Hotel services *Babysitting. Bar. Business services. Garden. Laundry. Limousine service. No-smoking rooms. Parking. Restaurant.*
Room services *Dataport. Iron. Minibar. Room service (24hrs). Telephone. TV: cable/pay movies/web TV.*

Palace Hotel

Rådhuspladsen 57, 1550 Copenhagen K (33 14 40 50/fax 33 14 52 79/www.palace-hotel.dk). **Rates** 1,525kr single; 1,725kr-1,925kr double; 2,495kr Ambassador Room. **Credit** AmEx, DC, MC, V. **Map** p310 O12.

This huge luxury hotel stands adjacent to Rådhuset (the Town Hall) at the western end of Strøget. The Palace was built in 1907-10 (by Anton Rosen), just after the Town Hall was finished, to provide prestigious accommodation for visiting officials coming for business at the then-new Rådhuset. The Ambassador rooms have balconies overlooking Rådhuspladsen. All of the 162 rooms were refurbished in 1998 in an easy-on-the-eye-if-unremarkable generic hotel style.

Hotel services *Bar. Concierge. Laundry (self-service). No-smoking rooms. Restaurant.*
Room services *Dataport. Iron. Minibar. Room service (24hrs). Telephone. TV: pay movies/satellite.*

Nyhavn & around

71 Nyhavn

Nyhavn 71, 1051 Copenhagen K (33 43 62 00/fax 33 43 62 01/www.71nyhavnhotelcopenhagen.dk). **Rates** 1,250kr-1,495kr single; 1,495kr-1,795kr double. **Credit** AmEx, DC, MC, V. **Map** p312 N17.

Perched at the end of Nyhavn within a splendid early 19th-century warehouse, this relaxed, well regarded hotel enjoys a prime location. Thoroughly refurbished in 1997, the small, modern bedrooms are given character by their wood-beamed ceilings. Be sure to ask for a view over the water or you could find yourself facing the neighbouring building at the rear. Good breakfasts.

Hotel services *Babysitting. Bar. Concierge. Laundry. No-smoking floor. Parking (free). Restaurant.*
Room services *Dataport. Iron. Minibar. Room service (noon-midnight). Telephone. TV: cable.*

Clarion Hotel Neptun

*Sankt Annæ Plads 14-20, 1250 Copenhagen K
(33 13 89 00/fax 33 96 20 66/www.choicehotels.dk).*
Rates 1,385kr single; 1,490kr-1,865kr double;
2,170kr suite. **Credit** AmEx, DC, MC, V.
Map p312 N16.

Located just north of Nyhavn and close to
Amalienborg Slot (the Queen's gaff), the Neptun is
a classy hotel with an atmosphere of restrained elegance. Among its highlights are superb views from
its roof terrace and the French-provincial style
Gendarmen restaurant, renowned for its Danish
regional specialities and its excellent lunches.
The (pricier) Nordic Light Executive rooms are
'environmentally and allergy tested'. The Neptun
lives up to its well-established reputation for ser-
vice, style and comfort. Affiliated to the Best
Western chain.
Hotel services *Bar. Laundry. Limousine service.
No-smoking floors. Restaurant.* **Room services**
*Iron. Minibar. Room service (7am-10pm). Telephone.
Turndown. TV: cable/pay movies.*

Kong Arthur

*Nørre Søgade 11, 1370 Copenhagen K (33 11
12 12/fax 33 32 61 30/www.kongarthur.dk).*
Rates 1,095kr-1,195kr single; 1,320kr-1,520kr
double; 1,900kr-2,900kr suite. **Credit** AmEx, DC,
MC, V. **Map** p306 L11.

Inaugurated by Christian IX in 1882, the Kong
Arthur stands alone in its class: a charming family-
run hotel that offers quality accommodation at
a competitive price. This beautiful 107-room mansion, filled with antique furniture, is conveniently
located: one side overlooks the lakes, while the
other faces one of Copenhagen's liveliest streets,
Nansensgade, and its hip cafés.
Hotel services *Air-conditioning. Bar. Laundry.
Limousine service. No-smoking floors. Parking (free).
Restaurant.* **Room services** *Iron. Minibar. Room
service (24hrs). Telephone. Turndown. TV: cable.*

Phoenix Copenhagen

*Bredgade 37, 1260 Copenhagen K (33 95 95 00/
fax 33 33 98 33/www.phoenixcopenhagen.dk).*
Rates 1,290kr-1895kr single; 1,650kr-2,495kr double;
3,000kr-6,000kr suite. **Credit** AmEx, DC, MC, V.
Map p308 L16.

Housed in a massive building dating back to 1780,
the Phoenix is one of Copenhagen's classiest and
most extravagant hotels: the flashy foyer has tall
mirrors, a fountain, huge candelabras and paintings.
Its chic location, between Kongens Nytorv and
Amalienborg Slot, means the hotel is surrounded by
some of Copenhagen's hottest modern art galleries
and antique dealers. Favoured by showbiz types and
jet-setters with good taste (as opposed to nouveau-
riche show-offs), the hotel has elegant bedrooms,
decorated 'à la Louis XVI', and the owner, who is
passionate about art, displays only originals on his
walls. The hotel is appropriately named since it has
closed and reopened three times, arising from its
ashes most recently in 1991, when it was entirely
refurbished under the present management.

Hotel services *Air-conditioning. Babysitting. Bar.
Business services. Concierge. Cooking facilities.
Garden. Laundry. Limousine service. No-smoking
rooms. Parking. Restaurant.* **Room services**
*Dataport. Iron. Minibar. Room service (24hrs).
Telephone. TV: pay movies/satellite.*

Moderate (750kr-1,300kr)

Tivoli & around

Alexandra

*HC Andersens Boulevard 8, 1553 Copenhagen V (33
74 44 44/fax 33 74 44 88/www.hotel-alexandra.dk).*
Rates 995kr-1,095kr single; 1,195kr-1,295kr double.
Credit AmEx, DC, MC, V. **Map** p310 O11.

The Alexandra is an above average three-star
hotel, well located close to Rådhuspladsen. Its eco-
friendly policies have earned the hotel a Green Key
Award for environmental achievement, which
means, among other things, that you'll find only
organic products on the breakfast buffet. Many of
the bedrooms are of a good size, and all are decorated in a light, bright modern style. The location is
very convenient for most sights and attractions.
Hotel services *Bar. Beauty salon. Laundry.
No-smoking floor. Parking. Restaurant.*
Room services *Dataport. Iron. Room service (3-
9pm). Telephone. Turndown. TV: cable/pay movies.*

Hotel du Nord

*Colbjørnsengade 14, 1652 Copenhagen K (33 31 77
50/fax 33 31 33 99/reservations@hoteldunord.dk).*
Rates 700kr-990kr single; 990kr-1,200kr double.
Credit AmEx, DC, MC, V. **Map** p310 P10.

This formerly economy-class hotel was transformed
by a major renovation in spring 2000. It's located in
the middle of the red light district (a five-minute
walk to Central Station), the most popular neighbourhood for Copenhagen hotels. The rooms are
agreeably decorated in light colours, and the hotel
is notable for its friendly service. Ask for a room
overlooking the courtyard at the back if you want
to avoid the traffic noise.
Hotel services *Disabled: adapted rooms. Laundry.
No-smoking floor.* **Room services** *Iron. Telephone.
TV: cable/pay movies.*

Nyhavn & around

Copenhagen Strand

*Havnegade 37, 1058 Copenhagen K (33 48 99 00/
fax 33 48 99 01/www.copenhagenstrand.dk).*
Rates 995kr-1,095kr single; 1,195kr-1,295kr double.
Credit AmEx, DC, MC, V. **Map** p312 N17.

One of Copenhagen's newest posh hotels, the
Copenhagen Strand is located overlooking the water
towards Christianshavn, just south of Nyhavn. Most
of the city's attractions are within easy walking distance, and boats to Sweden, and the only direct bus
to the airport, stop just outside. All rooms are decorated in a rustic maritime style, the lounge is warm
and cosy and the TV room has an open fireplace.

Hotel services *Bar. Laundry. Limousine service. No-smoking floor.* **Room services** *Iron. Minibar. Room service (7am-10am). Telephone. Turndown. TV: cable/pay movies.*

Rosenborg & around

Hotel Christian IV

Dronningens Tværgade 45, 1302 Copenhagen K (33 32 10 44/fax 33 32 07 06/www.christianivhotel copenhagen.dk). **Rates** 1,020kr single; 1,220kr double. **Credit** AmEx, DC, MC, V. **Map** p307 L15.
A small, cosy and peaceful 42-bedroom hotel by Kongens Have (the King's Garden; *see p98*), the Christian IV is the only hotel in this central residential area. It also stands out for a charm and intimacy that is rare among Copenhagen's three-star hotels, and for the modern Danish designer furniture with which all rooms are equipped. The location is a chic one for a hotel in this category – Rosenborg Slot (*see p100*), built by the eponymous Danish king, is at the end of the street, while the royal residence of Amalienborg Slot (*see p88*) is the same distance in the opposite direction.
Hotel services *No-smoking rooms.*
Room services *Iron. Telephone. TV: satellite.*

Ibsens

Vendersgade 23, 1363 Copenhagen K (33 13 19 13/ fax 33 13 19 16/www.ibsenshotel.dk). **Rates** 845kr-945kr single; 1,050kr-1,250kr double; 1,900kr suite. **Credit** AmEx, DC, MC, V. **Map** p306 L12.
Ibsens is a lovely three-star hotel with a brand-new reception, breakfast room and bar. It's a romantic place, with flowery curtains and flowers on the balconies of this typical Danish 19th-century building. The location (near Nørreport station) is about as central as you can get in Copenhagen (only the uninformed think the area around Tivoli is the centre).
Hotel services *Laundry (self-service). No-smoking floor.* **Room services** *Iron. Minibar. Telephone. TV: cable.*

Cheap (under 750kr)

The **Cab-Inn** chain has two hotels in the city. Neither is especially well located (though only a 10 to 15-minute walk from the centre), and the 'cabin' style rooms are basic, but they are useful standbys. They are: **Cab-Inn Scandinavia** (Vodroffsvej 55, Frederiksberg, 35 36 11 11, www.dkhotellist.dk/cab-inn); **Cab-Inn Copenhagen** (Danasvej 32-34, 33 21 04 00). A two-bed room is 595kr.

Tivoli & around

Hotel Centrum

Helgolandsgade 14, 1653 Copenhagen K (33 31 31 11/fax 33 32 51/www.centrumhotel.dk). **Rates** 550kr-680kr single; 700kr-920kr double. **Credit** AmEx, DC, MC, V. **Map** p310 P10.

Hotel Centrum is one of the few two-star hotels in Copenhagen, with very basic rooms. It's safe and clean enough, though, and the staff are very welcoming. Located in the hotel-dense area just west of Central Station, it has a connecting Thai restaurant that serves good, cheap food. Note that not every room has its own TV, and that only 50 of the 79 rooms are en suite.
Hotel services *Bar. Restaurant.* **Room services** *Iron. Telephone. TV: cable.*

Hotel Selandia

Helgolandsgade 12, 1653 Copenhagen K (33 31 46 10/fax 31 31 46 09/www.hotel-selandia.dk). **Rates** 450kr-975kr single; 540kr-1,150kr double. **Credit** AmEx, DC, MC, V. **Map** p310 P10.
The Selandia is located just behind Central Station, at the eastern edge of lively Vesterbro, and is very popular due to its cheap rates and friendly service. The rooms are simple and functional.
Hotel services *Babysitting. Business services.* **Room services** *Telephone. TV: cable.*

Rosenborg & around

Hotel Jørgensen

Rømersgade 11, 1362 Copenhagen K (33 13 81 86/ fax 33 15 51 05/www.hoteljoergensen.dk). **Rates** 115kr dorm; 425kr-525kr single; 525kr-650kr double. **Credit** DC, MC, V. **Map** p306 L12.
The Jørgensen has a few tiny double and single rooms with their own toilet/bath, and a clean but uncharming dormitory in the basement. The main points here are the low rates and the very convenient location, near Nørreport Station, close to the centre, and with plenty of groovy cafés and bars nearby.
Hotel services *Bar. Restaurant.* **Room services** *Iron. Telephone. TV: cable.*

Vesterbro & Frederiksberg

Family Hotel Valberg

53 Sønder Boulevard, 1720 Copenhagen V (33 25 25 19/fax 33 25 25 83/www.valberg.dk). Bus 10. **Rates** 450kr-600kr single; 600kr-800kr double. **Credit** AmEx, DC, MC, V. **Map** p111 S8.
A young Icelandic couple started up this hotel (on the top floor of a century-old building) in 1998, pitching the place somewhere between a *pension*, a sleep-in and a hotel. The atmosphere is cool and cosy with a nice café and a fine views from the fifth floor. Some rooms are en suite, and a number have good views over the rooftops. A good place for visitors of all ages.
Hotel services *Laundry (self-service).*
Room services *Iron. Telephone. TV.*

Hotel Euroglobe

Niels Ebbesens Vej 20, 1911 Frederiksberg C (33 79 79 54/fax 33 79 79 54/www.euroglobe.dk). **Rates** 350kr single; 475kr double; 575kr triple; 675kr quad. **Credit** AmEx, DC, MC, V. **Map** p111 N8.

This cheery 48-room hotel has the air of a youth hostel and some of the cheapest rooms in town. All facilities are shared, including a kitchen. Located in an agreeable residential area in Frederiksberg, west of the centre, it's only a five-minute walk from the lakes. **Hotel services** *Babysitting. Cooking facilities. Parking (free). Payphone.* **Room services** *Iron.*

Hotel Sct Thomas
Frederiksberg Allé 7, 1621 Copenhagen V (33 21 64 64/fax 33 25 64 60/www.hotelsctthomas.dk). **Rates** 295kr-525kr single; 475kr-725kr double. **Credit** V. **Map** p111 P7.
This small family hotel is one of our favourites: low rates, a welcoming atmosphere and a great location. The services offered are very limited, and there are only 26 rooms, but Frederiksberg Allé is one of the most sought-after residential areas in town. Tivoli and Rådhuspladsen are a ten-minute walk away, and Vesterbro's trendy cafés are close by. For those looking for a sightseeing tour, the manager told us he would gladly take guests around the city on the back of his bicycle.
Hotel services *Garden. No-smoking floor. Parking. Payphone. TV room: cable.* **Room services** *Iron.*

Further afield

Hotel Copenhagen
Egilsgade 33, 2300 Copenhagen S (32 96 27 27/fax 32 96 83 08/www.hotelcopenhagen.dk). **Rates** 440kr single; 540kr double; 640kr-740kr family room; 980kr-1,500kr suite. **No credit cards**.
This unremarkable hotel is only of note for its low prices. It's located in a part of Amager (south-east of the city centre) that is becoming increasingly appealing, with the art galleries of Njalsgade 19 and the various developments of Islands Brygge. Rådhuspladsen is about 15 minutes' walk away. **Hotel services** *Bar. Disabled: adapted rooms. Parking. TV room: cable.* **Room services** *TV.*

Hostels

Copenhagen has two hostels that are part of the International Youth Hostel Association, but both are four kilometres (2.5 miles) from the city centre. This is where you'll find the real backpacker atmosphere. Prices start from around 90kr per person per night without breakfast. Sleep-ins are essentially the same as hostels, but aren't part of an international organisation. Note that **Use It** (Rådhusstræde 13, 33 73 06 49, www.ui.dk) can provide help and information to young travellers on a budget.

Vesterbro & Frederiksberg

City Public Hostel
Absalonsgade 8, 1658 Copenhagen V (33 31 20 70/fax 33 23 51 75). **Rates** from 140kr per person. **No credit cards**. **Map** p111 Q9.

The eco-friendly **Sleep-In Green**.

A small hostel that provides no more than the bare essentials, but is the most centrally located, being in the Vesterbro hotel district, west of Central Station. Note that this hostel is closed from September to April.

Løven
Vesterbrogade 30, 3, 1620 Copenhagen V (21 80 67 20/www.loeven.dk). Bus 6. **Rates** 250kr-350kr single; 350kr-450kr double; 170kr 3-6 bed room. **No credit cards**. **Map** p310 P10.
Løven offers basic but clean hostel-style accommodation on busy Vesterbrogade, a five-minute walk from Tivoli. There are three- to six-person dorms, but also single and double rooms. Shower and toilets are shared, and guests can make use of the kitchen. Buy breakfast for 40kr, or make it yourself. A good alternative to some of the less conveniently located hostels.

Sleep-In Heaven
Peter Bangs Vej 30, 2000 Frederiksberg (38 10 44 45). Bus 1. **No credit cards**. **Map** p110 N1.
Only under-35s are allowed at this friendly sleep-in, not far from Frederiksberg Have. The city centre and the buzzing area of Nørrebro, which attract plenty of young people and arty types, are a short bus ride away. Breakfast is not included in the price.

Nørrebro & Østerbro

Sleep-In
Blegdamsvej 132A, 2100 Copenhagen Ø (35 26 50 59/fax 35 43 50 58). Bus 14, 16. **Rates** 90kr per person. **No credit cards**. **Map** p121 F12.
This sleep-in is near to lively Fælledparken, 15 minutes from the city centre, but within the city boundaries and with plenty of bus connections. Usually very crowded, and the dormitories are huge. Breakfast is not included in the rate. Note that this hostel is closed from September to June.

Sleep-In Green
Ravnsborggade 18, 2200 Copenhagen N (35 37 77 77/fax 35 35 56 40). Bus 4E, 5, 16, 350S. **Rates** 85kr per person. **No credit cards**. **Map** p306 J10.

The only ecologically-minded sleep-in: start the day with an organic breakfast (30kr). Located in a very lively street with plenty of antiques shops, and Nørrebro's lively bar/café life just round the corner.

Further afield

Belægningen/Advedørelejren
Avedøre Tværvej 10, 2650 Hvidovre (36 77 90 84/ fax 36 77 95 87/belaegningen@hvidovre.dk). **Train to Avedøre/650S bus.** **Rates** 100kr per person. **Credit** MC, V.
This former military camp houses both a sleep-in and the 'Danish Hollywood', the studios of Zentropa film (which produced all the Dogme movies, as well as Lars von Trier's *Dancer in the Dark*). It boasts barbeque and Internet facilities and offers easy access to bus or trains (it's a 25-minute journey into the centre of town). Breakfast is not included in the price.

Copenhagen Amager DanHostel
Vejlands Allé 200, 2300 Copenhagen S (32 52 29 08/fax 32 52 27 08). **Rates** 90kr dorm; 240kr double. **No credit cards.**
A modern hostel on the island of Amager, south-east of the centre, near the future town of Ørestad currently being built between the airport and the centre of Copenhagen. It's just 15 minutes by bus from the city centre and web facilities. A Youth Hostel membership card is required to stay here, but these can be purchased at the hostel for 160kr.

Copenhagen Bellahøj DanHostel
Herbergvejen 8, 2700 Brønshøj (38 28 97 15/fax 38 89 02 10). Bus 2, 11. **Rates** 90kr dorm; 240kr double. **No credit cards.**
Located on the edge of the Copenhagen suburbs, but well connected to the centre (a 20-minute bus ride away). Phone, fax and web facilities. You need a Youth Hostel membership card to stay here, but these can be purchased from the hostel for 160kr. Note: closed mid January until the end of February.

Bed & breakfast

B&Bs are not numerous in Copenhagen, but **Bed & Breakfast in Denmark** can help you find a congenial home in which to lay your head. Prices are usually 200kr-350kr for a single room, 300kr-400kr for a double, with extra beds about 120kr and breakfast at 25kr-45kr.

Bed & Breakfast in Denmark
Postbox 53, 2900 Hellerup (39 61 04 05/fax 39 61 05 25/www.bbdk.dk).

Rosita Ternstrøm
Gammeltoftsgade 8, 1355 Copenhagen K (33 15 90 93). **Rates** 350kr per room. **No credit cards.** **Map** p306 J12.
Rosita Ternstrøm is the hostess and a colourful character: she will probably tell you about her daughter making films in Hollywood and introduce you to

Emma and Sascha, her two Cuban dogs. The bedrooms are brightly decorated, and the location (close to the Botanisk Have near Nørreport Station) is handy. Breakfast is not included in the price.

Camping

Denmark's unreliable climate means that camping is always a risky option. Danes are good at comfort though, and campsites are well kept and have plenty of facilities.

Bellahøj Camping
Hvidkildevej 66, 2400 Copenhagen NV (38 10 11 50/ fax 38 10 13 32). Train to Fuglebakken/11 bus. **Rates** phone for details. **No credit cards.**
A cheap campsite with few services, but the closest to the centre (6km/3.5 miles to the north-west). There are cabins for two people at 200kr per night.

Camping Charlottenlund Fort
Strandvejen 144B, 2920 Charlottenlund (39 62 36 88/fax 39 61 08 16/http://home6.inet.tele.dk/ camping/uk/uk.html). Train to Charlottenlund/6 bus. **Rates** 65kr adults; 25kr children. **No credit cards.**
The best campsite around Copenhagen, located 8km (5 miles) north of the centre of town around a disused military sea-front fort. The beach is 50 metres away, and, on the other side of Strandvejen, starts the most expensive residential area in Denmark. The pleasant, upmarket suburb of Hellerup is a ten-minute walk away, while the city centre is accessible by bus 6 (every 20 minutes) or train in under half an hour. If the sun is shining, this is the area everybody in Copenhagen wants to go to: the east coast beaches start here.

Apartments

Citilet Apartments
Fortunstræde 4, 1065 Copenhagen K (33 25 21 29/fax 33 91 30 77/www.citilet.dk). **Rates** 950kr-2,100kr double. **Credit** AmEx, DC, MC, V. **Map** p311 N14.
The only organisation for short-stay serviced apartments in Copenhagen offers superb quality accommodation at excellent prices. All flats (from 30 to 160 sq m) are fully furnished with luxury bathrooms, fine furniture and kitchens. All the 26 Citilet flats are in the centre of town. Breakfast and a beer are included in the price, and the telephone charges are much lower than in regular hotels. Each hotel-apartment is comparable to suites in hotels (if not better) for the price of a room in a 3-4-star hotel.

Hay 4 You
Vimmelskaftet 49, 1, 1161 Copenhagen K (33 33 08 05/fax 33 32 08 04/www.scanhomes.com). **Rates** 300kr-500kr. **Credit** MC, V. **Map** p311 N13.
With a three-night minimum stay, Hay 4 You is a booking service for longer-term (usually at least one month) rental of apartments in Copenhagen. The flats all belong to temporarily absent residents, and are fully furnished.

Sightseeing

Sightseeing

A panoply of attractions with a minimum of legwork.

Although the medieval centre of Copenhagen is a mere four kilometres (one and a half miles) square, contained within its old ramparts and lake defences are more (and more varied) attractions than in many far larger European cities. Whether you are looking for museums, galleries, fine architecture, blissful café squares, waterfront walks, parks or, simply, a good time, you'll find it all in Copenhagen, and all a short walk away in this most accessible of cities.

COPENHAGEN CARD

If you're planning on doing a lot of sightseeing, then it may well save you money to invest in a **Copenhagen Card**. The cards (valid for 24, 48 or 72 hours) offer free travel by public transport and free entry into more than 60 museums and attractions in the greater Copenhagen area, as well as discounts on car hire, ferries to Sweden and admission to some attractions in Sweden.

Prices for 2001 are – 24hrs: 175kr; 75kr children (10-15s) – 48hrs: 295kr; 145kr children – 72hrs: 395kr; 195kr children. The cards are available from travel agents, hotels, main railway stations and the **Wonderful Copenhagen** office on Bernstorffsgade (*see page 292*). Call 33 25 74 00 for information.

However, you will have to do a fair amount of sightseeing to get your money back, and bear in mind that the majority of Copenhagen's

Ways to see the city

By bike

City Safari Bike Tours
33 23 94 90/www.citysafari.dk.
From Reventlowsgade, by Central Station.
Duration 2hrs. **Available** *June-Aug* 10am, 1pm daily. *Sept-May* by appointment.
Price 150kr. **No credit cards**.
A range of bike tours, including a Danish design tour, a night tour and a historical tour.

By boat

Kajak-Ole
40 50 40 06/www.kajakole.dk. **From** Gammel Strand. **Duration** 1.5-3hrs. **Available** *May-Sept*. **Price** 165kr. **No credit cards**.
Excellent guided kayak tours, including a stop at a café in Christianshavn.

DFDS Canal Tours
33 42 33 20/www.canal-tours.dk.
From Nyhavn. **Duration** 50mins. **Available** *1 Apr-22 June, 28 Aug-22 Oct* 10am-5pm half-hourly daily. *23 June-27 Aug* 10am-7.30pm half-hourly. **Price** 50kr. **No credit cards**.
DFDS also runs a hop-on, hop-off water bus.

Netto-Bådene
32 54 41 02/38 87 21 33/www.netto-baadene.dk. **From** Holmens Kirke.
Duration 1hr. **Available** *Apr-Oct* 10am-7.30pm 2-5 times per hour daily. **Price** 20kr; 10kr concessions. **No credit cards**.

By bus

Open-top yellow-and-pink tour buses run frequent hour-long tours from Rådhuspladsen daily. Call 32 66 00 00 or 32 54 06 06.

Copenhagen Excursions
32 54 06 06/www.copenhagen-excursions.dk.
A range of bus tours of Copenhagen and elsewhere in Denmark. Phone for details.

By foot

If you want a personal authorised guide, contact **Guide Danmark** (33 11 33 10/ www.guides.dk).

Christiania Tours
32 57 96 70/www.christiania.org.
From main entrance, Princessegade.
Duration 1.5hrs. **Available** *1 May-19 June, 1 Sept-31 Oct* 3pm Sat, Sun. *20 June-31 July* 3pm daily. **Price** phone for details.
No credit cards.
Get the inside story on the Free State.

Jazz Guides
35 26 65 15/www.jazzguides.dk.
A variety of tours of the city's jazz venues.

Wonderful Copenhagen Guided Tours
32 97 14 40/www.woco.dk. **From** Tourist Bureau, Bernstorffsgade 1. **Duration** 2hrs.
Available *May-Sept* 10.30am Mon-Sat.
Price 50kr. **No credit cards**.

The best of Copenhagen

The following list is our pick of the city's best sights, attractions, museums, galleries and historic buildings.

Amusements

Bakken p270 – amusement park.
Museum Erotica p68 – naughty but nice.
Tivoli p57 – legendary pleasure gardens.
Zoologisk Have p113 – zoo in Frederiksberg.

Applied arts & design

Dansk Design Center p62 – contemporary Danish design.
CL Davids Samling p99 – ancient Islamic art.
Kunstindustrimuseet p92 – decorative and applied arts.

Art

See also chapter **Galleries**.
Arken p124 – modern art museum.
Bakkehus Museet p115 – 19th-century literary and artistic relics.
Den Hirschsprungske Samling p95 – 19th-century Danish paintings and sculpture.
Den Kongelige Afstøbningssamlingen p89 – 4,000 years of international sculpture.
Lousiana p272 – world-class modern art.
Ny Carlsberg Glyptotek p64 – ancient Mediterranean and 18th- and 19th-century sculpture and painting.
Statens Museum For Kunst p98 – the Danish national gallery.
Thorvaldsens Museum p81 – Denmark's finest sculptor.

Churches & cemeteries

Alexander Newsky Kirke p91 – Russia comes to Copenhagen.
Assistens Kirkegård p120 – last resting place of many famous Danes.
Frederikskirken (Marmorkirken) p88 – the city's grandest church.
Grundtvigs Kirke p122. – striking 20th-century church.
Vor Frelsers Kirke p103 – Christianshavn's spiralling spire.
Vor Frue Kirke p73 – Copenhagen's modest cathedral, with Thorvaldsen sculptures inside.

Gardens & parks

Biblotekshaven p86 – exquisite small garden by the Royal Library.
Botanisk Have p97 – botanical garden.
Frederiksberg Have p113 – large, rambling park in Frederiksberg.
Kongens Have p98 – park by Rosenborg Slot.

History & warfare

Amalienborg Museum p88 – historic royal living rooms.
Frihedsmuseet p93 – history of the Danish resistance.
Frilandsmuseet p123 – open-air museum of domestic architecture.
Københavns Bymuseet & Søren Kierkegaard Samlingen p108 – Copenhagen city museum & small Kierkegaard collection.
Nationalmuseet p62 – Viking and Renaissance riches.
Nyboders Mindestuer p99 – picturesque old navy cottages.
Orlogsmuseet p104 – Denmark's maritime history and model ships.
Tøjhusmuseet p85 – arms and armour.

Miscellaneous

Carlsberg Museum & Visitors Center p117 – beer, beer and more beer.
Musikhistorisk Museum og Carl Claudius' Samling p98 – musical history, instruments and curios.
Tobacco Museum p70 – quirky history of the weed.

Palaces & historic buildings

Amalienborg Slot p88 – Queen Margrethe II's appropriately majestic home.
Børsen p82 – Christian IV's charming stock exchange with its dragon-tail spire.
Christiansborg Slot p84 – the monumental palace/parliament on Slotsholmen.
Kastellet p93 – remains of fortifications.
Det Kongelige Bibliotek & the Black Diamond p86 – the Royal Library and modern extension.
Rådhuset p65 – the Town Hall.
Rosenborg Slot p100 – Christian IV's Renaissance palace.
Ruinere Under Christiansborg p84 – the ruins of Bishop Absalon's castle.
Rundetårn p69 – art within and views from on top of Christian IV's unique Round Tower.

Natural history & science

Danmarks Akvarium p122 – aquarium, north of the city.
Experimentarium p122 – innovative hands-on science museum.
Medicinsk-Historisk Museum p92 – history of medicine, with gruesome exhibits.
Tycho Brahe Planetarium p108 – explore the galaxy and watch an Imax film.
Zoologisk Museum p121 – stuffed animals.

attractions are within easy walking distance of the centre, so taking a bus or train is rarely necessary. Also, be aware that many museums offer free entry on Wednesdays (*see page 55* **Something for nothing**).

COPENHAGEN IN 48 HOURS

If you are only in Copenhagen for a couple of days and want to cram in as much of the city as possible, here is our suggestion for an intensive 48 hours. Most of this can be accomplished easily on foot. For details of the museums and sights described, see the index.

Day 1: Rosenborg & Frederiksstaden

Begin at **Kongens Nytorv**, the city's grandest square, fronted by **Det Kongelige Teater** (the Royal Theatre), the **French Embassy** and **Magasin du Nord**, Scandinavia's largest department store. With the famous **Hotel d'Angleterre** behind you, cross over to the historic canal of **Nyhavn**, once home of Hans Christian Andersen.

Walk down the north side of the canal (which will be on your left), past **Charlottenborg**, a former royal palace, now an art space with temporary exhibitions, on the opposite side of the canal. You will pass Nyhavn's bustling (or not, depending on the weather) cafés, restaurants and bars, as well as the ships from the Nationalmuseet's collection. At the end of the canal turn left and walk north along the harbour front until you come to the waterside **Amaliehaven** gardens.

If you head inland from here into grand Amalienborg Slotplads, you come to the residence of Denmark's much-loved queen, Margrethe II, **Amalienborg Slot**. There is a small museum here, which recreates the royal chambers of previous monarchs.

Back on the harbour front, walking north, you come to a replica of Michelangelo's *David*, standing outside the **Det Kongelige Afstøbningssamlingen** (the Royal Cast Collection; a kind of Madame Tussaud's of the history of sculpture). A few minutes further on is the stunning **Gefion Springvandet** (Gefion Fountain). Walk inland here, past the flint English church, **St Alban's Church**, and **Frihedsmuseet** (the Museum of the Danish Resistance), and enter **Kastellet**, former home of the Danish army. Climb the ramparts to the east and walk north. At the north-east corner of the fortress you will be able to see **Den Lille Havfrue** (the Little Mermaid) reclining on rocks beside the water.

Head back across Kastellet and walk south along Bredgade. On your left you soon pass the elegant **Kunstindustriemuseet** (the Museum of Decorative and Applied Art), the **Medicinsk-**

Historisk Museum (Medical History Museum) and **Skt Ansgars Kirke**, the Roman Catholic church. A little further up are the golden minarets of the Russian church, **Alexander Newsky Kirke**. Turn right at Frederiksgade and you arrive at Copenhagen's most impressive church, **Frederikskirken** (better known as **Marmorkirken**, the Marble Church).

Continue west from Marmorkirken and you come to the junction with Store Kongensgade; turn left. Take the first right on to Dronningens Tværgade, then at the end, cross over Kronprinsessegade and enter **Kongens Have** (the King's Gardens), the gardens surrounding **Rosenborg Slot**. Walk across the gardens, via the palace (home to the crown jewels), and exit at the northern gate. Turn right and walk over the busy crossroads. Here, in Øster Anlæg park, is **Statens Museum For Kunst**, Denmark's impressive national gallery.

Beyond Statens Museum, but still within the park, is another excellent art museum, **Den Hirschsprungske Samling** (the Hirschsprung Collection), containing works from Denmark's so-called Golden Age (the early 19th century). Opposite Statens Museum is the **Geologisk Museum** (Geological Museum), standing in one corner of the **Botanisk Have** (Botanical Garden), with its 19th-century greenhouses.

Day 2: Strøget, Slotsholmen, Tivoli & Christianshavn

Start in Kongens Nytorv again, this time facing the Hotel d'Angleterre. The pedestrianised street to the left of the hotel is **Strøget**, the backbone of Copenhagen and its main shopping area. Walk down what is Strøget's 'posh' end, past the flagship stores of **Bang & Olufsen** (on your left) and **Bodum** (right) and the **Guinness**

World Records Museum (right). Turn left just before the electronics store Fona 2000, and you come to Nikolaj Plads and **Skt Nikolaj Kirke** (now an art gallery). Back on Strøget, walk past **Illum** department store on your right, and you soon arrive at **Amagertorv**, and the elegant **Storkespringvandet** (Stork Fountain). The square is fronted by two great cafés, Europa and Norden, as well as some of the finest shops in the city: the silversmith **Georg Jensen**, **Royal Copenhagen Porcelain**, **Holmegaard** glassware and the design temple, **Illums Bolighus**. Opposite, is the tobacconist **WØ Larsen**, dating from 1864, with a tobacco museum in the basement.

From Amagertorv, head north along the shopping street Købmagergade (also pedestrianised) past the **Museum Erotica** on your right. After a few minutes the extraordinary **Rundetårn** observatory tower looms on your right, built by Christian IV and abutting **Trinitatiskirke**. Climb the tower for superb views over medieval Copenhagen. Take Store Kannikestræde (opposite the tower's entrance) and walk through what is sometimes known as Copenhagen's 'Latin Quarter', where the oldest part of the city's university is located. At the end of the street you come to Vor Frue Plads, a large cobbled square with, on the right, the red brick university buildings, and in its centre to your left, **Vor Frue Kirke**, Copenhagen's relatively modest neo-classical cathedral. Turn left down Nørregade and walk down to **Gammeltorv** and **Nytorv**, two ancient squares bisected by Strøget at its western end. Here you'll find another fine neo-classical building, **Domhuset**, the city court.

The last leg of Strøget, Frederiksberggade, brings you to **Rådhuspladsen** and **Rådhuset** (the Town Hall). Cross the square and busy HC Andersens Boulevard and a few hundred metres along Vesterbrogade on the left is the entrance to **Tivoli**, the world-famous amusement park. If you return to HC Andersens Boulevard and head south you pass the **Dansk Design Center**, on the left, and, further down on the right, the **Ny Carlsberg Glyptotek**, one of the city's finest art collections, just across Tietgensgade to the south of Tivoli. From here is a short hop across HC Andersens Boulevard, along Ny Vestergade to the former royal palace which now houses **Nationalmuseet** (the National Museum), with its breathtaking Viking and Renaissance treasures.

The rear of Nationalmuseet overlooks Marmorbroen (the Marble Bridge) to **Slotsholmen**, the island on which the city was founded almost 1,000 years ago. Today, the area features several major attractions: **Christiansborg Slot** (containing the

Danish parliament) and **Kirke** (church); **Tøjhusmuseet** (the Royal Arsenal Museum); the royal stables; **Thorvaldsens Museum** (containing the work of Denmark's greatest sculptor); **Børsen** (the former stock exchange, with its beguiling dragon tails spire); and Copenhagen's most striking modern building, the new extension to the national library, the '**Black Diamond**'.

From here it is a ten-minute walk across Knippelsbro (a bridge linking Slotsholmen with **Christianshavn**), to another of the city's most recognisable landmarks, **Vor Frelsers Kirke**, whose remarkable spiralling copper spire overlooks the **Free State of Christiania**. As fine a place as any to unwind after an intensive weekend in Copenhagen.

Something for nothing

If money is tight, then don't despair. Many of Copenhagen's main attractions don't charge admission, while some of the major museums are free one day a week.

Always free

None of the city's churches or parks charge entrance fees.
Assistens Kirkegård p120.
Black Diamond p86.
Carlsberg Museum & Visitor Center p117.
Christiania p105.
Dansk Skolemuseum p74.
CL Davids Samling p99.
Folketinget p83.
Frihedsmuseet p93.
Geologisk Museum p97.
Kastellet p93.
Livjægermuseet p94.
Tobacco Museum p70.

Free on Wednesday

Den Hirschsprungske Samling p95.
Nationalmuseet p62.
Ny Carlsberg Glyptotek p64.
Post & Tele Museum p68.
Statens Museum For Kunst p98.
Thorvaldsens Museum p81.

Free on Friday

Københavns Bymuseet & Søren Kierkegaard Samlingen p108.

Free on Sunday

Ny Carlsberg Glyptotek p64.

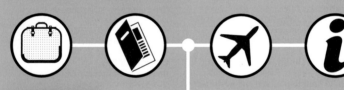

Tivoli & Around

The Danes' beloved pleasure garden and the bustling town hall square.

Tivoli

Tivoli (*listings page 61*) is the jewel of Copenhagen's family attractions, Denmark's biggest tourist draw and a must for any visitor to the city. A few years ago the American entertainment giant Disney began to make rumblings about buying the venerable pleasure park (founded in 1843) in the centre of Copenhagen. There was an outcry among the public, press and in parliament, just as there was when Michael Jackson was also rumoured to be buying the park after falling in love with it during a concert tour in the early '90s. In fact, there was an outcry whenever there were rumours that owners Carlsberg wanted to sell up to anyone, which made it all the more surprising when, in June 2000, the brewery sold its 43.4 per cent stake in the park to the Scandinavian Tobacco Company (the rest remains with a Danish bank and small investors). For Danes, Tivoli is an oasis of comforting constancy in a cynical, fast-changing world, and the sale generated endless column inches in the newspapers.

Tivoli holds an almost mystical place in the hearts of Danes; it's as if each and every one of them is umbilically linked to the place, and they never quite shrug off the childhood urge to make the pilgrimage each May when the park opens (the season lasts from May to September, with a special Christmas Market in December). As the Vikings yearned for Valhalla, so too do their modern-day ancestors dream of the ice-cream and candy floss innocence of this historic amusement park. Tivoli is Denmark's number one tourist attraction and an incredible 4.5 million visitors pass through the gates each summer in search of an Elysian escape – not bad for a country whose population is only just over five million. In all, over 300 million people have visited in a century and a half.

So what's so special about this relatively small 80,000-square metre (20-acre) plot of land, sandwiched between Central Station and Rådhuspladsen? By day, Tivoli is undoubtedly charming, with its picturesque lake, thrilling (though not that thrilling) rides, classy restaurants and riotous flower beds. It possesses a unique atmosphere – part traditional beer garden, part Victorian pleasure

park, part, whisper it, Disneyland. But it isn't really until night falls, when the 100,000 specially-made soft-glow light bulbs and over a million standard bulbs are switched on, and the scenery becomes a kaleidoscope of diffused colour (there is no neon here, and the place is a mecca for lighting technicians from all over the world), that the magical transformation from amusement park to dreamland takes place. Passers-by can only glimpse through the trees the wondrous world within and hear the distant squeal from the rollercoasters, as Tivoli enters its nightly childhood Twilight Zone. Something genuinely peculiar happens when night falls; somehow the place seems to expand exponentially inside.

The main entrance to **Tivoli**.

Det Gyldne Tårn – here comes dinner.

A tour of Tivoli

There are three entrances to Tivoli, but by
far the grandest is the main gate (on
Vesterbrogade), a Renaissance-inspired
confection decorated with Corinthian columns
and a dome, dating from 1889. On the right as
you enter is a statue to the garden's architect
George Carstensen. In front of you, beside the
extraordinary Moorish façade of **Restaurant
Nimb** (breathtaking at night) is a remarkable
perspex fountain, with bubbling tubes, rather
like a gigantic lava lamp. It was designed by
the Nobel Prize-winning Danish physicist
Niels Bohr (*see page 74* **Great Danes: Niels
Bohr**). On your left is the **Peacock Theatre**,
while before you is **Plænen** (the Lawn; *see
page 232*), the open-air concert venue. Beyond
that is the 1956 **Tivolis Koncertsal** (*see page
222*), a pastel orgy in wood.

There are 29 rides to choose from in Tivoli,
from tame roundabouts decorated with
winsome HC Andersen characters, to the mad
exhilaration of **Det Gyldne Tårn** (the Golden
Tower) vertical drop. The tower was likened
by one sniffy critic to a high tension pylon,
but few rides in the world can unleash the
butterflies with quite the force of this terrifying
63-metre (207-feet) vertical drop. At night, you
can see Sweden twinkling in the distance from
the top. Predictably, the tower, which, like
everything in this corner of Tivoli, is designed
in a faux Muslim style, has prompted
allegations of Disneyfication from the older
generation of Tivoleans. They would much
rather that time had stood still with the far
more tepid rollercoaster, constructed in 1914
and still running.

All the traditional fun of the fair is here too,
including shooting alleys, electronic arcade
games, a hall of mirrors, bumper cars, a test-
your-strength machine, an execrable chamber
of horrors, the deeply surreal HC Andersen
fairytale ride, and Det Muntre Kokken (the
Crazy Kitchen), where you can vent pent-up
frustration by hurling tennis balls at crockery
targets. The hot air balloon Ferris wheel,
dating from 1943, is a traditional focus for
courting couples.

Many visitors, particularly the elderly who
flock here in their thousands, come simply to
enjoy the flora. Tivoli has hundreds of trees
(predominantly lime, chestnut, weeping willow
and elm) and many more flowers within its
perimeter fence. The flowers help keep the park
visually fresh throughout the season – if you
visit in May the tulips will be out, then come
the roses, lilacs and laburnum in summer, and,
by the time the park closes for winter, the
chrysanthemums are in bloom.

Slightly contrary to its fairytale image, Tivoli has its own nightclub, open Thursday to Saturday. Although it can hardly be said to push the envelope of contemporary club culture, **Mantra Night-club** is still fun for teens, and, for many Danes, it's their first taste of clubbing.

In 1994, a new tradition was inaugurated at Tivoli: the **Christmas Market**. The market has since become a fixture on Copenhagen's calendar, with hundreds of thousands of visitors a year braving the often sub-zero temperatures. Though many of the rides don't run at this time of year, there are cabarets, shows and concerts, and many of Tivoli's food outlets serve traditional roast pork, rice pudding and *æbleskiver* (a kind of mini doughnut), all washed down with *glögg* (mulled red wine). The gardens also play host to a large market, selling decorations and gifts, and Father and Mother Christmas administer seasonal cheer.

Performance venues

Tivoli is a collage of architectural styles, from Moorish palaces to Chinese towers, with just about everything else in between. The oldest building in the park is the remarkable outdoor Chinese-style **Peacock Theatre**, designed by Vilhelm Dahlerup (also responsible for Det Kongelige Teater; *see page 223 and 225*) in 1874, which stages classical pantomime in

Little China in Tivoli: the **Peacock Theatre**.

the tradition of *commedia dell'arte*. The performances are complex, often hard-to-follow dumb shows, starring Pierrot, Harlequin and Columbine, but are worth a look if only to see this extraordinary theatre, operated by cords and pulleys. The theatre's 'curtain' is a peacock, whose tail feathers fold to reveal the stage. The Oriental theme is echoed elsewhere in the park – a legacy of George Carstensen's peripatetic childhood, which fuelled a love of exotic cultures – in the **Chinese Pagoda**.

Plænen (*see page 232*) is Tivoli's largest venue. Most of its (potentially) 50,000-strong audience stand in the open air before the circus-like stage. This is where returning Danish heroes, like the 2000 Eurovision Song Contest winners the Olsen Brothers, are feted by the crowds, and where Tivoli celebrates big events and hands out its various honours. Performances – musical and otherwise – are twice nightly (international acrobats are a speciality). A recent, popular innovation has been the **Friday Rock Concerts**, which also take place on the Plænen stage. Danish bands (such as Aqua) usually headline, but each year an international star (Phil Collins and Cher have

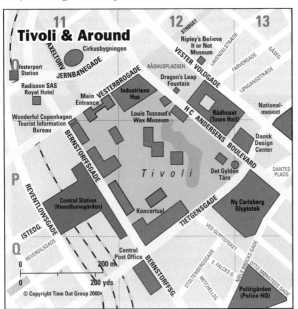

History of a pleasure garden

Like most of Copenhagen's landmarks, Tivoli has royal roots. In 1841, King Christian VIII was much vexed by the burgeoning civil unrest in his country and his increasingly untenable position as absolute monarch, and, so the story goes, he allowed the Danish architect **George Carstensen** to build the park as a distraction: 'When people amuse themselves they forget politics,' the king is reputed to have said.

Carstensen, a self-made publishing magnate and son of a diplomat, was born in Algiers in 1812. Tivoli grew out of a carnival he arranged for his readers in Kongens Nytorv, whose success is thought to have swayed the king in favour of a permanent site for public pleasure. His new park would blend three main ingredients: light, fairytales and music, the king's only condition being that the park would not contain 'anything ignoble and degrading'. The original Tivoli, little changed today since Carstensen's time, was based on similar gardens in Paris and London, and named after the Italian town near Rome known for its fountains.

The park opened on 15 August 1843 and welcomed 16,000 visitors in its first day, Hans Christian Andersen among them. But for Carstensen the park's success was bittersweet. Buoyed by its popularity, he attempted to repeat the formula abroad, but failed abjectly. The board of directors at Tivoli became increasingly concerned about his outlandish and expensive projects until, finally, after one argument too many,

Carstensen left in high dudgeon for America. Legend has it that upon returning years later, the guard at the turnstiles failed to recognise him and he had to pay to get in. Carstensen died a bankrupt, aged 45.

Unlike many other amusement parks, Tivoli is now slap-bang in the centre of the city. But it wasn't always so. When it was built, the park stood in the countryside among the cattle and crops, on land that was once part of the old fortifications of the city, donated by the government. Tivoli lake is today the model of picturesque charm with flower borders, weeping willows, and, at night, illuminated dragonflies, but it used to be part of the city's defensive moat (the continuation of which can can be seen in the lakes of Ørsteds Parken, Botanisk Have and Østre Anlæg park).

In 1944, Tivoli's peace was shattered by the occupying forces of Nazi Germany who were quick to recognise the significance of the park to the Danish people. They used it as a target for retaliatory attacks following the increased activity of the Danish resistance. The main victim was the original Concert Hall. Within a week the resilient Danes had erected a tent in the grounds to replace it. A permanent, new hall (still standing) was built in 1956.

Many of the buildings erected in Tivoli in the post-war era were seen by Denmark's architects as an opportunity to let their creative hair down, and so the park is packed with boisterous structures. Elsewhere many might have been outlawed on grounds of taste, but in Tivoli they somehow seem appropriate.

played here in recent years) is booked as a treat, free of charge to visitors to the park.

Every Wednesday and Saturday at 11.45pm visitors to Tivoli are treated to a firework display, choreographed by the Barfoed family since the park opened. Produced in a special factory, the highlight of the Tivoli firework display is the Blue Chrysanthemum bombshell.

Throughout the summer you can catch parades and performances by the **Tivoli Garden Guard**, a children's marching band, founded in 1844, and made up of a hundred or so local boys aged between nine and 16. The Guard is on holiday for two weeks in mid-July.

The renowned **Tivolis Koncertsal** (see page 222), which seats 1,900, is home to the **Sjælland Symphony Orchestra** and visiting orchestras, ballet companies, ensembles and soloists of world repute also play here. You'll recognise the hall by the row of Danish flags along the front of its roof.

Restaurants

Tivoli has over 25 sit-down eateries, from the exclusive gourmet cuisine of **Divan 1** and **Divan 2** (among the best and most expensive food in the city is served here), and the Moorish splendour of **Restaurant Nimb**, to more humble fast food outlets. **La Crevette** offers often spectacular fresh seafood, while the emphasis is more on traditional Danish dishes at **Restaurant PH**. More basic Danish fare is available at **Færgekoren**, beside the lake, while the more sensible prices at **Grøften** usually ensure that it is the most popular restaurant in the garden. A more recent addition to Tivoli's restaurants is the hilarious **Valhal**, a back to basics (though that doesn't extend to the prices) Viking-style dining hall, which, predictably, is good for steaks. Then, of course, there are the candy floss stalls, hot dog sellers, ice-cream and sweet vendors, not to mention cigar and cigarette kiosks.

Without exception, all of Tivoli's caterers are more expensive than their 'real world' equivalent, sometimes 30 per cent more. Tivoli is not a destination that ranks highly in terms of value for money, and it is a shame that the park seems to take such blatant advantage of its captive audience.

Tivoli

*Vesterbrogade 3 (33 15 10 01/ticket centre 33 15 10 12/www.tivoli.dk). **Open** Apr-late Sept 11am-midnight Mon-Thur, Sun; 11am-1am Fri, Sat. Christmas Market late Nov-Christmas noon-9pm daily. Ticket Centre 10am-8pm daily. **Admission** Late June-Aug 49kr; 25kr concessions. Sept-mid Nov, Jan-Mar 39kr; 20kr concessions. Christmas Market 20kr. **Credit** AmEx, DC, MC, V. **Map** p59/p310 P12.*

Around Tivoli

From Tivoli's gates you can see Arne Jacobsen's world-famous, 22-storey **Radisson SAS Royal Hotel** (see page 43; see also page 38 **Great Danes: Arne Jacobsen**). It dates from 1960, though that's hard to believe, given its uncompromising functionalist lines. Jacobsen designed not only the exterior but the interior too, right down to the cutlery originally used in the roof-top restaurant. (Customer complaints about its impracticality led to its eventual withdrawal, although you can see the cutlery in use by characters in the film *2001: A Space Odyssey*.)

Round the corner on Bernstorffsgade is the **Wonderful Copenhagen Tourist Information Bureau** (with plenty of material in English; see page 292). A little further down the street stands **Hovedbanegården** (**Central Station**), from where you can catch trains to the airport, the rest of the country and beyond. The station, which dates from 1911, has a centre for Interrailers with showers and lockers, as well as several food outlets, a bank, a police station, newspaper and magazine kiosks and a bookshop.

Close by is the **Hotel Plaza** (see page 42), with its wood-panelled **Library Bar** (see page 147), redolent of a London St James's gentlemen's club (though, this being Denmark, women are, of course, also admitted).

Immediately north of the main entrance to Tivoli is Copenhagen's cinema district. Here you'll find several cinemas – the biggest are **Scala**, **Palads** (in a frightful multicoloured building), **Imperial** and **Palladium** – within a few minutes walk (see page 200). Scala is on the top floor of the Scala shopping mall on Axeltorv (the square in front of Tivoli). The mall also has numerous fast food outlets. Behind it is the **Cirkusbygningen**, once one of the world's few permanent circus buildings, now a middlebrow concert and theatre venue. The original building, dating from 1886, burned down in 1914 (although the walls survived). During its reconstruction a frieze, depicting scenes from ancient Rome, was added.

To the south-east of Tivoli is the **Ny Carlsberg Glyptotek** (see page 64). As a member of Sjælland's quartet of world-class art collections (the others are **Arken** – see page 124; **Louisiana** – see page 272; and **Statens Museum for Kunst** – see page 98), the Ny Carlsberg Glyptotek has much to live up to. But with a breathtaking line-up of ancient sculptures, the largest collection of Etruscan art outside of Italy, as well as an exceptional array of more recent Danish and French paintings and sculpture, it more than holds its own in such vaunted company. And with the opening in 1996 of a well-received extension by the Danish architect Henning Larsen (most famous for his Foreign Ministry building in Saudi Arabia), the Glyptotek can now, like its rivals, boast a thoroughly modern, sympathetic space for its impressive collection of French Impressionist paintings.

A little further up HC Andersens Boulevard is the **Dansk Design Center** (*listings below*). Bearing in mind Denmark's rich and renowned design heritage, not to mention Copenhagen's current standing as one of the world's leading design capitals, this 86 million kroner, five-storey education, research, conference and exhibition complex, which opened in January

2000, is a bit of a disappointment. To be fair, its public spaces were never intended to house a comprehensive display of contemporary Danish design, or a museum to past glories, so the DDC's small displays of current products and, admittedly, often innovative temporary exhibitions are unlikely to be placed high on many a casual tourist's must-see list. The centre has a pleasant café and a small shop that sells books (some English) and Danish-designed products.

Dansk Design Center

HC Andersens Boulevard 27 (33 69 33 69/ www.ddc.dk). **Open** 10am-5pm Mon-Fri; 11am-4pm Sat, Sun. **Admission** 30kr; 20kr concessions. **Credit** DC, MC, V. **Map** p59/p311 P13.

Nationalmuseet

Housed in a sumptuous former royal palace, boasting some of the finest rooms in the city, and extensively modernised in recent years, Denmark's Nationalmuseet surpasses the equivalent institutions of many nations, both in terms of its content and its skilful presentation. The collection, which had its beginnings as Frederik II's Royal Cabinet of Curiosities (c1650), focuses, of course, on Danish culture and history, but there are also world-class Egyptian, Greek, Roman and ethnographic departments. All exhibits have excellent English captions. The museum's main home is in **Prinsens Palæ** (the Prince's Palace), built by Nicolai Eigtved (see page 91 **Great Danes: Niels 'Nicolai' Eigtved**) in 1743-4, but it has several other outposts elsewhere in the city and in Sjælland (**Frilandsmuseet**, see page 123; **Lille Mølle**, see page 105; **Brede Værk**, see page 123).

Visitors enter Prinsens Palæ via a large, airy main hall, once a courtyard but now enclosed with a glass roof, which also acts as a venue for concerts. On the first floor landing overlooking the hall is the museum's excellent café.

To the right, on the ground floor, you enter the **prehistoric wing**, encompassing Denmark's history from the reindeer hunters of the Ice Age to the Vikings. Here you can marvel at the wealth of archaeological finds from the Early Bronze Age, unearthed in Denmark's bogs – the most impressive of which is the collection of large bronze horns, known as **lurs** (some still playable), once used to appease the sun god. Also in this wing is another of the museum's most

recognisable exhibits – the statue of a horse pulling a **sun chariot**, dating from c1200BC and unearthed by a Trundholm farmer ploughing his field in 1902. The sun chariot is only a small representation of a much larger cult figure that was used by farmers to bless new crops, but it is exquisitely beautiful, and still has some of its gold leaf. Slightly less edifying, but no less fascinating, are the grave chamber finds and a nearby display of skulls with various injuries (and evidence of trepanning). The **Runic Stone Hall** is the highlight of the **Stone Age era displays**, while the **Hjortespring Boat** from c300 BC is an evocative example of a war canoe, and the oldest plank-built vessel in northern Europe. The **Golden Age Room** (AD 400-1000), meanwhile, is a jaw-dropping display of gold artefacts.

Upstairs, the **Medieval and Renaissance department** covers the pre- and post-Reformation periods and majors on ecclesiastical and decorative art. This is the era of the great Renaissance kings: Christian III, Frederik II and Christian IV. The surviving example of Frederik's tapestries of kings, made for the Great Hall of Kronborg Slot (see page 265), are a breathtaking sight, as are the richly carved bourgeois interior from Aalborg (c1660) and the splendid State Room.

The museum's eclectic and fascinating ethnographical collection is housed in the **Peoples Of The World exhibition**. It includes exhibits from Java, Central America, West Africa, Papua New Guinea and India, and is said to be the oldest of its kind in the world. It is augmented by a **Please Touch exhibition**

Rådhuspladsen

Tivoli's neighbour to the east is the usually frenetic **Rådhuspladsen** (Town Hall Square). Though the square is less architecturally appealing than Kongens Nytorv (*see page 77*) at the other end of Strøget, Denmark's answer to Times Square and Piccadilly Circus is far more pedestrian-friendly, and, at night, when the hundreds of adverts on the surrounding offices are lit up, far more spectacular. This large square, stretching out from **Rådhuset** (the Town Hall; *see page 65*) bustles unceasingly with commuters (the city's bus terminus is here), shoppers, sightseers, *pølser* (Danish hot dog) sellers, and, on weekends and holidays, street performers, gatherings and protests. It remains an important focal point for the people of Copenhagen, and is the prime New Year's Eve gathering point. A gigantic Christmas tree is lit in the square on the first Sunday in advent.

Rådhuspladsen is part of the original site of Havn, the small fishing village that stretched to Gammeltorv and down to the sea, before Bishop Absalon set it on its course to regional domination (*see page 8*). By the 13th century, the city rampart, protected by a moat, stretched from Vester Voldgade on the eastern side of the square, along Nørre Voldgade and down Gothersgade to what is now Kongens Nytorv, in a defensive arc that still marks the boundaries

of fur and crafts from Greenland, and the **Eldorado rooms** dedicated to the Native Americans, and the peoples of the Amazon and Andes.

The **Royal Collection of Coins and Medals**, though one of the more specialist rooms in the museum, is still intriguing. The room itself (Room 146) is definitely worth a visit. It is said to be one of the most beautiful in Copenhagen, and has views over Marmorbroen (the Marble Bridge) and Christiansborg Slot. The museum has removed the various layers of paint from the walls in places, to expose the decoration from past centuries that lies beneath.

On the top floor is the museum's **Collection of Antiquities**, a mini British Museum, with pieces from Egypt, Greece (including two fragments from the Parthenon, bought by a Danish naval officer in 1687) and Italy. On the same floor is a charming toy museum, which begins with a mention of a rattle in Saxo Grammaticus' *Gesta Danorum* and continues through early 16th-century German toys, a spectacular array of doll's houses, Lego (of course) and toy soldiers. Though the main museum is excellent for kids, in the basement is a **Children's Museum**, which attempts to condense the rest of the museum into an exhibition for four- to 12-year-olds (see also page 192). Last, but certainly not least, the highly inventive temporary exhibitions at Nationalmuseet are invariably worth paying the extra entrance charge to see.

Nationalmuseet

Ny Vestergade 10 (33 13 44 11/ www.natmus.dk). **Open** 10am-5pm Tue-Sun; closed Mon. **Admission** 40kr; 30kr concessions; free under-16s. Free to all Wed. **Credit** AmEx, DC, MC, V. **Map** p59/p311 O13.

The **Dragon's Leap Fountain**. See p65.

of medieval Copenhagen. All that remains of those medieval fortifications today is **Jarmers Tårn**, a small ruin on a roundabout in Jarmers Plads (at the north end of Vester Voldgade). The square itself lay outside the ramparts as it was used (up until 1850) as a haymarket, and there was a risk of fire. The layout of the streets within the medieval ramparts also remains pretty much intact from that period – a blind Copenhagener from the 14th century could probably still find his way from Rådhuspladsen to Købmagergade (if he didn't become disorientated by the smells from kebab and waffle vendors).

Rådhuspladsen is also where the last western city gate stood until the middle of the 19th century. In 1888, the square hosted over a million visitors at a huge exhibition of industry, agriculture and art. At that time, the square was designed in a shell shape, like the main piazza in Siena, but the internal combustion engine soon rendered it impossible to negotiate and its corners were squared off.

There's lots to look out for in and around Rådhuspladsen. On HC Andersens Boulevard, on the corner of the square nearest Tivoli, is a

Ny Carlsberg Glyptotek

The original sculpture collection ('glyptotek' means 'sculpture collection') was donated in 1888 to the city of Copenhagen by the philanthropist-brewer **Carl Jacobsen** (son of the founder of the Carlsberg brewery, IC Jacobsen) and his wife Ottilia. He intended the museum to have 'a beauty all its own, to which the people of the city would feel themselves irresistibly drawn', and pretty much got his way. His vision has been financed, run and much expanded by the Ny Carlsberg Foundation for more than a hundred years, and is housed in a building rich in architectural delights that was specially designed for the original collection by Vilhelm Dahlerup and Hack Kampmann. The highlight of the old building is the glorious, glass-domed **Winter Garden** – a steamy palm house bursting with monster subtropical plants and graced by Kai Nielsen's unsettlingly beautiful fountain piece *Water Mother With Children*. The Winter Garden's excellent café (open 10am-3.30pm daily, and great for cakes) is a popular meeting place for art-loving Copenhageners, and is an excellent spot in which to thaw out during winter.

The Glyptotek's thousands of pieces of art can be roughly divided into two groups: **ancient Mediterranean**, and **18th- and 19th-century French and Danish**. The first four rooms are dedicated to the museum's oldest pieces, some up to 5,000 years old (the Egyptian hippopotamus is a favourite of many). The exhibits proceed to trace the history of sculpture from the Sumerians, Assyrians, Persians and Phoenicians, through to a collection of ancient Greek pieces (one of the best in Europe), and some highly entertaining, privately commissioned (and therefore far more lifelike than officially commissioned) Roman busts. Jacobsen's unrivalled Etruscan collection – including bronzes, vases and stone and terracotta sculptures – is another highlight in the old building.

The French painting collection, housed in Henning Larsen's intriguing extension (ask for directions if you can't find its entrance off the Winter Garden), includes 35 works by the Post-Impressionist **Paul Gauguin**, who married a Danish woman in 1873 and lived in Copenhagen before moving on to the Pacific, and somewhat younger companions. As well

large statue of, appropriately enough, Hans Christian Andersen (*see page 255* **Great Danes: Hans Christian Andersen**). In front of that stands the striking **Dragon's Leap Fountain**, by Joachim Skovgaard. Nearby is a small carved stone pillar which marks the centre or 'zero point' of Copenhagen. Across the street, high on the corner of the Unibank building on Vesterbrogade and HC Andersens Boulevard, is a barometer featuring a girl on a bicycle (if it's fair) or under an umbrella (if it's not).

Also on the Tivoli side of the square, in a building nicknamed 'Little Rosenborg', is **Louis Tussaud's Wax Museum** (*listings page 66*), founded by Marie Tussaud's great-grandson. Slavishly following the model of Madame Tussaud's tourist honey jar in London, this smaller collection of celebrity wax effigies (200 in total) opened in 1974. As with the original museum, the likenesses are erratic to say the least (Madonna is a dead ringer for Barbra Streisand; Yasser Arafat and Ringo Starr are interchangeable), but at least an effort has been made to incorporate figures from Danish history into the collection.

Towering over the opposite side of the square is a pillar crowned by a bronze statue of two Vikings blowing lurs (S-shaped bronze horns), similar to the ones you can see in Nationalmuseet (*see page 62*). The statue, by Siegfried Wagner, was erected in 1914. Next to the pillar across Vester Voldgade is the elegant façade of the Anton Rosen-designed **Palace Hotel** (*see page 46*), which dates from 1910. Next door is **Ripley's Believe It Or Not Museum** (*listings page 66*), part of a world-wide chain of freak shows based on an idea by the American showman Robert Ripley. Weird and wacky exhibits include a matchstick Taj Mahal, two-headed animals, various optical illusions, voodoo dolls and Papua New Guinea penis sheaths. Jumped-up bric-a-brac, basically.

Rådhuset (*listings page 66*), situated on the southern side of Rådhuspladsen, is Copenhagen's administrative and political heart, as well as a venue for exhibitions, concerts, and the home of an horological masterpiece, **Jens Olsens Verdensur** (Jens Olsen's World Clock; *see page 66*). Denmark's second tallest tower (105.6 metres/346 feet;

as this unique collection (donated by Jacobsen's son Helge in 1927), the Glyptotek is home to one of only three complete sets of **Degas** bronzes in the world (including an insouciant ballerina in an original, evocative tulle costume), paintings by the leading lights of the Impressionist movement, including Corot, Manet, Renoir, Monet, Pissarro, and a remarkable Cézanne self-portrait. The rest of the Post-Impressionist movement is represented by Van Gogh, Toulouse-Lautrec, Bonnard and Signac.

Over 30 works by **Auguste Rodin** dominate the French sculpture rooms, but don't overlook the extremely sexy pieces by his contemporaries. A further pleasant surprise awaits those who think that Danish sculpture began and ended with Bertel Thorvaldsen in the collection of Danish sculpture (the largest after **Thorvaldsens Museum**, see page 81), and, while the collection of **Danish paintings from the Golden Age** (1815-50) is surpassed by those of **Statens Museum for Kunst** (see page 98) and **Den Hirschsprungske Samling** (see page 95), the leading lights (Dahl, Købke and Eckersberg among them) are well represented.

On Sundays, from October to March, the Glyptotek hosts a variety of music events; for details contact the museum.

Ny Carlsberg Glyptotek

Dantes Plads 7 (33 41 81 41/ www.glyptoteket.dk). **Open** 10am-4pm Tue-Sun; closed Mon. **Admission** 30kr; 20kr concessions; free under-16s; free to all Wed, Sun. **Credit** MC, V. **Map** p59/p311 P13.

there is a lift – the tallest, just, is part of Christiansborg Slot, *see page 84*), located on its eastern side, is almost incidental to the decorative splendour of this, the sixth town hall in Copenhagen's history.

Completed in 1905, Rådhuset has been the site of numerous elections (polling takes place in its central hall); home to as many city administrations; endured occupation by the Germans during World War II; and welcomed the returning football heroes from the 1992 European Championships, when Schmeichel, Laudrup and company famously brought the city to a standstill during their appearance on the balcony overlooking Rådhuspladsen (*see page 23*).

At first glance Rådhuset, inspired, like the square, by its Sienese counterpart, looks imposing, monolithic and perhaps a little dull, but at close quarters this national romantic masterpiece by architect Professor Martin Nyrop reveals its often witty, occasionally gruesome, but invariably exuberant architectural detail. The balcony is above the front door, and above that is a golden statue by CGV Bissen of Bishop Absalon. Even higher up, lining the front of the roof, stand six watchmen, separated by the city flag pole (watch for a swallow-tailed flag on special occasions, such as the Queen's birthday). This rises from the city's coat of arms, presented in 1661 by King Frederik III in thanks for the people's support during a city siege. Across the façade, and indeed all around the building, are countless gargoyles, reliefs, and individually crafted stone and iron figures (check out the hilarious walruses guarding the back door), while standing just in front of the right-hand side of the entrance are three grotesque bronze dragon-gargoyles, hunched as if ready to spring into action.

Inside, Rådhuset's endless corridors, halls, council chambers and meeting rooms offer a decorative feast to inquisitive visitors, who can roam with surprising freedom. Highlights include busts of HC Andersen, the physicist Niels Bohr, Professor Nyrop and sculptor Bertel Thorvaldsen (in the central hall), the library, the banqueting hall, various mosaic floors, chandeliers, reliefs, intricate brickwork and painted ceilings.

Jens Olsens Verdensur cost one million kroner to build (and 27 years to make; it was set going in 1955; *listings below* **Rådhuset**) and is extremely accurate, losing only milliseconds each century. Its display features the local time, sidereal time (gauged by the motion of the earth relative to distant stars, rather than the sun), firmament and celestial pole movement, the movement of the planets, and sunrises and sunsets. The clock is in a room on the right as you enter through Rådhuset's main door. An information office, where you can also buy tickets to the clock, the tower and for tours, is on the left.

On Ny Vestergade (off Vester Voldgade), five minutes' walk south-east from Rådhuspladsen, is **Nationalmuseet** (the National Museum; *see page 62*), northern Europe's largest museum, and one of most worthwhile places to pass an afternoon in the city.

The best Views

Frederiksberg Hill
View the city from the west. See page 113.

Det Gyldne Tårn
See Tivoli spread out beneath you, before plunging 63 metres. See page 58.

Rundetårn
Gaze out on central Copenhagen from Christian IV's observatory. See page 69.

Top of the Town Wine Bar
See the city from Amager while sipping at this sky-high hotel bar. See page 156.

Vor Frelsers Kirke
Climb the spiral spire of Christianshavn's famous church for vertiginous vistas. See page 103.

Louis Tussaud's Wax Museum
HC Andersens Boulevard 22 (33 11 89 00/ www.tussaud.dk). **Open** *Apr-mid Sept* 10am-11pm (last entry 10pm) daily. *Mid Sept-Mar* 10am-7pm (last entry 6pm) daily. **Admission** 65kr; 25kr-45kr concessions. **Credit** MC, V. **Map** p59/p310 O12.

Rådhuset
Rådhuspladsen (33 66 25 82/83/ www.copenhagencity.dk). **Open** 8am-5pm Mon-Fri; 9.30am-1pm Sat; closed Sun. *Guided tour* (English only) 3pm Mon-Fri; (English & Danish) 10am, 11am Sat. *Rådhuset Tower tour* June-Sept 10am, noon, 2pm Mon-Fri; noon Sat; Oct-May noon Mon-Sat. *Jens Olsens Verdensur* 10am-4pm Mon-Fri; 10am-1pm Sat; closed Sun. **Admission** *Rådhuset guided tour* 30kr. *Rådhuset Tower tour* 20kr. *Jens Olsens Verdensur* 10kr; 5kr concessions. **No credit cards.** **Map** p59/p310 O12.

Ripley's Believe It Or Not Museum
Rådhuspladsen 57 (33 91 89 91/www.ripleys.dk). **Open** *June-Aug* 9.30am-9.30pm daily. *Sept-May* 10am-5pm Mon-Thur, Sun; 10am-8pm Fri, Sat. **Admission** 66kr; 33kr-56kr concessions. **Credit** DC, MC, V. **Map** p59/p310 O12.

Sightseeing

Strøget & Around

The pedestrianised heart of the city, with shops, bars and restaurants aplenty.

Bishop Absalon and the spire of **Sankt Nikolaj Kirke**. *See p70 and p68.*

Sightseeing

Strøget, (pronounced 'stroll', meaning 'stripe', and often referred to as 'the walking street') is the main shopping street and backbone of Copenhagen. In fact Strøget is actually made up of five streets – Østergade, Amagertorv, Vimmelskaftet, Nygade and Frederiksberggade – running from Kongens Nytorv at its eastern (posher) end, almost two kilometres (one mile) to Rådhuspladsen in the west. Since 1962 it has been Europe's longest pedestrian shopping street, home to some of the world's grandest retailers (as well as some not so grand), and scattered with restaurants, arcades, cafés, churches, fountains and squares. In the 1820s the shops at the Kongens Nytorv end were among the pioneers of window displays. Despite its cosmopolitan feel, stylish shop fronts and near-24-hour bustle, Strøget's medieval foundations have ensured that it has retained an intimate charm that make Oxford Street or the Champs-Elysées seem like motorways in comparison. Its presence helps make Copenhagen one of the most user-friendly shopping cities in the world.

As well as the usual international clothing chains found in most cities, Strøget has many other more unique stars. Turn down practically any side street and these world-class clothes, design, food, jewellery, ceramics, art and other specialist shops (many with long histories) multiply exponentially (*see chapter* **Shops & Services**). At the Kongens Nytorv end of Strøget lies Kronprinsensgade (actually off Købmagergade), which is probably the best street for fashion, and has some great cafés, but most of the streets north of Østergade – such as Pilestræde, Grønnegade, Ny Adelgade and Ny Østergade – are eminently wanderable. The great thing about Copenhagen is that these shops are all within a few minutes' walk of each other, and, if your feet do tire, a cosy, grand, hip or historic café or bar is never far away.

Strøget even has several museums. The first you arrive at, as you walk from Kongens Nytorv, past the desirable minimalist electronica in the Bang & Olufsen shop (*see page 164*) on your left, is the **Guinness World Records Museum** (*listings page 75*), on your right. Part of a chain, the Guinness museum unaccountably lures the passing crowds of tourists most days with its 13 galleries dedicated to human achievements of dubious worth.

Hermaphroditic delights at the Museum Erotica.

not for the faint-hearted, the museum offers a genuinely fascinating trawl through the history of pornography from Roman and oriental decorative erotic art to *Playboy* and rather more extreme genres (animal lovers should stay away!). Like the highest shelf in a newsagents, it doesn't get *really* sleazy until you reach the top, where an entire wall of TVs screening non-stop hardcore porn videos awaits. The museum has excellent English captions, best employed in the salacious room dedicated to the sex lives of the famous (where we discover the secret of Toulouse-Lautrec's success with the ladies, and that Rousseau used to wait in dark alleys with his trousers round his ankles in the hope that passing women might spank him).

A little further up Købmagergade on your left is Denmark's **Post & Tele Museum** (*listings page 75*), a new and clearly very expensive museum dedicated to Denmark's communications services. Sadly, all the state-of-the-art museum know-how in the world can't make stamps and telephones *that* interesting, but do make the effort to visit the excellent roof-top café with views of old Copenhagen to rival the Rundetårn's (*see page 69*), only this time there's a lift. It's open late on Wednesdays when it serves an à la carte menu of Danish and international cuisine.

Further down Strøget, if you take a detour left behind the electrical store Fona2000, you come to **Sankt Nikolaj Kirke** in Nikolaj Plads. The church is no longer used for services, but holds temporary exhibitions and also houses a café. It originally dates from the 13th century, but the fire of 1795 (*see page 14*) destroyed all but the tower; it was rebuilt in 1917. The square has several restaurants and cafés, and during the summer is a main venue for the Copenhagen Jazz Festival (*see page 219*).

Back on Strøget, as you walk past famous names like Vuitton, Versace, Gucci and Hermés, you come to the Illum department store on your right (*see page 158*). Illum stretches for a short block to the corner of Købmagergade (on your right), which runs north-west to Nørre Voldgade and is another excellent shopping street. Between Købmagergade and the (almost) parallel Nørregade lies the heart of what's sometimes ambitiously termed Copenhagen's '**Latin Quarter**' (on account of its narrow alleyways, cobbled café squares and student life).

If you take a detour off Strøget for a while you will find that Købmagergade is also home to Copenhagen's most infamous museum, **Museum Erotica** (*listings page 75*), founded by Ole Ege (son of a Chief of Police). Though

Christian IV's Rundetårn. *See p69.*

Københmagergade's other main draw is the
Rundetårn (Round Tower; *listings page 75*),
beside **Trinitatiskirke** (Trinity Church;
listings page 75). Built in 1642 at the behest of
Christian IV for the astronomer Tycho Brahe,
the red-brick Rundetårn was originally intended
as an observatory for the nearby university,
and is still the oldest functioning observatory
in Europe. Christian is commemorated on the
front in a red and gold wrought iron lattice; the
letters RFP stand for the famously lecherous
king's unlikely motto: *Regna Firmat Pietas* –
Piety Strengthens the Realm. The Rundetårn is
unique in European architecture for its cobbled
spiral walkway which winds for 209 metres
(686 feet) almost to the top of the tower, 34.8
metres (114 feet) above the city. There are
only a few stairs at the very top where the
view, as you'd expect, is superb. Czar Peter the
Great is said to have ridden in his carriage all
the way in 1716; while a car once drove up in
1902. Halfway up is an exhibition space.
Trinitatiskirke was built in 1637 and boasts
a baroque altar by Friedrich Ehbisch as well
as a three-faced rococo clock (1757). The
observatory at the top of the tower is often
open, with an astronomer on hand to explain
what you can see through the telescope.

Opposite the Rundetårn is **Regensen**,
built in 1616 as a student hall of residence
for the nearby University, and still in use as
such today. Around the corner on Krystalgade
is Copenhagen's **Synagogen** (synagogue);
it dates from 1833. On the parallel Store
Kannikestræde is one of Copenhagen's
loveliest old buildings, **Admiral Gjeddes
Gard**, at No.12. Its half-timbered oak walls,
dating from 1567, were made from trees
grown on the site.

Towards the end of Købmagergade is
Kultorvet, a pretty, leafy square which, though
desolate in winter, becomes gridlocked in
summer with café tables, fruit and veg stalls
and beer stands. It also houses Copenhagen's
main municipal library. Continue on over
Nørre Voldgade (the northern boundary of
the old city ramparts), and you arrive at two
more excellent areas for summer cafés:
Nansensgade and Israels Plads. The latter,
situated beside the very pretty **Ørsteds
Parken** (a cosy park, laid out around a small
lake and named after the Danish physicist Hans
Christian Ørsted, famous for his discovery of
electromagnetism), hosts a large fruit and veg
market and, on Saturdays in the summer, an
antiques and flea market.

Sightseeing

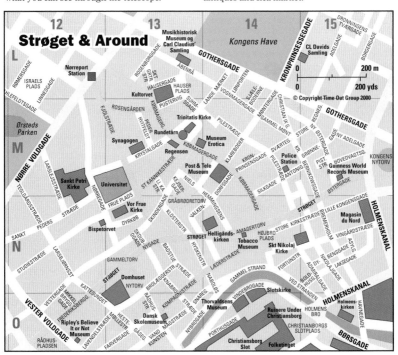

In 1985, three venerable Strøget institutions on Amagertorv (back at the junction of Østergade and Købmagergade), amalgamated to form **Royal Copenhagen** (*see page 165*). Located opposite the elegant, unusual **Storkespringvandet** (the Stork Fountain, erected in 1894 amid much public protest at its then-radical design), the silversmiths **Georg Jensen**, the **Royal Copenhagen Porcelain**, and glass nirvana **Holmegaard** make an impressive triumvirate of high quality but fiercely expensive retailers. Next door is **Illums Bolighus** (*see page 165*), which stocks a mouth-watering selection of the finest Danish-designed products.

Since 1911, Royal Copenhagen Porcelain (founded in 1780) has had a shop here at No.6 (built in the Dutch Renaissance style in 1616 for the mayor Mathias Hansen – check out the fabulous copper drainpipes); on its first floor is a small museum. Lord Nelson coolly bought gifts for Lady Hamilton at an earlier shop after the English fleet had bombarded the city to smithereens (*see page 17*). There is also a small Georg Jensen Museum through a courtyard to the rear of the shop at No.4.

Amagertorv's origins date back at least to the 14th century. In the 17th century a law was passed that meant all the produce grown on Amager island (south-east of the centre, where the airport is now located) had to be sold at the market here, and soon a number of shops grew up around it. It has always been one of

Copenhagen's main markets and meeting places, and though the stalls have long gone, the fountain is still very much used as a rendezvous point and attracts a constant throng of people. Many move on to one of the two adjacent cafés – **Café Norden** and **Café Europa** (for both, *see page 147*), if they are blessed enough to find an empty table.

Adjoining Amagertorv, in the direction of Slotsholmen, is another busy square, Højbro Plads. Its main feature is a 1902 equestrian statue of **Bishop Absalon** (*see page 8*), the founder of Copenhagen, by Vilhelm Bissem, with an inscription that reads: 'He was courageous, wise and far-sighted, a friend of scholarship, in the intensity of his striving a true son of Denmark.'

Running parallel to Strøget from Højbro Plads to Nybrogade is **Gammel Strand** (Old Beach; *see page 71*), home to some pricey and exclusive restaurants, prime among them the fish-focused **Krogs Fiskerestaurant** (*see page 133*). One of Copenhagen's leading art spaces, **Kunstforeningen** (*see page 205*), is located here. It houses an often-changing programme of contemporary art exhibitions over three floors.

A little further down from Amagertorv, on the opposite side of the street from Royal Copenhagen, is the beautiful black and gold 19th-century shop front of tobacconist **WØ Larsen**, dating from 1864. In the basement is a **Tobacco Museum** (*listings page 75*),

Chilling out in **Ørsteds Parken**. *See p69.*

Static and dynamic distractions on Strøget: **Storkespringvandet** and break-dancing.

charting the history of the weed from the 16th century onwards, and packed full of fascinating smoking ephemera.

The next major sight as you continue west along Strøget from Amagertorv is **Helligåndskirken** (Church of the Holy Spirit; *listings page 75*), on your right, the oldest church in Copenhagen. It dates from 1400 and was originally part of the Greyfriars monastery, founded in 1238. The early monks were hardy, destitute souls and their devoted piety earned them much respect. Over the years, however, their standards relaxed somewhat, to the point where they were expelled from the city by the Protestant reformers of the 16th century (some stones from the monastery can still be seen in Peder Oxe restaurant (*see page 134*) on Gråbrødretorv – Greyfriars Square, a short walk up Niels Hemmingsens Gade by the side of the church). The current neo-Renaissance structure dates from 1880. In the churchyard is a memorial to the Danish victims of Nazi concentration camps.

Gråbrødretorv itself is a delightful restaurant square, a kind of Nyhavn without a canal, in the heart of the 'Latin Quarter'. It comes alive in summer as tables and parasols from its (generally excellent but costly) restaurants spill out onto the cobbles. It was created in 1664 after Corfitz Ulfeldt, the secretary of war and husband of Eleonore Christine (daughter of Christian IV), had his mansion torn down as a punishment for attempted high treason. A monument to Ulfeldt's infamy was erected in the square, it now stands in the courtyard of Nationalmuseet (*see page 62*). After the fire of 1728, many houses in the now-pedestrian square were rebuilt with the typical triangular gable-ends of the period.

From here, Strøget starts to become slightly more downmarket (though this is Denmark, so that's a comparative term), with various cheap eateries serving pizzas, kebabs, ice-cream and waffles. The watershed comes at **Gammeltorv**

and **Nytorv**, two adjoining cobbled squares, beyond which things start to get really touristy. The squares themselves are extremely pretty, however. During the 14th century Gammeltorv, the oldest square in the city, was the hub of Copenhagen, a busy market and

Gammel Strand

In the time of Bishop Absalon, and for many centuries afterwards, **Gammel Strand** was the fish-selling centre, and therefore commercial centre, of Copenhagen. It was here that the Øresund herring were landed, before being transported throughout Catholic Europe. Gammel Strand remained part of Copenhagen's sea front, which stretched from what is today Fortunstræde, along Gammel Strand to Snaregade, Magstræde and Løngangstræde until well into the Middle Ages. By the bridge from Højbro Plads to Slotsholmen is a stout stone statue (dating from 1940) of one of the notoriously foul-mouthed and quarrelsome fishwives grasping a huge flounder by the gills, in memory of this trade which continued into the 20th century. There is still a fishmongers' nearby on Højbro Plads, though its swift trade in sushi indicates that it has moved with the times. Cross to the other side of the bridge and look into the water and you'll see the sculpture of the *Merman With His Sons*; at its best when illuminated at night. All of Gammel Strand, except for No.48, burned to the ground in the fire of 1795.

During the summer you can take a canal tour or harbour trip to the Little Mermaid from Gammel Strand. The more adventurous might like to try the excellent kayak tour (for both, see page 52).

Vor Frue Kirke.

In 1848, Nytorv was the starting point for the relatively peaceful march by 10,000 Copenhageners on Christiansborg Slot, demanding the end of absolute monarchy. Frederik VII had conceded defeat before they even arrived (*see page 19*). Søren Kierkegaard (*see page 112* **Great Danes: Søren Kierkegaard**) lived for a while in Nytorv in a house on a site now occupied by Den Danske Bank. Look out, too, for the outline of Copenhagen's first town hall (before it moved to Rådhuspladsen) traced in the paving of Nytorv beneath the fruit sellers who usually pitch here. Mozart's widow Constanze lived with her second husband (Georg Nikolaus Nissen, a Danish diplomat) at No.1 Lavendelstræde, which runs from Nytorv's southern corner towards Rådhuspladsen.

Café Europa on Amagertorv. *See p146.*

meeting place for the 5,000 residents of an expanding and prosperous trading town that was probably the largest settlement in northern Europe. It also held jousting competitions. The two squares became one (though they are bisected by Strøget) after the fire of 1795 destroyed the town hall that once separated them.

Arriving in Gammeltorv today your eye is immediately drawn to the extraordinary **Caritas Springvandet** (Charity Fountain), dating from 1608. This Renaissance masterpiece is made from copper and depicts a pregnant woman and two children with fishy gargoyles at their feet. The Caritas Springvandet is one of the earliest surviving pieces of art of its kind; it was rebuilt and remounted in the 1890s. On royal birthdays golden apples dance on the water jets.

Of interest chiefly because of its grand neo-classical façade (restored in 1993), featuring six Ionic columns, Copenhagen's imposing and elegant **Domhuset** (Court House; open 8.30am-3pm Mon-Fri; closed Sat, Sun) on Nytorv was built in 1805-15 (work had to be suspended for a while in 1807 due to the bombardment by the English). The dusky pink Domhuset was designed by CF Hansen, who was also responsible for the city cathedral, Vor Frue Kirke (*see below*), which is a short walk away up Nørregade. Domhuset was built on the site of the former town hall, which burned down in the great fire of 1795 (*see page 14*), and, up until 1905, it served as both courthouse and town hall. Today, it houses court rooms, conference rooms and chambers and is the largest of Denmark's town courts. The nearby Slutterigade (Prison Street) annexe was built as a prison in 1816 and converted to house court rooms and chambers in 1944. It is attached to Domhuset via two arches, one of which is known as the Bridge of Sighs, as this is where prisoners are taken to and from the court rooms.

In total six churches have stood on the site of **Vor Frue Kirke** (Church of Our Lady; just north of Gammeltorv, on Nørregade; *listings page 75*) since 1191, and over the years they have suffered from a variety of misfortunes. The destruction of Vor Frue Kirke's art treasures by the Lutherans during the Reformation in the 16th century stands as one of their more barbaric acts. The current neo-classical cathedral by CF Hansen replaced the church destroyed by the British bombardment in 1807 (they used its 100 metre/328 feet spire as a target). The interior's spartan whitewash is relieved by several figures by Thorvaldsen, including his famous depiction of Christ. The church frequently hosts musical events. A short way up Nørregade is **Sankt Petri Kirke**, the church of the German community in Copenhagen (not open to the public, other than for services), dating from 1450.

Next to Vor Frue Kirke is a large cobbled square, **Frue Plads**, often used for public performances during summer. The rather grimy building lined with busts of famous Danes (including physicist Niels Bohr; *see page 74* **Great Danes: Niels Bohr**) opposite the church is part of the **Universitet** founded by Christian I in 1479. The present building stands on the same site as the original (itself built over the Bishop's Palace, but long since lost to a variety of fires), and was designed by Peter Malling and inaugurated by Frederik VI in 1836. The fabulously ornate great hall, through the door on Frue Plads, is worth a look (concerts are often held here), and, if you have time, pop into the University Library round the corner in Fiolstræde. Halfway up the stairs is a small glass cabinet containing some fragments of a cannon ball and the book they were found embedded in after the British bombardment (*see page 17*). The title of the book, by Marsilius of Padua (at that time kept in Trinitatiskirke's loft) is *Defender of Peace*.

Sightseeing

Great Danes Niels Bohr

Between the years of 1903 and 1997 Denmark could boast an extraordinary 13 Nobel Prize-winners. Probably the most famous of them all was the atomic physicist **Niels Bohr**, a Danish Jew born in Copenhagen in 1885. Bohr won the Nobel Prize for Physics in 1922 for his explanation of the periodic system of elements. His work advanced our understanding of atomic structure and quantum mechanics and, as a result, Bohr is generally considered one of the 20th century's greatest physicists.

Bohr grew up in a scientific hothouse. He was the son of a professor of physiology, and, in 1916, became professor at the University of Copenhagen, a post he held until 1955. While at university Bohr constructed the basic model of atomic structure, developing his colleague Ernest Rutherford's atomic model into the Bohr atomic model (1913) by proposing that electrons travel only in certain successively larger orbits around the nucleus. He went on to found the Institute of Theoretical Physics (later renamed the Niels Bohr Institute) in 1920, and to formulate the principle of atomic fission, which led directly to the creation of the atom bomb. The Institute became known as the

Copenhagen School, and during the 1920s and '30s was the world centre for theoretical physics. Bohr's understanding of quantum mechanics thus became known as the Copenhagen Interpretation, one of its main tenets being his theory of 'complementarity'.

Bohr's relationship with Einstein during this time has become the stuff of science legend, partly due to Bohr's habit of highlighting discrepancies in his friend's theories. On one occasion he famously pointed out that Einstein had overlooked the fact that his own theory of relativity states that clocks run slower under the influence of a gravitational field.

In 1943 Bohr was a part of the miraculous exodus by the majority of Denmark's Jews to Sweden (he left disguised as a fisherman; see page 21 **Jewish exodus**), from where he travelled to England and the USA. There, at the atomic research centre in Los Alamos, he worked with some of the world's leading scientists (Einstein included) to produce the first atom bomb.

Despite this pioneering work, Bohr frequently warned against the dangers of atomic power, and attempted to persuade both Churchill and Eisenhower to share the West's findings with the Soviet Union. In

---

On the nearby corner of Store Kannikestræde is **Det Lille Apotek** (The Little Pharmacy), probably Copenhagen's oldest restaurant, which dispensed drugs before devoting itself to gastronomy in 1720. It was a favourite haunt of HC Andersen.

In Rådhusstræde, just off Nytorv near Rådhuspladsen, is the **Dansk Skolemuseum** (*listings page 75*), dedicated to the history of Danish education. It includes old classrooms and exhibitions divided by subject. The museum's pride and joy are 12,000 period educational illustrations from the first half of the century, many of which are on show. That said, the museum is really only for those with a special interest in education.

The final stretch of Strøget is along Frederiksberggade, which opened up between Nytorv and Rådhuspladsen when the fire of 1728 razed buildings here to the ground. On the right as you approach Rådhuspladsen is the hideous Club Absalon, built on the site of the city's first church, **Sankt Clemens Kirke**. The church was probably built by Absalon in the 1160s, but was demolished in the early

16th century. Some of its foundations can be seen in the bar's toilets.

Running parallel with Strøget at this end, to the south, are a network of narrow, medieval streets (including Farvergade, Magstræde, Snaregade, Kompagnistræde and Læderstræde), packed with a range of excellent independent shops, as well as some superb cheaper restaurants and cafés.

To the north of Frederiksberggade, in an area bookended by Nørregade and Vester Voldgade, lies the liveliest area around Strøget, known as **Pisserenden**. 'Piss' means the same in Danish as it does in English, and this district was thus called due to its notoriety as an odoriferous dwelling for prostitutes and criminals, until it was purged by the first great fire of 1728. Today, Pisserenden is one of the youngest and most vibrant areas of Copenhagen, full of the coolest (but relatively cheap) clothes, skateboarding, book and record shops. Most of the streets (which include Kattesundet, Vestergade, Larsbjørnsstræde and Teglgårdstræde) have a few bars along their length too.

Sightseeing

1950 he published an open letter to the United Nations pleading for international co-operation on the issue of nuclear weapons and free exchange of information.

Bohr is typically described as a gentle, kind man with a sharp wit and charming modesty; he was a philospher-scientist in the great tradition. In 1947 he received Denmark's oldest and most distinguished order of chivalry, the grand cross of the Order of the Elephant, and in 1957 he was appointed chairman of the Danish Atomic Energy Commission.

Bohr's son, Aage, with whom Niels often worked, also won the Nobel Prize for physics (jointly) in 1975. He took over the direction of the Bohr institute after his father's death.

In 1998 English playwright Michael Frayn's play *Copenhagen* made its debut in London's West End. In it

Frayn offers his various hypotheses for what might have occurred during a meeting in the Danish capital in 1941 between Bohr and his former colleague and friend, the German physicist Werner Heisenberg (of 'uncertainty principle' fame). The play won numerous theatrical awards and has subsequently played in Denmark.

Famous Bohrisms:

'An expert is a man who has made all the mistakes which can be made in a very narrow field.'

'Anyone who is not dizzy after his first acquaintance with the quantum of action has not understood a word.'

'Prediction is very difficult, especially about the future.'

Einstein: 'God does not play dice.'
Einstein: 'God is not malicious.'
Bohr: 'Einstein, stop telling God what to do.'

Sightseeing

Dansk Skolemuseum
Rådhusstræde 6 (33 15 58 10/www.skolemuseum.dk). **Open** 10am-4pm Mon-Fri; noon-4pm Sun; closed Sat. **Admission** free. **Map** p72/p311 O13.

Guinness World Records Museum
Østergade 16 (33 32 31 31/www.guinness.dk). **Open** *June-Aug* 9.30am-9.30pm daily. *Sept-May* 10am-6pm daily. **Admission** 66kr; 33kr-56kr concessions. **Credit** DC, MC, V. **Map** p72/p311 M15.

Helligåndskirke
Amagertorv (no phone). **Open** noon-4pm Mon-Fri; closed Sat, Sun. **Admission** free. **Map** p72/p311 N14.

Museum Erotica
Købmagergade 24 (33 12 03 11/ www.museumerotica.dk). **Open** *May-Sept* 10am-11pm daily. *Oct-Apr* 11am-8pm daily. **Admission** 65kr. **Credit** AmEx, DC, MC, V. **Map** p72/p311 M14.

Post & Tele Museum
Købmagergade 37 (33 41 09 00/www.ptt-museum.dk). **Open** 10am-5pm Tue, Thur-Sun; 10am-8pm Wed; closed Mon. *Café* 11am-5pm Tue, Thur-Sun; 11am-8pm Wed; closed Mon. **Admission** 30kr; 15kr concessions; free under-12s. Free to all Wed. **Credit** MC, V. **Map** p72/p311 M14.

Rundetårn
Købmagergade 52A (33 73 03 73/ www.rundetaarn.dk). **Open** *June-Aug* 10am-8pm Mon-Sat; noon-8pm Sun. *Sept-May* 10am-5pm Mon-Sat; noon-5pm Sun. *Observatory* 1 Oct-25 Mar 7-10pm Tue, Wed; closed Mon, Thur-Sun. *26 Mar-30 Sept* closed. **Admission** 15kr; 5kr concessions; free under-5s. **Credit** AmEx, DC, MC, V. **Map** p72/p311 M13.

Tobacco Museum
WØ Larsen, Amagertorv 9 (33 12 20 50). **Open** 10am-6pm Mon-Thur; 10am-7pm Fri; 10am-5pm Sat; closed Sun. **Admission** free. **Credit** AmEx, DC, MC, V. **Map** p72/p311 N14.

Trinitatiskirke
Landemærket 2 (33 12 91 00). **Open** 9.30am-4.30pm daily. **Admission** free. **Map** p72/p311 M13.

Vor Frue Kirke
Nørregade 8 (www.koebenhavnsdomkirke.dk). **Open** *Apr-Sept* 9am-5pm Mon-Thur, Sat; 9-10.30am, noon-5pm Fri; noon-4.30pm Sun. *Sept-Mar* 9am-5pm Mon-Thur, Sat; 9-10.30am, noon-5pm Fri; noon-1.30pm, 3-4.30pm Sun. **Admission** free. **Map** p72/p311 N13.

Nyhavn & Around

The city's photogenic tourist magnet and its grandest square.

Touristy but undeniably pretty: **Nyhavn**.

Nyhavn

At the north-east corner of Kongens Nytorv
lies **Nyhavn** (New Harbour), a bustling,
colourful and exceptionally pretty Dutch-style
canal lined with cafés, bars, restaurants, the
odd tattoo parlour (Ole at No.17 is the most
famous) and ships from Nationalmuseet's
collection. If the sun so much as peeps
momentarily from behind the clouds, hundreds
of these establishments' tables and chairs
(and, in the autumn months, the all-important
umbrella heaters) pour out onto the quayside.
You know summer has arrived in Copenhagen
when Nyhavn starts to buzz, and an evening
stroll here is an essential part of the city
experience. Nyhavn is immensely popular
with tourists, and, on Friday nights, the
place throngs with tipsy Swedes who have
disembarked from the Malmö ferry (which
docks here at the Scanlines Ferry Terminal)
with the sole intention of buying what is for
them cheaper booze. Thus, crowds are virtually
guaranteed throughout the summer, so try and
book ahead at restaurants or arrive early to
bag a table at weekends. It has to be said that
the restaurants along Nyhavn – be they

Danish, Russian, Mexican, Italian, American,
Scottish or French – vary from decent to
dreadful (**Cap Horn** at No.21 is probably the
best; *see page 139*) and none are especially
good value, but the harbourside is always
a great place for a beer or two before going
on elsewhere.

The canal was dug by soldiers in 1671-3 to
allow trading ships access to Kongens Nytorv.
After the British bombardment of 1807,
Nyhavn's so-called 'Palmy Days' of prosperity
were brought to a rude end, and the wealthy
merchants moved out. Its quayside saw service
as one of the city's red light districts and was
notorious for its high crime rate and confidence
tricksters. But it is somehow more fitting that
this most *hygge* (*see page 79* **The essence
of *hygge***) of streets is also remembered as
the home for over 20 years to Hans Christian
Andersen (*see page 255* **Great Danes: Hans
Christian Andersen**), who lived, variously,
at Nos.18, 20 and 67. At the head of the canal a
large anchor commemorates the Danish sailors
who died during World War II. If you stand at
the end of Nyhavn, looking out to sea, you are
confronted on the other side of the harbour by
12 statues. These were erected in 1996, during

Idiosyncratic museums

CL Davids Samling
Mecca for Islamic-art lovers. See page 99.

Experimentarium
Inventive hands-on science extravaganza.
See page 122.

Medicinsk-Historisk Museum
Weird and wonderful medical exhibits.
See page 92.

Museum Erotica
Naughty but nice. See page 68.

Copenhagen's reign as European City of Culture, and are the work of 12 different artists from seven countries, sharing the theme of 'living in exile'.

Two excellent shopping streets, Store Strandstræde (where you'll find the restaurant **Els**; *see page 140*) and Lille Strandstræde, are good for antiques, art and ceramics and lead off Nyhavn on the north side. On the quieter south side, the main draw is the 17th-century Dutch baroque palace of **Charlottenborg**, home to **Det Kongelige Kunstakademi** (the Royal Academy of Fine Arts) since 1754. Charlottenborg, originally built in 1683 as a royal palace, offers a constantly changing programme of exhibitions of contemporary art in the **Charlottenborg Udstillingsbygning** (Charlottenborg Exhibition; *see page 201*).

Kongens Nytorv

Windswept and stately, **Kongens Nytorv** (1680) has the potential to be Copenhagen's grandest square, but since Dutch elm disease robbed it of its trees in 1998, it has taken on a rather barren appearance (the hideous Eastern Bloc-style street lighting doesn't do it any favours either). Nevertheless, the square is still graced by a number of the city's finest buildings, and a large, faintly absurd statue (by Abraham-César Lamoureux; 1687) of its architect, Christian V, which stands in its centre (inspired by the statue of Louis XIII in Paris, it depicts him as a Roman general astride his horse). The vast weight of the lead statue eventually proved too much for the horse's legs to bear and it had to be recast in bronze in 1946.

Kongens Nytorv was built on the site of former ramparts that ringed the city in an arc all the way from Rådhuspladsen. It is an excellent starting point for a tour of the city (*see page 54* **Copenhagen in 48 hours**), as Bredgade, Nyhavn and Strøget, among many other streets, all radiate from it, and most of the other main sights of central Copenhagen are within a few minutes' walk. Around Christmas time, its artificial ice rink is a major draw.

The square is dominated to the south-east by the commanding bulk of **Det Kongelige Teater** (the Royal Theatre; *see page 223*

Map: **Nyhavn & Around**

Odd Fellow Palæ · Garnisons Kirke · PALÆGADE · GOTHERSGADE · AMALIENGADE · SANKT ANNÆ PLADS · Amber Museum · STORE STRANDSTRÆDE · LILLE STRANDSTRÆDE · BREDGADE · Hotel d'Angleterre · KONGENS NYTORV · STRØGET · Charlottenborg Nye Scene · NYHAVN · TOLDBODGADE · KVÆSTHUSGADE · LILLE KONGENSG. · HOLMENSKANAL · SGADE · HEIBERG · HERLUF · TROLLES · GADE · Magasin du Nord · VINGÅRDSTRÆDE · Det Kongelige Teater · PEDER · TORDENSKJOLDSGADE · HOLBERGSGADE · CORT ADELERS GADE · SKRAMS GADE · HAVNEGADE · Inderhavnen · HOLMENS KANAL · Nationalbanken

N · 0 — 200 m · 0 — 200 yds

© Copyright Time Out Group 2000

Sightseeing

The essence of *hygge*

Danes are, generally, a clear-headed, logical-thinking lot, not easily fazed, or given to fits of bluster. But ask them to explain the meaning of the innocuous Danish word *hygge*, and the response usually goes something like this: there'll be a short pause, a few aborted attempts, 'Well, it's kind of like when...' or 'Erm, you know how if you...'; perhaps a quick, heated discussion with another Dane nearby; but, invariably they will shrug and concede that there is no direct English equivalent.

Definitions for *hygge* are many and varied. The simplest is 'cosy', but that is woefully inadequate; *hygge* is so much more than being simply warm and snug. *Hygge* is a state of being. Trouble is, the more you try to define the word, the more indefinable the phenomenon becomes.

It is probably more productive to examine what exactly Danes mean when they describe an occasion or event as being *hygge* (pronounced 'hooga'): it usually involves a gathering of two or more people (to *hygge* oneself is regarded as a sign of desperation, or worse, mental illness), almost always friends or family. Those gathered will be happy and convivial, perhaps slightly drunk, definitely generous of spirit and, yes, cosy. Toasts will be raised on the flimsiest

of premises, good food consumed and bonhomie exchanged. Subjects of seriousness or controversy will be outlawed to avoid unnecessary friction, but a song or two may well be sung. In summary, *hygge* means unchallenging, relaxing, feel-good, convivial. Tell a Dane that you had a *hygge* time with him or her and you will have a friend for life.

A *hygge* event can take place out of doors (on a beach during a long summer evening, for instance), or inside, usually with candlelight and an open fire. And, though the guests will be familiar with each other, the mood won't necessarily be intimate – the Danes have another word for that: *råhygge*, meaning, literally, raw *hygge*, which is more applicable to couples.

The ultimate *hygge*-fest comes, of course, during Christmas, when the Stygian Danish winter brings optimum *hygge* weather – long dark nights, short gloomy days, thunder, wind and rain. Traditional Danish comfort food like rice porridge, roast pork, mulled wine and sugary cakes are served, candles are lit, and for once they actually have an excuse for the communal singing. You can't help thinking that if only Danes exported *hygge* along with their beer and bacon, the world would be a much nicer place.

Romantic Copenhagen

Though it hasn't enjoyed quite the PR campaign of Paris or Venice, Copenhagen is undoubtedly one of the most romantic cities in Europe. With its fairy tale architecture, swoonsome gardens and cosy candlelit restaurants, the city is an aphrodisiac in itself. Here's where and how you'll best discover that loving feeling.

Rowing on the lake in **Frederiksberg Have**. See page 113.

A picnic beside Rosenborg Slot in **Kongens Have**. See page 98.

A walk along the windswept beach at **Tisvildeleje**. See page 275.

Sunset over Marmorkirken, as seen from the harbourside at groovy al fresco bar **Thorsen**. See page 151.

A springtime stroll along poplar alley in **Assistens Kirkegård**. See page 120.

Cocktails at the **Top of the Town** wine bar. See page 154.

Watching the windsurfers from a bench beside the **Sortedams Sø**. See page 118.

Enjoying an inventive dinner for two at the **Schultz**. See page 140.

La Traviata at **Det Kongelige Teater**. See page 77.

The fireworks at **Tivoli**. See page 57.

and 225). Denmark's national theatre is unique in that it produces opera, ballet and theatre together in two auditoria – Gamle (old) Scene and Nye (new) Scene – seating a total of 2,550 people. The main neo-Renaissance building (the fourth on this site), by Vilhelm Dahlerup and Ove Petersen, dates from 1872, but the theatre was founded in 1748. The Nye Scene was added in 1931, connected via an archway to the other side of Tordenskjoldsgade. The inscription '*Eì blot til lyst*', outside, is taken from the original building designed by Nicolai Eigtved (*see page 91* **Great Danes: Niels 'Nicolai' Eigtved**), and translates as 'Not just for pleasure'. This may suggest that Royal Theatre productions are rather worthy affairs, and they can be; but that doesn't stop most selling out way in advance, hence the theatre's need for other venues like the **Turbinehallerne** at Adelgade 10, and **Baron Bolten** in Boltens Gård.

Det Kongelige Teater. *See p77.*

The theatre's most famous former employee was Auguste Bournonville, director of the Danish Ballet from 1830 to 1877. Outside stand statues of two other significant figures from the theatre's history, the playwright Ludvig Holberg (the father of modern Danish theatre) and the poet Adam Oehlenschläger.

Working your way clockwise round the square from the theatre you come to Denmark's first department store, the grand **Magasin du Nord** (*see page 159*), which replaced the Hotel du Nord in 1894; **Vinstue**, a venerable drinking den dating from 1723; the eastern end of Strøget (*see page 67*); and the posh and fusty **Hotel d'Angleterre** (*see page 43*). On a corner of the square opposite the hotel is an ornate kiosk, selling soup and drinks and decorated by a gold relief depicting Denmark's early aviators. At No.4 is another of the square's finest buildings, the Dutch Palladian-style **Thotts Palais** (1685), named after a previous owner, Count Otto Thott. These days, the pretty pink stucco palace houses the French Embassy.

On the other side of Bredgade from Thotts Palais is **Ravhuset**, home to a small shop (*see page 175*) selling jewellery made from Baltic amber. Above the shop is the equally diminutive **Amber Museum** (*listings below*) with a rather monotonous display of pieces of amber (petrified tree resin) and various prehistoric insects trapped inside more lumps of amber.

Amber Museum

Ravhuset, Kongens Nytorv 2 (33 11 67 00).
Open *June-Aug* 10am-8pm daily. *Sept-Dec, Apr, May* 10am-6pm daily. *Jan-Mar* 10am-6pm Mon-Sat; closed Sun. **Admission** 20kr; 10kr concessions. **Credit** AmEx, DC, MC, V. **Map** p77/p312 M16.

Slotsholmen

The island birthplace of the city is still its monumental heart.

A tangle of dragons' tails form the spire of **Børsen**. *See p82.*

Slotsholmen is the ancient heart of Copenhagen. This island (though it is barely recognisable as such) is the city's most important piece of real estate, the place where it all began. It was on this site in the 12th century that Bishop Absalon built his original fortress as a base from which to defeat the Wendish pirates who had been plaguing the Baltic for many years (*see page 8*). Over time Slotsholmen has expanded, and is now defined by canals on three sides (dating from Christian IV's time) and the harbour facing Christianshavn to the east. The original castle, and the many later versions, are long gone but you can still see remnants of their foundations – including, amazingly, the ruins of Bishop Absalon's castle – in the bowels of the current **Christiansborg Slot** (Christiansborg Palace). The palace is also where the Danish parliament, **Folketinget** (*see page 83*), is housed, along with the High Court, several ministries, the prime minister's department, the Royal Reception Chambers (De Kongelige Repræsentationslokaler; *listings page 85* **Christiansborg Slot**), and the Queen's

Reference Library. It is somehow also fitting that the oldest remains of the city share the island with its most striking modern sight, the 'Black Diamond' (Den Sorte Diamant) extension to the Royal Library (Det Kongelige Bibliotek; *see page 86*). The other great thing about Slotsholmen today is that many of its delights are tucked away behind small doors or in unlikely corners, which somehow makes them all the more rewarding – that's a polite way of saying that the whole place is somewhat confusingly laid out, and its main attractions are very poorly signed. (It is worth timing your visit to Slotsholmen for a Sunday afternoon when all the attractions are open at the same time.)

There is, however, no missing the classical stuccoed mausoleum (by Gottlieb Bindesboll) that houses a definitive collection of the works by Denmark's master sculptor Bertel Thorvaldsen (*see page 82* **Great Danes: Bertel Thorvaldsen**). **Thorvaldsens Museum** (*listings page 87*), situated behind Christiansborg Slotskirke (*see below*), and housed over three floors, is a must, not only for sculpture fans but for all art lovers. It opened in 1848 and is the oldest art gallery in Denmark. The museum itself is a charming blend of sparkling blue ceilings (painted in part by Christen Købke), elegant colonnades and mosaic floors. Although the monumental scale of Thorvaldsen's work and his prolific output is often hard to take in, perseverance is certainly rewarded. His subjects include not only figures from Greek and Roman mythology, his epic studies of Christ and numerous self portraits, but busts of contemporaries such as Byron, Walter Scott and the Danish poet Adam Oehlenschläger. Also featured are Thorvaldsen's private collections of Egyptian and Roman artefacts, contemporary Danish art, his sketches and some personal belongings. Outside, a fresco depicts the return of the sculptor and his works from Rome. Some English information is available.

Immediately behind the Thorvaldsens Museum is **Christiansborg Slotskirke** (Christiansborg Palace Church; *listings page 87*), one of CF Hansen's notable neo-classical masterpieces (others include the Domhuset in Nytorv and Vor Frue Kirke; *see page 73*), with a columned façade and a beautiful white stucco interior and dome. It was completed in 1829 and survived a fire in 1884, but the roof was destroyed by another fire that started during the Whitsun carnival in 1992. The restoration work was completed just in time for the 25th anniversary of Queen Margrethe's coronation in 1997. A small exhibition charts the building's remarkable restoration to its current grandeur.

Børsen (the Old Stock Exchange), on the other side of Christiansborg Slotsplads, is the oldest stock exchange in Europe, built between 1619 and 1640. It still serves as a business centre and home to Copenhagen's Chamber of Commerce, and, as such, is not open to the public. However, the exterior of this Renaissance wedding cake is a riot of stonework, embellished gables and green copper. Above it towers one of Copenhagen's most recognisable landmarks – a fantastical 54-metre (177-foot) copper spire made of four intertwined dragon's tails, built in 1625 to a design by Ludvig Heidritter. The three gold

Great Danes Bertel Thorvaldsen

echelons of neo-classical sculpture, came with the piece *Jason*, completed in 1803, and now housed in **Thorvaldsens Museum** (see page 81). His figure of Christ, which can be seen in **Vor Frue Kirke** (see page 73), became the model for statues of Christ the world over.

After his time in Rome, during which he forged an international reputation and ran a large studio with many pupils, Thorvaldsen returned to a Copenhagen that was broken and wearied by war. His return, as well as the general artistic revival of the time, helped boost morale and contributed to the emergence of a cultural and social character that is still recognisably Danish today. In 1833, he was appointed director of the Danish Academy of Fine Arts. Before his death in March 1844, Thorvaldsen bequeathed his works (plaster moulds, sketches and finished works in marble), and a collection of ancient Mediterranean art to the city, and, in return, the royal family built Thorvaldsens Museum. Thorvaldsen is buried in the centre of the museum, but don't let that cast a shadow over your enjoyment.

Denmark's greatest sculptor **Bertel Thorvaldsen** was born in Copenhagen on 19 November 1768, and studied at the Academy of Art where he won the Gold medal. In 1797, a scholarship saw him off to Rome, where he lived for 40 years, developing a style that was heavily influenced by Greek and Roman mythology, and creating works of a majestic, classical beauty, frequently on an epic scale.

His major international breakthrough, which catapulted him into the highest

Guns galore at **Tøjhusmuseet**. *See p85.*

crowns topping the spire represent the three
Nordic nations: Denmark, Sweden and Norway.
Børsen (which literally translates as 'the
covered market') was built at the behest of
Christian IV, who desperately wanted
Copenhagen to become the financial capital of
Europe (it didn't). When it was first built, ships
could moor right at its doors to unload cargo
into the downstairs trading hall, while upstairs
were shops and businesses. In 1634, the French
diplomat Charles Ogier wrote of Børsen that,
'Everything decorative and practical for all
male and female purposes is for sale here. It is
a new and splendid building much visited by
people of quality, as many women as men.'

An unusually ostentatious (for a Lutheran
church) altarpiece is the main draw of
Holmenskirken (*listings page 87*), a church
dedicated to sailors, which lies on the opposite
side of the canal from Børsen. Denmark's tallest
pulpit (it extends right to the roof, and has just
been restored) is worth a look too. Converted,
aptly, from an anchor smithy in 1619 under the
orders of Christian IV, the church's rather bland
exterior was augmented by the main portal
(on the east side), originally from Roskilde
Cathedral. Holmens Kirke is often used for
royal occasions – in 1967 Queen Margrethe and
Prince Henrik were married here. Walk through
the side door on the left of the altar and you
enter a room dedicated to Denmark's sea heroes
and graced by numerous ornate sarcophagi.
It has an excellent view of Børsen. Next door
is a forbidding concrete building housing
Nationalbanken (the National Bank), the
work of famed Danish architect and designer
Arne Jacobsen (*see page 38* **Great Danes:
Arne Jacobsen**).

The imposing copper-roofed building
fronting Christiansborg Slotsplads, beside
Børsen, is the present-day **Christiansborg
Slot**, built directly above the ruins of
Absalon's fort. Christiansborg Slot is home to
Folketinget (*listings page 87*), the Danish
parliamentary chamber, where the 179
members of the Danish parliament meet to
debate and adopt
laws. (The second
chamber, Landstinget,
was abolished in
1953.) Members sit
in a semi-circle in
their party groups
facing the speaker.
The Social Democrats
sit on the left, and
so are known as
'left wing'; the
Conservatives, seated
on the right, are
'right wing'. The
other parties sit in
between. Government
ministers sit on the
right-hand side of
the chamber with
the prime minister
closest to the platform.
Folketinget is
opened annually in
a ceremony attended
by members of the
royal family on the
first Tuesday in
October. A public

Christiansborg Slot

For many centuries **Christiansborg Slot** (Christiansborg Palace) effectively *was* Copenhagen, so central was it to the lives of the townspeople, and so dominant was it as a power base for the region. Understandably, its history mirrors that of Denmark. Its development can be divided into three stages: Absalon's fortress dating from 1167; the 17th century; and the current palace.

The warrior-bishop Absalon built his fortress on what was then the small islet of Strandholmen, in the channel separating the island of Amager from Sjælland (see page 7). The fortress was ringed by a strong, thick wall of limestone blocks, with its internal buildings made from brick and timber – the first time bricks had been used in Denmark. Bishop Absalon's fortress was badly damaged in 1259 by the avenging Wends, and then burned to the ground in 1369 by an alliance of forces led by the Lübeckers against King Valdemar Atterdag. It was replaced by the first Copenhagen Castle. From 1416, when Erik of Pomerania moved in, the castle became the permanent home of the royal family (until they moved to Amalienborg Slot in 1794).

The castle's best-known feature during the Middle Ages was the **Blå Tårn** (Blue Tower), used to house prisoners of note for several centuries – most famously Eleonore Christine, the daughter of Christian IV. She wrote what was probably the most important piece of 17th-century Danish prose, *Jammersminde*, while imprisoned here on suspicion of being involved in her husband's treason plot.

As was his way, Christian IV had the first castle demolished (though not the Blue Tower), and replaced it with a typically over-the-top baroque building, the first Christiansborg Slot, with its own chapel and very grand stables. During Frederik II's reign the castle very nearly fell to the Swedes who, following a two-year siege, in February 1659 advanced towards it across the frozen sea south of Slotsholmen, dressed in white cloaks to camouflage themselves. Luckily, the boiling oil, tar and water that the Danes rained down upon their enemy managed to drive the Swedes away. They gave up and eventually went home when their king, Karl Gustav X, died suddenly at the beginning of 1660. Soon afterwards Frederik III instructed the Dutch military engineer Henrik Ruse to build a new rampart where the Swedes had advanced. This became known as **Vestervold** (Western Rampart), and between it and Slotsholmen a new quarter, **Frederiksholm**, grew up. **Prinsens Palæ**, which now houses Nationalmuseet (see page 62), stands on land between the rampart and Slotsholmen.

Frederik IV extensively modernised the castle between 1710 and 1729, but, in 1732, Christian VI tore it all down on aesthetic grounds (the place was a mess of styles), and because its foundations were weak. The baroque replacement was one of the biggest palaces in Europe; its foundations

viewing gallery is open when parliament is in session, and there are English-language tours of the building.

Down some steps, through a door on the right-hand side of the main archway of Christiansborg Slot as you walk from Christiansborg Slotsplads (we told you this was tricky) are the enjoyably spooky **Ruinere Under Christiansborg** (Ruins under Christiansborg; *listings page 87*) and a museum dedicated to the 800-year history of the current castle site. Housed in three large underground rooms are excavations of the various older castles' foundations, including stonework from Absalon's fortress, the foundations of Denmark's most famous prison, the **Blå Tårn** (Blue Tower) and what is called **Absalon's Well** (though it probably dates from the 19th century). Viewing this jumble of ancient masonry is like trying to put together the

discarded pieces from several jigsaw puzzles, but the exhibition works hard to help you decipher the rubble (with English captions).

If you turn right as you come out of the ruins museum door and walk for a few hundred metres, you will find yourself at the equestrian arena. Over in the colonnades on the left are the entrances to two particularly enchanting royal attractions: the **Kongelige Stalde og Kareter** (Royal Stables and Coaches; *listings page 87*) and **Teatermuseet** (the Theatre Museum; *listings page 87*). If you can endure the horsey odours, the royal stables, with their vaulted ceilings and marble columns, offer a glimpse into an extravagant royal past. The queen's horses and coaches are still kept in grand style here, and are often used for state occasions (as is a rather dusty Bentley convertible from 1969). Teatermuseet, which opened in 1922, is housed in the old Royal Court

during its design they demanded to have at least the same number of windows overlooking the palace square as the king. Its central tower is the tallest (by 40 centimetres) in Denmark at 106 metres (358 feet). Frederik VIII laid the foundation stone for the current castle in 1907, and the museum displays several amazing photographs from that time.

Over the years, the various castles/palaces on Slotsholmen have come in for a bit of stick from European visitors, as the ruins exhibition (see page 84) also records. In 1588, a French traveller commented, 'It is remarkable more for its age than its magnificence.' A German visitor of 1600 said that, 'It resembles the dwelling of a little prince rather than a great king.' Englishman William Bromley, writing in 1699, agreed: 'The King's palace is one of the meanest that I ever saw, with a foul stinking ditch about it,' while Erik Pontoppidan wrote in the Danish Atlas of 1764 of his concerns for the building's structural integrity: 'A piece of the old building, which I remember seeing before and which was said to have been Bishop Absalon's house did not look as though it could bear all the masonry set on top of it.'

Christiansborg Slot

Slotsholmen (33 92 64 92/www.slotte.dk). **Tours** (in English) *May-Sept* 11am, 1pm, 3pm daily. *Oct-Apr* closed. **Tickets** 40kr; 10kr-30kr concessions. **No credit cards**. **Map** p83/p311 O14.

alone cost three million rigsdalers, then equivalent to the entire value of Sjælland's arable land.

On the night of 26 February 1794 the whole lot burned down (bar the stables, which are still in use today). The royal family finally gave up on Slotsholmen and, like monarchical magpies, bought Amalienborg Slot (see page 88). Work on the next Christiansborg Slot didn't start until 1803 due to the national bankruptcy under Frederik VI, and the building, a neo-classical masterpiece, was completed in 1828. That, too, was badly damaged by a fire (which could be seen from Jylland) in October 1884.

You would hardly term the present-day copper-roofed Christiansborg Slot a castle. Its neo-baroque granite and concrete façade, more like that of a town hall, was designed by Thorvald Jørgensen. It was the first Christiansborg to have been built by the people's representatives, who were apparently still quite touchy about the monarchy, as

Theatre, designed by the French architect Nicolas Henri Jardin. It dates from 1766 and was modernised in 1842 – HC Andersen once performed in a ballet here in his youth. The exhibits include costumes, set designs and art works. There is also a special cabinet of objects connected with the Royal Ballet choreographer Auguste Bournonville. Incidentally, this is also where Count von Struensee (*see page 16* **The cunning count and the crazy king**) was arrested in 1772 on trumped-up charges of treason, and not so trumped-up allegations of an affair with the queen.

Continue across the equestrian arena to the archway beyond and you come to Frederiksholms Kanal, forded by **Marmorbroen** (the Marble Bridge). Quite a fuss is made over this bridge, designed by Nicolai Eigtved (*see page 91* **Great Danes: Niels 'Nicolai' Eigtved**) for Christian IV and

completed in 1745, but, frankly, aside from some decorative sandstone portraits, it isn't all that special (and it isn't even all marble).

Back on Slotsholmen, another tucked-away treat is **Tøjhusmuseet** (the Royal Arsenal Museum; *listings page 87*), founded in 1838. It's a couple of minutes' walk back in the direction of the castle. Comprising an endless vaulted Renaissance cannon hall (the longest in Europe, modelled on the one in Venice), and a mind-boggling number of arms and armour in an upstairs display, this is the finest museum of its kind in the world. On the ground floor of what was Christian IV's original arsenal building (dating from 1589-1604), within walls four metres (13 feet) thick, are a vast number of gun carriages, cannons, a V-1 flying bomb from World War II and the teeniest tank you ever saw (from 1933). Upstairs, the glass cases, containing everything from 15th-century swords and pikes

Flying free over Slotsholmen.

to modern machine guns, seem to go on forever. Many items, such as the beautiful ivory inlaid pistols and muskets, are works of art, and the royal suits of armour are equally stunning. The small arms section of the museum is housed in **Kongens Bryghus** (the King's Brewery), a vast, red-brick warehouse that has the largest tiled roof in Denmark; it's just south of Tøjhusmuseet. The Bryghus, erected during Christian IV's reign (probably to quench the king's herculean thirst, as well as that of his navy) was never actually used for brewing beer, merely to store it. (Look out for plunging bungee jumpers just outside by the water.)

Copenhagen's most beautiful 'hidden' garden, **Bibliotekshaven** (the Library Garden; *listings page 87*), just around the corner, lies tucked away behind the old ivy-covered **Det Kongelige Bibliotek** (the Royal Library; *listings page 87*), through a gateway on Rigdagsgården, opposite the entrance to Folketinget. Arranged in a square around a fountain and fishpond, the garden, on the site of what was once a dockyard giving access to the armoury and **Proviantshuset** (the Supply Depot), blooms beautifully in summer, when even the bronze statue of Søren Kierkegaard looks cheerful. You can see some of the old ships' mooring rings from Christian IV's time on the walls surrounding it.

The Danes love nothing more than to juxtapose old and new styles, particularly where architecture is concerned, but when the designs for the new extension to the Royal Library, by architects Schmidt, Hammer and Lassen, were first unveiled, they weren't prepared for something this radical. There are several ways to approach Denmark's new national library extension (opened in September 1999). Perhaps the best is to walk through the old library's garden so that when you round the corner of the 1906 red-brick building (by Hans Holm), you are suddenly confronted with the enormity of the new structure close up. This malevolent parallelogram (nicknamed the '**Black Diamond**'), made from glass, black Zimbabwean granite (cut in Portugal and polished in Italy), Portuguese sandstone, silk concrete and Canadian maple, abuts the old building with little consideration for the clash of styles that ensues. Its reflective surfaces interact constantly with the sky and water around it, altering the building's colour and shape by the second. The 500 million kroner library houses 200,000 books, an exhibition space, a shop, a concert hall (*see page 221*), the **National Photography Museum** (with regular temporary exhibitions in the basement), a restaurant (**Søren K**; *see page 140*), a canteen, espresso bar and conference rooms. The old library, the largest in Scandinavia, with its glorious reading room (open to non-members) is accessed through a glass walkway from the first floor.

The '**Black Diamond**' – a literary jewel.

Bibliotekshaven.

Bibliotekshaven
Rigdagsgården (33 92 65 86/www.slotte.dk).
Open 6am-10pm Mon-Sat; closed Sun.
Admission free. **Map** p83/p311 O14.

Christiansborg Slotskirke
Christiansborg Slotsplads (33 92 64 51/www.ses.dk).
Open noon-4pm Sun; closed Mon-Sat.
Admission free. **Map** p83/p311 O14.

Folketinget
Rigdagsgården (33 37 55 00/www.folketinget.dk).
Tours *Late Aug-late May* (in Danish) hourly 10am-
4pm Sun (2pm in English); closed Mon-Sat. *Early
June-mid Aug* (in Danish) hourly 10am-4pm Mon-Fri
(2pm in English); closed Sat, Sun. **Admission** free.
Map p83/p311 O14.

Holmenskirken
Holmens Kanal (33 13 61 78/www.holmenskirke.dk).
Open 9am-2pm Mon-Fri; 9am-noon Sat; closed Sun.
Admission free. **Map** p83/p311 O15.

The best Parks

Bibliotekshaven
Exquisite 'hidden' garden. See page 86.

Frederiksberg Have
Hilly park, west of the centre. See page 113.

Kongens Have
Around Rosenborg Slot. See page 98.

Ørsteds Parken
Small park, with a cool café. See page 69.

Det Kongelige Bibliotek
*Søren Kierkegaards Plads 1 (33 47 47 47/
www.kb.dk).* **Open** *Main building* 10am-11pm
Mon-Sat; closed Sun. *Library* 10am-9pm Mon-Fri;
10am-7pm Sat; closed Sun. *Exhibitions* 10am-7pm
Mon-Sat; closed Sun. **Admission** *Main building &
library* free. *Exhibitions* 30kr; 10kr concessions.
Concerts prices vary. **No credit cards**.
Map p83/p311 P14.

Kongelige Stalde og Kareter
Christiansborg Ridebane 12 (33 40 26 77).
Open *May-Sept* 2-4pm Fri-Sun; closed Mon-Thur.
Oct-Apr 2-4pm Sat, Sun; closed Mon-Fri.
Admission 10kr; 5kr concessions.
No credit cards. **Map** p83/p311 O14.

Ruinere Under Christiansborg
Christiansborg Slot (33 92 64 94/www.ses.dk).
Open *Jan-Sept* 9.30am-3.30pm daily. *Oct-Dec*
9.30am-3.30pm Tue, Thur, Sat, Sun; closed Mon,
Wed, Fri. **Admission** 20kr; 15kr concessions.
No credit cards. **Map** p83/p311 O14.

Teatermuseet
*Christiansborg Ridebane 10/18, southern wing of
Christiansborg Slot (33 11 51 76).* **Open** 2-4pm
Wed; noon-4pm Sat, Sun; closed Mon, Tue, Thur, Fri.
Admission 20kr; 10kr concessions. **No credit
cards**. **Map** p83/p311 O14.

Thorvaldsens Museum
Porthusgade 2 (33 32 15 32). **Open** 10am-5pm Tue-
Sun; closed Mon. **Admission** 20kr; free under-15s.
Free to all Wed. **Credit** MC, V. **Map** p83/p311 O14.

Tøjhusmuseet
Tøjhusgade 3 (33 11 60 37/www.thm.dk).
Open noon-4pm Tue-Sun; closed Mon.
Admission 20kr; 5kr-10kr concessions.
No credit cards. **Map** p83/p311 P14.

Frederiksstaden

A fine example of 18th-century urban planning, the wide, straight streets of the city's stately northern district are lined with palaces, churches and museums.

Head north from cutesy Nyhavn into Bredgade and the architecture changes dramatically, from quaint, multicoloured gabled houses to the straight, wide, French-influenced streets of **Frederiksstaden**, a residential area (now mainly offices) laid out in the 18th century for Copenhagen's nobility and nouveau riche. Frederiksstaden was the vision of Frederik V, who wished to celebrate the 300th anniversary of the House of Oldenburg in 1749 with a grand new building project. The king didn't, however, fancy paying for it, so, instead, he donated the land on the condition that selected members of Copenhagen's nobility commission the rococo architect Nicolai Eigtved (*see page 91* **Great Danes: Niels 'Nicolai' Eigtved**) to build a uniform quarter. Today, Bredgade is a street packed with treasures, some more obvious than others.

The main auction houses are based here, as are numerous art and antiques dealers from the higher end of the market. A short way down Bredgade on the right is Sankt Annæ Plads, a quiet tree-lined square with a dull, red-brick church, **Garnisons Kirke**. Inside, the church is equally uninspiring, apart for some pretty silver chandeliers and a profoundly vulgar gold and red organ. Another, far more impressive, church, **Frederikskirken**, better known as **Marmorkirken** (the Marble Church; *listings page 94*), awaits a short walk away.

Although today it is one of Copenhagen's most breathtaking sights, the circular, domed Marmorkirken very nearly didn't get built. Work on the church, designed by Nicolai Eigtved as the focal point of the new quarter, began in 1749, but was halted in 1770 by Count von Struensee (*see page 16* **The cunning count and the crazy king**) due to its exorbitant expense, with the walls only 10-15 metres (33-49 feet) high. It wasn't until the deep-pocketed industrialist CF Tietgen intervened in the late 1800s that the church (by then a grass-covered ruin) was completed in Danish limestone, instead of Norwegian marble. It was topped with a 46-metre (151-foot) dome (inspired by St Peter's in Rome; from the top you can see Sweden), by the architect Ferdinand Meldahl. Outside, the church is surrounded by statues of great Danes including Grundtvig and Kierkegaard.

Down Frederiksgade, directly opposite the main entrance to Marmorkirken, are the four rococo palaces surrounding a grand cobbled square, which together make up **Amalienborg Slot** (Amalienborg Palace). Home to the royal family since 1794 (a raised flag indicates their presence), the palaces were originally built by four wealthy traders, as part of Frederik V's scheme for the area. The royal family commandeered it after a fire destroyed Christiansborg (*see page 84*). As you enter the square along Frederiksgade from Marmorkirken, the palaces are (clockwise from the left) **Levetzau Palace**, **Brockdorff Palace**, **Moltke Palace** and **Schack Palace** (originally Løvenskjold Palace).

The **Amalienborg Museum** (within Levetzau Palace; *details page 94*) is an extension of the Royal Collections at Rosenborg Slot (*see page 100*) and features several private rooms and studies belonging to the Royal Glücksborg family, from 1863 to 1947, starting with Christian IX (the so-called Father-In-Law of Europe). Note Frederik IX's amazing pipe collection, Queen Louise's rococo drawing room and a number of quite abysmal pieces of art created by members of the family over the years (in contrast to the works by the current, more gifted queen).

In the square stands French sculptor Jacques Saly's 12-metre (39-foot) statue of Frederik V, modelled on the equestrian statue of Marcus Aurelius on the Capitol in Rome. It took 20 years to complete due to a financial wrangle over payment from backers the East Asiatic Company, but remains an important piece of European sculpture. Every day, when the queen is in residence, the square is the venue for the changing of the Royal Guard. You can follow the soldiers, who start their parade at 11.30am from the barracks beside Rosenborg Slot, and continue along Gothersgade, Frederiksborggade, Købmagergade, Østergade, around Kongens Nytorv and down Bredgade, until reaching Frederiksgade and the palace square. If you miss it, don't worry, because several soldiers remain on guard in the square, wearing their distinctive blue, red and white uniforms with bearskins around the clock – primarily, you can't help suspecting, to provide photo opportunities.

Behind the mighty statue of Frederik V is **Amaliehaven**, a small harbourside park donated by the industrialist AP Møller in 1983. In the summer, the walk from the shadows of the vast cruise ships that dock here, past a number of 18th-century warehouses, the Royal Cast Collection, the spectacular Gefion Fountain and on to the (far from spectacular) Little Mermaid (for all, *see below*) is extremely popular among Copenhagen's perambulators, dog walkers and joggers. You may even bump into Queen Margrethe or Prince Henrik, who walk their daschunds here.

The exterior of **Den Kongelige Afstøbningssamlingen** (the Royal Cast Collection; *listings page 94*) is marked by an incongruous bronze replica of Michelangelo's *David*. Inside, 2,000 plaster casts of the world's most famous and outstanding sculptures cover a period of 4,000 years.

A short walk along the old harbour brings you to Copenhagen's most spectacular piece of public statuary, **Gefion Springvandet** (the Gefion Fountain). Built in 1909 by sculptor Anders Bundgaard and financed by the Carlsberg Foundation, the statue of the

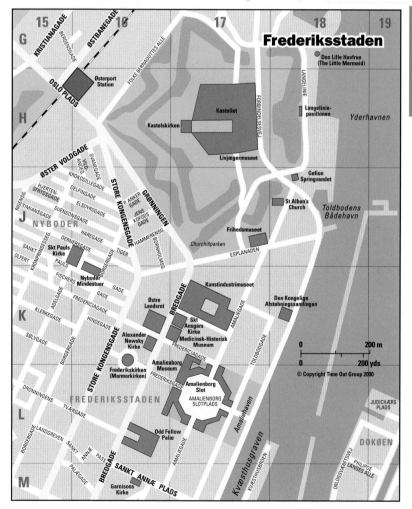

The gilded onion domes of **Alexander Newsky Kirke**. *See p91.*

goddess Gefion commanding four ploughing bulls (her sons, conveniently transformed for the purpose), is inspired by the ancient Norse saga about the birth of Sjælland – Gefion was told by the King of Sweden that she could keep as much land as she could plough in a night, and that hard night's labour earned her Sjælland.

Finally, after passing the ramparts of Kastellet along Langelinie, you arrive at **Den Lille Havfrue** (the Little Mermaid). This winsome bronze sculpture, created by Edward Eriksen in 1913, and, again, paid for by Carlsberg, has, through sheer repetition of its image, become the international symbol of Copenhagen. Many wish it hadn't, so utterly does it fail to evoke either the spirit of the city or the poignancy of HC Andersen's fable (about the daughter of the sea king who gave up her sea legs for a human prince), so pitifully small is it, and so remote is its location (in winter the seafront walk to reach it is a particular challenge). No wonder the poor dear has had her head hacked off a couple of times.

Back on Bredgade a few of those hidden treasures await. Just around the corner from Marmorkirken is another smaller, but equally fascinating church, **Alexander Newsky Kirke** (*listings page 94*). The only Russian Orthodox church in Denmark is easily identified by its three incongruous gold onion domes; to step inside is to travel back into pre-Revolutionary Russia, as your eyes adjust to

The inexplicably popular **Little Mermaid**.

the Byzantine gloom, and begin to take in the gold icons that glimmer on the walls. The church was built between 1881 and 1884 at the behest of Princess Dagmar, daughter of Christian IX, who married Grand Duke Alexander, later Emperor Alexander III, and converted to the Russian Orthodox faith. She apparently needed somewhere to worship when she visited Copenhagen (and the fact that Newsky, Prince of Novgorod, once famously defeated a Swedish army in the 13th century can only have helped get the project through). On the right-hand side of the church an icon of the Holy Virgin, painted in a monastery on Mount Athos in Greece in 1912, and mounted on its own stand, is said, occasionally during spring, to weep real tears. If you doubt it, you can see for yourself where water has run from

Great Danes Niels 'Nicolai' Eigtved

The architect **Niels 'Nicolai' Eigtved** was Denmark's leading rococo architect, responsible for many of Copenhagen's most impressive buildings. Having learned about the fashionably light, decorative style while working in Germany and Poland, Eigtved returned to Copenhagen in 1735 where his knowledge was immediately exploited by Christian VI who appointed him court architect. In this capacity he began working on the interiors of Christiansborg, before designing **Marmorbroen** (the Marble Bridge, which crosses the Frederiksholm Canal on the west side of Slotsholmen), the original Royal Theatre on Kongens Nytorv (no longer there),

Frederiks Hospital (which now houses Kunstindustrimuseet and the Medicinsk-Historisk Museum, see page 92), and **Prinsens Palæ**, now home to Nationalmuseet (see page 62). By far his greatest achievement was the plan for an entire new quarter, **Frederiksstaden**, ordered by Frederik V in 1749, with the present **Amalienborg Slot** and **Marmorkirken** (see page 88) at its centre. He designed the four palaces of Amalienborg around an octagonal square and personally oversaw the lavish interior of one of them, **Moltke Palace**, which is still used for state occasions. Eigtved died in 1751, and is commemorated by a stone relief in a wall on Frederiksgade as you enter Amalienborg from Bredgade.

her eyes and tarnished the paint. The nearby icon of St Nicholas is said to have been the only item to have survived the wreck of a Russian warship.

Across the street lies Copenhagen's small neo-Romanesque Catholic cathedral, **Sankt Ansgar Kirke** (*listings page 94*), built in 1841. The cathedral is flanked by Kunstindustrimuseet and the Medicinsk-Historisk Museum (for both, *see below*).

Housed around a grand courtyard in the old Frederiks Hospital (by Nicolai Eigtved; *see page 91* **Great Danes: Niels 'Nicolai' Eigtved**), the 300,000 items in **Kunstindustrimuseet** (the Museum of Decorative and Applied Art; *listings page 94*) focus on living rooms from the Middle Ages to the present day, with the emphasis on Danish design and craft. As you'd expect, chairs dominate (a rare and fragile chair from a Glasgow tearoom, designed by Charles Rennie Macintosh, is a highlight and probably one of the most valuable chairs in the world), but there are also textiles, carpets, clothing, ceramics, cutlery, silverware, glassware, art and other furniture on display. The exhibits from Asia are particularly good. The strength of the museum is its blending of the old with the contemporary in a pleasant, soothing rococo setting. This is yet another of Copenhagen's museums funded by the Ny Carlsberg Foundation. It was founded in 1890, and moved to this site in 1926. There are English captions throughout, as well as an excellent café and shop.

It is easy to miss the **Medicinsk-Historisk Museum** (Medical History Museum; *listings page 94*), housed in the Royal Academy Of Surgeons (1787), Titken's House (1754) and Panum's Physiological Institute (1867), all once part of the old Frederiks Hospital, but it is definitely worth taking in a guided tour (the only way to see the museum). Tours last around an hour, during which visitors are shown all manner of grisly exhibits, starting in the old lecture hall, modelled on Gondouinin's anatomical auditorium in Paris. If chairs used to examine syphilis patients, the faeces from a cholera patient, amputation tools, enema syringes and dental equipment worthy of the Spanish Inquisition sound appealing, this is the museum for you. The interior from a 19th-century apothecary is another notable attraction. In July and August the 1pm tour is in English.

Bredgade ends at a diminutive park, **Churchillparken**, located in front of Kastellet (*see page 93*), and named after Britain's wartime leader (there's a small, curmudgeonly bust of him here). Maintaining the British theme, you'll also find **St Alban's Church** (*listings page 94*), a perfect English Gothic flint church (bizarrely part of the Anglican Diocese of Gibraltar), which looks like it's been lifted straight from the Sussex countryside, and Frihedsmuseet (*see page 93*).

Continue towards the harbour and you pass the offices of Maersk, the international oil and shipping conglomerate, owned by AP Møller,

Great Danes Queen Margrethe II

The Danes' affection for their Queen is one of their most touching and, given the general attitude of determined equality that pervades Danish society, puzzling characteristics. That's not to say that **Queen Margrethe II** isn't worthy of such adoration; by all accounts she is a sensitive, modern monarch, whose artistic talents put a certain other European royal's watercolour efforts in the shade. Literally every single Dane you meet, while perhaps might not wholeheartedly endorsing the abstract notion of a royal family, won't have a bad thing to say about Queen Margrethe II.

Margrethe Alexandrine Porhildur Ingrid was born during the dark days of Denmark's occupation by Germany, on 16 April 1940. The daughter of King Frederik IX and Queen Ingrid, she was born at Amalienborg and was heralded as a beacon of hope during that

troubled time (her very name harked back to the first Margrethe, who unified the region under the Kalmar Union; see page 8).

Margrethe went to school in Denmark before going on to study at the universities of Copenhagen, Cambridge, Århus, London and the Sorbonne in the 1960s. Her main subject was political science, but she also developed a keen interest in archaeology and the arts. She also spent time in the Women's Flying Corps and the WAAF in England.

In 1967 she married a French diplomat, Henri, Comte de Laborde de Monpezat (now Prince Henrik), by whom she had two sons, Frederik (born 1968), an adventurer and one of Europe's most eligible bachelors, and Joachim (born 1969), married with one son.

When Margrethe was born, Denmark's royal accession law still forbade female inheritance of the throne, but in 1953 a referendum on your right, and eventually arrive at the old harbour buildings and the southern end of Langelinie. Here are also two pentagonal, green-roofed gazebos, where the royal family wait to board their yacht.

The entrance to **Frihedsmuseet** (the Museum of Danish Resistance; *listings page 94*) is marked by a battered armoured car, once used by the plucky minority that constituted the Danish Resistance during World War II. Inside this purpose-built wooden hall, arranged around an open courtyard, are numerous moving testimonies to the endeavours of the Danish Resistance and the suffering of their country under occupation. The museum is divided into four areas: 1940-1 Adaptation; 1942-3 Resistance; 1943-4 Terror; and 1944-5 Liberation. The letters (translated into English), from Resistance fighters to their mothers before their execution, and indeed the very execution stakes they stood against to face the firing squads, are here, as are the various home-made weapons and sabotage equipment used by the resistance. There are biographies of the movement's leaders and displays about the boys' groups who were the first to rebel.

Denmark was something of a military backwater during World War II, of use chiefly as Germany's larder, and, as such, it was in the occupier's interest to allow life here to continue as normally as possible. However, when in 1942 Hitler took offence to King Christian X's terse response to his birthday greeting, the German

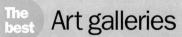

The best Art galleries

Arken
Contemporary art. See page 124.

Den Hirschprungske Samling
Denmark's Golden Age. See page 95.

Louisiana
Stunning location, stunning modern art. See page 272.

Ny Carlsberg Glyptotek
Sculpture and Impressionism. See page 64.

Statens Museum For Kunst
Denmark's National Gallery. See page 98.

leader sent Werner Best, one of the architects of the Gestapo, to run the country. That year saw numerous uprisings, the largest of which came in August. In the same year, around 7,000 Danish Jews were spirited away to neutral Sweden after news got out that Best was about to round them up for deportation to concentration camps (*see page 21* **Jewish exodus**).

Frihedsmuseet is overlooked by **Kastellet** (the Castle; *listings page 94*), a remnant of even older conflicts. Built by Frederik III in 1662 after the Swedish siege of 1658 on the St Annæ entrenchment from Christian IV's time,

endorsed the overturning of this centuries-old policy to enable her to one day become queen. When her father died in January 1972, she ascended the throne and revolutionised the Danish monarchy with her frank interviews, open stance on various social issues, and a spirited attack on Janteloven (see page 15 **Janteloven**). She meets with representatives of the government weekly, and her well-informed New Year's broadcast to the nation is awaited with respect by the populace.

Margrethe's various artistic achievements are near-legendary (as is her cigarette habit). She has created textile designs; illustrated a version of *Lord Of The Rings*; together with her husband she translated Simone de Beauvoir's *Tout Les Hommes Sont Mortelle* into Danish; and designed sets for the 1987 TV production of HC Andersen's *The Shepherdess and the Chimney Sweep* and the ballet *A Popular Legend* (1991).

In 2000 Margrethe celebrated her 60th birthday with her popularity undiminished.

Amalienborg Slot. *See p88.*

this vast star-shaped fortress with its five bastions was the base for the Danish army for many years, and still houses troops in pretty red terraces inside the ramparts. Kastellet was designed partly to protect the harbour and partly as a safe haven for the royal family and military in case Copenhagen Palace were to be attacked again. Ironically, it was right in front of Kastellet, that the Germans landed many centuries later in 1940. Its prison (1725) housed Count von Struensee (*see page 16* **The cunning count and the crazy king**) before he met his grisly end.

These days the path around the ramparts makes a good jogging track. From its north-easterly bastion you get a good view of the Little Mermaid and the Swedish coast. Turn around and you get an equally good view of Marmorkirken's dome and the windmill on nearby Kongens Bastion. There is a tiny museum of army regalia, **Livjægermuseet** (*listings below*), at the southern gate.

Alexander Newsky Kirke
Bredgade 53 (33 13 60 46/Tours 26 65 23 74).
Open 11.30am-1.30pm Tue-Thur; closed Mon, Fri-Sun. **Admission** free. **Tours** by arrangement only, 25kr; 20kr concessions. **No credit cards.**
Map p89/p308 K16.

Amalienborg Museum
Levetzau Palace, Amalienborg Plads (33 12 08 08/ www.slotte.dk). **Open** *May-Oct* 10am-4pm daily. *Nov-Apr* 11am-4pm Tue-Sun; closed Mon. **Admission** 40kr; 5kr-25kr concessions; free under-5s. **Credit** MC, V.
Map p89/p308 L17.

Frederikskirken (Marmorkirken)
Frederiksgade 4 (33 15 01 44). **Open** 10am-5pm Mon, Tue, Thur, Fri; 10am-6pm Wed; noon-5pm Sat, Sun. *Dome 1 Sept-14 June* 1pm, 3pm Sat, Sun; closed Mon-Fri. *15 June-31 Aug* 1pm, 3pm daily. **Admission** free; *dome* 20kr; 10kr under-12s. **No credit cards.** Map p89/p308 K16.

Frihedsmuseet
Churchillparken (33 13 77 14/www.natmus.dk/ frihedsmuseet). **Open** *1 May-15 Sept* 10am-4pm Tue-Sat; 10am-5pm Sun; closed Mon. *16 Sept-30 Apr* 11am-3pm Tue-Sat; 11am-4pm Sun; closed Mon. **Admission** free. Map p89/p308 J17.

Kastellet
Langelinie (33 47 95 00). **Open** 7am-10pm daily. **Admission** free. Map p89/p308 J17.

Den Kongelige Afstøbningssamlingen
Vestindisk Pakhus, Toldbodgade 40 (33 74 85 85/ www.smk.dk). **Open** 10am-4pm Wed, Thur; 1-4pm Sat, Sun; closed Mon, Tue, Fri. **Admission** 20kr; free under-16s. **Credit** DC, MC, V. Map p89/p308 K18.

Kunstindustrimuseet
Bredgade 68 (33 14 94 52/www.mus-kim.dk). **Open** *Middle Ages to 1800* 1-4pm Tue-Fri; noon-4pm Sat, Sun; closed Mon. *1800 to present day, café, library & temporary exhibitions* 10am-4pm Tue-Fri; noon-4pm Sat, Sun; closed Mon. **Admission** 35kr; 20kr concessions; free under-16s. **Credit** MC, V. Map p89/p308 K17.

Livjægermuseet
Kastellet (33 47 95 00). **Open** *May-Sept* noon-4pm Sun; closed Mon-Sat. *Oct-Apr* closed. **Admission** free. Map p89/p308 H17.

Medicinsk-Historisk Museum
Bredgade 62 (35 32 38 00/www.mhm.ku.dk). **Open** *guided tours only* 11am, 1pm Wed-Fri, Sun (1pm tours in Aug are in English). **Admission** 30kr; 20kr concessions. **No credit cards.** Map p89/p308 K17.

St Alban's Church
Churchillparken (tours, ring 1 wk in advance 33 15 60 62). **Open** *May-Sept* 10am-4pm daily. *Oct-Apr* for services only, 10.30am Wed; 9am, 10.30am Sun. **Admission** free; *tours* prices vary. Map p89/p308 J18.

Sankt Ansgar Kirke
Bredgade 62 (33 13 37 62). **Open** 8am-6pm daily. **Admission** free. Map p89/p308 K17.

94 Time Out Copenhagen Guide

Rosenborg & Around

A clutch of superb art and curiosity museums lie within a few minutes of Christian IV's fascinating palace.

As with most of Renaissance Copenhagen, the impetus for the development of the area surrounding Rosenborg Slot came from King Christian IV. In the early 17th century this area lay beyond the northern side of the city's ramparts and, at first, Christian contented himself with a summer pavilion here, laid out within the ornamental gardens of Kongens Have (*see page 98*). However, this subsequently became Rosenborg Slot (*see page 100*), the fantastical Renaissance palace that stands here today, while around it grew up a new district, which eventually doubled the size of Copenhagen. The Nyboder (*see page 99*) system of cottages, built to house Christian's naval personnel, alone increased the population by a couple of thousand.

Statens Museum For Kunst (the National Gallery; *see page 98*), on the corner of Øster Voldgade and Sølvgade, is Denmark's national gallery and its largest art museum, a position that it consolidated in 1998 with the opening of a new extension by architect Anna Maria Indrio. Inside are works that chart the cultural identity of the country over a period of 700 years, from pictorial art from the 14th century to the most contemporary installations. Other important international works also feature strongly, including many by Dutch and Italian 16th- and 17th-century masters, and the big names of the 19th and 20th centuries, such as Van Gogh, Matisse and Picasso.

Hidden, both literally and metaphorically, in the shadow of the monolithic Statens Museum For Kunst is another remarkable art museum, **Den Hirschsprungske Samling** (the Hirschsprung Collection; *listings page 101*), a collection of art from the 19th and early 20th centuries that is particularly strong on the Danish Golden Age (1800-50; *see page 18*). It was created by the tobacco manufacturer Heinrich Hirschsprung (1836-1908), who during his life crammed the paintings and sculptures into his home on Højbro Plads. Before he died, Hirschsprung donated the entire collection to the Municipality of Copenhagen on condition that they be displayed in similarly intimate surroundings, hence the series of small rooms around three larger halls that make up the museum building (by architect HB Storck).

Eckersberg at **Den Hirschsprungske Samling**.

The museum opened in 1911, three years after Hirschsprung's death, and it has continued to purchase works ever since.

The father of the Golden Age of painters was CW Eckersberg, who was appointed Professor of Painting at the Academy of Fine Arts in 1818. Eckersberg was part of Thorvaldsen's circle in Rome (*see page 82*) and his rejection of the rules governing historical painting, and his focus on 'real' subjects, influenced pupils like the child prodigy Christen Købke and Wilhelm Bendz. The museum has examples of both Eckersberg's enjoyably frank portraits of Copenhagen's bourgeoisie and his serene seascapes, while Købke's and Bendz's (who lived on nearby Esplanaden) at times almost photo-realistic landscapes also feature strongly. Several of the other leading landscape painters of the time studied under Professor JL Lund, and their works feature in room five. Of these, JT Lundbye's are the most effective at evoking the

late summer light in Denmark. Many of the rest are typified by clouds scudding across icy blue skies, with rolling, golden corn fields below. As the 19th century drew to a close, an increasing awareness of social inequality began to influence Denmark's artists. Neither Ejnar Nielsen nor Erik Henningsen, for instance, shied away from difficult subjects, while the symbolist Vilhelm Hammershøi reflected the grim lives of his subjects with a fittingly sombre palette. The museum is packed with pensioners on Wednesdays, when entrance is free.

Across Sølvgade from Statens Museum is the large **Geologisk Museum** (Geological Museum; *listings page 101*), with displays of fossils, dinosaurs, and Denmark's and Greenland's geography. There are several English-language leaflets, but the museum is showing its age, and is really only for those with a special interest.

Adjoining the museum is the **Botanisk Have** (Botanical Garden; *listings page 101*), providing Elysian relief from the city's intense medieval streets in summer, while its balmy Palmehus (Palm House), modelled after the one at Kew in London, can provide a welcome rest from the arctic frost of winter. There is also a **Botanisk Museum** (*listings page 97*) here, open only in summer. The garden was laid out in 1871 to designs by HA Flindt with a lake that was once part of the city moat as its centrepiece.

Inside the **Botanisk Have**'s Palmehus.

Here, you'll find examples of most of Denmark's wild flora as well as the more exotic plants that could be persuaded to grow this far north.

Just south of the Botanisk Have, on Rømersgade, is **Arbejdermuseet** (the Workers' Museum; *listings page 101*), whose entrance is guarded by a statue of Lenin that looks like it's come straight from a provincial Soviet town square. (As it turns out, the statue is here because the Danish co-operative, the Workers' Fuel Suppliers, helped pay for Lenin's passage from exile in Switzerland home to Russia). This rather dry, and sometimes muddled, museum, housed in the atmospheric former headquarters of the Social Democratic Party, attempts to show how Danish workers' lives have changed over the century. Its political bias is a little oppressive, and the exhibits overpoweringly sepia-toned, but the glimpses it offers into how Danes used to live are fascinating. The most interesting exhibit is an entire apartment that remained unaltered through the course of the last century, and was donated to the museum in 1990. The various rooms tell the moving story of the real-life Sørensen family, who occupied them for two generations. The rooms chart the progress of the family's escape from rural poverty, the father's work at a

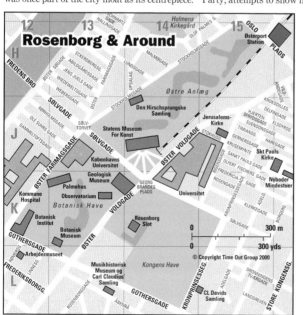

Statens Museum For Kunst

Sightseeing

As with Nationalmuseet, the world-class collection of **Statens Museum For Kunst** (the National Gallery), though founded in 1824, has its origins in royal collections from centuries earlier. During the 19th century, the collection was based in Christiansborg Slot, until a fire meant it had to move to the current specially-designed building by Vilhelm Dahlerup (also responsible for Ny Carlsberg Glyptotek and Det Kongelige Teater, see pages 64 and 77) in 1896.

Unlike Henning Larsen's acclaimed extension to the Ny Carlsberg Glyptotek, Anna Maria Indrio's glass and stone extension has proved to be a controversial space for the museum's large collection of Danish and European art from the 20th century onwards. Some say the new gallery fails to provide appropriate rooms in which to exhibit the paintings, others find its mixture of vast glass windows (overlooking Østre Anlæg park) and unrelenting stone offers a pleasing spacial puzzle. It's certainly

not quite the neutral backdrop the museum claims it to be, more a grand piece of 'event' architecture, against which the artworks themselves can sometimes struggle to be heard (the acoustics, incidentally, are terrible).

These days, Danish art museums tend to attract as much architectural discourse as they do artistic appreciation, but what of the works themselves? The museum's main focus is of course Danish art, and as you'd expect the artists from the so-called Golden Age of the early 19th century figure prominently (see also page 95 Den Hirschsprungske Samling). These rooms are dedicated to the old Danish masters, such as CW Eckersburg, and his pupils Christen Købke (see page 202) and Constantin Hansen. The landscapes of JT Lundbye, the stark portraits of Vilhelm Hammershøi, the powerful portraits by LA Ring and the symbolist pieces by PC Skovgaard (whose mighty canvas, *Christ in the Kingdom of Death*,

---

brewery, the parents' deaths, and how one of their eight children, their daughter Yrsa, took over the home in 1964. Be warned, it swarms with school trips on weekdays.

Diagonally across the crossroads outside Statens Museum is the entrance to the oldest park in Copenhagen, **Kongens Have** (the King's Garden), and **Rosenborg Slot** (Rosenborg Palace; *see page 100*). A glimpse of this fairytale, Dutch Renaissance castle right in the heart of Copenhagen never fails to surprise, and many more pleasures await inside, not least the crown jewels.

Just south of the park, on Åbenrå, is the **Musikhistorisk Museum og Carl Claudius' Samling** (Musical History Museum and Carl Claudius' Collection; *listings page 101*), another of Copenhagen's great curio museums,

founded in 1898. Here, in three 18th-century houses, you'll find just about every musical instrument from Europe, Asia and Africa that you can imagine. Oddities abound in this collection, and include King Frederik IX's zither, Prime Minister HC Hansen's mandolin and a life mask of Beethoven, as well as many other fantastically ornate 17th- and 18th-century instruments. Carl Nielsen's piano, or one of them at any rate, is another star among the 2,000 or so exhibits. (Some English information is available.)

Alongside Kongens Have, on Kronprinsessegade (built on land donated by the king after the fire of 1795; *see page 14*), is hidden yet another treasure house of a museum, one that is often overshadowed by its neighbours. Actually, as you climb the first

If you haven't seen them before, allow as much time as you can in these rooms.

In the new wing, the astounding collection of 25 paintings by Henri Matisse, as well as works by Braque, Munch and Picasso, are highlights, as is the Danish modernist collection featuring the painters Giersing and Isakson, and sculptors Kai Nielsen and Astrid Noack. In the old wing the Italians are well represented by Titian, Tintoretto, Filippino Lippi, Mantegna and Guardi. Dutch and Flemish 15th- to 17th-century masters here include Rubens, Bruegel, Rembrandt, Van Dyck and Van Goyen. French 18th-century works are by Fragonard, Poussin and Lorrain, among others.

Statens Museum also has one of the world's oldest collections of European prints and drawings (some 300,000), by artists including Degas, Toulouse-Lautrec, Picasso, Giacometti, Rembrandt and Piranesi.

On the ground floor is a children's art museum (see page 193) with hands-on displays (compensation perhaps for the loss of the great toboggan hill – one of the few in Copenhagen – that the new extension now covers), and the museum also has a large bookshop and a decent café (with interior also by Indrio).

a milestone in Danish art, has just been restored; *pictured above*), and their forerunners from the 18th century, like Nicolai Abildgaard and Jens Juel, are among the biggest treats in the museum.

The Skagen artists (Michael and Anna Ancher and PS Krøyer), who were specialists in everyday scenes and light, summery landscapes, and the Fyn painters (Peter Hansen and Frits Syberg), are also well represented. No-one before or since has quite captured the unmistakable, crisp Danish light as these artists did, but their paintings often also depict brutal, beautiful and compelling stories concerning 'real' people's lives, be they butchers, maids, schoolchildren, farmers or fishermen.

Statens Museum For Kunst

Sølvgade 48-50 (33 74 84 94/www.smk.dk).
Open 10am-5pm Tue, Thur-Sun; 10am-8pm Wed; closed Mon. **Admission** 40kr; 25kr concessions; free under-16s. Free to all Wed. **Credit** AmEx, DC, MC, V. **Map** p97/p307 J14.

three floors of **CL Davids Samling** (CL David's Collection; *listings page 101*; David was a barrister in the Danish High Court; he died in 1960), whose highlights are a meagre collection of paintings by Abildgaard, Juel, Eckersberg and Købke, and some French and English furniture and porcelain, you can understand why this museum of art objects might not rank too highly on most people's itineraries. But if you persevere to the top floor (there's no lift), one of the most surprising displays in the whole city awaits. Here you'll find the largest collection of ancient Islamic art in Scandinavia, featuring pieces from the entire geographic span of the Islamic world, from Spain to west India. These entrancing displays, including a superb range of textiles, texts, pottery, weaponry, glassware and

silverware from the 8th to the 19th centuries, are definitely worth the climb.

A short walk along Kronprinsessegade on Gothersgade is **Filmhuset** (the Film House; *see page 199*), a world-class complex devoted to Danish and international cinema.

At the north end of Store Kongensgade (the other grand avenue of Frederiksstaden, running parallel to Bredgade) is **Nyboder**. While Kastellet (*see page 93*) was for centuries home to the Army, the Royal Navy lived just a stone's throw away in the Lilliputian, ochre terraces of Nyboder. Nyboder was actually built before Kastellet in 1631-41, during Christian IV's time, to house over 2,200 naval staff (a purpose it still serves). A small museum, **Nyboders Mindestuer** (Nyboder Memorial Rooms; *listings page 101*) opened here in 1926,

Rosenborg Slot

Though it was built at the same time as Frederiksborg Slot (see page 269), Rosenborg was Christian IV's favourite residence, and was very much his pet project. Towards the end of his life, he literally pulled up the palace drawbridge to escape the harsh fiscal realities of Denmark's ruin.

The castle started its existence as a small summer house. Christian extended it over a period of time from 1606 to 1634, completing the development of what was now his full-time spring-to-autumn residence with the large, octagonal staircase tower, by the fantastically named Hans van Steenwinckel the Younger. Rosenborg is still jammed full of the king's fancies: toys, architectural tricks, inventions, art objects and jewellery, which he gathered from around Europe like a regal Mr Toad. A source of great pride to him was the castle basement, where his personal orchestra would perform, their music travelling up through a complex system of pipes connected to his living quarters. (Rose Tremain's novel *Music And Silence* gives an imaginative account of the strange world of the palace musicians.)

These days, the basement houses the Treasury, the stronghold of the Crown Jewels. It is a collection in which quality, not quantity, is the watchword. The star is the Golden Crown of the Absolute Monarchy, decorated with sapphires, diamonds and rubies, made by Poul Kurtz in 1670, and used by Denmark's kings for 170 years. Christian IV's crown (1595) and ornate gold, pearl and jewel-encrusted saddle are, as you'd expect, jaw-dropping.

Rosenborg was a royal residence up until 1838, when these collections were opened to the public, along with the many rooms which had remained intact over several generations from the time of Christian IV (1588-1648) to Frederik IV (1699-1730);

later rooms were recreated. The decision to arrange the rooms chronologically was, at the time, radical, and, consequently, Rosenborg claims to be the first museum of contemporary culture in Europe.

The 24 rooms currently on show offer an insight into the lives of Renaissance kings that is perhaps unparalleled in Europe for its atmosphere and intimacy. Christian IV's toilet, covered in beautiful blue Dutch tiles, for example, is as fascinating a treasure as the jewels in the basement. Other must-sees include Christian's study with his beautiful writing desk; Frederik III's marble room; the breathtaking Mirror, Porcelain and Venetian Glass Cabinets; and the last room to be completed (in 1624), the Long Hall, with an amazing throne made from narwal horns, and guarded by three solid silver lions from 1670 (they somehow escaped being melted down to fill the bottomless pit of Denmark's finances in the late 17th century).

Despite existing quite happily for more than a century without it, electricity has now been installed at Rosenborg. That's a great shame, because the castle's Stygian gloom is a major part of its appeal. It remains to be seen whether the very special torch-lit, night-time tour that takes place here once a year on Kulturnat (see page 190) will continue.

Rosenborg Slot

Øster Voldgade (33 15 32 86/ www.kulturnet.dk/homes/rosenb). **Open** *Jan-Apr* 11am-2pm Tue-Sun; closed Mon. *May-Sept* 10am-4pm daily. *Oct* 11am-3pm daily. *Nov-mid Dec* 11am-2pm Tue-Sun; closed Mon. *27-30 Dec* 11am-3pm daily. *Mid Dec-26 Dec* closed. **Admission** 50kr; 10kr-30kr concessions. **Credit** AmEx, MC, V. **Map** p97/p307 K14.

Islamic art at **CL Davids Samling**. See p99.

and is staffed by naval veteran Commander, Thor Temler. It's located on St Pauls Gade and houses the cramped 19th-century rooms of a typical family who would have lived here, plus a small naval exhibition.

Arbejdermuseet
Rømersgade 22 (33 93 25 75/ www.arbejdermuseet.dk). **Open** *Nov-June* 10am-4pm Tue-Sun; closed Mon. *July-Oct* 10am-4pm daily. **Admission** 35kr; 15kr concessions. **Credit** MC, V. **Map** p97/p306 L12.

Botanisk Have & Museum
Gothersgade 128 (35 32 22 40/www.botanic-garden.ku.dk). **Open** *Garden May-Sept* 8.30am-6pm daily. *Oct-Apr* 8.30am-4pm Tue-Sun; closed Mon. *Palm house* 10am-3pm daily. *Cactus greenhouse* 1-2pm Wed, Sat, Sun; closed Mon, Tue, Thur, Fri. *Orchid greenhouse* 2-3pm Wed, Sat, Sun; closed Mon,

Tue, Thur, Fri. *Museum June-Aug* noon-4pm daily, but times vary, phone to check. *Sept-May* closed. **Admission** free. **Map** p97/p307 K13.

CL Davids Samling
Kronprinsessegade 30 (33 73 49 49/ www.davidmus.dk). **Open** 1-4pm Tue-Sun; closed Mon. **Admission** free. **Map** p97/p307 L15.

Geologisk Museum
Øster Voldgade 5-7 (35 32 23 45/ www.nathimus.ku.dk). **Open** 1-4pm Tue-Sun; closed Mon. **Admission** 25kr; free-15kr concessions. No credit cards. **Map** p97/p307 K13.

Den Hirschsprungske Samling
Stockholmsgade 20 (35 42 03 36/ www.hirschsprung.dk). **Open** 11am-4pm Mon, Thur-Sun; 11am-9pm Wed; closed Tue. **Admission** 25kr; 15kr concessions; free under-16s. Free to all Wed. **Credit** AmEx, DC, MC, V. **Map** p97/p307 J14.

Musikhistorisk Museum og Carl Claudius' Samling
Åbenrå 30 (33 11 27 26/www.kulturnet.dk/homes/ mhm). **Open** *May-Sept* 1-3.50pm Mon-Wed, Fri-Sun; closed Thur. *Oct-Apr* 1-3.50pm Mon, Wed, Sat, Sun; closed Tue, Thur, Fri. **Admission** 30kr; 10kr concessions. No credit cards. **Map** p97/p307 L13.

Nyboders Mindestuer
Skt Pauls Gade 24 (33 32 10 05/ www.kulturnet.dk/homes/orlm/nybod.HTM). **Open** 11am-2pm Wed; 11am-4pm Sun; closed Mon, Tue, Thur-Sat (except by prior arrangement). **Admission** 10kr; 5kr concessions. No credit cards. **Map** p97/p308 K16.

Sightseeing

Nyboder's naval cottages. See p99.

Christianshavn

A spectacular church, an ancient windmill, some great bars and restaurants, and the Free State of Christiania: Christianshavn is nothing if not intriguing.

Panoramic views from the top of **Vor Frelsers Kirke**'s spiralling spire. *See p103.*

Christianshavn is an idyllic, bohemian patchwork of canals and pastel-shaded 18th-century houses, home to an eclectic bunch of artists, young professionals and families, as well as probably the greatest concentration of crusties in Denmark. It's an enchanting area in which to wander on a warm afternoon, stopping off at a canal-side café, climbing the Hitchcockian spire of Vor Frelsers Kirke (*see page 103*) for a spectacular panorama of the city, before your nose leads you to the fragrant temptations of the Free State of Christiania.

Christianshavn was built to the east of Slotsholmen in the first half of the 17th century, partly to protect Christian IV's burgeoning city from attack, and partly to ease overcrowding within the city walls. The king's initially complex plan, inspired by Amsterdam's grid of canals (Christianshavn is sometimes referred to as Little Amsterdam), was eventually simplified for reasons of cost, but remains pretty much intact today following sympathetic

renovation in the '80s and '90s. Christianshavn's charming houses and courtyards also escaped most of the fires that ravaged Copenhagen over the centuries.

The area is partially ringed by massive, star-shaped, grass-covered fortifications (or Volden, meaning 'the Ramparts') and a large moat (Stadsgraven), and is connected to Sjælland via two bridges, Knippelsbro and Langebro.

To the north of Christianshavn is **Holmen**, the old dockland area which was built on reclaimed land in the 17th century. Holmen still has its naval base, but the rest of the area has been transformed in recent years, and now throngs with students from the various educational institutions based here (which teach drama, architecture and music). The pioneering mega-club and restaurant complex, **Base Camp** (*see page 152*), compliments the youthful vibe. Holmen is a fascinating place to explore by bicycle (*see page 283*) or on Rollerblades.

Christianshavn's dominant landmark is **Vor Frelsers Kirke** (Church of Our Saviour; *listings page 105*), whose fabulous 90-metre (295-foot) high copper and gold spire can be seen from most parts of the city centre. The church, on Sankt Annægade, was built by architect Lambert van Haven for Christian V in 1682 in the Palladian Dutch baroque style, from red brick and sandstone. Don't be taken in by Danes who try to tell you that the spire's architect, Laurids de Thurah, threw himself off the top because it wound the wrong way – he actually died in poverty seven years after its

completion. The spire was inspired by the lanterns on the Church of Sant'Ivo alla Sapienza in Rome, and was completed in pine with copper cladding and gilt decoration in 1752. On the day of its dedication King Frederik V climbed to the top to receive a 27-gun salute as crowds cheered below. This extraordinary spire is open to any visitors who feel they can conquer their vertigo and its 400 or so steps, which spiral narrower and narrower at the summit in the manner of the Yellow Brick Road. Inside, Vor Frelsers Kirke is airily spacious but prosaic in the typical Lutheran manner, though

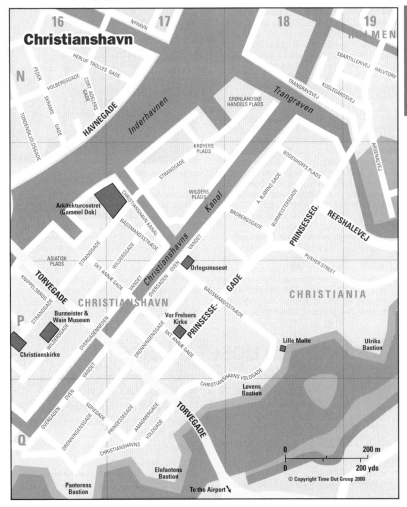

its immense three-storey organ, which was completed in 1698, is fairly stupefying.

Christianshavn's other significant church is **Christianskirke** (*listings page 105*), on Strandgade. It is notable for its unique interior, laid out in the style of a theatre. The rococo church, with its neo-classical spire, was built to designs by Nicolai Eigtved (*see page 91* **Great Danes: Niels 'Nicolai' Eigtved**) in 1755 for the German population of Christianshavn. It was financed by a lottery, and was known for a long time as the Lottery Church.

Two museums on Christianshavn attest to its important role in Denmark's naval history. **Orlogsmuseet** (the Royal Danish Naval Museum; *listings page 105*) has an extensive collection of fantastically detailed model ships. The collection was started by Christian IV, and originally exhibited in Sankt Nicolaj Kirke; it was moved to the current site of Søkvæsthus, the old naval hospital, in 1989. The oldest model, of a man of war (originally from Holmens Kirke), dates from 1680, and there are countless replicas of later ships (including the interior of a submarine, with sound effects), as well as a comprehensive history of the Danish Royal Navy (founded by King Hans in the 15th century), and several historic battle scenes recreated in model form. One gallery contains a splendid ornate state barge from 1780, another is dedicated to marine archaeology. Orlogsmuseet will delight model-making enthusiasts and naval historians; it's also popular with children, who are catered for with a well-equipped play room.

The **Burmeister & Wain Museum** (*listings page 105*), on Strandgade, has a more specialist collection that deals with the history of the diesel engine (of which the company was a pioneer), featuring numerous cut-away models of everything from early 40 horse power motors to monster 93,000 horse power ship engines. The museum also has 50 model ships, if

Lille Mølle. *See p105.*

Orlogsmuseet hasn't sated you on that front. The shipbuilders Burmeister & Wain was founded in 1843 in Købmagergade by Hans Heinrich Baumgarten, and the company has played an important role in the city's economy ever since, so much so that its Christianshavn factory, where U-boat engines were made, was a target of British bombers during World War II. It still has offices in Copenhagen, and employs 2,500 people across Denmark.

Further along historic Strandgade (where NFS Grundtvig lived at No.6; *see page 124*

Ten ways to upset a Dane

Say any of the following phrases to a Dane, and they may be your last…

'So, let's get this straight, you used to own Norway, southern Sweden, the top part of northern Germany, England, Greenland. So what happened?'

'Are you a natural blond?'

'Sweden was great!'

'I thought Helena Christensen was Norwegian.'

'You paid *how* much for your car?'

'Who exactly is this Victor Borge guy?'

'I know it's red, but I'm crossing anyway.'

'Surely there's no place for a monarchy in a modern, liberal society.'

'Precisely how much do you have left after tax?'

'… but I guess, at least you can be sure your government's going to spend it wisely.'

Great Danes: NFS Grundtvig), on the other side of Torvegade, are Asiatisk Plads and Gammel Dok, the location for a series of converted warehouses and home to, among other things, **Arkitekturcentret** (the Architecture Centre; *listings below*). The changing exhibitions here tend to be fairly technical and not for the casual grazer, which is a shame given Denmark's rich architectural heritage and its current status in this field. Exhibitions are often accompanied by debates and conferences, which the café on the main floor has more than enough room to host.

One of Christianhavn's easily overlooked sites is **Lille Mølle** (*listings below*), a windmill dating from 1669, situated on the ramparts to the south-east of Christiania. It was converted into a private home in 1916 and the interior, with numerous antiques and art objects, has been perfectly preserved by the Nationalmuseet which now owns the site. Next door is **Bastionen & Løven**, an excellent café (*see page 152*), and a very popular meeting place during summer.

Arkitekturcentret
Strandgade 27B (32 57 19 30/www.gammeldok.dk). **Open** 10am-5pm daily. **Admission** free. **Map** p103/p312 O16.

Burmeister & Wain Museum
Strandgade 4 (32 54 02 27/www.manbw.dk). **Open** 10am-1pm Mon-Fri & 1st Sun of the month; closed Sat, Sun. **Admission** free-30kr. **Map** p103/p312 P16.

Christians Kirke
Strandgade 1 (35 54 15 76). **Open** *Mar-Oct* 8am-6pm daily. *Nov-Feb* 8am-5pm daily. **Admission** free. **Map** p103/p312 P16.

Lille Mølle
Christianshavns Voldgade 54 (33 47 38 38/www.natmus.dk). **Open** *May-Sept* 1-4pm Tue-Sun; closed Mon. *Nov-Apr* tours by appointment; phone for details. **Admission** 40kr; 30kr concessions; free under-16s. **No credit cards**. **Map** p103/p312 P18.

Orlogsmuseet
Overgaden Oven Vandet 58 (31 54 63 63/www.kulturnet.dk/homes/orlm). **Open** noon-4pm Tue-Sun; closed Mon. **Admission** 30kr; 20kr concessions. **No credit cards**. **Map** p103/p312 P17.

Vor Frelsers Kirke
Sankt Annægade (32 57 27 98/www.vorfrelserskirke.dk). **Open** *Church* 9am-5pm daily. *Spire Apr-Nov* 11am-5.30pm daily; *Dec-Mar* closed. **Admission** free; *spire* 20kr; 10kr concessions. **No credit cards**. **Map** p103/p312 P17.

Christiania

Christiania, or the Free State of Christiania to give it its full title, is a living paradox of people, principles and practices. This idyllic mess, which straddles the defensive moat and 17th-century ramparts to the east of Christianshavn, can beguile, enchant and inspire, as well as repulse, infuriate and bore (one can, after all, only stomach so much self-satisfied recycling and soya-centric cuisine). What is indisputable is its fascination for visitors, who number around three quarters of a million a year (don't be surprised to see Saga-age tour groups being led by guides through the assembled dope dealers), and flock through the gates on Prinsessegade and Bådsmandsstræde to taste a life they are too chicken, or too savvy, to live themselves.

Christiania is unique, a community that exists within a capital city, but outside of its laws and conventions. It is both integrated into Copenhagen (the tourist board promote it enthusiastically) and shunned by it (the neighbours haven't yet stopped complaining). After 30 turbulent years, you can at least say that Christiania is a survivor, and that its residents are unquestionably committed to their 'alternative' lifestyle – though, as recycling and other environmentally conscious practices have been adopted by the mainstream over the years, and attitudes to soft drugs have changed, just how alternative Christiania is, is open to debate.

Up until 1971, the 34-hectare (840-acre) site that Christiania now occupies was an army barracks. When the army moved out, a group of like-minded Christianshavn residents decided to knock down the fence on Prinsessegade and access the land for use as a playground and open space. Meanwhile, an exhibition at Charlottenborg, 'Noget for Noget' (Give and

Keeping the area's maritime heritage alive.

Take), which examined the burgeoning interest in the hippy movement, and an alternative lifestyle newspaper, *Hovedbladet* ('Head Magazine'), further galvanised Copenhagen's experimentalists. The paper ran an article on the barracks with various proposals for its use, including as housing for the young. This was all the encouragement that hundreds of 'drop-outs' from across Denmark needed, and soon the site began to fill up. On 13 November 1971, the new residents founded the Free State, which was promptly declared illegal by the authorities. However, the number of residents had already grown to the extent that, despite their best and often most violent efforts, the police failed to clear the barricades.

In subsequent years, as the community formed its own system of government, built schools, shops, cafés, restaurants, various co-operatives and music venues, and embarked on recycling programmes and nascent solar and wind power projects, the debate about Christiania raged. The bulldozers and batons were never far away. Charity records, concerts, PR stunts and the election to the local council of some of its residents ensured Christiania remained in the headlines, and, eventually,

in 1991, an uneasy truce was met with the authorities. Christiania agreed to pay rent and cover the cost of water and electricity supplies, as well as to look after the buildings that were of historical importance, while the city council agreed to allow it to continue as a 'social experiment'. In truth, were Christiania to be closed down tomorrow, the ensuing housing crisis and city-wide crime wave would prove a far greater political hot potato. And anyway, polls show that the majority of Copenhageners would like it to stay. The site is technically still owned by the Ministry of Defence.

Drugs continued to be a stumbling block in relations with the police, however, and in 1992 the authorities attempted to purge the area of dealers. Eventually an agreement was reached in which the residents ensured that hard drugs were outlawed, while the sale of hashish and marijuana on 'Pusher Street' was tolerated. It should be stressed, however, that though Pusher Street's eye-poppingly brazen array of resin, grass and mushrooms suggests otherwise, all drugs remain illegal both inside and outside Christiania.

Christiania is still very much associated with drugs and crime in the minds of many, much to

Picture postcard images of **Christiania**.

Ten ways to charm a Dane

If you want a friend for life, try any of the following conversational gambits...

'Yes, but if you include Greenland, Denmark's really big!'

'Tell me again about the '92 European Championships.'

'Can we swap queens?'

'Would you like a cigarette?'

'I don't know about you, but I find a few candles make a place so much more cosy.'

'Sweden was great... in the '70s.'

'Hey, neat flags!'

'Hey, great chairs!'

'Can I get you a beer?'

'Tusind tak.'

the chagrin of the more idealistic residents, who would prefer the area to be known as a pioneer of ecological principles. Over the years, the governments of Sweden, Norway and Finland have complained that Christiania is the hub of Scandinavia's drug problem and a refuge for runaways, and there is some truth in that. Christiania does, however, have a good record in policing itself, and weapons and violence are uncommon.

Today, the community exists on a shoestring, earning money from its restaurants and bars, as well as the sale of its unique Christiania bicycles, handicrafts and, of course, the sale of drugs. The 1,000 or so residents (around 70 per cent of whom receive some kind of government benefit) pay rent, which goes towards the upkeep of buildings, city taxes and services. A complex system of self-government is headed by the Common Meeting, the ruling body, with power devolved through 15 local Area Meetings. Decisions are arrived at via consensus, as opposed to majority vote, and new arrivals must be approved by the House Meeting.

Christiania is divided by the moat into two distinct areas – the main commercial centre, where you'll find **Pusher Street**, the music venues and various shops, restaurants and bars; and **Dysen**, a quiet residential area on the eastern side of the moat.

Pusher Street is Christiania's main draw (if you'll excuse the pun), offering a frisson of the exotic in an entirely tame and sociable atmosphere (the truth is that Vesterbro and some of Copenhagen's less salubrious suburbs harbour far more sinister characters than Christiania). Stalls here tout 'African' and 'Thai Pot', 'Silverhaze Superskunk' and other varieties of marijuana; great slabs of cannabis resin, like unwrapped milk chocolate bars; hallucinogenic mushrooms; a variety of smoking paraphernalia; and ready-rolled spliffs for the lazy or legless. Compared to the soft drugs markets in other European cities it is all sold at knock-down

prices – from 50kr for 100 grams of grass. Photography is banned around the stalls.

Flower power is still alive and well in Christiania and, by way of evidence, no wall is left undaubed with murals, graffiti and, well, daubs. Large, shaggy dogs of indeterminate breed roam unhindered, as a rich tapestry of residents (known as Christianites) mingle amid the purple haze and pungent aromas. Several small bars and cafés, where your purchases can be enjoyed freely (though, we should again say, illegally), lie within a minute's walk. The vegetarian café **Morgenstedet** is good for lunch (*see page 143*), but **Spiseloppen** (spise means 'eat'; loppen means 'the flea'; *see page 142*) is Christiania's best eatery by far, and can, in fact, hold its own against many more salubrious venues in the city. **Grønsagen**, the organic produce store, is also nearby. In the same building as Spiseloppen is the atmospheric music venue **Loppen**, while the 2,000-capacity **Den Grå Hal** (the Grey Hall; for both, *see page 219*) is Christiania's largest music venue, and has hosted gigs by the likes of Blur, Manic Street Preachers, Portishead and Bob Dylan. Christiania holds a thoroughly festive Christmas market from around 12 December in Den Grå Hal, with over 100 small stalls and two restaurants.

All of Christiania is open to tourists (though obviously not the private dwellings), and it is a shame that many visitors never venture further than the pot stalls. An enjoyable time can be passed wandering around the quieter parts of Christiania, inspecting the extraordinary variety of housing – from pyramids, railway carriages and treehouses, to sophisticated wooden chalets and the original 17th-century barracks. An exhibition space, **Det Grønne Rum**, will tell you all you need to know about Christiania's solar power, ecological laundry, recycling and horticultural projects, while daily guided tours give an excellent inside view into the workings of this remarkable community.

Vesterbro & Frederiksberg

Sleaze and swank; a wander west of centre reveals two sharply contrasting neighbourhoods.

Sightseeing

Vesterbro

Vesterbro, stretching west from Tivoli and Central Station, is Copenhagen's eternal bridesmaid. Talk of the area's rejuvenation has been ceaseless over the last ten or so years, but still the shabby sex shops and the strip shows remain, like an indelible stain that no amount of trendification or political rhetoric can erase. Come to think of it, 'rejuvenation' suggests a past glory that Vesterbro, in truth, never had. Since the 18th century, when it was the site of numerous music halls and drinking dens, and the second half of the 19th century, when the area south of Vesterbrogade was filled by an immense block of inhuman corridor flats (to ease overcrowding in the city), Vesterbro has revelled in its image of sleaze and squalor, and, thankfully, it still does.

This is one of Copenhagen's more flavoursome districts, as well as being its most ethnically mixed. Immigrants from Asia and Africa, who came here in the 1960s and '70s when Denmark was suffering from a labour shortage, remain today to give Vesterbro a unique atmosphere and diversity. At the Central Station end of Istedgade, for example, there is a fascinating concentration of food shops selling produce from Hong Kong, Thailand, India and Afghanistan. Istedgade, however, is not best known for its grocers. This is also Copenhagen's notorious 'sex street' (*see page 174* **Sex street**), where the window displays of its many sex shops leave little to the imagination.

In fact, meat markets, literal and metaphoric, have always been Vesterbro's speciality. Until very recently it was the butchers' quarter of Copenhagen. Their trade was centred on Værnedamsvej (linking Vesterbrogade across the border into Gammel Kongevej in sedate Frederiksberg), which at one time had Europe's highest concentration of meat sellers. Today, Værnedamsvej's specialist food vendors will tell you that things aren't what they were ten or so years ago before the clothing boutiques moved in, but this is still the place to source hard-to-find

delicacies, from obscure cheeses to smoked fish or homemade chocolates (*see page 180* **Food street**).

Apart from these independent retailers, some great bars, and a lively cosmopolitan atmosphere, there are few specific tourist attractions in Vesterbro, other than the city museum and planetarium.

Københavns Bymuseet & Søren Kierkegaard Samlingen (Copenhagen City Museum & Søren Kierkegaard Collection; *listings page 109*) is about halfway along Vesterbrogade on the south side. The museum gives an excellent overview of the capital's history, and includes old shop fronts and displays depicting how Copenhageners have lived over the last millennium. A special 'Copenhagen Underground' exhibition tells you more than you'd probably like to know about all things subterranean – sewers, gas pipes and, metaphorically, prostitution and crime. There is a particularly good model of Copenhagen as it was in 1660, which shows how far out of the city Rosenborg and Kastellet once were. The Søren Kierkegaard Samlingen is disappointingly small – do not expect a definitive exposition of the life and work of the archetypal Copenhagener (although the information in English is excellent; *see also page 112* **Great Danes: Søren Kierkegaard**).

Tycho Brahe Planetarium (*listings page 109*), on Gammel Kongevej, at the southern end of Sankt Jørgens Sø, shows a variety of Imax movies and interplanetary displays. The largest planetarium in western Europe, it was opened in 1989 in a cylindrical building designed by the architect Knud Munk, and is named after the great Danish (although his home town of Knudsrup is now in southern Sweden) astronomer Tycho Brahe. Brahe was born in 1546 and developed an interest in astronomy which led to him discovering a new star, Cassiopeia, in 1572. In an age before telescopes, he also paved the way for later discoveries about the orbit of the planets. What's more, he had a false nose made of silver.

Københavns Bymuseet & Søren Kierkegaard Samlingen

Vesterbrogade 59, Vesterbro (33 21 07 72/ www.kbhbymuseum.dk). Bus 6, 28, 550S. **Open** *May-Sept* 10am-4pm Mon, Wed-Sun; closed Tue. *Oct-Apr* 1-4pm Mon, Wed-Sun; closed Tue. **Admission** 20kr; 10kr concessions; under-14s free. Free to all Fri. **Credit** V. **Map** p111 Q9.

Tycho Brahe Planetarium

Gammel Kongvej 10, Vesterbro (33 12 12 24/ www.tycho.dk). **Open** 10.30am-9pm daily, but times may vary; phone to check. **Admission** *Exhibition* 25kr. *Exhibition & film* 75kr; 56kr concessions. **Credit** AmEx, DC, MC, V. **Map** p310 P10.

Frederiksberg

Further west of Vesterbro, bordering Nørrebro to the north, lies an area which, like Christiania (*see page 105*), is a separate town within the city of Copenhagen, albeit one with a very different character to the alternative Free State. **Frederiksberg** is an independent municipality of just over 90,000 people, with its own mayor, town hall and administration. Its leafy, wide avenues, grand parks and elegant 18th-century royal palace make this one of the city's most desirable residential areas (slightly lower taxes for residents helps), as well as a popular destination at weekends for those who live more centrally. Apartments here tend to be larger and more expensive than elsewhere in the city, especially those along Frederiksberg Allé, a long, tree-lined boulevard, which could have been lifted straight from one of the more affluent arrondissements of Paris. Until the 19th century, Frederiksberg lay well outside Copenhagen, with views from its moderate hill ('berg' means hill) over the fields, where

China in your hands

May 2000 saw the 225th anniversary of the founding of the **Royal Copenhagen Porcelain Manufactory**, celebrated with an exhibition at Kunstindustrimuseet (see page 92). The Manufactory was founded by the chemist Frantz Müller on behalf of the royal family, who owned it for many years. As well as a huge range of porcelain products (most typically decorated with the trademark

delicate Blue Fluted or Blue Flower patterns), since 1789 the company has produced the world's most expensive dinner service, the famous Flora Danica, with designs based on the 700 or so drawings of the eponymous pioneering botanical encyclopaedia of Danish plants. A single dinner plate currently costs around 5,000kr, while larger examples of these extremely labour-intensive works of art cost over 100,000 kroner. Why so expensive? Well, Flora Danica artists must train for over ten years to be able to reproduce the paintings of flowers to the appropriate standard; and the process by which the porcelain is produced takes many days of firings at extreme temperatures. Understandably, these services tend only to be wheeled out for state occasions.

The first Flora Danica service, consisting of over 2,500 hand-painted pieces, was commissioned by Prince Frederik as a gift for Catherine II of Russia (who died before it was finished). The service was finally inaugurated by Christian VII in 1803.

The factory moved to its current site in Frederiksberg in 1884, where public tours operate daily. See also page 114.

Royal Copenhagen Porcelain Manufactory

Smallegade 47, Frederiksberg (38 14 92 97). Bus 1, 14. **Open** *Guided tours* 9am, 10am, 11am, 1pm, 2pm Mon-Fri; closed Sat, Sun. **Admission** 25kr. **Credit** AmEx, DC, MC, V. **Map** p110 N2.

Sightseeing

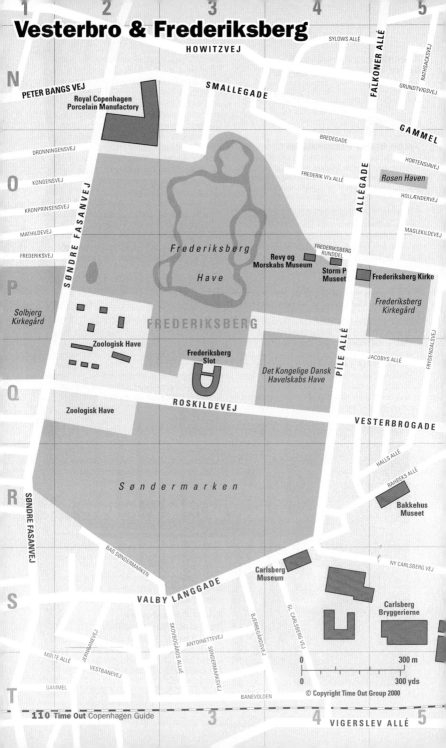

Vesterbro & Frederiksberg

HOWITZVEJ

SYLOWS ALLÉ

FALKONER ALLÉ

RATHSACKSVEJ

N

PETER BANGS VEJ

SMALLEGADE

GRUNDTVIGSVEJ

Royal Copenhagen
Porcelain Manufactory

GAMMEL

BREDEGADE

DRONNINGENSVEJ

O

KONGENSVEJ

FREDERIK VI's ALLÉ

HORTENSIAVEJ

Rosen Haven

KRONPRINSENSVEJ

ALLÉGADE

HOLLÆNDERVEJ

SØNDRE FASANVEJ

MATHILDEVEJ

MAGLEKILDEVEJ

FREDERIKSVEJ

Frederiksberg

FREDERIKSBERG
RUNDDEL

Revy og
Morskabs Museum

P

Have

Storm P
Museet

Frederiksberg Kirke

*Solbjerg
Kirkegård*

*Frederiksberg
Kirkegård*

FREDERIKSBERG

FRYDENDALSVEJ

Zoologisk Have

JACOBYS ALLÉ

PILE ALLÉ

Frederiksberg
Slot

Q

*Det Kongelige Dansk
Havelskabs Have*

Zoologisk Have

ROSKILDEVEJ

VESTERBROGADE

HALLS ALLÉ

RAHBEKS ALLÉ

R

SØNDRE FASANVEJ

Søndermarken

Bakkehus
Museet

BAG SØNDERMARKEN

NY CARLSBERG VEJ

Carlsberg
Museum

Carlsberg
Bryggerierne

S

VALBY LANGGADE

SKOVBOGÅRDS ALLÉ

ANTOINETTEVEJ

BJERREGÅRDSVEJ

SØNDERMARKSVEJ

GL. CARLSBERG VEJ

JERNBANEVEJ

MØLLE ALLÉ

VESTBANEVEJ

0   300 m

T

GAMMEL

0   300 yds

BANEVOLDEN

© Copyright Time Out Group 2000

VIGERSLEV ALLÉ

6
7
8
9

Det Kongelige
Veterinær of
Landbohøjskoles
Have

ØRESVEJ

BULOWSVEJ

AMALIEVEJ

J.M. THIELES VEJ

H C ØRSTEDS VEJ

FORCHHAMMERSVEJ

DANASVEJ

N

UNDTVIGSVEJ

KASTANIEVEJ

NIELS EBBESENS VEJ

VODROFFSVEJ

ONGEVEJ

LINDEVEJ

URANIAVEJ

LYKKESHOLMS ALLÉ

SKT KNUDS VEJ

TÅRNBORGVEJ

FORHÅBNINGSHOLMS ALLÉ

SCHØNBERGSGADE

O

AMICISVEJ

NYVEJ

FREDERIKSBERG

Skt Jørgens Sø

MADVIGS ALLÉ

MARTENSENS ALLÉ

MYNSTERSVEJ

ALHAMBRAVEJ

HAUCHSVEJ

SKT THOMAS ALLÉ

GAMMEL KONGEVEJ

VÆRNEDAMSVEJ

P

FREDERIKSBERG ALLÉ

KINGOSGADE

CARIT ETLARS VEJ

CARL BERNHARDS VEJ

SAXOGADE

OEHLENSCHLÆGERSGADE

VESTERBROGADE

**Københavns Bymuseet
& Søren Kierkegaard
Samlingen**

WESTEND

DANNEBROGSGADE

GASVÆRKSVEJ

Q

KOCHSVEJ

HENRIK IBSENS VEJ

PLANTEVEJ

VESTERBROGADE

SUNDEVEDS-
MATTHÆUSGADE

TØNDERGADE

VALDEMARSGADE

ESKILDSGADE

ABSALONSGADE

AMERIKAVEJ

HEDEBYGADE

SUNDEVEDS · MATTHÆUSGADE

FREDERIKSSTADGADE

VESTERBRO

ISTEDGADE

SKYDEBANEGADE

R

VESTERFÆLLEDVEJ

CARSTENSGADE

KÜCHLERSGADE

LYRSKOVGADE

ENGHAVEVEJ

HADERSLEVGADE

FLENSBORGGADE

OEHLENSCHLÆGERS
GADE

ESTLANDSGADE

VALDEMARSGADE

DANNEBROGSGADE

SØNDER BOULEVARD

SOMMERSTEDGADE

NY CARLSBERG VEJ

EJDERSTEDVEJ

Enghaven

CARLSBERG

VEJ

DYBBØLS

GADE

KRUSAGADE

GODSBANEGADE

S

VESTERFÆLLEDVEJ

ALSGADE

SLESVIGSGADE

DANNEVIRKEGADE

HADERSLEVGADE

FLENSBORGGADE

ASGER RYSS GADE

ARKONAGADE

ANGELGADE

SØNDER BOULEVARD

INGERSLEVSGADE

T

6

Enghave
Station

7

Great Danes Søren Kierkegaard

Søren Kierkegaard is generally held to be the founding father of the existentialist movement. He was born in Copenhagen on 3 May 1813, and though he spent time in Berlin, where he began the work that was to outline his main philosophical tenets, Kierkegaard was a Copenhagener at heart, and he lived at several addresses in the city during his life.

He was born the seventh child of a wealthy, but puritanical, hosiery shopkeeper and wool trader, and grew up in a house on Nytorv (now the site of a bank). This most self-confident of men, who considered himself a genius from a very early age, fell out with his father while he was studying theology at Copenhagen University. Kierkegaard's 'drop-out' phase was characterised by a fervent pursuit of pleasure, during which time he was often to be found at the restaurants and Swiss-run bakeries on Østergade (in 1836 his pastry debts alone were said to equal the annual income of a contemporary craftsman).

This rather dissolute period of Kierkegaard's early life ended when the young hedonist experienced a religious awakening in 1838. That same year his father died, leaving him a substantial inheritance. He returned to his studies in earnest, receiving a doctorate in theology in 1841 (though the theatre, literature, politics and philosophy also occupied him during this time). Another watershed, the termination of his engagement to the younger Regine Olsen, followed. Kierkegaard felt he could promise himself only to God, and the end of the relationship begat a major emotional crisis.

That crisis was to be the spur for his future writing career. In 1843, he wrote his philosophical novel, *Enten/Eller* (*Either/Or*), which outlined his philosophy of 'life stages', in which human existence was divided into what Kierkegaard called the 'three spheres of existence': the aesthetic, the ethical and the religious, concluding that man cannot exist truly, or reach any kind of peace, without first professing a faith in God and, more importantly, living a Christian life.

This most religious of writers drew inspiration, not just from the stimulus of life in the capital, but also from his wanderings throughout the countryside of Sjælland. He often visited Gilbjerg Hoved, the northernmost point of the island, or took a carriage to the Gribskov forest in the north of the island, whose eight-road intersection was, for him, a potent symbol of the issues of free choice and decision that recurred in his writing.

Kierkegaard's works can be roughly divided into two periods: the first included pieces like *Fear And Trembling*, *The Concept Of Anxiety* and *Philosophical Fragments*; the second, more religious, phase included *Works of Love*, *Christian Discourses* and *The Sickness Unto Death*. In 1963, his collected works, all 20 volumes of them, were published for the first time.

Kierkegaard collected enemies like others collect silverware, and during his life he struck out at HC Andersen (his first published work was a critical analysis of Andersen's novel *Only A Fiddler*), the Danish church (whose preachings he ultimately rejected) and his fellow philosopher Georg Hegel (one of his most important works, *Concluding Unscientific Postscript To The Philosophical Fragments*, published in 1846, was a direct assault on Hegelianism), among others. His endless confrontations are thought to have hastened the illnesses that finally led to Kierkegaard's collapse on the street, often described as a burnout, and his subsequent death five months later in October 1855 at the age of 42. He is buried in Assistens Kirkegård in Nørrebro (see page 120).

Though neglected during his lifetime, and in the years following his death, after World War I Kierkegaard's writings began to gain an international following. Towards the end of the 20th century he underwent a further popular revival, as issues of science and philosophy became increasingly interlinked. Today, Kierkegaard is recognised as one of the major figures in the history of philosophy.

Vesterbro has since spread, to the city beyond. Today, its borders are largely invisible, but the area still has a quiet, refined atmosphere that is in stark contrast to Vesterbro's chaotic hubbub.

While conservative Frederiksberg's nightlife is hardly a giddy whirl of cafés, clubs and bars, it does have a few sights that are certainly worth the short bus ride (or when it opens in 2002, the underground rail link) from the centre of town. It also has a few good shops, mostly located on Gammel Kongevej and Falkoner Allé, where you'll also find one of Copenhagen's very few shopping malls, Frederiksberg Centret (*see page 158*).

The heart of the quarter is **Frederiksberg Have** (Frederiksberg Park; *listings page117*), a large, rambling park that was laid out in the formal French style in the 18th century, before being given a more informal English restyle at the turn of the 19th century. When the flowers bloom from early spring onwards, Frederiksberg Have, with its tree-lined paths, canals and lake, is transformed into the city's most romantic open space. In its grounds are a Chinese pavilion, numerous statues and an impressive avenue of linden trees, dating from the 1730s. The greenery extends across Roskildevej to **Søndermarken** common, another (more informal) park that, together with Frederiksberg Have, forms the largest urban park in northern Europe.

In the south-east corner of Frederiksberg Have, bordering Pile Allé (with the entrance on Frederiksberg Runddel), is **Det Kongelige Danske Haveselskabs Have** (the Royal Danish Horticultural Society's Gardens; *listings page 117*), a formal, oriental-influenced water garden, founded in 1884. In the summer this is one of the **Copenhagen Jazz Festival**'s most idyllic outdoor venues (*see page 219*), while the orange stucco Spa Room is used year-round for exhibitions and concerts.

Frederiksberg has two other small parks, less frequently visited by tourists. Sheltering behind a cluster of apartment blocks on Hollændervej is the tiny **Rosen Haven** (the Rose Garden), which is home to a variety of roses including the Ingrid Bergmann and Queen Elizabeth. **Det Kongelige Veterinær of Landbohøjskoles Have** (the Royal Danish Veterinary and Agricultural University's Garden; *listings page 117*) on Bülowsvej was laid out in 1858 at the time of the university's foundation. This garden positively explodes in a riot of flora come spring, with aconite, snowdrops, crocuses and 10,000 tulips appearing in April. In summer they are complimented by roses and 700 different summer flowers, as well as 100 or so medicinal plants and exotic trees.

On the south side of Frederiksberg Have, on top of **Frederiksberg Hill** (formerly Valby Hill), lies **Frederiksberg Slot** (Frederiksberg Palace; *listings page 117*), a royal summer residence from the early 18th century until the mid 19th century. The yellow stucco palace was built for Frederik IV. The king had been very much taken by the villas he had seen while on a visit to Frascati, and, between 1699 and 1703, he instructed architect Ernst Brandenburger to build a palace in the Italian style, with ornate rococo interiors. The two side wings, designed by Laurids de Thurah, were added between 1733 and 1738, on the instruction of Christian VI. Today, this simple, symmetrical building is home to the Danish Military Academy, and, as such, not open to the public, other than for guided tours.

Beside Frederiksberg Slot on Roskildevej is the **Zoologisk Have** (Zoological Garden; *listings page 117*), Denmark's national zoo. Founded in 1859, it is one of the oldest in the world, and has a good reputation for breeding animals in captivity. The zoo is modest by international standards, but nevertheless has the usual remit of exotica, including polar bears, tigers, lions, apes and elephants. An impressive indoor tropical zoo houses butterflies, crocodiles and tropical birds. The children's zoo is also a major attraction (*see page 194*), and its main landmark is the

Tycho Brahe Planetarium. *See p108.*

Bucolic, hilly **Frederiksberg Have**.

This is hardcore

What constitutes pornography? Should the State prosecute those who consume and produce it? What harm does the availability of explicit sexual images have on society? In the late 1960s, these questions were being debated earnestly and rationally in Copenhagen's Folketing (parliament) while the rest of the world, and in particular the puritans in America and Britain, either looked on in Victorian-style disgust, or were nudge-nudge, wink-winking about those free-loving Scandinavians.

Denmark's racy reputation was borne out of the same pragmatism that would drive the country into innovative and progressive social policies. The Danes were tackling issues such as gay rights, drug use and green matters years before other countries acknowledged such things even existed.

Denmark became notorious as the first state to legalise pornography, but the story began rather prosaically in the 1950s, when Danish courts were finding it increasingly difficult to decide whether to prosecute the publishers of so-called 'obscene literature'. The difficulty was attributable to two main factors: firstly, both prosecutors and judges found it near-impossible to define what constituted obscenity; and secondly, when teams of criminologists, psychiatrists, psychologists and sociologists were brought in to assess the risks of harmful effects on individuals, a consensus was hard to find. In fact, very little systematic research had been carried out, and the experts were forced to base their findings on a handful of cases.

Under pressure from the legal authorities, the Minister of Justice initiated the reform of Denmark's laws on pornographic literature (though not images) in December 1964. There followed a three-year period of intense public debate, particularly concerning the distinction between literature and the more provocative pictorial material. Some of the arguments from these debates now seem rather absurd. For example: 'Pictures may have a more direct psychological effect than literature,' contended one politician, 'because a reader will have plenty of opportunity to stop reading when he finds that he does not like a book.'

The first groundbreaking piece of legislation was passed in June 1967, when restrictions on the sale of pornographic literature were completely abolished. The floodgates seemed to open at this point, and a number of new amendments soon followed: reducing the legal age of consumption from 18 to 16, decriminalising gay prostitution (heterosexual prostitution was already tolerated) and, most importantly for the nascent Danish porn industry, the abolition of restrictions on pictorial pornography.

Not surprisingly, the market for pornographic stories was soon superseded by increasingly hardcore images. Under the frowning glare of international attention, the Danish Ministry of Justice defended their reforms as rights of personal freedom: 'Liberalisation will, we hope, reduce interest in these images... By leaving the matter to individuals it encourages personal responsibility.'

40-metre (131-foot) tower, built in 1905, which, on a clear day, affords spectacular views as far as the Swedish coast.

Moving around Frederiksberg Have in a clockwise direction along Søndre Fasanvej, you come to the **Royal Copenhagen Porcelain Manufactory** (*see page 109* **China in your hands**). The factory is open for guided tours only (conducted in English and Danish, lasting about an hour), and even if you think seeing porcelain being made is about as interesting as watching paint dry (which, in fact, is part of the process), a tour of this vast factory, and a glimpse of its highly skilled artists at work, should change your mind. There are also two shops on site, one selling the entire range of products made in the factory, the other selling cheaper seconds (*see page 163*).

Further around the park, at the top of Frederiksberg Allé on Frederiksberg Runddel, are two small museums that offer a unique, and at times perplexing, insight into the Danish sense of humour.

Danes seem to be divided as to the merits of the Frederiksberg-born artist and cartoonist Robert Storm Petersen (1882-1949), better known as Storm P. For older Danes he typifies a traditional, aphoristic strain of Danish humour, for younger Danes he is a dusty relic of a bygone era, and about as funny as a hospital visit. At **Storm P Museet** (*listings page 117*) you can judge for yourself whether his many social-critical cartoons display any genuine comedic merit, or whether his symbolist-influenced paintings hold any profound philosophical meaning. You can also

Opinion polls among the Danish population seemed to vindicate the government's rather controversial stance. In 1965, only 46 per cent of Danes agreed with the liberalisation of pornography but by 1970 this figure had leapt to 57 per cent.

Copenhagen soon established itself as a global centre for pornography. Estimates in 1969 put the industry's value at US$50 million, with about 60 per cent of the magazines and films produced for export. 'Made in Denmark' became the hallmark of quality in the world's porn market.

While the Danish porn industry accrued huge sums of money, many psychologists and politicians regarded Copenhagen as a testcase for liberal policies. Berl Kutschinsky, a psychologist commissioned by the US Presidential Commission on Obscenity and Pornography, was despatched to Copenhagen and produced an influential report in 1970.

The 1970-report entitled *Pornography and Sex Crimes in Denmark* found that most young people (regarded as the most vulnerable sector of the population) were virtually unaffected by the reforms. The great majority of pornography consumers were men between 25 and 45 years old. Also, more crucially, the number of sex crimes registered by Danish police actually fell from 4,364 (1964) to 2,819 (1969). Kutchinsky concluded that 'in two types of sex crime – peeping and physical indecency – the abundant availability of hardcore pornography in Denmark was a direct cause in the decrease in these crimes.'

During the 1970s, Denmark's forward-thinking policies were gradually adopted by other European nations, and Copenhagen's reputation as the home of pornography became more myth than reality. Many Danes, however, remember the exciting period of the late 1960s with pride: when their government took a brave step for personal freedom.

Today, in this era of Internet porn, there are few signs of the Danish porn industry around Copenhagen. The few tatty remnants of the scene are around Istedgade, a long street running west from Central Station, where a few rather sad sex shops and strip shows mingle uneasily with the local kebab takeaways and Indian restaurants.

However, **Museum Erotica** (Købmagergade 24; see page 68), which opened at the height of the pornography controversy in 1968 as the world's first erotic museum, is still a popular city attraction and definitely worth a not-so-sneaky peak.

inspect the old misanthrope's extensive pipe collection upstairs. There are English captions.

Behind the Storm P Museum you'll find the even more idiosyncratic **Revy og Morskabs Museum** (Museum of Light – or 'Revue' – Theatre; *listings page 117*), containing two hundred years' worth of memorabilia from traditional Danish revue theatre. The assorted photographs, programmes and costumes will be largely meaningless to foreign visitors, however, as there is no English information.

Opposite Frederiksberg Runddel stands the small, octagonal **Frederiksberg Kirke** (not to be confused with the far more significant Frederikskirken, also known as Marmorkirken), dating from 1734. The pretty Dutch Renaissance church regularly holds concerts, and has an altar piece depicting the Eucharist, painted by

CW Eckersberg, while in its cemetery you'll find the grave of poet Adam Oehlenschläger.

On the south side of Frederiksberg, over near the Carlsberg Brewery, is **Bakkehus Museet** (the Bakkehus Museum; *listings page 117*), a converted 17th-century apartment containing souvenirs of Denmark's Golden Age (1780-1830; *see page 18*). This small, eclectic collection is housed in the former home of a renowned professor of literature and publisher of the period, Knud Lyhne Rahbek. The display includes everything from death masks to the poet Adam Oehlenschläger's dressing gown, as well as antique furniture and art.

Bakkehus Museet lies literally in the shadow of the headquarters of what is undoubtedly Copenhagen's and Denmark's best-known international brand: Carlsberg. The vast

Carlsberg: probably the most famous Danish brand in the world

The **Carlsberg Brewery** in Valby is one of the largest in the world. The brewer's parent company, Carlsberg A/S, has over 100 subsidiaries and associated companies world-wide, who together are responsible for the production of over ten billion bottles of beer per annum in 40 countries.

The story of this corporate giant begins with the brewer Christen Jacobsen (1773-1835), who learned his craft as a brewer's boy at Kongens Bryghus (the King's Brewery, on Slotsholmen; see page 86) after migrating to Copenhagen from Vendsyssel in 1801. Jacobsen founded his own brewery, which rapidly expanded to become the largest in the city. In 1847 his son, Jacob Christian Jacobsen, moved production to a new site nearer the fresh water and open air on Valby Hill, where he continued to develop his Bavarian brewing techniques. He named the new brewery Carlsberg (Carl's Hill) after his son. By 1871, production had reached a staggering 17 million bottles, and the Carlsberg name was already internationally known. Jacobsen was among the richest men in Denmark, but his keen social conscience ensured that his work force was also among the best looked after in the country, with unprecedented healthcare and pension provision. Between 1860 and 1890 each worker also had a daily beer allowance of four litres.

Unfortunately, that great success was soured somewhat by a row that broke out between JC and his son Carl Jacobsen who split to found his own brewery, **Ny Carlsberg**

(New Carlsberg) in 1881; at the same time his father's brewery changed its name to **Gamle Carlsberg** (Old Carlsberg).

Carl did at least inherit his father's fondness for philanthropy. In 1876, JC had used over two million kroner to found one of Europe's first private foundations, the Carlsberg Foundation, to invest in Danish scientific research (through the Carlsberg Laboratory) and take care of the Museum of National History at Frederiksborg Slot. His son Carl, meanwhile, decided to direct his charity towards the arts and, in 1902, founded the **Ny Carlsberg Foundation**, responsible for the creation of the Ny Carlsberg Glyptotek (see page 64), numerous statues and monuments throughout Copenhagen, and, until recently, the running of Tivoli Gardens (see page 57).

In 1970, Carlsberg merged with old rivals Tuborg (whose brewery is still based in Hellerup, in the north of Copenhagen). Today they produce a vast array of beers (øl in Danish): the most common are Tuborg's Grøn and Carlsberg's Hof, both light lagers. Ascending in strength are the Red Tuborg and Gammel Carlsberg (Old Carlsberg), which are slightly darker, then come Guld Tuborg and Carlsberg Guld Export, and the heavy hitters Carlsberg's Elephant Beer and 47, and Tuborg's FF and Påskebryg (6.2 per cent alcohol content). In addition, both breweries cash in on Easter and Christmas with special seasonal beers, whose release on to the market are eagerly awaited as a signal to commence festivities.

Vibrant **Vesterbro**.

Carlsberg Bryggerierne (Carlsberg
Brewery) compound is, strictly speaking, just
over the border from Frederiksberg in Valby,
but the rich, sweet smell of fermenting hops
does not respect municipal boundaries, and the
company's hedquarters dominate this whole
region of the city where Valby, Frederiksberg
and Vesterbro meet.

The **Carlsberg Museum** (*listings below*)
on Valby Langgade is a must for beer buffs,
featuring a pictorial overview of the company's
international operations in over 130 countries,
as well as providing scientific displays about
brewing and a few relics of the Jacobsen
dynasty. In the entrance hall are photographs
of the many VIP visitors who have sampled
Carlsberg's hospitality over the years. It's
certainly an eclectic bunch, including Danny
Kaye, Kenneth Branagh, Victor Borge and a
smattering of European royalty. The museum
also has an amusing display of promotional
material from the last century, and a large
1:10 scale model of the brewery. Outside the
museum, a little further down Ny Carlsberg
Vej, are the famous Elephant Gates, flanked
by two stone Indian elephants, designed
by Vilhelm Dahlerup.

Around the corner from the gates is the
entrance to the **Carlsberg Visitors Center**
(*listings below*). The centre used to run guided
tours, but these days visitors are allowed to
wander freely through the various displays on
the history of beer and the brewing processes
used at Carlsberg, which are housed in the
old brewery buildings. Naturally, visits
conclude at the stables and Bar Carlsberg
with a complimentary sample.

Bakkehus Museet

*Rahbeks Allé 23, Frederiksberg (33 31 43 62/
www.bakkehusmuseet.dk). Train to Valby/6, 18 bus.*
Open 11am-3pm Wed, Thur, Sat, Sun; closed Mon,
Tue, Fri. **Admission** 10kr; 1kr concessions.
No credit cards. Map p110 R5.

Carlsberg Museum

*Valby Langgade 1, Valby (33 27 13 14/
www.carlsberg.dk). Bus 6, 18.* **Open** 10am-3pm Mon-
Fri; closed Sat, Sun. **Admission** free. **Map** p110 S4.

Carlsberg Visitors Center

*Gamle Carlsberg Vej 11, Valby (33 27 13 14/
www.carlsberg.dk). Bus 6, 18.* **Open** 10am-4pm Mon-
Fri; closed Sat, Sun. **Admission** free. **Map** p110 S4.

Frederiksberg Have

*Main entrance: Frederiksberg Runddel,
Frederiksberg (33 92 63 00/www.ses.dk). Bus 18, 28.*
Open *Gardens* 6am-sunset daily. *Chinese Island
May-Sept* 2-4pm Sun; closed Mon-Sat. *Oct-Apr*
closed. **Admission** free. **Map** p110 P3.

Frederiksberg Slot

*Roskildevej 32, Frederiksberg (36 16 22 44). Bus 28,
550S.* **Open** *Guided tours* 11am, last Sat of month.
Admission 25kr; under-14s free, if accompanied by
adult. **No credit cards. Map** p110 Q3.

Det Kongelige Danske Haveselskabs Have

*Frederiksberg Runddel 1, Frederiksberg
(36 44 98 99) Bus 18, 26.* **Open** 24 hours daily.
Admission free. **Map** p110 Q4.

Det Kongelige Veterinær of Landbohøjskolens Have

*Grønnegårdsvej 15, Frederiksberg (35 28 21 18/
www.ibh.kul.dk). Bus 1, 14, 29.* **Open** *Oct-Mar*
7.30am-4pm Mon-Fri; 10am-4pm Sat, Sun. *Apr,
May, Sept* 7.30am-7pm Mon-Fri; 10am-7pm Sat, Sun.
June-Aug 7.30am-8pm Mon-Fri; 10am-8pm Sat, Sun.
Admission free. **Map** p111 N6.

Revy og Morskabs Museum

*Frederiksberg Runddel, Frederiksberg (38 10 20 45/
www.morskabsmuseet.dk). Bus 18, 28.* **Open** 11am-
4pm Tue-Sun; closed Mon. **Admission** 25kr; 15kr
concessions. **No credit cards. Map** p110 P4.

Storm P Museet

*Frederiksberg Runddel, Frederiksberg
(38 86 05 23/www.stormp-museet.dk). Bus 18, 28.*
Open *May-Sept* 10am-4pm Tue-Sun; closed Mon.
Oct-Apr 10am-4pm Wed, Sat, Sun; closed Mon, Tue,
Thur, Fri. **Admission** 20kr; 1kr-10kr concessions.
No credit cards. Map p110 P4.

Zoologisk Have

*Roskildevej 32, Frederiksberg (36 30 20 01/
www.zoo.dk). Bus 28, 39, 550s.* **Open** *Mar* 9am-4pm
Mon-Fri; 9am-5pm Sat, Sun. *Apr, May, Sept* 9am-
5pm Mon-Fri; 9am-6pm Sat, Sun. *June-Aug* 9am-6pm
daily; 9am-6pm Sat, Sun. *Oct* 9am-5pm daily.
Nov-Feb 9am-4pm daily. **Admission** 70kr;
35kr concessions. **Credit** DC, MC, V. **Map** p110 Q2.

Sightseeing

Nørrebro & Østerbro

Bars, boutiques and a refreshing ethnic mix, north and west of the lakes.

A fairy-tale ending: Hans Christian Andersen is buried at **Assistens Kirkegård**. *See p120.*

The boundary of Copenhagen city centre is marked to the north and west by a sequence of three exceptionally beautiful man-made lakes: **Sankt Jørgens Sø**, **Peblinge Sø** and **Sortedams Sø**. The lakes, which stretch from Østerbrogade in the east to Gammel Kongevej in the west, are fronted by some of the most most expensive apartment blocks in Copenhagen, whose views over the water and proximity to the city centre make them highly sought after. Three bridges cross the lakes, and around them runs a footpath, which is a popular jogging track. Immediately beyond the lakes to the north and west lie two very different residential areas, **Nørrebro** and **Østerbro**.

Although there are few specific sights or attractions in either area, each has a distinct character and something to offer visitors to the city who want to get a feel for how Copenhagers live. Both quarters also have a good range of shops, restaurants, cafés, clubs and bars.

Nørrebro

Over the last couple of years **Nørrebro** has overtaken Vesterbro as the hippest area of the city in which to live, thanks to its trendy clothes shops, vibrant cafés and burgeoning nightlife. Happening Nørrebro centres on Sankt Hans Torv, with its two swinging cafés, **Sebastapol Café** and **Pussy Galore's Flying Circus** (*see pages 153 and 154*), and the boutiques and cafés on Blågårdsgade. But the area, with its dark streets and tightly packed housing, has more than its share of social problems and, as such, is probably central Copenhagen's least safe (as opposed to 'most dangerous') neighbourhood at night – though that statement should be qualified by saying that it is still a relatively secure night-time destination, particularly compared with many other European capitals.

As with Vesterbro, many younger Copenhagers have found that Nørrebro's ethnic mix is a major element of its appeal as an up-and-coming residential area. But unlike

Residential **Østerbro**. See p121.

Vesterbro's so-called 'second generation Danes' who are more established, Nørrebro's ethnic inhabitants seem less integrated into the community and are generally less prosperous. As a result, the area has suffered from that most un-Danish phenomenon, social unrest, and has even experienced the odd riot on the occasion of a deportation or some heavy-handed policing.

It is fairly ironic then that Nørrebro's only museum is the **Politihistorisk Museum** (Police History Museum; *listings page 120*). This well-presented museum would potentially

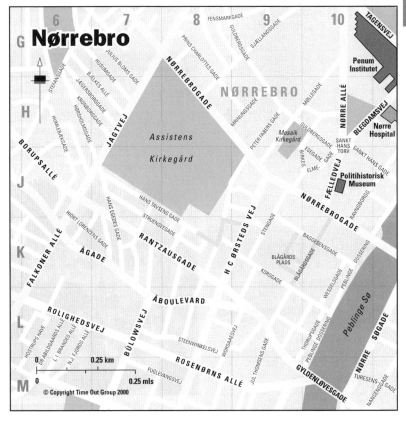

Nørrebro

An urban idyll by **the lakes**.

be of interest to foreign visitors but for the lack of any significant English information. As well as covering the history of the police force, with old uniforms, equipment and ephemera, the building also houses the **Museum of Crime**, which documents Copenhagen's nefarious residents (including various infamous murderers) from past centuries.

Nørrebro also has two historic cemeteries. The Jewish cemetery, **Mosaik Kirkegård**, on Peter Fabers Gade is surrounded by a high wall and gates, and is only open for private visits arranged through the local Jewish community. **Assistens Kirkegård** (*listings below*), on the other hand, is open year-round and, for a place of eternal rest, is fairly lively, used by many as a local park and picnic place (rehearsing musicians are a common sight). Buried among the hundreds of varieties of trees

in this graceful cemetery is just about everyone of any note from Danish history over the last two centuries, including Hans Christian Andersen, Søren Kierkegaard, Niels Bohr, Carlsberg patriarch Christen Jacobsen and the artists Christian Købke, CW Eckersberg, Jens Juel, Herman Bissen and Peter Skovgaard.

Of all Nørrebro's shopping attractions, the best known are its antique shops, which can be found scattered throughout the quarter. The trade centres on Ravnsborggade and Ryesgade, where just about every store sells old clothes, furniture, porcelain, art, glassware, silverware, gold or lesser bric-a-brac from the last three centuries or so (*see page 159*).

Assistens Kirkegård
Entrances on Jagtvej & Nørrebrogade, Nørrebro. Bus 5, 16. **Open** *Mar, Apr, Sept, Oct* 8am-6pm daily. *May-Aug* 8am-8pm daily. *Nov-Feb* 8am-4pm daily. **Admission** free. **Map** p119 H8.

Politihistorisk Museum
Fælledvej 20, Nørrebro (35 36 88 88). Bus 5, 16. **Open** 11am-4pm Tue, Thur, Sun; closed Mon, Wed, Fri, Sat. **Admission** 20kr. **No credit cards.** **Map** p119 J10.

Østerbro

The area of **Østerbro**, which runs from the eastern side of Nørrebro across to the docks on the coast, is dominated by Denmark's national stadium, **Parken** (the Park) located in a park of the same name. Bordered by Nørre Allé, Blegdamsvej, Østerbrogade and Jagtvej, Parken is a large, open, municipal park with a small lake. A more practical open space than most of Copenhagen's other more historic or

Retro chic on Nørrebro's **Blågårdsgade**.

The best Churches

Alexander Newsky Kirke
Russia in Copenhagen. See page 91.

Frederikskirken (Marmorkirken)
The city's finest church. See page 88.

Grundtvigs Kirke
A majestically stark 20th-century yellow-brick monument. See page 122.

Vor Frelsers Kirke
Christianshavn's spiral spire. See page 103.

Zoologisk Museum.

ornamental gardens, this is where locals come for a game of football or hockey, to play tennis, cycle, Rollerblade, go skateboarding or jog. During the summer, there are often free concerts here: larger scale pop and rock concerts by international bands and artists take place in the big concrete stadium, better known as the home of **FC København** (*see page 237*), one of the country's premier football teams (though you would never guess, given the last couple of seasons' results).

To the west of Parken, across Nørre Allé, is the **Zoologisk Museum** (Zoological Museum; *listings below*), the perfect place to come if the animals at the zoo in Frederiksberg (*see page 113*) have proved elusive – the mammals and birds from around the world that are displayed here are stuffed and static. The museum's

standout attractions are the polar bear and cub, its various African wildlife and the enormous whale skeletons.

Østerbro itself is a prosperous residential area with a mixture of century-old apartment buildings and newer high-rise blocks. There is a good mix of shops, cafés and restaurants along the length of Østerbrogade, as well as the embassies of several nations, most prominently Russia and the United States.

East of Østerbro is a large dock area that in recent years has seen a considerable amount of development at its southern end (Frihavnen) near Kastellet (*see page 93*), to provide exclusive and expensive waterside apartments. Further north, the docks become far more industrial, dusty and inhospitable, with various warehouses, power stations and railway lines, though here you will find the cavernous modern furniture store **Paustian** (*see page 164*) and a couple of stylish restaurants, as well as Copenhagen's yacht basins.

Zoologisk Museum

Universitetsparken 15, Østerbro (35 32 10 01/ www.zoologiskmuseum.dk). Bus 18, 42, 43, 72E, 79E, 184, 185. **Open** 11am-4pm Tue-Sun; closed Mon. **Admission** 25kr. **No credit cards.**

Sightseeing

Further Afield

Copenhagen's immediate environs aren't packed with interest, but there are a few compelling attractions within easy reach of the city.

Hellerup & Charlottenlund

As you leave central Copenhagen, via Østerbro to the north, you come to the affluent coastal suburb of **Hellerup**. Though it has some good shops and restaurants, there isn't much to delay you in here, except for one superb and tremendously fun museum.

Beside the mighty Tuborg Brewery (not open to the public) is **Experimentarium**, Denmark's radical, inventive and endlessly fascinating interactive science museum. You soon notice as you wander around this large, aircraft hanger-style exhibition hall, filled with imaginative displays and hands-on experiments that, though they are aimed at children, the exhibits attract as many adults, and all are trying out the latest virtual technology, programming robots, experiencing a human-size gyroscope or staring entranced at an optical illusion. Experimentarium renders apparently mundane topics like alternative power, recycling, aerodynamics and genetics fascinating and accessible. Nothing is static in this place; everything invites investigation. One day all science museums will be like this. Until then, however, adults visiting Experimentarium may care to take along a few aspirin, as the noise levels can be deafening.

Continue northwards through the suburbs and you soon reach the greenery surrounding **Charlottenlund Slot** (Charlottenlund Palace), the site of a royal residence since 1690. The current baroque palace, with its leafy gardens, was built for Princess Charlotte Amalie in 1730, and subsequently found favour as a popular destination for Sunday outings for city dwellers. Various other royals have lived in the palace, but since the 1930s it has been home to the Danish Institute for Fisheries, so the house is not open to the public.

Danmarks Akvarium located in the palace grounds, is one of Copenhagen's perennially popular attractions. Though not the most modern of aquariums, the 90 or so tanks here contain all the usual marine attractions including sharks, piranhas, turtles and tropical fish. The building dates from 1939, but was enlarged in 1974. It's worth a look if you are visiting **Charlottenlund Fort** (not much more than a grassy hillock, with a nice campsite and

Charlottenlund Beach (*see page 123 Beaches close to the city*) and the weather has taken a turn for the worse. All are a short walk from Charlottenlund station.

Probably more appealing to adults will be **Ordrupgaard**, an often overlooked art museum containing some excellent French Impressionist and Danish art from the 19th and 20th century. Significant works by the likes of Manet, Renoir, Matisse and Gauguin, many collected contemporaneously by wealthy Copenhageners, are displayed in a charming house dating from 1908.

Danmarks Akvarium

Kavalergården 1, Charlottenlund (39 62 32 83/ www.danmarks-akvarium.dk). Bus 6. **Open** *Mid Feb-mid Oct* 10am-6pm daily. *Mid Oct-mid Feb* 10am-4pm Mon-Fri; 10am-5pm Sat, Sun. **Admission** 60kr; 30kr-45kr concessions. **No credit cards.**

Experimentarium

Tuborg Havnevej 7, Hellerup (39 27 33 33/ www.eksperimentarium.dk). Bus 6, 21, 650S. **Open** 9am-5pm Mon,Wed-Fri; 9am-9pm Tue; 11am-5pm Sat, Sun. **Admission** 79kr; 57kr-70kr concessions. **Credit** AmEx, DC, MC, V.

Ordrupgaard

Vilvordevej 110, Charlottenlund (39 64 11 83/ www.ordrupgaard.dk). Train to Klampenborg or Lyngby/388 bus. **Open** 1-5pm Tue-Sun; closed Mon. **Admission** 25kr; 20kr concessions; free under-16s. **Credit** MC, V.

Bispebjerg

Undoubtedly the most striking landmark among Copenhagen's otherwise fairly monotonous suburbs is **Gruntvigs Kirke** (Gruntvig's Church) in Bispebjerg, 15 minutes' drive north-west of central Copenhagen. Named after the Danish writer, composer and educational pioneer Nicolai Frederik Severin Grundtvig (*see page 124 **Great Danes: NFS Grundtvig***), the building of the church was very much a family affair – it was designed by PV Jensen-Klint and, after his death, completed by his son, the designer Kaare Klint. The massive yellow brick church took almost 20 years to complete (it was finished in 1940), and though devoid of embellishment both inside and out, it does possess a certain stark beauty.

Grundtvigs Kirke

På Bjerget, Bispebjerg (35 81 54 42/
www.grundtvigskirke.dk). Train to Emdrup/10, 16
bus. **Open** *May-Sept* 9am-4.45pm Mon-Sat; noon-4pm
Sun. *Oct-Apr* 9am-4pm Mon-Sat; noon-1pm Sun.
Admission free.

Lygnby

One of Copenhagen's more leafy and attractive
suburbs is Lyngby, eight kilometres (five
miles) north of the centre, and it's also home
to Denmark's largest open-air museum,
Frilandsmuseet. Not to be confused with
Frihedsmuseet (the museum to Denmark's
resistance movement; *see page 93*),
Frilandsmuseet covers an area of 35 hectares
(86 acres), and is home to 110 buildings from
Denmark, southern Sweden and northern
Germany, all dating from the 17th to the
19th century. To see and appreciate them
all takes the best part of a day, but to get a
good cross-section of architectural styles the
museum's curators suggest you visit buildings
34, 42, and 60-72.

Frilandsmuseet was one of the first
museums of its kind in the world. It opened
in Kongens Have in Copenhagen in 1897, but
was relocated to the present site in 1901 and
was subsequently much expanded under the
auspices of Nationalmuseet. In fact, buildings
continue to be added to the collection, which

already features wind and water mills, farm
buildings, fishermen's cottages, peasants'
houses, factories, and even a 19th-century
fire station, all perfectly preserved with
appropriate interior furnishings and
decoration. There aren't even any information
signs to spoil the atmosphere (though there
is a useful guide book in English). Other
attractions include rare Danish cattle breeds,
folk music performances and excellent
guided tours.

On the down side, as it's an open-air museum,
an enjoyable day out relies heavily on the
weather, and, thanks to diabolical signposting
(typical of Denmark), it is very difficult to find
the museum by car. However, you can catch the
train to Greve Station and walk the ten minutes
or so to the entrance.

Adjacent to Frilandsmuseet is **Brede
Vaerk**, once the Brede cloth mill industrial
complex, and now preserved as a complete
industrial village (with workers' and
craftsmen's cottages, the owners' country
house, a nursery school and gardener's lodge).
It's also run by Nationalmuseet (the factory
closed in 1956). At one time, this whole
region was the centre for Denmark's early
industry, and there were once many factories
and mills like this, stretching all the way from
Lyngby to the coast. **Brede House** is a neo-
classical manor, built in 1795 for the owner

Beaches close to the city

Sjælland's finest beaches are along its north
coast (see page 274), but if you need a quick
dose of sea and sand, and want a minimum
of travelling, the following three options are
more accessible. (Bear in mind that Malmö in
Sweden, just across the Sound, also has a
good beach, Ribban; see page 245.)

Amager Strand (Amager Beach; on the
east side of the island of Amager; see page
125) is the closest beach to the centre of
Copenhagen. Unfortunately, its proximity –
about 15 minutes by bus from Rådhuspladsen
– is about all there is to recommend it.
With a backdrop featuring suburban housing
interspersed with factory units and gas works,
Amager Strand is never going to win any
beauty contests, but on a hot summer day it
is extremely popular, and its shallow waters
are ideal for children. There is some sand,
and grass areas for picnics, ball games and
barbecues, while in the distance looms the
mighty Øresund Bridge to Sweden.

North of the city, the first beach you arrive
at is **Charlottenlund** (small but pleasant),
though it is worth the extra five minutes' drive
to **Bellevue** at Klampenborg, as this is the
best beach close to Copenhagen (20 minutes
by line C train from the city). On sunny days
Bellevue's small, well-groomed patch of sand
becomes very crowded, but it does offer
shallow, clean water, a large grass picnic
area, volleyball nets and beach huts.
Immediately south of Copenhagen the
pickings are less rich. Within striking
distance of the city is the beach at **Ishøj**,
20 minutes south from Central Station,
then a short bus ride from Ishøj station to
the beach. The large (7-km/4-mile long) white
sandy beach here is artificial (it was created
in 1980), but it is set among unspoiled
wetlands that are rich in bird life. More
significantly, this is also the location of
Arken Museum For Moderne Kunst, the
contemporary art museum (see page 124).

Great Danes NFS Grundtvig

Nicolai Frederik Severin Grundtvig is one of Denmark's most influential figures. This deeply religious man was born in a parsonage in 1783 and graduated from Copenhagen University, where he studied theology, in 1803. Though few Danes have actually read many of his books, the impact of his ideas and his pioneering educational work is still keenly felt. It was the zealous Grundtvig who established the folk high schools with their radically new syllabuses that eschewed narrow vocational training for a broader range of topics. He was also a prolific writer of hymns, poetry and books, many of which were suffused with his characteristic brand of nationalism. It was these works that many Danes latched on to during the identity crisis following Britain's attack on Copenhagen in 1807 (see page 17), and his slow, formal hymns are still a fundamental part of all the Christian celebrations.

Despite his often heavyweight themes, Grundtvig appealed to the 'ordinary' Dane.

In a time of high ideas and artistic evolution, he spoke in plain Danish and, unlike his written works, with clarity. Privately, though, he was plagued by mental crises, the first of which was provoked by a disastrous love affair.

As a politician he advocated moves towards democracy and generally opposed authority, but his most significant achievement was the introduction of the art of compromise to Danish politics. Perhaps his greatest blight upon future generations, however, was the defining Grundtvigian attitude towards ambition and aspiration, best expressed in the following spirit-crushing couplet from one of his poems: 'Too much pomp and striving will bring us no rest/keeping our feet firmly on the ground is the best.' It was this attitude that would later be parodied in the fictional 'Jantelov' of 1933 (see page 15); unfortunately by that time it was too late. The Danish character had been well and truly cast.

of the mill, Peter van Hemert, and has an exquisite and largely complete Louis XVI interior. The house was intended to be a summer residence for his family, but van Hemert went bankrupt in 1805. Ironically, that bankruptcy, and the detailed inventory of the house that was made at the time, allowed Nationalmuseet to accurately restore the interior.

There is also a superb restaurant, **Brede Spisehuset** (IC Modewegs Vej; see page 144), nearby. It was once used as the canteen for the local textile factory and its beautiful interior, with ornate tiling and opal glass ceiling, has been sensitively restored.

Brede Vaerk

IC Modewegs Vej, Lyngby (33 13 44 11/ www.natmus.dk). Train to Jægersborg then train to Brede/184, 194 bus.
Open *Easter-mid Oct* 10am-4pm Tue-Sun; closed Mon. *Nov-Easter* closed. **Admission** 40kr; 30kr concessions; free under-16s; free to all Wed. **Credit** AmEx, DC, MC, V.

Frilandsmuseet

Kongevejen 100, Lyngby (45 85 02 92/ www.natmus.dk). Train Sorgenfri/184, 194 bus.
Open *Easter-mid Oct* 10am-4pm Tue, Thur-Sun; closed Mon, Wed. *Mid Oct-Easter* closed.
Admission 60kr; free under-16s; free to all Wed. **Credit** AmEx, DC, MC, V.

Ishøj

The fourth of Sjælland's world-class art museums (the others being Louisiana, *see page 272*; Statens Museum For Kunst, *see page 98*; and Ny Carlsberg Glyptotek, *see page 64*) is found in the unprepossessing suburb of Ishøj, 15 minutes by train south along the coast from Copenhagen. **Arken Museum For Moderne Kunst** (Arken Museum of Modern Art) was built to celebrate Copenhagen's year as European City of Culture in 1996, and is almost as famous for its architecture as its exhibits.

Arken is housed in an extraordinary concrete, glass and steel building, designed by the Danish architect Søren Robert Lund when he was aged only 25 and still a student of the Royal Danish Academy of Fine Arts. Lund's compelling and perplexing construction, with its echoes of marine architecture (both inside and out), won a competition for the design of the new gallery in 1988, and has divided critics ever since. Some applaud its apt maritime references (the museum is metres from the beach), which give it the appearance of an abstract shipwreck, while others feel that a visit to an art museum should focus more on the art than the building that houses it. Most artists are unanimous on the subject: they hate it, claiming the exhibition spaces compete with, rather than enhance, their work. Visitors, though, are usually won over by Lund's skewed vision.

Arken's permanent collection of paintings, sculpture, graphic art and installations includes 260 post-war works, although, rather disappointingly, only 50 or so of these are usually on show. This display, however, is augmented by superb temporary exhibitions, which have often been transferred from other major European museums.

Many pieces in the permanent collection are by Danish artists but there are also numerous foreign works. There is something to surprise everyone here, from major works by Asger Jørn and Per Kirkeby to the unsettling installation *The Beds* by Christian Boltanski. Probably the most famous piece in the permanant collection (in Denmark at least) is the photograph *Flex Pissing/Bjørk er en nar* (aka *Bringing It All Back Home*) by Claus Carstensen and the art group Superflex (popularly known as the mildly controversial Danish Art Mob; *see page 207*).

Arken also has a small cinema (which usually shows films connected with the temporary exhibition), an excellent concert hall and a café on the first floor.

Unfortunately, these days the museum's exterior has a slightly neglected air, exhibiting tell-tale signs of dishevelment, like rust spots and weeds. Looking at it now, you can't help thinking that it was built with the short-term goal of providing a flagship building for the City of Culture celebrations.

Arken lies just a few metres from **Ishøj Strand** (Ishøj Beach), an artificial but very attractive stretch of white sandy beach (*see page 123* **Beaches close to the city**).

Arken Museum For Moderne Kunst

Skovvej 100, Ishøj (43 54 02 22/www.arken.dk). Train to Ishøj then 128 bus. **Open** 10am-5pm Tue, Thur-Sun; 10am-9pm Wed; closed Mon. **Admission** 50kr; 20kr-40kr concessions. **Credit** MC, DC, V.

Amager

Amager is the small island immediately to the east of Copenhagen. It is home to the city's international airport, but aside from that, it's mostly a flat, uninteresting area of bleak industrial estates, cheap housing and farmland. Currently, the island is redeemed only by the fairytale fishing village of Dragør, though it also boasts the nearest beach to the centre of Copenhagen, **Amager Strand** (Amager Beach; *see page 123* **Beaches close to the city**), on the coast road to the airport. However, significant developments are planned for Amager following the completion of the new

Øresund Fixed Link to Sweden (*see page 246*), which terminates here on the Danish side. A new mini-metro system will link Amager to the city centre and beyond, while numerous grand building projects, including an entire new town and artificial beach, are mooted.

On the east coast of Amager, among salt flats and farmland bustling with bird life, lies the historic and exceptionally pretty village of **Dragør**. About half an hour's bus ride from Copenhagen, Dragør is a well-preserved fishing and farming town, with a maze of cobbled lanes bursting with hollyhocks, and fronted by traditional yellow-walled, orange-tiled cottages. Like many coastal settlements in this area it was founded upon the humble herring and prospered during the 14th century as a fishing port. In the 19th century, it found a new lease of life as a centre for shipping and salvage, trading throughout the Baltic and as far away as England. That came to an end with the advent of steam ships, and little has changed since.

However, Dragør's sleepy idyll can be misleading. Property prices here are among the highest in the Greater Copenhagen area – the village is popular with affluent young professionals who commute into the city. They ensure that Dragør remains an improbably lively, almost cosmopolitan village, for most of the year. There are also some smart shops on its short high street (open on Sundays during the summer), as well as several excellent restaurants and beer gardens which help make Dragør popular with foreign tourists and holidaying Danes. The town has a marina, a small cinema, and an equally small museum (**Dragør Museum**), housed in the town's oldest fisherman's house (dating back to 1682). If you fancy staying in Dragør, a great choice is the **Dragør Badehotel** (Drogdensvej 43, 32 53 05 00, www.badehotellet.dk, 895kr double).

Five minutes to the south, inland, is the village of Store Magelby, founded by Dutch settlers in the early 1500s. The village is home to the **Amager Museum**, which traces the history of the Dutch immigrants in the area.

Amager Museum

Hovedgade 4 & 12, Store Magleby, Amager (32 53 02 50/www.dragor-information.dk). Bus 30, 350S. **Open** *May-Sept* noon-4pm Tue-Sun; closed Mon. *Oct-Apr* noon-4pm Wed, Sun; closed Mon, Tue, Thur-Sat. **Admission** 20kr; 10kr concessions. **No credit cards**.

Dragør Museum

Havnepladsen, Dragør, Amager (32 53 41 06/ www.dragor-information.dk). Bus 30, 350S. **Open** *May-Sept* noon-4pm Tue-Fri; noon-6pm Sat, Sun; closed Mon. *Oct-Apr* closed. **Admission** 20kr; 10kr concessions. **No credit cards**.

Eat, Drink, Shop

Restaurants

Throw your preconceptions out of the window – Copenhagen is one of Europe's best cities for eating out.

Copenhagen is a foodies' paradise, whether your fancy is for traditional Danish, classical French, Asian or modern Scandinavian or European cuisine. You could easily spend a fortnight here and eat at a different world-class restaurant each night. Despite Scandinavia's reputation for pricey dining, you can also eat cheaply and well in the Danish capital, though, of course, you can just as easily pay 800kr per head for abysmal food and grumpy service.

Roughly speaking the city's culinary landscape is laid out as follows: along the quayside at Nyhavn you will find traditional Danish and seafood restaurants, whose main clientele are tourists. The quality is variable and the prices are high but it is a beautiful spot for an al fresco beer if the weather's nice, and even in winter the bars and restaurants are the very definition of *hygge* (*see page 79* **The essence of *hygge***). The finer French and modern Scandinavian restaurants are mainly to be found in the area just west of Kongens Nytorv, though there are notable exceptions. Istedgade in Vesterbro has a number of Thai and Indian restaurants, while Nørrebro is quite good for cheaper dining.

Traditional lunch cafés are a unique element of the Danish restaurant scene; open only for weekday lunch and serving *smørrebrød* (open sandwiches), herring and *frikadeller* (traditional Danish meatballs). You'll find them all over the city, and though they don't always look particularly inviting, they are the best places to sample old-fashioned, traditional Danish food, and you can be assured of a warm welcome.

Copenhagen's restaurant staff tend to be paid far more highly than those in other European countries and so, while a tip is naturally appreciated, don't feel obliged to load on an extra 15 per cent for each meal; five per cent or 10kr for meals under 100kr will do fine. Danes are thoroughly mean tippers; in fact, many don't tip at all.

> ▶ **Note**: the line between café, restaurant and bar is not always clear in Copenhagen. Be aware that many of the establishments in the **Bars & Cafés** chapter also serve excellent food.

It is always worth asking for an English menu in Danish restaurants, more have them than don't. Finally, you should note that, as extraordinary as this sounds, some of the better restaurants close in July for a holiday.

Tivoli & around

For restaurants within Tivoli itself, *see page 61*.

Contemporary

Alex Vinbar & Køkken

First Hotel, Vesterbrogade 27, Vesterbro (33 78 80 25/www.alexvinbar.com). **Open** *Restaurant* noon-11pm daily. *Bar* noon-1am daily. **Main courses** 150kr-250kr. **Set menus** 245kr-360kr. **Credit** AmEx, DC, MC, V. **Map** p310 P10.
Though the design and atmosphere may be slightly too Scandinavian cool (to the point of chilly, if it isn't busy), young Swedish chef Alexander Magnusson's restaurant in the rear of the First Hotel still serves sumptuous food to warm the heart of even the most demanding gastronome. With a kitchen (which opens on to the dining area) staffed by young, inventive graduates of some of Sweden's and London's top restaurants (including Vong, the Square, Le Caprice and The Ivy), the food is bound to excite. European and Asian styles are fused seamlessly in dishes such as sashimi of tuna and salmon with rice, mango and papaya spring roll, and ravioli of scallop and lobster with roasted sweetbreads. Recommended mains include the carpaccio of beef with aged parmesan and red wine risotto, and pan-fried redfish with baby squid, pesto linguini and tomato confit.

Passagens Spisehus

Vesterbrogade 42, Vesterbro (33 22 47 57/ www.passagens.dk). **Open** 5-11pm Mon-Thur; 5pm-midnight Fri, Sat; 5-10pm Sun. **Main courses** 145kr-235kr. **Set menus** 189kr-250kr. **Credit** MC, V. **Map** p111 P9.
When it opened in October 1999, this modern Nordic restaurant received rave revues from the local and national press for its imaginative use of rare game, and it remains one of the best restaurants (for meat eaters at least) in town. Reindeer from Lapland and musk ox from Alaska are highly recommended specialities, while grouse and salmon also feature regularly. The interior of this former cancan bar beside Det Ny Teater may be a little austere (it's all mirror-finish wood panelling, parquet floor and crisp, white

linen tablecloths), and the clientele more reserved than Vesterbro's other more fashionable eateries, but once the food arrives, you'll hardly notice. What's more, the wine list offers unusually good value (for such a classy joint) and the service is impeccable.

Indian

Taj Indian Restaurant

Jernbanegade 3-5 (33 13 10 10/www.indiantaj.dk). **Open** noon-midnight daily. **Main courses** 85kr-155kr. **Set menus** from 160kr. **Credit** AmEx, DC, MC, V. **Map** p310 O11.

The outlandish interior of what, when it opened in 1973, was Scandinavia's first Indian restaurant, has to be seen to be believed. Smoked glass windows conceal a homage to Delhi's Red Fort and the Taj Mahal in the form of a marble waterfall centrepiece complemented by lavish wood carvings and ornate metal relief chairs throughout the rest of the room. And the food's not bad either; in fact, at its best, the Taj, which specialises in Moghul food, is the finest Indian restaurant in town.

Strøget & around

American

Chili

Vandkunsten 1 (33 91 19 18). **Open** 11am-midnight Mon-Sat; noon-11pm Sun. **Main courses** 59kr-90kr **No credit cards**. **Map** p311 O13.

Expect rough and ready burgers and chicken in this American-style diner located in a former hippy enclave, within two minutes of Nationalmuseet and the western end of Strøget. If you want a quick, cheap meal this beats the usual chains hands down.

Contemporary

Konrad

Pilestræde 12-14 (33 93 29 29/ www.konrad.living.dk). **Open** noon-midnight Mon-Wed; noon-1am Thur; noon-3.30am Fri, Sat; closed Sun. *Food served* noon-3pm, 6-10pm Mon-Thur; noon-3pm, 6-11pm Fri, Sat; closed Sun. **Main courses** 175kr-195kr. **Set menu** 445kr. **Credit** AmEx, DC, MC, V. **Map** p311 M14.

There are some who find Copenhagen's most self-consciously cool restaurant a bit of a turn-off, but as long as you don't take its tyrannical stylishness too seriously Konrad remains one of the city's finest restaurants. Disappointing desserts apart, the Scandinavian/French food is sublimely prepared and artfully presented. Peerless service is further compensation for the high prices, as are the people-watching opportunities afforded by the centrally located bar – a honey pot for Copenhagen's hip thirtysomethings and the city's more mature jet set. A DJ plays from 11pm Friday and Saturday. Booking is advisable.

TyvenKokkenHansKoneog-HendesElsker

Magstræde 16 (33 16 12 92). **Open** 6pm-2am Mon-Sat; closed Sun. **Set menu** 395kr; 400kr-550kr with wine. **Credit** AmEx, DC, MC, V. **Map** p311 O13.

Though it is rather disturbingly named after Peter Greenaway's cannibalistic *The Cook, The Thief, His Wife and Her Lover*, this gastronomic pantheon, located in a converted 18th-century townhouse (formerly a brothel) near Rådhuspladsen, could very well be Copenhagen's finest restaurant. It's certainly its most inventive. Diners are offered one

The best Restaurants

For al fresco dining
Cap Horn (p139); **Peder Oxe** (p134); **Pussy Galore's** (p155); **Sebastapol Café** (p155); **Thorsen** (p153); **Zeleste** (p139).

For budget dining
Ban-Gaw (p143); **Cascabel Madhus** (p141); **Galathea Kroen** (p149); **Den Græske Taverna** (p144); **Kate's Joint** (p155); **Propaganda** (p155); **Shark House Deli** (p144); **Spicey Kitchen** (p143).

For day trips
Bio Bistro, Tisvildeleje (p276); **Jacobsen**, Klampenborg (p273); **Nokken**, Rungsted (p273).

For glamour
Café Victor (p148); **Etcetera** (p150); **Konrad** (p130); **Schultz** (p140).

For going local
Cap Horn (p139); **Ida Davidsens** (p141); **Huset Med Det Grønne Træ** (p133); **Passagens Spisehus** (p129).

For Sunday brunch
Amokka (p156); **Base Camp** (p152); **Bastionen og Løven** (p152); **Café Klimt** (p151); **Café Sorte Hest** (p153).

For vegetarians
Atlas Bar (p147); **Cascabel Madhus** (p141); **Morgenstedet** (p143).

For views
Café Norden (p147); **Café à Porta** (p150); **Restaurant Wiinblad** (p139).

Simply the best
TyvenKokkenHansKoneogHendesElsker (p130); **1th** (p138); **formel B** (p143); **Konrad** (p130); **Kommandanten** (p140); **Schultz** (p140); **Le Sommelier** (p141).

Eat, Drink, Shop

TyvenKokkenHans-
KoneogHendesElsker.
See p130.

Eat, Drink, Shop

Classical gastronomy in the heart of old Copenhagen

Restaurant Nico welcomes you to dinner or lunch in the middle of Copenhagen's charming Latin quarter.

Enjoy our French/Italian inspired kitchen, where first class ingredients and classical gastronomy are our aim.

Enjoy Restaurant Nico's stylish decor and superb service.

- First class French/Italian kitchen of international standard
- Classic Danish lunch - all homemade from the best ingredients.
- More than 100 wines from selected wine houses.
- à la Carte
- Seperate floors for smokers and non-smokers

Kultorvet 5 • 1175 Copenhagen K
Kitchen open noon-11pm • Sunday closed
Tel. 33 91 09 49 · Fax 33 69 05 81
www.nicos.dk · mail@nicos.dk

Krogs Fiskerestaurant resists the vagaries of fashion, and concentrates on its fish quota.

fixed menu (you choose the number of courses), but from the first mouthful you'll realise that proprietor Anders Selmer's confidence in his kitchen's ability to excite even the most jaded palate is totally vindicated. The menu changes weekly but will typically feature dishes like lamb with Madagascar pepper, bulgar and oyster cream, or wild boar salad with winter vegetables served with a white wine sorbet (you can see why chef Claus Jørgensen cites Marco Pierre White as an influence). If you go for the full menu, then we recommend you place the choice of wine in the hands of Anders, who will regale you with the stories behind them as he pours. The team behind this restaurant have recently opened Delicatessen (*see p154*), a 'fast food' outlet on Vesterbrogade also named after an art house movie with a cannibalistic theme. Advance booking is advised. Note: a 5% surcharge is added to all credit card payments.

Danish

Huset Med Det Grønne Træ

Gammeltorv 20 (33 12 87 86). **Open** *Apr-Aug* 11am-3pm Mon-Fri; closed Sat, Sun. *Sept-Mar* 11am-3pm Mon-Sat; closed Sun. **Main courses** 35kr-115kr. **Credit** MC, V. **Map** p311 N13.

A kind of working man's Ida Davidson's (*see p141*), this old-style lunch restaurant is frequented by journalists, local businessmen and lawyers from the nearby courthouse. Offering traditional Danish *smørrebrød* in a small, spartan cellar café with yellowed ceilings and wood-panelled walls, this is an authentic taste of basic Danish cuisine. Owner Peter Damgaard has run the place for over 20 years and is happy to talk you through the menu (English version available), which includes a decent range of typical open sandwich toppings. If you think you can stomach it, why not sample a traditional beef tartar garnished with raw egg yolk, onion and radish on rye, washed down with an akvavit and Tuborg?

Fish

Krogs Fiskerestaurant

Gammel Strand 38 (33 15 89 15/www.krogs.dk). **Open** 11.30am-4pm, 5.30-10.30pm Mon-Sat; closed Sun. **Main courses** 280kr-450kr. **Set menus** 415kr-825kr. **Credit** AmEx, DC, MC, V. **Map** p311 N14.

Krogs Fiskerestaurant, on historic Gammel Strand, is a constant in Copenhagen's ever-shifting culinary landscape, standing proudly aloof from the frivolities of fashion. Its French-influenced Danish kitchen performs to exacting standards, though whether it can justify the exorbitant prices is a moot point, and you'll struggle to find much on the menu that is light. Krogs does, however, have one of the most extensive wine lists in the city – it runs to 50 pages and bottles start at around 230kr. Krogs' clientele tend not to be in the first flush of youth (although you get a lot of wealthy, aged Americans who dress as though they were), but then, with these prices, and decor from the maiden aunt school of interior design, that's hardly surprising. If it were in Paris the staff would be rottweilers, but this being Denmark the service is only slightly chilly. A fine restaurant, but, ultimately, overrated.

French

Albert & Co

Læderstræde 11 (33 93 53 53). **Open** noon-10pm Mon-Sat; closed Sun. **Main courses** 98kr-145kr. **Set menu** 225kr. **Credit** DC, MC, V. **Map** p311 N14.

This superior brasserie combines a warm atmosphere with an exceptional and very reasonably priced menu. The food is mainly French-influenced (the wine list is diverse), but the decor is characteristically Danish (white walls, wooden floors, candles). Owner Henrik Lazlo's enthusiasm ensures that the quality of the food remains as high as that of many of Copenhagen's pricier restaurants, but the atmosphere is far from stuffy, attracting a fairly young, trendy crowd. In summer the charming courtyard to the rear is opened, and you may find yourself dining next to Prince Joachim and Princess Alexandra who are regulars.

L'Education Nationale

Larsbjørnsstræde 12 (33 91 53 60/www.leduc.dk). **Open** 11.30am-midnight Mon-Sat; 4pm-midnight Sun. **Main courses** 110kr. **Set menu** 238kr. **Credit** AmEx, DC, MC, V. **Map** p310 N12.
Having spawned several chefs who have gone on to work in French restaurants elsewhere in Copenhagen, this standard issue French café/restaurant in Pisserenden continues to serve amply proportioned portions of regulation French fare (duck, mussels, steaks, etc) to an appreciative local crowd. The genuine gallic atmosphere is reinforced by an unsettlingly large wooden caricature of Serge Gainsbourg that greets you as you enter, ceilings and walls plastered with posters of obscure (and by the looks of it, deservedly so) French pop stars, and surly service.

La Gallette

Larsbjørnsstræde 9 (33 32 37 90). **Open** noon-11pm Mon-Fri, Sat; 4-10pm Sun. **Main courses** 50kr-60kr. **Credit** MC, V. **Map** p310 N12.
Secreted down an alleyway in the heart of the so-called 'Latin Quarter', it's worth searching out this charming little Breton crêperie and café. Within, there are two compact levels, while tables spill into the alley in fine weather. The genuine buckwheat gallettes come with a variety of fillings and are very reasonably priced around the 50-60kr mark. Wash them down with real Brittany cider, drunk, as tradition dictates, from an earthenware cup.

Restaurant Godt

Gothersgade 38 (33 15 21 22). **Open** 5.30pm-midnight Tue-Sat; closed Mon, Sun. **Set menus** 325kr-445kr. **Credit** DC, MC, V. **Map** p311 M15.
Owned and run by chef Colin Rice (from Middlesborough) and his Danish wife Marie Ann Ravn, this tiny, two-storey, classical French restaurant received a hallowed Michelin star in 2000, and was promptly booked up for weeks in advance. Things have cooled a little, but you still need to phone a few days ahead to be sure of a table (there are under ten). Colin uses only the very finest, freshest ingredients available and his kitchen's attention to detail is breathtaking. A harmonious, heavy duty treat, not for the casual grazer, but slightly marred by a lack of atmosphere.

Restaurant Grønnegade

Grønnegade 39 (33 93 31 33/www.groennegade.dk). **Open** 5-11pm daily. **Main courses** 200kr. **Set menus** 368kr-468kr. **Credit** AmEx, DC, MC, V. **Map** p311 M15.
Grønnegade tends to be overshadowed by its more showy neighbours like Konrad, Capo and Kommandanten, but this small, intimate and exceptionally charming Franco-Danish restaurant,

located in a 17th-century town house, deserves applause for its beguiling menu and smiley service. Expect to be tempted by dishes such as consommé with frog's legs baked in puff pastry with fresh herbs, and fillet of lemon sole poached in white wine, served with sun-dried tomatoes and olives, marinated in truffle sauce and a dill bouillon. Go for the fixed menu of three courses, or more, for optimum value.

Global

Illum

Østergade 52, Strøget (33 18 28 00). **Open** 11am-7pm Mon-Thur; 11am-8pm Fri; 11am-5pm Sat; closed Sun. **Main courses** 59kr-98kr. **Credit** AmEx, DC, MC, V. **Map** p311 M15.
If Café Norden and Café Europa on nearby Amagertorv are full (which they invariably are) you could do worse than take the lift to the top floor café/bar/restaurant in the Illum department store. Bargain wok food, salads and pizzas are the backbone of the menu (as opposed to the pricier restaurant food they used to serve here) in this very pleasant dining area beneath the store's majestic glass roof. The pagers that you receive when you make your order at the bar, which then flash to tell you when it's time to go and pick up your food from the open kitchen, are a neat gimmick.

Peder Oxe

Gråbrødretorv 11 (33 11 00 77/www.pederoxe.dk). **Open** 11.30am-1pm daily. *Food served* 11.30am-10.30pm Mon-Wed, Sun; 11.30am-11pm Thur-Sat. **Main courses** 78kr-165kr. **Credit** DC, MC, V. **Map** p311 N13.
Located on charming and historic Gråbrødretorv, Peder Oxe is one of Copenhagen's best-known restaurants, and is very popular with tourists. A wide-ranging menu covers all bases, from steaks and burgers (made from organic or free-range beef), to light, fresh Asian-influenced dishes such as tuna tartare with avocado and mango, all of which are well presented and reasonably priced. But Peder Oxe's trump card is its romantic interior featuring original wooden floors and exquisite Portuguese tiling – ample compensation should the few tables outside be taken. At lunchtime there's an extensive *smørrebrød* menu. *See also p148.*

Italian

Pasta Basta

Valkendorfsgade 22 (33 11 21 31/ www.pastabasta.dk). **Open** 11.30am-3am Mon-Thur, Sun; 11.30am-5am Fri, Sat. **Main course** 69kr-159kr. **No credit cards. Map** p311 M14.
Above average, centrally located pasta restaurant that offers a fine all-you-can-eat buffet for 69kr. Alternatively, the à la carte menu includes a collection of verbose dishes such as 'Siam prawns and angler fish skewer, grilled and served with a shell-

fish gravy and fine soba pasta turned in spinach, fresh chilli, black olives and spring onions'. Excellent quality, reasonably quick service and well priced. A great place to take kids.

San Giorgio

Rosenborggade 7 (33 12 61 20). **Open** 6pm-midnight Mon-Sat; closed Sun. **Main courses** 198kr. **Set menu** 380kr. **Credit** AmEx, DC, MC, V. **Map** p307 L13.

If you don't fancy Era Ora (*see p143*), this cosy, romantic restaurant, housed in an 18th-century half-timbered house serves the next best Italian food in town, and at far more reasonable prices. San Giorgio's service is particularly good, too. A short walk from Kultorvet.

Spisehuset/La Bella Notte

Magstræde 14 (33 32 61 73/33 14 52 70/ www.spisehuset.aok.dk). **Open** 6-10pm Tue-Sat; closed Mon, Sun. **Main courses** 78kr-140kr. **Credit** AmEx, DC, MC, V. **Map** p311 O13.

The one-room restaurant in this excellent arts venue attracts a creative crowd who bring with them an enjoyable hubbub. The menu is limited but generally of a high standard. Service comes at the speed of a glacier, however. But wait! Come summer, and a butterfly-like transformation takes place when Huset opens out into the adjacent narrow alleyway to become a classic Neapolitan restaurant, La Belle Notte, inspired by the alleyway scene in the Disney animation *Lady And The Tramp*, and serving simple, cheap Italian food on small, check-clothed tables. Diners sit beneath washing lines strung out for that special Italian feel. Funny and charming.

Meditteranean

Riz Raz

Kompagnistræde 20 (33 15 05 75/ www.rizraz.dk). **Open** 11.30am-midnight daily. **Main courses** 89kr-179kr; *buffet* 49kr-59kr. **Credit** DC, MC, V. **Map** p311 O13.

This convivial cellar restaurant, just a salad's toss from Strøget, is a favourite with tourists and Copenhageners and consistently wins over reviewers from the Danish press. Riz Raz always seems to be packed to the gunwales with fascinating folk, in for a quick bite before heading somewhere more groovy. The bargain-priced southern Mediterranean food is imaginative, and invariably fresh and light. The buffet, which in many other places is usually an excuse to stuff punters with low-overhead salads, is, in Riz Raz's case, utterly delectable, and probably the best value food on offer here. As if that wasn't enough, the service is extremely friendly and the young staff are always happy to make recommendations on how to spend the rest of your evening. A place to return to, particularly in summer when there is outdoor dining.

Oriental

Flyvefisken

Larsbjørnsstræde 18 (33 14 95 15/www.aok.dk). **Open** 5.30-10.30pm Mon-Sat; closed Sun. **Main courses** 99kr. **Credit** DC, MC, V. **Map** p310 N12.

This adorable Thai restaurant is located above the Atlas Bar in the epicentre of funky Pisserenden. The prices aren't as cheap as those in the Thai restau-

Eat, Drink, Shop

Firmly on the tourist trail, but none the worse for it: **Peder Oxe**. *See p134.*

All the best ingredients

Though a correctly prepared *smørrebrød* or the traditional herring buffets down on Nyhavn will always have their place, in the last few years Copenhagen's dynamic and creative restaurant scene has blossomed with a whole raft of modern, inventive and unutterably stylish restaurants opening to widespread acclaim. In the process, these revolutionary kitchens, led by a new generation of clued-up entrepeneurs and chefs, have overturned outdated preconceptions of Danish cuisine and enticed the city's palate towards a fusion future. Today, a clutch of wonderful restaurants – Schultz, Konrad, Etcetera, formel B, Passagens Spisehus, Le Sommelier, TyvenKokkenHansKoneogHendesElsker and 1th among them – have helped make Copenhagen a mecca for discerning foodies. Typically, their menus marry traditional Danish country ingredients and recipes with contemporary, foreign cooking styles, and when that's combined with interiors and clienteles straight from the pages of *wallpaper**, it usually ensures that a meal at any of these venues is not quickly forgotten (particularly, of course, by your accountant).

At 24, young chef **Nikolai Kirk** was one of the pioneers of this new Danish cuisine. Working at Kirk restaurant (now reborn as Schultz), spikey-haired Kirk became a local hero by using his grandmother's recipe book and updating the recipes for cosmopolitan Copenhageners. In fact, Kirk was so successful that he is now a TV celebrity chef and a successful cookbook author. Today, he reigns over one of the most accomplished kitchens in Denmark, that of Vesterbro's **formel B** (see page 143).

Schultz (see page 140) has taken up where Kirk left off. The head chef and owner **Allan Schultz** has used his experience as a former chef at Pantina (the trendy Beverly Hills restaurant) to incorporate fresh Danish ingredients into an international menu (for example, granita of cucumber with vodka, and aubergine ravioli with cockles, leek, ginger and beurre blanc). Schultz masterfully melds Californian, Danish, French and Asian styles and, unlike Kirk, the gregarious Harley Davidson-riding Schultz loves nothing more than an enthusiastic discussion about food with guests.

'Danes have high standards when it comes to food,' believes **Jacob Blom**, the 27-year-old entrepreneur behind **Konrad** (see page 130), another super hip eaterie that delivers both in terms of style and content. 'But Konrad has taken things further. It was originally inspired by Terence Conran's philosophy that the best food must be matched by the quality of service and decor. We've managed to come a long way, very quickly.' The menu at Konrad focuses on Danish cuisine with some inventive twists – from relatively simple dishes (summer venison with beetroot and onions) to the more ambitious (grilled seabass, oyster gazpacho and warm fennel salad). Chef **Petter Nillson**'s philosophy is to make each ingredient stand out. 'Some Danish chefs are trying to do some strange things to food without thinking about the seasons,' he explains. 'This could be the consequence of reading too many foreign magazines and cookbooks. The link between traditional and modern Danish cooking is to let the food taste of every single ingredient.'

However, in striving to attract Copenhagen's beautiful people, Konrad, whose bar and weekend DJs are almost as popular as its restaurant, has been accused of elitism by

Eat, Drink, Shop (side tab)

---

rants on Istedgade (west of Central Station) and the food is not as authentic (there is a distinct Danish element in many dishes), but if you are looking for Thai food that won't ignite your mouth, Flyvefisken is a cosy, intimate venue in which to find it.

Sushi Time

Grønnegade 28 (33 11 88 99). **Open** noon-3pm, 5-9pm Mon-Fri; noon-7pm Sat; closed Sun. **Main courses** from 75kr. **Credit** DC, MC, V. **Map** p311 M15.

A no-frills, decent value, sushi takeaway with a small dining area upstairs, though if the weather is nice it's far better to go and enjoy your nigiri in nearby Kongens Have.

Steakhouses

Bøf & Ost

Gråbrødretorv 13 (33 11 99 11/www.boef-ost.dk). **Open** 11.30am-1am daily. **Main courses** 147kr-179kr. **Credit** DC, MC, V. **Map** p311 N13.

The wooden tables and stone floor of this quality cellar restaurant in lively Gråbrødretorv reflect the simplicity of its food. That's not to say this is a paper napkin/beer-in-the-bottle kind of place – appetisers like terrine of black truffles (95kr), and mains such as turbot with a lobster sauce and tabbouleh (179kr), as well as the various cuts and preparations of beef

some locals more used to egalitarian door policies. 'Konrad and Kirk were the first restaurants in Denmark to have a guest list,' says Jacob Blom. 'Some people have criticised us for this – it's an unusual thing in Denmark, but our regulars understand what we are trying to do.' Whatever people think of the filtering out of undesirables (and if you book a day or two ahead you should have no problem getting a table), it has certainly paid off for Konrad. David and Victoria Beckham are among the visiting celebrities who have recently dined here (not necessarily a recommendation for the efficacy of its kitchen, but still a useful barometer of the restaurant's international status), and for

the past few years it has been a favoured meeting place for Copenhagen's in-crowd.

Konrad lies at the heart of Copenhagen's swanky restaurant quarter with the venerable **Café Victor** (still drawing the Chanel and Gucci crowd after all these years; see page 147), the businessmen's favourite **Kommandanten** (see page 140), the classic French temple **Restaurant Godt** (see page 134) and the super cool North African lounge bar **Etcetera** (see page 149), all within glass chinking distance. Together with the dozens of world-class restaurants and distinctive cafés scattered throughout the city, they have helped to make Copenhagen an irresistible dining destination.

(charcoal-grilled is the house speciality), swiftly disavow you of that notion. As you'd guess from the name ('Beefsteak & Cheese'), the cheese board is one of the best in Copenhagen, with a broad range of Danish and foreign cheeses. The restaurant is situated on the southern side of the square in the oldest of the so-called 'Fire Houses', built after the great fire of 1728. As with all the cafés and restaurants in this square, in summer Bøf & Ost's parasols and tables spill out riotously onto the cobbles, creating a great atmosphere in the evening. Shame about the really uncomfortable chairs though. Note: if you pay by credit card, a 3.5% surcharge will be added to your bill (except Visa).

Jensen's Bøfhus

Gråbrødretorv 15 (33 32 78 00/www.jensens.com). **Open** 11am-10.30pm Mon-Thur, Sun; 11am-11.30pm Fri, Sat. **Main courses** *lunch* 45kr-75kr; *dinner* 84kr-160kr. **Set menus** 168kr-218kr. **Credit** AmEx, DC, MC, V. **Map** p311 N13.

Don't dismiss these excellent family restaurants just because they are a chain. Expect a decent range of grilled steak and chicken dishes (particularly good value at lunch-time), and attentive and friendly service. There are a few variations on the standards (such as the Tex-Mex 'Sombrero Steak'), but Jensen's classic whisky sauce is a deserved long-standing favourite, as is the all-you-can-eat ice-cream bar.

A surrealist plague of lobsters descends on **Zeleste**. *See p139.*

Branches: Kultorvet 15 (33 15 09 84); Axeltorv (33 12 16 66); Vesterbrogade 11A, Vesterbro (33 25 03 66); Amagerbrogade 84, Amager (32 84 85 03).

Turkish

Strøgets Shawarma og Café
Frederiksberggade 5, Strøget (33 13 72 84).
Open 11am-1am daily. **Main courses** 27kr-62kr.
No credit cards. Map p310 O12.
You can't move for Turkish shawarma restaurants at the western end of Strøget, but this one has the edge due to its small first-floor terrace, which is great for watching the world go by on the pedestrian shopping street below (assuming you can get one of the three tables with a view). Food-wise, however, it's nothing out of the ordinary, serving the usual kebabs, filled pittas, burgers and chips at rock-bottom prices.

Nyhavn & around

Contemporary

1th
Herluf Trollesgade 9, 1th (33 93 57 70/www.1th.dk).
Open from 7pm Wed-Sat; closed Mon, Tue, Sun.
Set menu 900kr. **Credit** V.
Map p312 N16.

This unique and really rather splendid restaurant behaves more as if it were a private dinner party (or, at times, a piece of performance art), than a commercial catering enterprise. You pay in advance when you book (two to three weeks in advance to be sure of a table) and receive an invitation by return of post. When you arrive, ('promptly at seven'), in the quiet residential street adjacent to Nyhavn, you buzz a discretely labelled intercom before being shown into a drawing room in which other 'guests' are mingling over an aperitif. After a while doors are opened with a theatrical flourish to reveal a spacious and light dining room with an open kitchen. The ten or so innovative, contemporary European dishes in the fixed menu more than live up to this elaborate preamble, but an evening at 1th can occasionally hit a few bum notes. The wine is part of the fixed menu but is rationed to around one glass every 40 minutes; some ingredients recur a little too often; and the staff, though efficient and unstuffy, don't quite live up to the general sense of occasion. That said, dishes like golden fried pumpkin with frissée salad and diced, crisp-fried pigs' trotters, or cold virgin lobster soup with rillette of lobster, cherry tomatoes and fennel are sublime, and the remarkably calm kitchen (the chefs are female, so there's none of that macho pan bashing) is a pleasure to watch. The evening lasts around five hours including, if you're lucky, an a capella interlude.

Barock

Nyhavn 1 (33 33 01 51/www.barock.dk). **Open** noon-11pm daily. **Main courses** 170kr. **Credit** AmEx, DC, MC, V. **Map** p312 M16.

Forget the cheesy name and gaudy red sign outside, and ignore the little voice inside your head that tells you that this is on Nyhavn so it can't be any good, Barock has an unexpectedly appealing restaurant on its first floor, as well as bearable prices. This is predominantly a tourist place but they still make an effort with the food, which is passable Modern European fare. The service is friendly and quick, while Barock's interior is enjoyably decadent. From April to October there is seating on the quayside.

Zeleste

Store Strandstræde 6 (33 16 06 06/www.zeleste.dk). **Open** 11am-midnight daily. **Main courses** 150kr-170kr ('small' dishes 69kr-95kr). **Set menu** 285kr. **Credit** MC, V. **Map** p312 M16.

Why fight for a table and inferior food on Nyhavn when this gem of a restaurant lies just around the corner? Ask the staff and they will describe their kitchen as 'confusion rather than fusion', and it's true the menu is the very definition of eclecticism, though the end result is generally skilfully prepared, fascinating fare. Service is friendly and efficient (a rare combination in Copenhagen), and in summer

FREDSFONDENS HUS

Cap Horn – a *smørrebrød* and herring haven.

they close the first-floor dining room and open the delightful cobbled courtyard to the rear. Check out the plastic lobsters which smother the front of the building – sounds tacky, but like the food here, somehow they pull it off. Worth booking at weekends, especially if you want to sit outside. Note: there's a 3.5% charge for paying by credit card.

Danish

Cap Horn

Nyhavn 21 (33 12 85 04/www.caphorn.dk). **Open** 9am-1am daily. *Food served* 11.30am-11pm daily. **Main courses** 150kr. **Set menu** 255kr. **Credit** MC, V. **Map** p312 M16.

When Danes think of Nyhavn they usually think of herring and *smørrebrød*, and few restaurants along the canal do it better than Cap Horn. In the evenings the menu becomes rather more adventurous, with a Mediterranean influence. This is the most commonly recommended venue on the quayside, so it is popular with tourists, but Danes come here too, which is always a good sign. There's outdoor seating during the summer.

Restaurant Wiinblad

Hotel d'Angleterre, Kongens Nytorv 34 (33 37 06 45/www.remmen.dk). **Open** 11.30am-10pm Mon-Thur, Sun; 11.30am-11pm Fri, Sat. **Main courses** 169kr-220kr. **Credit** AmEx, DC, MC, V. **Map** p311 M15.

The Hotel d'Angleterre's restaurant is not quite as expensive as you might expect, given its excellent location overlooking Kongens Nytorv and a virtually captive, not to mention loaded, audience (platinum-carded American businessmen and their freeze-dried wives, corpulent German tourists, boisterous conference guests, and the like). Though Wiinblad's antediluvian clientele can sometimes make it seem like a scene from the movie *Coccoon*, they do make for highly entertaining eavesdropping. The food, meanwhile, is a revelation – excellent Modern Scandinavian cuisine presented with great flair, and created from luxurious and fresh ingredients like Norwegian lobster, Russian caviar and guinea fowl. Thankfully, the whimsical work of the Danish artist, Bjørn Wiinblad, after whom the restaurant is named, is unobtrusive.

Fish

Skipperkroen

Nyhavn 27 (33 11 99 06/www.skipperkroen-nyhavn.dk). **Open** noon-11pm daily. **Main courses** 150kr. **Set menus** 168kr-238kr. **Credit** AmEx, DC, MC, V. **Map** p312 M16.

Skipperkroen (meaning Sailor's Inn) is one of the nicer seafood restaurants on Nyhavn serving traditional herring dishes for lunch and production line French staples in the evening. Good value by Nyhavn standards, but not the kind of place to linger in the memory.

French

Egoisten

Hovedvagtsgade 2 (33 12 79 71/www.egoisten.dk).
Open *Jan-Sept* noon-3pm, 6-11pm Mon-Fri; closed
Sat, Sun. *Oct-Dec* noon-3pm, 6-11pm Mon-Sat; closed
Sun. **Main courses** 198kr-228kr. **Credit** AmEx, DC,
MC, V. **Map** p311 M15.
The exquisite cooking at this French restaurant is,
regrettably, largely eclipsed by dire interior decor
(very '70s, but not fashionably so), and execrable
muzak. However, Egoisten knows its market –
essentially business account suits from Hotel
d'Angleterre opposite – and perhaps there are those
who will brave the ambience for the imaginatively
sourced ingredients and peerless game on offer here.

Els

Store Strandstræde 3 (33 14 13 41).
Open noon-3pm, 5.30-10pm Mon-Sat; 5.30-10pm Sun.
Main courses 185kr-240kr. **Set menu** 388kr.
Credit AmEx, DC, MC, V. **Map** p312 M16.
There is no doubting the excellence of the cooking
at this posh (and a tad stuffy) restaurant just off
Nyhavn and across Kongens Nytorv from Hotel
d'Angleterre. The food at Els is steeped in the classical French tradition, and its rich, original mid 19th-
century interior underscores the mood, which is
more 'well-heeled tourist on a spree' than 'regular
local in for a treat'.

Kommandanten

Ny Adelgade 7 (33 12 09 90/
www.kommandanten.com). **Open** noon-2pm,
5.30-10pm Mon-Fri; 5.30-10pm Sat; closed Sun.
Main courses from 250kr. **Credit** AmEx, DC, MC,
V. **Map** p311 M15.
One of Copenhagen's top five restaurants, double
Michelin-starred Kommandanten is, sadly, usually
packed to the rafters with stern, fat men with equally fat cigars and even fatter expense accounts.
That's a great shame because, though the prices
may induce angina, the service is jolly and not at all
snooty; the interior is blissful (with sky blue wood
panelling and glorious steel frame thrones, courtesy
of neighbouring flower artist Tage Andersen); and
the predominantly French food, well, let's just say
that once eaten it's never forgotten. The menu
changes fortnightly, but you can be sure that dense,
sticky reductions lapping wild, flavoursome vegetables and light, tender meats sourced from
Denmark and France, will feature strongly.

Slotsholmen

Contemporary

Søren K

Søren Kierkegaard Plads 1 (33 47 49 50/
www.soerenk.dk). **Open** 11am-10.30pm Mon-Sat;
closed Sun. **Main courses** 200kr. **Set menus**
315kr-395kr. **Credit** DC, MC, V. **Map** p311 P15.

For a brief period when the 'Black Diamond' extension to the Royal Library (*see p86*) opened in 1999,
this small, minimalist Scandinavian restaurant on
its ground floor was the hottest ticket in
Copenhagen. Although it is still a popular lunch
venue with visitors to the library and exhibitions,
and with concert-goers in the evening, there are
more atmospheric destinations for a night out in the
city than this slightly frosty eaterie. The food is wonderful, however, and the views across the water to
Christianshavn are pleasant (though you always
have the sense that the opposing view is better).
Watch out for the sea breeze (the wind, you understand, not the cocktail) if you choose to sit outside.

Frederiksstaden

Contemporary

Schultz

Store Kongensgade 15 (33 16 12 13).
Open 6-10pm Mon-Thur; 6-11pm Fri, Sat; closed Sun.
Main courses 225kr; tapas 75kr-95kr. **Credit** DC,
MC, V. **Map** p308 L16.
This vogueish restaurant is dominated by celebrity
chef Allan Schultz (formerly of Konrad; *see p130*),
who, by turns, works front of house and slaves in
the kitchen to produce inventive, rich and costly
modern Italian/French/Danish/Californian food of
exceptional quality. Formerly known as Kirk (one
of the city's swankiest eateries during the '90s; *see
p136* **All the best ingredients**. The eponymous
and masterful Kirk now works at formel B, *see p143*,
by the way), this small, artificially lit restaurant is
located in a kind of jazzy concrete corridor, and
attracts a wealthy, international melange of diners.
Choose from up to five courses selected from three
memorable menus, 'Petit' (which might include
roasted sweetbreads with lime-parsley glace, fried
courgettes and pimento sauce), 'Fish' (aubergine
ravioli with cockles, leek, ginger and beurre blanc,
for example) or 'Grand' (stuff like marinated ten-
derloin of ox, salsa with grilled corn and chipolta on
naan bread with spicy oxtail consommé with dim
sum and shiitake), but whichever you select you'd
better be prepared for a blow-out and a bill (wines
start at around 350kr a bottle) of epic proportions.

Danish

Olsen

Store Kongensgade 66 (33 93 91 95/www.living.dk).
Open noon-1am Mon-Sat; closed Sun.
Main courses 95kr-185kr. **Set menu** 275kr.
Credit AmEx, DC, MC, V. **Map** p308 L16.
When it opened in 1995, Olsen was one of
Copenhagen's hippest and priciest gourmet restau-
rants. It's still fairly cool, but these days, with the
culinary spotlight elsewhere, it has transformed into
a reasonably priced, stylish cellar restaurant serv-
ing simpler, but still superb, modern Danish food.

According to manager Michel Reimann, the owners' aim was to revamp the image of traditional Danish cooking. The chef's lunch plate of herring, smoked salmon, duck breast, and minute steak on a bed of diced, fried swede and bacon pieces, is a good example of an updated classic (and good value at 125kr).

Restaurant Amadeus
Store Kongensgade 62 (33 32 35 11).
Open 11am-11.30pm daily. **Main courses** 68kr-189kr. **Set menu** 199kr. **Credit** AmEx, DC, MC, V. **Map** p308 L16.
This upmarket bakery/café/restaurant, a few steps from Ida Davidsen's (*see below*), is run by chef Allan Otto, the self-proclaimed 'Master of Danish Food', who has made it his mission to prove that the best Danish cooking can match anything the French have to offer. Though he fails to triumph in what was always going to be a rather David and Goliath confrontation, the food in this intimate cellar (great for eavesdropping) is of a consistently high standard, and his *smørrebrød*, though not as varied as Ida's, are excellent. Lunch tends to be better value than dinner.

Restaurant Ida Davidsen
Store Kongensgade 70 (33 91 36 55). **Open** 10am-4pm Mon-Fri; closed Sat, Sun. **Main courses** *smørrebrød* 45kr-150kr. **Credit** AmEx, DC, MC, V. **Map** p308 L16.
Ida Davidson is generally regarded as the queen of *smørrebrød* and a visit to her poky, unostentatious cellar restaurant is the perfect introduction to the art of the open sandwich. Ida, who works behind the counter most days and is the fifth generation of her family to run this 100-year-old lunch restaurant, is the Carl Fabergé of the *smørrebrød* world, concocting ornate sandwiches that could rank as works of art in any gourmand's book. She piles high her home-made rye bread with a multiplicity of well-matched toppings, including smoked salmon, caviar, herring, tomato, dill, akvavit, beef tartare, raw egg yolk and just about any other ingredient that will fit. From the 250 or so sandwiches on offer, the Victor Borge, featuring fresh salmon, lumpfish roe, shrimps, crayfish and dill mayonnaise is always popular with a clientele that includes everyone from royalty (from their gaff round the corner in Amalienborg) to local office workers.

French

Le Sommelier
Bredgade 63-5 (33 11 45 15/www.lesommelier.dk). **Open** noon-3pm, 6-10pm Mon-Fri; 5.30-10pm Sat, Sun. **Main courses** from 145kr. **Credit** DC, MC V. **Map** p308 L16.
Bredgade's top eatery is also one of Copenhagen's finest restaurants, offering a limited but superb menu of French-inspired dishes fortified with a welcome Danish robustness. This relaxed but stylish restaurant/brasserie (which opened in 1997) has won several awards for its wine list and has one of the finest

cellars in Copenhagen, stocked with over 800 bottles (more than 50 reds are sold by the glass). Consequently, despite being located in a fairly quiet part of town, Le Sommelier is constantly busy and booking is essential at weekends and in the evenings. At lunchtime it is chock full of expense account suits and visitors to the nearby Kunstindustrimuseet; in the evenings it draws a more mixed crowd.

Mexican

Chico's Cantina
Borgergade 2 (33 11 41 08/www.aok.dk). **Open** noon-midnight Mon-Sat; 5pm-midnight Sun. **Main courses** 100kr. **Credit** DC, MC, V. **Map** p307 L15.
This is probably Copenhagen's most popular Mexican restaurant, and it's always full at weekends. That's not entirely a reflection on the food, which, though it comes in plentiful portions and is better than the average Copenhagen Mexican fare, is far from outstanding. What does draw the crowd is Chico's bubbling atmosphere and extraordinary decor. Groups of six or more have the option (if there is a table free) of dining in their own little beach alcove, amid plastic parrots and dense foliage, around a table with its own serve-yourself beer pump. Those with dicky tickers might like to know that, periodically through the evening, Chico's lets rip with a simulated thunder storm. The service is usually exemplary. Great for kids.

Russian

Restaurant KGB & Vodka Bar
Dronningens Tværgade 22 (33 36 07 70/www.k-g-b.dk). **Open** 5.30pm-midnight Mon-Thur; 5.30pm-1am Fri, Sat; closed Sun. **Main courses** 170kr-190kr. **Credit** DC, MC, V. **Map** p307 L15.
Despite the portraits of old Soviet leaders that line the walls, this swanky vodka bar and restaurant is definitely more new Russian than old Kremlin. Diners who experienced pre-Gorbachev Russian cuisine will probably be grateful for this, although others may be disappointed by the token blinis and borscht on a menu that otherwise could be from any of a dozen restaurants in town. Nevertheless, the staff make an effort, dressing in military clothes; they serve caviar (though admittedly it's Iranian); and the bar boasts 60 different blends of vodka, the recipes supposedly gleaned from a book left to the owners by an elderly Russian lady who once visited. Stylish in a chilly way.

Vegetarian

Cascabel Madhus
Store Kongensgade 80-82 (33 93 77 97/www.cascabel.dk). **Open** 11am-9pm Mon-Fri; closed Sat, Sun. **Main courses** 90kr-125kr. **Credit** MC, V. **Map** p308 L16.

Top takeaways

If you need to fill yourself up on the hoof, there's no shortage of fast food joints in town, as well as the ubiquitous Danish hot dog (*pølser*) sellers. But there are far superior offerings available for those who just want a quick snack.

The **längos takeaway** on the east side of Nørreport Station (10.30am-7pm Mon-Fri) serves delicious Hungarian längos, fried (in cholestrol-free oil, incidentally) potato-based bread, with sweet and savoury toppings, for about 30kr a piece.

If you fancy soaking up the atmosphere down on Nyhavn but aren't in the mood to pay 180kr for a 20kr piece of smoked salmon and a heap of lettuce, just around the corner in Toldbodgade is **Jasmin**, an above average Thai takeaway serving basic curry and rice dishes for 40kr a time. There are couple of tables inside, but if the weather is fine it's far better to take your polystyrene box and sit on the quayside.

Should you need to rest your feet, but want a major fill up for minimal cost, you could do worse than drop by the Turkish/Mediterranean restaurant **Broadway** (Linnésgade 14, overlooking Israels Plads, just north of Nørreport Station). Despite its less than pleasant appearance, the all-you-can-eat buffet is the cheapest in town (39kr).

It may not look much from the outside, or indeed inside for that matter, but despite its anti-*hyggelige* decor, Cascabel is highly recommended for its fresh, light, delicious vegetarian food. Above all, it's very cheap. You can fill up on healthy pastas, salads and muffins for under 90kr – the sun-dried tomato pasta salad with aubergine, olives, jalapeño peppers and sunflower seeds (50kr) is a meal in itself. Understandably, Cascabel draws a loyal, local Frederiksstaden crowd of Danes and expats.

Rosenborg & around

Oriental

Sticks 'n' Sushi
Nansensgade 47 & 59 (33 16 14 07/www.sushi.dk).
Open 6pm-midnight daily; *takeaway* noon-10pm daily. **Main courses** 200kr. **Credit** MC, V.
Map p306 L11.
If you can forgive the heinous abbreviation in the name, you will find this to be one of the city's best, and certainly most stylish, sushi restaurants (it was also the first). Divided into a posh, sit-down place and a fast food/takeaway (at Nos.59 and 47 respectively), Sticks 'n' Sushi's menu varies, depending on the fish of the day, but the quality remains consistantly high (as do the prices).
Branch: Øster Farimagsgade 16B (35 38 34 63).

Christianshavn

Contemporary

Schiøtt's
Overgaden Neden Vandet 17 (32 54 54 08).
Open noon-3pm, 5.30-10pm Mon-Fri; 5.30-10pm Sat; 5-9pm Sun. **Main courses** 180kr. **Set menus** 265kr-395kr. **Credit** AmEx, DC, MC, V. **Map** p312 P16.

If ever a restaurant tried a little too hard, Schiøtt's is it. After all, being confronted with a choice of four different kinds of water before you've even sat down is a little overbearing and, although it's well meant, the over-attentive service does not compensate for an eerie lack of atmosphere. The food, however, is decent, Modern European stuff – rather plain but fresh and skilfully cooked and presented. The decision to paint this large cellar space all-white hasn't done it any favours in terms of ambience, and a sedate, middle-aged clientele only compound the problem.

Global

Spiseloppen
2nd floor of Loppen building, Bådsmandsstræde 43, Christiania (32 57 95 58/www.spiseloppen.com).
Open 5-10pm Tue-Sun; closed Mon.
Main courses 110kr-170kr. **Credit** MC, V.
Map p312 P18.
What do you get when you cross an Englishman, an Irishman, a Scotsman, a Dane, a Lebanese and an Italian? Spiseloppen's constantly changing rota of international kitchen staff create a different menu every night, but for once this isn't a case of 'too many cooks spoil the broth' – the myriad influences at work here rarely fail to conjure something really special (the vegetarian dishes are particularly impressive). The entrance to Spiseloppen, through an anonymous-looking door and up some shabby stairs in one of the Free State of Christiania's warehouses, promises little, but once you enter its low-ceilinged, candlelit dining hall its true worth becomes clear: this is a very special restaurant. Diners tend to be young and arty, though Spiseloppen is just as much a destination for anyone who loves good food as for those seeking an alternative nirvana (assuming the occasional waft of an exotic cheroot doesn't offend).

Indian

Spicey Kitchen
Torvegade 56 (32 95 28 29). **Open** noon-11pm Mon-Sat; noon-10pm Sun. **Main courses** 40kr-60kr. **No credit cards. Map** p312 P16.
The number of customers usually found waiting for a table inside this frantic and cramped one-room curry house is a testament to the excellent value offered by its menu. The choice of chicken, lamb or fish curries is fairly limited (the chicken and spinach curry is highly recommended), but that hasn't stopped Spicey Kitchen, a short walk from Christiania, building a reputation as one of Copenhagen's best cheap and fast eats. Expect to battle with regulars for a seat.

Italian

Era Ora
Overgaden Neden Vandet 33B (32 54 06 93). **Open** 6pm-midnight Mon-Sat; closed Sun. *Food served* 6-10pm Mon-Sat; closed Sun. **Set menus** 495kr-750kr. **Credit** AmEx, DC, MC, V. **Map** p312 P16.
The starting point for Copenhagen's grandest Italian restaurant is the food of Umbria, but most Umbrians will recognise little in the ten elaborate, but rather one-note appetisers (the note being balsamic vinegar), two pasta dishes, one main course and dessert that make up the fixed menu, the only option on offer here. They'll be even more confused by the exhorbitant cost of it all, and the surreptitious methods used to bump up the bill. Don't be surprised, for example, to discover that the extra glass of what you thought was simply house wine has cost you 200kr. If you come prepared to blow 1,800kr or so for two, however, the chances are you will leave satisfied by Era Ora's rather secretive ambience (it lies hidden behind a dull, anonymous frontage on the unfashionable perimeter of Christianshavn), and the obvious dedication of the kitchen, apparent in the presentation of unusual dishes such as thinly sliced marinated roast beef in parsley, citrus zest, garlic and herbs, the squash with sun-dried tomato pesto, or veal on a bed of puréed chickpeas.

Vegetarian

Morgenstedet
Bådmandstræde 43, Christiania (no phone). **Open** noon-9pm daily (sometimes closed Thur). **Main courses** 30kr. **No credit cards. Map** p312 P18.
You might have guessed that one of Copenhagen's best vegetarian restaurants (and indeed one of its best bargain eateries) lies in the heart of hippy heaven. This simple but charming one-room diner serves wonderful fresh salads, breads and various chickpea and lentil concoctions – all made from organic produce in its open kitchen. Two huge cauldrons (usually full of delicious-smelling vegetable hot pots or spicy stews) simmer throughout the day on antique stoves. Salads start from as little as 12kr. Addresses are enigmatic in Christiania, so to find Morgenstedet walk down Pusher Street, turn left past Manefiskeren (the commune's wonderful coffee house), and walk for about 100 metres. You may care to know that Morgenstedet is an alcohol- and smoke-free zone.

Vesterbro & Frederiksberg

Contemporary

formel B
Vesterbrogade 182, Frederiksberg (33 25 10 66/ www.formel-b.dk). Bus 6. **Open** 6pm-midnight Mon-Sat; closed Sun. **Set menu** 495kr; wine menu 295kr-375kr. **Credit** AmEx, DC, MC, V. **Map** p110 Q5.
Tucked away in leafy, bourgeois Frederiksberg is this bold, breathtaking jewel of a restaurant serving the best Modern Scandinavian-with-a-French-accent food in town. That's a juggling act you'll find attempted less successfully elsewhere with a frequency that will eventually drive you to the nearest Burger King, but the kitchen at formel B couldn't be boring even if it tried. There is no menu, instead diners place themselves in the hands of celebrity chef Nikolai Kirk (*see p136* **All the best ingredients**), who, over the course of the evening, beguiles you with seven courses, each a veritable symphony of flavours. These might include lobster soup with julienne of raw leek and roasted pumpkin seeds; or cod roasted with its skin and garnished with lentils and reduced balsamico, served with a small piece of basil oil toast and seared foie gras. Specially selected wines accompany the menu which, almost unbelievably, changes nightly. It is all delivered to your table by staff who seem to genuinely relish talking about the food and pampering guests. During the summer you can dine outside under parasol heaters, but when the temperature drops the stylish polished sandstone interior, with its open kitchen framed by a stunning black granite bar, is equally inviting. Ambitious, extravagant, but never pompous, you won't find a better restaurant than this anywhere in Copenhagen.

Oriental

Ban-Gaw
Istedgade 27, Vesterbro (33 22 84 38/33 22 85 33). Bus 16. **Open** noon-11pm daily. **Main courses** 85kr-95kr. **Credit** MC, V. **Map** p310 Q10.
In the heart of grubby Istedgade is this gem of a Thai restaurant which, though somewhat cramped and shabby inside, has compelling views of the streetlife outside. More importantly, Ban-Gaw's authentic, occasionally sensational food and extensive menu rank this as the city's most rewarding Thai restaurant.

Nørrebro

French/Californian

De Gaulle
Kronborggade 3, Nørrebro (35 85 58 66/
www.de-gaulle.dk). Bus 18. **Open** *Jan-June, Aug-Dec*
6pm-1am Mon-Sat; closed Sun. *July* varies, phone for
details. **Main courses** 170kr. **Set menus** 300kr-
750kr. **Credit** AmEx, DC, MC, V. **Map** p119 H6.
This intimate Californian/French haute cuisine
restaurant is cheaper than Godt (*see p134*) and
benefits from warmer service and a generally more
relaxed vibe. The food, though not as complex or
accomplished as Gothersgade's finest, still comes
close to matching its Michelin-starred rival in terms
of the quality of its ingredients and presentational
flair. There are even some realistically priced wines
on the menu. If you're in the area (Assistens
Kirkegård is opposite), this will prove a entirely
pleasant conclusion to the evening .

Global

Shark House Deli
Blågårdsgade 3, Nørrebro (35 35 51 35).
Bus 5, 7E, 16, 350S. **Open** 11am-9pm daily.
Main courses 45kr-80kr. **No credit cards.**
Map p119/p306 K9.
Jesper Dillon's superb little cellar deli and sandwich
bar is just the ticket for a quick lunch served at its
mahogany bar or, during the summer, at tables outside. For lunch try the spicy couscous with a marinated chicken kebab for just 45kr, or one of its famed
sandwiches with French, Danish or Dutch cheeses,
sausage and hams wrapped in Italian bread. In the
evening they barbecue outside. Jesper and chef
Marco Sganzerla are enthusiastic foodies, always
keen to chat about their latest obsession. The deli
also sells a small selection of wines.

Østerbro

French

Le Saint-Jacques
Sankt Jakobs Plads 1, Østerbro (35 42 77 07/
www.aok.dk). Bus 4, 16. **Open** noon-3pm; 6-10pm
daily. **Main courses** 95kr-195kr. **Credit** DC, MC, V.
Map p121 D13.
This pricey but inviting French restaurant, run by
accomplished chef Daniel Letz, is just across
the street from the national stadium Parken in a
quiet square off the busy shopping street of
Østerbrogade. Impeccable service, crisp white linen
tablecloths and evocative candlelight that flickers
enigmatically across the religious icons on the
walls ensure that this is a place that the locals return
to for special treats or well-earned blow-outs.
Home-smoked salmon is Le Saint-Jacques' speciality, and the brunch costs 89kr.

Theodors
Østerbrogade 106, Østerbro (35 26 66 66/
www.theodors.dk). Bus 4,16. **Open** *Nov-Apr*
11am-midnight Mon-Wed; 11am-2am Thur;
11am-4am Fri, Sat; noon-7pm Sun. *May-Sept*
11am-midnight Mon-Wed; 11am-2am Thur;
11am-4am Fri, Sat; noon-midnight Sun.
Set menus 238kr-428kr. **Credit** AmEx, DC, MC, V.
Map p121 D13.
Immediately opposite Le Saint-Jacques on Sankt
Jacobs Plads (*see above*) is Theodors, a pleasant
café/restaurant that makes for a slightly more informal alternative to its elegant French rival. At
lunchtimes you can choose from a menu of typical
bistro food featuring moules, soups and salads (68-
88kr), while in the evening you can dine beneath art
deco lamps and sample an enjoyably eclectic menu
of fish and meat courses. The staff provide excellent
service to boot.

Greek

Den Græske Taverna
Rosenvængets Allé, Østerbro (35 26 74 43/
www.dengraesketaverna.aok.dk). Bus 1, 6, 14.
Open 1pm-midnight daily. **Main courses** 93kr-
129kr. **Set menu** 139kr. **Credit** DC, MC.
Map p121 E14.
Greek food is one of Copenhagen's hidden jewels,
and Den Græske is a particularly charming and
cosy taverna. It is always packed, so it is essential
to book ahead, but you won't regret it. Delicious
lamb, beef and fish dishes, and holiday favourites
like souvlaki, moussaka and tzatziki, all wonderfully prepared, fresh and authentic, easily earn this
small restaurant just along the street from the hip
Circus (*see p156*) the title of best Greek restaurant
in Copenhagen. If you fancy trying their highly
recommended game dishes, you'll need to let them
know when you make your reservation.

Further afield

French/Danish

Brede Spisehuset
IC Modewegs Vej, Lyngby (45 85 54 57).
Open 11.30am-9.30pm Tue-Sun; closed Mon.
Main courses 142kr-168kr.
Credit MC, V.
If you are wondering whether to pay a visit to
Denmark's largest open-air museum, the excellent
Frilandsmuseet (*see p123*), then Brede Spisehuset,
just down the road, may tip the balance. Housed in
a glorious 19th-century building that was once the
canteen for the old Brede Værk textile mill next door
(now also run by Nationalmuseet), Spisehuset's
(meaning 'eating house') beautiful period interior is
graced by decorative tiles and an opal glass ceiling.
Its Franco-Danish food is above average, too. The
restaurant is particularly popular with families for
Sunday lunch.

Bars & Cafés

With alcohol flowing and a steady supply of food served day and night, the cafés of Copenhagen often blur the boundary between bar and restaurant.

Copenhagen is the Paris of the north, or so the cliché goes, and nowhere is this more apparent than in the city's glorious cafés. A good Copenhagen café will always be a match for any of the city's restaurants both in terms of the quality of food they serve and the atmosphere, plus of course they are generally cheaper. And there are hundreds to choose from, located all over the city. Virtually all of the city's cafés serve alcohol and food (both throughout the day), from sandwiches and salads to complex fusion dishes and traditional Danish staples, and in the last five years or so most have jumped on the brunch bandwagon. Brunch is big in Copenhagen, and the best cafés vie to see who can offer the most elaborate and exotic mid-morning platter (usually for around 80kr). The super-club **Base Camp** (*see pages 150 and 213*) deserves a special mention for its Sunday buffet brunch, which though not necessarily the best food-wise, has a unique army mess atmosphere.

Copenhagen's café scene is dominated in the centre of town by **Café Europa** and **Café Norden** (for both, *see page 146*), facing each other on Amagertorv, but they can't hold a candle to the city's best cafés which are slightly further out of the centre – places like **Café Klimt** (*see page 150*), **Bankeråt** (*see page 149*), **Amokka** (*see page 154*), **Café Wilder** (*see page 151*) or **Bastionen og Løven** (*see page 150*) – whose captivating, quirky ambience and superb, reasonably priced food guarantees crowds of satisfied punters most days. You can eat well in a café here for under 100kr.

The line between café, bar, restaurant and, occasionally, club is frequently blurred in Copenhagen; in some cases the same venue can fulfil all four roles within a day. As all (or very nearly all) cafés sell alcohol, they often have a bar-like atmosphere (come to that, many actually have bars, too), and numerous cafés change their menus in the evening to serve slightly more expensive restaurant food. You'll often find a DJ in the cooler places at weekends.

Though it's not nearly as costly as in the other Scandinavian countries, alcohol is expensive everywhere in Denmark, spirits especially so (though, curiously, wine is cheaper in Danish

Isn't that Michael Laudrup? Go celebrity spotting at **Café Victor**. *See p147.*

supermarkets than in British ones). As a rule, the further the café or bar is from the centre of town, the cheaper the booze becomes. You can usually expect to pay 20-30kr for a glass of wine or a small beer; this rises to 30-40kr on Nyhavn and in places like Norden and Europa.

Tivoli & around

For eating and drinking options within Tivoli itself, *see page 61*.

Bjørgs

Vester Voldgade 19 (33 14 53 20). **Open** 11am-midnight Mon-Wed, Sun; 11am-1am Thur; 11am-2am Fri, Sat. **Main courses** 90kr. **Credit** AmEx, MC, V. **Map** p310 O12.

This L-shaped café/bar does a passable impression of the famous Edward Hopper painting of a New York bar, with its large windows, red sofas and mirrored walls. Although it's from the same stable as Sommerkso (*see below*) and Dan Turèll (*see p147*), Bjørgs is far less showy and pretentious and serves as both a local bar and a trendy Saturday night stop-off. Understated and cool.

Hotel Plaza Library Bar

Hotel Plaza, Bernstorffsgade 4 (33 14 15 19/ www.living.dk). **Open** 3.30pm-1am Mon-Sat; 3.30pm-midnight Sun. **Credit** AmEx, DC, MC,V. **Map** p310 P11.

Though elsewhere some of the more salubrious gentlemen's clubs of London's St James's will be underwhelmed by the scale of this quiet and faux-exclusive bar within the Plaza Hotel (though this being Denmark, it is open to all), most visitors swoon at its characterful wood panelling, crystal chandeliers, book-lined walls and Chesterfield-style sofas. This was voted one of the finest gentlemen's bars in the world by *Forbes Magazine*, and, inverted snobbery aside, it is a wonderful place to escape the plebs and blow money on a cognac or two. If you've any money left over you may care to nibble at sybaritic snacks like oysters and parma ham. Cocktails start at 60kr.

Strøget & around

Akvavit

Gammel Strand 44 (33 32 88 44/www.akvavit-cafe.dk). **Open** 10am-midnight Mon-Fri; 10am-10pm Sat, Sun. **Main courses** 135kr. **Credit** AmEx, DC, MC, V. **Map** p311 N14.

Akvavit's unique selling point is that each course comes with a recommended akvavit (or schnapps), from around 18kr a shot, and chosen to complement your choice of *smørrebrød*, sandwich or fish dish. Also in its favour is a fine location on Gammel Strand, with outside tables during summer overlooking the canal and Christiansborg, plus exceptionally charming waitresses. However, prices are virtually in orbit, and we have yet to find meaner portions than those served here.

Atlas Bar

Larsbjørnsstræde 18 (33 15 03 52). **Open** 11am-10pm Mon-Thur; noon-10pm Fri, Sat; closed Sun. **Main courses** 80kr-100kr. **Credit** DC, MC, V. **Map** p310 N12.

Appropriately enough, given its international theme, Atlas Bar's food ranges in influence from Asia (they do a decent Manila Chicken) to Mexico (humungous burritos), encompassing fishy Danish staples along the way. To underscore the point, the table tops are decorated with a variety of maps. Well located in the heart of bustling Pisserenden, Atlas is one of the city's most pleasant and popular cellar venues. It's great for a mid-shop lunch, and popular with vegetarians.

Café Europa

Amagertorv 1 (33 14 28 89). **Open** *Apr-Sept* 9am-midnight Mon-Thur; 9am-1am Fri, Sat; 10am-midnight Sun. *Oct-Mar* 9am-midnight Mon-Thur; 9am-1am Fri, Sat; 10am-7pm Sun. **Main courses** 55kr-119kr. **No credit cards. Map** p311 N14.

Opposite Café Norden on Amagertorv is this marginally more hip, smaller café, which is very popular as a meeting place for younger Copenhageners. As with its glitzy rival across the square, Europa's prices can be high and the service frosty, but the food isn't bad and it's a nice place to stop off for a drink during an afternoon's shopping. Sandwiches are reasonable value at around 49kr. There is seating outside on the square during the summer.

Café Lazlo

Læderstræde 28 (33 33 88 08). **Open** 11am-1am Mon-Sat; noon-1am Sun. **Main courses** 42kr-90kr. **Credit** AmEx, DC, MC, V. **Map** p311 N14.

Well-established and popular cellar café in beautiful Læderstræde (which runs parallel with Strøget on its south side). Lazlo offers excellent sandwiches and salads at lunchtime, and has outdoor seating in warm weather.

Café Norden

Østergade 61, Strøget (33 11 77 91). **Open** 9am-midnight Mon-Sat; 10am-midnight Sun. **Main courses** 68kr. **No credit cards. Map** p311 M15.

This grandest and largest of all Copenhagen's cafés (it seats 350 on sunny days) overlooks Amagertorv in the heart of Strøget, but despite its vast, two-storey, Parisian-style interior (with chandeliers and wood panelling), it's usually a challenge to find a table. Sadly, the service here is fairly grouchy, but the food is adequate (salads, sandwiches, steaks and so forth), though you will pay around 20 per cent more for everything by virtue of Norden's prime location.

Café Sommersko

Kronprinsensgade 6 (33 14 81 89/ www.sommersko.dk). **Open** 8am-midnight Mon-Wed; 8am-1am Thur; 8am-2am Fri; 9am-2am Sat; 10am-midnight Sun. **Main courses** 49kr-105kr. **Credit** DC, MC, V. **Map** p311 M14.

Eat, Drink, Shop

Sommersko has been resting on its reputation for several years now and we've heard plenty of complaints about the food and service. There was a time when this was a compulsory pit-stop on a Saturday night, but these days trendy Copenhageners scoff at the out-of-town parvenus who frequent the place at weekends. Still, Sommersko retains a certain charisma, and its wonderfully glamorous tacky decor (mirror mosaics, baby grand piano, red vinyl banquettes) is distinctive, which is more than you can say for most cafés in town. The menu is predictable (burgers, moules, salads) and the food is usually a disappointment when it finally arrives. Many of the staff, meanwhile, seem to believe part of their job description is to be as hostile to the customers as possible. But it's still fine for a beer or two.

Café Victor

Ny Østergade 8 (33 13 36 13/www.cafevictor.dk).
Open *Café* 8am-2am daily. *Restaurant* noon-3pm, 5.30-11pm Mon-Fri; noon-3pm, 5.30pm-midnight Sat, Sun. **Main courses** 195kr-245kr. **Credit** AmEx, DC MC, V.
Map p311 M15.
A Copenhagen institution, Café Victor is one of the city's prime see-and-be-seen venues for celebrities, football stars, politicians, journalists and the jet set. At lunchtime it is packed to the rafters with lunching ladies, weighed down with gold and wrapped in fur or Gucci. The food is classic French; sturdy, creamy and fine enough (the menu is a lengthy read), but hardly outstanding. However, you don't come here just for the food, but more to soak up the atmosphere, marvel at the mirrored, art deco interior and do battle with the supercilious staff. If you don't fancy a full meal, half a dozen oysters at the bar (110kr), washed down with a glass of champagne will give you a good taste of the Victor experience. Note: A 3.5% surcharge is added to credit card payments (except Visa).

Copenhagen Jazzhouse

Niels Hemmingsens Gade 10 (33 15 26 00/ 33 15 47 00/www.jazzhouse.dk). **Open** 6pm-5am Thur-Sat; closed Mon-Wed, Sun. **Credit** AmEx, DC, MC, V. **Map** p311 M13.
The old stalwart of the Copenhagen nightlife scene, this superb two-floor bar and live jazz venue has a large dance floor downstairs and is a dead cert most nights for an excellent atmosphere, interesting clientele and superb music (*see also page 217*). Blessedly free of jazz snobs.

Dan Turèll

Store Regnegade 3-5 (33 14 10 47/ www.danturell.dk). **Open** 9am-midnight Mon, Tue; 9am-1am Wed; 9am-2am Thur; 9am-4am Fri, Sat; 10am-midnight Sun. **Main courses** 80kr-100kr. **Credit** AmEx, DC, MC, V.
Map p311 M15.
One of Copenhagen's most celebrated cafés and a pioneer in its day, Dan Turèll lies in the heart of Copenhagen's throbbing nightlife area (Café

Sommersko, Zoo Bar, Konrad and Café Victor, among others, are nearby) and has been one of *the* places to visit on a Friday or Saturday night for as long as anyone can remember. Named after a famous (in Denmark, at least) Danish poet, writer and iconoclast (*see p297*), Dan Turèll is also known as DTs or, as one crowd we know has it, the Gonorrhoea Aquarium (on account of its pick-up potential, large plate glass windows, and mirrored walls). The food here is middling (salads and sandwiches during the day), and the drinks expensive, but that's the price you pay to mingle with the beautiful people.

Det Elektriske Hjørne

Store Regnegade 12 (33 13 91 92/www.deh.aok.dk).
Open 11.30am-2am Mon-Wed; 11.30am-4am Thur; 11am-5pm Fri, Sat; 3pm-1am Sun. *Food served* 11.30am-4pm Mon-Fri; 11am-4pm Sat; no food Sun. **Main courses** 40kr-70kr. **Credit** AmEx, DC, MC, V.
Map p311 M15.
This exceptionally stylish café, with a grand double aspect frontage dating from the 1890s, is well located, with dozens of the city's best bars and restaurants nearby. Wisely, the Hjørne doesn't attempt to outdo its neighbours on the food front (workmanlike sandwiches and salads, served only until 4pm), but instead trades on its chilled, hospitable vibe and welcome spaciousness. The basement houses table football, darts and pool.

Drop Inn

Kompagnistræde 34 (33 11 24 04).
Open 11am-5am Mon-Fri; 2pm-5am Sat, Sun.
Credit MC, V. **Map** p311 O13.
With live music every night (jazz, blues and folk; *see also p218*), and an open front with pavement seating in summer, Drop Inn is one of those places that never seems to rest. Hardly cool or trendy, Drop Inn tends instead to attract the more dedicated drinkers, so things can get a little lively towards the end of the evening. Food is available in the form of sandwiches (25kr-30kr), and it is worth noting that a beer before 7pm costs 17kr.

Fogtdals Fotocafé

Østergade 22, Strøget (33 16 28 30).
Open 11am-6pm Mon-Fri; 11am-5pm Sat; closed Sun. **Main course** *lunch* 42kr-72kr.
No credit cards. **Map** p311 M15.
With an excellent vantage point overlooking the upmarket end of Strøget, this relaxed and refined first floor café is very popular with the more mature shoppers. The sandwiches are excellent – fresh, amply proportioned and reasonably priced (around 72kr) – and there is a small range of cakes and pastries. A mini photographic gallery adjoins the eating area.

Galathea Kroen

Rådhusstræde 9 (33 11 66 27/www.galathea.dk).
Open 4am-2am Mon-Thur; 4pm-5am Fri, Sat; closed Sun. **Main courses** 80kr-120kr. **Credit** MC.
Map p311 O13.

Named after a celebrated poet, **Dan Turèll** is now a celebrated café. *See p147.*

The moment you enter this charismatic, eclectic mess of a bar, past the totem poles that guard the entrance, you instinctively know that Galathea Kroen is rather special. Maybe it's the groovy jazz playing on the turntable (this is a strictly vinyl-only joint); or the affable and intriguing clientele, from trendy teens to bohemian oldies; or perhaps it's the engagingly dishevelled decor – Galathea Kroen is named after a ship that was used as a base for exploration of Pacific sealife, and inside it is decorated with momentoes from its journeys, while zebra skins and Indonesian carvings loom over you in the intimate corners. It could be, of course, the superb curries, served with a huge tray of spices and sauces. You decide.

La Glace

Skoubogade 3 (33 14 46 46). **Open** *Sept-Apr* 8am-5.30pm Mon-Thur; 8am-6pm Fri; 9am-5pm Sat; 11am-5pm Sun. *May-Aug* 8am-5.30pm Mon-Thur; 8am-5pm Fri; 9am-5pm Sat; closed Sun. **No credit cards. Map** p311 N13.

Copenhagen's most vaunted and venerable bakery and pâtisserie was founded in 1870, and is famous for its delectable cream cakes (around 25kr a slice), which would tempt even the most fanatical calorie counter. The speciality is the Sports Kage (Sport Cake), an OTT cream, caramel and nougat mousse confection, but chocolate fans will be in heaven here, too. Skoubogade is just off the west end of Strøget, which makes it perfect for weary shoppers, but also means that you usually have to fight your way through the scrum of elderly groupies that gathers in La Glace's café most afternoons.

Krasnapolsky

Vestergade 10 (33 32 88 00/www.krasnapolsky.dk). **Open** 10am-2pm Mon-Wed; 10am-5am Thur-Sat; 2pm-midnight Sun. **Main courses** 30kr-79kr. **Credit** AmEx, DC, MC, V. **Map** p310 O12.

A star during the '80s, this bar/restaurant/club is looking decidedly tatty around the edges these days, and one can't help feel that it's living on past glories. However, weekend evenings still see it packed with Copenhagen's pre-clubbers, apparently unbowed by the extortionate cocktail prices and grim-faced staff.

The food is pretty basic fare; in fact you're unlikely to find anything more extravagant than pasta or chilli, and at lunchtimes it has all the atmosphere of a concrete barn. *See also p210.*

Kreutzberg Café & Bar

Kompagnistræde 14A (33 93 48 50). **Open** 9am-2am Mon-Sat; noon-8pm Sun. **Main courses** 42kr-68kr. **No credit cards. Map** p311 O13.

Located on one of the city centre's most charming streets, Kreutzberg is a relative newcomer to Copenhagen's eclectic café scene but hasn't lost any time in carving a cosy niche for itself as a friendly, buzzing basement venue serving classic café sandwiches and salads.

Mojo

Løngangstræde 21c (33 11 64 53/www.mojo.dk). **Open** 8pm-5am daily. **No credit cards. Map** p311 O13.

If you like your blues bars smoky, pokey and steamy, the venerable Mojo should do the trick. It's the kind of place that feels like it's underground, even though it is on the ground floor. An unashamedly plain candle-lit interior (exposed heating ducts, simple wooden tables, parquet floor) and an unpretentious clientele help make it a relaxed, informal venue in which to enjoy invariably excellent live music. *See also p218.*

Peder Oxe Vinbar

Gråbrødretorv 11 (33 11 00 77/www.pederoxe.dk). **Open** noon-1am daily. **Credit** DC, MC, V. **Map** p311 N13

Located in the vaulted cellars beneath the venerable Peder Oxe restaurant (*see p134*), this stylish wine bar near the centre of Strøget opened in 1978, since when it has become one of the city's more sociable and cosy cellar bars.

Studenterhuset

Købmagergade, Copenhagen University (35 32 38 60/www.studenterhuset.dk). **Open** *Sept-May* noon-6pm Mon; noon-midnight Tue; noon-2am Wed-Fri; closed Sat, Sun. *June-Aug* closed. **No credit cards. Map** p311 M13-14.

This well-subsidised student drinking den and live music venue is adjacent to the Rundetårn in the heart of town. Predictably, the decor is grotty-chic to match the clientele's dress sense, but prices are set for those on an SU (Statens Udannelsesstøtte – government grant) budget. The beer is cheap and there is usually something groovy happening of an evening – most notably jazz on Thursdays and rock on Fridays. It is also a participating venue in the city's annual jazz festival (see p219).

Thorvaldsen Gourmetbar & Café
Gammel Strand 34 (33 32 04 00/www.nouvelle.dk). **Open** 11.30am-10pm Mon-Thur, Sat, Sun; 11.30am-11pm Fri. **Main courses** 58kr-135kr. **Set menus** 145kr-195kr. **Credit** AmEx, DC, MC, V. **Map** p311 N14.
Advantageously located on historic Gammel Strand, Thorvaldsens is a sophisticated and stylish cellar bar and café whose tables spill out on to the cobbles beside the canal during summer. Any place calling itself a 'Gourmetbar' has much to live up to, and Thorvaldsens does struggle to offer consistency throughout its menu, though it excels at its more traditional Danish fare. Prices are favourable, too – at lunchtime, it's not difficult to eat well here for under 100kr.

Nyhavn & around

Café à Porta
Kongens Nytorv 17 (33 11 05 00/www.aporta.dk). **Open** 10am-midnight Mon-Thur; 10am-1am Fri, Sat; 10am-10pm Sun. *Food served* 11.30am-4.30pm, 5.30-10.30pm daily. **Main courses** 125kr-185kr. **Set menus** 250kr-280kr. **Credit** AmEx, DC, MC, V. **Map** p311 M15.
When the underground railway station on Kongens Nytorv is finally finished in 2003, Café à Porta should emerge from its billboard chrysalis to become one of the city's finest cafés. In fact, with its stunning, mirrored interior (recently restored at a cost of ten million kroner), exceptionally good service and reliably tasty French/Danish bistro cooking (in ample portions), it's almost there already. This is one of the city's oldest cafés, dating to 1792, when it was a popular haunt for the actors of the day. It was renovated to its current magnificent condition in 1999, when the original bar was rescued from a venue on Christianshavn. Today, it attracts the more mature tourists passing on their way to the theatre or the excellent shopping on nearby Strøget.

Etcetera
Hovedvagtsgade 8 (33 33 99 97). **Open** *Restaurant* 6-11pm Tue-Sat; closed Mon, Sun. *Bar* 6pm-midnight Tue-Thur; 6pm-4am Fri, Sat; closed Mon-Sun. **Set menus** 295kr-345kr. **Credit** AmEx, DC, MC, V. **Map** p311 M15.
This gorgeous, hyper-hip Moroccan-style lounge bar and restaurant is packed at weekends with money-to-burn fashion victims, models (occasionally of the

'super' variety), young blades-about-town and all the rest of Copenhagen's glamorous gadflies. You can either prop up the long bar with an extortionately priced cocktail in hand, or descend to the sunken lounge area, where you can recline on vast, squashy sofas around communal tables and be served inventive and luscious North African-inspired food. The five-course menu is recommended, if you can stomach the price. DJs play at weekends until 3am. Painfully cool but immense fun – a must.

Fisken
Nyhavn 27 (33 11 99 06/www.skipperkroen-nyhavn.dk). **Open** 9am-3am Mon-Thur; 9am-5am Fri, Sat; 9am-2am Sun. **Credit** AmEx, DC, MC, V. **Map** p312 M16.
One of Nyhavns most *hygge* (see p79) pubs is located in the cellar underneath Skipperkroen. The decor is heavy on maritime references (it's hard to tell how authentic any of it is) and there is live folky, guitar-based music every night.

Palæ Bar
Ny Adelgade 5 (33 12 54 71). **Open** 10am-1am Mon-Wed; 10am-2am Thur-Sat; 4pm-1am Sun. **No credit cards.** **Map** p311 M15.
This esteemed boho bar, just around the corner from Hotel d'Angleterre, tends to appeal to more mature drinkers who prefer its unrushed, understated mood and rich, old-fashioned boozer interior. Popular with writers and journalists, Palæ exudes a kind of old-world intellectualism (though that may just be the wine talking).

Rosenborg & around

Bankeråt
Ahlefeldtsgade 27-9 (33 93 69 88). **Open** 9.30am-midnight Mon-Fri; 10.30am-midnight Sat, Sun. **Main courses** 70kr. **No credit cards.** **Map** p306 L11.
Monster brunches, great tortillas and pasta dishes, plus an atmosphere that is defiantly unique among Copenhagen's cafés, set this grungy, boho cave apart from the rest of the café crowd. Brace yourself for a sobering encounter when you descend to the basement loos, as a ghoulish assortment of gothic taxidermy tableaux (a match even for the idiosyncratic characters usually found huddling in Bankeråt's cosy corners) awaits. Unusually for egalitarian Denmark, a hardcore collage awaits in the men's toilets, but there's no reciprocation in the women's.

Café Creme
Vendersgade 5 (33 93 29 00). **Open** 9am-10pm Mon-Fri; 10am-6pm Sat; closed Sun. **Main courses** 40kr. **No credit cards.** **Map** p306 L12.
An austere, raised ground floor café near to Israels Plads' excellent fruit and veg market, decorated with atrocious travellers' art and serving an uninspired range of lasagnes and omelettes. Popular with

Palæ Bar. See p149.

Danish actors, whose union is just around the corner, Café Creme is inoffensive, but you'd do far better to walk a little further to Café Klimt, Leopold's or Bankeråt. Some pavement tables.

Café Klimt

Frederiksborggade 29 (33 11 76 70/
www.cafeklimt.dk). **Open** *Café* 10am-midnight Mon-Wed, Sun; 10am-2am Thur-Sat. *Restaurant* 10am-10.30pm daily. **Main courses** 50kr-99kr.
Credit AmEx, DC, MC, V. **Map** p306 L12.
You are advised to book ahead if you want to sample the fabulous brunch (one of the best in the city), at this deservedly popular, arty café in Frederiksborggade (not to be confused with Frederiksberggade, which is part of pedestrianised Strøget). Teas, coffees, fresh juices and cognacs complement a café menu that is far superior to most, featuring a little bit of Mexican, Asian, Italian and even a dash of Cajun cooking. Klimt attracts a young-ish, local, fashionable crowd who tend to linger longer than usual amid the palm trees and homemade art.

Hacienda

Ørsteds Parken, near Farimagsgade 6 (33 33 85 33).
Open *May-Aug* 11am-7pm Mon-Fri; 10am-7pm Sat, Sun. *Sept-Apr* closed. **No credit cards**.
Map p310 M11.
This seasonal café, run by Kate Kamil of Kate's Joint (*see p153*), is located in a wooden hut in one of the city's prettiest parks (named after the Danish physicist HC Ørsted), beside the children's play area in the park's northern corner. Salads and sandwiches cost around 50kr. Look out for the frequent live jazz or DJs who play to the chilled out locals. Perfect for a cold beer on a hot day.

Leopold's

Nørre Farimagsgade 57 (33 11 33 63/
www.leopolds.dk). **Open** 10am-2pm Mon-Sat; 10am-midnight Sun. **Main courses** 85kr-160kr.
Credit DC, MC, V. **Map** p310 M11.
An elegant, sophisticated café/restaurant with large glass windows from which to watch the world go by. Nearby rivals tend to eclipse Leopold's, both in terms of atmosphere (Bankeråt) and the quality of its cuisine (Café Klimt), but it has found its own niche with a decent array of cocktails and an inviting spaciousness. The clientele is young, trendy and affluent.

Christianshavn

Base Camp

Halv Trolv, Building 148, Holmen (70 23 23 18/
www.basecamp.dk). Bus 8. **Open** 6pm-1am Mon-Thur; 11am-5am Fri, Sat; 11am-3pm Sun.
Main courses 150kr; *brunch* 80kr. **Credit** DC, MC, V. **Map** p313 N19.
Denmark's biggest nightclub (*see p213*) is also a great place to visit on a Sunday lunchtime when its chaotic family brunch is in full swing. Served from a long, open kitchen to the accompaniment of live jazz, Base Camp's brunch features all the usual cheeses, meats, fish and fruits, and at 80kr for all you can eat, it's a steal. Diners (up to 600 at a time) mingle sociably at long tables. A great place to mull over the Sunday papers or meet up with friends. Kids love it too (*see also p102*).

Bastionen og Løven

Christianshavn Voldgade 50 (32 95 09 40).
Open *Apr-Sept* 10am-midnight daily. *Oct-Mar* noon-midnight daily. **Main courses** 130kr-772kr.
Set menu 285kr. **Credit** DC, MC, V. **Map** p313 Q17.

This delightful, if hard to find, garden café is situated in an extension of Nationalmuseet's Lille Mølle (Little Windmill; *see p105*) on the ramparts of Christianshavn. It's well off the tourist trail and during the summer is usually packed with locals, but if you fancy trying one of the city's great culinary institutions – a traditional Copenhagen brunch (a simple but satisfying array of cheeses, herring, bread, fruit and cold meats; 95kr) – in idyllic surroundings, this is the place. Highly recommended, so booking is advised at weekends.

Café Luna

Sankt Annæ Gade 5 (32 54 20 00/www.cafeluna.dk).
Open 10am-11pm Mon-Thur; 10am-1am Fri; 10am-1am Sat; 10am-11pm Sun. **Main courses** 105kr-195kr. **Set menus** 225kr-250kr. **Credit** AmEx, DC, MC, V. **Map** p312 P17.
If you can't get a table at the usually more popular Café Wilder opposite (*see below*), Cafe Luna offers equally high quality cuisine, as well as cheap salads, pasta dishes and more traditional Danish café fare. An extensive wine list is an added bonus.

Café Wilder

Wildersgade 56 (32 54 71 83/www.cafewilder.dk).
Open 9am-2am daily. **Main courses** 70kr-135kr; *brunch* 85kr. **Credit** MC, V.
Map p312 P16.
Christianshavn's best café/bar is located a short walk from the chaos of Christiania, from which Wilder is an oasis of mellow sophistication. The food is fresh, cheap and simple (pasta, salads and sandwiches) and the service perfectly charming. This

small, L-shaped room is usually crowded to bursting point at weekends, arty locals at weekends, so arrive early to be sure of a seat.

Christianshavn Bådudlejning & Café

Overgaden Neden Vandet 29, (32 96 53 53).
Open *May-Sept* 11am-midnight daily.
Food served May-mid Aug. **Main courses** 100kr.
No credit cards. Map p312 P17.
Located on the canal itself, this outdoor café is a wonderful spot from which to watch the (water) world go by, as the canal tour boats pass this way. Bådudlejning means boat rental, incidentally; you can rent rowing boats here too. Decent sandwiches (from 45kr) and salads are also on offer.

Thorsen

Fabriksmestervej/Judichær Plads, Holmen (70 23 23 18/www.basecamp.dk). **Open** *June-Sept* 10am-1am daily. *Oct-May* closed. **Main courses** 100kr.
Credit AmEx, DC, MC, V. **Map** p309 L19.
If location is all, then Thorsen could probably get away with serving cardboard salads (actually they're not far off, but we'll come to that) and screwing its customers with the booze prices (which to its credit it doesn't), so sensational is its site beside the harbour, opposite Amalienborg Slot. Once you've reclined in Thorsen's deck chairs beneath the long-defunct harbour cranes, and watched the sun set behind the green and gold dome of Marmorkirken, all other cafés will seem unbearably conventional by comparison. The food is grilled fish or steak (both rather chewy), served on a bed of all-purpose salad which you order at the bar, before a chef summons you to collect it by shouting a number through a loud hailer. While you are waiting, you can swim in the dock, or take part in a game of water polo, or dance to the DJs who play on Fridays and Saturdays. Thorsen could well be one of the most charismatic venues in Europe, with the grooviest clientele to match, so it's a shame that the Danish climate restricts it to summer opening only, and, more worryingly, that the land is perilously close to the site of Copenhagen's proposed new opera house.

You lookin' at me? **Bankeråt.** *See p149.*

Vesterbro & Frederiksberg

Bang og Jensen

Istedgade 130, Vesterbro (33 25 53 18/www.aok.dk).
Bus 16. **Open** 8am-2am Mon-Fri; 10am-2am Sat; 10am-midnight Sun. **Main courses** 40kr-50kr.
No credit cards. Map p111 R9.
This intimate, kitschy Vesterbro café is popular with the area's recently arrived fashionable types and can usually be relied upon to serve up a bit of life most nights. Though the food is the usual Copenhagen café fare, it doesn't detract from Bang og Jensen's appeal as an alluring place to while away an evening (slumped, if you're lucky, in their great squashy sofas). The breakfast, served until 4pm daily, is good value with sausage, cheese, yoghurt, eggs and coffee all for 65kr.

Thorsen. *See p151.*

Café Sorte Hest

Vesterbrogade 135, Vesterbro (33 25 20 08). Bus 6.
Open 11am-midnight Mon-Thur; 11am-1am Fri;
10am-1am Sat; 10am-10pm Sun. **Main course** 55kr;
brunch 60kr. **Credit** AmEx, MC, V.
Map p111 Q6.
This really super little one-room café/bar at the quiet end of Vesterbrogade (near the Carlsberg Brewery) has an unbeatably good value brunch. For 60kr you get a plateful of cheeses, chorizo, pancakes, warm quiche and fresh fruit, and you couldn't hope for a nicer atmosphere in which to consume it, particularly on Sundays, and in the evenings, when the place is full of affable young locals. This is up there with the most enticing cafés in the city.

Café Viggo

*Vernedamsvej 15, Vesterbro (33 31 18 21/
www.cafe-viggo.dk). Bus 6.* **Open** 10.30am-midnight
Mon-Wed; 10.30am-1am Thur; 10.30am-2am Fri;
11am-1am Sat; 11am-6pm Sun. **Main courses** 80kr-
130kr. **Credit** MC, V. **Map** p111 P8.
This cheap, bustling, bohemian French café on the famous 'food street' (*see p180* **Food Street**) is a focus for the French community in Copenhagen. Sandwiches, omelettes and salads are served during the day, while the dinner menu includes heartier fare like rabbit stew and roast duck. The Moby Dick (smoked salmon, crème fraîche and dill on a large crêpe; 49kr) is recommended.

Delicatessen

*Vesterbrogade 120, Vesterbro (33 22 16 33/
www.delicatessen.dk). Bus 6.* **Open** 11am-
midnight Mon-Wed, Sun; 11am-3am Thur-Sat.
Main courses 35kr-145kr. **Credit** V.
Map p111 Q7.

An innovative and ambitious attempt to serve high quality fusion cooking as fast food, at reasonable prices. Located in newly hip Vesterbro, Delicatessen is the latest project from the folks behind the terrific TyvenKokkenHansKoneogHendesElsker (*see p130*) and its menu is equally as challenging, though not nearly as consistent, as its upper class sibling. Wok-fried horse with oyster cream, maki rolls with banana and basil, or Bloody Mary soup with sugar salted celery are just some of the convention-bashing dishes on offer. Sandwich fillings include duck marinated in truffle oil and the perplexing 'Lee Van Cleef (version original)', a macho beef affair. It's a promising venture, although the 'fast' element of the concept needs work. Those hoping for a quiet meal should note that there's a DJ spinning jazzy and ambient vinyl from 9pm, Thursdays to Saturdays (Club D nights), to warm up clubbers on their way to serious dancing at nearby Vega (*see p216*).

Obelix

Vesterbrogade 53, Vesterbro (33 31 34 14). Bus 6.
Open 8.30am-2am daily. **Main courses** 35kr-45kr.
No credit cards. Map p111 P9.
The cartoon-adorned café/bar Obelix dominates Vesterbrotorv, half way up Vesterbrogade, and is an agreeable place to stop off while exploring the area, either at night or during the day. The beer and sandwiches are cheap, the staff reasonably welcoming.

Nørrebro

Barcelona

Fælledvej 21, Nørrebro (35 35 76 11). **Open** 11am-
2am Mon-Wed; 11am-5am Thur-Sat; 11am-5pm Sun.
Main courses 170kr **Credit** AmEx, DC, MC, V.
Map p119 H10.

This Spanish café/bar/club with a first-floor restaurant lies within seconds of hip Sankt Hans Torv. The restaurant only opens in the evenings and serves substandard, costly Italian and French food (the veggie options are particularly poor), while during the day tapas are on offer in the café/bar. When the local bars close at around 2am, Barcelona fills up with undiscerning types who are not willing to queue for Rust (*see p218*), but want to carry on drinking. Weekends see local DJs playing soul and disco in the corny, womb-like cave designated for dancing, which was recently given the name Club Bar'cuda in an attempt to perk up its reputation for outdated disco.

Frontpage

Sortedam Dossering 21, Nørrebro (35 37 38 27/ www.frontpage.dk). Bus 1, 6, 14. **Open** *Café* 11am-1am Mon-Wed, Sun; 11am-2am Thur-Sat. *Restaurant* 5.30-9.45pm Mon-Wed, Sun; 5.30-10.15pm Thur-Sat. **Main courses** 45kr-89kr. **Credit** *Restaurant only* AmEx, DC, MC, V. **Map** p306 J11.

It's a bit of a mystery why there aren't more cafés and bars located beside Copenhagen's historic and beautiful lakes to the west of the city centre. It seems such an obviously picturesque spot to dine and drink. So we should be grateful for Frontpage, an appealing cellar bar (with outdoor tables during summer), and with a separate cellar restaurant serving excellent Franco-Danish delights next door.

Kate's Joint

Blågårdsgade 12, Nørrebro (35 37 44 96). **Open** 5.30pm-11.30pm daily. **Main courses** 60kr-75kr. **Credit** MC, V. **Map** p119/p306 K10.

This small, one-room local 'taverna' run by Kate Kamil on trendy Blågårdsgade is one of the best cheap eats in town. The young clientele dress down to dine in this laid-back and basic curry house which is usually packed at weekends. Kate's Caribbean/Indonesian/Indian fusions are particularly popular with students.

Propaganda Spisehus og Bar

Nørrebrogade 13, Nørrebro (35 39 49 00). Bus 5, 16. **Open** 5pm-midnight Mon-Wed, Sun; 5pm-3am Thur; 5pm-5am Fri, Sat. **Main courses** 74kr-118kr. **Credit** DC, MC, V. **Map** p119/p306 J10.

This Japanese-styled venue is among Copenhagen's grooviest hangouts. Formerly known and loved as Banana Republic, this recently refitted two-floor bar-cum-restaurant serves excellent noodles and other Thai/Chinese dishes at refreshingly sensible prices (desserts like melon soup or deep-fried bananas are also striking). The kitchen closes around 11pm, but at weekends the downstairs bar/club stays swinging with soul, funk and R&B DJs until the wee small hours.

Pussy Galore's Flying Circus

Sankt Hans Torv 30, Nørrebro (35 24 53 00/ www.pussy-galore.dk). Bus 3. **Open** 8am-2am Mon-Fri; 9am-2am Sat, Sun **Main courses** 80kr-100kr. **Credit** DC, MC, V. **Map** p119/p306 H10.

At the heart of what is currently the hippest part of Copenhagen (the area surrounding Sankt Hans Torv in Nørrebro) lies Pussy Galore's, the archetypal modern Copenhagen café. This busy L-shaped bar and dining area decorated in a '90s minimalist style (replete with Arne Jacobsen chairs), is the trendy counterpart to the more conventional French food offered by Sebastapol next door (*see p154*). The menu boasts a collection of enticing, exotically named fusion dishes including Mekong Delta Darling, Impression of Marrakech and China Chilli Chill Out, as well as cheap salads and hearty burgers. As with Sebastapol, come spring, Pussy Galore's tables sprawl out into the square to create

Delicatessen. *See p152.*

Eat, Drink, Shop

a convivial continental atmosphere. The cocktails are very reasonably priced (a Caipirinha is 60kr) compared to the bars in the centre of town, too.

Sebastopol Café.

Sankt Hans Torv 32, Nørrebro (35 36 30 02). Bus 3.
Open 8am-1am Mon-Wed, Sun; 8am-2am Thur-Sat.
Main courses 100kr. **Credit** AmEx, DC, MC, V.
Map p119/p306 H10.
The menu may be more conservative than its fusion-crazy neighbour Pussy Galore's *(see p153)*, but Sebastopol's superb French staples offer tempting, good value competition. Service is exemplary, while a young and groovy clientele (musicians, journalists, advertising creatives, designers, students and young professionals) provide constant visual entertainment. It's a bit like Café Victor *(see p147)* without the attitude or the prices. Sebastopol gets very crowded on summer weekends when, like Pussy's, it bursts exuberantly outside onto the square.

Østerbro

Amokka

Dag Hammarskjölds Allé 38-40, Østerbro (33 25 35 35/www.amokka.com). Bus 6, 14.
Open 11am-11pm Mon-Wed, Sat, Sun; 11am-midnight Thur, Fri. *Food served* 11am-10pm Mon-Sat; 11am-9pm Sun. **Main courses** 80kr-155kr.
Set menus 195kr-245kr. **Credit** AmEx, DC, MC, V.
Map p307 G14.
This glorious temple to the coffee bean is *the* meeting place in upcoming Østerbro. Combining an exceptional restaurant (lorded over by chef Carsten Pedersen, formerly of London's esteemed Sugar Club), with one of the city's best coffee bars, it is no surprise that Amokka is hugely popular, particularly at weekends. The cakes, it should be stressed,

are spectacular, while the home-roasted coffee blends and definitive expressos entice quivering caffeine freaks from all corners of the city. Good brunch, too.

Circus

Rosenvængets Allé 7, Østerbro (35 55 77 72). Bus 6, 14. **Open** 11am-1am Mon-Thur; 11am-2am Fri, Sat; 11am-6pm Sun.
Main courses 100kr. **Credit** AmEx, MC, V.
Map p121 E14.
Leading the charge towards the transformation of Østerbro into the city's newest fashionable district is Circus, part café/bar, part delicatessen, part, ahem, hairdressers. With a charming, cosy interior graced by original 19th-century cow-themed frescoes (from the time when this was a butchers) as well as some outdoor seating, Circus serves tapas with a Danish twist plus a top-notch brunch to a young, trendy clientele who can't be bothered to schlep into town just to stand posing in some costly, crowded bar all evening.

Further afield

Top of the Town Wine Bar

Radisson SAS Scandinavia Hotel, Amager Boulevard 70, Amager (33 96 58 58). Bus 6, 14.
Open 6pm-midnight Tue-Sat; closed Sun, Mon.
Set menus 395kr-525kr. **Credit** AmEx, DC, MC, V.
Apart from Copenhagen Airport there isn't much to lure visitors to Amager, the small island adjacent to the city to the east, but the wine bar on the 25th floor of the SAS hotel does have one of the city's best views, particularly at night when you can see Sweden twinkling in the distance. A large selection of wines are sold by the glass. Predictably, though, the clientele are mainly well-heeled, middle-aged tourists, so don't expect a riotous party atmosphere.

Sebastopol Café: don't mention the (Crimean) war.

Shops & Services

Welcome to a shopaholic's paradise.

Copenhagen is one of the best shopping cities in Europe. Rather an extravagant claim? Well, firstly, you should forget all your prejudices about how expensive Scandinavia is supposed to be; Copenhagen's prices are very often on a par with London's and New York's, if not cheaper. Keep an eye on exchange rates and cheap flight offers and you could bag yourself some real bargains.

There are several areas in which Copenhagen particularly excels, chief among them being interior and furniture design, glassware and ceramics. And, in the Danish capital's clothing and jewellery stores, you'll find unique items with a distinctive, modern Scandinavian flair.

Copenhagen's trump card, however, is its outstanding range of small independent retailers who, for now at least, seem to have the big name high street stores licked in terms of consumer satisfaction. Even on Strøget, the city's main shopping artery (car-free, by the way), big international chains are blessedly absent, while the city's two main department stores – Illum and Magasin du Nord – are on a comparatively modest scale.

This is a city whose layout makes life easy for shoppers. In the centre at least, everything is within a few minutes' walk from Strøget, while the other rich shopping seams, Nørrebro, Vesterbro and Frederiksberg, are only a five-to ten-minute bus ride away. What's more, you often find that similar shops tend to congregate in the same area to a much greater extent than in other cities. The best women's and men's fashion, for example, is pretty much contained within the area bordered by Gothersgade, Strøget, Købmagergade and Landemærket; while Ravnsborgade and its neighbouring streets in Nørrebro are excellent for antiques. Værndemsvej, in Vesterbro, is good for gourmet food products; the area around the university has some wonderful bookshops (new, second-hand and antiquarian); Pisserenden (the area contained by Frederiksberggade – the western end of Strøget – Nørre Voldgade and Nørregade) has some superb record shops, musical instrument stores and younger, 'streetwear' clothes stores (surfing, skateboarding gear and the like); while Kompagnistræde and Læderstræde have a little of everything. The city's fine art galleries, antique dealers and auction houses are on Bredgade, but let's not

also forget Istedgade in Vesterbro, the street of a hundred (well, a fair few) sex shops for which Denmark became justly notorious in the '60s. For camping and outdoor pursuits (a huge market in Denmark), Frederiksborggade has several large stores that cater for hunters, walkers, campers and climbers. The only bad news is Denmark's draconian opening hours that see most stores close early on Saturdays (although many shops are open later on the first Saturday of each month) and pretty much all of them closed on Sundays. Late opening times on Fridays is some compensation and, thankfully, Vesterbro's ethnic food stores seem to keep their own hours, regardless of the regulations.

But shopping in Copenhagen is as much about the environment as products and prices. In the centre of town you'll find the most modern stores within the most historic of buildings, alongside cobbled streets, around chilled-out café squares or in grand town houses dating from as far back as the 17th century. As with its restaurants and cafés, Copenhagen's shops – many of them in semi-subterranean basements – are among the cosiest and most welcoming in the world. If you don't get in the buying mood here, it ain't going to happen.

Art supplies & stationery

Fyldepenne Depotet

Nygade 6, Strøget (33 11 33 22/ www.fyldepennedepotet.dk). **Open** 10am-5.30pm Mon-Thur; 10am-7pm Fri; 10am-2pm Sat; closed Sun. **Credit** AmEx, DC, MC, V. **Map** p311 N13.
The number one Danish stockist of Mont Blanc pens (from 700-104,000kr plus), as well as other leading prestige pen brands like Schaeffer, Waterman and Parker. Also stocks quality paper, inks, filofaxes and Mont Blanc accessories.

Kontor Partner

Nikolaj Plads, Store Kirkestræde 1 (33 12 12 43/ www.kontorpartner.dk). **Open** 9am-5.30pm Mon-Fri; 10am-2pm Sat (until 3pm 1st Sat of month); closed Sun. **Credit** DC, MC, V. **Map** p311 N14.
Decent sized, one-stop stationers and art supply store close to the centre of town.

Ordning & Reda

Østergade 11, Strøget (33 32 30 18/www.ordning-reda.com). **Open** 10am-6pm Mon-Thur; 10am-7pm Fri; 10am-5pm Sat; closed Sun. **Credit** AmEx, DC, MC, V. **Map** p311 M15.

COPENHAGEN

THE OFFICIAL GUIDE TO WONDERFUL COPENHAGEN

THISWEEK 2001

Subscription: www.ctw.dk

Delectable designer paper, folders, photo albums and other stationery from this super-cool Swedish chain. The most desirable note pads in Copenhagen.

Auctions

Bruun Rasmussen Kunstauktioner
Bredgade 33 (33 43 69 11/www.bruun-rasmussen.dk). **Open** 9am-5pm Mon-Fri; closed Sat, Sun. **Credit** MC, V. **Map** p312 M16.
Denmark's top auction house also happens to be one of the world's top ten auctioneers, serving the prime end of the antiques and art market. Usually themed, Rasmussen's sales of art, antiques, furniture, wine and just about everything else, take place at least a couple of times a week (the frequency depends on the time of year). As with other such institutions, the knowledgeable collector stands a good chance of finding a bargain. Founded in 1948 by Arne Bruun Rasmussen, the business remains a family concern and is now run by Arne's son Jesper.

Sotheby's
Bredgade 6 (33 13 55 56/www.sothebys.com). **Open** 10am-5pm Mon-Fri; closed Sat, Sun. **Map** p312 M16.
The Copenhagen intake office of the world-famous London art and antiques auction house doesn't hold sales, but gives valuations, and recommendations on where to sell.

Books

General

Arnold Busck
Købmagergade 49 (33 73 35 00/ www.arnoldbusck.dk). **Open** 10am-6pm Mon; 9.15am-6pm Tue-Thur; 9.15am-7pm Fri; 10am-4pm Sat; closed Sun. **Credit** DC, MC, V. **Map** p311 M13-14.
Busck's is one of Denmark's leading book retailers and this three-storey shop on Købmagergade, adjacent to the university, is its largest outlet (though the interior is fairly charmless and uninviting). There's a large English paperback department on the ground floor, and elsewhere there are strong art, architecture, photography and CD-Rom sections. Busck Antikvariat at Fiolstræde 24 is its second-hand and antiquarian books branch.

Atheneum
Nørregade 6 (33 12 69 70/www.atheneum.dk). **Open** 9am-5.30pm Mon-Thur; 9am-6pm Fri; 10am-2pm Sat; closed Sun. **Credit** DC, MC, V. **Map** p310 M12.
Another of the many bookshops serving the university students in this so-called 'Latin Quarter' of town, Atheneum has a large quantity of (new) books in the English language and is particularly strong on English literature. This excellent general bookshop also attracts major international authors for book signings and readings (Seamus Heaney drops by when he's in town).

GAD
Vimmelskaftet 32, Strøget (33 15 05 58/ www.gad.dk). **Open** 9.30am-7pm Mon-Fri; 9.30am-5pm Sat; closed Sun. **Credit** AmEx, DC, MC, V. **Map** p311 N13.
One of Denmark's largest bookshop chains, with a general cross-section of titles, many in English. The centrally located Strøget branch is particularly good for travel books and dictionaries, as well as contemporary English fiction.
Branches: Illum (*see p158*); Fiolstræde 31-33; Central Station; Frederiksberg Centret (*see p158*).

Politikens Boghallen
Rådhuspladsen 37 (33 11 85 11/www.pol.dk). **Open** 9.30am-5.30pm Mon-Thur; 9.30am-6.30pm Fri; 10am-2pm Sat; closed Sun. **Credit** AmEx, DC, MC, V. **Map** p310 O12.
If the book you seek isn't here, you probably won't find it in Copenhagen. Along with Busck's (*see above*), this is one of the city's biggest bookshops, with a good stock of paperback Penguins (in English), as well as plenty of other English-language titles. It also has an antiquarian department, known as Politikens Antikvariat, in the basement (33 47 27 63/www.polantik.dk).

Antiquarian/second-hand

Harcks Antikvariat
Fiolstræde 34 (33 12 13 44). **Open** 9am-5.30pm Mon-Thur; 9am-7pm Fri; 9.30am-2pm Sat (until 4pm 1st & last Sat of month); closed Sun. **Credit** DC, MC, V. **Map** p311 M13.
Fiolstræde has several antiquarian and second-hand bookshops catering to the needs of the university students nearby (Paludan and Arnold Busck, both a few doors down, are two rivals). Harcks is one of the largest, and has specialised in the humanities for 85 years, as well as also selling rare books. Around 40% of its stock is in English.

Peter Grosell
Læderstræde 15 (33 93 45 05/www.grosell.dk). **Open** 10am-5pm Mon-Fri; by appointment Sat; closed Sun. **Credit** AmEx, DC, MC, V. **Map** p311 N14.
This large dealer in rare, second-hand and antiquarian bookshop is particularly strong on art and design books (it also has some graphic art, posters and drawings), as well as Scandinavian first editions. Around 20% of the 4,000 titles are in English.

Comics

Fantask
Sankt Peders Stræde 18 (33 11 85 38/ www.fantask.dk). **Open** 11am-6pm Mon-Thur; 11am-7pm Fri; 11am-3pm Sat; closed Sun. **No credit cards.** **Map** p310 N12.
This large cellar shop covers pretty much the entire gamut of anoraky collectibles, though its stock is mainly comprised of US comics, fantasy books and

Eat, Drink, Shop

Illum: Strøget's premier department store.

role-playing games. *Marvel* comics, Terry Pratchett novels and *Star Wars* and *Star Trek* merchandise are the predictable best sellers.

Newsagents

Turist Kiosken
Jorcks Passage, Vimmelskaftet 42, Strøget (33 13 05 41). **Open** 6.30am-5.30pm Mon-Fri; 6.30am-3pm Sat; closed Sun. **No credit cards**. **Map** p311 N13.
Probably the best range of international magazines and up-to-date newspapers in Copenhagen, but much more expensive than prices back home.

Specialist

Filmhusets Bog- og Videohandel
Filmhuset, Vognmagergade 10 (33 74 34 21/ www.dfi.dk). **Open** 11am-6pm Mon-Fri; 1-6pm Sat; closed Sun. **Credit** AmEx, DC, MC, V. **Map** p311 M14.
Most of the books in the Danish Film Institute's bookshop (round the back of the Institute's radical headquarters, which also features a library, café and screens – *see p199*) are in English, and though the stock isn't that extensive, this is the only haven for literary cinefiles in the city. The bookshop also sells posters and videos.

Nordisk Korthandel
Studiestræde 26-30 (33 38 26 38/www.scanmaps.dk). **Open** 10.30am-5.30pm Mon-Fri; 10am-2pm Sat; closed Sun. **Credit** DC, MC, V. **Map** p310 N12.
Copenhagen's best source of maps, travel books and globes, this comprehensively stocked shop, near to Rådhuspladsen, is staffed by friendly and knowledgeable travel enthusiasts. This is the place to come for those detailed geological maps before setting out for the North Pole, or Jylland even.

Department stores & malls

Fisketorvet Shopping Center
Kalvebod Brygge, Vesterbro (no phone/ www.fisketorvet.dk). Train to Dybbølsbro/46, 150S bus. **Open** 10am-8pm Mon-Fri; 9am-3pm Sat; closed Sun. **Credit** varies. **Map** p311 Q13.
Constructed on the site of a former fish market, Copenhagen's largest shopping centre is sandwiched between an attractive canal on one side and a four-lane highway on the other. For those who like to shop by numbers, there are upwards of 100 stores, ten cinemas and 2,000 parking places making up the complex.

Fona 2000
Østergade 47, Strøget (33 15 90 55/www.fona.dk). **Open** 10am-6pm Mon-Thur; 10am-7pm Fri; 10am-5pm Sat; closed Sun. **Credit** AmEx, DC, MC, V. **Map** p311 M15.
Denmark's largest home entertainment store sells DVDs, CDs, computer games, cameras, and well-known TV and stereo brands.

Frederiksberg Centret
Falkoner Allé 21, Frederiksberg (38 16 03 40). Bus 18, 29. **Open** 8.30am-9pm Mon-Fri; 7.30am-6pm Sat; closed Sun. **Credit** varies. **Map** p110 N5.
A charmless mall whose only redeeming feature is that it's open later at night than most other shops.

Illum
Østergade 52, Strøget (33 14 40 02). **Open** 10am-7pm Mon-Thur; 10am-8pm Fri; 9am-5pm Sat; closed Sun. **Credit** AmEx, DC, MC, V. **Map** p311 M15.
One of Copenhagen's two mighty department stores (the other being Magasin du Nord; *see p159*). There is little to distinguish the two, though Illum is smaller, more modern and perhaps the more upmarket of the pair, with a spectacular interior and a marvellous glass dome. Cosmetics and food are on the lower floors; designer mens- and womenswear (a wide range of labels, from chic to sporty with everything in between) on the first and second floors; household goods are on the third, along with a small and pricey antiques market; and the fourth floor houses young fashions and sportswear (and the city's only Gap outlet) as well as an excellent café and restaurant.

(sidebar) **Eat, Drink, Shop**

Magasin du Nord

Kongens Nytorv 13 (33 11 44 33/www.magasin.dk).
Open 10am-7pm Mon-Thur; 10am-8pm Fri; 9am-5pm Sat; closed Sun. **Credit** AmEx, DC, MC, V.
Map p311 M15.
With its original ornate façade, Magasin du Nord very nearly upstages Det Kongelige Teater (the Royal Theatre) opposite on Kongens Nytorv. This was Scandinavia's first department store, and it is still the largest, with six floors of clothes, cosmetics, household goods and food. Its toy department has the widest range of Lego in town, the book department is excellent, and the ground floor has a wonderful food hall. Womenswear is also good, featuring a good spread of labels, such as Esprit, Mexx, Bruuns Bazaar, French Connection and Part II. Though rather chaotic, Magasin can be a surprisingly rich hunting ground for bargains.

Interiors

For **Georg Jensen**, **Royal Copenhagen Porcelain**, **Holmegaard** and **Illums Bolighus**, *see page 165* **Royal Copenhagen**.

Antiques, classics & decorative art

Boasting over 30 antique shops, each with its own speciality and price range, **Ravnsborggade** in Nørrebro is a browser's paradise. And the street's relaxed and friendly atmosphere means you don't have to be an expert – or fabulously wealthy – to enjoy checking out the merchandise; anyone with even a passing interest in Danish design furniture will find plenty to get excited about.

10 A Modern

Ravnsborggade 10a, Nørrebro (24 41 47 48). Bus 4E, 5, 16, 350S. **Open** 3-5.30pm Mon-Fri; noon-2pm Sat; closed Sun. **No credit cards. Map** p119/p306 J10.
This occasional supplier to uncompromisingly named London retro interiors shop eatmyhandbagbitch has excellent examples of mid-range, good quality stylish Danish designs dating from the '50s to the '70s.

Antik 37

Kompagnistræde 37 (33 13 37 75/ www.antikringen.dk). **Open** 11am-5pm Mon-Thur; 11am-6pm Fri; 11am-3pm Sat; closed Sun.
Credit MC, V. **Map** p311 O13.
One of several excellent antique shops in this area south of Strøget. Antik 37 is packed with a wide range of Danish collectibles including silver, porcelain and cutlery. Good for a nose around, but watch the prices.

Antikhallen

Courtyard at Ravnsborggade 12, Nørrebro (35 35 04 20). Bus 4E, 5, 16, 350S.
Open 4-6pm Mon-Fri; 11am-2pm Sat; closed Sun.
No credit cards. Map p119/p306 J10.

Follow the sandwich board signs through two courtyards to reach this unpretentious treasure trove of antique and second-hand furniture. The shop is piled high with great deals: goods range from posh 19th-century mahogany tables to orange 1970s moulded plastic chairs and an unbeatable selection of hanging lamps.

Antique Toys

Store Strandstræde 20 (30 12 66 32/www.antique-toys.suite.dk). **Open** 3-6pm Wed-Fri; closed Mon, Tue, Sat, Sun. **Map** p312 M16.
This has to be one of Copenhagen's more enchanting antique shops, selling, as you will have guessed from the name, antique toys of all shapes, some dating from as far back as the 17th century. Good for old model cars, dolls and their furniture, trains and teddy bears. Not particularly cheap though.

L'Art

Ravnsborggade 12b, Nørrebro (22 34 94 53). Bus 4E, 5, 16, 350S. **Open** noon-5.30pm Tue-Fri; 11am-2pm Sat; closed Mon, Sun. **No credit cards. Map** p119/p306 J10.
This little shop has good deals on an eclectic range of specialties: antique silk kimonos, bathroom fixtures and Danish naval paraphernalia.

Caso

Refshalevej 2, Christiania (32 95 30 51/www.caso-ovne.dk). **Open** 10am-5pm Mon-Fri; 11am-3pm Sat; closed Sun. **No credit cards. Map** p313 O19.
Part of the alternative community of Christiania (*see p105*) for almost 30 years, this one-of-a-kind shop is an unexpected find, and worth a visit if you're in the neighbourhood. Its main trade is the unglamorous-sounding field of old stoves, but these impeccably restored wood-burning ovens – often sporting elaborate metalwork designs and porcelain tiling – are strangely beautiful pieces. The shop has two interesting sidelines: turn-of-the-century Scandinavian wood furniture and inexpensive Italian glass vases.

H Danielsens Eftf

Læderstræde 11 (33 13 02 74). **Open** 9.30am-5.30pm Mon-Fri; 9.30am-1pm Sat; closed Sun.
Credit AmEx, MC, V. **Map** p311 N14.
This family firm, founded in 1907 and currently run by the fourth generation, is a unique find. Possessing the original moulds of countless designs of cutlery, H Danielsens can reproduce to order long-extinct silverware by companies such as Michelson and Georg Jensen. Danielsens also maintains a good supply of antique Royal Copenhagen Porcelain, particularly the highly collectible Christmas plates (from 100-5,000kr each).

Dansk Antik

Ravnsborggade 20B, Nørrebro (35 37 30 37). Bus 5, 4E, 16, 350S. **Open** 10am-5pm Mon-Fri; 10am-2pm Sat; closed Sun. **No credit cards. Map** p306 J10.
All manner of Royal Copenhagen Porcelain dishes and figurines.

Design classics at **Dansk Møbelkunst**.

Dansk Møbelkunst
Bredgade 32 (33 32 38 37/www.dmk.dk).
Open 10am-6pm Mon-Fri; 10am-2pm Sat;
closed Sun. **No credit cards. Map** p312 M16.
The majority of classic furniture sold in this huge
shop in Bredgade is by Danish designers; the stellar
cast includes Poul Henningsen, Arne Jacobsen, Hans
J Wegener, Finn Juhl and Kaare Klint. Illustrious
international names might include Charles Eames
and Charles-Edouard Jeanneret, better known as Le
Corbusier. Given the location, you wouldn't expect
bargains and there are few here, but it's great for a
covetous browse and probably the best place to pick
up an example of the famous model 3107 chair by
Arne Jacobsen. Designed in 1955, five million have
been made, none more famous than the one posed
upon by Christine Keeler for a photograph by David
Bailey that was to become one of the iconic images
of the 1960s.

Jørgen L Dalgaard
Bredgade 28 (33 14 09 05). **Open** 1-6pm Mon-Fri;
closed Sat, Sun. **Credit** MC, V. **Map** p312 M16.
Specialising in a diverse and high quality range of
20th-century decorative art, Dalgaard is one of the
big hitters on Bredgade's art and antiques scene. His
showroom could be considered something of a mini-
Kunstindustrimuseet (Museum of Decorative and
Applied Art, *see p92*).

Kim Antons & Co
Ravnsborggade 14d, Nørrebro (35 37 00 68).
Bus 4E, 5, 16, 350S. **Open** 9am-5.30pm Mon-Fri;
closed Sat, Sun. **Credit** V. **Map** p119/p306 J10.

Luxurious 18th- and 19th-century European furniture is Kim Anton's forte. Head straight to the basement: a cavernous room that feels like the forgotten
wing of an old castle.

Kirstens Antik
*Ravnsborggade 17, Nørrebro (35 37 00 68). Bus 4E,
5, 16, 350S.* **Open** 10am-5.30pm Mon-Fri; 10am-2pm
Sat; closed Sun. **Credit** AmEx, DC, MC, V.
Map p119/p306 J10.
An elegant boutique dealing in high-end French art
deco and modern Danish furniture, Holmegaard
glass and Just Andersen ceramics.

Mads Lang
*Landemærket 9 (33 32 42 24/madslang@
wanado.dk).* **Open** 2-6pm Mon-Fri; 11am-3pm Sat;
closed Sun. **No credit cards.**
Map p307 L14.
Assuming you find it open (not likely), Mads Lang's
cellar shop, just off Købmagergade, offers a sumptuous array of groovy, psychedelic '60s and '70s furniture, lighting and glassware. Very retro chic; very
Austin Powers.

Maritime Antiques
Toldbodgade 15 (33 12 12 57). **Open** 10am-5.30pm
Mon-Fri; 10am-2pm Sat; closed Sun. **Credit** AmEx,
MC, V. **Map** p312 M17.
This magical basement antiques shop (which has
been here for over 20 years) is, appropriately enough
given its watery theme, just around the corner
from Nyhavn. It's packed with maritime collectibles,
from magnificent 19th-century diving bells (from
16,000kr), to model lighthouses, and just about every
other boat fixture and fitting. A one-off.

Moving Furniture
Silkegade 5 (33 15 30 90). **Open** noon-6pm Mon,
Wed-Fri; 11am-3pm Sat; closed Tue, Sun.
No credit cards. Map p311 M14.
The only shop of interest in what was once the centre of the city's rag trade (there's only one fabric shop
here now, Giselles at No.13, and that's not up to
much), this rather dingy but well-stocked shop sells
unusual furniture, lighting, ceramics and glassware
from the last century (as we must now learn to call
it). Plastic moulded chairs from the '60s and '70s
dominate. *See also p40.* Owner Jacob Noring is also
the proprietor of the Stereo Bar (*see p40 and p215*).

Permanent Design
Bredgade 36 (33 15 13 50/www.permanentdesign.dk).
Open noon-5.30pm Mon-Fri; 11am-2pm Sat; closed
Sun. **Credit** MC, V. **Map** p312 M16.
Collector and dealer Bente Friborg specialises in
20th-century Danish furniture, lighting and decorative art (particularly from the '50s and '60s), though
there's also the odd Swedish and Italian piece
('Anything I like, really,' she says) in her large, sham-
bolic, two-storey showroom on Bredgade. You can
pick up a simple, battered Jacobsen chair for around
850kr, but for a better idea of Bente's stock, her website is an excellent guide.

Sølvkælderen

Kompagnistræde 1 (33 13 36 34).
Open 9am-5.30pm Mon-Fri; 9am-2pm Sat;
closed Sun. **Credit** V. **Map** p311 O13.
This breathtaking L-shaped cellar shop has dealt
in antique silverware, mostly Danish, for over a
hundred years. Pieces date as far back as 1700, but
there are also candlesticks, plates and cutlery from
the 20th century, as well as a selection of newly
manufactured pieces.

Something Special

Løvstræde 10 (33 14 51 31). **Open** 10am-7pm
Mon, Thur-Fri; 10am-6pm Tue, Wed; 10am-5pm Sat;
closed Sun. **Credit** AmEx, MC, V. **Map** p311 M14.
Ali Al-Awssi is one of Copenhagen's more engag-
ing shopkeepers. Originally from Iraq, Ali opened
Something Special in the early '80s, and within a
few years was designing lamps, bar stools and mirrors. Today, his sizeable furniture and lighting shop
sells art deco originals and his own-designed striking art deco-style chrome furniture. The shop's centrepiece is Ali's angular, chrome dining table and
chairs, which you will probably be persuaded to try
for yourself.

Spunk & Co

*Kompagnistræde 21 (33 12 79 77/www.soelberg-
antik.dk).* **Open** 11am-5.30pm Mon-Fri; 11am-2pm
Sat; closed Sun. **Credit** MC, V. **Map** p311 O13.
One of the most eclectic shops on this most eclectic
of streets, the unfortunately-named Spunk gathers
together under one roof (well, two connected cellar
stores) the likes of fabulous Russian Orthodox
icons, military memorabilia, and fascinating ethno-

graphic items from the Inuit and Eskimo cultures.
Customers might be found wrestling with improbable conundrums like whether to go for the antique
pith helmet or a Greenlandic shamanist soapstone
talisman, known as a Tupilak.

Art

Designer Zoo

*Vesterbrogade 137, Vesterbro (26 81 18 26/
www.dzoo.dk).* Bus 6. **Open** 10am-6pm Tue-Thur;
10am-7pm Fri; 10am-3pm Sat; closed Mon, Sun.
No credit cards. **Map** p111 Q6.
An exceptional open-concept shop/gallery featuring
creative, contemporary Danish design. The four
young artisans who own Designer Zoo produce
handmade clothes, jewellery, furniture and glass, on
site – they each have a studio where you can watch
them at work through windows.

Qvindesmedien

*Bådsmandsstræde 43, Christiania (32 57 76 58/
www.kvindesmedien.dk).* **Open** 9am-5pm Mon-Fri;
11am-3pm Sat; closed Sun. **No credit cards.**
Map p312 P17.
This warehouse-like space in Christiania is both a
metalwork shop full of noisy, dirty machines, where
you can watch the three female blacksmiths at work,
and a gallery selling their creations – industrial-look
iron candleholders, lamps, tables and sculptures.
The back of the workshop is given over to
Christiania Bikes, the company responsible for those
enormous cart-bicycles you see Danish parents
hauling their kids around in.

Fascinating for young and old: the eclectic **Spunk and Co.**

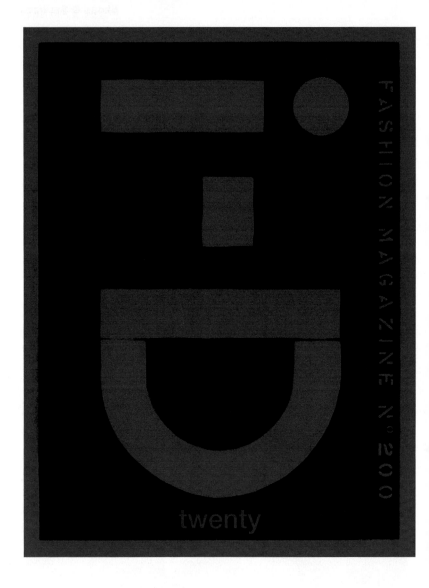

FASHION MAGAZINE N° 200

twenty

subscribe

subscribe and get i-D Magazine monthly. 11 issues per year uk £30.00 europe £45.00 world £60.00

For further information go to: www.i-dmagazine.com

cast themselves and their message live and interactive over the Internet. Broadcast times are limited to a few hours a week, but you can drop by the studio almost anytime of day or night and talk to the forward-looking people who run the place. Superflex has also helped set up similar studios in Liverpool, Amsterdam, Vienna and Edinburgh. *See also p207.*

Ceramics

Galleri Nørby
Vestergade 8 (33 15 19 20/www.galleri-noerby.dk).
Open noon-5.30pm Tue-Thur; noon-6pm Fri; 11am-2pm Sat; closed Mon, Sun. **Credit** AmEx, DC, MC, V.
Map p310 O12.
Denmark's largest ceramics gallery holds ten exhibitions a year in its beautifully spartan showroom near Gammeltorv. Nørby promotes the work of Danish and international ceramic artists and potters working at the forefront of the media, and the results are often challenging and invariably beautiful. Note that there's a 10% surcharge for any credit card payments.

Royal Copenhagen Porcelain
Factory shop: Smallegade 47 (38 14 48 48).
Open 9am-5.30pm Mon-Fri; 9am-2pm Sat;
closed Sun. **Credit** AmEx, DC, MC, V.
Map p110 N3.
The fairly interesting and inexpensive (25kr) half-hour tour of the Royal Copenhagen factory is rounded-off by a visit to the gift shop/discount outlet, where you can take advantage of good prices on slightly damaged and discontinued crockery, figurines and crystal. If you want to skip the tour, the shop entrance is also accessible around the corner on Søndre Fasanvej. You'll find even cheaper pieces in the tent outside, but it's a bit depressing, even for dedicated bargain-hunters. *See also p165.*

Strandstræde Keramik
Lille Strandstræde 14 (33 11 99 46/
www.beate-andersen.dk). **Open** 10am-5.30pm
Tue-Fri; closed Mon, Sat, Sun. **Credit** MC, V.
Map p312 M16.
Within earshot of the buzzing tattoo parlours opposite, and just around the corner from Nyhavn, is this wonderful basement ceramics studio and gallery that sells the works of Gunhild Aarberg, Jane Reumert and Beate Andersen. Exquisite, modern vases and bowls are the main attraction, although you may find the prices an equally strong deterrent.

Udstillingssted For Ny Keramik
Kompagnistræde 25 (33 91 05 91). **Open** 1-5.30pm
Wed-Fri; 11am-2pm Sat; closed Mon, Tue, Sun.
No credit cards. Map p311 O13.
This is one of the most exciting showrooms in Copenhagen for contemporary ceramics. The work displayed here is often brilliant, usually experimental, and certainly never boring. The collection features a mix of functional and decorative pieces by young artists, both Danish and international.

Sleek, chic **Casa Shop**. *See p164.*

Starving Artistz
Elmegade 17, Nørrebro (26 16 07 16). Bus 3, 4E, 5, 16, 350S. **Open** 2-6.30pm Mon-Fri; noon-5pm Sat; closed Sun. **No credit cards. Map** p306 J10.
A democratic gallery concept that gives young artists a chance to show, and hopefully sell, their work in a relaxed setting (for instance, paintings might be piled up on the floor). *See also p208.*

www.superchannel.org
Blågårdsgade 11B, Nørrebro (22 76 47 61).
Bus 4E, 5, 16, 350S. **Open** 2-4pm Mon; 4-6pm
Wed; 8-10pm Fri; closed Tue, Thur, Sat, Sun.
Map p119/p306 J10.
Started by the local artist group Superflex and supported by the Culture Ministry, superchannel is a studio that anyone can use, free of charge, to broad-

Eat, Drink, Shop

Desirable ceramics at **Galleri Nørby**. *See p163.*

Contemporary furniture

For **Ichinen Design**, *see page 175* **Sex street**.

Casa Shop
Store Regnegade 2 (33 32 70 41/
www.casagroup.com). **Open** 10am-5pm Mon-Thur,
10am-7pm Fri, 10am-3pm Sat; closed Sun.
Credit DC, MC, V. **Map** p311 M15.
Casa Shop is one of the country's premiere contemporary furniture retailers. Although most of the stock is Italian, of the type usually found in Sunday newspaper supplements (and nowhere else), there are plenty of smaller, quirkier pieces, such as Nemo lamps and Ron Arad's clever flexible Bookworm bookshelf to tempt those on a tighter shopping budget. The equally stunning, and equally expensive, **Casa Køkken og Bad Studio**, a few doors down Gammel Mønt, caters to your kitchen and bathroom needs in similar, contemporary style (needless to say, stainless steel abounds).

Paustian
Kalkbrænderiløbskal 2, Østerbro (39 16 65 65/
www.paustian.dk). Train to Nordhaven then 29 bus.
Open 9am-5.30pm Mon-Thur; 9am-6pm Fri; 10am-2pm Sat; closed Sun. **Credit** MC, V.
For aficionados of modern furniture design there is only one shop to visit in Copenhagen (though unfortunately it is stuck out in the rather inhospitable docks area). The stunning warehouse, designed by Jørn Utzon (the Danish architect behind Sydney's Opera House), alone makes the trip worthwhile. Inside is an unprecedented range of achingly stylish chairs, tables, cabinets and other pieces by Aalto, Eames, Starck and top Danish designers, including Arne Jacobsen. Next door, Paustian's restaurant provides the perfect environment in which to ponder a purchase.

Steel
Blågårdsgade 2a, Nørrebro (35 35 55 11). Bus
4E, 5, 16, 350S. **Open** 11am-5.30pm Mon-Fri;
10am-2pm Sat; closed Sun. **No credit cards.**
Map p119/p306 K10.
Danish steel designs for the home. Storage-on-wheels for small city apartments is a speciality.

Home accessories

B&B Bed And Beauty
Købmagergade 26 (33 69 00 71/www.bedand
beauty.dk). **Open** 10am-6pm Mon-Thur; 10am-7pm
Fri; 10am-5pm Sat; closed Sun. **Credit** DC, MC, V.
Map p311 M13-14.
A kind of Danish Muji, but without the consistency of style (or in fact any style, come to think of it), B&B sells a hotchpotch of gifts and bedroom items, from inflatable armchairs to picture frames and storage containers. Good for cheap bedding and presents.

Bang og Olufsen
Østergade 35, Strøget (33 15 04 22/
www.bang-olufsen.com). **Open** 10am-5.30pm
Mon-Thur; 10am-6pm Fri; 10am-2pm Sat;
closed Sun. **Credit** AmEx, DC, MC, V.
Map p311 M15.

Eat, Drink, Shop

With its recent radical redesign, featuring changing colour slides projected onto corrugated glass, bare walls and acoustically perfect listening rooms, the world-famous Danish hi-fi and TV manufacturer's flagship store is now more alluring than ever. Fans of B&O's minimal, modernist masterpieces will be pleased to learn that prices for its hi-fis, TVs and telephones are 10-15% lower than abroad; Hi-fis start at 10,000kr, TVs at 10,500kr. Second-hand B&O can be found at AA Audio (Gothersgade 58, 33 14 14 53).

Bodum Hus
Østergade 10, Strøget (33 36 40 80/ www.bodum.com). **Open** 10am-6pm Mon-Thur; 10am-7pm Fri; 10am-5pm Sat; closed Sun. **Credit** AmEx, DC, MC, V. **Map** p311 M15.

Royal Copenhagen

In 1985 three of Copenhagen's top design companies merged under the title of **Royal Copenhagen**. Today, the three connecting shops: silversmith **Georg Jensen**, **Royal Copenhagen Porcelain** and glass makers **Holmegaard**, plus **Illums Bolighus** (which sells products by all of the above plus a miscellany of other well-designed household items and clothing), dominate the centre of Strøget at Amagertorv.

Georg Jensen
Amagertorv 4, Strøget (33 11 40 80/ www.royalshopping.dk). **Open** *May-Sept* 10am-6pm Mon-Thur; 10am-7pm Fri; 10am-5pm Sat; noon-5pm Sun. *Oct-Apr* 10am-6pm Mon-Thur; 10am-7pm Fri; 10am-5pm Sat; closed Sun. **Credit** AmEx, DC, MC, V. **Map** p311 N14.
Jensen dates back to 1904, and over the years has attracted the best Danish designers (Arne Jacobsen and Kay Bojsen among them). Today, it still sells fine jewellery, cutlery, watches and many other more functional pieces made from silver. Photo frames start at 310kr; a dinner place setting of one knife, spoon and fork will typically cost around 334kr; or, as a souvenir, you could buy a cute elephant bottle opener key ring for 160kr. As with all of Royal Copenhagen, it's not that Georg Jensen is particularly expensive, it's just that, without wanting to state the obvious, it sells expensive things. Like its grandiose neighbours, it's definitely worth a visit, even if you haven't the slightest intention of buying anything.

Holmegaard
Amagertorv 8, Strøget (33 12 44 77/ www.royalshopping.dk). **Open** 10am-6pm Mon-Thur; 10am-7pm Fri; 10am-5pm Sat; 10am-5pm Sun. **Credit** AmEx, DC, MC, V. **Map** p311 N14.
An utterly breathtaking array of glassware by local artists and internationally known names is displayed to optimum effect in this lavish store. Staff are courteous and patient (and must have nerves of steel to cope with the hordes of rucksacked tourists that stampede through each day). With glass sculptures, vases, glasses, bowls and the odd item that tries to be all four, you're sure to find something here. And with pieces priced from 120kr for simple wine glasses and 105kr for a perennially popular flowerhead candle holder, it's even possible for budget shoppers to come away with a tasteful souvenir.

Illums Bolighus
Amagertorv 10, Strøget (33 14 19 41/ www.royalshopping.dk). **Open** 10am-6pm Mon-Thur; 10am-7pm Fri; 10am-5pm Sat; 10am-5pm Sun. **Credit** AmEx, DC, MC, V. **Map** p311 N14.
Do you get paranoid about issues of home decor? You can be confident that most products at Illums Bolighus accord with commonly held principles of good taste and sophistication. Almost a match for its department store cousin further up Strøget (see page 158), the shop's range encompasses stationery, cutlery, glassware, silverware, porcelain, clothing, kitchenware, toys, bed linen and furniture – all of the highest quality and all pricey (though it's not so stuck up that it won't stock the odd lava lamp). Illums strives to epitomise the Danish design ethic of form and function combined in quality products. Mostly it succeeds.

Royal Copenhagen Porcelain
Amagertorv 6, Strøget (33 13 71 81/ www.royalshopping.dk). **Open** 10am-6pm Mon-Thur; 10am-7pm Fri; 10am-5pm Sat; 10am-5pm Sun. **Credit** AmEx, DC, MC, V. **Map** p311 N14.
Top of the desirability stakes among the Danish-produced porcelain on sale at this recently-refurbished showroom is, of course, the Flora Danica range. With individual pieces costing up to an otherwordly 115,500kr (even the mugs are frightfully expensive at 175kr). Tours of the factory can be arranged. See also page 109 **China in your hands**.

Eat, Drink, Shop

Royal Copenhagen. *See p165.*

Worshipped by coffee drinkers the world over for their cafetières, the famous Danish kitchenware chain, Bodum, has its remarkable flagship store in Copenhagen. The awe-inspiring, multi-floored, glass-fronted temple to tea-time is a short walk down Strøget from Kongens Nytorv and is, of course, laden with coffee and tea-making parapher-nalia, as well as other practical, simply designed, domestic glassware.

Gubi

Grønnegade 10 (33 15 63 88/www.gubi.dk).
Open 10am-5.30pm Mon-Thur; 10am-7pm Fri; 10am-4pm Sat; closed Sun. **Credit** DC, MC, V.
Map p311 M15.
An exceptional but not easily categorised store, Gubi looks like it could have been transported straight from the pages of *wallpaper** magazine. Founded in 1976 by Lisbeth and Gubi Olsenpart, it's part modern furniture and home decor and part men's and women's designer fashions. The likes of Prada, Dior, Burberry and Dolce & Gabbana cloth-ing is stocked downstairs, while Cappellini and other Italian furniture brands dominate the upper floors. Gubi describes itself as a 'lifestyle' store, though whoever can afford to buy wholesale into this lifestyle probably has someone else doing their shopping for them. The shop has an excellent web magazine, now in English.

Le Klint

Store Kirkestræde 1 (33 11 66 63/www.leklint.com).
Open 10am-5.30pm Mon-Thur; 10am-6pm Fri; 10am-2pm Sat; closed Sun. **Credit** MC, V. **Map** p311 N14.
The doyen of Danish furniture design is Kaare Klint (*see p37*), part of the Klint family of designers and architects (mostly famous for Grundtvig's Kirke; *see p122*), and this is the main stockist for his trademark concertina-style lampshades and accompanying lamps. His best-known design is 'Model 1' (535kr), but many of Klint's shades are variations on a sim-ilar theme (though, conversely, he has also designed some fiendishly complex pieces). Made in Denmark, these most Lutheran of lampshades (reminiscent of a ruff collar) have been folded by hand (hence the price) – since 1943. No Danish home is complete without a Klint lampshade.

Kunst og Køkkentøj

Østergade 26, Strøget (33 13 29 28). **Open** 10am-5.30pm Mon-Thur; 10am-6pm Fri; 10am-2pm Sat; closed Sun. **Credit** 10am-5.30pm Mon-Thur; 10am-6pm Fri; 11am-2pm Sat; closed Sun. **Map** p311 M15.
For professional, semi-professional and serious ama-teur cooks this is the best shop in Copenhagen in which to buy high-quality, no-nonsense kitchen utensils, pot and pans. Copper pans (from 870kr) tend to be cheaper here than in London, and there is also a dazzling array of kitchen knives.

Rosenthal Studio Haus

Frederiksberggade 21, Strøget (33 14 21 01).
Open 10am-6pm Mon-Thur; 10am-7pm Fri; 10am-5pm Sat; closed Sun. **Credit** AmEx, DC, MC, V.
Map p310 O12.
The main outlet for Bjørn Winblad's grotesque but popular porcelain plates, bowls and figures (for instance, flower pots with faces for thousands of kro-ner), Rosenthal also sells a large range of glassware, Lin Utzon vases (from 199kr), Versace and Bulgari tableware and high-class cutlery and kitchenware. Despite its frequent lapses of taste, there is bound to be something here that appeals, whether it's a Philippe Starck lemon squeezer (390kr) or a Mendini pepper mill.

Søstrene Grene

Amagettorv 29, Strøget (no phone/www.grenes.dk).
Open 10.30am-6pm Mon-Thur; 10.30am-7pm Fri; 10am-4pm Sat; closed Sun. **No credit cards.**
Map p311 N14.
Søstrene Grene tends to polarise opinion like no other store in the city. People either love its lucky dip bargain potential, or loath its frustrating one-way- system layout, and often brazenly poor qual-ity stock. Chances are, though, that you'll find at least one gem among the oddball crockery, toys, bedding, glassware, basketware, DIY tools, obscure food items and miscellaneous gifts (much of it Chinese- or Japanese-sourced), and more than like-ly it will be at a rock-bottom price. Perhaps not the classiest shop in town, but where else can you find a Panama hat for sale alongside a jar of marmalade?

Vi Ses

Valkendorfsgade 3 (33 12 33 15). **Open** 11am-5pm
Mon-Fri; 10am-2pm Sat (until 4pm 1st Sat of month);
closed Sun. **No credit cards**. **Map** p311 M14.
Visit Vi Ses once and you'll wonder how you've done
without a shop like this all your life. Whether it's for
bottles, clothes, hair or nails, Vi Ses, which is run by
the Danish Association for the Blind, has the brush
for you – in fact, it has a whole wall of them. Great
for obsessive compulsives with a cleaning complex.

Second-hand

Utopia

*Baggesensgade 18, Nørrebro (35 36 61 67). Bus 4E,
5, 16, 350S.* **Open** noon-5.30pm Tue-Fri; 11am-7pm
Sat; closed Mon, Sun. **Map** p119/p306 K10.
A homey shop with the vibe of a 1970s suburban liv-
ing room. Utopia has some good finds in '50s to '70s
Danish household goods and furniture.

Fashion

Budget

Hennes & Mauritz

Amagertorv 23 (33 73 70 90). **Open** 10am-6pm
Mon-Thur; 10am-7pm Fri; 10am-1pm Sat; closed Sun.
Credit AmEx, DC, MC, V. **Map** p311 N14.
With two gargantuan branches on Strøget alone,
H&M is undoubtedly the king of the Danish high
street, selling reasonably fashionable casualwear
and accessories for women and men. Bargains
abound at H&M: it's great for simple stuff like T-
shirts, shirts, jeans and underwear. The Big is
Beautiful corner at Amagertorv 23 is one of the only
collections of larger sizes for women on Strøget.
Branches: Cityarkaden, Østergade 32-34, Strøget
(33 48 31 00); Kultorvet, Købmagergade 69 (33 36 84
84); Metropol, Frederiksberggade 16 (33 14 90 00);
Amagercentret 115 (32 57 03 12); Frederiksberg
Centret, Falkoner Allé 21 (38 16 00 70).

Indiska

Amagertorv 33, Strøget (33 91 20 00). **Open** 10am-
6pm Mon-Thur; 10am-7pm Fri; 10am-5pm Sat; closed
Sun. **Credit** AmEx, DC, MC, V. **Map** p311 N14.
This century-old Swedish company, carrying mainly Indian-made goods, has inexpensive women's
clothes in two styles: plain and hippy. You can also
find cheap, beautifully beaded jewellery and purses,
and house linens in gorgeous imported textiles.
Branch: Købmagergade 60 (33 91 07 03).

Children

Exit

Østergade 21, Strøget (33 14 70 15). **Open** 10am-
6pm Mon-Thur; 10am-7pm Fri; 10am-5pm Sat; closed
Sun. **Credit** AmEx, DC, MC, V. **Map** p311 M15.
A well-stocked children's clothes shop with the
emphasis on fashion rather than frugality.

Medusa's Børn

Torvegade 33 (32 96 07 90). **Open** 11am-6pm Mon-
Thur; 11am-7pm Fri; 10am-2pm Sat; closed Sun.
Credit DC, MC, V. **Map** p312 P16.
Indisputably adorable and stylish designer togs in
bright candy colours for babies and kids. Most of
the clothes are Danish-designed, with a few high
quality imports like Osh Kosh.

Pluto Børne Sko

Rosengården 12 (33 93 20 12). **Open** 10am-5.30pm
Mon-Fri; 10am-2pm Sat; closed Sun. **No credit
cards**. **Map** p311 M13.
If your child is beginning to notice the cut of your
Patrick Cox shoes or is casting envious glances at
your Manolo Blahniks it's time for a trip to Børne
Sko. For nascent foot fetishists this child's shoe
shop is hard to beat, offering trendy, stylish
footwear for kids whose parents are prepared to
cough up designer prices for something that will
have a practical life for about as long as a paper hat
in a monsoon.

Pure Baby

*Willemoesgade 4, Østerbro (35 55 11 62).
Bus 6, 14.* **Open** 10am-5.30pm Mon-Fri; 10am-2pm
Sat; closed Sun. **No credit cards**. **Map** p121 E15.
Stylish baby clothes, toys and bedding, all fashioned
from organic materials.

Søstjernen

*Østerbrogade 50, Østerbro (35 55 46 90/
www.sostjernen.com). Bus 6, 14.* **Open** 10am-
5.30pm Tue-Thur; 10am-6pm Fri; 10am-2pm
Sat; closed Mon, Sun. **No credit cards**.
Map p121 D13.
Danish-designed shoes for trendy tots.

Toddlers and Juniors

*Birkegade 1, Nørrebro (35 34 10 37). Bus 5, 16,
350S.* **Open** noon-5.30pm Mon-Thur; noon-6pm Fri;
10am-3pm Sat; closed Sun. **No credit cards**.
Map p119/p306 J10.
Toddlers and Juniors specialises in end-of-stock,
marked down kids' clothes, especially jeans, by the
trendy Italian streetwear label Diesel.

Clubwear/streetwear

For **Asfalt**, **Donn Ya Doll** and **Yvonne
Foght Designs**, *see pages 174-5.*

Flying A

Kronprinsensgade 5 (33 33 90 63). **Open** 10am-6pm
Mon-Wed; 10am-7pm Thur, Fri; 10am-5pm Sat;
closed Sun. **Credit** MC, V. **Map** p311 M14.
A funky and laid-back two-storey streetwear shop
that sells new and recycled clothing, fun accessories,
backpacks and lots of tight little T-shirts.

Funky D Tail

*Elmegade 17, Nørrebro (21 33 13 33). Bus 4E, 5,
16, 350S.* **Open** 11am-5.30pm Mon-Thur; 11am-6pm
Fri; 11am-4pm Sat; closed Sun. **No credit cards**.
Map p119/p306 J10.

Eat, Drink, Shop

Funky D Tails carries a wide range of spirited, imaginative club- and streetwear, from trendy styles to exclusive, one-of-a-kind creations.

Tracks/Tracks Surf & Snow

Larsbjørnsstræde 23 & 26 (33 33 83 83/www. tracks.dk). **Open** 10am-6pm Mon-Thur; 10am-7pm Fri; 9.30am-4pm Sat; closed Sun. **Credit** MC, V. **Map** p310 N12.

Tracks has two outlets opposite each other on funky Larsbjørnsstræde, each catering to two very different markets. One is the best shop in town for surf gear – hallucinogenically patterned short-sleeved shirts, T-shirts and clothing by the likes of Quicksilver and Rip Curl. The other store, meanwhile, caters to a slightly more mature market, selling pseudo-outdoors clothing (leather cowboy hats, wax jackets, suede trousers and so forth). Neither shop is especially good value.

Mid-range

Benetton

Købmagergade 19 (33 32 14 32/www.benetton.dk). **Open** 10am-6pm Mon-Thur; 10am-7pm Fri; 10am-3pm Sat; closed Sun. **Credit** AmEx, DC, MC, V. **Map** p311 M13-14.

The Italian clothing company's main Danish store is here on Købmagergade. A prize goes to anyone who can spot the difference between this and any other Benetton outlet in the world.

Blues

Østergade 59 (33 13 10 41). **Open** 10am-6pm Mon-Thur; 10am-7pm Fri; 10am-4pm Sat (until 5pm 1st & last Sat of month); closed Sun. **Credit** AmEx, DC, MC, V. **Map** p311 M15.

Sombre but stylish Danish-designed clothes for men and women. Customers tend to be in their mid 20s to mid 30s.

Blue Willi's

Frederiksberggade 32, Strøget (33 12 90 06). **Open** 10am-6pm Mon-Thur; 10am-7pm Fri; 10am-5pm Sat; closed Sun. **Credit** AmEx, DC, MC, V. **Map** p310 O12.

Pricey, pseudo yachtwear in the worst possible taste, for men and women.

Diesel

Købmagergade 19 (33 32 90 70/www.diesel.com). **Open** 10am-6pm Mon-Wed; 10am-7pm Thur, Fri; 10am-5pm Sat; closed Sun. **Credit** AmEx, DC, MC, V. **Map** p311 M13-14.

Diesel's vast, glass-fronted shop opened to great acclaim in 1999 and offers pretty much the same, slightly skewed streetwear that you can buy in any of its branches anywhere in the world. Still, it keeps the young 'uns happy.

Earth A Wear

Sankt Peders Stræde 37 (33 11 21 41). **Open** 10am-6pm Mon-Fri; 10am-2pm Sat; closed Sun. **Credit** MC, V. **Map** p310 N12.

This laid-back shop specialises in environmentally friendly casual wear for men, women and children. Mainly organically grown cotton and linen, with some wool and silk.

Golman

Frederiksberggade 40, Strøget (33 14 50 80/ www.golman.dk). **Open** 10am-6pm Mon-Thur; 10am-7pm Fri; 10am-5pm Sat; closed Sun. **Credit** AmEx, DC, MC, V. **Map** p310 O12.

Above par, contemporary high street fashion and casual wear for men, with middle-brow labels like YSL and Versace Jeans, plus better value own-brand items (trousers cost from 999kr) and Gucci-esque footwear. This modern, glass-fronted, three-storey store is at the Rådhuspladsen end of Strøget.

Hemp House

Larsbjørnsstræde 22 (33 91 41 71/ www.hempvalley.dk). **Open** 11am-5.30pm Mon-Thur; 11am-6.30pm Fri; 11am-3pm Sat; closed Sun. **Credit** MC, V. **Map** p310 N12.

All your hemp needs (except *that* one, try Christiania) are catered for in this fascinating store, which sells mainly clothing (you can buy a hemp suit, should you wish) but also some food products. The hemp is sourced in China but most products are finished in Denmark.

Invasion

Vestergade 10 (33 11 00 26). **Open** 11am-6pm Mon-Thur; 11am-7pm Fri, 10am-4pm Sat (until 5pm 1st Sat of month); closed Sun. **Credit** DC, MC, V. **Map** p310 O12.

Rugged outdoor types and surf dudes make for **Tracks** and **Tracks Surf & Snow**.

Eat, Drink, Shop

A seemingly endless fashion store, with startling red floors and minimal white walls, where even the most confident fashion victim might feel a pang of self-consciousness. Invasion has a huge stock of painfully trendy clothes that only skinny teenagers can get away with, but more often than not only the over-20s can afford.

Inwear/Matinique

Østergade 27, Strøget (32 66 77 10/33 14 20 41/ www.inwear.com). Open 10am-7pm Mon-Thur; 10am-8pm Fri; 10am-5pm Sat; closed Sun. Credit AmEx, DC, MC, V. Map p311 M15.

More modern Scandinavian twentysomethings' clothing. InWear (for women) and Matinque, upstairs (for men), could be thought of as kind of a bland version of Sand (*see p172*), but prices are often significantly lower.

Monsoon

Amagertorv 16, Strøget (33 14 31 31). Open 10am-6pm Mon-Thur; 10am-7pm Fri; 10am-5pm Sat; closed Sun. Credit AmEx, DC, MC, V. Map p311 N14.

British chain of something-for-everyone womenswear; colourful clothes and accessories.

Noa Noa

Østergade 16, Strøget (33 13 06 08). Open 10am-6pm Mon-Fri; 10am-5pm Sat; closed Sun. Credit AmEx, DC, MC, V. Map p311 M15.

This popular Danish chain puts comfort first: loose-fitting, colourful women's casual wear in body-friendly fabrics.
Branches: Købmagergade 5 (33 14 08 57); Larsbjørnsstræde 16 (33 14 23 02).

Part II

Købmagergade 42 (33 11 55 25). Open 10am-7pm Mon-Fri; 10am-5pm Sat; closed Sun. Credit AmEx, DC, MC, V. Map p311 M13-14.

Quality daywear for grown-ups; classic cuts and subdued colours for men and women.

Sweater Market

Frederiksberggade 15, Strøget (33 15 27 73/ www.sweatermarket.com). Open 9.30am-6pm Mon-Thur; 9.30am-7pm Fri; 9.30am-5pm Sat; closed Sun. Credit AmEx, DC, MC, V. Map p310 O12.

If the wind is whistling down Strøget, as it does most of the year, dive inside this wonderful woollens store where you'll find traditional Scandinavian jumpers that would deflect a Force 10 if required. This densely patterned chunky knitwear (which includes socks, gloves and scarves) from Norway, Iceland, the Faroe Islands and Denmark would hardly set the pulses racing on the catwalks of Milan, but try braving a Danish winter without it. Very popular with more mature tourists.

Vero Moda

Østergade 7-9, Strøget (33 15 88 15). Open 10am-6pm Mon-Thur; 10am-7pm Fri; 10am-4pm Sat; closed Sun. Credit AmEx, DC, MC, V. Map p311 M15.

This classic Danish dayware collection shares the store with its streetier little-sister label ONLY.

Designer

Aña

Sankt Peders Stræde 25 (33 13 43 13). Open 11am-6pm Mon-Thur; 11am-7pm Fri; 11am-3pm Sat; closed Sun. Credit DC, MC, V. Map p310 N12.

Smart, stylish women's daywear in delicious fabrics and colours, at surprisingly good prices.

Birger Christensen

Ny Østergade (33 11 55 55). Open 10am-6pm Mon-Thur; 10am-7pm Fri; 10am-4pm Sat; closed Sun. Credit DC, MC, V. Map p311 M15.

A beautiful store with beautiful clothes, Birger Christensen stocks a range of top designer names, including Gaultier, Prada, Chanel and Reiss. Expect to pay a little more than you would in London or New York, however.

Bruuns Bazaar

Kronprinsensgade 8 & 9 (33 32 19 99/69/ www.bruunsbazaar.com). Open 10am-6pm Mon-Thur; 10am-7pm Fri; 10am-4pm Sat (until 5pm 1st & last Sat of month); closed Sun. Credit AmEx, DC, MC, V. Map p311 M14.

Set up by the two brothers Bruun in the mid '90s, Bruuns Bazaar quickly established itself as a label to be reckoned with, not only in Denmark, but also on the Paris catwalks. Its mainstays are creative but wearable designs in attractive colours and top-of-the-range fabrics; close-fitting, simple but effortlessly stylish in a uniquely Scandinavian way. If you pass a late twentysomething on the street in Copenhagen and find yourself admiring what he or she is wearing, chances are it's from Bruuns Bazaar. The shop also stocks costly labels like Gucci (it's the only Gucci menswear stockist in Denmark) and Ann Demeulemeester.

Cerutti

Østergade 17-19, Strøget (33 91 00 23). Open 10am-6pm Mon-Thur; 10am-7pm Fri; 10am-4pm Sat; closed Sun. Credit AmEx, DC, MC, V. Map p311 M15.

The only Danish outlet for the perenially-stylish Italian clothes designer often receives new collections earlier than London stores. As you'd expect, the stock is mainly men's suits, but you will find some womenswear in the basement. Prices are on a par with London.

Companys

Frederiksberggade 24, Strøget (33 11 35 55). Open 10am-7pm Mon-Thur; 10am-8pm Fri; 10am-5pm Sat; closed Sun. Credit AmEx, DC, MC, V. Map p310 O12.

In Wear, Paul and Joe, Diesel, Part II and Bruuns Bazaar can all be found under one roof at this one-stop shop for label-hounds. Prices are roughly the same as in the individual boutiques and shopping here will save you legwork. The dingy bargain basement (*kældershop*) has some spectacular reductions on last season's leftovers.

Effortless Danish style from **Fillipa K**.

Fillipa K

Ny Østergade 13 (33 93 80 00). **Open** 11am-6pm
Mon-Thur; 11am-7pm Fri; 10am-4pm Sat; closed Sun.
Credit DC, MC, V. **Map** p311 M15.
Fillipa Kihlborg's low-profile, minimalist store is a
honeypot for Copenhagen's style-conscious twentysomethings. This Swedish designer has a knack
for creating cool, understated clothes with a distinct,
but internationally-relevant, Scandinavian style that
many other Copenhagen designers have been quick
to pick up on. Great for something subtly different
to take back home.

Frankk's Darling

Købmagergade 40 (33 33 73 24). **Open** 10am-6pm
Mon-Thur; 10am-7pm Fri; 10am-5pm Sat.
Credit AmEx, DC, MC, V. **Map** p311 M13-14.
Seductive and playful women's casual and dressy
clothes at reasonable prices. Asian-inspired fabrics
and designs dominate the collection: beaded fringes,
embroidered details, sheer layers and sequins.
Highly recommended.

Gianni Versace

Østergade 15, Strøget (33 33 83 81). **Open**
10am-5.30pm Mon-Thur; 10am-6.30pm Fri; 10am-
4pm Sat; closed Sun. **Credit** AmEx, DC, MC, V.
Map p311 M15.
The usual flashy, decadent men's and women's gear
(couture and first line). Hard to believe, but it's often
substantially cheaper than in Italy.

Hugo Boss

Kristen Bernikows Gade 4 (33 93 13 49).
Open 10am-6pm Mon-Thur; 10am-7pm Fri; 10am-
4pm Sat; closed Sun. **Credit** AmEx, DC, MC, V.
Map p311 M15.
Frequented by German (and Danish) businessmen,
this large Hugo Boss outlet is just a few seconds
away from Strøget.

Ivan Grundahl

Østergade 4, Strøget (33 93 40 10). **Open**
10am-6pm Mon-Thur; 10am-7pm Fri; 10am-
4pm Sat; closed Sun. **Credit** AmEx, DC, MC, V.
Map p311 M15.
Immaculate Scandinavian lines in neutral colours
for women. Some cuts are generous enough for
extra-tall builds.

Kenzo

Østergade 57, Strøget (33 14 01 10/www.kenzo.dk).
Open 10am-6pm Mon-Thur; 10am-7pm Fri; 10am-
4pm Sat; closed Sun. **Credit** AmEx, DC, MC, V.
Map p311 M15.
The recently-opened Danish branch of the distinctive Kenzo design house divides its stock 50/50
between the 'classic' lines and 'trend' lines. Prices
can often be slightly cheaper than in other countries,
with men's suits starting at 3,800kr, and women's at
4,200kr. Copenhagen's Gucci and Louis Vuitton
stores can be found nearby.

Mads Nørgaard

Amagertorv 13 & 15, Strøget (33 32 01 28).
Open 10am-6pm Mon-Thur; 10am-7pm Fri; 10am-
5pm Sat; closed Sun. **Credit** AmEx, DC, MC, V.
Map p311 N14.
A plethora of international designer labels – Prada,
Miu Miu, Dries Van Noten, John Smedley and
Carhartt – are the main attractions in this tidy men's
clothing store in the middle of Strøget, although
Mads also produce some excellent own-label cloth-
ing. Streetsmart women's jeans, T-shirts and dress-
es by Comme des Garcons, Diesel and Levi's,
amongst others, are held next door.

Masai

Esplanaden 14 (33 32 23 33). **Open** 10am-6pm
Mon-Thur; 10am-7pm Fri; 10am-2pm Sat; closed Sun.
Credit AmEx, DC, MC, V. **Map** p308 K16.
Masai stocks casual and formal women's clothing
in interesting textures and prints. The look is drapey
and elegant without being matronly and so is great
for statuesque proportions.
Branch: Grønnegade 3 (33 91 30 29).

Munthe plus Simonsen

Kronprinsensgade 11 (33 32 03 12). **Open** 10am-
6pm Mon-Thur; 10am-7pm Fri; 10am-4pm Sat; closed
Sun. **Credit** AmEx, DC, MC, V. **Map** p311 M14.
Reportedly the favourite shop of Danish supermodel
Helena Christensen, this expensive boutique stocks
fun, inspired designs in intriguing fabrics.

Sabine Poupinel

Kronprinsensgade 12 (33 14 44 34). **Open** 10am-
6pm Mon-Thur; 10am-7pm Fri; 10am-5pm Sat;
closed Sun. **Credit** V. **Map** p311 M14.

Stig P's cool casuals. *See p172.*

Eat, Drink, Shop

A small shop with gorgeous Danish designs for women and a slightly unorthodox approach (there's no sign outside and there are no price labels on the clothes). This might be because prices are pretty steep, but the clothes are hand-crafted and tailored for the individual customer.

Sand
Østergade 40, Strøget (33 14 21 21). **Open** 10am-7pm Mon-Thur; 10am-8pm Fri; 10am-5pm Sat; closed Sun. **Credit** AmEx, DC, MC, V. **Map** p311 M15.
Divine men's and women's clothes from this archetypal Copenhagen designer store. Sand's simple, elegant style is the epitome of modern Scandinavian clothing design, but it doesn't come cheap.

Sneaky Fox
Larsbjørnsstræde 15 (33 91 25 20). **Open** 11am-6pm Mon-Fri; 10am-4pm Sat; closed Sun. **Credit** AmEx, DC, MC, V. **Map** p310 N12.
Flirty, feminine party dresses and irresistible designer stockings, for trendy, well-heeled gals. Labels include Betsy Johnson, Patty Shelabarger and Bettina Bakdal.

Stig P
Kronprinsensgade 13 & 14 (33 14 42 16).
Open 10am-6pm Mon-Thur; 10am-7pm Fri; 10am-5pm Sat; closed Sun. **Credit** DC, MC, V.
Map p311 M14.
With women's and men's clothing outlets on opposite sides of Kronprinsensgade, Stig P dominates Denmark's trendiest street. In the menswear department you'll find names like Paul Smith, Birkenstock, Diesel and DICO rubbing alongside Stig P's highly desirable own-label products.

Storm
Elmegade 13, Nørrebro (35 36 00 79). **Open** 11am-5.30pm Mon-Thur; 11am-7pm Fri; 10am-3pm Sat; closed Sun. **Credit** AmEx, DC, MC, V. **Map** p306 J10.
High-end men's casual wear: classic to sporty cuts with occasional designer flourishes. Levi's Red, Dirk Schönberger and Burberry are just some of the labels stocked here.

Fetish & erotic

Lust
Mikkel Bryggers Gade 3A (33 33 01 10/www.lust.dk).
Open 11am-7pm Mon-Thur; 11am-10pm Fri; 11am-5pm Sat; closed Sun. **Credit** AmEx, DC, MC, V.
Map p310 O12.
When it opened in 1999, Sabine Elvstam-Johns and Rosa Lind, the two Swedish women behind this ground-breaking store, finally dragged Copenhagen's sex shop scene out of the dark ages where it had stuck since being thrust to world prominence in the '60s (*see p114* **This is hardcore**). The sleazy old stores still remain on Istedgade, of course, but it can only be a matter of time before more follow suit and mimic Lust's mainstream, high street, open-armed attitude. Lust welcomes all shapes, sizes

Spice up your life at **Lust**.

and sexual preferences, and its mission (to bring sensual and erotic products, clothing, magazines, videos, sex toys and DIY manuals to a wider audience) is well served by this still relatively discrete and self-assured shop just off Strøget. Check out the theme nights every Thursday.

Schwartz' Mode & Piercing Studio
Studiestræde 27 (33 32 33 03/www.schwartz-mode.com). **Open** 10am-6.30pm Mon-Thur; 10am-7pm Fri; 10am-4pm Sat; closed Sun. **Credit** AmEx, DC, MC, V. **Map** p310 N12.
A specialty S&M shop with heaps of leather and rubberwear, including top-notch Danish label Latexa. The 19th-century drawing room décor (check out the changing area) is leagues above anything on seedy Istedgade, as is the quality and, unfortunately, the prices.

Lingerie

Illum and **Magasin du Nord** (*see pages 158 and 159*) both have large lingerie departments whose range takes in designer labels such as Calvin Klein and DKNY.

Donna i
Østergade 59, Strøget (33 93 29 13).
Open 10am-6pm Mon-Fri; 10am-4pm Sat; closed Sun. **Map** p311 M15.
Expensive Italian unmentionables.

Wunderwear

Vimmelskaftet 49, Strøget (33 14 72 20).
Open *May-Aug* 10am-7pm Mon-Fri; 10am-5pm Sat;
closed Sun. *Sept-Apr* 10am-6pm Mon-Thur; 10am-
7pm Fri; 10am-5pm Sat; closed Sun. **Credit** AmEx,
DC, MC, V. **Map** p311 N13.
Popular underwear chain dealing in the lacy basics.

Second-hand

The best second-hand pickings are in the 'Latin
Quarter', north of Strøget, especially on and
around Studiestræde.

Kbh K

Studiestræde 32B (33 33 03 60). **Open** 11am-6pm
Mon-Thur; 11am-7pm Fri; 11am-4pm Sat; closed Sun.
Credit DC, MC, V. **Map** p310 N12.
Because of its location in a courtyard you could easily miss Kbh K, but you really shouldn't. Most of the
stock is carefully chosen and cleaned men's and
women's second-hand kit ('60s to '80s), but there are
also some new designer clothes, bags and shoes, and
some funky homewares thrown into the mix. Comfy
chairs, magazines, good music and up-to-date club
flyers are provided for customers, which makes this
a great place to stop during a day of shopping in the
'Latin Quarter'.

Kitsch Bitch

Læderstræde 30 (33 13 63 13). **Open** noon-6pm
Mon-Fri; 11am-4pm Sat; closed Sun. **Credit** MC, V.
Map p311 N14.
A fabulous shop loaded with '50s, '60s and '70s vin-
tage fashion (including pieces by Danish designers),
kitschy Swedish kitchenwares and classic '70s
Holmegaard hanging lamps.

The Second Way

Studiestræde 11 (no phone). **Open** varies.
No credit cards. **Map** p310 N12.
With old clothes piled almost to the ceiling and
touches of retro-kitsch decor, this shop is like the
overcrowded attic of somebody's cool aunt. You can
sometimes liberate good finds from the tightly
packed racks, but only after some digging.

UFF

Vestergade 14 (33 32 34 31). **Open** noon-6pm Mon-
Thur; noon-7pm Fri; noon-4pm Sat; closed Sun.
No credit cards. **Map** p310 O12.
Spacious volunteer-staffed charity shop selling
donated hand-me-downs. There are a few branches,
but the Vestergade store gets all the funkiest goods.
Vintage winter coats are a specialty.

Suit hire

Amorin

Vesterbrogade 45, 1st floor, Vesterbro (31 21 20 21/
www.amorin.dk). Bus 6, 28. **Open** 9am-5.30pm Mon-
Fri; 9am-1pm Sat; closed Sun. **Credit** DC.
Map p111 P9.

Formalwear and costume rentals; Amorin's range
covers everything from tuxes, tails and evening
dresses, to gorillas, pirates and French maids.

Tailors

Bellini

Grønnegade 27 (33 11 01 06/www.bellinishirts.com).
Open 10.30am-5.30pm Tue-Thur; 10.30am-6.30pm
Fri; 10.30am-3pm Sat; closed Mon, Sun. **Credit** MC,
V. **Map** p311 M15.
Small, traditional Italian shirt makers, offering both
off the peg and tailored shirts and accessories. Made
to measure shirts cost from 800kr.

Unusual sizes

There are small sections of clothes in large sizes
at **Hennes & Mauritz** (*see page 167*) and
Magasin du Nord (*see page 159*).

Søstrene Nielsen

Christian IX' Gade 1 (33 16 30 08). **Open** 11am-
6pm Mon-Thur; 11am-7pm Fri; 10am-2pm Sat;
closed Sun. **Credit** DC, MC, V. **Map** p311 M14.
The only shop in the city centre devoted to large-
sized women's fashion. The impressive selection
takes in inexpensive jeans and T-shirts, higher-end
formalwear and designer pieces (Denmark's
Benedikte Utzon is a favourite), as well as bathing
suits, underwear and designer accessories.

Fashion accessories

Bags

Neye

Vimmelskaftet 28, Strøget (33 69 28 33/
www.neye.dk). **Open** 10am-6pm Mon-Thur; 10am-7pm
Fri; 10am-4pm Sat; closed Sun. **Credit** AmEx, DC,
MC, V. **Map** p311 N13.
The city's largest bag shop, with bags, handbags,
luggage and those most Copenhagen-ish of accessories, rucksacks, to suit most mainstream tastes.
Well-known brands include Samsonite (suitcases
from 799kr), Carlton and Florentine manufacturer
the Bridge, who make highly desirable leather brief-
cases and satchels.

Hats

Chapeaux Petitgas

Købmagergade 5 (33 13 62 70). **Open** 10am-5.30pm
Mon-Thur; 10am-6pm Fri; 10am-2pm Sat; closed Sun.
Credit AmEx, DC, MC, V. **Map** p311 M13/14.
Nothing much has changed over the 144 years that
Chapeaux Petitgas has been furnishing the heads of
Copenhagen's gentlemen. But that, of course, is all
part of its old-fashioned charm and part of the rea-
son why it is the perfect place to pick up a quality
Panama or old duffer's flat cap.

Eat, Drink, Shop

Q-Hats

Ny Adelgade 4 (33 33 83 28). **Open** 10.30am-5.30pm
Mon-Fri; 10.30am-2pm Sat; closed Sun. **Credit** DC,
MC, V. **Map** p311 M15.
Women's hats, from dressy ladies' numbers to cloth
caps, in a range of prices.

Samarkand

Dag Hammarskjölds Allé 32 (35 38 14 45). **Open**
Sept-Mar noon-6pm Mon-Sat; closed Sun. *Apr-Aug*
by appointment. **No credit cards**. **Map** p307 G14.
Jane Eberlein's boutique/workshop is rarely open in
the summer, but it's worth taking a peek in her display window, especially if you're stopping for a coffee at nearby Amokka (*see p154 and p178*). Eberlein
makes only 100 luxurious Mongolian-look embroidered silk and fur hats a year, and Queen Silvia of
Sweden and Hillary Clinton are among the well-to-
do heads she has covered.

Susanne Juul

Store Kongensgade 14 (33 32 25 22). **Open** 11am-
5.30pm Tue-Thur; 11am-6pm Fri; 10am-2pm Sat;
closed Mon, Sun. **No credit cards**. **Map** p308 L16.
Gorgeous handmade women's headgear. Designs
range from Tibetan-inspired wool beanies to
impossibly wide-brimmed chic *chapeaux*. First-
class craftsmanship at prices lower than you
might expect.

Jewellery

Carré

Læderstræde 18 (33 12 92 18/www.carre.dk).
Open 11am-6pm Mon-Thur; 11am-7pm Fri; 10am-
4pm Sat; closed Sun. **Credit** MC, V. **Map** p311 N14.
Carré specialises in romantic, Victorian-inspired
sterling silver and gold-plated jewellery adorned

Sex street

An ambitious government-sponsored
urban renewal programme, coupled with
skyrocketing rents in the 'Latin Quarter'
(see page 68), has made the working class
neighbourhood of Vesterbro into an attractive
alternative for students and young designers,
who have recently started settling in
comfortably alongside the area's traditional
population of immigrants, prostitutes and
porn merchants.

Vesterbro is one of the fastest changing
neighbourhoods in the city, especially along
Istedgade, the core of Copenhagen's red
light district. Shortly after 1969, when
Denmark became the first country in the
world to legalise pornography (see page 114
This is hardcore), Istedgade was lined chock-
a-block with sex shops trying to keep up with
the steady influx of prurient tourists. But this
wave has been subsiding for some time in
the face of competition from the Internet,
along with other stores all over the city
(try buying a pack of cigarettes anywhere
in Copenhagen without brushing by a rack
of girlie mags).

The remaining sex shops are clustered
around the east end of the street close to
Central Station, and are still popular with
tourists (according to one shop assistant,
the Japanese browse but the Brits buy),
perhaps explaining the red light district's
otherwise puzzling abundance of tacky
souvenir shops selling cutesy porcelain
figurines. Despite attempts at improvement –
such as hiring attractive, well-scrubbed
young assistants – the sex shops still have

a pretty seedy atmosphere, which is hiked
up a notch to really seedy later at night
(most sex shops are open until 2am) when
the area's drug and prostitution trades
become more visible.

A little further west, past the hotels,
the middle section of the street supports
a considerable Middle Eastern and Asian
community. This lively patch is dominated
by busy shawarma takeaways, halal
butchers, Thai restaurants (**Bam-Gaw** is
excellent, see page 143) and low-end
'international import' shops packed with
household bric-a-brac.

From here to Enghave Plads, at the
western end, the newer face of the street
starts to become evident, particularly around
the ultra-hip **Bang & Jensen** café (see
page 151), where the furnishings and the
clientele's clothes seem to have been
plucked from the same cool retro boutique.
Trendy cafés and shops run by creative
young designers are opening all the time
along this stretch of Istedgade, and just
around the corner on Enghavevej is one of
Copenhagen's most popular night spots,
Vega (see page 216).

This latter group is the fastest growing in
the neighbourhood and represents its future,
perhaps a mixed blessing for those drawn
to the street in the first place by the cheap
rents and urban grit. It will be a while before
Istedgade is entirely transformed – if it is
ever – and at the moment it's one of those
fascinating streets that wears its history
on its sleeve.

with semi-precious stones and freshwater pearls. The well-crafted, almost fairy tale-like designs are fit for a princess (especially the tiaras), but without the hefty price tag.

Creol

Sankt Peders Stræde 33 (33 15 30 03). **Open** 10am-6pm Mon-Thur; 10am-7pm Fri; 10am-4pm Sat; closed Sun. **Credit** DC, MC, V. **Map** p310 N12.
Classic silver jewellery with an exotic flavour. A wide range of beautiful but inexpensive designs, most featuring semi-precious stones. High quality craftsmanship from Indonesia, India and Nepal.

Ravhuset

Ravhuset, Kongens Nytorv 2 (33 11 67 00).
Open *Apr, May, Sept-Dec* 10am-6pm daily. *June-Aug* 10am-8pm daily. *Jan-Mar* 10am-6pm Mon-Sat; closed Sun. **Credit** AmEx, DC, MC, V. **Map** p311 M15.

This amber shop is a landmark at the west end of Nyhavn on the corner of Kongens Nytorv. Together with its sister branch on Strøget, Ravhuset sells a range of Baltic amber products: mainly jewellery, made from the petrified resin from trees that died 35-55 million years ago. You can also buy examples of amber with prehistoric insects preserved inside, for a price. There's a small museum upstairs (*see p80*).

tactus 2

Kronprinsensgade 12 (33 15 30 02).
Open 11am-5.30pm Mon-Thur; 11am-7pm Fri; 11am-3pm Sat; closed Sun. **Credit** AmEx, DC, MC, V. **Map** p311 M14.
Contemporary elegance and creativity rule at this exclusive little shop/gallery, displaying carefully selected gold and silver jewellery by Danish and international designers.

Asfalt

Istedgade 83, Vesterbro (33 22 51 74/ www.asfalt-online.dk). Bus 16. **Open** 11am-6pm Mon-Thur; 11am-7pm Fri; 11am-3pm Sat; closed Sun. **No credit cards**. **Map** p111 R9.
Two young designers with their own lines of men's and (mostly) women's considerably priced street- and clubwear, featuring fun prints and fresh combinations of textures and colours.

Donn Ya Doll

Istedgade 55, Vesterbro (32 22 66 35/ www.donnyadoll.dk). Bus 16. **Open** 11am-6pm Mon-Fri, 11am-3pm Sat; closed Sun. **No credit cards**. **Map** p111 R9.
The most playful clubwear shop in town and a must for devotees of sci-fi kitsch. Labels like Cyberdog hang alongside original designs – Barbarella-inspired men's and women's clubwear in silver, neon and transparent ultra-synthetic fabrics – created by the two twenty-something owners. It also stocks a wide range of UFO-themed toys and accessories, such as alien-head frisbees, R2D2 phones and 3-D effect pencil cases.

Ichinen Design

Istedgade 59, Vesterbro (33 79 47 17/ www.ichinendesign.com). Bus 16. **Open** 11am-6pm Mon-Thur; 11am-7pm Fri; 11am-3pm Sat; closed Sun. **No credit cards**. **Map** p111 R9.
Inviting designer beanbag chairs and hip floor-to-ceiling lamps are the mainstay of this relaxed little shop, which also does a side in funky imported T-shirts.

Plan E

Istedgade 30, Vesterbro (33 21 99 30).
Bus 16. **Open** 10am-2am Mon-Sat; noon-2pm Sun. **Credit** MC, V.
Map p310 Q10.
This sex shop is typical of what you'll find in the area: white, fluorescent-lit rooms filled with raunchy magazines, videos, fetish clothes and sex toys. A cooler filled with lube by the entrance adds to the supermarket atmosphere. Popular spot for earnest-looking browsers and wide-mouthed gawkers alike.

Thailandsk Supermarked

Istedgade 134, Vesterbro (33 79 43 45).
Bus 16. **Open** 10am-7pm Mon-Fri; 10am-6pm Sat; noon-5pm Sun. **No credit cards**.
Map p111 R9.
A bright, spacious supermarket that sells a wide variety of fresh and frozen Thai and oriental foods, spices, curry pastes, sweetmeats and wines, as well as some huge ceramic vases.

Yvonne Foght Designs

Istedgade 44, Vesterbro (33 79 16 40/ www.subwave-design.dk). Bus 16.
Open noon-5.30pm Mon-Thur; noon-7pm Fri; 11am-3pm Sat; closed Sun. **No credit cards**.
Map p310 Q10.
This hip shop stock techno, fetish and rococo clubwear and lingerie, with some original biker-inspired leatherwear. Yvonne, sensing a trend, recently relocated from the 'Latin Quarter'.

Eat, Drink, Shop

Shoes

A Pair
Ny Østergade 3 (33 91 99 20/www.apair.dk).
Open 10am-6pm Mon-Thur; 10am-7pm Fri; 10am-4pm Sat; closed Sun. **Credit** AmEx, DC, MC, V.
Map p311 M15.
A fun, trendy collection of mostly French and Italian brands, just half a block from Strøget. Gianni Barbato and Plein Sud are just two of the labels you might find here.

Billing/Bally
Østergade 55, Strøget (33 12 35 11/www.billing.dk).
Open 10am-6pm Mon-Wed; 10am-7pm Thur, Fri; 10am-5pm Sat; closed Sun. **Credit** AmEx, DC, MC, V. **Map** p311 M15.
This chain gets top marks for selection: dressy, casual and sporty footware for men, women and kids.

Bruno & Joel
Store Strandstræde 9 (33 13 90 90/www.bruno-joel.com). **Open** 11am-6pm Mon-Thur; 11am-7pm Fri; 10am-4pm Sat; closed Sun. **Credit** AmEx, DC, MC, V. **Map** p312 M16.
Unbelievably chic Danish-designed, Italian-made women's foot candy for true shoe junkies.
Branch: Kronprinsensgade 2 (33 13 87 78).

Ecco
Frederiksberggade 1, Strøget (33 13 47 58/ www.ecco.com). **Open** 9am-5.30pm Mon-Thur; 9am-7pm Fri; 9am-2pm Sat; closed Sun. **Credit** AmEx, DC, MC, V. **Map** p310 O12.
The flagship store for this most sensible of Danish shoe manufacturers, who specialise in prosaic but extremely comfortable and durable sandals (from 549kr).
Branch: Vimmelskaftet 39, Strøget (33 14 43 80).

Frogeye
Blågårdsgade 2a, Nørrebro (35 37 01 39). Bus 5, 16, 7E, 350S. **Open** 10am-6pm Mon-Thur; 10am-7pm Fri; 10am-4pm Sat; closed Sun. **No credit cards** .
Map p119/p306 K10.
A trendy yet easygoing shop with stylish labels such as Camper and Trippen, and Pom d'Api for kids.

Lædersmeden
Vestergade 15 (33 11 60 48). **Open** 11am-6pm Mon-Thur; 11am-7pm Fri; 11am-3pm Sat; closed Sun.
No credit cards. Map p310 O12.
Lædersmeden has been selling high quality Danish-designed cowboy boots in the 'Latin Quarter' for 23 years, and is a favourite stop for rock stars after their regular fix of hand-crafted leather and snakeskin. It also carries belts, purses, sandals and walking shoes.

Sut Sko
Birkegade 7, Nørrebro (35 39 68 86). Bus 3, 5, 16, 7E. **Open** 10am-5.30pm Mon-Fri; 10am-1pm Sat; closed Sun. **No credit cards. Map** p119/p306 J10.
In this modest boutique, Tom Larsen sells his simple handmade slippers, crafted out of discarded fabric and carpet scraps – a practice that his father

started after World War II when materials were scarce. Now the inexpensive rough-look slippers have a sort of recycled eco-caché, and have been special-ordered for performances at Det Kongelige Theater, as well for a Bruuns Bazaar catwalk show.

Watches

Gullacksen Ure
Frederiksberggade 8, Strøget (33 13 17 64).
Open 10am-6pm Mon-Thur; 10am-7pm Fri; 10am-3pm Sat; closed Sun. **Credit** AmEx, DC, MC, V.
Map p310 O12.
A superior high street watch shop that stocks CK, Tag Heuer and Adidas watches as well as more formal wrist wear by Seiko and Omega. The current owner, Niels Gullacksen, is the third generation from this family of watchmakers and he prides himself on the attentive service offered in what was formerly his father's store.

Flowers

There are lots of impromptu outdoor flower stalls around the city centre all summer long. For price and selection **Kurt Kirkeby Blomster** (8am-6pm Mon-Thur; 8am-7pm Fri; 7.30am-3.30pm Sat; closed Sun), in front of Den Danske Bank on Købmagergade across from Nørreport Station, is as good as it gets.

Paradis Blomster
Overgaden Oven Vandet 48 (32 54 35 51).
Open 10am-6pm Mon-Fri; 10am-3pm Sat; 11am-3pm Sun. **No credit cards**.
Map p312 P17.
Located beside a charming boat-filled canal and around the corner from the spiral tower of Vor Frelsers Kirke (*see p73*), Paradis carries a luxurious and fragrant assortment of gorgeous flowers. The owners also started a gift shop next door worth peeking into: it has a beachy sand-covered floor and assorted colourful kitschy knick-knacks like beaded candelabras and Bodum cozies.

Tage Andersen
Ny Adelgade 12 (33 93 09 13). **Open** 10am-5pm Mon-Thur; 10am-7pm Fri; 10am-7pm Sat; closed Sun.
Credit AmEx, MC, V. **Map** p311 M15.
To call Tage Andersen a florist is rather like calling the *QE2* a boat; the term just isn't quite grand enough for what is one of Copenhagen's most astonishing, and it has to be said, pretentious, shops (you've got to laugh at the audacity of trying to charge 40kr entry fee). Opulent and over the top, Andersen's is part-florist, part-garden gallery, selling sculptures, ironwork, bonsai and flower arrangements in its labyrinthine emporium. It's worth a visit just to wander among the caged tropical birds and ornate flower sculptures, then out to the courtyard gazebo to the rear. Keep your Beta Blockers to hand when asking the prices though.

The artery-clogging pâtisserie heaven of **Kransekagehuset**.

Food & drink

For the various food and drink shops along Værndedamsvej ('food street') in Vesterbro, *see page 180* **Food street**.

Bakeries & pâtisseries

For **Marie-France**, *see page 181* **Food street**.

Kransekagehuset

Ny Østergade 9 (33 13 19 02). **Open** 8am-6pm Mon-Fri; 9am-4pm Sat; closed Sun. **No credit cards.** **Map** p311 M15.
In the heart of fashionable Ny Østergade lies this marvellous pâtisserie with an on-site bakery. If you adore marzipan, bring a suitcase with you as the fresh confections Kransekagehuset's lovely ladies prepare are the probably the best in town. Kransekagehuset's speciality is the eponymous kransekage, an indulgent special occasion (usually wedding) cake made from up to 21 thin hoops of marzipan-laden sponge. It also sells homemade Italian ice-cream, and excellent freshly baked bread, of course.

Sattvabageriet

Frederiksborggade 29 (33 14 62 26). **Open** 6.30am-6pm Mon-Fri; 6.30am-4pm Sat, Sun. **No credit cards.**
One of the few organic bakeries that goes beyond selling bread. It also does delicious pastries and cakes, as well as a few vegan and wheat-free goodies. **Branch**: Istedgade 98 (33 24 66 02).

Butchers

Marburger Charcuterie

Cityarkaden, Østergade, Strøget (33 13 57 67). **Open** 10am-5.30pm Mon-Thur; 10am-7pm Fri; 10am-2pm Sat; closed Sun. **Credit** DC, MC, V. **Map** p311 M15.
Great little kiosk in the Cityarkadan (where you'll also find a large bakers and Super Brogsen supermarket), specialising in sausages and salamis from around Europe. The place to come for that souvenir Danish salami.

Cheese

Czar

Købmagergade 32 (33 12 94 03/www.aok.dk). **Open** 10am-6pm Mon-Thur; 10am-7pm Fri; 9am-3pm Sat; closed Sun. **Credit** MC, V. **Map** p311 M13.
Denmark's largest cheese shop by a long chalk, the odours from Czar's open-fronted shop beckon cheese-aholics from hundreds of metres away on Købmagergade. Though it stocks the full range of Danish Danbo cheeses (an impressive 400 different types in all, and the store's most popular line), you will also find rare and not-so-rare cheeses from across Europe (including a decent range of British cheeses), as well as some meats, sausages and wines in the small delicatessen department. Czar was founded in 1885, and is the oldest cheese firm in the country.

Chocolate & confectioners

In Copenhagen you're never more than a few steps away from some truly delectable treats. For a quick fix, pop into any sweetshop or newsagent and seek out the Danish brand Toms – a superior bar of chocolate. More discerning chocophiles should consider heading west and trekking from **Bojesen** (*see p180* **Food street**) to **Frederiksberg Chokolade** via Frederiksberg Allé – the grandest tree-lined boulevard in the city.

Chocoland

Nygade 24, Strøget (33 12 12 35). **Open** 10am-9pm Mon-Sat; noon-3pm Sun. **Credit** MC. V. **Map** p311 N13.
A tempting blend of connoisseur chocolates and mass-produced rubbish are on sale in this fab chocoholic's supermarket. At the posh end of the range there are the likes of cocoa-heavy Valrhona bars and indulgent fresh cream Belgian chocolates, as well as marzipan chocolates by Copenhagen-based Anthon Berg. But you'll also find traditional Danish liquorice (an acquired taste if ever there was one), Haribo candies, soft ice-cream and an extensive pick 'n' mix.

Eat, Drink, Shop

Unique shops

You won't find anything quite like the following anywhere else in the world:

Dansk Møbelkunst. Danish furniture design's greatest hits. See page 160.

Gubi. Super-cool furnishing and clothing store. See page 166.

Le Klint. The definitive Danish lamp shade shop. See page 166.

Kransekagehuset. One of Copenhagen's leading bakers; the European marzipan mountain starts here. See page 177.

Lust. Dragging Denmark's sex shop industry kicking and screaming into the 21st century. See page 172.

Munthe plus Simonsen. The doyen of Copenhagen fashion. See page 171.

Royal Copenhagen. The best in glassware, silverware, porcelain and home furnishings in four deluxe stores. See page 165.

Samarkand. Idiosyncratic hats by appointment to royalty, politicians and movie stars. See page 174.

Spunk & Co. Fascinating eclectic miscellany – from military memorabilia to Greenland shamanist talismans. See page 161.

Tage Andersen. Flower arranging as art, with an admission charge. Pretentious? Moi? See page 176.

Frederiksberg Chokolade

Frederiksberg Allé 64, Frederiksberg (33 22 36 35).
Bus 28. **Open** 11am-6pm Mon-Fri; 10am-2pm Sat; closed Sun. **No credit cards**.
Map p111 P6.
Unrepentant chocoholics can press their noses against the glass next door to watch Frederiksberg Chokolade's goods being made. For a sugar high of a truly Danish variety, try the frothy cream-filled chocolate dome known as a *flødebolle*. The shop also produces its own boiled sweets.

Sømods Bolcher

Nørregade 24 & 36 (33 12 60 46/www.soemods-bolcher.dk). **Open** 9.15am-5.30pm Mon-Fri; 10am-2pm Sat; closed Sun. **Credit** AmEx, DC, MC, V.
Map p310 M12.
There has been a traditional boiled candy factory and shop here on Nørregade (running north from Gammeltorv) since 1891. You can still watch the multicoloured sweets being made by the fourth generation of the Sømod family, before walking a little further down the street to purchase a bag from their small shop (17kr for 100g). Sweets are boiled nine times a day. A magical taste of old Copenhagen, with no additives or preservatives.

Coffee & tea

AC Perchs Thehandel

Kronprinsensgade 5 (33 15 35 62/www.perchs-the.dk). **Open** 9am-5.30pm Mon-Thur; 9am-7pm Fri; 9.30am-2.30pm Sat; closed Sun. **Credit** MC, V.
Map p311 M14.
Copenhagen's most venerated and venerable tea emporium dates back to 1834 and is currently in the hands of the sixth generation of the Perch family. A glorious, wood-panelled interior lined with old-fashioned jars of tea leaves invites you to stand and enjoy the fragrance as you pass by. Don't be intimidated by the almost reverential esteem in which locals hold Perchs; the staff are friendly and happy to help guide you through the complexities of their own blends and some of the more exotic leaves on offer (green tea is a current favourite). The Darjeeling First Flush is highly recommended.

Amokka

Dag Hammerskjolds Allé 38-40, Østerbro (35 25 35 35/www.amokka.com). Bus 4, 14. **Open** 10am-6pm Mon-Thur; 10am-7pm Fri; 10am-5pm Sat; noon-4pm Sun. **Credit** AmEx, DC, MC, V.
Map p307 G14.
Attached to a popular local coffeehouse with a large outdoor patio, this shop carries roasted-on-site Java and assorted paraphernalia imprinted with its designer coffee bean logo. *See also p154.*

Delicatessens

For **The Fisherman** and **Ostegården**, *see page 181* **Food street**.

Charcuterie Rita

Larsbjørnsstræde 22 (33 13 52 59).
Open 10am-6pm Mon-Thur; 10am-7pm Fri; 10am-4pm Sat; closed Sun. **No credit cards**.
Map p310 N12.
Scrummy, dreamy deli specialising in sausages and salamis from across Europe (and even some from South America), but also serving delicious sandwiches, cheeses and hard-to-find comestibles.

Shark House Deli

Blågårdsgade 3, Nørrebro (35 35 51 35). Bus 5, 16, 7E, 350S. **Open** 11am-9pm daily. **No credit cards**.
Map p119/p306 K10.
This hip Nørrebro spot does mostly takeaway food. Warm dishes, cold salads and sandwiches are made from a small, but considered, selection of Danish, French and Italian meats and cheeses. *See also p144.*

Fish

Højbro Fiskehus

Højbro Plads 19 (33 33 72 62/www.aok.dk).
Open 9am-5.30pm Mon-Thur; 9am-6pm Fri; 9am-
2pm Sat; closed Sun. *Sushi Bar* 11am-4pm Mon-Fri;
11am-2pm Sat; closed Sun. **Credit** AmEx, DC, MC,
V. **Map** p311 N14.
The last remnant of Gammel Strand's fishing heritage has cunningly moved with the times and now
has a great sushi bar out back. This ancient fishmongers, dating from 1876, hasn't entirely done
away with all of its traditions, however, and you can
still buy prime fresh and smoked fish and roe, as
well as delicious fish pies to take away.

Health & organic food

McGrail's Naturmagasin

Gammeltorv 6 (33 13 20 43). **Open** 10am-4pm Mon-
Thur; 10am-7pm Fri; 10am-4pm Sat; closed Sun.
Credit DC, MC, V. **Map** p311 M13.
This is the best centrally located source for a diverse
range of organic and natural health food products,
including vitamins, cosmetics, wine, detergents, tea,
coffee, rice, pasta and even single malt whisky.
McGrail's most popular range is Urtekram sham-
poos, lotions and cosmetics.

Solsikke

*Blågårdsgade 33, Nørrebro (35 39 53 11). Bus 5,
16, 7E, 359S.* **Open** 9am-6pm Mon-Thur; 9am-7pm
Fri; 9am-4pm Sat; closed Sun. **Credit** MC, V.
Map p119/p306 K10.
A neighbourhood shop with lots of organic food
including baked goods and wine.

International

For **Thailandske Supermarked**, *see
page 175* **Sex street**.

Americana Company

Peder Hvitfeldts Stræde 13 (33 93 78 70).
Open 10am-5.30pm Mon-Thur; 10am-7pm Fri;
10am-2pm Sat; closed Sun. **No credit cards.**
Map p311 M13.

This small subterranean mini-mart does a roaring
trade in root beer, cereals, peanut butter and candy
from across the Atlantic. It doesn't just sell to expats,
but also to Danes who've sampled the joys of
American cuisine while on holiday and, apparently,
those who want to try out weird products they've
seen in the movies. Aunt Jemima's pancake mix is
its number one draw, however.

Samson Kosher

Rørholmsgade 3 (33 13 00 77). **Open** 9.30am-
5.30pm Mon-Fri, Sun; closed Sat. **No credit cards**.
Map p307 J13.
This small kosher grocery store draws customers
from all over Scandinavia with its modest but varied selection of foods that includes meats, dairy
products and a good assortment of Israeli wines.

Scott's

*Peder Hvitfeldts Stræde 17 (33 91 25 04/
www.scotts.dk).* **Open** 10am-5.30pm Mon-Thur;
10am-7pm Fri; 10am-2pm Sat; closed Sun.
Credit AmEx, MC, V. **Map** p311 M13.
Who'd have thought there'd be a market for selling
British sweets, canned foods, pickles and chocolate
to Danes? But there is, and Brummie Phil Mason
has exploited it for four years from his small cellar
shop a few doors down from the Americana
Company (*see above*). In case you were wondering,
the Danes tend to go for marmalades and jams,
while Faroe Islanders can't get enough of
Tunnock's Tea Cakes. Finding that your salt 'n'
vinegar cold turkey is a little too much to endure?
Then come on down.

Special Købmanden

Cityarkadan, Østergade 32, Strøget (33 15 12 88).
Open 9.30am-6pm Mon-Thur; 9.30am-7pm Fri;
9.30am-4pm Sat; closed Sun. **Credit** DC, MC, V.
Map p311 M15.
A real gourmet's treasure trove that stocks a bewil-
dering range of culinary curios, from exotic teas
(a Pina Colada blend, among them), to flavoured
cooking oils, mustards, pickled vegetables, jams
and candy. One of the best sources for speciality
food products in the centre of town. Particularly
good for cake-making and decorating materials
and ingredients.

Vertical text: **Eat, Drink, Shop**

Kjær Sommerfeldt's venerable temple for oenophiles. *See p180.*

Food street

Danes share a collective memory of **Værnedamsvej** as a charming little street lined with family-owned butchers, fishmongers, greengrocers, cheese shops and bakeries, catering to happy housewives from another era. Even though the rise of the supermarket in the 1970s – that double-edged sword of convenience and unflattering lighting – changed the face of the street forever, this small patch of pavement connecting serene, middle-class Frederiksberg and hipper, livelier Vesterbro, is still known affectionately as 'the food street'.

Today, the street is mostly a mishmash of different businesses that seem to change every few months or so. However, a few of the shops from the food street's golden era have tenaciously hung on, most having changed hands at least once along the way. And many of the new owners were drawn by – and have a vested interested in preserving – Værnedamsvej's reputation for high-quality edibles and old-fashioned friendliness. It may be a little soon to start talk of a food street renaissance, but there's a whiff of something in the air, and it's not just old cheese.

Of course, where there's a reputation for good food, the French are not far behind. The francophone school Lycée Prins Henri (named after the queen's French-born husband) is right around the corner, and **Café Viggo** (see page 152) is the only place, besides the French Embassy and Amalienborg Slot, where one is guaranteed to hear the language of Molière spoken at any time of day or night.

Food street is a good place for a quick browse before lunch – both **Bojesen** and Café Viggo are excellent. Or pick up wine, cheese, meat, bread and chocolate along the way – turn the corner and walk a couple of blocks up tranquil, tree-lined Frederiksberg Allé, and find a good bench for a picnic. If you're on a bicycle, continue up Frederiksberg Allé to Frederiksberg Have (see page 113), a sprawling park complete with a former palace, gardens and a zoo.

Bojesen
Værnedamsvej 10 (33 31 70 55/ www.bojesen.dk). Bus 1, 6, 14, 28. **Open** 11am-midnight Mon-Fri; 10am-midnight Sat; 11am-11pm Sun. **Main courses** 55kr-195kr. **No credit cards. Map** p111 P8.
This trendy restaurant/café/takeaway is located in a renovated slaughterhouse, and offers a creative assortment of salads and sandwiches, and a counter full of expertly prepared takeaway dishes. Delectable handmade chocolates (although the more adventurous flavours like chilli and curry are, to say the least, an acquired taste) and French-style mousse desserts.

Wines, beers & spirits

For **Juuls Vinhandel**, *see page 181* **Food street**.

Højbro Vin
Frederiksborggade 6 (33 14 03 87). **Open** 10am-6pm Mon-Fri; 10am-2pm Sat; closed Sun. **Credit** DC, MC, V. **Map** p306 L12.
Large wine merchants that also sells a decent range of spirits and whiskies. Not quite Sommerfeldt's, though (*see below*).

Kjær Sommerfeldt
Gammel Mønt 4 (70 15 65 00/www.kjaer-sommerfeldt.dk). **Open** 10am-5.30pm Mon-Thur; 10am-6pm Fri; 10am-2pm Sat; closed Sun. **Credit** AmEx, DC, MC, V. **Map** p311 M14.
This is Denmark's (and that probably means Scandinavia's) leading wine and spirit importer and retailer. Worth a look, even for teetotallers, Sommerfeldt's wondrous wood-panelled interior is more library than off-licence – add a couple of Chesterfields and a waiter and you could be in a St

James's gentleman's club. Sommerfeldt's speciality is wines from Bordeaux, but it also has an entire (and really rather dazzling) room dedicated to single malts from Scotland and Ireland – the only one of its kind in the country – while another room houses collectors' wines, including a Château Margaux at 6,500kr. And if you expected the staff in this 125-year-old firm to be wine snobs, far from it – you'd be hard pushed to find friendlier experts than these.

Gifts & souvenirs

København Souvenir
Frederiksberggade 2, Strøget (33 14 74 00). **Open** *Jun-Aug* 9am-9pm daily. *Sept-Dec* 10am-7pm Mon-Fri; 10am-5pm Sat; 11am-4pm Sun. *Jan-Mar* 10am-7pm Mon-Fri; 10am-5pm Sat; closed Sun. *Apr, May* 10am-7pm Mon-Fri; 10am-6pm Sat; 11am-5pm Sun. **Credit** AmEx, DC, MC, V. **Map** p310 O12.
Your one-stop shop for cheesy souvenirs, such as dolls in national costume, plastic Viking helmets, T-shirts, mugs and replicas of the Little Mermaid. A good range of postcards, though.

Juuls Vinhandel

Værnedamsvej 15 (31 31 13 29/
www.juuls-vinhandel.dk). Bus 1, 6, 14, 28.
Open 9am-5.30pm Mon-Thur; 9am-7pm Fri;
9am-1pm Sat; closed Sun. **Credit** DC, MC, V.
Map p111 P8.
This is an old shop (est 1926) with a new
owner and a large selection of European
wines for any budget, French brandies,
cognacs, champagnes and a staggering
number of single malt Scotch whiskies.

The Fisherman

Værnedamsvej 10 (33 31 61 62/
www.thefisherman.dk). Bus 1, 6, 14, 28.
Open 9am-6pm Tue-Thur; 9am-7pm Fri; 8am-
2pm Sat; closed Mon, Sun. **No credit cards**.
Map p111 P8.
A newish shop combining traditional goods,
like marinated herring and Faroe Islands
smoked salmon, with more modern fare;
namely fresh takeaway sushi.

Kiwi & Mango

Værnedamsvej 5 (33 23 23 64/
www.vaernedamsvej.dk/kiwi_mango).
Bus 1, 6, 14, 28. **Open** 8am-7pm Mon-Fri;
9am-5pm Sat, Sun. **No credit cards**.
Map p111 P8.
A good place for inexpensive fruit and veg,
and Greek and Spanish olives.

Marie-France

Værnedamsvej 2 (33 24 72 46). Bus 1, 6,
14, 28. **Open** 5am-6pm Mon-Thur; 4am-6pm
Fri-Sun. **No credit cards**. **Map** p111 P8.
This bakery does both French and Danish
cakes, pastries and breads, as well as full-on
French croissants and quiches.

Ostegården

Værnedamsvej 4A (33 21 71 99). Bus 1, 6,
14, 28. **Open** 9am-7pm Mon-Thur; 9am-
7.30pm Fri; 9am-4pm Sat; 10am-3pm Sun.
Credit AmEx, DC, MC, V. **Map** p111 P8.
A friendly shop in an appealing courtyard,
Ostegården encourages (nay, insists upon)
sampling – a good chance to get experimental
with Danish cheese. If you want, you can have
your purchases made into a sandwich on the
spot. Wine tastings at weekends.

Slagteren pi Værnedamsvej

Værnedamsvej 14 (33 21 25 45). Bus 1, 6,
14, 28. **Open** 8.30am-5.30pm Mon-Fri;
8am-1pm Sat; closed Sun. **No credit cards**.
Map p111 P8.
Food street was also once known as 'the
butcher street' for its many meat markets.
This superior-quality shop, serving traditional
cuts, is the sole survivor of that era. Try the
homemade *rullepølse* (pork cold cuts swirled
with pepper) or *frikadeller* (meatballs).

Tibet Shop

Sankt Gertruds Stræde 8 (39 76 68 88). **Open** noon-
4pm Mon-Thur; noon-5pm Fri; 11am-2pm Sat; closed
Sun. **No credit cards**. **Map** p307 L13.
Incense, herbal products, clothing and books,
all from Tibet, are on sale in this small cellar shop
a couple of minutes' walk from Kultorvet. Good
for gifts.

Health & beauty

Beauty services

Bliss Copenhagen

Store Regnegade 3 (33 93 99 56/
www.blissonline.net). **Open** 11am-6pm Mon-Wed;
11am-8pm Thur; 11am-6pm Fri; 11am-3pm Sat;
closed Sun. **Credit** DC, MC, V. **Map** p311 M15.
Swish salon with everything from haircuts and man-
icures to cellulite and permanent make-up treatments. Nars cosmetics, bumble & bumble hair
products and Comme des Garçons fragrances are
just some of the treats at Bliss.

The Body Shop

Cityarkaden, Østergade 32, Strøget (33 12 56 60/
www.bodyshopdirect.dk). **Open** 10am-7am Mon-
Thur; 10am-8pm Fri; 10am-5pm Sat; noon-5pm Sun.
Credit AmEx, DC, MC, V. **Map** p311 M15.
Perenially popular British chain stocking ethically
produced, deliciously scented bodycare products
and accessories.

Green

Sankt Hans Torv 3, Nørrebro (35 37 68 37). Bus 3,
5, 16, 7E, 350S. **Open** 10am-6pm Mon-Fri; 8am-3pm
Sat; closed Sun. **No credit cards**. **Map** p306 H10.
A great-smelling shop with a selection of enormous
blocks of specially made soap, and all-natural body
and haircare products. It also does facials, massages
and aromatherapy in a down-to-earth, rather than
glam, salon atmosphere.

Nordic Center of Chinese Medicine

Sølvgade 85 (33 11 80 01). **Open** 10am-7pm Mon;
10am-6pm Tue-Thur; 10am-8pm Fri; closed Sat, Sun.
Credit MC, V. **Map** p307 J13.
Chinese teas, tonics and acupuncture treatments.

Eat, Drink, Shop

Market values

Copenhagen's outdoor markets are modest affairs compared to those of other countries, but can nonetheless yield generous bounty in terms of kitschy souvenirs and other garage-sale type finds. Some of them also provide a diverting pastime for early birds waiting for the rest of the city to wake up on a Saturday morning, and can be combined with visits to different parts of the city.

Blågårds Plads Eco-Market

Blågårds Plads, Nørrebro (35 35 35 40). Bus 4E, 5, 8, 12, 13, 16, 67, 68, 69. **Open** *May-Sept* 11am-4pm Sat. *Oct-Apr* closed. **Map** p119 K9.
True to the square's laid-back reputation, this outdoor market starts a little later than others in the city. Its mainstay is organic food, but you'll also find other assorted environmentally friendly products. The surrounding hip little shops and cafés make this area well worth visiting, but watch your timing: a lot of places start to lock up around 2pm on Saturday.

Det Blå Pakhus

Holmsbladsgade 113, Amager (32 95 17 07). Bus 2, 9, 19, 28, 73E, 350S. **Open** 10am-5pm Sat, Sun.
Inside an old warehouse, this vast three-floor indoor fleamarket has over 100 stalls selling everything from clothes to car parts. Nominal entrance fee (10kr).

Gammel Strand Bric-a-Brac Market

Gammel Strand (33 14 05 18). **Open** *May-Sept* 8am-4pm Fri, Sat; closed Mon-Thur, Sun. *Oct-Apr* closed. **Map** p311 N14.
This central bric-a-brac market runs along busy Gammel Strand and is at its best on sunny days when the street's popular cafés and restaurants are packed with diners. Merchandise is similar to that of Israels Plads market (see below) – silver, ceramics, glassware, furniture, clothes and a fair amount of junk.

Frederiksberg Rådhusplads

Smallgade, Frederiksberg (38 21 21 21). Bus 1, 14. **Open** *Apr-Oct* 8am-2pm Sat. *Nov-Mar* closed. **Map** p110 N3.
The market behind Frederiksberg town hall is strong on second-hand clothing, furniture and kitchen goods, with some organic produce available in front of the building. The nearby Frederiksberg Have is a gorgeous urban oasis of greenery, gardens and waterways, and boasts its own zoo and castle (see page 113).

Israels Plads

Israels Plads (44 99 41 11). **Open** *May-Oct* fruit & vegetables 8am-5pm Mon-Sat; closed Sun. *Antiques & bric-a-brac* 8am-5pm Sat; closed Mon-Fri, Sun. *Nov-Apr* closed. **Map** p306 L12.
This medium-sized market, just north of Nørreport Station, is the best place in town to buy fresh fruit and veg. The produce is invariably fresher and considerably cheaper than what's on offer in the city's sub-standard supermarkets, and there's a decent range of vendors (including a flower stall). On Saturdays, across the street, the city's myriad bric-a-brac and antiques traders set out their trestle table stalls for one of the most pleasurable browses in town. There's quite a decent selection of Royal Copenhagen Porcelain, nostalgic bric-a-brac, silver and glassware, as well as some furniture, clothing and the inevitable piles of random old tat. Extremely popular if the weather is fine.

Nørrebrogade

Nørrebrogade (35 35 01 73). Bus 4E, 5, 16, 350S. **Open** *Apr-Nov* 8am-2pm Sat; closed Mon-Fri, Sun. *Dec-Mar* closed. **Map** p119 H8.
'Copenhagen's longest market' is the dubious claim to fame of this rather rag-tag bunch of vendors lining the wall of Assistens Kirkegård every Saturday. The goods are solidly low-end, but worth a walk-by if you're planning an outing to Nørrebro's famous cemetery (see page 120) and topless sunbathing mecca.

Hair salons

The city is thick with hair salons, especially around the 'Latin Quarter'. You can usually just drop in on Monday to Thursday, but you'll have a hard time getting clipped on Friday or Saturday without an appointment.

Capaldi

Nørrebrogade 45, Nørrebro (35 39 36 39). **Open** 10am-6pm Mon-Wed; 10am-7pm Thur, Fri; 9am-2pm Sat; closed Sun. **No credit cards. Map** p306 J10.
This stylish salon has young, friendly staff who offer either far-out or classic cuts for men and women. **Branch**: Østerbrogade 142 (35 38 68 37).

Oz

Hyskenstræde 12 (33 15 63 14/www.oz-frisoer.dk).
Open 11am-7pm Mon-Fri; 10am-3pm Sat; closed
Sun. **No credit cards. Map** p311 N13.
Environmentally friendly salon that favours natural products over harsh chemicals.

X-Salonen

Sankt Peders Stræde 45 (33 32 32 76).
Open 1-8pm Mon-Sat; closed Sun. **No credit cards.**
Map p310 N12.
A den of industrial glam that does it all, especially extensions, make-up and styling wigs-as-art.

Pharmacies

Natur Medicin

Cityarkaden, Østergade 32, Strøget (33 32 75 60).
Open 9.30am-6pm Mon-Thur; 9.30am-7pm Fri;
9.30am-5pm Sat; closed Sun. **Credit** AmEx, DC, MC,
V. **Map** p311 M15.
Small cubbyhole in Cityarkadan selling a range of natural health products, including vitamins and herbal medicines.

Steno Apotek

Vesterbrogade 6C, Vesterbro (33 14 82 66).
Open 24 hours daily (ring the bell if the door is locked). **No credit cards. Map** p310 P11.
This 24-hour pharmacy (right across from Central Station) is the only place in town to go if your allergies flare up at 3am. There is a small surcharge (15kr) on late-night purchases.

Hobbies & crafts

Eva Rosenstand

Østergade 42, Strøget (33 13 29 40).
Open 10am-5.30pm Mon-Thur; 10am-6pm Fri;
10am-4pm Sat; closed Sun. **No credit cards.**
Map p311 M15.
Dedicated entirely to needlecraft, Rosenstand's large store is the place to stock up on your raw materials, or purchase finished embroidery 'art'.

Grønlændernes Hus

Løvstræde 6 (33 91 12 12/www.ghsdk.dk).
Open 10am-6pm Mon, Wed-Fri; 10am-7pm Tue;
closed Sat, Sun. **No credit cards.**
Map p311 M14.
The best source for Greenlandic handicrafts and information, this shop sells books, jewellery, art and – animal rights supporters be warned – seal-fur products from Denmark's northerly frontier.

Panduro Hobby

Nørre Farimagsgade 74 (33 15 44 21/www.pandurohobby.dk). **Open** 10am-6pm Mon-Thur; 10am-7pm
Fri; 10am-2pm Sat; closed Sun. **Credit** DC, MC, V.
Map p310 M11.
Copenhagen's one-stop hobby and craft shop caters for just about every handicraft and artistic genre imaginable, from flower arranging to oil painting and needlecraft. Ranged over three floors are depart-ments dedicated to sculpture, model-making and decoupage, while in the basement is an excellent children's section.

Stof 2000

Frederiksberggade 19, Strøget (33 32 27 37).
Open 9.30am-7pm Mon-Fri; 9.30-5pm Sat; closed
Sun. **Credit** MC, V. **Map** p310 O12.
The largest fabric and needlecraft supplier in the centre of the city. Here you'll find everything from up-to-the-minute exotic animal prints to plain cottons, as well as zips, cotton thread and any other materials that you might possibly require for sewing.

Teater Hjørnet

Vesterbrogade 175, Frederiksberg (33 22 22 47/
www.drama.suite.dk). Bus 6. **Open** 10am-5.30pm
Mon-Fri; 10am-2pm Sat; closed Sun. **Credit** MC, V.
Map p110 Q5.
Theatre make-up, wigs and masks for professionals or amateurs.

Markets

See page 182 **Market values.**

Musical instruments

Aage Jensen

Landemærket 27-29 (33 18 19 00/www.aage.dk).
Open 10am-5.30pm Mon-Thur; 10am-7pm Fri; 10am-
2pm Sat; closed Sun. **Credit** AmEx, DC, MC, V.
Map p307 L14.
With the Musikhistorisk Museet (*see p98*) and Sony's Danish HQ nearby, this area rivals Pisserenden for the title of Copenhagen's most musical quarter. It's here that you'll also find Aage Jensen, Denmark's largest musical instrument store. Guitars, keyboards and drums are, of course, the most significant ranges, but you'll find just about everything else that shakes, rattles and rolls.

Caravan

Blågårdsgade 17, Nørrebro (35 37 80 80).
Bus 5, 16, 7E, 350S. **Open** noon-6pm Mon-Fri;
closed Sat, Sun. **No credit cards.**
Map p119/p306 K10.
From simple wooden flutes and tambourines to beautifully crafted and enamel-inlaid Middle Eastern drums and strings. There's also a nice assortment of Turkish sazes (guitars).

Super Sound

Skindergade 27 (33 32 50 88). **Open** 10am-5.30pm
Mon-Thur; 10am-7pm Fri; 10am-2pm Sat; closed Sun.
Credit MC, V. **Map** p311 N13.
Another of Copenhagen's larger muso hangouts, Super Sound is in the centre of Pisserenden. Opposite you'll find **Guitar Bygger** (a basement dedicated solely to guitars) and, nearby, specialist drum, bass guitar and wind instrument stores. There are also countless dingy basement record shops to hand for inspiration.

Wood Sound

Blågårdsgade 16a, Nørrebro (35 35 74 13/
www.woodsound.dk). Bus 5, 16, 7E, 350S.
Open 11am-5.30pm Tue-Thur; 11am-7pm Fri; 10am-
2pm Sat; closed Mon, Sun. **No credit cards.**
Map p119/p306 K10.
Electric and acoustic guitars – new and vintage.
Most of the goods are imported from the US or
Spain, but the shop also carries its own handmade
brand, the Kehlet guitar.

Music shops

See also page 214.

Baden Baden

Larsbjørnsstræde 15 (33 15 40 30/
www.badenbaden.dk). **Open** 10am-6pm Mon-Thur;
10am-7pm Fri; 10am-3pm Sat; closed Sun.
Credit DC, MC, V. **Map** p310 N12.
Larger-than-usual cellar CD store with an exceptional electronic section and a wide range of second-
hand CDs. Strong on indie and dance music and very
good for recent chart stuff.

Bånd & Plade Centret

Vognmagergade 9 (33 11 22 51/www.sinfonia.dk).
Open 10am-5.30pm Mon-Thur; 10am-6pm Fri; 10am-
2pm Sat; closed Sun. **Credit** MC, V. **Map** p311 M14.
Unpretentious, mildly chaotic, but about as comprehensive as you'll get, this is Scandinavia's largest
classical music store. Stock is mainly new CDs
(priced from as little as 20kr), but there's also some
second-hand vinyl.

Danmusik

Vognmagergade 7 (33 15 78 88). **Open** 9.30am-
5.30pm Mon-Fri; 10am-1pm Sat; closed Sun.
Credit DC, MC, V. **Map** p311 M14.

Scandinavia's largest sheet-music shop stocks individual tunes – pieces as well as books – from easy
guitar pop-by-numbers to proper grown-up symphonies. This is the best source in the world for
works by Danish composers, from Nielsen to Aqua.

Guf

Nørrebrogade 51, Nørrebro (35 35 29 29/
www.gufmusik.dk). Bus 5, 16, 7E, 350S. **Open** 9am-
7pm Mon-Thur; 9am-8pm Fri; 9am-5pm Sat; noon-
5pm Sun. **Credit** DC, MC, V. **Map** p306 J10.
One of several enticing cellar CD shops in this area.
Guf sells mainly chart pop and jazz CDs, often at
more favourable prices than at the high street stores.
Branch: Vester Farimagsgade 4 (33 93 71 71).

Jazzcup

Gothersgade 107 (33 15 02 02/www.jazzcup.dk).
Open 10am-6pm Tue-Thur; 10am-7pm Fri; 10am-
2pm Sat; closed Mon, Sun. **Credit** MC, V.
Map p307 L14.
This stylish and friendly jazz CD store and café
opposite Rosenborg Slot is the perfect place to
peruse the racks and chew the fat with knowledgeable staff who are only too eager to help. But the
most convivial aspect of Jazzcup is that you can sip
a chilled beer or frothy coffee while contemplating
your new purchase. There's also live jazz each week.

Moskito Music World

Nørregade 38 (33 93 28 00). **Open** 11am-5.30pm
Mon-Thur; 11am-6pm Fri; 11am-2pm Sat; closed Sun.
No credit cards. Map p310 M12.
Since it opened six years ago Moskito has been the
country's leading world music CD store, covering
just about every style and trend of music from across
the planet, both contemporary and classic. Acid,
gospel, New Age, bhangra, cajun, salsa, reggae, you
name it, it's here. CDs cost from under 100kr.

Sunday shopping: the Swedish alternative

Shoppers anxious for a Sunday fix will have
a hard time in Copenhagen: the city's
Draconian closing laws are rigidly enforced.
Fortunately, the ultra-liberal Swedes have no
such rules, and thanks to the recently opened
Øresund Fixed Link (see page 246), the land
of Abba is more accessible than ever.

An attractive city (Sweden's third largest) of
about a quarter million people, **Malmö** has a
fully stocked pedestrian shopping street with
a robust range of goods.

The prices are similar to those found in
Copenhagen: in other words, not cheap.
However, if you're spending a little time in
Copenhagen, it's well worth the effort to see

a bit more of Scandinavia, not only to get a
better handle on the intricacies of Nordic
identity but also to get a taste of the
seductively musical Swedish language.

A lightweight shopping excursion across
the Øresund can also be combined with
redeeming cultural activities: the **Rooseum**
is a first-rate centre for contemporary
Scandinavian art; and the **Malmö Museum**,
housed in a 16th-century castle, features
exhibitions about the the city, which for much
of its history was under Danish rule.

For more details on Malmö's attractions,
including information on how to get there,
see page 234.

Music And Movie Shop (M&M)

Nygade 1-3, Strøget (33 12 43 50). **Open** 10am-6pm Mon-Thur; 10am-7pm Fri; 10am-5pm Sat; closed Sun. **Credit** AmEx, DC, MC, V. **Map** p311 N13.

Standard issue high street chart music and video store. Not very big by London or New York standards, but about as large as they come in Denmark. Also stocks DVDs and Playstation games.

Paul's Books and Records

Frederiksborggade 50 (33 11 94 60/ www.paulsbooksnrecords.com). **Open** 11am-6pm Mon-Thur; 11am-7pm Fri; 11am-3pm Sat; closed Sun. **Credit** MC, V. **Map** p306 L12.

This enticing jazz record shop was for 22 years known as Steve's Books and Records. Today it boasts the largest vinyl jazz collection in Scandinavia, as well as a decent range of rare soul and many new CDs. The main draw, however, is the second-hand and rare jazz recordings that make up the majority of the stock. Books, videos and art works are also sold. Paul's keeps alive the flame ignited by the internationally-renowned Copenhagen jazz scene in the '60s and, as you would expect, is a hub of activity during the Jazz Festival in July.

Street Dance Records

Vestergade 17 (33 15 90 70/www.streetdance.com). **Open** noon-6pm Mon; 11am-6pm Tue-Fri; 11am-2pm Sat; closed Sun. **Credit** AmEx, DC, MC, V. **Map** p310 O12.

One of Pisserenden's better record basements, particularly for DJs, as it boasts a large stock of soul, funk, techno, house and electronic music on vinyl.

Opticians & eyewear

Synoptik

Købmagergade 22 (33 15 05 38/www.synoptik.dk). **Open** 9.30am-6pm Mon-Thur; 9.30am-7pm Fri; 9.30am-4pm Sat; closed Sun. **Credit** DC, MC, V. **Map** p311 M13-14.

Large, modern chain of opticians and eyewear retailers with branches throughout Denmark. Stocks most major designer labels including Chanel, Dolce & Gabbana, Ray Ban and Moschino, as well as cheaper ranges.

Branch: Nørre Voldgade 15 (33 93 38 61).

Photography & film processing

Kontant Foto

Købmagergade 44 (33 12 00 29/ www.kontantfoto.com). **Open** 9am-5.30pm Mon-Thur; 9am-7pm Fri; 10am-2pm Sat; closed Sun. **Credit** AmEx, DC, MC, V. **Map** p311 M13-14.

In terms of floor space this is Denmark's largest photographic retailers, and its central location makes it convenient for dropping films in while shopping. Film processing is not particularly cheap in Denmark, however.

Photografica

Skindergade 41 (33 14 12 15/ www.photografica.com). **Open** 10am-5.30pm Mon-Thur; 10am-6pm Fri; 10am-3pm Sat; closed Sun. **Credit** AmEx, DC, MC, V. **Map** p311 N13.

An Aladdin's cave for camera collectors awaits at the top of the spiral staircase in this large photographic store (which caters to happy snappers and professionals alike). This is the only store in Copenhagen in which you'll find vintage Leicas, Rolleiflexes, Nikons and the like from 3,000kr to over 100,000kr. Friendly, helpful staff.

Repairs

Keys & shoe repairs

Hælebaren

Cityarkaden, Østergade 32, Strøget (33 91 02 20). **Open** 8am-6pm Mon-Thur; 8am-7pm Fri; 9am-3pm Sat; closed Sun. **Credit** DC, MC, V. **Map** p311 M15.

Large, centrally-located key cutter and shoe repairer.

Watches

Vintageure & Urmager

Kompagnistræde 10 (33 12 10 94). **Open** 11am-5.30pm Mon-Thur; 11am-7pm Fri; 11am-3pm Sat; closed Sun. **Credit** V. **Map** p311 O13.

Clock and watch repairs, plus a small but exquisite range of vintage watches from Jaegre le Coutre, Cartier, Rolex and others.

Sex shops

See page 172 **Lust**, *page 174* **Sex street** and *page 114* **This is hardcore**.

Sport

Christiania Cykler

Refshalevej 2, Christiania (32 95 45 20). **Open** *Sept-May* 10am-5.30pm Mon-Thur; 10am-6pm Fri; closed Sat, Sun. *June-Aug* 10am-5.30pm Mon-Thur; 10am-6pm Fri; 10am-2pm Sat; closed Sun. **No credit cards**. **Map** p313 O19.

Christiania Cykler stocks a range of touring and mountain bikes, but its most interesting item is the idiosyncratic Pedersen bike. Based on a design from the early 20th century, the original inventor Mikael Pedersen was tired of getting a sore backside from riding, so he devised a swinging hammock-like leather seat, then built a unique pyramid-like frame to support it. Today the shop builds 40-50 specially ordered Pedersen bikes a year, about half of which are bought by cycling enthusiasts from abroad.

Eat, Drink, Shop

Eventyr Sport

Nørre Voldgade 9 (33 93 66 21). **Open** 10am-5.30pm
Mon-Thur; 10am-7pm Fri; 10am-3pm Sat; closed Sun.
Credit AmEx, DC. MC. V. **Map** p310 M12.
There are several excellent outdoor pursuits stores
on the streets to the north of Nørreport Station (particularly on Frederiksborggade), but Eventyr Sport
is one of the most comprehensive. It sells camping
equipment, climbing gear, clothing for heavy duty
outdoor use, as well as all the usual accoutrements
required for survival in the wilderness.

Intersport

Nørregade 36 (33 11 41 48/www.intersport.dk).
Open 10am-5.30pm Mon-Thur; 10am-7pm Fri; 10am-
2pm Sat; closed Sun. **Credit** AmEx, DC, MC, V.
Map p310 M12.
An international sports franchise selling a
reasonable range of internationally homogenous (ie
American-style, Asian-made) sports clothing
and equipment.
Branch: Købmagergade 60 (33 14 43 48).

Planet Football

Frederiksberggade 2, Strøget (33 12 90 81).
Open 10am-6pm Mon-Thur; 10am-7pm Fri; 10am-
5pm Sat; closed Sun. **Credit** AmEx, DC, MC, V.
Map p310 O12.
If you want to blend in around the bars of
Copenhagen on a Saturday afternoon you'll have
to get kitted out in an FC København strip, and
Planet Football is the place to buy it. This small
store sells other Danish strips as well as scarves,
boots and balls. A full Danish national strip is
around 800kr.

Pro Shop Danmark

Bredgade 21 (33 93 14 77/www.proshopdanmark.dk).
Open 10am-6pm Mon-Thur; 10am-7pm Fri; 10am-
4pm Sat; closed Sun. **Credit** AmEx, DC, MC, V.
Map p312 M16.
One of Copenhagen's largest golf clothing and equipment stores (the sport is very popular in Denmark),
selling international brands and labels, and located
right in the heart of posh Bredgade.

Tobacconist

WØ Larsen

WØ Larsen, 9 Amagertorv, Strøget (33 12 20 50).
Open 10am-6pm Mon-Thur; 10am-7pm Fri; 10am-
5pm Sat; closed Sun. **Credit** AmEx, DC, MC, V.
Map p311 N14.
If you hang around this fantastic tobacconist (dating from 1864) long enough, who knows, you may
even bump into Her Majesty Queen Margrethe II
who buys her non-filtered Greek fags here (though
for photos she smokes the Danish brand Prince).
While you wait, you can do all sorts of damage to
yourself by trying the extensive selection of cigars,
tobacco, and cigarettes from around the world.
Alternatively, pop down to the basement museum
(*see p70*).

Toys, games & magic

Bridge Butikken

Møntergade 12 (33 93 63 12/www.bridgebutikken.dk).
Open noon-5.30pm Tue-Fri; 10am-2pm Sat; closed
Mon, Sun. **No credit cards**. **Map** p311 M14.
Talk about niche retailing, this cellar shop is dedi-
cated solely to the art of bridge playing. There's a
huge variety of playing cards and accessories, plus
books with titles such as *How To Play A Bridge
Hand* and *How The Experts Win At Bridge.*

Dansk Håndværk

Kompagnistræde 20 (33 11 45 52). **Open** 11am-
5.30pm Tue-Thur; 11am-6pm Fri; 11am-3pm Sat;
closed Mon, Sun. **No credit cards**. **Map** p311 O13.
Local craftsman Lars Jensen has been producing
these traditional wooden toys for almost 30 years
and this small cellar shop is full of a wide range of
brightly coloured playthings for under-fives.

Faraos Cigarer

Skindergade 27 (33 32 22 11/www.faraos.dk).
Open 10am-6pm Mon-Thur; 10am-7pm Fri; 10am-
3pm Sat; closed Sun. **Credit** MC, V. **Map** p311 N13.
Copenhagen's answer to Forbidden Planet is, as with
the London store, a great meeting place for like-
minded adolescents (of all ages) who collect comics,
role-playing figures, *Star Wars* merchandise and
Pokémon paraphernalia with a voraciousness that
borders on mania (check out the mezzanine café,
usually the scene of some intense swapsie action).

Fætter BR

*Frederiksberggade 11, Strøget (33 13 74 04/
www.br-leg.dk).* **Open** 10am-6pm Mon-Thur; 10am-
7pm Fri; 10am-5pm Sat; closed Sun. **Credit** AmEx,
DC, MC, V. **Map** p310 O12.
Denmark's biggest toyshop chain with, obviously,
lots of Lego (kits from 69kr), as well as well-known
international brands like Barbie, Action Man,
Nintendo and Playstation.
Branches: Bremerholmen 4 (33 14 08 73);
Købmagergade 9 (33 14 74 64).

Krea

Vestergade 4-6 (33 32 98 58/www.krea.dk).
Open 9.30am-5.30pm Mon-Thur; 9.30-7pm Fri; 9.30-
3pm Sat; closed Sun. **Credit** AmEx, DC, MC, V.
Map p310 O12.
Usually found echoing with squeals of delight from
its excitable clientele, Krea caters mainly to under-
tens, and does so with a broad range of educational
and fun toys for boys and girls.

Travel

STA Travel

Fiolstræde 18 (33 14 15 01/www.statravelgroup.com).
Open 10am-5.30pm Mon-Thur; 10am-5.30pm Fri;
10am-1pm Sat; closed Sun. **Credit** MC, V.
Map p311 M13.
The Student Travel Association's Copenhagen HQ,
located near to the university.

Eat, Drink, Shop

Arts & Entertainment

By Season

From summer jazz to fairy-tale Christmases, Copenhagen has the year covered.

The events listed in this chapter are just the highlights of the year. See individual chapters within this Guide for a wider selection and more information. For further details and precise dates of the year's events in the city, the **Wonderful Copenhagen Tourist Information Bureau** (*see page 292*) publishes an annual booklet as well as more up-to-date seasonal guides and *Copenhagen This Week*, a weekly magazine containing detailed listings of sporting and cultural events. All are in English and are available free from tourist information centres, hotels, libraries, etc.

Danish school holidays begin in the middle of June and usually end in the first week of August. For a list of public holidays in Denmark, *see page 289*; for information on the best time to visit, *see page 292* **When to go**.

Spring

The opening of **Tivoli** (*see page 57*) at the end of April (until the end of September) is a symbolic moment for the city. The **Bakken** amusement park (*see page 270*), north of the city, is less famous, but its season starts at the end of March (until the end of September) and is just as appreciated by Copenhageners.

Junge Hunde
Østerfælled Torv 37, Østerbro (35 43 20 21/tickets: BILLETnet 70 15 65 65 or Kanonhallen 35 43 20 21/www.kanonhallen.net/www.jungehunde.dk). Bus 6, 14, 18. **Date** between Feb & June. **Box office** 2-6pm Mon-Fri; 1hr before performances daily. **Tickets** varies. **No credit cards. Map** p121 B12.
Junge Hunde (Young Dogs) international dance festival features many of the stars of tomorrow.

The Queen's Birthday
Date 16 Apr.
The Danes are united by their fondness for their multi-talented Queen (*see p93* **Great Danes: Queen Margrethe II**) and her birthday is cause for celebration across the country. The Queen herself makes an appearance on a balcony at Amalienborg Slot (*see p88*) at noon, while the royal guards mark the occasion by parading in their finest ceremonial dress.

Ballet & Opera Festival
Tordenskjoldsgade 7 (main box office 33 69 69 69/www.kgl-teater.dk). **Date** mid May-end June.
Box office 1-7pm Mon-Sat; closed Sun.
Tickets varies. **Credit** DC, MC, V. **Map** p311 N15.

The Gamle Scene of Det Kongelige Teater (the Royal Theatre) hosts a season of classical and modern dance performances, plus two major opera productions.

Sophienholm Concerts
Sophienholm, Nybrovej 401 (45 88 40 07). Train to Lyngby, then 191 bus. **Date** May-end Aug. Open *for exhibitions* 11am-5pm Tue-Sun; closed Mon. Closed between exhibitions. **Admission** *concerts free; exhibitions* 30kr. **No credit cards.**
Classical music promenade concerts are held every Sunday during summer, with a special children's programme. Sophienholm (15km – 9 miles – north-west of the city) is an early 19th-century lakeside house, which holds art exhibitions three or four times a year.

Wonderful Copenhagen Marathon
35 26 69 00/www.sparta.dk. **Date** last Sun in May.
Admission 300kr-350kr.
Professional and amateur runners from around the world pound the cobbles for 42km.

Copenhagen Whitsun Carnival
Østerbrohuset, Århusgade 103, Østerbro (35 38 85 04/www.karneval.dk). **Date** Whitsun weekend.
Admission free. **Map** p121 E12.
Founded by students and community groups in the early '80s, this is Copenhagen's stab at a Rio Carnival-type event with lashings of South American spirit, costumes, parades and floats. The three-day festivities are held in Østerbro's Fælledparken.

Summer

Sommerscene
(33 15 15 64/www.kit.dk). **Date** June-Aug.
Tickets phone for details.
A huge annual three-month festival of international dance, theatre and circus, Sommerscene takes place in venues across the city. The lineups are usually impressive (and have included the likes of Le Cirque Invisible and the Royal Shakespeare Company).

Danish Derby
Klampenborg Galopbane, Klampenborgvej, Klampenborg (39 96 02 02/www.galopbane.dk). Train to Klampenborg/388 bus. **Date** late June.
Admission 60kr. **No credit cards.**
Denmark's premier equine event takes place at Klampenborg racecourse, to the north of the city.

The Round Sjælland Yacht Race
Helsingør. Train to Helsingør. **Date** late June.
Over three days sailors compete in one of Europe's largest yacht races, which circumnavigates Sjælland, starting and finishing at Helsingør.

Arts & Entertainment

The **Copenhagen Jazz Festival**.

St Hans Eve

Date 23 June.

One of the most *hygge* (*see p79* **The essence of hygge**) events of the year takes place on the evening of Denmark's longest day. At around 9-10pm most Danes gather together across the country to build bonfires (in Copenhagen many build theirs on the beaches to the north of the city), and watch the sunset – the idea being that the flames of the fires will help keep the sun alive to prolong summer for as long as possible. There is much singing, dancing and feasting, not to mention more than a few glasses of schnapps and Tuborg consumed. At the end of the evening a home-made witch on top of the bonfire catches light and 'flies off', legend has it, to the Brocken Mountain in Germany – apparently the home of all witches. St Hans Eve is probably Denmark's most atmospheric and enjoyable celebration, and one to which foreigners are typically welcomed heartily (the Danes love nothing more than when others take an interest in their traditions).

Roskilde Festival

Roskilde (www.roskilde-festival.dk).
Train to Roskilde. **Date** 4 days over last weekend in June. **Tickets** within Denmark: 70 15 65 65 10am-9pm daily/www.billetnet.dk; from UK: The Way Ahead 0115 912 9116/9000. Phone for details of prices.

Denmark's answer to Glastonbury is the largest rock festival in northern Europe, and it boasts a stronger line up as each year passes. Blur, Bjork, Bob Dylan and the Beastie Boys have all played here before crowds of 70-90,000 (and that's just artists beginning with 'B'). Each year about 150 acts perform in fields on the outskirts of this ancient town in the centre of Sjælland. (A shuttle bus runs from Roskilde station to the festival grounds.) The 2000 festival lineup included Lou Reed, the Cure, Roni Size, Groove Armada, Gomez, Oasis, Nine Inch Nails, Pearl Jam, Travis and the Pet Shop Boys, as well as a good representation of Scandinavian bands, DJs and African and Latin American music. Yet it was, unfortunately, remembered instead for the tragic death of nine people during Pearl Jam's set. *See also p260.*

Copenhagen Jazz Festival

33 93 20 13/33 93 25 45/www.cjf.dk. **Date** 1st Fri-2nd Sun in July. **Tickets** varies; phone for details.

The Copenhagen Jazz Festival is a major event, not only in the Danish musical calendar but world-wide. Each year, since it began in 1979, the festival, like the rock festival at Roskilde, seems to boast bigger names than before. During this enjoyable and relaxed nine days Copenhagen really lets its hair down with a huge range of performances (over 500) taking place in just about every indoor or outdoor venue, public park or square. Impromptu jam sessions in which established stars join jobbing musicians and amateurs are a highlight. *See also p219.*

Copenhagen Summer Festival

35 38 60 69. **Date** early Aug. **Tickets** 25kr-45kr. **No credit cards.**

A two-week programme of chamber and classical music concerts in various venues across the city.

DCCP Images of the World Festival

33 17 97 00/www.dccd.dk. **Date** Aug-Sept. **Tickets** varies; phone for details.

An annual celebration of the non-Western world, including theatre, dance, music, visual arts, handicrafts, photography, architecture and literary events. The festival is held in various venues around Copenhagen and in other Danish towns.

Dancin' World

33 15 15 64/www.kit.dk. **Date** Aug 2002 (biennial). **Tickets** phone for details.

Scandinavia's biggest modern dance festival attracts performers and audiences from across the world, and provides a fascinating snapshot of global trends in dance.

Ny Carlsberg Glyptotek Concerts

Dantes Plads 7 (33 41 81 41/www.glyptoteket.dk). **Date** mid Aug. **Credit** MC, V. **Map** p311 P13.

A season of classical music concerts is held within this exceptional art museum. *See p64 and p223.*

Copenhagen Ballet Festival

Landbokijshoten, Bülowsvej, Frederiksberg (39 90 15 00/www.xproduction.com). **Date** mid Aug-1 Sept. **Tickets** phone for details. **Map** p111 N6.

Featuring the world's finest ballet dancers from Den Kongelige Ballet (the Royal Danish Ballet) and international companies.

Golden Days in Copenhagen

'Golden Days in Copenhagen', Stockholmsgade 21 (35 42 14 32/tickets: BILLETnet 70 15 65 65/ www.goldendays.dk/english). **Date** 2wks late Aug-early Sept. **Tickets** varies; phone for details.

A wistful remembrance of the first half of the 19th-century, when Denmark enjoyed a particularly rich and productive cultural life (*see p18*). This annual festival features exhibitions, concerts, poetry readings and ballet from the Golden Age period. The 2001 festival is the fifth to take place.

Arts & Entertainment

Autumn

PRIMO

35 43 83 00/box office 35 43 58 58/
www.dansescenen.dk. **Date** Sept-Oct 2002 (biennial).
This festival of Nordic modern dance is held every
two years in venues in Malmö and Copenhagen.

Amager Musikfestival

Churches around Amager (33 16 01 31/
www.kulturnet.dk). **Date** mid Sept-early Oct.
Admission free.
A programme of church concerts held on the island
of Amager, south-east of the city.

Kulturnatten

www.visitcopenhagen.dk. **Date** 1st night of
the Autumn half-term holidays in mid Oct.
Tickets varies.
Kulturnatten ('The Night of Culture') is pretty much
the city's last cultural hurrah before the shutters
come down for winter. With everything from classical concerts in churches, special performances in
museums, open-air shows, and theatre and cinema
events, there is guaranteed to be something to whet
most appetites. All museums, galleries and other
public buildings and palaces have free admission
from 6pm until midnight.

Copenhagen Choir Festival

Greiff Musik, Gammeltoftgade 16 (33 13 55 70/
www.kultunaut.dk). **Date** late Oct. **Tickets** varies.
A festival held across Øresund, in Tivoli's concert
hall and in churches across Copenhagen and Malmö,
featuring the cream of Denmark's choirs plus
numerous international groups.

Copenhagen Gay & Lesbian Film Festival

www.gayfilm.dk. **Date** late Oct. **Tickets** phone
for details.
A ten-day festival showcasing mainstream and
underground gay and lesbian films.

Winter

Autumn Jazz Festival

33 93 20 13/www.jazzfestival.dk. **Date** 1st Thur-
1st Sun in Nov.
A smaller, more low key version of the famous summer jazz festival. *See p189.*

Copenhagen Irish Festival

N Zahles Seminarium, Nørre Voldgade
(36 45 08 02/tickets: 70 15 65 65/
www.billetnet.dk./www.ashplant.dk).
Date early Nov. **Tickets** phone for details.
Events with an Irish theme held throughout the city
over four days.

Tivoli's Christmas Season

Tivoli (33 15 10 01/www.tivoli.dk). **Date** late Nov-
Christmas. **Admission** 20kr. **No credit cards.**
Map p310 P12.

This recent innovation, introduced in 1994, transforms Tivoli into a vast Christmas grotto with a special Christmas market, ice skating (on the artificially
frozen lake), plenty of Yuletide grub and an
infestation of *nisser* (Danish Christmas pixies).
Guaranteed to give you that seasonal feel.

Christmas Fairs & Parade

www.visitcopenhagen.dk. **Date** from end Nov.
Like most European cities Copenhagen is decked out
in decorations and illuminations at this time of year,
but unlike most, the atmosphere is less commercial
and somehow more authentically 'Christmassy'
(maybe the sub-zero temperatures have something
to do with it). On a night towards the end of
November Father Christmas parades through the
city in the Great Christmas Parade. And in past
years a hugely popular artificial ice rink has been
constructed in the centre of Kongens Nytorv.

Christmas

www.visitcopenhagen.dk. **Date** 24 Dec.
The Danes give a great Christmas, both in the pri-
vacy of their owns homes with elaborate rituals,
feasting and decorations, and on a more grand public scale. Like all Danes, Copenhageners celebrate on
Christmas Eve, and judge other nations to be perfectly bizarre for doing otherwise. Having already
gone out into the woods to chop down their own tree,
Danes will decorate it the night before Christmas
and hang it with real candles. Once these are lit, the
family dances around the tree holding hands and
singing carols, before settling down to a traditional
Christmas dinner of roast duck, potatoes and red
cabbage followed by a rice pudding with a hidden
almond (whoever gets the almond wins a present).

Fastelavn

www.karneval.dk. **Date** late Feb.
Fastelovn could be considered the Danes' Halloween,
in which children dress up in all manner of costumes
and gather together wielding sticks with which they
beat the hell out of a wooden barrel. This is mild
compared with what used to happen: in more barbaric times the barrel, containing a live cat, would
be suspended from a tree by a rope so that the
youths of a town could gallop past it on a horse and
wallop it until the bottom fell out. These days it is
not a traumatised feline that falls from the broken
barrel, but huge quantities of sweets.

Antiques Fair

Børsen, Slotsholmen (45 86 17 45/www.danfair.dk).
Date last weekend in Feb. **Map** p311 O15.
Large antiques fair held in Børsen, the old stock
exchange building.

Night Film Festival

www.natfilm.dk/english. **Date** between Feb & Apr.
Over 140 international films shown in the original language with Danish subtitles over a nine-day period.
Every cinema in town gets involved, and often the
directors themselves turn up to talk about their work.

Children

The Danes love kids, and their capital is packed with great things for youngsters to see and do.

Being a parent in Copenhagen is really quite enjoyable. The parks, pedestrian streets, cycle lanes and canals make it easy to get around the city with children without having to cope with too many cars.

You will rarely find a restaurant that doesn't have a children's menu, and almost every museum has either a special activity centre for children or offers educational exercises designed in such a way that kids understand the exhibitions in their own terms.

Danish children are highly valued and fully integrated into life in the capital. Freedom with responsibility characterises the Danish way of bringing up kids. In practice, this means that children are allowed to be both seen and heard, and are treated as cogent individuals.

Most Danish women work and maintain active social lives when they become mothers. You will see plenty of babies in the streets of Copenhagen, and more than the occasional breastfeeding mother. You will also get used to seeing babies in prams left outside shops or cafés, while the mothers are inside. In a well-publicised case, a Danish woman in New York was sent to jail for leaving her sleeping baby outside a café; apparently, then, the Danish way of life is not transferable to all cultures.

Great days out

A good way to see Copenhagen with a child is to adopt a geographical approach, and base a day's activities around one area of the city.

Tivoli & around

A must for every child visiting Copenhagen is **Tivoli** (*see page 57*). Located right next to Central Station, the old amusement park can still make every Danish kid's heart beat faster. The rollercoaster, the shooting galleries, Valhala Castle and the Pantomime Theatre are among the attractions that provide action and fun for kids and (many) adults, while the flowers and gardens, open-air cafés and restaurants offer parents some tranquility and time to breath. For children of nappy age, Tivoli provides a family amenity centre with baby-changing tables, free nappies and microwave ovens for heating baby food.

There are a couple of diverting museums in the area. Next to Tivoli is **Louis Tussaud's Wax Museum** (*see page 65*), a strangely fascinating little cousin to London's Madame Tussaud's. Here you can meet the Danish Royal family, see the characters created by Hans Christian Andersen come to life and get close to icons like Michael Jackson and Marilyn Monroe. At the end of Strøget, across Rådhuspladsen from here is the less impressive freak show fodder at **Ripley's Believe It or Not Museum** (*see page 65*).

At the other end of the scale, the heavyweight **Nationalmuseet** (the National Museum; *see page 62*) is actually a very interesting place to take children (who can resist the Vikings at any age?). Every new exhibition is accompanied by a children's area, with specially designed activities. Youngsters learn about the displays through interactive games and educational materials.

West of Tivoli is **Tycho Brahe Planetarium** (*see page 108*), with its small exhibition on astronomy and space travel, but the real attraction here is the Imax cinema. (Ask for headphones with English narration at the ticket office.)

South of Tivoli is a place for pure relaxation. The ultra-popular swimming centre **Vandkulturhuset** (within the **DGI-Byen** sports complex; *see page 238*) contains a baby pool with fountains, an ellipse-shaped swimming pool, water slides, diving boards, climbing walls and a spa, where parents can recharge their batteries.

Strøget & around

The long pedestrian street **Strøget**, running from Rådhuspladsen to Kongens Nytorv, is fun for kids, partly because of its shops, but mostly because of the myriad mime artists, musicians and comedians who perform on the street. At Christmas time most of the shops on Strøget have window displays featuring trolls and elves; the display at Royal Copenhagen Porcelain on Amagertorv is especially worth a look.

Towards the Kongens Nytorv end of the street is the **Guinness World Records Museum** (*see page 67*), which features such eclectic delights as replicas of the tallest and the smallest men in the world, a violin made of matches, a shrunken Indian head and a man who can swallow a billiard ball.

Get away from the noise of the street by climbing the 17th-century **Rundetårn** (Round Tower; *see page 69*) on Købmagergade. The tower, the oldest functioning observatory in Europe, rises 34.8 metres (114 feet) above street level and offers a magnificent view of the old part of Copenhagen. Instead of steps there is a 209-metre (686-feet) long ramp, which spirals up inside the tower. Apparently, this was designed so that King Christian IV could ride his carriage all the way to the top.

For something completely different rent out a kayak from **Kajak-Ole** on Gammel Strand (book in advance if you want to to be sure to get a boat; *see page 52*). A guide leads the group through the canals, telling local anecdotes and historical facts about the buildings on the way; a drink at a café in Christianshavn is included in the price. No experience is necessary to take part, as the kayaks are very stable, but children must be 11 or older for a two-person kayak and 15 for a single-person kayak.

South of Gammel Strand on Slotsholmen, the double-handed swords, suits of armour and other military paraphernalia at **Tøjhusmuseet** (the Royal Arsenal Museum; *see page 85*) nearby are also an unexpected hit with kids, especially boys. Also on Slotsholmen, older children might like the spooky atmosphere of the **Ruinere Under Christiansborg** (*see page .* The excavated ruins of the original castle of Bishop Absalon (the founder of Copenhagen; *see page 84*), jumbled together with those of later castles on the site, are situated directly below the current **Christiansborg Slot**.

Rosenborg & around

Five minutes' walk north of the east end of Strøget lies **Kongens Have** (the King's Garden; *see page 98*). This is a wonderful place for a picnic if the weather is good. (If it's not, the Mexican food and jungle flora and fauna of nearby **Chico's Cantina** – *see page 141* – are always a hit with kids.) The park has a unique wooden playground for one- to four-year-olds, and alongside this is one of the most charming traditional attractions in Copenhagen: the **Marionet Teater** (Marionette Theatre; *see page 229*). Performances for children up to five years of age take place every day in the summer (except Monday) at 2pm and 3pm.

Rosenborg Slot (Rosenborg Palace; *see page 100*) at the other end of the park is packed with historical treasures, but is also the place to

Going over the top at **Bakken**. See p194.

watch the Queen's Life Guards in training. The soldiers can be seen marching and playing military tunes outside the palace, while inside there are rooms dedicated to each of the Danish kings, from Christian IV to Frederik VII, furnished with authentic objects from the time. The rooms of special interest to children are the Treasury, the Long Hall and Room 10. The atmospheric Treasury houses the Danish crown jewels, while the impressive Long Hall is decorated in golden stucco and has three silver lions guarding the thrones of the king and queen. Room 10 features a curious picture that shows the children of Frederik IV – when you look at it from the left, you see a girl; from the right, you see a boy.

Two minutes' walk south of Rosenborg is the **Musikhistorisk Museum** (Musical History Museum; *see page 98*). If your kids are interested in music, this is a fun place to visit. Audio sets play the sounds of old instruments, including Highland pipes from Scotland, launeddas from Greece and hurdy-gurdys from the Czech Republic. Unfortunately, you cannot play the painted cembalos or the other historical instruments, but the museum does have a kids' room where children can use up some of their energy on drums, stringed instruments and xylophones.

A couple of minutes' walk north of Rosenborg is the excellent **Statens Museum For Kunst** (the National Gallery; *see page 98*). It features a children's gallery, a cinema and a workshop, and offers guided tours for children on Saturdays, Sundays and throughout the Danish school holidays. Tours start at 1pm, and are followed by a workshop from 2-4pm, where children can create sculptures, drawings and paintings (they can take all their artwork home afterwards). The guided tours are mainly in Danish, but English-speaking children are well catered for in the post-tour workshops.

Behind the gallery stretches **Østre anlæg** park containing some of the best playgrounds in Copenhagen, and some fun and amusing wooden sculptures.

Christianshavn

Vor Frelsers Kirke (*see page 103*), close to Chistianshavns Kanal has a unique tower with a spiral staircase that twists around the outside of the spire. Children find it fun (and a little scary) to climb up the 400 steps and are rewarded by a great view of Copenhagen from the top.

Nearby is **Christiania** (*see page 105*). Older children might find it interesting to visit the Free State (although you'd have to be extraordinarily liberal-minded not to worry

about all the dope on display on Pusher Street), while younger children can commune with the dogs and horses, and romp in the playgrounds. There are some lovely green spaces and intriguingly constructed houses to gawp at, too.

On Wednesdays (4-10pm) don't miss dinner at **Base Camp** (*see pages 102 and 152*), a restaurant in the old cannon hall at Holmen, a former naval base, just north of Christianshavn). Wednesday is children's day, and there are lots of activities on offer, including a disco, cartoons, indoor hockey and football matches. Moreover, the children's buffet is free for kids under ten years of age. Base Camp is also child-friendly during the rest of the week, with a permanent play- and videoroom and lots of space. Brunches on Saturdays and Sundays are very popular with parents with prams. From Holmen you have a great view across the water to **Amalienborg Slot**, the royal palace (*see page 88*), which can be reached by harbour bus. The changing of the guards takes place at Amalienborg every day at noon.

If you need some open space for a ball game, try **Christianshavns Vold** (Christianshavns Voldgade 36). Alternatively, hire a rowing boat from **Christianshavn Bådudlejning & Café** (*see page 151*) and take to the canals.

Frederiksberg

West of central Copenhagen lies **Frederiksberg Have** (*see page 113*), a beautiful garden that is ideal for a picnic. To find out more about the royal gardens, take one of the guided boat trips on the lake. The neighbouring **Zoologisk Have** (Zoological Garden; *see page 113*) is one of the most attractive in Europe, with a lot of space for the animals. It has a special children's zoo for the smallest children, where they can touch and play with not-so-dangerous beasties from all over the world. Other kiddie attractions include riding a pony, climbing the zoo tower or just looking at the numerous baby animals.

If you want somewhere to eat in Frederiksberg, **MG Petersens Familiehave** (Pile Allé 23, 36 16 11 33) is a family garden restaurant that welcomes prams, and has a big play area for children.

Østerbro & further north

In Østerbro, north of the lakes, lies extensive **Fælledparken**, which has several playgrounds, but is more renowned for its skateboard park and open-air swimming pool. In the summer, several festivals, carnivals and playdays for children are held here. Another

Arts & Entertainment

summer attraction in the park is **Pavillionen**, an outdoor café and restaurant that does very good barbecues.

Older children might find the stuffed animals a little dusty, but for younger kids the **Zoologisk Museum** (*see page 121*), just west of Fælledparken, is a hit. Exhibits from Greenland, Africa and the rest of the world are accompanied by educational games.

The **Experimentarium** (*see page 122*), further north in Hellerup, on the other hand, is for children of every age. This science centre explores nature and technology, environment and health through more than 300 interactive exhibits. Among other things you can solve puzzles, measure the air in your lungs or try out the gyroscopes. In the kids' pavillion – aimed at children between three and six – there are crazy mirrors, water wheels and other delights to explore.

You shouldn't miss spending a day along the coast, north of Copenhagen. Scenic views, beaches and beautiful forests are only part of the experience. You will also find some good museums, and some of the biggest and cheapest ice-creams in Denmark at **Lydolphs Isbar** in Hellerup (Strandvejen 167).

In **Danmarks Akvarium** (the Danish Aquarium; *see page 122*) in Charlottenlund, you can learn about the sealife that inhabits polar seas and tropical waters. On Saturdays and Sundays, when the touch pool is open, children can get up close and personal with marine life. Don't miss feeding time at 2pm on Wednesdays, Saturdays and Sundays, and daily during the school holidays.

The oldest amusement park in the world, **Bakken** (*see page 270*) is located in the forest of **Dyrehaven**, further north of the city at Klampenborg. Since 1583, a trip to Bakken has been a popular excursion for Copenhageners. It has all the usual amusement park attractions, including rollercoasters, shooting galleries and daily shows for children, but you should note that although entrance to the park is free, most of the attractions are not. A pleasant way to see the rest of Dyrehaven is by pony. Very small ponies, which can be led by parents, are available at **Fortunens Ponyudlejning**. Alternatively, take a horse and cart ride or simply stroll around in the forest. Next to Dyrehaven is the best beach in the Copenhagen area – **Bellevue** (*see page 123*).

Further north, the beautifully situated **Louisiana Museum For Moderne Kunst** (Lousiana Museum of Modern Art; *see page 272*) has a children's wing offering lots of artistic activities every day. Artwork produced by visiting children is sometimes exhibited in the children's wing or online on the Louisiana

homepage. Louisiana also has a wonderfully designed park, perfect for a picnic, and there's a small swimming beach in front of the museum.

Fortunens Ponyudlejning

Ved Fortunen 33, Lyngby (45 87 60 58). Train to Klampenborg, then bus 388 towards Lyngby or train to Lyngby, then bus 388 towards Helsingør. **Open** noon-6pm Mon-Fri; 9am-6pm Sat, Sun. **Rates** *Horse rides* 100kr/hr. *Pony rides* 85kr/hr; 50kr/30mins. **No credit cards**.

Annual events

In addition to those events listed here, annual events such as the **Copenhagen Jazz Festival** (July; *see page 219*), the **Images of the World Festival** (Aug-Sept; *see page 230*), **Golden Days in Copenhagen** (Aug-Sept; *see page 233*), and film and music festivals all over the country include plenty of child-friendly activities. For further details, *see* chapter **By Season**.

Fastelavn

Date Feb or Mar.
The Danish equivalent of Hallowe'en is celebrated seven weeks before Easter, when fastelavn parties are held all over the city. Kids dress up as princesses, Zorros, tomatoes, teddy bears and the like, and hit a barrel hanging from a string. Originally, there was a cat inside the barrel, but thankfully nowadays it is filled with sweets, fruit and chocolate. The child who makes the bottom fall out of the barrel is 'King of the cat'. The one who fells the last board is 'Queen of the cat'. *See also p190.*

Copenhagen Whitsun Carnival

35 38 85 04/www.karneval.dk. **Date** Whitsun weekend. **Admission** free. **Map** p121 B15.
During Whitsun, Fælledparken boils with hot samba rhythms and dancing people. Children turn up in facepaints and fancy dress to enjoy three days of parades, music and dancing. *See also p188.*

Autumn holiday

Date Oct.
The schools' autumn holiday normally involves lots of activities for children. The holiday begins on Friday evening with **Kulturnatten** ('The Night of Culture'; *see page 190*), when lots of museums and shops are open late and have special displays and events.

Other attractions

Axelborg Bowling

Axeltorv 3A (33 32 00 92/www.axelborg-bowling.dk). **Open** 11am-midnight Mon-Wed, Sun; 11am-1am Thur; 11am-5am Fri, Sat. **Admission** 40kr-240kr; *shoe hire* 10kr. **Credit** AmEx, DC, MC, V. **Map** p310 O11.
For other bowling alleys, *see p238.*

Street entertainers are a fixture on **Strøget** during the summer. *See p191.*

Park Bio Cinema

Østerbrogade 79, Østerbro (35 38 33 62/ www.parkbio-kbh.dk). Bus 6, 14. **Open** 10.30am Sun. **Tickets** 30kr. **No credit cards. Map** p121 C13.

Alongside the normal screenings, this cinema offers so-called 'baby screenings' for parents with small children. You can take your baby into the cinema, or leave it outside where the staff will look after it. There's a nappy-changing break in the middle of the film, and nappies are provided free of charge.

Professor Olsens Spilleland

Scala, Axeltorv 2 (33 11 50 00). **Open** 11am-midnight daily. **Admission** 30kr minimum. **No credit cards. Map** p310 O11.

Electronic video games, pinball machines, slot machines and more. The place is a noise inferno and a money-eater. Admission is free but you have to change at least 30kr into 'game coins' in order to play (a free fizzy drink is included in the exchange).

Resources

Babysitters

ABC Babysitting

39 20 43 46. **Open** *Office* 8-9am, 2-5pm Mon-Fri; closed Sat, Sun. **Rates** 40kr/hr, plus 40kr booking fee and travel expenses.
A 24-hour service.

Studenternes Babysitters

Lykkesholm Allé 33 C (70 20 44 16/babysitters @mail.tele.dk). **Open** *Office* 10am-3pm Mon-Wed, Fri; 1-6pm Thur; closed Sat, Sun. **Rates** *8am Mon-6pm Fri* 40kr/hr, plus 40kr booking fee. *6pm Fri-8am Mon* 50kr/hr, plus 40kr booking fee.
A 24-hour service.

Online information

www.aok.dk

Almost all the information you could wish for on events in Copenhagen. Music, drama, sport, cultural events, restaurants and more.

www.karneval.dk

Information on activities for children during Copenhagen's yearly carnival, but also details of the Roskilde Festival, the children's biennale festival in Kongens Have and several other musical and entertainment events.

www.kidlink.org

Global site 'Empowering kids and youth to build global networks of friends', with mailing lists and online art exhibitions.

www.kulturdanmark.dk

Cultural sights and events in Denmark for children and adults, split into seven themes.

Film

Danish movie makers have a long and distinguished pedigree.

For a tiny country with a language that is unique to its shores, Denmark has had an extraordinary influence on the world of cinema, both in the early days of silent movies and in more recent years.

The Danish government was comparatively quick to recognise the PR value of a vibrant and internationally successful film industry and since the mid '60s has been extremely supportive of its movie makers (to the tune of 420 million kroner in 2001, for example), particularly of the art house variety. That support, coupled with a glut of talented, innovative film makers – more often than not graduates of **Den Danske Filmskole** (the Danish Film School) – has brought Danish cinema several notable triumphs over the last two decades. Production of feature films in Denmark is currently running at around a very healthy 20 features a year.

IN THE BEGINNING...

The first moving pictures in Denmark were shown in June 1896 in the Panorama cinema on Rådhuspladsen. In the same year **Peter Elfelt** had made the first Danish film, *Kørsel med Grønlandske Hunde* (Travel With Greenlandic Dogs), a short documentary. Elfelt was also responsible for the first Danish feature film, *Henrettelsen* (The Execution, 1903).

Denmark's film makers were among the key pioneers in European cinema, and in the decades leading up to World War II were notably influential in the development of the media in a whole host of areas. The establishment of **Den Nordisk Film Kompagni** in 1906 galvanised the industry, and its success (in 1912 it gave shareholders a 60 per cent dividend) spawned numerous imitators. Nordisk Film was the first studio in Europe to focus solely on feature films, and it thrived (until the emergence of the American film industry, in around 1913), thanks to its technical superiority and the talent of its directors. As extraordinary as this sounds, for a while in the early days of cinema, Denmark was the world's biggest film producer.

After facing near-bankruptcy with the advent of sound, Nordisk Film re-established itself in 1929 as a producer of talkies, and it still flourishes as the oldest working film studio in the world. Trivia fans may like to know that its polar bear logo is said to have inspired the use of a lion as MGM's symbol.

Denmark's first leading movie actress **Asta Nielsen** is fondly remembered in her home country as the Danish Garbo, though, for a time, she was even more popular, both at home and throughout the continent. Nielsen caused a stir with an unprecedented erotic screen kiss with one of the greatest Danish actors of the century, **Poul Reumert**, and a saucy dance in the 1910 film *Afgrunden* (The Abyss) directed by the legendary Danish filmmaker **Urban Gad**. The film transformed Nielsen into Europe's first great female film star, and today she is thought of as one of the greatest ever silent actors.

MOVIE PIONEERS

Among the most important innovators of early cinema was **Carl Theodor Dreyer** (1889-1968), generally considered the greatest of all Danish directors. Much inspired by the American director DW Griffith Dreyer played a significant role in devising the language of narrative cinema, with his use of the close-up and fast, dramatic cutting techniques. His first film *Præsidenten* (The President, 1920) was made for Nordisk Film, but was deemed too dark for them, so the perfectionist Dreyer made his next five films in Sweden, Germany and with other Danish companies. Dreyer's acknowledged masterpieces include *Master of the House* (1925), *La Passion de Jeanne d'Arc* (made in French, 1928) and *Vredens Dag* (Day of Wrath, 1943), a courageous allegorical attack on the occupying Nazis, which ultimately led to Dreyer fleeing to Sweden. Dreyer made his last film, *Gertrud*, in 1964, and died in 1968.

In the realm of comedy, the 1920s Danish slapstick duo **Fy og Bi** (translated into Long and Short for English audiences), played by Carl Schenstrøm and Harald Madsen, are often seen as the precursors of American double acts like Laurel and Hardy and Abbott and Costello. In fact, their straight man/funny man, short and fat/tall and thin formula would be endlessly replicated by double acts around the world. Their finest hour was probably the classic *Lykkehjulet* (The Wheel of Fortune), directed by Urban Gad for Lau Lauritzen and his Palladium studio. Less innovative, but still extremely popular in Denmark, Norway and the former East Germany, were the **Olsen Gang**; three

Top ten · Danish films

Dancer in the Dark
(Lars von Trier, 2000)
Controversy for von Trier (not least regarding
the casting of, and his relationship with, his
star, singer and costume-consumer Björk)
with this award-winning melodrama-musical.

Festen
(The Celebration, Thomas Vinterberg, 1997)
The international breakthrough Dogme movie;
one of the most talked-about films of the year.

Breaking The Waves
(Lars von Trier, 1996)
A Best Actress Oscar nomination launched
the career of the then-unknown Emily Watson
and confirmed the status of von Trier as one
of the world's most distinctive auteurs.

Babette's Feast
(Gabriel Axel, 1987)
Axel's sublime rendering of Blixen's gently
comic tale of an exiled culinary genius toiling
for a religious community in darkest Jylland
had them drooling at the Academy.

Dancer in the Dark

Babette's Feast

Pelle The Conqueror

Pelle The Conqueror
(Pelle Erobreren, Bille August, 1987)
A Best Foreign Film Oscar and Best Actor
nomination for Max von Sydow were no less
than this heart-rending tale deserved.

Ordet
(The Word, Carl Theodor Dreyer, 1954)
This brilliant adaptation of Kaj Munk's
rural family drama, and in particular its
extraordinary closing scene, cemented
Dreyer's reputation.

La Passion de Jeanne d'Arc
(Carl Theodor Dreyer, 1928)
Made in France, but directed by Dreyer,
this remains a milestone of the silent era.

Vester Vov Vov
(People of the North Sea,
Lau Lauritzen, 1927)
Comedy duo Fy and Bi at the height of
their powers; it influenced a generation of
screen comics.

Blade af Satans Bog
(Leaves From Satan's Book, Carl Theodor
Dreyer, 1921)
Dreyer advanced the pioneering work of
DW Griffith with his innovative use of
dramatic cutting.

Afgrunden
(The Abyss, Urban Gad, 1910)
Hugely popular and influential silent movie
which created Europe's first screen heroine,
Asta Nielsen.

Arts & Entertainment

petty criminals who, with 13 light comedies made between 1968 and 1981, entertained the masses with their misadventures.

The popularity of cinema – particularly documentaries – exploded in Denmark during the 1930s, and as a result a Film Act was passed in 1938 establishing the Film Council, the Film Fund and the National Film Board. During the German occupation the industry also flourished, thanks to a ban on imported films. A consequence unforeseen by the Nazis was that during this time Danish films became a potent symbol of resistance for the Danish people.

Between World War II and the early '80s Danish cinema experienced something of a lull in international terms. In the post-war years the country's film makers more often focused their energies on television production, and when feature films were made they were often worthy social dramas, or soft porn (the industry having been derestricted in 1969).

The Film Act of 1964 went some way to address the problem by introducing government subsidies for film production, and by the mid '70s most Danish films were made with some element of government aid. By 1989 an even more radical system was introduced, whereby a film maker could demand 50 per cent of his budget (with no creative strings attached) from the government if he could match it with private funding.

GLOBAL RECOGNITION

In 1985, the American Motion Picture Academy gave the Best Picture award to the Robert Redford/Meryl Streep movie Out of Africa, which was based on the work of the Danish writer Karen Blixen (see page 271). Danish cinema duly prepared its Beverley Hills landing party, but had to wait a further three years for genuine home-grown success with Gabriel Axel's film adaptation of Karen Blixen's short story Babette's Feast, which won the Oscar for Best Foreign Language Film in 1988. Danish cinema then scored an unprecedented double triumph when Bille August's Pelle Erobreren (Pelle The Conqueror) won in the same category the next year; its leading man, Max von Sydow, receiving a nomination in the best actor category. August also won the Golden Palm at Cannes for this grindingly bleak tale of Swedish immigrants coping with life in 19th-century Bornholm, adapted from Martin Andersen Nexø's novel. The director went on to consolidate his position as one of the leading lights of Danish cinema with the thriller Smilla's Feeling For Snow (1997), set partly on Christianshavn, and his adaptation of Les Misérables, starring Liam Neeson and Uma Thurman (1998).

Not content with these successes (which eclipsed the efforts of many other larger European movie industries), Danish cinema continued to hog the limelight in the 1990s with the international success of director Lars von Trier, and the advent of Dogme 95, the cinema-ascetic movement of which he was a co-founder.

Von Trier's 1996 film Breaking The Waves starred Emily Watson as a retarded woman living in an extremist religious community in a remote coastal area of Scotland. With this torrid, and occasionally crudely manipulative, film (the first of his so-called 'Trilogy of Goodness') von Trier cast the die for his future relationship with the world's film critics, who continue to be violently polarised in their opinions of his work. The film did, however, win him the top prize at Cannes (to add to the Palm d'Or he received there in 1991 for an earlier film, Europa), and Watson was nominated for the Best Actress Oscar. Von Trier's 2000 release, the musical Dancer in the Dark, starring Björk and Catherine Deneuve as probably the most unlikely mid-West American factory workers ever, similarly divided the critics, but again went on to win at Cannes for both director and star.

Intriguingly, von Trier, who lives in Copenhagen's suburbs with his wife and four children, has also revealed that he is working on a 'cinema monument', a film called Dimension, which he is making at a rate of three minutes per year, and is scheduled for release in 2025 (if he dies in the meantime von Trier has arranged for someone else to complete the film).

DOGME 95

Despite von Trier's successes, Danish cinema in the 1990s was not the domain of just one director. Founded in Copenhagen, the Dogme collective was the brainchild of four Danish directors – von Trier, Thomas Vinterberg, Søren Kragh-Jacobsen and Kristian Levring. Dogme was a movement with a mission: to discard the 'trickery' of modern film making, refocus on the character's emotional journeys and democratise the process of film making.

The Dogme directors declared that Hollywood movies deceived their audience, mythologised the process of film making in order to render it inaccessible and neglected the human aspect of the stories they told. But to set themselves aside from all the other bleating, underfunded independent directors, they made it clear that their creed (called the Vow of Chastity, see page 199) need not preclude Hollywood-sized budgets, as Vinterberg commented: 'The Dogme 95 Manifesto does not concern itself with the economic aspects of

The Dogme Vow of Chastity

1. Shooting must be on location only, with no additional sets or props.
2. Sound and images must be recorded simultaneously, never separately (ie no dubbing).
3. No tripods; cameras must be hand held.
4. Film stock must be colour, with no special lighting.
5. No filters or other optical affects can be used.
6. There must be no superficial action.
7. The film should take place 'here and now'.
8. Films can not be of a specific genre.
9. The film format must only be Academy 35mm.
10. The director can receive no credit.

Festen

film-making. A Dogme film could be low-budget or it could have a $100m budget.'

Nitpickers enjoyed highlighting the Dogme directors' transgressions of their own code and pointing out similarities with the French New Wave of the 1960s, but in doing so ultimately missed the point. Dogme came as a breath of fresh air for many cinema-goers, reflecting the disillusionment they felt at the homogeneity of American blockbusters. Ironically, Hollywood pricked up its ears to this new notion of film making, and even Spielberg was at one time rumoured to be intrigued by the possible limitations inherent in the Dogme code.

The movement spawned several notable successes, prime among them Vinterberg's second feature film, *Festen* (The Celebration), a disturbing tale of family secrets, set against the backdrop of a 60th birthday party. *Festen* swept to success in America and Europe, and won the Special Jury Prize at Cannes 1998. Vinterburg's first feature film, *De Største Helt*

(The Greatest Heroes, 1996), a kind of modern day Danish *Butch Cassidy and the Sundance Kid*, had also won accolades at festivals in Madrid and Rouen.

Meanwhile, Kragh-Jacobsen's darkly humourous Dogme drama *Mifune* (his eighth film) won the Grand Jury Prize at the Berlin Film Festival in 1999, and von Trier stirred up further controversy with *The Idiots* (1999), being accused by some of tastelessness in his portrayal of the disabled. As usual, he lapped up the attention.

Danish Oscar success has continued more recently with a short film Best Oscar for *Election Night* (Anders Thomas Jensen, 1999), while Danish actors like Ulrich Thomsen (*Festen, The World Is Not Enough*), Connie Nielsen (*Gladiator*) and Iben Hjejle (*High Fidelity*) continue to fly the Dannebrog (the Danish national flag) in Hollywood.

CINEMA-GOING

There is an abundance of top quality cinemas in Copenhagen's city centre, both multiplexes and art house, as well as a dynamic Film Institute, housed within **Filmhuset** (*see below*) overlooking Kongens Have. Within five minutes' walk of Rådhuspladsen alone, there are six cinemas to choose from, all with top-quality sound and seating, and there's even a drive-in on Amager. This all points to the locals' insatiable appetite for film, which means that even the largest cinema in Scandinavia, the Imperial, will usually be packed to capacity in the first week of a new blockbuster opening. Almost four million people go to the cinema annually in Copenhagen.

But cinephiles have learned to be patient in this town. There seems to be no rhyme or reason to when foreign films make it to Danish screens. Occasionally, American movies can take up to a year to arrive; at other times Copenhageners get to see major releases a week or two before Londoners. In general though, you should be able to see the latest Will Smith or Julia Roberts flick within a couple of months of its release in America.

Blessedly, the vast majority of foreign films are shown in their original language with Danish subtitles. Even better is the fact that you are allowed to take alcohol into cinemas, like proper grown-ups. Tickets usually cost no more than 70kr, and at off-peak times are considerably less.

Filmhuset/Den Danske Filminstitut Cinemateket

Gothersgade 55 (33 74 34 00/www.dfi.dk).
Open *Café Sept-June* noon-midnight Tue-Fri; 1.30-midnight Sat, Sun; closed Mon. *July, Aug* noon-10pm Tue-Sun; closed Mon. *Bookshop* 11am-6pm Mon-Fri;

The polychrome monstrosity of the **Palads** cinema.

1-6pm Sat; closed Sun. *Documentary archive* noon-7pm Tue-Sun; closed Mon. *Library* noon-7pm Tue; noon-4pm Wed-Fri; closed Mon, Sat, Sun. **Admission** free; prices vary for cinema. **Map** p307 L13.
This world-class film complex is devoted to Danish and international cinema. Among its facilities are a shop selling books, posters and videos, a café, a documentary archive (open to non-members) and three cinemas, all wrapped up in some super-cool architecture.

Multiplexes & big screens

Dagmar Teatret
Jernbanegade 2 (33 14 32 22/www.dagmar.dk). **No credit cards. Map** p310 O11.

Imperial
Ved Vesterport 4 (70 13 12 11/www.film.eon.dk). **Credit** DC. **Map** p310 O10.

Palads
Axeltorv 9 (70 13 12 11/www.film.eon.dk). **Credit** DC. **Map** p310 O11.

Palladium
Vesterbrogade 1 (70 13 12 11/www.film.eon.dk) **Credit** DC. **Map** p310 O11.

Park Bio
Østerbrogade 79, Østerbro (35 38 33 62). Bus 6, 14. **No credit cards. Map** p121 D13.

Scala Biograferne
Axeltorv 2 (33 13 81 00/www.scalabiograferne.dk). **No credit cards. Map** p310 O11.

Tycho Brahe Omnimax
Gammel Kongevej 10 (33 12 12 24). **Credit** AmEx, DC, MC, V. **Map** p310 P10.

Art house cinemas

Gloria
Rådhuspladsen 59 (33 12 42 92/www.gloria.dk). **No credit cards. Map** p310 O12.

Grand Teatret
Mikkel Bryggers Gade 8 (33 15 16 11/ www.grandteatret.dk). **No credit cards. Map** p310 O12.

Husets Biograf
2nd Floor, Magstræde 14 (33 32 40 77). **No credit cards. Map** p311 O13.

Vester Vov Vov
Absalonsgade 5, Vesterbro (33 24 42 00/www.vester-vov-vov.dk). Bus 6, 16, 28. **No credit cards. Map** p111 Q9.

Drive-ins

Drive In Bio
Refshalevej 114, Amager (32 54 00 33/ www.drivein.dk). **No credit cards. Map** p309 K21.

Galleries

Copenhagen boasts a remarkably rich and diverse art scene.

As in so many other European cities, the Copenhagen art scene exists on three separate levels. The first is the trade houses – firms buying and selling art, hosting only the occasional exhibition. The second is the managers: galleries built up around a stable of artists, managing and promoting them, and using the venue as a showroom. The third level is the one you read about in the art magazines, galleries devoted to examining and analysing art as a social phenomenon, a philosophical commentary on our world – these galleries also serve the purpose of meeting places for all parties interested in contemporary art.

It's also important to note that Copenhagen is a very Internet-oriented place, and that more and more guides to the cultural life of the city are popping up on the web. The most relevant here are **www.kulturnet.dk** for the established, museum-oriented art and culture news; **www.crafts.dk** for all design-related news and events; **www.artaround.dk** for updates and total info service focusing on galleries and exhibitions in Copenhagen (artaround.dk is an Internet portal representing only galleries with the highest standards in contemporary and modern art, as well as independent artists. It will soon open its own gallery space in Copenhagen); and finally **www.oddresort.com** which likens galleries to resort destinations, and combines the two subjects in a unique tableau of art and culture. General culture listings can always be found on **www.aok.dk**, which is listing more and more things in English, and the website of the English-language newspaper *Copenhagen Post* at **www.cphpost.dk**.

A recent development in the Copenhagen art scene has been the mass migration of cutting-edge galleries to the last undeveloped region of the city, Islands Brygge, south of Christianshavn on Amager. With large loft spaces still being rented out at affordable prices, this area of town could (with a little imagination) be regarded as Copenhagen's own little SoHo, anno 1970, though the cafés and trendy restaurants are yet to arrive.

> ▶ **Note:** the major public art galleries are listed within the sightseeing chapters; see page 53.

Centre

Bie & Vadstrup

Store Strandstræde 19B (33 91 14 91/www.bie-vadstrup.com). **Open** noon-6pm Tue-Fri; 11am-2pm Sat; closed Mon, Sun. **Credit** DC, MC, V. **Map** p312 M16.

With seven or eight exhibitions yearly, this gallery primarily concentrates on the efforts of younger Danish artists. The focus of the gallery is on painting, installation and video art.

Black Diamond

Søren Kierkegaards Plads 1 (33 47 47 47/tours 33 47 48 80/www.kb.dk). **Open** 10am-7pm Mon-Sat; closed Sun. **Admission** 30kr; 10kr concessions. **No credit cards. Map** p311 P15.

The Black Diamond is the nickname for the new extension to the Royal Library, which also contains two galleries: one for cultural history exhibitions, the other an exhibition space of the National Photography Museum. In addition, there is a rare book room, a fine restaurant (Søren K; *see p140*) and a concert hall with 600 seats.

Charlottenborg Udstillingsbygning

Nyhavn 2 (33 13 40 22/www.charlottenborg-art.dk). **Open** 10am-5pm Mon, Tue, Thur-Sun; 10am-7pm Wed. **Admission** 20kr; 10kr concessions. **No credit cards. Map** p312 M16.

Exhibiting Danish and international contemporary art, this huge gallery is host to spring and autumn exhibitions widely considered to be the most important group shows in Denmark. The hall was built in 1883 at the request of an influential group of Danish artists, and is now run by the Danish Ministry of Culture. The gallery is located in the rear of Charlottenborg Slot, home of the Royal Danish Academy of Art.

Clausens Kunsthandel

Toldbodgade 9 (33 15 41 54/ www.clausenskunsthandel.dk). **Open** 11am-5pm Mon-Sat; closed Sun. **No credit cards. Map** p308 K17.

Clausens has been working the art trade since 1953, and has built up an impressive selection of graphic work by some of Denmark's most established artists. The two-floor building also houses a gallery with regular exhibitions, but Clausens is best known for its collection of affordable signed prints.

Copenhagen Art Gallery

Rådhusstræde 3A (33 12 89 80/www.copenhagen-art.dk). **Open** 1-5pm Wed-Fri or by appointment. **No credit cards. Map** p311 O13.

Arts & Entertainment

Dealing everything from abstract expressionism to documentary photography, Copenhagen Art Gallery is open to the trade by appointment only. Among the artists represented here are Per Kirkeby, Carl-Henning Pedersen, Poul Janus Ipsen and Gérard Venturelli.

Danske Grafikeres Hus
Sølvgade 14 (33 13 31 85). **Open** 1-6pm Tue-Fri; closed Mon, Sat, Sun. **No credit cards.**
Map p307 K15.
In addition to an exhibition space for Danish graphic artists, Grafikeres Hus also runs a graphic art information centre, hosting a number of meetings and symposiums on graphic art, and an archive of over 500 works.

Fotografisk Center
Gammel Strand 48 (33 93 09 96/www.photography. dk/www.digitalroom.org). **Open** 11am-5pm Tue-Sun; closed Mon. **Admission** 25kr; 20kr concessions; free under-12s. **Credit** MC, V. **Map** p311 N14.
Six exhibitions yearly of mostly modern photographic art. The Fotografisk Center also functions as the only art book shop in the country specialising solely in the photographic arts.

Galerie Asbæk
Bredgade 20 (33 15 40 04/www.asbaek.dk).
Open 11am-6pm Mon-Fri; 11am-4pm Sat; closed Sun. **Credit** AmEx, DC, MC, V. **Map** p312 M16.

Since its inception in 1975, Asbæk has been one of Denmark's leading galleries. Patricia and Jacob Asbæk have collected an impressive stable of modern artists, and their prices are commensurately high, with works easily running up to 100,000kr. In the gallery's shop, graphic works, books and posters, as well as international art magazines line the walls. The Asbæk café is a good place to stop for a cup of coffee while doing the gallery crawl.

Galleri Bo Bjerggaard
Pilestræde 48, 2nd floor (33 93 42 21/ www.bjerggaard.com). **Open** noon-6pm Tue-Fri; 11am-3pm Sat; closed Mon, Sun. **No credit cards.**
Map p311 M14.
Well-established gallery with a tendency towards exhibiting the 'sure thing'. With artists like Baselitz, Kirkeby and Picabia in its stable, Bjerggaard is recognised as one of the better trade galleries, and hosts six to eight exhibitions a year.

Galleri Christian Dam
Bredgade 23 (33 15 78 78/www.gcd.dk).
Open noon-5pm Mon-Fri; noon-3pm Sat; closed Sun. Closed 3 weeks July. **No credit cards.**
Map p312 M16.
Christian Dam concentrates primarily on the COBRA artists, and their artistic heirs. The gallery owns a great deal of work by Robert Jacobsen, Asger Jørn and Lise Malinovsky, and hosts four to six exhibitions yearly.

Prominent Danish artists

Bertel Thorvaldsen (1770-1844)
Enrolled at the Royal Academy at the age of 11, Thorvaldsen is a national treasure in Denmark. For details of why, see page 81 **Great Danes: Bertel Thorvaldsen.**

Christen Købke (1810-48)
Growing up as a baker's son in the military settlement of Kastellet, Købke is best known for his paintings of the milieu in and around his workplace, which exhibit a very refined sense of characterisation. A pupil of Thorvaldsen's friend CW Eckersberg, Købke was an accomplished colourist and painter of domestic scenes and portraits. Although he achieved little recognition in his own time, he is now generally regarded as one of the finest Danish painters of the 'Golden Age', and is currently enjoying immense popularity on the international scene.

JA Jerichau (1816-83)
Jerichau tudied under Thorvaldsen in Rome in his early 20s, where he was heavily influenced by New Classicism. He quickly broke away from Thorvaldsen's style, and began to concentrate on a more dramatic, storytelling approach. At 33, Jerichau was elected to Rome's Academy, yet he wasn't accepted by Danish critics until well after his death. Some of Jerichau's more important pieces can be found at the Ny Carlsberg Glyptotek (see page 64).

Jens Ferdinand Willumsen (1863-1958)
Originally trained as an architect, Willumsen's first major contribution to the Danish art world was the designing of the Free Exhibition Hall in Copenhagen (1898). A naturalist until the late 1880s, Willumsen was greatly influenced by his meeting with Gauguin in Brittany in 1890, while the Dane was living in Paris. His most famous piece, *The Great Relief* (1893-1928) is currently on loan to Statens Museum for Kunst (see page 98). One of his last great works, *Tizian Dying* (1935-8), is a triptych self-portrait, which now hangs at the Willumsen Museum in Frederikssund. Many of his works are on view at Statens Museum for Kunst.

Galerie Mikæl Andersen.

Mostly an art trade showroom, Faurschou deals in contemporary art, and is regarded as one of the better galleries of its kind. Faurschou represents Michæl Kvium, Christian Lemmertz, Balder Olrik and Polish artist Zbigniew Libera. Occasionally it get its hands on a Monet, Picasso or Rauschenberg.

Galerie Frahm
Bredgade 73 (33 91 84 84). **Open** 11am-6pm Mon-Fri; 11am-4pm Sat; closed Sun. **No credit cards.** **Map** p308 K16.
A progressive modern art gallery concentrating on the COBRA artists, Frahm was started with a private collection, but has quickly grown into a major player in the art trade.

Galerie Egelund
Landemærket 12 (33 93 92 00/www.egelund.dk). **Open** 11am-6pm Mon-Fri; 11am-3pm Sat; closed Sun. **Credit** AmEx, DC, MC, V. **Map** p307 L14.
A contemporary art gallery with eight exhibitions yearly. Egelund's stable includes Poul Janus Ibsen, Anne Vilsbøll, Tom Krøjer, Grazyna Gots and Aaron Fink.

Galleri Faurschou
Store Strandstræde 21 (33 91 41 31). **Open** 11am-6pm Tue-Fri; 11am-2pm Sat; closed Mon, Sun. **No credit cards.** **Map** p312 M16.

Galleri Heede & Moestrup
Gothersgade 29 (33 14 64 74).
Open 1-5.30pm Tue-Fri; 10am-2pm Sat; closed Mon, Sun. **No credit cards.** **Map** p307 L14.
Galleri Heede & Moestrup specialises in modern art, and its four floors house everything from sculpture to sketches. The gallery also runs an in-house art publishing company, primarily producing exhibition catalogues.

Galerie Mikael Andersen
Bredgade 63 (33 33 05 12/www.gma.dk).
Open noon-5pm Tue-Fri; 10am-2pm Sat; closed Mon, Sun. **No credit cards.**
Map p308 L16.

Vilhelm Hammershøi (1864-1916)
Sometimes called the Whistler of Danish Art, Hammershøi worked with only a few simple subjects – his family, his home, and important buildings in Copenhagen and London – but was still considered scandalous in the rigidly conservative Danish scene. His paintings concentrate on the relationship of light and air to empty space, which was reflected in the blank expressions of his subjects. When his work was rejected twice in a row from the Royal Exhibition space at Charlottenborg Slot, a supporter of Hammershøi, Johan Rohde, took it upon himself to establish an alternative exhibition space, designed by popular painter and architect Jens Willumsen. Den Frie Udstillingsted (Free Exhibition Hall) was to be Hammershøi's haven for the rest of his career.

Rudolph Tegner (1873-1950)
Inspired by Rodin in the late 1800s, Tegner was later to develop his own style of sculptural symbolism, which never found favour with the public or the art world, but did result in Tegner building his own extraordinary museum to what he saw as his neglected genius. See also page 275 **Great Danes? Rudolph Tegner.**

Franciska Clausen (1899-1986)
A student of Fernand Léger in 1920s Paris, Clausen was profoundly influenced by his tight, abstract paintings. She became the first Danish artist to work solely with the abstract form. Clausen exhibited regularly with Léger, and earned extra money enlarging his works. Towards the start of the '30s, Clausen left Léger's side and began to find her influence in the Dutch De Stijl school, of which Piet Mondrian was a member. Her influence on the Dutch group was significant, redefining its geometric style and thereby earning its respect. Her return to Denmark, however, saw an end to experimentation. She lived as a portrait painter from the late '30s onward, though she did experiment with collage in the '50s and mosaic in the '70s.

Wilhelm Freddie (1909-95)
The son of the pathology lab director at the University of Copenhagen, Wilhelm Freddie was one of Denmark's leading surrealist painters. He worked with paintings, collages and objects characteristically made up of opposing elements in a dreamlike and hallucinatory universe. He had his first solo show at the age of 22, where he exhibited ▶

Galerie Mikæl Andersen opened in 1989, and has come to be a major force in the Copenhagen art world, representing a number of artists who debuted in the mid '80s, and who have gone on to be internationally significant. The gallery also exhibits selected 'classic' artists. Among the exhibited artists are Kaspar Bonnén, Mogens Andersen, fos, Günther Förg, Poul Gernes, Sonja Ferlov Mancoba, Øivind Nygård, and Tal R.

Galleri Nørby
Vestergade 8 (33 15 19 20/www.galleri-noerby.dk). **Open** noon-5.30pm Tue-Thur; noon-6pm Fri; 11am-2pm Sat; closed Mon, Sun. **Credit** AmEx, DC, MC, V. **Map** p310 O12.
Galleri Nørby is a ceramics gallery that has, for the last decade, represented the most celebrated ceramic artists in Denmark. With both a showroom and artists' studios on the premises, Nørby is the primary resource for ceramic-oriented art in Denmark. Note: a 10% charge will be added to all credit card payments (except Visa).

Galleri Søren Houmann
Sølvgade 9 (33 13 13 99). **Open** noon-5pm Tue-Fri; 11am-2pm Sat; closed Mon, Sun. **No credit cards.** **Map** p307 K15.
Houmann is one of the newcomers on the Copenhagen gallery scene. He comes from an institutional background (the conservative world of museums rather than the hip underground scene)

and often works with very young artists, still in, or just out of, the academies. His respected gallery is positioned at the top end of the quality range, and is sharply focused on Copenhagen artists, especially painters. John Kørner, Jacob Tell and Claus Carstensen are among the few artists in his stable. Houmann can always be counted on for good, stimulating exhibitions.

Galleri Specta
Peder Skrams Gade 13 (33 13 01 23/www.specta.dk). **Open** noon- 5.30pm Tue-Fri; 11am-2pm Sat; closed Mon, Sun. **No credit cards.** **Map** p312 N16.
Gallerist Else Johannesen was one of the most respected in the art scene in Århus, Denmark's second largest city. Her work there with the Baghuset project is recognised as having had tremendous influence on the Danish scene in general. She moved to Copenhagen in 1992 and established Specta, a gallery which today is well known throughout Europe; both because of its success on the international art fair scene, and due to the competent work Johannesen has done for her artists. She represents Sylvie Fleury, Clay Ketter, Anders Moseholm and the late Sven Daalskov – who has enjoyed quite a lot of success at the auctions recently. Specta sells well, thanks in large measure to its collection of smaller works and collectibles by some of the more cutting edge Danish artists.

▶ # Prominent Danish artists (continued)

readymades, or found objects in unusual, unpredictable combinations. He was invited to participate in the 1936 International Surrealist Exhibition in London, but due to the morbidly sexual nature of his art, all his pieces were seized by the British authorities and sent back to Denmark. In 1937, Copenhagen police seized three of his paintings from an exhibition, and he received a short prison sentence. Because of his outspoken criticism of the Nazis in the late '30s, Freddie was forced into exile in Sweden, where he remained until 1950.

Robert Jacobsen (1912-93)
Auto-didactic artist Jacobsen began making compositions in wood, and had his first major exhibition in 1945 at the Harvest Exhibition, where he exhibited nine gigantic sculptures under the name *Fable Animals*. Working primarily with granite until 1947, Jacobsen was forced to switch to welding iron when the risk of his sculptures crumbling to pieces was increased by his decision to investigate the empty space created when he hacked his way

through his work. Through Jacobsen's exploration of the air in and around his heavy, iron sculptures, he created a new, contradictory yet playful tendency in Danish art. In the mid '50s, Jacobsen introduced a polychromatic use of colours to his work. He was later named honorary professor at the academies in Munich and Florence, officer of the French Legion of Honour and Commander of the Order of Arts and Letters. He is represented in most of Denmark's museums.

Asger Jørn (1914-73)
Jørn debuted in 1933, and shortly thereafter left the country to study in Paris with Léger. Jørn, with artists from Belgium and Holland, founded the COBRA (COpenhagen, BRussels, Amsterdam) group. In 1953, after years in a sanatorium convalescing from severe TB, Jørn left Denmark, swearing that he was finished with Danish art. Relocated in Paris, Jørn's breakthrough was his 1958 painting *Letter to my Son*, now a part of the Tate Modern collection in London. Upon returning to Denmark in 1961, Jørn announced his intention to document 10,000 years of Scandinavian art in a 30-volume history. He was forced to give up the project in '66, after

Galerie Susanne Højriis

Bredgade 63, 1st floor (33 14 04 41). **Open** 11am-5pm Tue-Fri; 11am-2pm Sat; closed Mon, Sun. **Credit** MC. **Map** p308 K16.

Højriis ended her stint as curator of Gallerihuset on Studiestræde by opening this upmarket gallery specialising in established Danish contemporary artists like Thyra Hilden, Julie Sass and Kasper Holten. Højriis focuses on classically oriented artists producing figurative, realistic painting or sculpture. The gallery is located directly above Galleri Mikæl Andersen.

Galleri Susanne Ottesen

Gothersgade 49 (33 15 52 44). **Open** 10am-1pm, 2-6pm Tue-Fri; 11am-3pm Sat; closed Mon, Sun. **No credit cards. Map** p307 L14.

Like Galleri Asbæk on Bredgade, Ottesen represents the established generation of contemporary artists. The gallery opened its doors to the public in 1989, and has had an impressive string of exhibitions, including Per Kirkeby, Kirsten Ortwed, Cindy Sherman and Kehnet Nielsen.

Kunstakademiets Udstillingssted

Peder Skrams Gade 2 (33 74 46 18). **Open** 2-6pm Tue-Sun; closed Mon. **Admission** free. **No credit cards. Map** p312 N16.

The Royal Academy of Art's official exhibition space for students, offering a good-sized gallery for work of varying quality. The shows aren't on for long, so it's possible to catch a cross-section of the current stock of Danish artists over a short period of time.

Kunstforeningen

Gammel Strand 48 (33 36 02 60/ www.kunstforeningen.dk). **Open** 11am-5pm Tue-Sun; closed Mon. **Admission** 30kr; 20kr concessions. **Credit** DC, MC, V. **Map** p311 N14.

Kunstforeningen was built in 1825, and has been an institution in Danish art ever since. With five exhibitions a year, Kunstforeningen focuses its attention on presenting shows that reflect the age we live in, often through retrospectives or importing group shows from abroad. The building also houses a café and the Photographic Centre gallery.

Nikolaj Udstillingsbygning

Nikolaj Plads (33 93 16 26). **Open** noon-5pm daily. **Admission** 20kr; 10kr concessions; free under-14s & to all Wed. **No credit cards. Map** p311 N15.

Carlsberg Brewery founder Carl Jacobsen turned this fire-damaged church into a cultural centre in 1917. With a small permanent collection and four exhibition spaces, Nikolaj certainly has enough room for the constant flow of (mostly group) shows that pass through its doors. Fluxus artist Eric Andersen created a permanent installation here, *the crying room*, which is adorned with all kinds of things that can make you cry (onions, needles, etc). There's also a prose jukebox in the foyer containing 381 aural artworks.

having collected 25,000 photographs. The abstract nature of his paintings soon became a metaphor for his life, as he switched to writing, and produced a large body of work.

Albert Mertz (1920-90)

Via experimentation with pointillism and abstract art, Mertz established himself as one of the most important Danish artists of the 1940s. His experimental film collaborations with Jørgen Roos are considered turning points in Danish cinema. Working with a wide variety of media, Mertz excelled in everything from radical modernism to photo-montage and collage. A repeating theme in his work has been his critique of the more accepted art forms. In the '60s Mertz joined the Fluxus movement, and subsequently developed his colour system of only blue and red, which had been inspired by the concept art he had been so taken with while living in France. Despite his rejection of traditional art, the later part of his career was made up solely of works on canvas.

Per Kirkeby (born 1938)

Originally educated as a geologist, Kirkeby took part in scientific expeditions in Greenland throughout the 1960s, but also participated in the founding of the Danish Fluxus movement in 1962. Kirkeby's painting style moved steadily away from the figurative, and towards a concentration on black holes, or caves on canvas, and then on towards the architectonic, resulting in the red brick structures for which he is known today. Visitors to the Louisiana Museum For Moderne Kunst (see page 272) are greeted by one of Kirkeby's structures as they step off the train. In addition to his work as a fine artist, Kirkeby has contributed numerous essays and publications on Danish literary life, as well as two documentary films on the lives of Asger Jørn (1976) and Bertel Thorvaldsen (1980).

Olafur Eliasson (born 1967)

One of the most influential contemporary artists in Denmark, Eliasson commands a great deal of respect internationally. His medium is usually the classic installation, often with some relationship to nature, though he often works with engineers to alter natural laws, like his *Waterfall* (1998) which ran uphill, or his outdoor ice skating rink in Sao Paolo. His tendency to use one of the four elements, combined with modern technology, makes him an exciting artist to watch out for.

Arts & Entertainment

North Udstillingssted

Nørregade 7C, basement (33 93 94 60/www.north-udstillingssted.dk). **Open** 1-5pm Tue-Fri; 11am-3pm Sat; closed Mon, Sun. **No credit cards.** **Map** p310 M12.

North was recently taken over by a group of young Danish artists, and is dedicated to artistic dialogue with artists in other countries. The result is an interesting mix of styles and nationalities, as well as three yearly group shows representing the best of the three Danish art academies.

Rundetårn

Købmagergade 52A (33 73 03 73/www.rundetaarn. dk). **Open** Sept-May 10am-5pm Mon-Sat; noon-5pm Sun. *June-Aug* 10am-8pm Mon-Sat; noon-8pm Sun. **Admission** 15kr; 5kr-10kr concessions. **Credit** AmEx, DC, MC, V. **Map** p311 M13.

The Rundetårn (Round Tower; *see p69*), was originally built as an astronomy centre in 1642. Now it houses a unique exhibition space with six to eight shows each year, often concentrating on design and architecture or theological issues (the gallery is built on top of a church). There are often small ensemble classical concerts here as well. While visiting the Rundetårn, be sure to take a look at Copenhagen from the roof-top observatory.

Christianshavn

Art Salon

Strandgade 50 (32 95 85 98). **Open** 11am-5pm Tue-Fri; 11am-3pm Sat; closed Mon, Sun. **No credit cards.** **Map** p312 O16.

The Art Salon specialises in Danish and Nordic art, representing among others William Skotte Olsen and Niels Reumart. The gallery hosts 12 exhibitions each year, in a wide variety of disciplines.

Christiania Museum of Art

Loppen Building, Christiania (32 96 20 94). **Open** noon-5pm Tue-Sun; closed Mon. **Admission** free. **No credit cards.** **Map** p312 P18.

No visit to Copenhagen would be complete without a visit to Christiania, where hippy culture seems to have won its eternal battle with the authorities. The Christiania Museum of Art is no exception, often presenting work that in any other setting would be seen as unusual at best. Be sure to check out the nightclub and restaurant in the same building for some of Copenhagen's best nightlife.

Frederiks Bastion

Refshalevej 28 (32 57 08 51/www.arts.dk/gallerie/ bastion). **Open** noon-5pm Tue, Thur-Sun; noon-7pm Wed; closed Mon. **Admission** 20kr; concessions 10kr. **No credit cards.** **Map** p313 M21.

Frederiks Bastion was built in 1744 as part of Copenhagen's military defence against sea attacks. Today, it's a gallery with a large permanent collection and various temporary exhibitions. The Bastion concentrates its attention on Nordic art, and presents a wide variety of styles.

Galerie Edition Copenhagen

1st Floor, Strandgade 70 (32 54 33 11). **Open** 9am-5pm Mon-Fri; closed Sat, Sun. **Admission** free. **No credit cards.** **Map** p312 O16.

Galerie Edition Copenhagen is a gallery and lithographic workshop for contemporary Danish and German art, concentrating primarily on artists from the 20th century. The gallery also houses a collection of sketches by such noted artists as Michael Kvium and Lise Malinovsky, and even writer Günter Grass.

Overgaden

Overgaden Neden Vandet 17 (32 57 72 73/ www.kulturnet.dk/homes/overgaden). **Open** 1-5pm Tue-Sun; closed Mon. **No credit cards.** **Map** p312 P17.

Overgaden is a two-floor open exhibition space for younger experimental artists. It's previously hosted a series of exciting shows and the facilities are top notch. A three-person committee sifts through hundreds of applications a year, and the shows it sets up (often two at the same time) tend to be of a very high standard.

Islands Brygge

This fast-developing area lies by the waterside on Amager, just south of Christianshavn.

Galleri Nicolai Wallner

Njalsgade 21 Building 15 (33 13 09 70/ www.nicolaiwallner.com). **Open** noon-5pm Tue-Fri; noon-3pm Sat; closed Sun. **No credit cards.**

One of the most significant of the contemporary art galleries in Copenhagen, Wallner single-handedly changed the art scene here in the early '90s. Among Wallner's stable, artists like Joachim Koester, Jonathan Monk, Gitte Villesen, Jes Brinch, Henrik Plenge Jakobsen, Christian Schmidt-Rasmussen and Jens Haaning (the best conceptual artist of the younger generation), make sure that the gallery remains important. The gallery moved to Islands Brygge in 1999, to a building that has come to house many of the more hip galleries in town. Definitely worth a visit.

Galleri Nicolai Wallner.

Arts & Entertainment

Danish art movements

The **Fluxus** art movement began in 1960 as an offshoot of the Action Art and the Happenings scenes. As the name would imply, the Fluxus movement was based on flexibility, a constantly bubbling cauldron of impressions and ideas, involving dance, theatre, music, poetry, pantomime and the visual arts. The manifestation of a Fluxus event was dependent upon audience participation and intrusion. Fluxus was inspired by the courses in experimental composition that John Cage conducted at the end of the 1950s at the New School in New York. The high point of Danish Fluxus was the Tabernakel exhibition at the Louisiana Museum For Moderne Kunst (see page 272) in 1970, which featured works by German Josef Beuys, and Danes Kirkeby and Nørgård.

The **Nye Vilde** (New Wild) movement of the early '80s encompassed two groups of artists. The first were students at the Art Academy, whose breakthrough occurred with the infamous Knife on the Head exhibition at Tranegården in 1982. Among the artists exhibiting were Claus Carstensen and Peter Bonde, who later became professors at the academy, and who were, in 1999, taken to task by Denmark's leading tabloid newspaper *Ekstrabladet* which ran front page stories about the two artists for weeks, debating the integrity of their work. The second group was

made up of members of the now defunct atelier Værst, and included artists such as Erik A Frandsen, Christian Lemmerz and Ane Mette Ruge. This group was opposed to the more formal and theoretical approach of the Academy group and much more anarchistic in its approach to art and artistic expression. Not an actual, organised movement, the New Wild was more of a tendency in Danish art of the '80s. Most of the New Wild artists are featured in the collection of Statens Museum for Kunst (see page 98).

Working under the supposition that the art world has become so institutionalised that it no longer serves its societal function, **Superflex** was founded by three students at the Royal Academy in 1993. Bjørnstjerne Christiansen, Rasmus Nielsen and Jakob Fenger have created in Superflex an artistic form called Social Intervention: a comment on, or an intervention into, society at large. Superflex's work has encompassed a fascinating range of activity, from providing self-sustaining natural gas installations to African villagers to an Internet television station (www.superchannel.org, with extensive audio and visual archives) to transportable orange saunas. Superflex's new base is an office at Blågårdsgade 11B in Copenhagen, which is a combination atelier, TV studio and office/showroom called Situflex.

Galleri Tommy Lund
Njalsgade 21, Building 15 (32 57 79 57).
Open noon-5pm Tue-Fri; noon-3pm Sat; closed Mon, Sun. **No credit cards**.
Galleri Tommy Lund is one of the most successful of Copenhagen's newer contemporary art galleries. Lund is often applauded for his 'hands-on' approach to his exhibitions, and is among the most active gallery owners in the capital. Although already making an impact both internationally and locally with significant major shows and sales, what makes Lund's gallery so successful is his tireless dedication to his field and his stable of artists. Among the artists Lund represents are Ann Lislegaard, Knut Åsdam, Katja Sander and Klaus Tejl Jacobsen.

Jacob Fabricius/Recent Works
Njalsgade 21, Building 15 (32 57 09 79).
Open noon-5pm Tue-Fri; noon-3pm Sat; closed Mon, Sun. **No credit cards**.
Jacob Fabricius got his start as Nicolai Wallner's assistant, and now has his own space located inside the Wallner gallery. Occasionally, he can also be

found curating larger shows and different projects with artists around the city. Admirably, Fabricius falls for art, not potential sales, and his gallery is dominated by concept-oriented art, everything from painting to video, and a host of unknown up-and-coming artists from abroad. He is also known for his progressive and inventive thinking in exhibition form.

The Leisure Club Mogadishni
Artillerivej 40, Building 9 B, 4th floor (32 54 35 35).
Open noon-4pm Wed-Sat; closed Mon, Tue, Sun. **No credit cards**.
Mogadishni opened its doors in the Njalsgade complex on Islands Brygge in February 2000 as an exhibition space hosting long-term exhibitions of contemporary art. The gallery was established by students from the Jutland Art Academy, in a shrewd move to give their own art a showcase platform in Copenhagen. Also known for its innovative events, don't be surprised to find Mogadishni's gallery floor covered with grass and a pirate radio station set up in the corner by the self-service teaset.

Nils Stærk

Njalsgade 19C (32 54 45 62/www.nilsstaerk.dk).
Open noon-5pm Thur, Fri; noon-3pm Sat; other
times by appointment; closed Mon-Wed, Sun.
No credit cards.
Stærk is a relative newcomer, but has been successful in promoting his artists to the larger museum exhibitions in Denmark. A manager in the best
sense of the word, Nils Stærk's stable is one of the
strongest in Copenhagen, and is well respected
internationally. Representing artists like Martin
Bigum, Miriam Bäckström, Ingvar Cronhammer,
Jeremy Dickinson, Mads Gamdrup, Bjarne
Melgaard and Daniel Pflumm is a full-time job,
but Stærk is also able to run an established and
successful gallery.

Vesterbro

Galleri Trap

Vesterbrogade 111, Vesterbro (33 31 90 38).
Bus 6. **Open** noon-6pm Thur-Sun; closed Mon-Wed.
No credit cards. Map p111 Q7.
For dentist Jørgen Trap-Jensen, being a gallery
owner had been a lifelong dream, until, 27 years ago,
he actually opened one. When he eventually sold his
clinic-cum-showroom, he moved to Copenhagen and
established this combination trade and exhibition
establishment. Most of the major Danish old-school
players are represented here.

Øksnehallen

*Halmtorvet 11, Vesterbro (33 86 04 00/
www.oeksnehallen.dk).* **Open** 11am-6pm Tue,
Thur-Sun; 9am-9pm Wed; closed Mon; times vary,
depending on exhibition. **Credit** MC, V.
Map p310 Q10.
This was once the largest slaughterhouse in
Copenhagen, but, after many dormant years, it was
turned into a cultural centre in 1996. At a massive
5,000sq m (53,700sq ft), Øksnehallen is ideal for larger events, such as fashion shows, trade shows and
conventions. Exhibitions tend to concentrate on
photography and design.

Stalke Galleri

*Vesterbrogade 14A (backyard), Vesterbro (33 21 15
33/www.stalke.dk). Bus 6, 28.* **Open** 1-6pm Wed-Fri,
11am-3pm Sat; closed Mon, Tue, Sun. **No credit
cards. Map** p310 P10.
Since 1987, Stalke Galleri has played an important
role in the contemporary art scene in Copenhagen.
Named after the Tarkovski film *Stalker*, it is a very
international gallery, and has put on over 100 exhibitions since its inception. Stalke likes to consider
itself a 'cowboy-gallery' that hosts unexpected and
unconventional exhibitions; it has worked with a
large number of artists, in such a way as to be
collaborative rather than representational. Stalke
has exhibited international artists such as Lawrence
Weiner and Anastasi, among others, and always has
new works by internationally renowned Olafur
Eliasson (*see p205*).

Nørrebro & Østerbro

Den Frie Udstillingsbygning

Oslo Plads, Østerbro (33 12 28 03/www.denfrie.dk).
Open 10am-5pm daily. **Admission** 20kr.
No credit cards. Map p307 H15.
Built in 1891, as an alternative to Charlottenborg, it
houses a permanent exhibition of modern Danish
art, as well as hosting yearly exhibitions.

Gallerie Die Werkstatt

*Stockholmsgade 23, Østerbro (35 42 62 59/
www.gdw.dk).* **Open** noon-5pm Wed-Fri; noon-3pm
Sat; closed Mon, Tue, Sun. **Map** p307 H15.
Galleri Die Werkstatt concentrates its attention on
contemporary avant-garde art, with eight exhibitions yearly of everything from sculpture and painting to installations and experimental graphics.

Galleri Grønlund

*Sankt Jakobs Plads 6, Østerbro (35 43 20 07/
www.glassart.dk). Bus 6, 14.* **Open** 11am-5.30pm
Tue-Fri; 11am-2pm Sat; closed Mon, Sun.
No credit cards. Map p121 D13.
The only gallery in Copenhagen specialising solely
in glass art, and housing both a permanent collection and a showroom with moderately priced work.

Galleri Starving Artistz

*Elmegade 17, Nørrebro (26 16 07 16/26 18 07 16/
www.starving-artistz.dk). Bus 3.* **Open** noon-6pm
Tue-Fri; 11am-6pm Sat; closed Mon, Sun.
No credit cards. Map p306 J10.
At the Starving Artistz gallery you can afford to be
the owner of a piece of fine art – even if you're on
the dole. The gallery primarily sells drawings and
graphic pieces by younger artists, not all of whom
have attended the Royal Academy.

Other

N55

32 57 78 70/www.n55.dk.
N55 isn't exactly a gallery, but it is a dynamic and
significant presence in the Copenhagen art scene.
N55 is a group of artists that creates concrete
structures with fundamental significance to our
daily lives, which at the same time have aesthetic
and ethical consequences. These works are exhibited publicly, and, more often than not, in forms
resembling houses (which are both artworks in
themselves, and galleries containing other exhibits).
Check the group's website for updates.

OTTO

OTTO is a mobile exhibition forum that has been
making its mark in Copenhagen for several years. It
is run by four students from the Royal Academy and
an art historian. One of the trademarks of an OTTO
exhibition is its typically unusual choice of exhibition spaces, like a Halal butcher or the basement of
an apartment block. Check www.artnode.dk/otto for
updates on this exciting project.

Gay & Lesbian

Enjoy a small but perfectly formed scene.

Denmark is a frontrunner in many aspects of gay culture, so it's surprising to find a rather measly gay scene in Copenhagen. Part of the reason is that the Danes' live-and-let-live attitude gives gay Danes little to kick against. But what the Danish gay scene lacks in size, it makes up for in its unique charm and – surprisingly – warmth (that quintessential Danish concept of *hygge*; *see page 79*).

The oldest gay publication in Europe, the first male-to-female sex transplant, and the first gay marriage are just some of the big contributions of the egalitarian Danish society to gay culture. And it doesn't stop there: in 1998, a member of the Danish parliament made headlines when he brought his gay partner to Queen Margrethe's annual court ball (the queen, of course, welcomed the gay couple). During **Mermaid Pride** (*see page 212*) that summer, leather men were seen waltzing in the open air at Tivoli, along with other ballroom dance queens. The Danes smiled and took photos, along with bemused Japanese tourists. Such is the beauty of Hans Christian Andersen's fairytale homeland.

But all is not too well in gay Copenhagen. A *laissez-faire* attitude prevails among gay Copenhageners, which is causing damage to gay businesses here. The members of **Copenhagen Gay Life**, a young association of gay and gay-friendly businesses, are struggling hard to make local gays patronise their venues. Casualties are emerging: **Babooshka**, the only lesbian bar on the scene, closed in 2000, followed by **Café Size**, the largest gay café and bar.

Lesbian visibility is being promoted through an annual Lesbian Awards ceremony which honours lesbian achievers. At present, gay adoption rights are being debated in parliament, as well as the rights of lesbians to receive artificial insemination.

For a good overview of gay life in Copenhagen and plenty of useful information, see **www.copenhagen-gay-life.dk**.

Bars & clubs

Admission is free unless otherwise stated.

Amigo Bar

Schønbergsgade 4, Frederiksberg (33 21 49 15). Bus 1, 14. **Open** 10pm-5am daily. **No credit cards.** **Map** p111 O8.

Although this isn't really a gay bar, it is popular among the 'straight fetishists', and has a very relaxed and unpretentious feel. The sing-along side to Amigo Bar doesn't discourage off-key amateurs from trying a note or two, and the male regulars do not exactly complain about the attention they get from Versace-clad boyband wannabes insouciantly sipping G&Ts.

Badboyz

www.badboyz.dk

This monthly rave is taking gay Copenhagen by storm, and boasts lots of flesh, sweat and ecstatic floor thumpers. Buy tickets in advance to avoid long queues (also available online – check the website for the forthcoming venue). Recommended.

Centralhjørnet

Kattesundet 18 (33 11 85 49). **Open** 11am-1pm Mon-Fri; noon-1am Sat, Sun. **Credit** MC, V. **Map** p310 N12.

The venerable old grandpa of all gay bars in Copenhagen. Contagious high spirits and camaraderie define Centralhjørnet, which is popular among 'daddies' and their followers. Think *Cheers* in Danish.

Cosy Bar

Studiestræde 33 (33 12 74 27). **Open** midnight-6pm Mon-Wed, Sun; 11am-8am Thur-Sat. **No credit cards.** **Map** p310 N12.

Don't be fooled by the name. Dark, boisterous and untidy, this bar is infamous for its unkempt, uncompromising male crowd. One of the oldest gay bars on the scene, and popular for its cheap drinks and no-nonsense cruising. Women are welcome but should be wary about the activity in the ever-busy ladies' toilet.

Masken Bar

Studiestræde 33 (33 91 09 37). **Open** 4pm-2am Mon-Fri; 3pm-2am Sat, Sun. **Credit** AmEx, DC, MC, V. **Map** p310 N12.

The cheapest beer in town is one of the draws at Masken. Its down-to-earth atmosphere makes the bar a favoured meeting place for young gays. There's a lesbian night every Thursday in the basement area.

Men's Bar

Teglgårdsstræde 3 (33 12 73 03). **Open** 3pm-2am daily. **No credit cards.** **Map** p310 N12.

The only real men's club (butch, semi-leather, you know the sort of thing) on the scene. Surprisingly friendly, and popular for its cheap drinks and Sunday brunch.

Arts & Entertainment

Bums on (and off) seats at **PAN Disco**.

Never Mind

Nørre Voldgade 2 (33 11 88 86/www.aok.dk).
Open 10am-6am daily. **Credit** AmEx, DC, MC, V.
Map p310 M12.

An intimate bar characterised by kitschy interiors, folk pop, and a mixed crowd dominated by mature gay males. Always very lively and spontaneous, so don't be surprised to witness an impromptu striptease from a merry customer.

PAN Disco

Knabrostræde 3 (33 11 37 84/www.pan-cph.dk).
Open *June-Aug* 7.30pm-3am Mon, Tue; 7.30pm-5am Wed, Thur; 7.30pm-6am Fri-Sun. *Sept-May* 7.30pm-5am Wed, Thur; 7.30pm-6am Fri, Sat; closed Mon, Tue, Sun. **Admission** 50kr; free Wed, Thur. **Credit** AmEx, DC, MC, V. **Map** p311 N13.

Copenhagen's lone gay dance club also happens to be the hottest three-floor affair in town. PAN has been getting a lot of media promotion lately, which has generated quite a following from young and trendy straights – to the consternation of the regular gay patrons. But the tempo remains upbeat, and monthly party gimmicks still reflect the club's gay identity. The main floor plays house, the second floor classic pop. Admission is free before 10pm.

Restaurants

There are few restaurants where gay couples will not feel welcome, but the following are some of the most gay-friendly places.

Base Camp

Halv Tolv, Byg 148 (70 23 23 18/www.basecamp.dk).
Open 6pm-1am Mon-Thur; 11am-5am Fri, Sat; 11am-3pm Sun. **Main courses** 150kr. **Credit** MC, V. **Map** p313 N19.

Located in a defunct military barracks, Base Camp attracts a mixed group of 'adventurous elites'. One wonders whether the place is constantly undergoing renovation or the whole mix of open kitchen, minimalist table settings and dilapidated furnitures is just 'the concept'. Dishes fuse a disparate collection of cuisines and satisfy discriminating palates. Advanced booking is advisable, as this is a popular place. The nightclub starts up at 11pm at weekends. *See also page 213.*

Krasnapolsky

Vestergade 10 (33 32 88 00/www.krasnapolsky.dk).
Open 10am-2pm Mon-Wed; 10am-5am Thur-Sat; 2pm-midnight Sun. **Credit** AmEx, DC, MC, V. **Map** p310 O12.

Not entirely a gay venue, but so much frequented by gay patrons it might as well be officially gay. At the weekend, this artsy café turns into a bar and disco around 11pm. Food (the usual basic café fare) is the poorest excuse for Krasnapolsky's existence. Locals claim that it is the bisexuals' watering hole.

Queen Victoria

Snaregade 4 (33 91 01 91/www.aok.dk).
Open 5pm-midnight daily. **Credit** AmEx, DC, MC, V. **Map** p311 O13.

The selling point of this restaurant is that it is owned by a famous drag queen, but don't expect outlandish interiors, nor a menu (largely trad Danish), that shouts 'Fabulous!'. Still, you've got to give it to the Danes that places like this actually get regular customers. Not a place for the claustrophobic.

Sebastian Café & Bar

Hyskenstræde 10 (33 32 22 79). **Open** noon-2am daily. **Credit** MC, V. **Map** p311 N13.

The most popular gay venue on the scene, Sebastian is a must for first-timers in Copenhagen. Weekend revellers make their first stop here, since it's where everyone eyes the night's offerings. Gay guys hang out in the mezzanine area, while lesbians remain in the basement pool area, as if following an unwritten code. The menu consists of light dishes and salads, and drinks during happy hour shouldn't be missed.

Sauna

Amigo Sauna

Studiestræde 31, middle building (33 15 20 28/ www.copenhagen-gay-life.dk). **Open** noon-7am Mon-Thur, Sun; noon-8am Fri, Sat. **Admission** 90kr. **Credit** MC, V. **Map** p310 N12.

This friendly sauna has been running for more than 25 years and is now an institution. It has all the effects: cabin, dark maze, video rooms and café. There's 800sq m (8,600sq ft) of steamy action on three floors, especially on Saturday nights and early Sunday afternoons. The relaxed atmosphere is no doubt helped by free massages on Tuesdays.

Sex shops

Copenhagen Gay Center

Istegade 34-36, Vesterbro (33 22 23 00/ www.copenhagengaycenter.dk). Bus 16.
Open 10am-5am daily. **Credit** MC, V. **Map** p310 Q10.

One of Copenhagen's only two gay sex shops, located in Istegade, the long-standing red light district. It houses a good collection of videos, magazines, sex toys and other accessories, plus a small two-floor sauna. Not exactly the most discreet location, but the Danes are rarely put off anyway.

Arts & Entertainment

Men's Shop
Viktoriagade 24, (33 25 44 75).
Open 10am-2am Mon-Sat; noon-2am Sun.
Credit MC, V. **Map** p310 Q10.
Not much different to the Copenhagen Gay Center (*see p210*), only this place has a video cabin instead of a sauna. And there is free coffee for those who take too much time deciding whether to bring home a Falcon or Cadinot movie.

Private clubs

Body Bio
Kingosgade 7 (no phone). **Open** noon-1am daily.
Admission 30kr. **No credit cards**. **Map** p111 Q7.
There's always some action taking place at Body Bio, probably in the video rooms which are pleasure zones for the uninhibited. This seedy yet very popular club is advertised as a mixed venue, so women and transvestites are admitted free of charge.

Loke
Nørre Søgade 23 (no phone). **Open** 3pm-1am Mon-Fri, Sun; closed Sat. **No credit cards**.
Map p306 L11.
The latest addition to the men's club scene, Loke is the biggest of them all, with its three video rooms, a dark room and a maze.

SLM
Studiestræde 14A (33 32 06 01/www.slm-cph.dk).
Open 10pm-2am Fri; closed Mon-Thur, Sat, Sun.
Admission 15kr members. **No credit cards**.
Map p310 M11.
Home to Danish leather men, SLM is a members only club, although visitors can obtain a guest card for an additional 25kr. It's open every Friday, with occasional events staged on Saturday nights (check website for details). The leather dress code is strictly enforced.

Shops

Strøget is the longest pedestrianised shopping street in Europe, reason enough for label queens to go mad. But High Street fashion is a recent discovery for the Danes. Local shopping queens used to travel to London or Paris just to get their hands on the latest designer get-ups. The Danes are catching up though, as they now have streets like Studiestræde, Gothersgade, Kronprinsessegade and Pilestræde, which boast an impressive cluster of small, sharp and very Danish designer shops. *See also page 170.*

Retazo
Sankt Peder Stræde 43 (33 93 53 69).
Open 10am-6pm Mon-Fri; 10am-2pm Sat; closed Sun. **Credit** DC, MC, V. **Map** p310 N12.
Filipino designer Resty Nanta creates witty designs for the confident individualist – a unique fashion statement for a good price. Great club clothes.

Underwear for Gentlemen
Gothersgade 27 (33 14 04 84). **Open** 11am-6pm Mon-Thur; 11am-7pm Fri; 11am-3.30pm Sat; closed Sun. **Credit** MC, V. **Map** p307 L14.
Bold and very provocative underwear designs. The kind of second skin to wear at foam parties on Ibiza nights. Caution: the designs can be seriously body conscious. A huge amount of self-confidence and a reality check could be handy.

Fitness

Form & Fitness Scala
Vesterbrogade 2E, 5th floor (33 32 10 02).
Open 24hrs Mon-Fri; 8am-8pm Sat; 9am-9pm Sun.
Admission 75kr. **Credit** AmEx, DC, MC, V.
Map p310 O11.
It certainly wouldn't consider itself to be a gay gym, but if you want to see merchandise before you touch it, then this is where to go. Most of the gay guys in the scene work out here. Early afternoons is the best time to catch them. Serious bodybuilders work out in the wee hours.

Frederiksberg Svømmehal
Helgesvej 29, Frederiksberg (38 14 04 04/ www.frederiksberg.dk). Bus 2, 11, 29.
Open 8am-8pm Mon-Fri; 8am-2pm Sat; 9.30am-2.15pm Sun. **Admission** 35kr incl sauna; 25kr incl Turkish bath. **No credit cards**.
Indoor public swimming venues are popular among gays as rumours about cruisey shower rooms abound. Nudity is tolerated, since the males are separated from females. This Frederiksberg swimming venue is quite notorious on the scene, as it's located in a district where many gay people live. The cruising here is so notable that signs have been posted in the shower rooms encouraging 'proper behaviour' among the clientele.

Accommodation

At Carsten's
5th Floor, Christians Brygge 28, Vesterbro, Copenhagen V (33 14 91 07/www.copenhagen-gay-life.dk/atcarstens). **Rates** 125kr dormitory; 350kr single; 450kr double; 700kr-950kr studio; 1,250kr-2,800kr apartment. **Credit** MC, V. **Map** p311 P15.

A home away from home **At Carsten's**.

Never Mind. See p210.

Queens will definitely fall in love with this one: from the outside, it looks like a cake castle; inside it is a luxurious bed and breakfast that has an art studio feel to it (check out their impressive modern art collection). Within walking distance of the city centre. Warm, personal service, and surprisingly affordable. Former guests say only good things about its amicable proprietors.
Hotel services *Cooking facilities. Laundry (self-service). No-smoking rooms. Parking. Payphone.* **Room services** *Iron. Minibar. Turndown. TV: cable.*

Copenhagen Rainbow

4th Floor, Frederiksberggade 25, 1459 Copenhagen K (33 14 10 20/www.copenhagen-rainbow.dk). **Rates** 685kr-795kr double. **Credit** AmEx, DC, MC, V. **Map** p310 O12.
This friendly gay penthouse B&B opened in summer 2000 and has proved very popular. One reason is the prime location, right on Strøget. All rooms have their own bathrooms.
Hotel services *Laundry (self-service). No-smoking rooms.* **Room services** *TV.*

Hotel Windsor

Frederiksborggade 30, 1360 Copenhagen K (33 11 08 30/www.hotelwindsor.dk). **Rates** 450kr-550kr single; 550kr-650kr double; 700kr triple; 800kr quad. **Credit** MC, V. **Map** p306 L12.
The gay hotel in Copenhagen. It's very discreet, simple and kitschy and is located centrally, so you can just walk to the scene. Gay mags and posters abound, as if reminding you that you're in good company. The owners are very friendly and welcoming. Ørsteds Parken, the gay park-after-dark, is close by.
Hotel services *Bars. Concierge (8am-11pm daily). Parking. Payphone. Restaurant.* **Room services** *TV: cable.*

Events

Frøken Verden (Miss World)

Den Grå Hal, Christiania (www.christiania.org). **Date** varies.
An annual drag queen extravaganza very similar to New York's Wigstock, this unique beauty contest was started in 1985 by Nelly Nylon, a drag queen who resided in the (in)famous Bøssehuset (Gay House) in the Free State of Christiania. The event attracts a fair sized following, and, in 1999, it migrated to Den Grå Hal to accommodate the 1,500-strong audience. The most outlandish candidate wins the contest, voted for by the audience themselves. The date of the event varies from year to year, so check the website for details (click on the Bøssehuset link on the main page).

Mermaid Pride

Gammel Kongevej 89 (33 23 92 11/ www.mermaidpride.dk). **Date** summer.
Denmark's annual Pride event which takes place in the summer (usually August) includes a street parade and ballroom dancing at Tivoli, and special appearances by international celebrities (such as Jimmy Somerville).

Associations

Landsforeningen for Bøsser og Lesbiske (LBL)

Teglgårdsstræde 13, Baghuset, 1452 Copenhagen K (33 13 19 48/www.lbl.dk). **Phone enquiries** 11am-3pm Mon-Fri; closed Sat, Sun.
Denmark's national gay and lesbian association is more than 50 years old (founded 1948) and is one of the more active interest groups in Europe. It prides itself on being in the vanguard of gay politics, especially in Scandinavia, and its achievements (gay marriage et al) are what many other gay groups aspire to. It also incorporates **PAN Idræt**, a sports group that sent the highest number of athletes from Scandinavia to the recent Eurogames in Switzerland. Its first-rate handball and football teams take part in national tournaments, and its annual gay sports day attracts a huge audience.

Stop Aids

Amagertorv 33, 1160 Copenhagen K (33 11 29 11/ www.stopaids.dk). **Phone enquiries** 10am-4pm Mon-Fri; closed Sat, Sun.
Stop Aids has been promoting safe sex in Denmark since 1986 in ways that can only be defined as refreshing. This group was responsible for putting up pigeon holes-cum-condoms-and-lube compartments in cruising parks. It also puts on occasional sex shows, where dancers demonstrate safe sex procedures, and sends out friendly volunteers who circulate on the gay scene distributing safe sex kits. The group also employs qualified masseurs at Amigo Sauna every Tuesday to give free massage in exchange for a little safe sex chat.

Nightlife

Expect stylish, chilled surroundings ahead of musical innovation.

Hyggeligt is perhaps the best, if most overused, word to describe Danish culture and attitude (*see page 79* **The essence of *Hygge***), and it pervades much of the nightlife in Copenhagen, too. Comfortable, snug, cosy, homely and pleasant is the dictionary definition, which in terms of nightlife can translate into a lack of excitement and innovation. On a more positive note, it also means that a chilled and relaxed atmosphere permeates all social situations, even clubbing. It's true that Copenhagen does not foster new and progressive music; it is a follower not a world leader. On the other hand, there's a variety of decent clubs worth checking out. Many are aesthetically very stylish, borne out of the omnipresent Danish attention to design, and you'll see plenty of very trendy people frequenting them. Note, however, that *hyggeligt* can also mean cliquey; local clubbers may seem a little distant or unwelcoming, and tend to run in tight packs until the alcohol kicks in.

For a small city, Copenhagen has its fair share of night spots. Apart from the myriad clubs, bars and cafés in the centre, there is at least one serious club in each of the city's main districts: **Rust** in Nørrebro; **Vega** in Vesterbro; and **Park Café** in Østerbro. (For details of these, *see pages 218, 216 and 217* **The big three**). Additionally, there are many venues that don't fit the typical club mould; a new hybrid of club/café/bar/restaurant is emerging, creating an adaptable, inclusive scene more typical of larger capital cities (*see page 215* **Warm up and chill out**).

Variable factors such as season, weather, night of the week, as well as management policies, security arrangements and pre-event publicity all determine the atmosphere on a particular night, which can make going out in Copenhagen a hit-and-miss affair. Perhaps the key issue is the lack of hype surrounding the city's nightlife scene; in larger cities there are pirate radio stations promoting new music, and magazines specialising in topics such as music, fashion, art and clubbing. With only one million or so inhabitants, there are just fewer punters in Copenhagen than in other capital cities. After a few visits to a place you are likely to start bumping into the same people, which at best breeds a feeling of a clubbing community; at worst it becomes predictable and unexciting.

PRACTICALITIES

Copenhageners usually don't get going until late in the evening, so you shouldn't expect to move your hips with the glitterati before midnight. Luckily, there is a plethora of places to hang out before this (*see page 215* **Warm up and chill out**), and once they get started, many clubs and large bars stay open until 5am. The places listed here are the city's main nightlife venues, but it's also worth checking the local press for updates on regular nights and one-offs. For details of where to get information, *see page 214* **Finger on the pulse**). Entrance fees to most venues are not prohibitive (relative to the cost of living), as organisers tend to make most of their money on drinks instead. Finally, a word about the drug scene: it's present and growing, with a lot of recent media concern about ecstasy, but it is not all-pervasive, and certainly not comparable with the situation in cities such as London, Paris or Berlin.

Clubs

For details of Copenhagen's most influential dance clubs, *see pages 216, 217 and 218* **The big three**. *See also page 217* **Copenhagen JazzHouse**.

Base Camp

Holmen, Halv Tolv, building 148, Holmen (70 23 23 18/www.basecamp.dk). **Open** 6pm-1am Mon-Thur; 11am-5am Fri, Sat; 11am-3pm Sun. **Admission** varies depending on the event. **Credit** DC, MC, V. **Map** p313 N19.
This converted former cannon foundry on the harbour is Copenhagen's largest venue and claims to be the biggest bar/restaurant/nightclub in Scandinavia. Its size means it can host a variety of events, ranging from fashion shows and product launches to concerts and club nights. There's an outdoor sandy strip where you can catch your breath, and a less hectic DJ and bar site with beach decor to create a getting-away-from-it-all feel. The restaurant (*see p150*) has a vast seating area and offers fabulous Sunday brunches. Base Camp is slightly out of the way, but well worth seeking out. Check the press for one-off parties.

Discotek IN

Nørregade 1, Strøget (33 11 74 78/ www.discotekin.dk). **Open** 10pm-10am Wed-Sat; closed Mon, Tue, Sun. **Admission** 50kr-150kr. **Credit** AmEx, DC, MC, V. **Map** p311 N13.

Finger on the pulse

Here's where to pick up clubbing and gigging information:

Record shops

Record shops have flyers and posters advertising upcoming events and club nights. The staff are usually a good source of info, too. Try **Loud Music** (Hyskenstræde 9, 33 11 23 16/www.loudmusic.dk), **Baden Baden** (Larsbjørnsstræde 15, 33 15 40 30/www.badenbaden.dk), **Paul's Books & Records** (Jazz; Frederiksborggade 50, 33 11 94 60/www.paulsbooksnrecords.com), **Street Dance Records** (Vestergade 17, 33 15 90 70/www.streetdance.dk) or **Candy Vin & Vinyl** (Fælledvej 3, 35 35 65 60/ www.candyrecords.dk).

Publications & websites

AOK www.aok.dk
Excellent visitors' and listings website. Well designed, clear and up-to-date, with comprehensive listings for clubs, cafés bars and live music venues, as well as other visitor information.

Copenhagen Post www.cphpost.dk
Danish news in English, available from kiosks and some hotels. Good weekly listings guide In & Out, with daily club listings.

Gaffa www.g.dk
Another free (Danish-language) music paper, available from coffee shops and bars.

Musik Kalenderen
Bi-monthly leaflet, listing daily events at the main music venues in Copenhagen.

Nat & Dag www.natdag.dk
Danish-language free listings guide for music, club and film events. Available from most coffee shops and bars. Although in Danish, it can give useful tips as to which big names are playing and where.

Politiken/Berlingske Tiderne
Two of the nation's dailies provide weekly listings supplements (every Friday) with details of all concerts, from major gigs to smaller club events; in Danish, but reliable and complete.

A sparkling and bouncing inferno of dancing teens moving to the sound of pumpin' house and bangin' trance. Yes, it is provincial, but if commercial euro-techno, dry ice and cheesy decor is your bag, then this is a raving place. 'Live' performances from 666, Venga Boys and other European dance acts are an indication of this club's target audience.

Frame
Lyngbyvej 62, Østerbro (70 27 01 13).
Open *Nightclub* 6pm-6am Fri, Sat; closed Mon-Thur, Sun. *Restaurant* 6pm-midnight Fri, Sat. **Main courses** 150kr-160kr. **Set menu** 248kr-288kr. **Admission** 60kr. **Credit** DC, MC, V.
A mixed-use venue, encompassing a café, restaurant, club and gallery in an old cinema. The '80s music and soft pop aim to attract a more mature crowd. Note, there's a smart dress code (no trainers) and queueing is likely at weekends.

Mantra
Bernstorffsgade 3 (33 11 11 13/www.mantra.dk).
Open 11pm-4am Thur; 11pm-6am Fri, Sat; 6am-1pm Sun; closed Mon-Wed. **Admission** *Thur* 25kr; *Fri, Sat* 50kr. **Credit** DC, MC, V. **Map** p310 P11.
With its photographic wall panorama of the city, well-styled white loungey sofas and central location, Mantra could be one of Copenhagen's best nightspots. But with its slightly edgy Friday night crowd of predatory men and tarted up girls, there is a lot of room for improvement. Nonetheless, the music is good, if R&B and soul are your bag. Saturdays feature a more mature crowd, grooving to drum 'n' bass, followed by the ATT Club's Sunday morning techno fest from 5am to 1pm.

NASA/Fever/Slide
Boltens Gård, Kongens Nytorv (33 93 74 15/ www.nasa.dk). **Open** midnight-5am Fri, Sat; closed Mon-Thur, Sun. **Admission** *NASA* 100kr, subject to the doorman's discretion. *Fever, Slide* 60kr. **Map** p311 M15.
NASA is supposedly the cream of Copenhagen clubbing, but maybe that accolade only refers to the bio-morphic, all-white Barbarella-style interior, inspired by the glamour of space travel. It's basically a members-only nightspot, but you can always chance it on the door, if you're desperate to see and be seen. Is this the beau monde of Copenhagen? – more like hairdressers, aerobics instructors and clothes shop assistants, and incredibly snotty staff. NASA is not really a dancing place (it has possibly the smallest dancefloor in town) but the music is unobtrusive and smooth, and the crowd is good-looking. The Spice Girls, Peter Schmeichel and the Danish Crown Prince have all been spotted here (if that's any recommendation) and its reputation amongst Danes for being harder to get into than size eight hotpants ensures NASA maintains its high-profile image.

Admission into NASA also entitles you to slum it in the other two clubs in this complex. **Fever** and **Slide** are for the masses, with less fierce admission

Warm up and chill out

Ideal Bar.

As in many major cities, the distinction between clubs and bars in Copenhagen has become rather fuzzy, with many cafés, bars and restaurants featuring DJs or live music performances. Rather than causing an identity crisis, this has created a fluid and amorphous scene, in which venues experience waves of clientele who frequent the space at varying times, and for varying purposes.

Autobahn

Gammel Kongevej 51, Vesterbro (33 24 69 65/www.autobahn.dk). Bus 1, 14. **Open** 6pm-midnight Mon-Wed; 6pm-3pm Thur, Fri; noon-3am Sat; noon-4pm Sun. **Admission** free. **No credit cards. Map** p111 P8.

The Castrol oil drums, red vinyl seating and the depictions of racing cars make Autobahn a kitsch, themey but fun late-night bar. If you find yourself in the company of Elvis fans, cowboys or girls with '50s bouffants, you've landed in one of the Friday or Saturday theme parties. Leave your attitude at home and enjoy yourself. This place is lively enough, but the lack of a dancefloor may mean you won't want to stick around all night.

Barcelona

See page 153.

Café Bopa

Bopa Plads, Østerbro (35 43 05 66/www.bopa.dk). Bus 6, 14. **Open** 10.30am-midnight Mon, Tues; 10.30am-1pm Wed; 10.30am-3pm Thur; 10.30am-5am Fri; 10am-5am Sat; 10am-midnight Sun. **Admission** free. **Credit** DC, MC, V. **Map** p121 C14.

This warm, continental-style bar is tucked away in Østerbro's residential area, popular with a blend of young, trendy but individual working types and international students. The heavy wooden interior includes a small dancefloor, where disco and mainstream dance music is played. In summer, the café spills out onto

leafy Bopa Plads, where there are deckchairs, rugs and games of pétanque. Bopa can be a bit predatory on a Saturday night, but generally it has a very relaxed atmosphere – a gem.

Delicatessen

See page 152.

Ideal Bar

Enghavevej 40, Vesterbrø (33 25 80 12). Bus 3. **Open** 6pm-2am Wed; 6pm-4am Thur; 6pm-5am Fri, Sat; closed Mon, Tue, Sun. **Admission** *before 1am* free; *after 1am* 30kr. **No credit cards. Map** p111 S7.

Part of the Vega complex, this super-cool lounge bar in bohemian Vesterbrø is ideal for pre-club drinks. Music is often latin and world grooves. See also p216 **The big three: Vega**.

Saxon's

Jagtvej 71, Nørrebro (35 86 16 03/www.saxonscafe.dk). Bus 5, 16, 18, 350S. **Open** 8am-midnight Mon-Wed, Sun; 8am-3am Thur; 8am-5am Fri, Sat. **Admission** free. **No credit cards. Map** p119 H7.

This relaxed and ethnically diverse bar in the centre of Nørrebro fits the bill for early or all-evening drinking in a cramped but laid-back atmosphere. There are DJs and music gigs from Thursday to Saturday, playing everything from house and dance to latin and reggae, and live jazz every Sunday afternoon.

Stereo Bar

Linnésgade 16A (33 13 61 13/www.stereobar.com). **Open** 8pm-3am Wed-Sat; closed Mon, Tue, Sun. **Admission** *upstairs bar* free; *club* varies. **Credit** DC, MC, V. **Map** p306 L12.

With black walls and funky '60s lighting and loungey seats, Stereo Bar is modish without being pretentious, and retains an underground feel (the black walls and low lighting make everyone look mysterious and interesting). Stereo's music policy is eclectic, ranging from latin to drum 'n' bass, with house and electronica in between. Quality local DJs spin in the small and intimate downstairs club, where a mélange of arty, media and student types rub shoulders with the occasional celeb (Björk has been known to come here). The interesting crowd and uncharacteristically friendly bar staff make Stereo Bar a cornerstone of Copenhagen revelry. An original, not to be missed. See also page 40.

Arts & Entertainment

The big three Vega

Vega is one of Copenhagen's biggest and grooviest venues; a veritable department store of musical entertainment. The listed 1950s former union building, designed by architect Vilhelm Lauritzen, stood empty for years before being acquired in 1996. The subsequent refurbishment, retaining many original features, has created a unique environment: fashionable, simple and very Scandinavian. The emphasis is on quality music and clubbing, with several branded nights that underpin Vega's reputation for being the nightclub in Copenhagen with the best bookings.

Located in the bohemian Vesterbrø district, the venue has an overall capacity of 2,000, and is split into **Store Vega** (1,500 capacity), where concerts and big club nights take place; **Lille Vega**, the Friday and Saturday nightclub venue; and **Ideal Bar** (see page 215), a stylish, cosy lounge bar area, that typically has latin and rare groove DJs at the weekend, is the latest addition to the complex. This third floor area, with a capacity of 500 and a cocktail bar, acts as a showcase for new bands and promises a more sociable, less sweaty atmosphere than other parts of the club.

The concert programme and DJ line-up offers an impressive mix of leading national and international names from the rock, pop and electronic scene, with forays into jazz, folk and avant garde music. Artists who have performed at Vega include Björk, Fatboy Slim, David Bowie, Prince, Afro Cuban Allstars and Cesaria Evora.

Regular club nights include 'Vegatronic', a monthly electronic dance club in Store Vega, with guest DJs such as Derrick May, Aphex Twin and Dave Clarke, and house night 'Respect is Burning', a bi-monthly residency in collaboration with the Queen club in Paris.

Future plans are to create a new milieu of sensory experience within the club, with the

inclusion of dancers, food and art installations. Collaborations with other clubs in Scandinavia and France are also planned.

Vega attracts a hip crowd ranging from 18 to 35; it's a favourite place for aspiring art, theatre, design and media people. The clientele are fashionably dressed, but are more likely to be penniless fashion students than Louis Vuitton-toting daddy's girls.

Vega House of Music

Enghavevej 40, Vesterbrø (33 25 70 11/ www.vega.dk). Bus 3. **Open** *Ideal Bar* 6pm-4am Wed, Thur; 11pm-5am Fri, Sat; closed Mon, Tue, Sun. *Lille Vega* 11pm-5am Fri, Sat; closed Mon-Thur, Sun. *Store Vega* varies according to event. **Admission** *Ideal Bar, Lille Vega* free before 1am, 50kr after 1am Fri, Sat. *Store Vega* varies according to event; tickets from BILLETnet (70 15 65 65). **Credit** AmEx, MC, V. **Map** p111 S7.

The big three Park Café

Park rules supreme over in Østerbro (which is otherwise devoid of notable nightlife, excepting Café Bopa; see page 215). With three dance floors, a restaurant and grand surroundings, it's not surprising that Park attracts a dressed-up, sophisticated and classy crowd of law and business students and young professionals.

This venue used to be the function rooms of Parken, the national sport stadium (see page 120) and has a capacity of 2,000. The ground floor is home to the cosy **Kitty Club**, decorated in Arabian style with floor cushions and oriental furnishings, where live music can be heard from Sunday to Wednesday. From Thursday to Saturday (after the restaurant closes), the whole venue is used as a nightclub, featuring mainstream house and pop in mirrored and chandelier-decked surroundings. The faux-opulent renaissance-style decor is in sharp contrast to the currently fashionable pared-down interiors of other city nightspots, but this faded grandeur style seems to suit Park's corporate clientele.

Park doesn't attract big international names, and has an unadventurous musical policy, catering to the loyal crowd who keep coming back. The attempt at glamour attracts wannabe-chic girls and boys (there are handbags aplenty to dance round), so a fair amount of sharking goes on, but generally the party atmosphere is good.

Park Café
Østerbrogade 79, Østerbro (35 42 62 48/ 35 42 46 86/www.parkcafe.dk). Bus 6, 14. **Open** *11pm-midnight Mon, Sun; 11pm-2am Tue, Wed; 11pm-4am Thur; 11pm-5am Fri, Sat.* **Admission** *Mon-Thur, Sun free; Fri, Sat 50kr.* **No credit cards. Map** p121 C13.

---

policies. Fever is filled with ordinary folks, shaking to mainstream R&B and dance music in a typical DJ-altar disco set-up. Slide is at the bottom of this clubbing foodchain, with a DJ who has seen better days (fag in mouth), churning out mainstream dance music to a sparse dancefloor.

Sabor Latino
Vester Volgade 85 (33 11 97 66). **Open** *9pm-3am Thur; 9pm-5am Fri, Sat; closed Mon-Wed, Sun.* **Admission** *40Kr.* **No credit cards. Map** p311 P13.
During the salsa fever that hit Copenhagen in the late '90s, Sabor Latino made its name as the most authentic and popular salsa club in town. The Cuban owners make sure the music and drinks are authentic, and encourage people to dance, dance, dance. There is a lesson (in Danish) at 10pm, where novices can learn the basics of salsa from a well-built Cuban, before Sabor Latino turns into a disco at midnight. The crowd is varied, from real latino regulars to local Danes and visiting Swedes practising their newly-learned hip wiggles.

Stengade 30
Stengade 30, Nørrebro (35 36 09 38/ www.stengade30.dk). **Open** *Nightclub 9pm-2am Tue, Wed; 10pm-5am Thur-Sat; closed Mon, Sun. Stalingrad café 2pm-2am Tue, Wed, Sun; 2pm-5am Fri, Sat; closed Mon, Thur.* **Admission** *40kr.* **No credit cards. Map** p119 K9.
Events change a lot at this venue and music ranges from '80s goth to drum 'n' bass, plus unsigned bands and alternative DJs ('if it's been released, I won't play it'). There are more than 250 live concerts a year, and the very eclectic music policy means that events are rather hit and miss. If you don't catch a good night,

Sankt Hans Torv with its hip bars and nightspots is only a short walk away. Stengade is not a purpose-built venue, but there are three floors with pool tables, and a cosy, chilled bar area upstairs if the band isn't to your liking.

Subsonic
Skindergade 45-47 (33 13 26 25/www.subsonic.dk). **Open** *11pm-5am Fri, Sat; closed Mon-Thur, Sun.* **Admission** *50kr.* **Credit** AmEx, DC, MC, V. **Map** p311 N13.
Subsonic offers an unchanging menu of 1970s and '80s dance music (no techno or hip hop). The decor is inspired by air travel, and features aerodynamic post-modern styling, incorporating plenty of balconies and alcove seating. At the centre is a large bar serving original cocktails. The somewhat limited music policy continues to prevent this venue turning into a city centre Rust/Vega contender, but this doesn't seem to put off Copenhagen's unpretentious lovers of disco and the out-of-towners who regularly fill the place.

Live music venues

Jazz, blues & folk

Copenhagen JazzHouse
Niels Hemmingsens Gade 10 (33 15 47 00/ www.jazzhouse.dk). **Open** *Concerts 6pm-midnight days vary. Club JazzHouse midnight-5am Thur-Sat; closed Mon, Wed, Sun.* **Admission** *Club JazzHouse until midnight free; after midnight Thur 30kr; after midnight Fri, Sat 50kr. Concerts prices vary.* **Credit** AmEx, DC, MC, V. **Map** p311 M13.

The big three Rust

One of the city's best venues for live concerts and clubbing, Rust is an integral part of Copenhagen nightlife, having evolved over the years from political café to dubious rock club to polished and cool nightclub/concert venue. Rust claims to have been at the interface between rock and electronic music in the late 1990s, and has certainly been a key player in bringing electronica to the locals through its successful Wednesday club nights. Its renegade history, adventurous music policy and stylish interior attracts a good diversity of people; hip but not intolerably so.

Divided into three floors, Rust is more intimate than Vega or Park, yet large enough for most people to find the atmosphere they're looking for. The cocktail bar, **Living Room**, is a minimalist millennial interpretation of a '70s lounge, complete with groovy low seating, mellow lighting and a laid-back atmosphere. The **Main bar** is used as the concert venue; up-and-coming, recently signed Danish bands playing rock or pop, and lesser known international acts and DJs are Rust's main bookings. The stage is wide and well proportioned, yet the venue remains an intimate one, with enough space for the audience to stand and dance, or to sit in the higher bar area with a view over the mixing

desk. The **Bassment** is the key dancefloor, where various club nights happen from Thursday to Saturday.

Rust attracts a laid-back and approachable crowd: students from nearby Copenhagen University, musicians and residents of the funky Nørrebro district.

Rust
Guldbergsgade 8, Nørrebro (35 24 52 00/ www.rust.dk). **Open** *Living Room* 7.30pm-2am Tue; 7.30pm-5am Wed-Sat; closed Mon, Sun. *Main bar* 11pm-5am Wed-Sat; closed Mon, Tue, Sun. *Bassment* midnight-5am Fri, Sat; closed Mon-Wed, Sun. **Admission** *Mon, Tue, Sun* free; *Wed, Thur* 30kr; *Fri, Sat* 50kr. **Credit** DC, MC, V. **Map** p119/p306 H10.

The country's premier jazz venue is subsidised by the government and showcases both international and local musicians. It offers consistently good live concerts on Thursday, Friday and Saturday nights throughout the year, focusing on contemporary jazz. When the gigs finish, the large downstairs dancefloor is filled by a younger disco crowd, gyrating to mainstream soul, pop and worldbeat.

Drop Inn
Kompagnistræde 34 (33 11 24 04). **Open** 11pm-5am daily. **Admission** free-30kr. **Credit** AmEx, DC, MC, V. **Map** p311 O13.
This laid-back, friendly venue offers good-quality jazz concerts every Sunday afternoon.

La Fontaine
Kompagnistræde 11 (33 11 60 98/www.aok.dk). **Open** 8pm-4am daily. **Admission** *Mon-Thur, Sun* free; *Fri, Sat* 50kr. **No credit cards. Map** p311 O13.
Though it has a capacity of only 60 people, this cosy, dingy and low-key jazz venue is well known and respected for its legendary jam sessions. It attracts music students and other jazz lovers to its weekend swing and mainstream concerts, with performances from local and visiting artists. Happy hour is 8-11pm.

Mojo
Løngangstræde 21C (33 11 64 53/www.mojo.dk). **Open** 8pm-5am daily. **Admission** varies depending on performance. **No credit cards. Map** p311 O13.
Grubby little blues venue, featuring live entertainment (365 days a year) in a friendly environment. On busy nights, push your way to the bar to make the most of the happy hour (8-10pm) through a crowd of blues and booze enthusiasts. *See also p148.*

Rock & pop

For details of **Vega** and **Rust**, *see pages 216 and above* **The big three**.

Amager Bio
Øresundsvej 6 (tickets 70 15 65 65/info 32 86 02 00). Bus 2, 11, 12, 13, 28, 7E, 21N, 250S, 350S. **Open** times vary. **Admission** varies depending on event. **Credit** V.
One of the largest concert spaces in Copenhagen, with a capacity of 1,000. The programme includes theatre, opera and dance performances as well as mix of pop and rock concerts by local and international artists. Annual Muay Thai kick-boxing contests also take place here. There's a mediocre café/bar on site.

Den Grå Hal

Christiania. (32 54 31 35). **Open** times vary.
Admission varies depending on event.
No credit cards. **Map** p312 P18.
Originally built as a riding gallery for the nearby
military academy, this draughty hall has been used
as a gathering spot for cultural, theatrical and
musical events since the birth of Christiania in the
1970s (*see p105*). Big and small, local and international artists (such as Portishead, Bob Dylan and
Metallica) have played here, but the programme
encompasses a huge variety of acts. More recently,
the Grey Hall has been a favourite with visiting hip
hop performers, who create a feverish atmosphere.
Check the press for details of upcoming events.

Loppen

Christiania (32 57 84 22/www.loppen.dk).
Open 9pm-2pm Wed, Thur; 10pm-5am Fri, Sat;
closed Mon, Tue, Sun. **Admission** 40kr-100kr.
No credit cards. **Map** p312 P18.
Since its opening in 1973, Loppen has been putting
on live music in its dilapidated surroundings. The
booking policy is adventurous, covering the whole
spectrum from jazz to rock, incorporating some
world music, but with an strong emphasis on
alternative sounds. Loppen is unconcerned with
refinement, wallowing langourously in the unique

environment of Copenhagen's hippy enclave. The
after-performance disco attracts a high quota of
weirdos, mixing students, artists and always a few
incongruously glammed-up girls in an idiosyncratic
and friendly atmosphere.

Operaen

Christiania (32 57 29 09). **Open** varies according
to performance. **Admission** *Mon-Sat* 30kr-50kr;
Sun free. **No credit cards**. **Map** p312 P18.
This shabby concert venue in the heart of Christiania
hosts alternative rock, techno, hip hop, and reggae
gigs. During the winter season, there is a Sunday
afternoon blues session. There are usually a few
stoned but basically harmless characters inhabiting
the flea-ridden sofas, as would be expected in this
location. So laid back, you want to check for a pulse.

Pumpehuset

*Studiestræde 52, Vesterbro (33 93 19 60/
www.pumpehuset.dk).* **Open** times vary.
Admission varies. **Credit** MC, V. **Map** p310 O12.
This purpose-built music venue (600 capacity) hosts
local and international bands that are on the verge
of hitting the big time. The acoustics are good and
the former power station retains some of its original
features, giving the performance area an organic feel.
The downstairs bar is big and interesting enough for
people to use as a pre-concert meeting place.

Jazz in Copenhagen

Copenhagen is one of the most important
centres for jazz in Europe. The scene
is financially supported by the Danish
government and the city has an enviable
number of well-known venues, offering high-
quality jazz of all types by local names and
international stars (Denmark has the highest
percentage of active musicians in Europe).

In the 1950s, Copenhagen's **Montmartre
Jazz House** gained a legendary reputation,
attracting all the big names of cutting-edge
American jazz (Stan Getz, Dexter Gordon
et al), many of whom settled in the city.
Transatlantic inspiration led to a flourishing
native jazz scene, which continues today.
Major names include Jørgen Emborg, Bo
Stief, Aske Bentzon and Niels Thybo, who
all brought an essentially Danish, open,
optimistic, lyrical flavour to the idiom.

For an inside taste of the city's jazz scene,
join one of the tours run by **Copenhagen Jazz
Guides** (35 26 65 15/www.jazzguides.dk).
The evening tours include dinner and a visit
to three or four of the city's jazz venues,
accompanied by knowledgeable guides.

Copenhagen's long-standing love affair with
jazz culminates each year in the **Copenhagen**

Jazz Festival (information 33 93 20 13/
www.jazzfestival.dk). Founded in 1979,
the festival is now one of the largest in
the world, attracting a huge number of
performers and visitors. During ten days at
the beginning of July, the city hosts nearly
500 concerts by international artists and
local talent in venues ranging from cafés
to cellars to concert halls. The absence
of a central organisation controlling the
programme means the festival is a
delightfully ad hoc affair, with impromptu
gigs, jamming sessions, free outdoor
concerts and street parades happening all
over the city. The centrepiece of the festival
is **Giant Jazz**, a series of concerts featuring
a famous international jazz performer. These
upscale events take place in Cirkusbygningen
(see page 61) not far from Tivoli, and in
the past have showcased the likes of Roy
Haynes, Sonny Rollins, Oscar Peterson and
Wynton Marsalis.

Since 1994 Copenhagen has hosted a
second jazz festival at the beginning of
November. **Copenhagen Autumn Jazz** is a
smaller, four-day event focused around the
city's major jazz venues.

Arts & Entertainment

Performing Arts

From classical conservatism to contemporary innovation, Copenhagen's cultural life has never been in finer fettle.

Classical Music & Opera

Although Copenhagen is known the world over for its jazz scene (*see page 219*), the city also has much to offer the classical music-lover. Not only can you check out the acknowledged professional orchestras like the **Danish National Radio Symphony Orchestra** (which is central in Copenhagen's musical life), professional ensembles and the major concert venues, but there are also plenty of opportunities to experience some excellent amateurs and local ensembles. Some of the best music (and most atmospheric surroundings) can be enjoyed at the many concerts held in the city's numerous churches. Denmark's choral tradition is closely connected with its churches, and, whether your taste is for renaissance, baroque or modern music, Copenhagen usually offers a choral concert to suit your taste.

ENSEMBLES

Foremost among the professional choirs (and a great favourite of the royal family) is **Musica Ficta**, a chamber choir with professional singers, led by composer and conductor Bo Holten. Its repertoire is mostly renaissance and contemporary music. **Camerata Chamber Choir** is one of Denmark's oldest chamber choirs. Founded in 1965, it has been one of the country's leading choirs ever since, and has attracted some of the best choral singers in the country, mostly students at the conservatory or at the musical department of the University of Copenhagen. The choir has won numerous awards and prizes. Nevertheless, don't neglect the many excellent amateur choirs that you'll often find performing in Copenhagen's churches.

Concerto Copenhagen was formed in 1990 and quickly made a name for itself as Scandinavia's leading baroque orchestra, as well as one of the more interesting among the new early music groups in Europe. The ensemble has toured abroad and worked with renowned conductors such as Andrew Lawrence King.

FESTIVALS & COMPETITIONS

Relative to its size, Denmark hosts an impressive range of music festivals and major competitions. The most important Danish competition for conductors was named after **Nikolai Malko**, who conducted the Danish National Radio Symphony Orchestra in the 1940s. The orchestra was founded in 1925, and, in its early years, two conductors, Fritz Busch and Nikolai Malko, played a particularly important role. But it was Malko who brought the orchestra to prominence after World War II, and he is honoured every three years by the **International Nikolai Malko Competition for Young Conductors**. The next one will be held in 2001 at the Radiohusets Koncertsal (*see page 221*).

The flautist **Michala Petri** received the coveted **Sonning Music Prize** (awarded every June in Tivolis Koncertsal) of 500,000 kroner in 2000. Petri, a child prodigy now in her 40s, has played with all the great conductors and orchestras throughout the world. The Sonning Music Prize has previously been given to prominent international artists such as Leonard Bernstein, Gidon Kremer and Janet Baker. If you are able to catch a concert with Petri, jump at the chance, not least so as to hear an instrument not normally associated with concert halls and symphony orchestras.

Other pre-eminent Danish singers and musicians to look out for include baritone **Bo Boje Skovhus** (although he currently

Tickets

Denmark has a ticket sales system called **BILLETnet** (70 15 65 65, 10am-9pm daily, www.billetnet.dk) that allows you to buy tickets from a central phone number, from post offices or on the Web. Tickets are also available for most concerts at the relevant venue. Prices naturally vary hugely, depending on the performers and the venues. Many church concerts are free or cost 50-150kr, tickets to medium-sized venues are typically priced between 100kr and 300kr, while those for the Royal Opera range up to 500kr.

The **Danish National Radio Symphony Orchestra**.

lives in Vienna), soprano **Tina Kiberg** and tenor **Stig Fogh Andersen** (both world-renowned interpreters of Wagner) and the brilliant young violinist **Nikolaj Znaider**.

Copenhagen hosts a number of different festivals. In the summer you can usually find organ festivals; a baroque festival, held in association with Danish Radio, which assembles some of Europe's finest baroque ensembles; and Tivolis Koncertsal's season (from April to September) of mini festivals in which the focus is on a specific composer, artist/ensemble or instrument. Every second year Danish Radio puts on a competition for young ensembles and chamber music at Radiohusets Concertsal. In 2000 it was won by the youthful Trio Ondine; the next will take place in 2002. Contact the **Wonderful Copenhagen Tourist Information Bureau** (*see page 292*) for further details of all the above.

Major venues

Black Diamond

Søren Kirkegaards Plads 1 (33 47 47 47). **Box office** 1hr before performances. **No credit cards**. **Map** p311 P15.

The opening of the stunning 'Black Diamond' (Den Sorte Diamant) extension to the Royal Library has provided Copenhagen with a brand new concert hall. It's a typical example of contemporary Danish design: panelled with golden Canadian maple and ornamented with black tapestries woven with quotations from Andersen's fairytales. The Black Diamond's ensemble in residence, the splendid **Zapolski Quartet**, focuses on lesser-known Danish string quartets (while not ignoring more famous repertoire standards). The Diamond also has an agreement with **Athelas Sinfonietta Copenhagen** to play six to eight concerts a year. Athelas is a leading ensemble in the field of contemporary composition music and has been appointed as the Danish National Ensemble from 2000 to 2003. The ensemble's repertoire reflects the musical idioms of the last century, from modern classics through newly composed works to experiments in the borderlands between musical styles and genres. You'll find a concert of some sort at the Black Diamond every week.

Radiohusets Koncertsal

Julius Thomsens gade 1, Frederiksberg (35 20 62 62). Bus 2, 8, 11, 13, 14. **Box office** 10am-6pm Mon-Fri; 10am-1pm Sat. **No credit cards**. **Map** p119 M9.

Every Thursday the beautiful Radio Concert Hall hosts a concert by one of Denmark's finest orchestras – the **Danish National Radio Symphony Orchestra**. This is where you'll find the city's finest regular concerts, which are broadcast on the radio (channel P2). The orchestra celebrated its 75th birthday in 2000, and is currently under the baton of principal conductor Gerd Albrecht. Other regular conductors are Yuri Termikanov, Michael

Schønwandt and Thomas Dausgaard. There are also occasional concerts on Saturdays in the main hall, and smaller concerts in **Studio 2** (Rosenørns Allé 22, 35 20 62 62) and other adjacent studios, which specialise in modern music.

Tivolis Koncertsal

Tivoli, Tietgensgade (Tivoli info line 33 15 10 01/ ticket centre 33 15 10 12/www.tivoli.dk). **Box office** *May-mid Sept, mid Nov-Christmas* 10am-8pm daily. *Mid Sept-mid Nov, Christmas-May* 10am-7pm Mon-Fri; 10am-5pm Sat; closed Sun. **Credit** MC, V. **Map** p310 P12.

Throughout the summer (mid April to late September), there is a series of fine concerts in the venerable Tivoli gardens, so you can combine music with a pleasant walk among the flowerbeds and fairground rides. There is also jazz and other popular music in the various little pavilions around the park. The concerts in the Tivolis Koncertsal vary from musicals to chamber music, opera and orchestral music (the Sjælland Symphony Orchestra is based here), and feature both new talent and a host of world-famous artists. During the season, concerts are performed almost every day (both matinée and evening). *See also p233.*

Other venues

Christianskirke

Strandgade 2 (32 96 94 11). **No credit cards.** **Map** p312 P16.

German immigrants built this church in the 16th century. It may not look special on the outside, but it is quite unique once you step inside, with its galleries and boxes reminiscent of an old theatre. Concerts here vary from gospel to chamber music. The renowned English counter-tenor James Bowman is very attached to the church and has sung here on many occasions. At the end of September, look out for a mini Bach festival. Concerts are roughly every week.

Garnisons Kirke

Skt Annæ Plads 4 (33 91 27 06/www.folkekirken.dk). **No credit cards.** **Map** p312 M16.

Though the venue itself is unremarkable, Garnisons Kirken holds a number of enjoyable concerts, usually on Wednesdays and Sundays, throughout the year. It's gaudy gold and red organ may not be easy on the eye but it rarely fails to be pleasing to the ear.

Holmenskirken

Holmens Kanal (33 13 19 51/www.holmenskirke.dk). **No credit cards. Map** p311 O15.

Holmenskirken is one of Copenhagen's best-loved churches, and has a long musical tradition. All year round you can experience a multitude of concerts (at least one a week), and every Easter and Christmas you're in for a treat with top quality performances of JS Bach's Passions, oratorios and Handel's *Messiah.*

DNRSO conductor **Gerd Albrecht.** *See p221.*

Kastelskirken

Kastellet (33 15 65 58/www.kastelkirken.dk). **No credit cards. Map** p308 H17.

This beautifully restored yellow-painted church stands amid Kastellet's red military buildings. The church has an unique acoustic and is therefore often used for recordings. Concerts are held here a couple of times a month. Sometimes a military brass band performs on the cobblestoned square outside the church, playing not just military marches, but even (honestly) the odd Abba number.

Ny Carlsberg Glyptotek
Dantes Plads 7 (33 41 81 41/www.glyptotek.dk).
Credit MC, V. **Map** p311 P13.
After you've gazed at the Glyptotek's fantastic ancient Egyptian or post-Impressionist art, be sure to check out the museum's concert calendar. The concert hall is an experience in itself: a dark red room bordered with pillars and antique sculptures. Both the atmosphere and the acoustics are exceptional for recitals and chamber music. Some afternoons the Winter Garden, with its palm trees, fountains and sculptures, also hosts concerts. Performances are generally on a weekly basis, and many of the concerts are free. For admission prices and opening times of the museum, *see p64.*

Opera

The **Danish National Opera** is based in Århus in Jutland (89 31 82 60/89 31 82 10).

Den Anden Opera
Kronprinsensgade 7 (33 32 38 30/booking 33 32 55 56/www.denandenopera.dk). **Box office** 11am-3pm Mon-Fri; 1hr before performances. **No credit cards**. **Map** p307 L15.
'The Other Opera' opened in 1995 as a venue for contemporary chamber opera, music and experimental music drama. Supported by the Ministry of Cultural Affairs, the company has staged some 25 new chamber operas since opening. This is the place to come if avant-garde and contemporary music is your thing. In 2000, the biggest production was *Rejse Opereatorium Rejse*, an extravagant and grandiose modern opera, tracing the history of humanity and ending with an escape from earth to another planet. This is as good as it gets in Denmark – if you appreciate zing-bang-klong abstract tones.

Det Kongelige Teater
Kongens Nytorv (33 69 69 69/www.kgl-teater.dk). **Box office** 1-7pm Mon-Sat; closed Sun. **Credit** DC, MC, V. **Map** p311 N15.
It will be very interesting to see how the Royal Opera (founded 1874) develops under the leadership of Kasper Holten. This young talent took the helm in early 2000, aged only 27, following the departure of Elaine Padmore to London's Covent Garden. It seems likely that he will continue the Royal Opera's ambition to strengthen contemporary Danish opera. In March 2000, the company staged the first new Danish opera in many years, Poul Ruders' *A Handmaid's Tale*, inspired by Margaret Atwood's novel. It was a huge success (described by the *Guardian* newspaper as 'a work of genius'). The intention is to stage a new Danish opera every year, and the 2000/2001 season's contribution is a children's opera *Heksemutter Mortensen*. In the seasons to come the Royal Opera plans to produce both popular classics, such as *Carmen* and *La Bohème*, and rarer pieces, like the 1789 Danish opera *Holger Danske* by FLÆ Kunzen, in a modern, provocative interpretation, and a Brecht/Weill trilogy. Tickets are half-price on the day.

Theatre

Unlike that of a lot of big cities around the world, the Copenhagen theatre scene is highly experimental, with a multitude of performance groups and dance theatre companies, but relatively few traditional theatre troupes. There are also a number of excellent theatre and dance festivals that are well worth catching. What follows is an overview of all the organisations, venues, groups and festivals that make up the lively Copenhagen theatre landscape. Where possible, websites have been listed; they are often the best source of information on what is proving to be one of the fastest-growing scenes in Europe.

Companies

Most Danish theatre companies perform, not surprisingly, in Danish; the following appeal more to an international audience.

Holland House
33 15 26 40/holland_house@hotmail.com.
Holland House was founded in 1988 by Danish visual artist Ane Mette Ruge and Dutch opera director Jacob Schokking, following the pair's first collaboration, *The Holland House Opera*. Since then, Holland House has staged a whole slew of productions spanning a variety of genres, from documentary films and video art to contemporary festivals. They have managed to establish a name for themselves on the international scene thanks to successful appearances at numerous festivals, and have recently sold two television programmmes to Japan and the USA.

Hotel Pro Forma
32 54 02 17/www.hotelproforma.dk.
Hotel Pro Forma is the Danish performance theatre with the highest international profile. Kirsten Delholm, the founder of HPF, has been an influential and ground-breaking member of the Danish theatre community for decades. Since her early days with the experimental action group Billedstofteater, Delholm has always had her finger on the pulse of the international scene, and via Hotel Pro Forma she has done a great deal to put Danish theatre on the map. Hotel Pro Forma's performances span a number of genres, from opera, performance art and fine art to live concerts, classical theatre and even all of the above and more. Another unique feature of HPF is their site-specific nature – the space in which they perform must always be a part of the performance, just as if it were one of the actors. HPF's casting policies are also very progressive; performers are chosen on the strength of their personal qualities and qualifications, and are not necessarily professional actors or dancers.

Top Danish classical recordings

The following is a selection of the best recordings of works by Danish composers, and by Danish artists and orchestras.

Arias **Bo Boje Skovhus**
(Sony SK60035; 1998)
English National Opera Orchestra conducted by James Conlon.

The Danish baritone Bo Boje Skovhus, who has been the darling of Vienna since his sensational debut as Don Giovanni in 1998, has recorded numerous CDs. Skovhus' first operatic recording with Sony features arias from *Billy Budd*, *Hamlet*, *Tannhäuser*, *Eugene Onegin* and *Don Carlos*. The CD shows the singer's outstanding musical expressiveness, especially when he sings *Korngold* and Ambroise Thomas' breathtakingly beautiful opera *Hamlet*.

Six symphonies **Carl Nielsen**
Nos.2 & 3 (Dacapo 8.224126; 1999)
Nos.4 & 5 (Dacapo 8.224156; 1999)
Nos.1 & 6 (not yet released at the time this guide went to press)
Danish National Radio Symphony Orchestra conducted by Michael Schønwandt.

A superb new series of recordings of all six of Nielsen's symphonies was released in 1999-2000. Schønwandt has a real flair for Nielsen, extracting the passion and detail of the orchestration with great clarity. The CD of the second and third symphonies won the Danish classical Grammy.

Maskarade **Carl Nielsen**
(Decca 460 227-2; 1998)
Gert Henning Jensen, Bo Boje Skovhus, Henriette Bonde Hansen, Aage Haugland and the Danish National Radio Symphony Orchestra conducted by Ulf Schirmer.

The Decca recording of Carl Nielsen's hugely popular festive opera *Maskarade* is a joyous affair. The opera, written in 1906, is based on Danish playwright Holberg's classic comedy; it's an emphatic expression of Danish humour, and is the most frequently performed Danish opera of modern times. This recording sparkles with the stunning performances of top Danish singers Gert Henning Jensen as Leander, Bo Boje Skovhus as Henrik, Henriette Bonde Hansen as Eleonora, and an unforgettable Aage Haugland as the *pater familias* Jeronimus.

Årstidernes sange **Ars Nova**
(ExLibris 30048; 1992)
If you want to experience the essence of Danish sound and style listen to Ars Nova sing *Songs for the Seasons* (Årstidernes sange).This vocal group, consisting of 12 singers, is one of Scandinavia's leading

London Toast Theatre
33 22 86 86/www.londontoast.dk.
The LTT is one of the most successful English language theatre companies in Denmark, playing to audiences of more than 50,000 a year. The theatre was established in 1981 under the artistic direction of Vivienne McKee, an English expatriate trained at the Old Vic Theatre School in London. Its repertoire is quite broad, spanning the moderns to musical cabarets, Shakespeare to stand-up comedy and drama workshops. Its enormously successful Christmas cabarets have been a mainstay of Danish theatre since 1982, with sell-out runs every year.

Odin Teatret
97 42 47 77/www.odinteatret.dk.
After 35 years in existence, Odin Teatret is the oldest surviving contemporary theatre troupe in Denmark. In 2000, director Eugenio Barba was awarded the prestigious Sonning Prize, a biennial award from the University of Copenhagen Senate to an individual who has profoundly affected European culture. Previous winners include Albert Schweitzer, Dario Fo, Vaclav Havel and Winston Churchill. Odin Teatret was founded in Oslo in 1964, when Eugenio

Barba, on his return from three years' study with Jerzy Grotowski in Poland, gathered together a group of would-be actors who had been rejected by the State Theatre School. The theatre is internationally renowned for 'Odin Week', a seminar aimed at providing theoretical/practical knowledge of Odin Teatret and its activities. The programme includes training, rehearsals, performances, work demonstrations, films, lectures and discussions. Only 50 participants may attend, and the group usually includes directors, actors, university teachers, students, critics, anthropologists and sociologists.

Teatret
86 54 41 71/www.teatret.dk.
Teatret is a touring ensemble based in East Jylland, but performing at least once a year in Copenhagen. Founded in 1984 by artistic director Hans Rønne, Teatret produces theatre for both children and adults. From small solo performances to large ensemble pieces, Teatret plays around 80-100 performances every year, both in Denmark and abroad. Over the next two years, Teatret will tour the international festivals in Bergen, Helsinki and Zagreb, as well as Denmark.

chamber choirs in the field of polyphonic renaissance choral music and experimental vocal music of our own period. Ars Nova has recorded many internationally acclaimed CDs and has given more than a thousand concerts in Europe, Israel, Japan, Africa and South America. The group was started in 1979 by a number of singers and the conductor Bo Holten. Since 1996, Hungarian-born Tamás Vetö has been the principal conductor of the choir.

Complete Chamber Concertos **Vagn Holmboe**
Nos.1-3 (Dacapo 8.224038; 1997)
Nos.4-6 (Dacapo 8.224063; 1997)
Nos.7-9 (Dacapo 8.224086; 1997)
Nos.10-12 (Dacapo 8.224087; 1997)
Danish Radio Sinfonietta conducted by Hannu Koivula.

The Dacapo recordings of the collected chamber concertos of Danish composer Vagn Holmboe (1909-96) has aroused great attention both in Denmark and abroad – 'Excellent performances and sonics make this worthwhile release a musical delight', wrote one critic; 'Masterpieces. It's difficult to imagine finer performances and recording quality' wrote another. The Danish Radio Sinfonietta is an active participant in Danish musical life, and holds Danish music

particularly close to its heart, as can be heard in the many radio broadcasts, concerts and CDs the orchestra produces every year.

In addition to the Danish works listed above, anybody searching for notable Danish performances of non-Danish pieces should consider the following.

The charming pianist **Christina Bjørkøe** has been described as one of the most talented young pianists of the 1990s. She studied at the prestigious Julliard School in New York City and has recently released a CD on Classico of Chopin's 24 preludes, nocturnes and waltzes. Bjørkøe has received a number of awards including the Victor Borge Music Prize.

The talented young pianist **Nikolaj Koppels**' EMI recording of Brahms' Piano Concerto No.1, with the Danish National Radio Symphony Orchestra conducted by Thomas Dausgaard, is the only recording of this piece by Danish musicians.

Alternatively, If you like Richard Strauss, the Chandos recording of *Salome* with Inga Nielsen, Robert Hale and the **Danish National Radio Symphony Orchestra** conducted by Michael Schønwandt is a must. This recording was nominated at the Gramophone Awards 1999.

That Theatre Co

33 13 50 42.
Known for his searingly satirical, tragi-comic monologues, Ian Burns got his start in Denmark as an actor in the now defunct Mermaid Theatre and also had a stint at Vivienne McKee's London Toast Theatre before establishing his own company. One of the things that sets Burns' group apart from other theatres, besides his use of English, is the fact that he prefers working with film directors, as opposed to those experienced in theatre. His pieces are accordingly cinematic, with a slightly altered vision of continuity and blocking.

Von Heiduck

32 95 74 30/vonheiduck@mail.tele.dk.
Von Heiduck emerged from the ashes of legendary Danish performance theatre group Exment in the mid '90s. Originally founded in the early '80s in Århus by Kim Eden and Thomas Hejlesen, Exment was a physical theatre group with strong butoh influences. The group grew in size and established a second office in Copenhagen. The Århus group evolved into what is now known as Tin Box, under the direction of Kim Eden, while the Copenhagen

group became Von Heiduck with Hejlesen at the helm. Hejlesen's interest in esoteric sexuality is the basis for Von Heiduck's performances. Using peepshow aesthetics, combined with Nietzsche, Kierkegaard and Bataille, Hejlesen explores themes of angst, loneliness and codified body language with a mix of theatre, ballet and performance art. Hejlesen was awarded the Frankfurt Mouson Award in 1999. The Mouson foundation has also selected Von Heiduck as one of the four theatre groups they will represent internationally, which means the group will be touring for most of the year and so should gain further international recognition.

Venues

The price of tickets varies from theatre to theatre and from performance to performance; phone the relevant venue to check.

Café Teatret

Skindergade 3 (33 13 58 13/box office 33 12 58 14/ www.cafeteatret.dk). **Box office** 3-6.30pm Mon-Fri; 1-3pm Sat; closed Sun. **No credit cards.** **Map** p311 N13.

Bente Hansen in Anita Saij's
Fireflies at **Kanonhallen**.

With three independent stages, this little venue, which was founded in the '60s as an alternative to the more conservative side of the Copenhagen scene, has gradually turned into a highly productive institution. As the name would imply, there are regular dinner theatre evenings here, as well as both Danish and foreign cabaret, modern, tango and improv productions.

Edison

Edisonsvej 10, Frederiksberg (33 21 14 90/ www.bettynansen.dk). **Box office** 2-6pm Mon-Fri; 2-4pm Sat; closed Sun. **No credit cards. Map** p111 O5.

The Edison theatre is an experimental annex of the more traditional and established Betty Nansen Teater (which is around the corner on Frederiksberg Allé). The theatre is housed in a renovated power transformer station, and as such offers none of the amenities of a purpose-built venue. The raw interior is, however, extremely flexible, and many innovative set designers have been given free rein here to great effect in the past. The majority of the plays shown at the Edison are in Danish, but there are occasional guest performances in English, and a few performance theatre pieces are staged each year.

Kaleidoskop

Nørrebrogade 37, Nørrebro (theatre 35 39 92 95/ box office 35 36 53 02/www.kaleidoskop.dk). Bus 4E, 5, 16, 350S. **Box office** 10am-4pm Mon-Fri; closed Sat, Sun. **No credit cards. Map** p306 J10.

This 100-150 seat Nørrebro playhouse has recently received nationwide recognition for its highly innovative productions. Attracting particular interest are two festivals that it stages, the new international Monologue Festival and the Sand Sculpture Festival. In addition to staging theatre productions, Kaleidoskop also hosts regular drama workshops and boasts a number of practice rooms and writing studios, which are available for use by authors or new theatre groups.

Kanonhallen

Østerfælled Torv 37, Østerbro (35 43 20 21/ www.kanonhallen.net). Bus 6, 14, 18. **Box office** 2-6pm Mon-Fri; 1hr before performances daily. **No credit cards. Map** p121 B12.

Presenting modern performance art and theatre of the highest quality, as well as hosting frequent guest performances by foreign companies, Kanonhallen has been hugely influential in raising the Danish standard for contemporary theatre. Kanonhallen hosts a series of festivals, including the biennial Dancin' World festival, the PRIMO dance festival, the Junge Hunde theatre festival (*for all, see p233*) and the international Sommerscene festival (*see p230*) as well as seminars and workshops, and an average of 10-12 independent productions a year. The importance of Kanonhallen to Denmark's cultural life cannot be overestimated. *See also p232.*

Det Kongelige Teater

Tordenskjoldsgade 7 (main box office 33 69 69 69/ www.kgl-teater.dk). **Box office** 1-7pm Mon-Sat; closed Sun. **Credit** DC, MC, V. **Map** p311 N15.

The Royal Theatre was founded in 1748, and, as Denmark's national theatre, is required by law to present a varied repertoire of high artistic merit in drama, opera and ballet. It has three main buildings:

Gamle Scenen – Plush, posh, yet distinctively Scandinavian, the Old Stage is a class act boasting full houses nearly every night of the year. Used primarily for ballet and opera, there's an awful lot of Mozart, Wagner and Strauss here, with a healthy dose of Verdi, Puccini and Rossini thrown in for good measure. Very little attention is given to modern theatre at the Old Stage, though the opening of a new opera house in Copenhagen, expected to be completed in 2005, will no doubt change the theatre's focus.

Stærkassen (Tordenskjoldsgade 5) – The New Stage is primarily used for dramatic productions, and has a fair number of touring productions from abroad. Built in a period of economic recession, Stærkassen has cramped seats and is not very wide, which means that the first ten rows get a real earful from actors attempting to project their lines all the way to the back of this cavernous room. There has been debate about how to redesign Stærkassen for over 100 years, but every competition for its renovation ends in a political scandal; the most recent furore being over Norwegian architect Sverre Fehn's huge bird-shaped addition in 1996. Fehn built a full-scale model of his design later that year, but the public and governmental debate that followed was so vocal that the project was never realised.

Turbinehallerne (Adelgade 10) – The Turbine Halls were built as a power plant in 1892, and reopened in 1998 as the new wing of the Royal Theatre. Its repertoire is quite varied, though it focuses primarily on modern drama. The new theatre was built to appease a growing dissatisfaction among the theatre-going public with the endless red tape and scandal associated with Stærkassen. Turbinehallen boasts two stages, one seating 400 spectators, the other 200. The gigantic dimensions of the former power station afford great potential for experimental set design to accompany the progressive drama.

Det Ny Teater

Gammel Kongevej 29, Vesterbro (box office 33 25 50 75/www.detnyteater.dk). Bus 1, 14. **Box office** noon-6pm Mon; noon-7pm Tue Sat; noon-4pm Sun. **Credit** DC. **Map** p111 P9.

The New Theatre first opened in 1908, and was refurbished to the tune of 50kr million in 1994. This beautiful venue is best known for staging Danish versions of major international musicals, and, as such, its main productions are in Danish. However, the cellar stage is often used for English language cabaret-style productions by British director Vivienne McKee's London Toast Theatre (*see p225*).

Arts & Entertainment

The key Danish composers

Niels W Gade (1817-90)

Niels W Gade was one of the most prominent figures in Danish music in the 19th century, and was closely associated with the early romantic movement under the leadership of Spohr, Marschner and Mendelssohn. Gade started his musical career as a violinist in the Danish Royal Orchestra, and his first success as a composer came in 1840 with his overture *Echoes of Ossian*. His First Symphony was accepted by Mendelssohn and performed by the Gewandhaus Orchestra in Leipzig, where the composer met Mendelssohn and Schumann, succeeding the former as conductor of the Gewandhaus Orchestra in 1847. The following year he returned to Denmark, where he came to assume a leading position in the musical life of the country, writing music in a style greatly influenced by Mendelssohn and Schumann. Gade's much-loved magical choral piece *The Elf-King's Daughter* is charming and typically Scandinavian in the choice of subject and its treatment.

Carl Nielsen (1865-1931)

The principal post-romantic Danish composer, Carl Nielsen, was born in 1865, the son of a painter and village musician. Childhood experience as an amateur performer led to subsidised study at the Copenhagen Conservatory and a long career, during which he developed his own personal style of composition, in particular in a series of important symphonies. Nielsen wrote six symphonies. Of these, the best known are Symphony No.2, *The Four Temperaments*, and No.4, *The Inextinguishable*. Symphony No.5, written after World War I, represents in its two movements the composer's struggle to develop new and stronger rhythms and more advanced harmony. His concertos for clarinet, for flute and for violin have also found a place in the classical canon, as has the overture taken from the opera *Maskarade*. *Maskarade* is in many ways thought of as Denmark's national opera and is often played at the Royal Opera. Carl Nielsen's music has become thought of as the epitome of Danish sound and style.

Vagn Holmboe (1909-96)

Holmboe may not be widely known outside Denmark, but he was an influential composer and a central figure in Danish musical life, particularly during the 1940s. Born in Jylland, his parents were both amateur pianists, and it was at the recommendation of Carl Nielsen that Holmboe went on to study at Copenhagen's Royal Danish Music Conservatory. One of his major inspirations was the folklore tradition (both in Scandinavia and in Romania, where his wife was from), and his considerable output includes 13

Rialto Teatret

Smallegade 2, Frederiksberg (38 88 01 88). Bus 1, 14. **Box office** 4-7pm Mon-Fri; 2-4pm Sat; closed Sun. **No credit cards. Map** p110 N3.
With occasional guest productions in English, and an anarchistic series of events called Chefens Fridage (The Boss's Day Off) that feature seminars, lectures, jazz, folk songs, coffee and cake, Rialto Teatret certainly keeps its audiences on their toes.

Teatret ved Sorte Hest

Vesterbrogade 150, Vesterbro (33 31 06 06). Bus 6. **Box office** noon-7pm Mon-Fri; 2-4pm Sat; closed Sun. **No credit cards. Map** p111 Q7.
This small, intimate theatre was founded in 1978, next door to the then infamous (but now largely forgotten) Black Horse squatters collective. Though the squatters were removed in an explosion of police violence in the mid-'80s, the Black Horse Theatre remains. With a predilection for Dario Fo productions, Sorte Hest offers high quality, modern Danish theatre, but rarely in English.

Terra Nova Teater

Vesterbro Kulturhus, Lyrskovgade 4, Vesterbro (33 79 90 01/www.fast.dk/terranova). Bus 6. **Box office** 10am-4pm Mon-Fri; closed Sat, Sun. **No credit cards. Map** p111 R6.
Terra Nova was founded in 1985 by English director Peter Bensted, and works with what they call 'living cultural theatre confrontations'. Focusing on weighty themes such as Northern Ireland and asylum seekers, performance art and experimental theatre are key features of Terra Nova. It also arranges international theatre workshops, and works on projects with young adults from Vesterbro. Many of Terra Nova's productions are the result of international collaboration, and are frequently performed in English.

Children's theatre

Anemoneteatret

Suhmsgade 4 (theatre 33 32 19 49/box office 33 32 22 49/www.anemoneteatret.dk). **Box office** 10am-3pm Mon-Fri; 1½hrs before performances Sat, Sun. **Map** p311 M13.

symphonies, chamber concertos and a long series of extremely fine string quartets. A good starting point for those new to Holmboe is the 1992 Dacapo recording (DCCD 9203) of his String Quartets by the Kontra Quartet.

Per Nørgård (born 1932)

Per Nørgård started composing as a child, and as a young man was taught by Danish composer Vagn Holmboe. He studied composition at the Royal Danish Academy of Music and later in Paris. In 1987 he was appointed professor of music at the Jylland Academy of Music. Nørgård has composed in most musical genres: opera, orchestral works (including five symphonies), chamber music, pieces for choir and songs. Among Nørgård's works from the end of the 1980s, his concertos for a string instrument and orchestra deserve a mention – *Between* (for cello), *Remembering Child* (for viola) and *Helle Nacht* (for violin). Per Nørgård is a key figure in Danish musical life, not only as a composer and a teacher in composition, but also as an inspiring leader of seminars where his analytical talent can be witnessed at its most impressive.

Poul Ruders (born 1949)

Hardly any Danish composer living today is more internationally minded than Poul Ruders. Since he first made his mark in the 1980s with his brilliant orchestral works, there have been ever-increasing numbers of requests from abroad for more pieces from his pen. And Ruders, with joyous energy, has plunged into diverse demanding genres and forms. International recognition came in 1980 with his Symphony No.1, written for the BBC Symphony Orchestra, and *Psalmodies*, commissioned by the guitarist David Starobin and Speculum Musicae. In 1996 he achieved what must surely be the ultimate in the dissemination of a composer's music: his *Concerto in Pieces* was premiered at the Last Night of the Proms in the Royal Albert Hall.

Ruders began his career as an organist, and also studied composition with Ib Nørholm. His music is extrovert, exhuberant and accessible. His starting point was the Polish School (Lutoslawsky, Gorecki, Penderecki), but his later works are rather neo-romantic. Besides his sparkling use of sound, Ruders is also a master of his craft who can create brilliant instrumentation. Worth singling out among his most striking orchestral works are the apocalyptic *Saaledes saae Johannes* (Thus saw St John), the instrumental concertos, his Symphony No.1 and the tension-filled *Soltrilogi* (Solar Trilogy). He has also garnered attention with his works for guitar and organ.

Anemoneteatret was founded in 1988, and has been producing top-quality theatre for 3-12- year-olds ever since. Its shows are generally much more visual than textual, so English-speaking children can still enjoy the fun, despite most performances being in Danish only. Anemone frequently tours the country, and over the years directors Albert Nielsen and Lisbet Lipschitz have developed a large and loyal following. The company's theatre, a former bakery, has room for up to 60 people, whether large or small.

Bådteatret

Nyhavn 16 (33 12 14 60/www.baadteatret.dk). **Box office** noon-4pm Mon-Fri; closed Sat, Sun. **Map** p312 M16.
True to it's name, Bådteatret (the Boat Theatre) is indeed on a boat, which can be found moored in the old harbour at Nyhavn. In addition to being well known (and highly regarded) in Denmark for its varied repertoire of modern Danish-language theatre, Bådteatret also produces a variety of wordless plays for children.

Comedievognens Broscene

Nyhavn 16 (33 12 14 60/www.baadteatret.dk). **Box office** noon-4pm Mon-Fri; closed Sat, Sun. **Map** p312 M16.
Having experimented for years with gibberish as an art form, Comedievognen has finally begun to produce plays employing this universal language. Though one might expect these productions to be primarily comic, they can be also be poignant and touching. Comedievognen's popularity has become so great that it's recently established its own venue.

Kongens Have Marionet Teater

Kronprinsessegade 21 (35 42 64 72). **Open** *June-Aug* performances Tue-Sun; closed Mon. *Sept-May* closed. **Map** p307 L14.
From June to August, the King's Garden Marionette Theatre is an institution in Copenhagen. Its repertoire is primarily original, but it also performs satires of popular plays from the Royal Theatre's past and present. There are performances every day at 2pm and 3pm, but get there early, before the hordes of children from every school in Copenhagen descend.

Arts & Entertainment

Organisations

ARTE

38 88 22 22/www.arte.eon.dk.

An organisation whose sole purpose is to make theatre and concert tickets available to everyone in the greater Copenhagen area. Their homepage (in Danish only) is designed to make finding various cultural events easy, and tickets can be ordered online.

Danish International Theatre Institute and Theatre Union (DITITU)

Vesterbrogade 26 (33 86 12 10/www.image.dk/ ~dititu). **Open** *office* 10am-3pm Mon-Fri.

The Danish ITI is an umbrella organisation, established in 1948 to aid Danish theatre groups and venues. The centre offers both practical help and courses, and sponsors festivals in Denmark and abroad. The DITITU website is a useful resource, with an English-language link containing articles, information about upcoming events, and a comprehensive list of Denmark's theatres and their activities.

KIT

Vestergade 5, 3 (33 15 15 64/www.kit.dk).

In 1980, influenced by a similar festival in Amsterdam, a group of theatre people in Copenhagen arranged the first Festival of Fools, an event that grew over the years in size and complexity into the organisation now known as KIT (the Copenhagen International Theatre). At the time of KIT's inception, the theatre scene in Copenhagen was insular and inbred, but KIT's centralised secretariat ensured that the Festival of Fools would not be a one-off event. Since 1980, the group has organised over 40 international theatre and dance festivals in Denmark, and has launched cultural exchanges with performing arts communities all over the world. KIT's website is an extremely informative, one-stop affair wherein one can order tickets, sign up for mailing lists, access a calendar of the season's events, read reviews and search links to a host of related sites on the web.

Festivals

Scandinavia's biggest annual multi-cultural and multi-discipline arts festival is **Århus Fest Uge** (89 31 82 70/www.aarhusfestuge.dk), held over one week in late August/early September.

DCCP Images of the World Festival

Vestergade 5 (33 17 97 00/www.dccd.dk). **Date** Aug-Sept.

This ambitious festival focuses on various cultural and political elements of the non-Western world, including music, theatre and dance, visual arts, handicrafts, photography, architecture, literature, education, and research and development. The theme of the festival is the cultural consequences of globalisation. It's held annually in Copenhagen and other major towns in Denmark.

Sommerscene

33 15 15 64/www.kit.dk. **Dates** June-Aug.

This annual, three-month-long festival celebrates international theatre, dance and new circus and has in its short life managed to completely eclipse every other event of its kind in Denmark. Not really a festival, in that it isn't held in a concentrated week of reception and seminars, Sommerscene transforms Copenhagen into a cultural mecca for three months of the year. Guests to the festival have included Pina Bausch and the Wuppertal Tanz Teater, Le Cirque Invisible and the Royal Shakespeare Company. Keep an eye on the KIT website for updates and information. *See also p233.*

Dance

Gone are the days when Det Kongelige Theater and folk art festivals were the only venues for dance in Copenhagen. The cultural monopoly was broken in 1979 when the **Patterson** project was founded. Though it wasn't the first independent dance group in Copenhagen, it may very well have been the most important. In 1981, Patterson changed its name to **Nyt Dansk Danse Teater** (New Danish Dance Theatre). In 1982, American dancer and choreographer Warren Spears joined the company and began a tradition of inviting choreographers and dancers from abroad, which has become the lifeblood of the contemporary Danish dance scene. The influence of Lester Horton, José Limon, Merce Cunningham and Martha Graham are easy to spot on stage here, and the combination of these styles and a more Nordic, intellectual mentality defines New Danish Dance.

Companies

Dance companies in Copenhagen are highly dependent on funding from the state. This means that the dance scene here is always in flux, with groups coming and going all the time. The following list of dance companies covers the major players in the scene – the groups which have stood the test of time and gained the respect of critics and audiences, both at home and abroad.

Åben Dans

35 82 06 10.

Originally called Ricketts Dance Company, Åben Dans (Open Dance) is one of the favourites of the National Theatre Council, which decides how much funding the various groups receive. The name comes from the company's reliance on flow instead of form, which means their work is a combination of everything from contact improvisation and abstract realism to Japanese butoh.

BIDT
35 37 45 41.
BIDT is a dance and performance theatre group made up of six graduates of the now defunct Nordisk Teaterskole. The influence of their former professor, Bo Madvig, a founding member of Exment Theatre, is apparent in most of their work, but that is no bad thing. BIDT's unique physical theatre is winning it international recognition and awards. Here in Copenhagen, BIDT performs in a converted bakery, the only underground performance space in town, seating between six and 35 spectators, depending on the scenography. The group has existed since 1996, and if the response it's received so far is any indication, it will go on to lead a revival of grass roots, living theatre.

Body Brains Unlimited
38 88 91 00/www.bodybrainsunlimited.dk.
One of the oldest modern dance companies in Denmark, BBU was founded as the New Now Dancers by former Twyla Tharp and Pina Bausch dancer Nanna Nilson in 1982. Its aggressive, humorous style confused the Danish public at first, but now, after years of performing, BBU has found its niche.

Warren Spears. *See p230.*

Corona Danseteater
49 21 07 40/www.coronadanseteater.dk.
Founded in 1990 by Jørgen Carlslund, Corona produces dance pieces for children, young adults and grown-ups. The company mixes many different media in its productions, blurring the line between dance, acting, gymnastics and mime. Though it bases its pieces on traditional Danish children's theatre, Corona has managed to create an international language that has led to it touring most of Europe and beyond.

Dance Lab
32 96 90 30/www.dancelab.dk.
Dance Lab's choreographer Anita Saij is one of the most prolific experimental dance personalities on the Danish scene. Since her beginnings with the now defunct Exment Theatre in Århus in the early '80s, Saij has combined elements of Japanese butoh dance and social commentary into a moody, dark form of expression which at times verges on the apocalyptic. Dance Lab also offers a variety of courses in dance and butoh.

Kreutzmann Dance
33 16 15 50/www.kreutzmann.dk.
Choreographer Kenneth Kreutzmann started Kreutzmann Dance in 1996 with the horror-ballet *Lullaby*, but that wasn't the first time Kreutzmann's name was up in lights. After a successful career as a dancer all over Europe and in New York, he began choreographing in Copenhagen in 1990. The company has proved to be one of the more successful in Denmark, with a diverse, enthusiastic following. *Make Up*, a follow up to the successful 1999 production, *Reservoir* (about events in and around a men's restroom), premiers at Det Kongelige Theater's new extension venue, Turbinehallen, from 9-30 June 2001. *Make Up* takes up where *Reservoir* left off, with an investigation of the rituals and rites in a women's restroom. The set design is by Rikke Juellund, the new big star of stage design in Denmark.

Micado Danseensemble
33 12 12 62.
One of the oldest existing groups in Copenhagen. Like Nyt Dansk Danse Teater (*see below*), Micado Danseensemble has made its name by inviting guest choreographers and dancers from abroad. Its productions vary in quality, but they have been a focal point for the dance scene in Copenhagen for many years. Kenneth Kreutzmann (*see above*) got his start here, as well as Danish acting star Mads Mikkelsen. Incredibly productive.

Nyt Dansk Danse Teater
35 39 87 87/www.nytdanskdanseteater.dk.
Over the course of its 20-year history, NDDT has redefined modern dance and experimental ballet in Denmark. Originally established by Randi Patterson in 1981 as an alternative to Det Kongelige Teater's monopoly on ballet and modern dance productions,

NDDT achieved international recognition very quickly. Over the years, NDDT's practice of inviting choreographers and journalists from abroad has brought such luminaries as Jorma Uotinen (Finland), Rami Be'er (Israel) and Milton Myers (USA) to the Danish scene. Since 1999, NDDT's repertoire has been created by guest choreographers.

Peter Schaufuss Ballet

97 40 51 22/www.schaufuss.com.
It would be something of an understatement to say Peter Schaufuss has been an influence on the development of modern ballet in Denmark – Peter Schaufuss *is* modern Danish ballet. From his beginnings as a soloist at the Canadian National Ballet, he has worked with the Kirov, the American Ballet Theatre, the Paris Opera Ballet and the Royal Ballet in London. He also worked with the New York City Ballet and George Balanchine, who created two ballets specifically for him. In 1988 he was knighted in Denmark, and in 1995 was made an Officer of the Belgian Order of La Couronne. He was the star of a four-part BBC TV series, received the Olivier and *Evening Standard* Awards, and was named director of the London Festival Ballet (now English National Ballet) where he founded the English National Ballet School. His ballet company, based in Jylland, is a touring company, which presents two full-length productions every year. Plans for 2001 include a Danish tour, an appearance at the Hong Kong Arts Festival, the Maifestspiele in Wiesbaden and a new production at Sadler's Wells in London.

[Stilleben]

35 83 62 32/www.danceproduction.dk.
Anders Christiansen, the artistic director and choreographer of [Stilleben] (Still Life) has achieved cult status in the Copenhagen dance world. His deeply poetic, trance-like performances summon up images of sex, death, life and loneliness. On stage alone in one of his infamous solo pieces, audiences can't take their eyes off him. As a testament to the wide array of expression Christiansen manages to conjure up in his challenging, sometimes abstract work, pieces have been commissioned for the Royal Ballet.

Uppercut Danseteater

35 82 11 71.
One of Denmark's first entirely professional dance theatre groups, the pioneering Uppercut Danseteater has been around for decades. Anne Crosset, co-founder of the group, was instrumental in introducing modern dance to Denmark. She has since gone on to sit on the board of the Danish National Theatre Council.

WILDA Dance Productions

33 16 15 70/www.wilda.dk.
WILDA starts out the 2001 season with a tour of cities in Russia, Estonia, Finland and Norway, before returning to Copenhagen to premier its new work, *Black Tail*, in May 2001. Recently, chief choreographer and founder Tim Feldmann has been hard at work on a new, large-scale dance/music/live art performance based on Picasso's *Guernica*, with American composers Guy Yarden and Doug Henderson writing the piece's requiem. In addition to his work with WILDA, Feldmann has taken commissions since 1995 from groups ranging from the State School for Modern Dance in Denmark to the Ricochet Dance Co. in England. Feldmann's wife, Venezuelan dancer Sara Gebron, has her own company as well, called Public Eye.

X-Act

33 83 62 32/www.3dk.dk/www.dansenshus.dk.
X-Act has existed since 1992, with Danish choreographer Kitt Johnson and Swedish musician Sture Ericson at the helm. Kitt Johnson has made a big name for herself as a dancer, teacher and a choreographer, and has been a principle dancer in several other notable companies, including Dance Lab (*see page 231*).

Venues

Dansescenen

Østerfælled Torv 34, Østerbro (35 43 83 00/Box office 35 43 58 58/www.dansescenen.dk). Bus 6, 14. **Box office** 10am-noon, 1-4pm Mon-Fri; 1 hr before performances daily. **Tickets** 50kr-110kr. **No credit cards. Map** p121 B12.
Opened in 1993, Dansescenen is the result of many years of struggle on the part of the dance community in Copenhagen to establish a venue exclusively for dance. Dansescenen co-produces performances with KIT (Copenhagen International Theatre) and the Kanonhallen theatre, and is the co-host of SALTO! (*see p233*), a yearly regional children's dance festival, as well as the autumn Nordic dance festival PRIMO (*see p233*). Dansescenen is also host to yearly residencies of foreign and local choreographers or dance groups. In 2000 it was Tim Rushton, a Danish choreographer currently making big waves abroad. Dansescenen runs dance development programmes in Copenhagen and nearby Hvidovre for young dancers, and also boasts an in-house junior company, which performs once a year.

Kanonhallen

Østerfælled Torv 37, Østerbro (tickets 35 43 20 21/ administration 35 43 23 24/www.kanonhallen.net). **Box office** 2-6pm Mon-Fri; 1 hr before performances daily. **Tickets** 100kr-165kr. **No credit cards. Map** p121 B12.
Kanonhallen has existed since 1990, and is an integral part of Copenhagen's cultural life. There is no other venue in the city with as broad a repertoire as Kanonhallen, which has in the past presented everything from DV8 (UK) to Annie Sprinkle (USA) to le Cirque Invisible (France). Kanonhallen is also the site of several yearly and biennial festivals, such as Junge Hunde, Dancin' World and Sommerscene (*see p233*). See also p227.

Tivoli

*Vesterbrogade 3, (information 33 15 10 01/
www.tivoli.dk).* **Box office** *May-mid Sept, mid Nov-
Christmas* 10am-8pm daily. *Mid Sept-mid Nov,
Christmas-mid May* 10am-7pm Mon-Fri; 10am-5pm
Sat; closed Sun. **Tickets** 40kr-400kr. **Credit** DC,
MC, V. **Map** p310 P12.

Besides being an amusement park, Tivoli also
offers something for the more cultured palate. Its
summer season lasts from mid April to late
September. There are several venues in Tivoli for
dance, and the majority of performances cost no
more than the entrance fee to the park itself.
Plænen is a huge outdoor semi-covered stage
which hosts many international events, concerts
and award ceremonies, as well as receiving frequent visits from the Royal Ballet. The **Peacock
Theatre** is Tivoli's silent stage, where children's
favourites Harlequin and Columbine are among the
stars. **Tivolis Koncertsal** (1874) is revered
throughout Scandinavia as one of the finest institutions for symphonic music (*see p222*) and ballet.
The current structure was rebuilt in 1956, and seats
2,000 guests. Tivoli has booked the Royal Ballet for
performances of *The Nutcracker* from 2001-2004.
The Tivoli Symphony Orchestra will supply the
music, while Det Kongelige Teater will be responsible for the scenography, choreography and, of
course, the dancers (check their website for details;
see p227). Tickets for performances can be
purchased at the Tivoli ticket office, just outside
the main entrance. *See also p222.*

Festivals

Dancin' World

33 15 15 64/www.kit.dk. **Date** Aug 2002.
Dancin' World is the Nordic biennial festival of
world dance that takes place in Copenhagen during August, and focuses on 'non-western' dance
form with groups from Africa, Asia, Latin America
and the Middle East. Dancin' World is a collage of
traditions from all over the globe; it provides an
informative cross-section of current trends in
global dance. There are workshops and seminars
throughout the festival.

Golden Days in Copenhagen

*Tickets: BILLETnet 70 15 65 65 or
www.goldendays.dk.* **Date** Aug-Sept
Golden Days celebrates the Danish 'Golden Age'
from 1800-50, considered to be the most productive
period for culture in Denmark. The festival covers
every genre of art, from chamber music and exhibitions to theatre and ballet. Over 50 institutions
and theatres take part in Golden Days, which is
organised by the Wonderful Copenhagen tourist
organisation (*see p292*).

Junge Hunde

*Tickets: BILLETnet 70 15 65 65 or
Kanonhallen 35 43 20 21/www.kanonhallen.net/
www.jungehunde.dk.* **Date** between Feb & June.

Junge Hunde (Young Dogs) is an international festival made possible by a network of production
offices and theatres in nine European cities:
Kampnagel, Hamburg; BIT, Bergen; La Vilette,
Paris; Monty, Antwerp; Yorkshire Dance Centre,
Leeds; Bunker, Ljubljana; La Caldera, Barcelona;
Inteatro, Polverigi; and Kanonhallen. The objective
of the festival is to profile young stage artists, and
give them a chance to tour Europe. Over the years,
the festival has grown substantially in status and
reputation, and is now regarded as the last chance
to see the stars of tomorrow while they're still
performing on small stages.The festival is scheduled to take place at Kanonhallen in May and
June 2001, and updates as of programmes and
performers can be found on either Junge Hunde or
Kanonhallen's websites.

PRIMO

*35 43 83 00/box office 35 43 58 58/
www.dansescenen.dk.* **Date** Sept-Oct 2002.
A festival of Nordic modern dance, held every two
years in Malmö and Copenhagen. The PRIMO festival is made possible thanks to a collaborative
effort from Dansescenen in Copenhagen and
Dansstationen in Malmö, Sweden. The festival is
made up of performances, seminars, master classes and workshops, and is the best chance to
experience a concentrated dose of the leading
Nordic choreographers today.

SALTO!

*35 43 83 00/box office 35 42 58 58/
www.dansescenen.dk.* **Date** late Aug-mid Dec.
Salto means 'I'm dancing' in Latin, and is the name
of a regional dance festival for young adults and
children aged six and up. The festival includes a
wide variety of workshops and seminars run by professional dancers and choreographers , but specifically designed for children. The SALTO! festival is
featured at eight different venues, both in southern
Sweden and Sjælland, and lasts for nearly four
months between August and December.

Sommerscene

33 15 15 64/www.kit.dk. **Date** June-Aug.
The 2001 Sommerscene Festival will be the sixth
to be held. Since its inception, some 100 companies
have visited Copenhagen: Robert Lepage, LaLaLa
Human Steps, Robert Wilson, Peter Brook, The
Wrestling School, Sociètas Raffaello Sanzio, Peter
Greenaway, The Builders Association, Pina
Bausch, DV8, Les Arts Sauts, Cirque Invisible,
Cirque Anomalie/Joseph Nadj. Sommerscene 2001
is arranged by KIT (the Copenhagen International
Theatre) and financially supported by the City
Council of Copenhagen and the Theatre Council of
Denmark. The 2001 programme will probably
include Cirque de Soleil, Theatre du Soleil and an
English production of Hamlet at Kronborg
(Elsinore). The majority of the productions will be
at Kanonhallen and Albertslund Musikhuset, just
outside Copenhagen. *See also p230.*

Arts & Entertainment

Sport & Fitness

Their nicotine habit doesn't keep the Danes out of the gym.

Danes love to stay in shape, and as a result Copenhagen has no shortage of fitness clubs and other venues to let off steam. A healthy dose of physical activity is seen as vital to the national wellbeing, and all sport is practised with enthusiasm and gusto. Joggers monopolise public parks, swimming pools are plentiful and – surprisingly, considering their country's latitude – many Copenhagen residents are suspiciously well tanned.

To stay in top form, short-stay visitors need look no further than lavish central sports complexes such as Sport and Fitness at the Scala Centre, and DGI-Byen, the spanking new sports centre adjacent to the city's central station. In addition, many larger hotels have their own facilities – be sure to ask when you check in.

For those on a tighter budget, a trip to one of the many public sports centres (Idrætsanlæge) outside the city centre will be rewarded with excellent facilities at reasonable prices. Contact the main **Copenhagen Council Sports Office** (Københavns Idrætsanlæg, 35 42 68 60/www.ki-kbh.dk) for full details of public sports facilities.

A co-ordinated national network means every sport, from archery to yachting, is controlled by a well-oiled organisational machine. Opportunities to partake in all kinds of sports abound, and facilities are usually excellent. Whatever your preferred discipline, detailed information is just a telephone call away. If your sport is not listed here, call the **Danish Sports Council** (43 26 26 26/www.dif.dk).

When locals aren't participating in sport, the chances are they're watching it. Copenhagen boasts two 30,000-plus capacity football stadiums, two horse racing tracks, two top ice hockey clubs, an annual ATP tennis competition, and the city regularly co-hosts the Scandinavian Masters golf tournament. Football is by far the most popular spectator sport (for real passion, witness a derby game between FC Copenhagen and Brøndby) but all disciplines have their own devotees. These include handball (the women's game is highly popular), golf, tennis, cycling and horse racing. If this wasn't enough, the Swedish city of Malmö (35 minutes by train) has its own successful football team and hosts a regular top-class athletics meet.

Participation sports

Athletics

In mid-May, top-class runners mingle with visitors and locals in a carnival atmosphere as the Copenhagen Marathon signals the start of summer. Although not on the same scale as its counterparts in London or New York, the 26-mile test of endurance has become an attractive date in the international athletics calendar. For those in need of training, contact the Copenhagen Council Sports Office (35 42 68 60/www.dansk-atletik.dk) for details of the marathon and other public training facilities.

Badminton

Denmark has a proud tradition in this sport, and can boast many of the world's current elite. Copenhagen's Brøndby Arena recently hosted the world championships, with local favourite Camilla Martin taking the women's title. Call the Danish Badminton Association (43 26 21 44/ www.badminton.dk) for more details.

Copenhagen Badminton Club
Krausesvej 12, Østerbro (35 38 72 92/ www.kbknet.dk). Train to Nordhavn, then bus 3 to Randersgade. **Open** 7am-11pm Mon-Fri; 8am-4pm Sat, Sun. **Prices** *members* 110kr/month; *juniors* 80kr/month; *non-members* 60kr/hr. **No credit cards. Map** p121 C14.

Chess

Many cafés have a chessboard (*skakspille*) behind the bar. Alternatively, take a stroll down Strøget and play with the hustlers offering speed-chess outside Helligåndskirken (*see page 71*). Be prepared to wager 20kr-50kr on the outcome. For details of tournaments and private clubs, contact the Copenhagen Chess Association on 43 99 25 41.

Fitness centres

These modern temples to the body are highly popular, with prices generally ranging from 50kr-100kr for a single session. The **Form and Fitness** chain run a series of well-equipped clubs throughout the city and suburbs, including **Scala Form and Fitness** and **Parken**

The ultra-popular swimming pool at the central **DGI-Byen** sports complex. *See p238.*

Fitness Centre, based in the national stadium. DGI-Byen is a fine new modern edifice boasting a hotel, fitness centre, swimming pool, bowling alley, sauna, steam bath and climbing wall, but its convenient location and modern facilities are reflected in its prices. Another venue is **Sporting Health Club**. Cheapest, at around 50kr per session, are the smaller council-run clubs such as **Vesterbro Fitness Centre**, but these facilities can get crowded. If you are planning to stay any length of time, a monthly pass could be the economic answer.

Form & Fitness Parken

Øster Alle 42E, Østerbro (35 55 00 71). Bus 6, 14. **Open** 6am-midnight Mon-Thur; 6am-9pm Fri; 8am-6pm Sat; 8am-7pm Sun. **Prices** 75kr. **Credit** DC, MC, V. **Map** p121 D12.

Scala Form and Fitness

Vesterbrogade 2E, 5th flr (33 32 10 02). **Open** 24hrs Mon-Fri; 8am-8pm Sat; 9am-9pm Sun. **Prices** 75kr. **Credit** AmEx, DC, MC, V. **Map** p310 O11.

Sporting Health Club

Gothersgade 14, 2nd floor (33 13 16 12). **Open** 6.30am-9pm Mon-Thur; 6.30am-8.30pm Fri; 9am-6pm Sat; 10am-6pm Sun. **Prices** 75kr. **Credit** DC. **Map** p306 K12.

Vesterbro Fitness Centre

Angelsgade 4 (33 22 05 00/www.ki-kbh.dk). *Train to Enghave.* **Open** 10am-9pm Mon; 7am-7pm Tue-Thur; 7am-6pm Fri; 9am-2pm Sat.; closed Sun. **Prices** 50kr. **No credit cards. Map** p111 T6.

Football

Fælledsparken, in the shadow of the national stadium (Parken), holds amateur tournaments each Sunday from April to November. If you want to join a team – or can raise one – just show up around 10am. Alternatively, there are plenty of indoor and outdoor pitches throughout the city that can be booked for a kick-about. To find out more, call the Copenhagen Football Association on 39 27 71 44. To book pitches, call the Council Sports Office on 35 42 68 60.

Golf

Golf is a highly popular pastime and the excellent courses outside Copenhagen can get very busy. Be sure to book in advance, and expect to pay 100kr-150kr per person, plus equipment hire. Members are given preference at busy times, and most courses are a fair distance outside town. These include **Hørsholm Golf Club** and **Rungsted Golf Club**. Closer to the city centre you can practise your swing at **Copenhagen Indoor Golf Centre**. Malmö, 35 minutes across the water, boasts some excellent courses, which are also frequented by Copenhagen residents. The Copenhagen Golf Association can be reached on 43 26 27 00, while Malmö Tourist Information (00 46 40 30 01 50) will provide details of Swedish courses.

Arts & Entertainment

Copenhagen Indoor Golf Centre

Refshalevej 177B (32 54 43 32/www.cigc.dk). Bus 8.
Open *Mid Sept-mid Oct* 4-9pm Mon-Fri; noon-5pm
Sat, Sun. *Mid Oct-Apr* 11am-3pm Mon, Fri; 11am-
10pm Tue-Thur; 9am-7pm Sat, Sun. *May-mid Sept*
closed. **Prices** *non-members* 60kr-70kr/30min;
100kr-126kr/hr. **Credit** MC, V. **Map** p309 K21.

Hørsholm Golf Club

*Grønnegade 2, Hørsholm (45 76 51 50/
www.hoersholm-golf.dk). Train to Rungsted Kyst;
381 bus.* **Open** phone to check. **Prices** *Green fees*
330kr Mon-Fri; 440kr Sat, Sun; 180kr under-18s.
Credit DC, MC, V.

Rungsted Golf Club

*Vestre Stationsvej 16, Rungsted (45 86 34 44/
booking 45 86 34 14/www.rungstedgolfklub.dk).
Train to Rungsted Kyst.* **Open** 8.30am-dusk Mon-Fri;
noon-dusk Sat, Sun. **Prices** *Green fees* 375kr Mon-
Fri; 425kr Sat, Sun; 200kr under-18s. **Credit** AmEx,
DC, MC, V.

Go-karting

City Go Kart

*Retortvej 1, Valby (70 20 53 11/www.citygokart.dk).
Train to Valby, then bus 21/16 bus.*
Open 3-10pm Mon-Thur; 1-10pm Fri; 10am-10pm
Sat; noon-6pm Sun. **Prices** 2,300kr/hr per group of 5.
Credit MC, V.

Fart and Tempo Go Kart Bane

*Tempovej 35, Ballerup (44 66 60 04/
www.fartogtempo.dk). Train to Malmparken, then by
foot.* **Open** 10am-10pm daily. **Prices** 140kr/15min;
2,400kr/1hr per group of 6; 300kr per extra kart.
Credit AmEx, DC, MC, V.

Horse riding

Axel Mattsson's Riding School at
Klampenborg is a 20-minute train journey
from central Copenhagen. Private riding
lessons are also available.

Axel Mattsson's Riding School

*Bellevuevej 10, Klampenborg (39 64 08 22). Train to
Klampenborg.* **Open** phone for details. **Prices** *in the
forest* 300kr/hr; *with instructor in paddock* 260kr/hr.
No credit cards.

Ice-skating

Each winter, outdoor public ice-skating rinks
spring up at locations across the city, with hot
chestnut stalls and romantic lights adding to
the chocolate-box atmosphere. The most central
winter skating rink is situated on Kongens
Nytorv, where skate hire is available and a
small fee is charged. A little further out of town,
skating is free on the lakes bordering Nørre
Søgade, Øster Søgade and Vester Søgade. Do
not skate unless signs indicate it is safe. The

popular **Østerbro Indoor Skating Rink** is
located beside the national stadium charges
around 20kr plus skate hire, but is closed
during the summer months.

Østerbro Indoor Skating Rink

*PH Lings Allé 6 (35 42 18 65/www.ki-kbh.dk). Bus 6,
14.* **Open** noon-3pm Mon, Wed; noon-3pm, 8.15-
11pm Tue; noon-4.30pm Thur; 9.30am-12.30pm Fri;
3-7.30pm Sat; 4-6.30pm Sun. **Prices** 20kr; 10kr
under-16s; *skate rental* 25kr. **No credit cards.**
Map p121 D12.

Jogging

Copenhagen is relatively flat, making jogging
an attractive proposition. The city's numerous
parks are both safe and spacious, and joggers
can outnumber walkers in some areas. In
the city centre, try **Ørsteds Parken** near
Nørreport Station, or the lakes area at Nørre
Søgade. Further out, **Søndermarken** by the
zoo in Frederiksberg is also popular.

Pool & snooker

Many bars have a billiard table, but Danish
billiards (a game which features small skittles
as the centrepiece) is often the only game on
offer. However, American-style pool can also
be enjoyed at some central bars and cafés
including **Pub & Sport** (Vester Voldgade 9,
33 15 08 10). Snooker is growing in popularity,
and, while the standard is surprisingly high,
tables are still in short supply. **Albertslund
Billiards Club** (Hedemarksvej 14, 43 62 21 79,
train to Albertslund) is one venue, while the
Pool Pub (Rentemestervej 67, 38 88 00 29,
train to Nørrebro/5, 350S bus) also caters
for snooker enthusiasts. Call the Danish
Billiards Association on 43 26 20 82 for
further details.

Rollerblading/skateboarding

Experienced skaters can do as the locals do and
risk life and limb on the city's numerous cycle
paths. Those looking to live past 30 can use
the public facilities at **Fælledsparken** (Nørre
Allé; by the national stadium) or further out at
Vanløse Idrætspark (train to Jyllingevej).
For more information on facilities contact the
Council Sports Office on 35 42 68 60.

Rowing

Rowing clubs exist to the north and south of the
city centre. Beginners and experienced rowers
can contact the **Copenhagen Rowing Club**
(Tømmergravsgade 13, 33 12 30 75). To the
north, try **Gefion Ladies Rowing Club,**

Danish football

The Danish domestic football scene has progressed hugely since the introduction of the professional **Superliga** in the early 1990s. Until then, the game was very much an amateur affair, dominated by a handful of bookish clubs from Copenhagen (such as KB, B1903, AB and the like), playing in front of a couple of thousand souls huddled in rickety wooden stands. **KB**, in fact, were the first club to be formed in continental Europe, in 1876, and Denmark performed well in the Olympic competitions before World War I.

The game then passed Denmark by until the advent of the famous Danish Dynamite side of the 1980s, featuring Michael Laudrup, the country's first footballing superstar. Fans (Roligans) painted their faces red and white, and Denmark was back on the football map after 80 years. The surprise Danish triumph at the 1992 European Championships, featuring Michael's almost equally famous footballing brother Brian, was the spur that the game needed.

The knock-on effect of a higher international profile was the Superliga, and increased revenue from TV and sponsorship. In turn there was the rise of **Brøndby**, populist and successful, and the formation of media darlings **FC København** from the merger of KB and B1903. Now Copenhagen had a city rivalry more in keeping with the late 20th century than the late 19th, including even a little tension on the terraces – although in the main Danish football is as safe as any in Europe – and substantial media coverage.

The Danish season runs from late July to the end of November, and carries on from mid March to early June. Games generally take place on Sunday afternoons at 3pm, with live TV games on Sundays or Mondays. Standing tickets (*ståplads*) are around 80kr, seats (*siddeplads*) 100kr. Sausages (*pølser*) and beer are the staple diet on match days. The main stadium is **Parken**, which hosted the infamous Galatasaray v Arsenal UEFA Cup Final of May 2000 – but for most international fixtures is a sea of friendly faces; red-and-white ones, naturally.

Brøndby IF
Brøndby Stadion, Brøndbyvester Boulevard 8, Brøndby (43 63 08 10/fax 43 43 26 27/ www.brondby-if.dk). Train to Brøndby Øster or Glostrup, then bus 131. **Tickets** 90kr-110kr. **No credit cards.**

Denmark's leading club was only founded in 1964, a merger of two small clubs from this fairly salubrious industrial suburb west of Copenhagen. Backed by the local mayor Kjeld Rasmussen, Brøndby eventually won promotion to the top flight and, still semi-professional, won the league in 1985. Leading players included Peter Schmeichel and Brian Laudrup. The latter's father, Finn, was behind the club's decision to turn fully professional, a move that changed the face of Danish football (see page 239 **The Laudrup Dynasty**). The club then won seven titles in ten years, and performed credibly in Europe, including runs in the lucrative Champions League. The revenue helped pay for the reconversion of the stadium into a 30,000 capacity all-seater.

FC København
Parken, Øster Allé 50 (35 43 74 00/ www.fck.dk). Train to Østerport, then bus 1. **Tickets** *club matches* 100kr; *internationals* 100kr-300kr. **No credit cards. Map** p121 D12.
FCK are either a bold attempt to launch a major club in the city, or a businessman's folly. Formed by the merger of KB and B1903 in 1992, and proudly installed at the national Parken stadium, FCK swept all before them by winning the league title in 1993. Their most notorious fans were the 'Cooligans', yuppies from the milieu of TV and advertising, dressing down in black strides and shades. Not surprisingly, they were mocked by the gritty boys of Brøndby, and not surprisingly FCK couldn't sustain their initial success, nearly going bankrupt in 1996. Since then, apart from the high-profile signing of Brian Laudrup in 1998, FCK have disappointed, rising only for the tense tussles with their rivals, Brøndby.

AB (Akademisk Boldklub)
Gladsaxe Idrætspark, Gladsaxevej 200, Søborg (44 98 98 42/fax 44 98 97 33/ www.abforever.dk). Bus 250S. **Tickets** 760kr-80kr. **No credit cards.**
AB are a hark back to the early days of Danish football. Traditionally, with a team and fanbase from Copenhagen University, AB won the league title in every decade after World War I – until the 1970s. By then they had been plonked near a bleak running track in Gladsaxe, north-west Copenhagen, attracting only loyal anoraks, surviving off the regular sales of star players. A recent mini-revival, however, included their first cup win, in 1999.

(Strandvænget 47, 39 29 62 36). The Danish Rowing Association can be reached on 44 44 06 33/www.roning.dk.

Rugby union

The centrally situated **John Bull Pub** on Løngangstræde (33 12 65 70) is the spiritual home of one of Copenhagen's top teams, **The Exiles**. Games are played at various locations including the **Kløvermarken** playing fields on the island of Amager (Kløvermarksvej; bus 47). For more info call the Danish Rugby Association on 43 26 28 00/www.rugby.dk.

Squash

Courts can be hired at **Nørrebrohallen**. For more info, the Danish Squash Association can be reached on 66 13 01 98.

Nørrebrohallen
Bragesgade 5, Nørrebro (35 83 10 01). Train to Nørrebro/5, 16 bus. **Open** 6.30am-11pm Mon-Thur; 6.30am-9pm Fri; 8am-11pm Sat; 8am-10pm Sun. **Prices** 50kr/hr. **No credit cards.**

Swimming

The most central place for a swim is the **DGI-Byen** sports centre by Central Station. This state-of-the-art building is fine for a dip, but tends to be monopolised by families, and is pricier than council-run venues. **Gladsaxe Sports Centre** is some distance out of town, but is worth the journey, offering modern indoor and outdoor pools and a host of other facilities. Many baths close in the summer, so remember to call first.

DGI-Byen
Tietgensgade 65 (33 29 80 90/www.dgibyen.dk). **Open** 6.30am-9pm Mon-Thur; 6.30am-7pm Fri; 9am-5pm Sat, Sun. **Admission** *6.30-9am* 25kr; 15kr concessions. *9am onwards* 40kr; 25kr concessions. **Credit** DC, MC, V. **Map** p310 Q11.

Gladsaxe Sports Centre
Vandtårnsvej 55-57 (39 67 27 29/www.gladsaxe.dk). Bus 66, 166, 250S. **Open** 7am-8pm Mon-Fri; 8am-2pm Sat, Sun. **Prices** 20kr; 10kr concessions. **No credit cards.**

Hillerødgade Swimming Pool
Sandbjerggade 35, Nørrebro (35 85 19 55/www.ki-kbh.dk). Bus 5, 7, 9, 16. **Open** *Sept-Apr* 10am-4pm Mon; 7am-9pm Tue; 7am-4.30pm Wed; 7am-7pm Thur; 7am-4pm Fri; 8am-2pm Sat, Sun. *May-June, Aug* 10am-4pm Mon; 7am-7pm Tue-Thur; 7am-4pm Fri; 8am-2pm Sat, Sun. *July* closed. **Prices** 24kr; 11kr concessions. **No credit cards.**

Vesterbro Swimming Pool
Angelsgade 4, Vesterbro (33 22 05 00/www.ki-kbh.dk). Train to Enghave. **Open** 10am-9pm Mon; 7am-5pm Tue, Thur; 7am-7pm Wed; 7am-4pm Fri; 9am-2pm Sat; closed Sun. **Prices** 24kr; 11kr concessions. **No credit cards. Map** p111 T6.

Tennis

Tennis courts are in short supply in Copenhagen. With most venues charging 100kr-150 kr per hour (sometimes with an additional fee for non-members), a five-set marathon can prove an expensive business. Most central is the **Hotel Mercur**, which rents out its own private courts to non-residents. **KB Tennis Club** has indoor and outdoor courts available; reservations required. **B93 Sports Club** is another tennis-friendly venue. More information can be provided by the Danish Tennis Association on 43 26 26 60.

B93 Sports Club
Ved Sporsløjfen 10 (39 27 18 90/www.b93.dk). Train to Svanemøllen/1, 6, 14 bus. **Open** *May-Sept* 7am-10pm daily. *Apr-Oct* closed. **Prices** 75kr. **No credit cards.**

Hotel Mercur
Vester Farimagsgade 17 (33 12 57 11/www.accorhotel.dk). **Open** 8am-6pm daily. **Prices** 100kr per person/hr. **Credit** AmEx, DC, MC, V. **Map** p310 O10.

KB Tennis Club
Peter Bangsvej 147, Frederiksberg (38 71 41 50). Bus 1. **Open** 7am-10pm Mon-Fri; 8am-7pm Sat; 8am-5pm Sun. **Prices** 100kr per person/hr. **No credit cards. Map** p110 N1. **Branch**: Pile Allé 14 (36 30 23 00).

Ten-pin bowling

Ten-pin bowling, usually accompanied by drinks or a meal, is a popular night out. Large indoor bowling alleys can be found centrally at **DGI-Byen**, **Scala Bowling** and **Parken**. Remember to call and reserve a lane, especially at weekends. Traditional outdoor bowls is less popular. Call the Danish Bowling Association (43 26 22 11/www.dbwf.dk) for details.

Bowlehuset
DGI-Byen, Tietgensgade 65 (33 29 80 20/www.dgi-byen.dk). **Open** 2-11pm Mon-Thur; 2pm-1am Fri; 10am-10pm Sat; 10am-8pm Sun. **Prices** 50kr-65kr per person/hr. **Credit** AmEx, DC, MC, V. **Map** p310 Q11.

Parkens Sportscafé & Bowling
Øster Allé 46, Østerbro (35 27 82 00). Bus 6, 14. **Open** 11am-11pm Mon-Wed; 11am-midnight Thur; 11am-1am Fri, Sat; 11am-10pm Sun. **Prices** 110kr-275kr. **Credit** AmEx, DC, MC, V. **Map** p121 D12.

The Laudrup dynasty

One family governs Danish sport: the **Laudrups**. Surname of the nation's greatest ever footballer, **Michael**, his influential father **Finn**, and less talented but ultimately more successful brother, **Brian** (pictured below), Laudrup stands for style, sporting excellence and above all, high international profile. The Laudrups rule. Several books, two art house films and reams of glossy magazine articles have been dedicated to the two brothers, their wives and their lifestyles. Although Brian and Michael were essential to the Danish Dynamite team, which raised the game from an amateur kickabout to football's elite, it was their father, Finn, who was behind the mechanics of this transformation. Finn, a journeyman midfielder, was still playing for the amateur club KB while his son Michael, at 16, was shining as a phenomenal talent in the junior ranks. Finn got him into the first team – father and son on the same pitch – but doddery old KB were barely prepared to pay the boy his bus fare. There was cold water in the showers and no nets in the goals, so Finn took his son to then second division club Brøndby, persuading the more progressive management to introduce proper payment for his underage wonderboy. Finn would go on to introduce professionalism in this amateur game.

Michael was Brøndby's star turn. The club was transformed. And so was Danish football, until then a complete backwater. On his 18th birthday, Michael made his debut for Denmark. Two years later he was the key player in Denmark's unprecedented move into the international arena at the 1984 European Championships, and in 1986 he and they formed Europe's major contribution to the Mexico World Cup. By then Michael was playing in the world's most prestigious league in Italy, for the mighty Juventus, and he would subsequently star in Spain for both Barcelona and Real Madrid.

Meanwhile much was expected of his brother, Brian, five years his junior – but he could barely make the Brøndby first team. Finn and Michael pulled a few strings, and found him a club in Germany's Bundesliga, albeit unfashionable Bayer Uerdingen. He flopped. After a move to Italy he was relegated with Fiorentina, then hardly played for Milan. Michael was the diplomat, known as 'The Ambassador'; he was socially smooth, with a stunning wife, and the couple

became popular with politician and pub-goer alike. Brian was a rather sad figure, mocked because of his own domineering partner. Brian and Michael – the odd couple, Copenhagen's Cain and Abel.

At national level, Brian notched up a few caps, but was hardly thought to amount to much, especially when Denmark failed to qualify for the 1992 European Championships. However, war in the Balkans prevented Yugoslavia from taking part and allowed the Danes through to Euro '92 by default. After a tactical row with coach Richard Møller Nielsen, Michael refused to take part. Brian was simply a member of a mediocre side given no chance. And then, against all odds, Denmark went on to win the tournament, beating Germany in the final. The greatest night Danish football will ever see – Copenhagen on fire – and it was Brian in the spotlight, and not Michael.

By the time of the 1998 World Cup, both had made their peace with the management and were looking to retire from the international stage with style and dignity – together in the national team for the first time in a major tournament. Reaching the quarter-finals, Denmark almost overturned the great Brazil, in a heroic 3-2 defeat. On the final whistle the camera caught the pair as brothers in arms, chucking their boots into the crowd, stripped to the waist. The end of the great Laudrup dynasty, from boggy pitches to Brazil.

Walking

Plenty of picturesque walking routes exist just a short bus or train ride from the city centre. **Amager Nature Reserve** is a real wilderness just five kilometres (three miles) from the central station (train to Tårnby/28, 30, 35, 36 bus). Another alternative is **Dyrehaven** (*see page 276* **Walking in Sjælland**), a few minutes' walk from Klampenborg station, 25 minutes north of the city.

Spectator sports

Athletics

The annual **Copenhagen Marathon** (second week in May; 35 26 69 00/www.sparta.dk) attracts participants from across Europe and beyond (entrance fee 300-350kr). The route changes each year, but vantage points are numerous and easy to find. Athletics meetings take place at the city's **Østerbro Stadium** (Gunnar Nu Hansens Plads 11, Østerbro, 35 26 69 00, bus 6, 14), but Malmö, 35 minutes by train, is the place to catch the more famous names. Call Malmö Tourist Information on 00 46 40 30 01 50 for details of events.

Boxing

Banned in Sweden and Norway, professional boxing is popular in Denmark, although safety issues have recently come under close scrutiny. Bouts are regularly held in arenas such as **KB Hallen** (Peter Bangsvej 147). Call 38 71 14 18 for tickets or check local press for details.

Cricket

The gentleman's game is surprisingly popular in Denmark, and the national team is on the fringes of the European elite. Cucumber sandwiches may be in short supply, but devotees can catch a game of cricket throughout the summer months at a number of venues throughout the suburbs such as **Kløvemarken** (bus 47). Contact the **Danish Cricket Association** (43 26 21 60/www.cricket.dk) for details of match schedules.

Golf

Denmark's only golf tournament of any real international interest is the **Scandinavian Masters**, an invitational event that pits some of the world's top players against a Nordic select team. The competition takes place at different venues across Scandinavia in early

August, and the Copenhagen area rarely misses out. Both **Rungsted Golf Club** (*see page 236*) and Malmö's Barsebæk course have both recently hosted a stage of the three-day tournament. Call the Danish Golf Union on 43 26 27 00 or visit www.dgw-golf.dk for details of venues, or BILLETnet on 38 88 70 22 for tickets and availability.

Handball

One of the nation's favourite spectator sports, handball is unique in that the women's game is far more popular than the men's version. The rules are simple, and games are easy to follow, fast-moving and exciting. Copenhagen has a number of semi-professional clubs such as **Ajax Farum** (Bavnehøj Hallen, Enghavevej 90, 33 21 49 00). Contact the Danish Handball Association (43 26 24 00) or visit www.dhf.dk for up-to-the-minute information.

Horse racing

Two venues exist in Copenhagen, both located to the north of the city. For chariot-style racing, visit **Charlottenlund** (Traverbanevej 10, 39 96 02 02), while for flat racing, **Klampenborg** racetrack is located in the idyllic Dyrehaven park (39 96 02 02/www.galopbane.dk).

Ice hockey

When football breaks for winter, ice hockey takes over as the nation's top spectator sport. Denmark hosted the world 'B' Championships in 1999, and the national team has produced some impressive recent results. Top teams in the Copenhagen area are **Rungsted Cobras** north of the city (Stadion Allé 11, Rungsted Kyst, 45 76 30 31) and **Rødovre** (Rødovre Parkvej 425, Rødovre, 36 72 17 79) to the south. Semi-pro teams also exist in Hvidovre, Gladsaxe and Gentofte. For details of fixtures, call the Danish Ice Hockey Association on 43 26 26 26.

Tennis

Denmark's flagship event is the **Copenhagen Open**, held every February in the **KB Hallen** arena (Peter Bangsvej 147; 38 71 41 50). This ATP event is not the biggest on the circuit, but the venue allows spectators to get close to the action, and the tight atmosphere generally creates a few upsets. International matches are due to take place at a new 1,100-seat venue in the suburb of Farum. For details, call the Danish Tennis Association on 43 26 26 60.

Arts & Entertainment

Trips Out of Town

Feature boxes

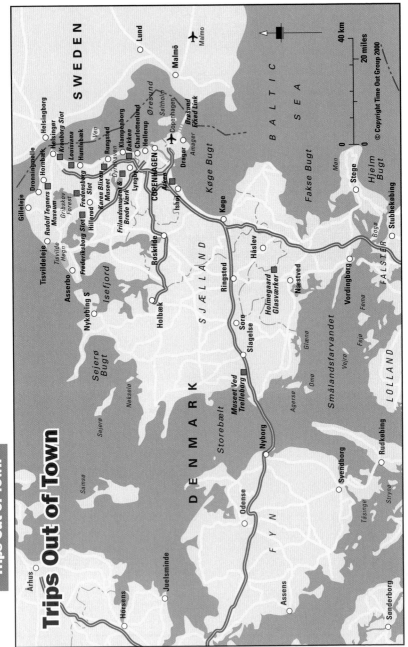

Trips Out of Town

SWEDEN

S W E D E N

Lund

Malmö

Malmö

Helsingborg

Helsingør

Helsingør

Kronborg Slot

Dronningølle

Hornbæk

Louisiana

Rungsted

Humlebæk

Klampenborg

Charlottenlund

Hellerup

Øresund

Saltholt

Øresund Fixed Link

Copenhagen

BALTIC

SEA

B A L T I C   S E A

© Copyright Time Out Group 2000

40 km

20 miles

Gilleleje

Tisvildeleje

Tisvilde Hegn

Rudolf Tegners Museum

Fredensborg Slot

Gribskov Forest

Karen Blixen Museet

Bakken

Dyrehaven

Lyngby

COPENHAGEN

Amager

Dragør

Køge Bugt

Fakse Bugt

Møn

Hjelm Bugt

Stege

Stubbekøbing

Asserbo

Frederiksborg Slot

Hillerød

Frilandsmuseet Brede Værk

Ishøj

Roskilde

Køge

Haslev

Ringsted

Holmegaard Glasværker

Næstved

Vordingborg

FALSTER

Nykøbing S

Isefjord

Holbæk

S J Æ L L A N D

Sorø

Slagelse

Giano

Smålandsfarvandet

Vejrø

Feijø

Femø

LOLLAND

Bøgø

Sejerø Bugt

Sejerø

Nekselø

Museet Ved Trelleborg

Storebælt

Nyborg

Agersø

Omø

Agersø

Tåsinge

Rudkøbing

Stryno

Samsø

D E N M A R K

Odense

F Y N

Svendborg

Århus

Juelsminde

Horsens

Assens

Sønderborg

Malmö & Lund

Geographically, Copenhagen is far closer to southern Sweden than the rest of Denmark, and these two fine Swedish cities make for rewarding day trips.

Malmö

If you're one of those people who don't really feel you've got your money's worth from a holiday unless you can tick two countries off your list, then you are in luck. Sweden is just a short hop away from Copenhagen, across the Øresund by ferry from Nyhavn, or by train or car across the spectacular new **Øresund Fixed Link** (*see page 246*). But a visit to Malmö, Sweden's third largest city situated directly opposite Copenhagen, is not just for geographical trainspotters; this historic fishing and trading town is probably the most appealing option for a day trip from Copenhagen.

Slottet Malmöhus. See p244.

Up until the mid 17th century, Malmö was an important settlement at the heart of the Danish empire. Copenhagen and Malmö have, thus, long been closely linked, and, even before the advent of the bridge/tunnel, there was constant traffic of workers and visitors between them.

Today, this prosperous and inviting city could be thought of as Copenhagen's little cousin (though the Swedes may not appreciate the comparison), offering a microcosm of the Danish capital's shops, restaurants and nightlife (Malmö has more pubs per head than any other Swedish city), in arguably even more beautiful surroundings. Malmö is sometimes known as the City of Parks, and its large, green open spaces, long, clean sandy beach, just a few minutes walk from the city centre, excellent cultural facilities (the wide-ranging **Malmö Festival** takes place at venues throughout the city in August each year; www.malmo.se) and an interesting ethnic mix (over a quarter of its total population of 250,000 are originally from Eastern Europe, Latin America, the Middle East and Africa), make it one of the most interesting towns in the region. Sweden's top pop band, the Cardigans, have set up their base in a studio here, and are frequently spotted in the town's bars and restaurants, augmenting an already trendy nightlife scene. In fact, with its café squares, lively restaurants and thriving beach culture Malmö has more in common with southern Europe than Scandinavia. A younger demographic, courtesy of a university population of 6,000 that is predicted to swell to 15,000 over the coming years (and that's not including the students of Lund University nearby), ensures that Malmö is a lively, fun and flirtatious party city, well worth checking out.

History

The first time Malmö crops up in any significant capacity is in 1260 when the town, then an integral part of the Danish empire, was included in the dowry of the Danish Princess Sophia for her marriage to King Valdemar of Sweden. As with Copenhagen, Malmö's prosperity and growth in the following years can mainly be attributed to the vast quantities of herring in the Øresund, and the strategic importance afforded by the town's sheltered bay.

For the next few centuries Malmö featured prominently in various Danish/Swedish squabbles, changing hands a number of times. During the 16th century Malmö grew to challenge Copenhagen as Denmark's premier city, and by the time of the disastrous (for Denmark and Malmö at least) Roskilde Treaty of 1658 it was Denmark's second biggest settlement. Swedish once more, Malmö's growth faltered as other cities supplanted it in importance, and a plague helped cull the population to just over 1,000 people in 1713. A turning point was the building of a proper harbour in 1775, under the guidance of Frans Suell (commemorated by a statue on Norre Vallgatan), which allowed vessels to dock practically in the centre of town. This had a dramatic affect on Malmö's economy. Shipbuilding, among other industries, commenced in earnest.

By 1800 the population had grown to 5,000, and though this still only made Malmö the fifth largest town in Sweden, King Gustav IV Adolf nevertheless considered it his unofficial capital, and for the second half of 1806 moved his family into buildings fronting Stortorget (the main square), in order to be nearer the front line in the war against Napoleon. The population became very excited at the prospect of Malmö becoming the royal seat, and even named a square after the king, but in the end it came to nothing.

However, exponential growth over the next century saw the population climb to 83,000, and today Malmö is home to around half a million people.

Sightseeing & shopping

The historic heart of Malmö is a beguiling mix of timbered buildings, wide canals, beautiful parks and a sizeable pedestrian shopping area, **Södergatan**, which connects the squares Stortorget and Gustav Adolfs Torg, before continuing down Södra Förstadsgatan to Triangeln, the triangular square in front of the Scandic Hotel. All are within easy walking distance of each other, as are the ferry terminals and the railway station.

While Södergatan is no Strøget, it does have a good range of international chain stores and independent shops, as well as numerous restaurants and bars. A little further south you find the immigrant area around Möllevångstorget, which has several Asian, African and Eastern European shops and restaurants, while to the north-west is the famous beach, Ribban (see page 245).

The historic heart of Malmö is criss-crossed by a series of canals and bridges, and a very

Kungsparken. *See p246.*

pleasant way to get your bearings is by taking a canal tour. **Rundan Canal Tours'** boats (*listings page 249*) leave every hour from a berth opposite the Central Station from May to August, and the tour takes 45 minutes. You can also hire pedalos from **City Boats**, based on Södertull between April and August, and do the tour under your own steam.

Malmö might not offer quite the rich cultural and historical tapestry of Copenhagen, but it does have one or two museums and galleries that are worth spending some time in. Conveniently for the day tripper, most of them are located in one site, within the walls of **Slottet Malmöhus** (Malmö Castle).

The Danish king Erik of Pomerania was the first to build a castle on the site (which at that time was right on the sea front) in 1434, and for a while afterwards it was the home of the Danish mint. In the 16th century the castle underwent a major rebuild under Christian III of Denmark, with the addition of ramparts, four red cannon towers (two of which are still standing) and a moat, in accordance with Malmö's strategic importance in the control of access to the Baltic. The castle's usefulness continued after the Swedes 'liberated' (as they still like to say) this part of their country from the Danes in 1658, so much so that Christian V tried unsuccessfully to take it back again in 1677. Up until 1937 the castle served as a prison, at which time it was converted to house the museums here today.

Today a rather stern, functionalist extension within the walls of Slottet Malmöhus contains the city's most important museums. **Naturmuseet** (the Natural History Museum; *listings page 248* **Malmö Museums**) features not only an enjoyably chaotic collection of stuffed animals (including one gargantuan moose) and birds from around the world, but also a small aquarium, various live insects and reptiles, and a fascinating nocturnal room.

Upstairs on the left, the **Malmö Konstmuseum** (Malmö Art Museum; *listings page 248* **Malmö Museums**) gives visitors a well presented bite-size tour through the history of art and design from the Renaissance through baroque, Regency, rococo to contemporary Scandinavian pieces. The museum is said to hold the largest collection of contemporary Scandinavian art in the world, featuring an impressive range of ceramics, paintings, sculpture, furniture, silverware and glassware. The F-Rummet houses a changing programme of contemporary, and often challenging and/or hilarious avant-garde installations from the region.

The **Stadsmuseet** (the City Museum; *listings page 248* **Malmö Museums**), to the right up the stairs, covers the history of Malmö from the flint miners and reindeer hunters of 1000 BC onwards. This leads into the castle itself, and its collection of tapestries, weaponry, art, furniture and other pieces from the 16th and 17th centuries (English information is available).

A short walk along Malmöhusvägen towards Ribban, Malmö's beach, on the other side of the road, is Malmö's **Teknik och Sjöfartsmuseet** (the Technology and Maritime Museum; *listings page 248* **Malmö Museums**), which opened in 1978. The Sjöfartsmuseet covers the region's naval history with boats, photographs, models and displays on shipbuilding. There are no English captions. The Teknikmuseet examines developments in aviation, steam power, motoring and submarine technology. The highlight is a 1943 U3 submarine – a claustrophobe's idea of hell.

Just before you reach Teknik och Sjöfartsmuseet, if you turn right into Banérskajen you will come to Fiskehoddorna. This row of pretty, coloured wooden fishermen's huts looks like a relic from the town's herring fishing past, but the local fishermen still sell their fresh catches from stalls in front of the houses most mornings.

Ribersborgs Stranden (Ribersborgs Beach, otherwise known as '**Ribban**'), Malmö's

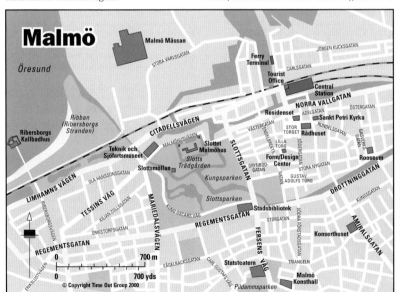

Øresund Fixed Link

On 1 July 2000 Denmark and Sweden finally put centuries of rivalry, war and ill-feeling behind them with the opening of the Øresund Fixed Link, 16 kilometres (10 miles) of tunnel, bridge and man-made island connecting Copenhagen and Malmö, on the south coast of Sweden. Not only do the bridge and tunnel now unite these two visitor-friendly cities and provide a fixed road and rail connection between the nations of Denmark and Sweden, but for the first time since the Ice Age the Scandinavian peninsula is connected to the European continent.

The effects of this historic event were already being felt before the opening, with new railway stations, motorways and towns being built on both sides of the water. Copenhagen Airport began the expansion needed to cope with the predicted growth of air traffic in the region with the opening of its new Terminal 3, and another terminal is in the pipeline. In Malmö, an underground rail link from the bridge to the centre of town (cutting out the current circuitous route) is planned for 2007.

The Link is a truly international project in the spirit of the new Europe (or so the PR spin would have it), created by five contractors

fine, two-kilometre (one-mile) long sandy beach, further west, is the town's unique selling point today, but it wasn't always the case. The beach is, in fact, a fake, constructed on a festering swamp in the 1920s. These days, however, it has given the city a very attractive sea front, the water is crystal clear and the sand slopes gently out into the sea, making it perfect for children. Unexpectedly, the first stretch of beach as you walk from the town centre is an unmarked nudist (and sometime gay cruising) area, but from then on there is a more family-oriented mix of sand, grass picnic areas, cafés and ice-cream vendors.

For an authentically Swedish experience, a visit to the **Ribersborgs Kallbadhus** (Ribersborgs Cold Bath House; *listings page 249*) is recommended. This charming green wooden bath house, dating from 1898, is situated at the end of a short pier off the eastern end of the beach, not far from the castle. Walk through the small café at the front, pay the entrance fee and you enter the segregated open-air deck areas (men to the left, women to the right), with their bracing sea water plunge baths and saunas. It goes without saying that

nudity is the norm here. Swedes use these kind of public saunas for socialising, catching up on their reading or just hanging out (so to speak). A masseur is on hand to pummel weary bodies, and there is also a solarium, should the sun be absent.

Malmö has several excellent and well used parks. The nearest to Ribban are the beautiful landscaped areas behind Slottet Malmöhus, **Slottsparken** and **Kungsparken** (the Castle Park and the King's Park), which feature lakes, canals and countless secluded corners, as well as **Slottsmöllan**, the castle windmill. **Pildammsparken**, a short walk down Fersens Väg to the south, is grander still, and has at its heart a large, picturesque lake framed with trees, flower beds and grass banks. It was created in 1914 to house the Baltic Exhibition. All three parks throng with nightingales during summer.

In the south-east corner of Kungsparken, in one of Malmö's grander quarters, is the town's answer to Copenhagen's Black Diamond (*see page 86*), the **Stadsbibliotek** (Town Library). As with the Black Diamond, Malmö's 19th-century red-brick library received an

Trips Out of Town

Ribersborgs Kallbadhus, and its view of the **Øresund Fixed Link** bridge.

from Denmark, Sweden, Holland, France and the UK. It consists of the largest immersed tunnel in the world, containing two rail tubes and two road tubes, stretching from an artificial peninsula at Kastrup to a four-kilometre (two and a half-mile) long artificial island midway, before emerging above ground on to a cable-stayed high bridge to the Swedish coast. The Øresund Bridge carries cars on a four-lane road on its upper deck, and a two-way rail link beneath on its lower deck. More relevant to visitors to the region is the fact that the bridge now renders Sweden a mere hop (well, a 35-minute train ride) away

from the Danish capital, with Stockholm a slightly more strenuous four and a half hours' train journey.

Facts & figures

Highest point: 57 metres (187 feet).
Deepest point: 20 metres (66 feet) below the surface of the sea.
Length of tunnel: 4.05 kilometres (2.5 miles).
Length of bridge: 7.8 kilometres (5 miles).
Volume of sea bed removed: 7 million cubic metres (9 million cubic yards).
Total cost: 3.6 billion euros (approx 27bn kr/£2.2bn/US$3.3bn).

uncompromising, modern glass extension in 1999, in this case designed by Danish architect Henning Larsen (most famous for his foreign ministry building in Riyadh, and also responsible for the Ny Carlsberg Glyptotek extension in Copenhagen; *see page 64*). A visit to this stunning, vertiginous glass construction, nicknamed the Cathedral of Light, is a must for anyone with a penchant for striking modern architecture.

Malmö's undisputed design temple is the **Form/Design Center** (*listings page 248*), housed in a converted warehouse. The first floor houses a changing programme of design-related exhibitions covering the fields of architecture, sculpture, design and art. On the second floor is an excellent Scandinavian design shop selling everything from garden furniture to jewellery, kitchenware and clothes.

The Center is located in a courtyard adjacent to Malmö's prettiest square, **Lilla Torg**. By night Lilla Torg is the hub of Malmö's lively nightlife scene. As well as its large number of pubs, the city also claims to have more restaurants per square kilometre than any other Swedish city, and this is where you'll find some of the best (*see page 249*). Lilla Torg dates back to 1591 when it developed as an overflow for Stortorget (*see below*). In 1903 the square was given a roof, but that was demolished in 1967 and the area was re-cobbled.

These days it is packed with busy and tremendously enjoyable bars and restaurants. You could liken Lilla Torg to Nyhavn (*see page 76*), except that its clientele tend to be younger, perhaps more affluent, and more fun than those who frequent Copenhagen's historic canal. When the temperature soars above freezing the café tables and parasol heaters move out onto

the cobbles to create a uniquely inviting and almost Mediterranean atmosphere.

In the north-east corner of Lilla Torg is the entrance to **Saluhallen** (10am-6pm Mon-Fri, 10am-4pm Sat), a cornucopia of world cuisine housed in a former indoor market. Stalls include a delicatessen, a fishmonger, a sushi bar, an Italian ice-cream parlour as well as Mexican, Turkish and Asian restaurants.

In the 16th century, nearby **Stortorget** was one of the largest market squares in Scandinavia. At its centre is a statue of the comically rotund King Carl X Gustav (responsible for the chain of events that climaxed with the Treaty of Roskilde), astride his horse Hannibal, while surrounding it are several grand old buildings. They include, on the east side, Malmö's Renaissance **Rådhuset** (the Town Hall) dating from 1546 but rebuilt in 1812 in the neo-classical style; on the western side, the 16th-century home of the former Danish mayor and controller of the Mint Jörgen Kock (in its basement you'll find one of the city's finest restaurants, **Årstiderna**; *see page 249*); and on the north side **Hotel Kramer** (*see page 250*), modelled on Copenhagen's Hotel d'Angleterre, and **Residenset** (the Governor's Residence) dating from the early 18th century, but rebuilt most recently in 1851. It was on the balcony here that the kings of Norway, Sweden and Denmark met in 1914, confirming their joint statement of neutrality. Shortly after the summit, the balcony was found to be on the brink of a collapse (it was, in fact, held on by a couple of rusty screws), which could have had serious repercussions, not only for Scandinavia but the whole of Europe. On the square's south-east corner is Malmö's oldest chemist, Apoteket Lejonet, founded in 1579 but now housed in an art nouveau building dating from 1890.

Trips Out of Town

During the 1650s an unsuccessful coup attempt by Danish sympathisers resulted in a number of grisly retaliatory executions in Stortorget, and in 1678 the Danish nobleman Jörgen Krabbe, who lived in the castle at Krageholm in Sweden, was beheaded here after being (probably wrongly) accused of plotting against Sweden. Much later, in 1811, executions and floggings took place here following an uprising by farmers and peasants opposed to conscription to fight Napoleon in Europe. During the August festival, Stortorget hosts another, slightly more palatable massacre: the world's largest crayfish party.

Behind Stortorget to the east is **Sankt Petri Kyrka** (St Peter's Church), Malmö's main place of worship, built at the beginning of the 14th century. It has many similarities with other Hanseatic churches of the period, particularly Marienkirche in Lübeck. Like most other Catholic churches at that time, Sankt Petri Kyrka suffered during the Reformation and, in 1555, its medieval frescos were whitewashed over (some have been restored and can be seen in the nearby **Krämer Chapel**).

As well as the Konstmuseum, Malmö has two other highly regarded art spaces. **Malmö Konsthall** (*listings below*), built in 1975, holds around ten temporary exhibitions of contemporary art a year in its capacious rooms (this is one of the largest contemporary art sites in Europe), and also has a fine courtyard café and hosts jazz concerts from time to time. Meanwhile, **Rooseum** (*listings page 249*) is Malmö's latest art space, located in a converted turn-of-the-century building that once housed the steam turbines of the local electricity company. Founded in 1988 by Swedish financier and collector Fredrik Roos (1951-91), and originally curated by Lars Nittve (also responsible for Louisiana – *see page 272* – and, latterly, another power station-cum-art museum, Tate Modern on London's South Bank), Rooseum is the place to find both radical modern art installations, themed exhibitions and mid-career retrospectives.

Malmö's striking **Stadsteatern** (the Town Theatre) was built on the corner of Fersens Väg and Östra Rönne in 1944 and is one of the largest theatres in Europe, with three stages. Ingmar Bergman was dramatic director here in the 1950s, and these days it is often visited by foreign ballet, opera and theatre groups and tends to offer a slightly more populist and international programme than Copenhagen's Det Kongelige Teater. In 1985 Malmö gained **Konserthuset** (the Concert House), on the corner of Föreningsgatan and Amiralsgatan, now home to the respected Malmö Symfoni Orkester (Malmö Symphony Orchestra).

What to see & do

Form/Design Center

Lilla Torg, Malmö (040 664 51 50/ www.formdesigncenter.com). **Open** *Jan-June, Aug-Dec* 11am-5pm Tue, Wed, Fri; 11am-6pm Thur; 10am-4pm Sat; noon-4pm Sun; closed Mon. *July* 11am-5pm Tue-Fri; 10am-4pm Sat; noon-4pm Sun; closed Mon. **Admission** free. **Map** p245.

Malmö Konsthall

St Johannesgatan 7, Malmö (040 34 12 93/ www.konsthall.malmo.com). **Open** 11am-5pm Mon, Tue, Thur-Sun; 11am-10pm Wed. **Admission** free; charges for some larger exhibitions. **Credit** MC, V. **Map** p245.

Malmö Museums & Art Museum

Malmöhusvägen, Slottet Malmöhus, Malmö (040 34 44 38/24-hr info 040 34 44 00/ www.museer.malmo.se). **Open** *Sept-May* noon-4pm daily. *June-Aug* 10am-4pm daily. **Admission** 40Skr; 10Skr-20Skr concessions; free under-7s. **Credit** MC, V. **Map** p245.

Lilla Torg. *See p247.*

Ribersborgs Kallbadhus

Ribersborgs Stranden, Malmö (040 26 03 66).
Open 8.30am-7pm Mon-Fri; 8.30am-4pm Sat, Sun.
Admission 30Skr; 25Skr concessions; free under-7s;
20Skr towel hire (30Skr deposit). **No credit cards.**
Map p245.

Rooseum

*Gasverksgatan 22, Malmö (040 12 17 16/
www.rooseum.se).* **Open** 11am-5pm Tue, Wed,
Fri-Sun; 11am-8pm Thur; closed Mon.
Admission 30Skr; 20Skr concessions; free under-
16s. **Credit** MC, V. **Map** p245.

Rundan Canal Tours

Central Station, Malmö (040 611 74 88).
Open *May-Sept* 10am-7pm daily. *Oct-Apr* closed.
Tickets 70Skr; 30Skr concessions. **No credit
cards.** **Map** p245.

Stadsbibliotek

Regementsgatan 3, Malmö (040 660 85 00).
Open *Apr-Aug* 10am-8pm Mon-Thur; 10am-6pm Fri;
noon-4pm Sat; closed Sun. *Sept-Mar* 10am-8pm Mon-
Thur; 10am-6pm Fri; noon-4pm Sat, Sun.
Admission free. **Map** p245.

Where to eat & drink

Årstiderna I Kockskahuset

*Frans Suellsgatan 3, Malmö (040 23 09 10/
www.arstiderna.se).* **Open** 11.30am-midnight Mon-
Fri; 5pm-midnight Sat; closed Sun. **Main courses**
195Skr-260Skr. **Credit** AmEx, DC, MC, V.
Map p245.
One of Malmö's most exclusive and expensive
restaurants, located in the atmospheric vaulted cellar of the former mayor Jorgen Kock's house. The
menu typically marries traditional Swedish ingredients, like reindeer or elk, with French influences.

Azteken

*Landbygatan 4, Malmö (040 12 50 45/
www.azteken.com).* **Open** 5pm-1am Mon-Sat; closed
Sun. **Main courses** 150Skr-196Skr. **Credit** AmEx,
DC, MC, V. **Map** p245.
This cosy courtyard restaurant, within a sombrero's
tilt of Lilla Torg, serves excellent modern and
traditional Mexican food. Parasol heaters mean you
can eat in the covered courtyard even when the
temperature drops.

Izakaya Koi

Lilla Torg 5, Malmö (040 757 00/www.koi.se).
Open 11.30am-1am Mon-Thur; 5pm-2am Fri, Sat;
5pm-1am Sun. **Main courses** 89Skr-265Skr.
Credit AmEx, DC, MC, V. **Map** p245.
Inventive, quality 'New Japanese' cuisine served,
when the weather is good, outside beneath parasols
in Lilla Torg. Said to offer the best sushi in Sweden.

Klubb Plysch

Lilla Torg 1, Malmö (040 12 73 60). **Open** 10pm-
3am Fri, Sat; closed Mon-Thur, Sun. **Admission**
50Skr. **Credit** AmEx, DC, MC, V. **Map** p245.

Located above Victors (*see p250*), this painfully cool
club/bar/lounge is arranged in a grand, five-room,
L-shaped apartment, decorated with lavish wallpa-
pers and opulent fabrics. A DJ plays at the bar,
beside which is an informal dance floor. A haven for
Malmö's beautiful people (models, media folk, musicians, millionaires), and trust us, they are beautiful.
Entrance is supposedly for members only (and members must be resident in Sweden), but you can get in
as a guest of a member, or, if you fancy a challenge,
through sheer guile.

Lemon Grass

*Grynbodgatan 9, Malmö (040 30 69 79/
www.lemongrass.se).* **Open** 6am-midnight Mon-Thur;
6am-1am Fri, Sat; closed Sun. **Main courses** 100Skr-
180Skr. **Credit** AmEx, DC, MC, V. **Map** p245.
More Asian-influenced fusion magic is on offer in
this stylish, minimalist eaterie.

Olgas

*Pildammsvägen, Malmö (040 12 55 26/
www.starta.net/olgas).* **Open** 11.30am-11pm Mon-Fri;
1-10pm Sat; 1-7pm Sun. **Main courses** 160Skr-
200Skr. **Credit** AmEx, DC, MC, V.
Map p245.
Olgas is one of Malmö's oldest and best-located
restaurants, by the lake in Pildammsparken. Not the
hottest night spot in town, it is, however, a great
place for a cool beer on a sizzling summer afternoon.

Petri Pumpa

*Savoy Hotel, Norra Vallgatan 62, Malmö (040 664
48 80/www.petripumpa.se).* **Open** 11.30am-2pm,
6-11pm Mon-Fri; 8-11pm Sat; closed Sun. **Main
courses** 140Skr-295Skr. **Credit** AmEx, DC, MC, V.
Map p245.
Consistently ranked in Sweden's top ten restaurants
(the chef won Michelin stars in his previous life), this
expensive but highly regarded restaurant is housed
in one of the city's top hotels, the Savoy.

Spot

*Stora Nygatan 33, Malmö (040 12 02 03/
www.restaurantspot.nu).* **Open** 9am-6pm Mon-Sat;
closed Sun. **Main courses** 55Skr-65Skr.
Credit AmEx, MC, V. **Map** p245.
Desirable and refreshingly modern Italian cooking
in a stylish setting close to the centre of town. As
with most of Sweden's restaurants, despite the chic
design, children are very welcome here. An in-house
delicatessen is a bonus.

Tempo Bar & Kök

Södra Skolgatan 30A, Malmö (040 12 60 21).
Open 5pm-1am daily. **Main courses** 150Skr.
Credit AmEx, DC, MC, V. **Map** p245.
Divided into an L-shaped bar and separate dining
area, Tempo is one of Malmö's hippest venues,
attracting a more studenty crowd than Lilla Torg.
Tempo is never going to win any awards for its inte-
rior design, but, you never know, you might catch a
glimpse of popsters the Cardigans, who are regulars.
Gets packed at weekends.

Trips Out of Town

Victors

Lilla Torg 1, Malmö (040 12 76 70). **Open** 11.30am-
1am Mon, Tue, Sun; 11.30am-3am Wed-Sat. **Main
courses** 110Skr-160Skr. **Credit** AmEx, DC, MC, V.
Map p245.
Experience modern Scandinavian cooking in this
trendy bar/restaurant that transforms into a club-
type space come night-time. Victors has its own
bar tending academy, so, as you would expect, the
cocktails are excellent.

Where to stay

If you want to stay overnight, and can't get into
the places below, contact **Destination Malmö**
(040 30 78 85/hotel@malmo.se).

Hotel Kramer

Stortorget 7, Malmö (040 20 88 00).
Rates 700Skr-1,495Skr single; 800Skr-1,695Skr
double. **Credit** AmEx, DC, MC, V. **Map** p245.
Malmö's poshest hotel is a smaller replica of
Copenhagen's swanky French château-style Hotel
d'Angleterre (*see p43*) and was built at the end of
the 19th century.

Hotel Temperance

*Engelbrektsgatan 16, Malmö (040 710 20/
www.temperance.se).* **Rates** 450Skr-890Skr single;
650Skr-990Skr double; 990Skr-1,090Skr family room.
Credit AmEx, DC, MC, V. **Map** p245.
Malmö's oldest hotel (dating from the turn of the
19th century) retains many of its period features and,
though not the finest hotel in town (that accolade
goes to the pricier Hotel Kramer), it is centrally
located and good value.

Scandic Hotel

*Triangeln 2, Malmö (040 69 34 700/www.scandic-
hotels.com).* **Rates** 1,299Skr-1,719Skr single;
1,709Skr-2,170Skr double. **Credit** AmEx, DC, MC, V.
Map p245.
Modern high-rise international hotel chain with a
decent restaurant, located at the southern end of
Malmö's pedestrian shopping area.

Getting there

Despite all the time, money and historical
brouhaha associated with the building of the
new fixed link across the Øresund, it is still
cheaper and more convenient for pedestrian
day trippers to Malmö to take the high speed
catamaran from Nyhavn instead of the new
train. The ferries, which run hourly, take
between 30 and 45 minutes depending on
whether you pay 89kr to take the high-speed
Scandlines Flyvebåden catamaran
(Havnegade 44, Copenhagen 33 12 80 88, Malmö
040 10 39 30, www.scandlines.dk), or 45kr
for the slower **Pilen** ferry (Havnegade 28,
Copenhagen 33 32 12 60, Malmö 040 23 44 11,
www.pilen.dk). Both prices are returns, and

both craft take you right into the central
harbour front of Malmö, a five-minute walk
from the town centre.

Tourist information

The Swedish krona tends to be worth around ten
per cent less than the Danish kroner. The international telephone code for Sweden is 00 46. The area
code for Malmö is 040.
You can rent a bicycle at **Fridhems Cyklar**,
(Tessinsväg 13, 040 26 35 50) or **Cykelkliniken**
(Carlgatan, behind the railway station, 040 611
66 66).

Malmö Tourist Office

*Centralstationen, Malmö (040 34 12 00/
www.malmo.se).* **Open** *June-Aug* 9am-8pm Mon-Fri;
10am-5pm Sat, Sun. *Sept-May* 9am-5pm Mon-Fri;
10am-2pm Sat; closed Sun. **Credit** AmEx, DC, MC, V.
Map p245.
The **Malmö Card** (one day 150Skr, two days
275Skr, three days 400Skr) is valid for one adult and
two children under 15 and gives discounts, free
entries and special offers.

Lund

Lund is a small, picturesque town about 20
minutes from Malmö by train. It predates
Malmö by several centuries and was an
important pre-Reformation religious centre
during its time as part of the Danish empire.
During the 11th century Lund was the final
destination of many pilgrims passing through
Copenhagen, and as such was the catalyst for
the Danish capital's initial growth. The
Reformation brought an end to all that in the
1530s, when the cathedral was relegated to
the status of parish church. Today, the town's
importance lies mostly with Lund University,
whose students (including many on exchange
from Europe and America), ensure that what
could be a quaint relic from the past –
many of its pretty cobbled lanes and half-
timbered houses are well preserved – is
actually a quietly buzzing, youthful town,
at least during term time.
Thanks to its impressive history, little Lund
can give Malmö a run for its money in terms
of tourist attractions. Lund's Cathedral
(*Domkyrkan; see page 251*) is one of the more
striking Lutheran churches in this part of the
world, and acts as the focus for the town, while
Lund's **Kultoren** (*listings page 253*) is a world-
class open-air museum, whose fascinating
collection of restored old buildings house
equally impressive permanent collections of
art, furniture and social history exhibits. The
town's shopping streets are centred on two
squares, **Stortorget** and **Mårtens Torget**.

Kultoren is an excellent place to commence a tour of Lund and get a feel for the history of the whole of southern Sweden. This cultural and historical museum is a ten-minute walk from Lund Station, down through the town's main shopping area. The museum was one of the first of its kind in the world when it opened in 1892 as a collection of Swedish folk culture. These days it can claim to be a kind of mini-national museum, so comprehensively does it cover Sweden's cultural, architectural, social and artistic history. Within the charming historic buildings you will find excellent exhibitions on the history of printing; Lund University (founded in 1668); the Modernist movement; ceramics and silver; and Lund in the Middle Ages, among other topics.

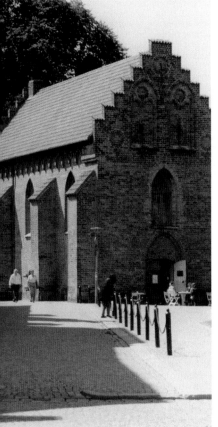

A quiet corner of **Lund**.

The real attractions, though, are the historic buildings from the 16th to 19th centuries, many with period furniture, fixtures and fittings. They include a vicarage, blacksmiths, farm buildings, various dwellings (ranging from a nobleman's house to a craftsman's workshop), and a remarkable wooden church dating from 1652. There is also a herb garden, children's play area and a café. Nearby on the corner of Sankt Annegatan is a period grocers' shop from the early 1800s (open from May to September) that sells old-fashioned sweets and souvenirs.

The exhibition on Lund University is housed in **Lindfors Hus**, the former residence of Pehr Henrik Ling, the so-called founder of Swedish gymnastics. If that whets your appetite, there is an entire, separate museum housing the University archive just across the square. Also notable is the museum's Modernism exhibition, **Metropolis**, charting the movement's influence across Europe from cities including Glasgow, Berlin, Paris and Stockholm; and an unexpected but evocative display of masks from around the world. Kultoren holds a wide variety of events, shows, lectures and performances throughout the year.

Adjacent to Kultoren in Lundagård is **Lunds Domkyrkan** (Lund Cathedral; *listings page 253*), at one time the largest and most important religious seat in Northern Europe. At the beginning of the 12th century Denmark still belonged to the diocese of Hamburg, but in 1103 Erik I visited the Pope and persuaded him to appoint the country its own archbishop, to be based in Lund. As a consequence Lund became the centre for the largest (in terms of area) diocese in Europe, positioning it as the religious centre for the whole of Scandinavia (including Greenland and Iceland).

Construction of the cathedral began on the site of the existing church (built by King Knud in 1085), under King Niels. The chief architect and master builder was a man known as Donatus, probably an Italian, and the cathedral was built in a Romanesque style from limestone quarried nearby. Donatus died in 1130 and the cathedral was consecrated in 1145 by Archbishop Eskil in honour of the Virgin Mary and St Lawrence. After a fire in 1234, the cathedral wasn't rebuilt until the early 1500s, just in time for the Reformation. The night of 11 August 1536, when Christian III imprisoned the Archbishop and all his bishops, and forced them to change allegiance to the Lutheran church, was to have dire consequences for Lund. The property and land that had once been the source of the Catholic church's power were confiscated, and with that went Lund's rank and importance within the Danish empire. Overnight, the town was reduced to a

A Dane, a Swede and a Norwegian walk into a bar...

The way in which the Danes rub along with the rest of their Scandinavian brethren is coloured by one simple, historical fact: they used to rule all of them, had a fight, and then lost everything in the most humiliating way possible. As a result, relations with Norway and particularly Sweden (who really rubbed the Danes' noses in it for a while), are understandably more complex than may at first be apparent.

This will probably come as a surprise to the rest of the world, which often sees Denmark, Norway and Sweden as one great, ultra-efficient, ultra-clean fjord, populated by cheery, bearded liberals who like nothing more than subjecting themselves to extremes of hot and cold in saunas and recycling anything that sits still long enough. Scandinavians, as a whole, are perceived as calm, laidback and, frankly, a little dull, but still waters, as they say, run deep.

The trouble really began in the 17th century, the Danes having lorded it over the region in not always the most sensitive of manners since the Viking era. But when they lost southern Sweden and the whole of Norway practically overnight (see page 13), the Danes faced a future of, as the euphemism goes, 'reduced circumstances'.

Understandably, some bitterness was inevitable, and no matter how nice they are face to face, and no matter how many splendid bridges they build across the Øresund, the Danes still gripe ceaselessly about the Swedes. They love, for instance, to point out the drunken Swedish day-trippers from Malmö, who stagger around Nyhavn's pubs and bars at the weekend ('They'd never behave like that at home,' goes the Danish chorus), or the Swedes who booze cruise from Helsingborg to Helsingør in their Volvo estates (rumour has it the cars are built around the dimensions of 10 crates of Tuborg). The Danes take great delight in mimicking the Swedes' singsong accents, and require little encouragement to dish the dirt on what a bunch of dull, law-abiding party poopers their fellow Scandinavians are.

The 1970s were a particularly stressful period for the Danes. The decade of Abba, muesli and Björn Borg was one of unprecedented glory for their neighbours across the Øresund. Thankfully for the Danes, the '90s kicked, with victory in the 1992

backwater, and the cathedral narrowly escaped demolition by becoming the local Lutheran church. More happily, a revival of kinds followed the reunification of Sweden in 1658 (*see page 13*), while the founding of Lund University in 1666 did much to bring prosperity back to the town, and its cathedral. In the 19th century the cathedral was extensively restored with its towers being rebuilt in the 1870s.

Today, the oldest surviving part of the cathedral is the crypt, dating from 1123. There you'll find the legendary Finn Pillars, mysterious carved stone pillars depicting the architect Donatus, the mythical giant Finn, Sampson, Abraham and Lazarus or even Christ, depending on who you believe. The cathedral's most popular attraction, however, is the Horologum Mirabile Lundense (astronomical clock), located on your left as you enter the west door. Built in 1380 and depicting a universe centred on the earth, this unusual clock features sun and moon indicators, showing their respective paths, as well as the 12 signs of

the zodiac. On the hour two knights clash swords, while the clock plays twice a day.

A short walk east of the cathedral is **Lunds Botaniska Trädgården** (Lund's Botanical Garden), an English-style park with unspectacular greenhouses (compared to those in Copenhagen's Botanisk Have; *see page 97*), and featuring over 7,800 plant species from around the world. The 20-acre garden was founded in 1690 and relocated here in the late 19th century.

Lund has little to offer in terms of restaurants or cafés, but the restaurant **Stortorget** (on Stortorget; *listings page 253*), which serves modern, Asian-influenced food, does come recommended. Otherwise, it's best to head into Malmö for an evening out.

Nearby, on Mårtens Torget, is Lund's **Konsthall** (Art Museum; *listings page 253*) housed in an austere functionalist red-brick building and Aura Krognoshuset, a tiny medieval house nearby. Admission is free to Konsthall, which hosts seven exhibitions of mainly contemporary art each year.

European Football Championships and their roaring mouse act that brought European federalisation screeching to a halt. Copenhagen became the hyper-cool design capital of the world, and Sweden found itself about as fashionable as a pair of elasticated beige leisure slacks. Denmark even won a Eurovision Song Contest.

For their part, the Swedes still look down upon the Danes as chain-smoking, underachieving, woolly liberals, with similarly lax attitudes towards drugs and sex as the Dutch. They have an unshakeable sense of self-belief that the Swedish way is best and all others should learn from them, which the Danes think makes them appear pushy and pretentious.

Even more damning within the Scandinavian fraternity is the accusation of 'being too much like the Germans', an insult that is hurled with equal conviction from all sides of the ramparts. The Danes cite the Swedes' regimented social behaviour as evidence of their Teutonic mindset, while the Swedes point to the Danes' closer cultural links with Germany, not to mention their sausage fetish. The Norwegians, meanwhile, stay quiet, grateful that no one is being horrid about them for once.

Norwegians know their place, and are more than content with it (as anyone would be with their balance of payments). They are less obviously high achieving, or, at least, don't

ram it down anyone's throats if they win a Eurovision or two, and therefore tend to be far better liked by the Danes. The relationship between Danes and Norwegians is more one of brotherly affection than regional rivalry; the Danes watch the Norwegian's backs, and vice versa. Though the Norwegians are significantly richer than the Danes (make that, 'than most of the planet'), thanks to their North Sea oil bonanza, the Danes think of them as rather naïve, innocent, and, if we're really honest, mentally disadvantaged country cousins. 'They've done rather well since we gave them their freedom,' the Danes joke. Norwegians are fiercely traditional, deeply religious and terrifyingly patriotic (as evidenced by their football commentators who become hyper-excitable in the event of a national team success), all of which the Danes find hilarious. However, the spectacular Norwegian scenery is much envied by the Danes, who only have a couple of cliffs and a sand dune to keep their amateur photographers happy. So they go to Norway to get away from it all and ogle the girls, with whom they can generally communicate better than with Swedish females. Danes feel at home with Norway's modest, inward-looking traditionalism and, secretly, covet their national costumes. This all makes the Norwegian's lack of humour and dull-wittedness (as the Danes see it) far easier to bear.

What to see & do

Konsthall
Mårtens Torget, Lund (046 35 52 95/www.lund.se). **Open** noon-5pm Mon-Wed, Fri; noon-8pm Thur; 10am-5pm Sat; noon-6pm Sun. **Admission** free.

Kulturen
Karlins Plats, behind the cathedral, Lund (046 35 04 00/www.kulturen.com). **Open** *Mid Apr-Sept* 11am-5pm daily. *Oct-mid Apr* noon-4pm Tue-Sun; closed Mon. **Admission** 40Skr; 30Skr concessions; free under-18s. **Credit** MC, V.

Lunds Botaniska Trädgården
Östra Vallgatan 20, Lund (046 22 27 320). **Open** *Mid May-mid Sept* 6am-9.30pm daily. *Mid Sept-mid May* 8am-8pm daily. *Greenhouses* noon-3pm daily. **Admission** free.

Lunds Domkyrkan
Kyrkogatan, Lund (046 35 88 80/ www.svenskakyrkan.se). **Open** 8am-6pm Mon-Fri; 9.30am-5pm Sat; 9.30am-6pm Sun. The clock chimes at noon, 3pm Mon-Sat; 1pm, 3pm Sun. **Admission** free.

Where to eat & drink

Stortorget
Stortorget 1, Lund (046 13 92 90). **Open** 11.30am-midnight Mon; 11.30am-1am Tue-Thur; 11.30am-3am Fri, Sat; 1-11pm Sun. **Main courses** 78Skr-166Skr. **Credit** AmEx, DC, MC, V. Contemporary Asian-slanted food.

Getting there

To get to Lund from Copenhagen by train, you'll need to change at Malmö. Lund is a 15-minute train journey from Malmö, which, in turn, is 35 minutes from Copenhagen's Central Station via the Øresund Fixed Link.

Tourist information

Lund Tourist Office
Kyrkog 11, opposite the cathedral, Lund (046 35 50 40/www.lund.se). **Open** *June-Sept* 10am-6pm Mon-Fri; 10am-2pm Sat, Sun. *Oct-May* 10am-5pm Mon-Fri; closed Sat, Sun. **Credit** AmEx, DC, MC, V.

Trips Out of Town

Odense

Midway between Sjælland and the Jylland peninsula, the island of Fyn's main town was once an unlikely artistic hotbed.

Odense is Denmark's third largest city (Århus on Jylland is the second), with a population of 185,000 inhabitants, but despite its size, its appeal to visitors lies almost entirely with two long-deceased natives: the writer Hans Christian Andersen (*see page 255* **Great Danes: Hans Christian Andersen** and the composer Carl Nielsen (*see page 258* **Great Danes: Carl Nielsen**), both born and brought up here.

It could have been so very different. Like Copenhagen, Odense has benefited from its location (in the centre of the central island of Fyn). Like Copenhagen, it is a city of historical importance that has been blessed with royal patronage, and was a religious centre of far greater significance for several centuries. Unfortunately for Odense, Copenhagen became favoured by the Danish kings of the Middle Ages, and Odense never quite recovered.

The name Odense dates to Denmark's pre-Christian era and is thought to derive from the Old Norse name for the god of war, Odin (or Woden). The town was an important trading post and religious site from well before its first written reference, in a document signed by Emperor Otto III of Germany in AD 998. During the Middle Ages, following the murder of King Knud in Odense's cathedral (*see page 257*) and his subsequent canonisation, the town became an important pilgrimage site. When a canal was built connecting Odense to the Storebælt (the stretch of sea between the islands of Fyn and Sjælland), its commerce also blossomed. In the 17th century the town suffered from high taxation (to cover the cost of Christian IV's various misadventures; *see page 11*) and looting by the Swedish army, and by the time of industrial expansion during the 19th century, which put the town back on its feet, Copenhagen and Århus had usurped it in the national rankings. Andersen once famously wrote that his somnambulant home town was 100 years behind the times. It still is.

Today, Odense is not exactly a riot of opportunity for visitors, but there are a few attractions that make a day's visit worthwhile (preferably on a Saturday, when the town's shopping streets have a little life).

Odense is very pretty in parts, with a medieval heart made up of winding alleys, colourful, wonky half-timbered houses, ample green spaces and picturesque waterways. Even today you can still sense some of the influences and atmosphere that shaped Andersen's fairy tale imagination.

As you leave Odense station the first site you see is **Kongens Have** (the King's Park), fronting the rather plain, 18th-century white stucco **Odense Slot** (Odense Castle). The castle was built by Frederik IV in 1720 as the royal family's base on Fyn; it was here that the king died from tuberculosis ten years later. Odense Slot is now a local government building and is not open to the public. HC Andersen's mother worked here for a while, and the author played as a child in its garden. To the left is an archway leading to **Sankt Hans Kirke** (St Hans' Church), whose main feature is an unusual external pulpit. Andersen was baptised here on Easter Monday 1805 (the writer is, in some way, connected with most historic sites in the city).

Just around the corner from Kongens Have on Jernbanegade is **Fyns Kunstmuseum** (Fyn Art Museum; *listings page 257*), all in all a poor effort given the town's prominence and the artistic heritage of the island. Here, ranged over three unimaginatively laid out floors, you'll find a meagre selection of works by the artists of the Golden Age (*see page 18*), with paintings by Eckersberg, Jens Juel, Dankvart Dreyer and Vilhelm Hammershøi, among others, plus some more recent abstract pieces.

A short walk away on Hans Jensensstræde is the city's main draw, **Hans Christian Andersens Hus** (Hans Christian Andersen's House; *listings page 257*), where the writer of fairy tales including *The Little Mermaid*, *The Nightingale* and *The Princess and the Pea* was supposedly born (though there is no documentary evidence) on 2 April 1805. The museum chronicles his life thoroughly, if rather prosaically, with photographs, manuscripts, letters, keepsakes and recreations of living rooms from the latter part of his life. A large book shop stocks English and other foreign language translations of his works. (*See also page 255* **Great Danes: Hans Christian Andersen.**)

Not far from the high street, on Munkemøllestræde, is **HC Andersens Barndomshjem** (HC Andersen's Childhood

Great Danes
Hans Christian Andersen

In Denmark they claim he is the most widely read author in the world, and they may well be right. The works of **Hans Christian Andersen** (1805-75), which include 190 fairy tales, travel writing, poems, a novel and dramatic works, have been translated into over 170 languages. His fairy tales continue to instruct and amuse across the generations with their psychological clarity, vivid characters and enchanting fantasy, while the man himself, a complex, often cantankerous mishmash of neuroses, sexual frustration and intrepid wanderlust, will always figure as one of literature's great enigmas.

In his home town, there is no doubting his hero status – he may as well have died yesterday, so fervently is his memory cherished. (No matter that his childhood here was miserable and he couldn't wait to escape.)

Once upon a time a little boy was born into grinding poverty. Andersen's home (now the main museum to his life; see page 254) was a small, half-timbered house in the poorer area of Odense, and soon his parents (a cobbler and a washerwoman who, rumour has it, were only married two months before his birth), moved on to an even smaller place in Munkemøllestræde (also now a museum; see page 254). Andersen's father died when he was 11, and he was then brought up by his grandmother.

Three years later Andersen left for Copenhagen intending to become either an actor or ballet dancer, and with hope in his heart he went knocking on the door of the Royal Theatre. All he achieved there, however, was a walk-on part as a troll, and he soon moved on to school in Helsingør.

There he slumped into a depression, exacerbated by an insensitive headmaster.

After school Andersen returned to Copenhagen where he made his literary debut with *A Walking Tour from Holmens Canal to the Eastern Point of Amager*, written in 1828. He quickly capitalised on its success with poems, stories and his first novel, *The Improvisatore*, written after his first visit to Italy. The success and immortality he would subsequently achieve through his fairy tales was predicted by his good friend the physicist HC Ørsted, though another famous contemporary, Søren Kierkegaard, had little respect for his fellow author and roundly criticised him at every opportunity.

Andersen fell in love a number of times during his life, but his sexuality has been the subject of much debate. He can probably best be summed up as a bisexual who never had either a heterosexual or homosexual experience. He died a virgin after enduring several unrequited loves, notably for Jenny Lind, a singer known at the time as the Swedish Nightingale (who inspired his story *The Nightingale*). She preferred to think of the gothic-faced writer as her brother.

Andersen was a restless soul, travelling frequently across Europe as far as Turkey, though his travel writing is perhaps under-appreciated today in comparison with his fairy tales. He never owned his own home, and indeed never even owned a bed until the age of 60. He died wealthy, acclaimed, but never quite content, at the age of 70 on 4 August 1875.

Trips Out of Town

Hans Christian Andersens Hus.
See p254.

Home; *listings page 257*), the house where
Andersen lived from 1807 to 1819, enduring
endless bullying from the neighbouring
children. 'House' is perhaps an overstatement,
as the museum consists of three diminutive
rooms (two houses knocked through),
only two of which actually housed the
Andersen family.

Fans of Odense's other famous son,
Carl Nielsen (*see page 258* **Great Danes:
Carl Nielsen**), are well catered for by the
Carl Nielsen Museet (*listings page 257*),
in the city's impressive modern concert hall.
The museum covers both the lives of Nielsen
(original scores, photographs, extracts from his
writings and recordings of his work), and his
talented sculptor wife Anne Marie.

A more general history of Odense and the
island of Fyn can be found in two museums,
Møntegården (*listings page 257*), and
Den Fynske Landsby (*listings page 257*).
Møntegården reveals Odense's urban history
within four idyllic 17th-century houses
arranged around a cobbled courtyard, featuring
interiors from the Middle Ages to the 20th
century as well as a large coin collection.
Den Fynske Landsby brings Fyn's rural past
to life, with 25 half-timbered 19th-century

buildings typical of the island (including
water and wind mills, a weaver's house, a
farm, a school, a jail, and a rector's house), all
authentically preserved and in working order.
During the summer months costumed staff
operate the machinery, and manufacture and
sell traditional crafts and foods – and the wood
smoke from these industries certainly enhances
the atmosphere.

Danmarks Jernbanemuseum
(Danish Railway Museum; *listings page 257*),
located in sheds behind the station, includes
locomotives and carriages from the country's
railway history. The royal coaches are the
main highlight, but there is also a large
model railway.

The original **Sankt Knuds Domkirke**
(*listings page 257*), built in the 12th century,
was ruined by fire in the 14th century and
latterly rebuilt in the current high Gothic style.
Today the most impressive feature of this
important cathedral is an extraordinary five-
metre (16-foot) high altar piece, made by the
woodcarver Claus Berg around 1521. It is
considered to be his finest work and is made
up of over 300 figures depicting the life of
Christ. More unexpected still is the 900-year-old
skeleton of King Knud (Canute) II which stands

in a glass case in the crypt. Next to Knud is another skeleton, believed to be that of his younger brother Benedikt. More steps take you to what's left of the foundations of the original Sankt Albans Kirke that stood here before Sankt Knuds. It was at the altar of Sankt Albans that Knud was murdered in 1035. HC Andersen was confirmed here in 1819.

Vor Frue Kirke (*listings page 258*) on Frue Kirkestræde is the city's oldest church. It was built towards the end of the 13th century (although a church has stood on the site since the 11th century).

Odense's cultural life centres around **Brandts Klædefabrik** (*listings below*), an imaginatively converted 19th-century textile mill which is home to the **Museet For Fotokunst** (the Museum of Photographic Art), **Danmarks Grafiske Museum** (Danish Printing Museum), **Danskepresse Museum** (Danish Press Museum), and **Kunsthallen** (the Art Hall).

When Brandts opened in 1987 it was Denmark's first international centre for art and culture, and it continues to hold around 40 challenging and original exhibitions a year in its pleasant, spacious rooms. Kunsthallen, its art gallery, is one of Scandinavia's largest, and usually hosts 12 exhibitions a year, majoring on contemporary art. The Museet For Fotokunst is the only one of its kind in Denmark, and it has a programme of changing exhibitions as well as a permanent collection of photography. The Grafiske Museum covers the development of printing in Denmark over three centuries and includes displays on lithography, papermaking, printing, bookbinding (often with professionals to demonstrate), while the Presse Museum chronicles the history of Denmark's newspapers. During the spring and summer the amphitheatre in the square in front of Brandts Klædefabrik buzzes with performances and shows.

Odense also boasts Denmark's second biggest zoo (**Odense Zoo**; *listings below*), but a less well-promoted curio is the **Elvis Presley Museum** (*listings below*), in the basement of the Superbowl complex. This one-room homage to the King's life and work is hardly going to challenge Graceland for breadth or quantity (or quality, come to that), but it does house over 1,500 pieces of memorabilia (record sleeves, photographs and letters, mainly).

What to see & do

Brandts Klædefabrik
Brandts Passage 37 & 43 (66 13 78 97/ www.brandts.dk). **Open** *Sept-June* 10am-5pm Tue-Sun; closed Mon. *July, Aug* 10am-5pm daily. **Admission** 50kr; 10kr-40kr concessions.

Kunsthallen 30kr; 10kr-25kr concessions. *Museet For Fotokunst* 25kr; 20kr concessions. *Danmarks Grafiske Museum/Danskepresse Museum* 25kr; 15kr concessions. **Credit** MC, V.

Carl Nielsen Museet
Koncerthus, Claus Bergsgade 11 (66 14 88 14/ www.odmus.dk). **Open** *Apr, May, Sept, Oct* noon-4pm Thur-Sun; closed Mon-Wed. *June-Aug* noon-4pm Tue-Sun; closed Mon. *Nov-Mar* 4-8pm Thur, Fri; noon-4pm Sat, Sun; closed Mon-Wed. Opening times may vary, phone for details. **Admission** 15kr; 5kr-10kr concessions. **Credit** MC, V.

Danmarks Jernbanemuseum
Dannebrogsgade 24 (66 13 66 30/ www.jernbanemuseum.dk). **Open** 10am-4pm daily. **Admission** 30kr; 7.50kr-22.50kr concessions. **Credit** MC, V.

Elvis Presley Museum
Superbowl, Grønkøkken 3 (66 19 16 40). **Open** 10am-6pm Mon-Fri; 2-6pm Sat; 10am-6pm Sun. **Admission** 35kr. **No credit cards.**

Den Fynske Landsby
Sejerskovvej 20 (66 14 88 14/www.odmus.dk). **Open** *Apr-mid June* 10am-5pm Tue-Sun; closed Mon. *Mid June-mid Aug* 9.30am-7pm daily. *Mid Aug-Oct* 10am-5pm Tue-Sun; closed Mon. *Nov-Mar* closed. **Admission** 35kr; 10kr-25kr concessions. **Credit** MC, V.

Fyns Kunstmuseum
Jernbanegade 13 (66 14 88 14/www.odmus.dk). **Open** 10am-4pm Tue-Sun; closed Mon. **Admission** 25kr; 5kr concessions. **No credit cards.**

Hans Christian Andersens Hus
Hans Jensensstræde 37-45 (66 14 88 14/ www.odmus.dk). **Open** *Sept-mid June* Tue-Sun 10am-4pm; closed Mon. *Mid June-Aug* 9am-7pm daily. **Admission** 30kr; 10kr-25kr concessions. **Credit** MC, V.

HC Andersens Barndomshjem
Munkemøllestræde 3-5 (66 14 88 14/www.odmus.dk). **Open** *Sept-mid June* 11am-3pm Tue-Sun; closed Mon. *Mid June-Aug* 10am-4pm daily. **Admission** 10kr; 5kr concessions. **No credit cards.**

Møntegården
Overgade 48 (66 14 88 14/www.odmus.dk). **Open** 10am-4pm Tue-Sun; closed Mon. **Admission** 15kr; 5kr-10kr concessions. **Credit** MC, V.

Odense Zoo
Sdr Boulevard 306 (66 11 13 60/www.odensezoo.dk). **Open** *Nov-late Mar* 9am-4pm daily. *Late Mar-Apr, Sept, Oct* 9am-5pm Mon-Fri; 9am-6pm Sat, Sun. *May, June, Aug* 9am-6pm Mon-Fri; 9am-7pm Sat, Sun. *July* 9am-7pm daily. **Admission** 65kr. **Credit**, DC, MC, V.

Sankt Knuds Kirke
Flakhaven (66 12 03 92). **Open** *Apr-Oct* 9am-5pm Mon-Sat; noon-3pm Sun. *Nov-Mar* 10am-5pm Mon-Sat; noon-3pm Sun. **Admission** free.

Trips Out of Town

Vor Frue Kirke

Frue Kirkestræde 12B (66 12 65 39/www.km.dk).
Open 10am-noon Mon-Sat; closed Sun.
Admission free.

Where to eat & drink

Odense is not blessed with many quality eating options. There are a number of unremarkable cafés in the main shopping area, a **Jensens Bøfhus** (*see page 137*) at Kongensgade 10, a pleasant café at **Brandts Klæderfabrik**, decent Thai fare at **Asia House** on the corner of Klostervej and Vestre Stationsvej, trad Danish grub at **Den Gamle Kro** at Overgade 23 (66 12 14 33) and first-rate French cuisine at tiny **Marie Louise** (Lottrups Gaard, Vestergade 70-72, 66 17 92 95, closed Sun).

Getting there

Odense is a 90-minute journey from Copenhagen's Central Station. Trains run approximately every half hour.

Tourist information

Odense Tourist Office

Rådhuset (66 12 75 20/www.odenseturist.dk).
Open *Mid June-Aug* 9am-7pm Mon-Sat;
10am-5pm Sun. *Sept-mid June* 9.30am-4.30pm
Mon-Fri; 10am-1pm Sat; closed Sun.
Credit DC, MC, V.
The **Odense Eventyr Pas** (24-hour 85kr, 48-hour 125kr, 40kr-60kr concessions) gives free admission to all sites listed on p257 except the Elvis Presley Museum and Denmarks Jernbanemuseum.

Great Danes Carl Nielsen

It is rather as if lightning struck in the same (extremely unlikely) place twice. Little Odense boasts two world-class artists who rose to dominate their fields nationally, and whose works are as popular and respected today, world wide, as they ever have been. Never mind that both couldn't wait to leave their home town, as far as Odense is concerned it's as if they never left, so regularly are they commemorated and celebrated in public performances and exhibitions.

Just like Hans Christian Andersen, the composer **Carl Nielsen** left Odense while in his teens to seek his fortune in Copenhagen, later returning to his birthplace in triumph.

Nielsen was born in the small village of Nørre Lyndelse, 10 kilometres (6 miles) from Odense, in 1865. His childhood was characterised by poverty. His father, a tradesman, was also a folk singer and fiddler and he would often incorporate his son into his performances. Already by the age of eight, young Carl was producing his first compositions, and at the age of 14 he joined Odense's Regimental Band, playing trombone. When he arrived in Copenhagen he joined the Royal Theatre

Orchestra as second violinist under the Swedish conductor Johan Svendson. Svendson encouraged the young man, whose formative heroes included Sibelius and Haydn, but particularly Mozart, to compose symphonies, folk songs, chamber music, opera and choral pieces, many still performed in schools and churches and concert halls throughout Denmark and Europe. (Appropriately enough, in 1982 an unknown symphony by Mozart was to be discovered in the city's archives. It was known thereafter as the Odense Symphony.)

Nielsen's finest works include the symphonies numbers 3-5, the operas *Saul and David* and *Maskerade*, and the vocal piece *Fynsk Foraar* ('Springtime on Funen'). They influenced several subsequent generations of Scandinavian composers. Nielsen was awarded the Knight Commander of the Order of the Dannebrog in 1925, and the same year he turned 60, amid great festivities in his home town. He died in 1931. Today, a small museum to his life and work is housed in the modern Koncerthus in the centre of town (see page 257).

Roskilde

Vikings, royal tombs and one of Europe's biggest rock festivals.

Roskilde is a peaceful town of 52,000 inhabitants, located at the southern end of the Roskilde fjord, 30 kilometres (22 miles) west of Copenhagen (25 minutes by train). A cursory visit could well leave you underwhelmed by Roskilde's sleepy high street and dull, commuter-town air. Delve deeper, however, and you'll soon discover that what was once the most important settlement in Scandinavia, as well as Denmark's premier ecclesiastical seat, still possesses a wealth of historical interest. Roskilde is the resting place for 38 Danish kings, as well as the site of the internationally famous **Vikingeskibshallen** (Viking Ship Museum; *see page 262*), which together make it worth a day trip from Copenhagen.

Before the monarchy and government moved to Copenhagen, Roskilde served as Denmark's first capital, as well as a major trading town. It was the site of the country's first Christian church, built in 980 by King Harold Bluetooth. In 1020, King Knud (Canute) the Great established a bishopric here, which meant that during the Middle Ages Roskilde was the destination for thousands of Catholic pilgrims (12 churches plus the cathedral stood within its ramparts and moat at that time). After the 16th-century Reformation, most of the churches and monasteries in the area were demolished, the stones being used to build Kronborg Slot in Helsingør (*see page 266*), among other notable buildings. By that time, however, Roskilde had long been supplanted as the country's capital, following Eric VII's move to Copenhagen in 1417.

In the 17th century Roskilde suffered the full force of Sweden's wrath as the old enemy marched on Copenhagen, while in 1711 a plague, followed later that century by two devastating fires, also took their toll. It wasn't until the railway arrived that a renaissance, of a sort, occurred.

The discovery of five Viking ships in Roskilde Fjord in 1957 gave the city an unexpected tourist boost, while in the 1970s Roskilde became known to rock music fans around the world as the location of one of the best outdoor music festivals in Europe (*see page 260* **Roskilde Festival**).

Roskilde's main shopping area (on Skomagergade and Algade) is typical of most provincial Danish towns, and offers a meagre range of stores, and even more meagre cafés and bistros. Things start to become more interesting when you reach **Roskilde Domkirke** (Roskilde Cathedral; *listings page 264*), which, at first glance, seems to be far too large a church for the town. It dominates the landscape for miles around, a testament to the Roskilde's former pre-eminence. Inside the cathedral you will find an extraordinary range of burial vessels containing the remains of 38 Danish kings, as well as many of their wives and children. Some lie in simple stone coffins, but many more have been laid to rest in elaborate, occasionally theatrical, sarcophagi.

The history of Roskilde has been closely linked to that of the Danish monarchy for many centuries. The tradition of burying Denmark's monarchs in Roskilde Domkirke began formally with the Reformation in the 1530s, but several kings and queens (including Harold Bluetooth and Margrethe I) had been buried here prior to that. Christians I, III, IV, V, VI, VII, VIII, IX and X are here, and there is almost a full deck of Frederiks, too. The latest royal incumbent is the current queen's father, Frederik IX, who lies in a simple, separate chapel in the north-west corner of the church.

The royal tombs in **Roskilde Domkirke**.

Roskilde Festival

The **Roskilde Festival** is held each year for four days towards the end of June/beginning of July in fields just outside the ancient former capital. The first festival, in 1970, was inspired by the 1969 Woodstock Festival in America, and was founded on similar sentiments of peace and love, and it remains a charitable event to this day.

Roskilde is renowned as Scandinavia's largest outdoor music event, regularly attracting crowds of 70,000 people and 150 or so internationally famous acts (Radiohead, Blur, Bob Dylan, the Rolling Stones, Iron Maiden and Lou Reed among them). The festival is famous for its relatively crime-free party atmosphere, in which events on the many and varied music stages (playing everything from hardcore techno to folk) are almost secondary to the carnival of New Age experiences, the multiplicity of food vendors, outlandish performers, and the beer and pot-fuelled hedonism surrounding them. Thanks in part to its reputation as a safe event, for many teenage Danes their first Roskilde Festival has been an important coming-of-age milestone.

Tragically, that reputation was to be seriously compromised by the deaths of nine people in 1999. On the night of Friday 30 June, during American rock band Pearl Jam's set on the main Orange Stage, a significant proportion of the 70,000-strong festival audience began to push forward to get closer to the band. Apparently some speakers had failed and the crowd at the back couldn't hear properly. The front rows slipped on the mud beneath them (it had been raining heavily beforehand), lost their balance and were crushed. Despite the pleadings of Pearl Jam's lead singer Eddy Vedder for the crowd to move back, their momentum continued. The resulting deaths of nine men (aged between 17 and 26, from Denmark, Germany, Holland, Sweden and Australia) who were at the front of the audience at the time, sent shock waves around the world's outdoor festivals. If it could happen in this usually most peaceful and amicable of festivals, then could it happen at any similar outdoor music event?

Despite the claims of festival manager Leif Skov – 'Nothing broke. Nothing collapsed. There was no chaos. People fell over and there was an accident' – criticism was levelled at the organisers. Safety barriers were said to be insubstantial (and of a type long banned in the UK); the amateur volunteer stewards were said to be too slow in responding; and the time it took to stop the music after the first crowd members fell (15 minutes) was deemed far too long.

Although most felt this was a freak accident, Oasis and the Pet Shop Boys, justifiably concerned about the safety arrangements for their gigs the following evening, pulled out. This prompted an extraordinary outburst from the event's organisers who, perhaps in the heat of the moment, accused the bands of showing

---

Being related to a Danish king in the 11th century was a perilous position, and mortality rates were high. The unlucky royal brother-in-law of 1026 was Ulf Jarl, who was assassinated in Roskilde church (St Luke's, as it was at the time), on the orders of King Knud I, for the apparently trivial matter of beating the king at chess. Ulf's widow, Estrid, had the church destroyed and the first stone church in Roskilde erected in its place (the foundations lie beneath the current Domkirke). Ironically, as the sister of the king, she is among the royalty buried here.

There are thought to have been at least two churches on this site before the first cathedral was built, at the behest of Bishop Absalon (founder of Copenhagen and Bishop of Roskilde at the time; *see page 8*), in 1170. The east section of the present-day cathedral was finished by the mid 13th century, the rest by 1282. The current red-brick building, with its slender twin spires, is the culmination of 800 years of extension, renovation and rebuilding and, as a consequence, architectural historians can spend many happy hours here. In 1968, a fire swept through the cathedral, but restoration work culminated with its addition to UNESCO's World Heritage List in 1995.

The Domkirke's main attractions are the royal chapels (which line the north and south aisles), with their hallowed residents and often stunning decoration, featuring frescoes, ornate ironwork and wood carving. In Christian I's chapel stands a column on which are marked the heights of several Danish kings. Christian himself is recorded as a mighty 6' 9" (2.06 metres), though his 6' 2" (1.88 metres) skeleton tells a different story.

As you would expect from Denmark's most bombastic monarch, Christian IV's chapel, built

(urine!). Choose the high ground to avoid the worst consequences of rain and mud. Pitch your tent in the middle of others to avoid having crowds tramping through the vicinity 24 hours a day.

2. There is almost no queue for the showers during late afternoon/evenings, as opposed to the mornings when the place can seem like a badly equipped refugee camp.

3. Bring your own dope from Christiania if you like, but it is very easy to come by at the festival and not that much more expensive. But don't forget, even at Roskilde, soft drugs are still technically illegal.

4. Even at this time of year the weather in Denmark can be volatile, so take clothing to cover all eventualities, from Mediterranean temperatures to Arctic winds and monsoons.

5. Do not leave without tasting the organic chocolate milkshakes in the organic food hall.

6. Check out the minor stages. The Orange Stage may play host to the headliners, but it rarely has the best vibe.

7. There is a cash machine on site, so you don't need to carry large amounts of cash with you (be prepared to queue, however).

8. Though crime is comparatively low, thefts from tents (and even occasionally of tents) do occur, so don't bring anything you couldn't bear to lose.

9. Take plenty of toilet paper and ear plugs (the two are not connected).

10. Under no circumstances wear a fuzzy felt jester's hat.

disrespect to the dead. Controversially, the next day's programme continued almost unaltered, save for a speech by the Bishop of Roskilde and a couple of sombre songs by a local singer.

At the time of going to press the Roskilde Festival is planned to go ahead in 2001 with, hopefully, extensively revised safety measures.

FESTIVAL TIPS

1. If you are camping come early. Check the site map on the Internet (www.roskilde-festival.dk) for good spots: close to entrances and facilities, but not too close to fences

in 1641 in the Dutch Renaissance style, is particularly striking, with a vaulted ceiling painted electric blue and covered in gold stars. It contains the surprisingly restrained coffin of the king, as well as his son, Prince Christian, and his wife, Anna Cathrine. Beside them are the brass coffins of Frederik III, Christian's successor, and his wife Sofie Amalie. The chapel is also graced by a rather camp statue of Christian by Bertel Thorvaldsen, and a typically self-glorifying painting by Wilhelm Marstrand, depicting Christian in 1644 aboard his flagship the *Trinity*, in the midst of a skirmish during the Battle of Kolbergerheide. Equally impressive is the decoration in Frederik V's chapel, which is the work of the neo-classical architect CF Hansen.

In addition, the Domkirke also has a characterful clock depicting St George slaying the dragon (it hangs inside the cathedral on its south wall, and every hour, on the hour, George makes the dragon howl) and an impressive organ, dating from 1554. The organ was recently restored and is said to be one of the most important historical musical instruments in northern Europe.

The ornately decorated pulpit was installed during Christian IV's reign, while the stunning gilded, winged altar piece, depicting the life of Christ in 21 scenes, predates that by 50 years. Legend has it that the altarpiece was confiscated from a ship travelling from Antwerp (where it was carved in 1560), past Helsingør en route to Danzig (now Gdansk) on the Baltic coast. The ship's captain claimed it to be worth a fraction of its true cost, so the harbour master, using a rule by which he was entitled to buy anything that passed through the port at its valuation price, purchased it for a song.

Trips Out of Town

The Vikings

It's become almost a cliché to say that the Vikings were not the bloodthirsty barbarians they are commonly perceived to be – but it's true, nonetheless. OK, so the Romans may have had the architects and the Byzantines better art, but none could match the Vikings for seamanship. And though no one is likely to claim that they were the most sensitive of souls, the Vikings' often superb craftsmanship and oral poetry tradition also mark them out as more complex people than they have often been given credit for. What's more, unlike many contemporary races, they bathed once a week on Sunday.

The Viking period began in the eighth century and lasted until the 11th. Though most Vikings were farmers, fishermen, tradesmen, craftsmen and hunters, the word Viking originally meant, simply, 'pirate' – a reference to their, at times, brutal domination of the seas of northern Europe. The Vikings were a Germanic race, unconquered by the Romans, and made up of Danes, Gauls, Norwegians and Swedes, all of whom spoke Danish. At the height of their power in the 10th century, the many small kingdoms of the north were amalgamated into the three Scandinavian countries – Sweden, Norway and Denmark. The name Viking, therefore, can refer to people from all three nations.

Their mastery of the oceans, aboard their super-fast longboats, took the Vikings as far as Greenland, North America, North Africa and the Caspian Sea, either trading with, or beating the hell out of, the races they encountered on the way. The wealthy Christian monasteries of the time were a favoured target, but the Vikings also ravaged entire regions of Spain, Italy, Portugal and Ireland. On one occasion, they travelled up the Seine to Paris, and had to be given a vast quantity of silver to leave.

By 1013, the whole of England had fallen to the Viking king Svend Forkbeard (as modern Danes are always just a little too quick to point out to English friends). Their notoriety as pagan rapists and pillagers stems from contemporary accounts of attacks on foreign settlements during this time, including the raid on the monastery at Lindesfarne in Northumberland, England, which took place in 793. Such writings tell of fearsome, bloodthirsty warriors descending like dragons from the north (they were known in England

---

There is a small museum charting the history of the Domkirke in the Great Hall above the Chapel of the Magi. The highlight is a replica of Margrethe I's golden dress (the original having been looted by the Swedes in 1659).

Beside the Domkirke is one of Roskilde's more unexpected attractions, **Museet For Samtidkunst** (Museum of Contemporary Art; *listings page 264*), which is made all the more unlikely for being housed within a pretty, baroque 18th-century palace by Laurids de Thurah. It's the last place you'd expect to encounter multimedia installations, with an emphasis on sound and video art, but it is definitely worth a visit if you are nearby. Also housed in the palace is **Palæsmalingerne** (the Palace Collections; *listings page 264*), featuring the 18th- and 19th-century paintings and decorative art collected by wealthy Roskilders of the period.

Roskilde Museum (*listings page 264*), in an old merchant's house a two-minute walk away, offers a well-presented history of the town, with archaeological finds as well as paintings, toys and decorative art on display. If it's raining you can perhaps kill half an hour or so here.

If you walk from the Domkirke towards the fjord through a meadow (the former site of the original medieval Roskilde, the outline of whose church, Sankt Hans Kirke, you can still see in the ground beside the footpath), you come to Roskilde's second most famous tourist attraction, **Vikingeskibshallen** (the Viking Ship Museum; *listings page 264*), located on the water front.

Here, five different 11th-century Viking ships are housed in an impressive concrete hall dating from 1969. The ships (used, variously, to carry cargo, passengers and soldiers) were discovered submerged in Roskilde Fjord 20 kilometres (12 miles) to the north of the town in 1957. They had been relatively well preserved in the mud, and were duly excavated amid great excitement in 1962. It is thought that the ships were deliberately sunk around AD 1000 (towards the end of the Viking period), in order to block the entrance to the fjord and protect Roskilde from marauding Norwegian Vikings. One of the vessels, a unique longship that could carry up to 50 Vikings (not the most petite of men) plus their weaponry at over ten knots, is of a type depicted on the Bayeux Tapestry.

as Northmen), accompanied by gigantic, ferocious dogs, known as Dane Dogs (possibly the forerunners of the Great Dane). A French account of a Viking attack on northern France tells of 'endless flocks of Vikings… Everywhere the Christians are massacred, burned and pillaged. The Vikings take everything that comes their way… A countless fleet moves up the Seine and all over the country viciousness is growing. Rouen has been devastated, plundered and sacked. Paris, Beauvais and Meaux are captured, the strong fortress of Melun has been razed to the ground, Chartres is occupied, Evreux and Bayeaux plundered and all towns besieged.' Europe had seen nothing like it.

Back home, Viking society was typified by social inequality. At the top were the kings and great lords, beneath them were the free peasants, and on the bottom of the pile were the 'thralls', virtual slaves. Most Vikings lived in communities of farmsteads within an enclosure around a central building. Much of what we know about the Vikings today has been deduced from burial site excavations which reveal that wealthy and important Vikings were buried with everyday goods

as well as their riches. One of the best repositories of this Viking treasure is the superb Nationalmuseet (see page 62) in Copenhagen.

Two Danish kings in particular stand out during the Viking period: Gorm the Old (who reigned from 883-940), and his son Harold Bluetooth (940-985). Together they united Denmark and conquered Norway, partly thanks to the conscientious efforts of the notorious Jomsburg Vikings, an elite fighting force based on the coast of Germany.

The end of the Viking era was heralded by the introduction of Christianity to Denmark by Harold in the late 10th century, proclaimed on the Jelling Stone, a large runic stone which still stands outside Jelling Kirke in Jylland. The Jelling Stone is seen by Danes both as a birth certificate for the new Christian Danish nation and an epitaph for the Vikings. It marked a new period in which Denmark was to have closer links with a more 'civilised' Europe.

The major destination for Viking-lovers on Sjælland are **Vikingeskibshallen**, Roskilde (see page 262), **Nationalmuseet**, Copenhagen (see page 62) and **Museet ved Trellebrog**, Trelleborg; (see page 278).

Of all their craft, this is the one that cemented the Viking's reputation as the terrible masters of the seas.

The ships' discovery came as a huge surprise to local historians. A local fisherman's tale had it that the wreckage was a single vessel sunk on the orders of Queen Margrethe I (who died in 1412), so the revelation that there were in fact five vessels, all Viking and, therefore, over 400 years older, was astounding. Marine archaeologists spent four months building a dam around the wrecks before draining the water and removing the huge mound of stones that had been used to sink them. The vessels, by now in pieces (they were probably near-wrecks when they were sunk), were then painstakingly preserved in polyethylene glycol before being rebuilt for display in the museum.

It was clear that the ships would require an appropriate exhibition site, and so an ambitious hall was built with floor to ceiling windows overlooking the fjord, in order to present them in as close proximity to the water as possible. It makes for an evocative experience, particularly if you join a guided tour led by one of the well-informed and enthusiastic students from Copenhagen University's History Department.

The hall is abutted by the **Viking Ship Museum Harbour & Workshops** (*listings page 264*), a complex of large wooden buildings, like overgrown fishing huts, which opened beside Vikingeskibshallen in 1997. During the complex's construction, two more Viking ships – one 38 metres (135 feet) long and built in Dublin – and seven more vessels from the Middle Ages were discovered. The island now contains various exhibitions, a picnic area, workshops, a boatyard building replica ships (with wonderful smells of fresh-cut spruce) and an information centre. Together with special exhibitions charting the influence of the Vikings around the world, it offers a comprehensive and accessible insight (with English information) into an era during which Denmark's maritime superiority helped it conquer large areas of northern Europe. During the summer you can also take a tour of the fjord aboard a replica Viking vessel.

There's a decent restaurant beside the yacht basin and fishermen's huts: **Restaurant Snekken** (*listings page 264*). Also nearby is **Glasgalleriet** (*listings page 264*), a glass workshop and gallery where you can watch the beautiful bowls, vases and artworks on sale here being hand-blown.

Trips Out of Town

Continue up the hill to the west and you come to what was once a separate village, **Sankt Jørgensbjerg**, originally the site of a leper hospital. The village church is one of Denmark's oldest, dating from 1100, and the area around it, made up of narrow, cobbled streets and small, thatched cottages, retains much of the charm of an old fishing village.

Around Roskilde

About 12 kilometres (7.5 miles) west of Roskilde, amid the woods, gentle hills and lakes of central Sjælland lies **Lejre Forsøgcenter** (Lejre Historical Archaeological Research Centre; *listings below*), a reconstructed Iron Age village that was founded in 1964. Intended to give a living, breathing insight into how Danes lived around the time of Christ, Lejre Forsøgcenter is a centre for practical historical and archaeological research. During the summer, Danish families live here as they would have done during the Iron Age. Visitors can try their hand at various crafts and activities, or even soak up the 2,000-year-old ambience of the sacrificial bog.

Lejre is also home to an exceptionally pretty rococo palace, **Ledreborg Slot** (*listings below*), home since 1739 of the Holstein-Ledreborg family. The house, approached along a seven-kilometre (four-mile) avenue of lime trees, is partly the work of architect Laurids de Thurah, and contains period furniture, art and decoration, as well as a chapel, maze and period kitchen. It is surrounded by formal gardens and wooded parkland. The highlight of what is one of the most attractive historic houses in Denmark is the Banqueting Hall, designed by Nicolai Eigtved (*see page 91* **Great Danes: Niels 'Nicolai' Eigtved**).

What to see & do

Glasgalleriet
Sankt Ibsvej 12, Roskilde (46 35 65 36/ www.glasgalleriet.dk). **Open** 10am-4.30pm Mon-Fri; noon-4.30pm Sat, Sun. **Credit** MC, V.

Ledreborg Slot
Ledreborg Allé, Lejre (46 48 00 38/ www.ledreborgslot.dk). **Open** *May-mid June, Sept* 11am-5pm Sun; closed Mon-Sat. *Mid June-Aug* 11am-5pm daily. *Oct-Apr* closed. **Admission** 50kr; 25kr-40kr concessions. **No credit cards.**

Lejre Forsøgcenter
Slangealleen 2, Lejre (46 48 08 78/www.lejre-center.dk). **Open** *1 May-24 June, 14 Aug-9 Sept* 10am-5pm Tue-Sun; closed Mon. *25 June-13 Aug* 10am-5pm daily. *10 Sept-30 Apr* closed. **Admission** 60kr; 30kr-50kr concessions. **No credit cards.**

Museet For Samtidkunst
Palæet, Stændertorvet 3, Roskilde (46 36 88 74/ www.mfsk.dk). **Open** 11am-5pm Tue-Fri; noon-4pm Sat, Sun; closed Mon. **Admission** 20kr; 10kr concessions; free under-16s. **No credit cards.**

Palæsmalingerne
Palæet, Stændertorvet 3, Roskilde (46 35 78 80/www.roskildemuseum.dk). **Open** *Mid May-mid Sept* 11am-4pm daily. *Mid Sept-mid May* 1-3pm Sat, Sun; closed Mon-Fri. **Admission** 10kr. **No credit cards.**

Roskilde Domkirke
Domkirke Pladsen, Roskilde (46 35 16 24). **Open** *Apr-Sept* 9am-4.45pm Mon-Fri; 9am-noon Sat; 12.30-4.45pm Sun. *Oct-Mar* 10am-3.45pm Tue-Fri; 11.30am-3.45pm Sat; 12.30-3.45pm Sun; closed Mon. **Admission** 15kr; 7.50kr-10kr concessions. **No credit cards.**

Roskilde Museum
Sankt Ols Gade 15 & 18, Roskilde (46 36 60 44/ www.roskildemuseum.dk). **Open** 11am-4pm daily. **Admission** 25kr; 15kr concessions; free under-15s. **No credit cards.**

Vikingeskibshallen & the Viking Ship Museum Harbour & Workshops
Vindeboder 12, Roskilde (46 30 02 00). **Open** *May-Sept* 9am-5pm daily. *Oct-Apr* 10am-4pm daily. **Admission** *May-Sept* 54kr; 30kr concessions. *Oct-Apr* 45kr; 28kr concessions. **Credit** AmEx, DC, MC, V.

Where to eat & drink

There are plenty of cafés, but few classy restaurants in Roskilde. One of the best is **Raadhuskælderen** (Stændertorvet, Fondens Bro 1, 46 36 01 00), in the cellar of the 15th-century town hall. There's a pleasant terrace too.

Restaurant Snekken
Museumsøen, Vindeboder 16, Roskilde (46 35 98 16). **Open** 11.30am-9pm daily. **Main courses** *lunch* 60kr-78kr. **Set Menu** 160kr. **Credit** DC, MC, V. This brasserie serves Mediterranean food in a large, airy glass building beside the dock.

Getting there

Roskilde is only a 25-minute train journey from Copenhagen's Central Station. Trains run approximately every ten minutes.

Tourist information

Roskilde Tourist Bureau
Gullandsstræde 15, Roskilde (46 35 27 00/ www.destination-roskilde.dk/fintrouk.htm). **Open** *Sept-June* 9am-5pm Mon-Thur; 9am-4pm Fri; 10am-4pm Sat; closed Sun. *July, Aug* 9am-6pm Mon-Fri; 9am-3pm Sat; closed Sun.

Helsingør

The home of mighty Kronborg Slot – Shakespeare's Elsinore.

Helsingør (Elsinore), 40 kilometres (25 miles) to the north of Copenhagen on the Øresund coast, is known the world over as the home of Hamlet, the (mostly) fictional troubled hero of William Shakespeare's most celebrated play. Mercifully, despite this notable claim to fame, the cult of Hamlet is not overly exploited by this seaside town of 56,000 people (around 40 minutes from Copenhagen by train). In fact, Helsingør, which dates back at least to the 13th century, is probably as well known among Danes as the source of the famous Sound Toll, extracted for several centuries from ships sailing between the town and Helsingborg, its neighbour four kilometres (two and a half miles) across the water in Sweden, on their way to and from the Baltic. The toll was in essence a legalised form of piracy, but it brought Denmark a significant proportion of its wealth from 1429, until its abolition in 1857.

Helsingør's major landmark is **Kronborg Slot** (*see page 266*), built in the 1420s. Renamed Elsinore Castle by Shakespeare (*see below*), this is what most visitors come to see (with the exception of the Swedes who take the 20-minute ferry crossing to buy cheap – for them – booze by the vanload).

In truth, despite the town's historic past and bustling harbour atmosphere, there is not much else. Helsingør does have an adequate shopping area in the lanes immediately inland from the railway station, while Axeltorv, the town's pleasant, quiet square (spoiled somewhat by all the parked cars) has a couple of cafés. There is a 15th-century church, **Sankt Mariæ Kirke** (*listings page 269*) on Sankt Annagade, with a nearby Gothic **Karmeliterklostret** (Carmelite Monastery; *listings page 268*). During Erik's day the town became a major ecclesiastical centre with three monasteries – Karmeliterklostret is the only one left, and is the best preserved monastery of its kind in Denmark.

One place we would recommend to visit is the town's best ice-cream parlour, which opened in 1922. **Brostræde Fløde Is** (on narrow Brostræde, just a couple of minutes from the station) serves excellent home-made ice-cream in home-baked waffle cones. If you look on the wall to the left as you enter you will see a framed magazine cover with a picture of Cary Grant – of all people – holding his Brostræde ice-cream proudly outside the shop (probably at some time during the mid '50s, judging by his suit).

Danmarks Tekniske Museum (the Danish Technical Museum; *listings page 268*) is a couple of kilometres north of the harbour. The museum has various exhibitions on transport, industry and science (including the world's first typewriter and tape recorder), as well as an exhibition dedicated to the physicist HC Ørsted, who discovered electromagnetism. It also has what is claimed to be the first aeroplane to have flown in Europe.

Helsingør Bymuseet (the Helsingør Museum; *listings page 269*), contains a dull collection of pottery fragments, art and dolls and is not really worth a visit unless you are desperate. **Øresundsakvariet** (The Sound Aquarium; *listings page 269*), to the west of Kronborg, is much smaller than Danmarks Akvariat in Charlottenlund (*see page 122*) and contains only local sea-dwellers. A ten-minute walk from the centre of town is the famous **Marienlyst Slot** (Marienlyst Palace; *listings page 269*), originally built by Frederik II in 1588 as a summer house, then called Lundegård. In 1759, the then-owner Count Adam Moltke enlarged the house with the help of the French architect Nicolas Henri Jardin, and today it is one of the earliest examples of neo-classicism in Denmark. The house was named after a subsequent resident, Queen Julianne Marie. The elegant gardens were also redesigned in the French style. Over the next two centuries the house changed hands privately several times, serving as a hospital, hydro-sanatorium and hotel. In 1953 it was taken over by the town council and opened as a museum and art gallery. The exhibits include some interesting paintings of the town as well as silverware and textiles, and the Louis XVI interiors are exceptionally pretty.

If you fancy staying overnight in Helsingør, and you've got some cash to splash, you could do a lot worse than the famous **Hotel Marienlyst** (Ndr Strandvej 2, 49 21 40 00, www.marienlyst.dk, 850kr-1,375kr single, 1,725kr-2,500kr double), founded in 1901 and enjoying splendid views over the Øresund.

HAMLET & ELSINORE

OK, he got the name wrong, but no one knows whether Shakespeare ever even visited 'Elsinore Castle', which makes it all the more astonishing that, even today, the castle's atmosphere of foreboding, and its labyrinthine layout still seem an entirely apt setting for his tragedy of intrigue, deceit and murder. It isn't difficult to conjure the tortured Dane brooding in the casemates, peering through the fog on the eerie ramparts or skewering Polonius in one of the royal chambers (though hopefully not damaging the tapestries). So how did Shakespeare get it so right, and what made him choose Kronborg in the first place?

The story of 'Amled', a prehistoric king of Denmark for 65 years from 3507 BC, is referred to in Saxo Grammaticus's *Gesta Danorum*, the 12th-century history of Denmark commissioned by Copenhagen's founder, Bishop Absalon. Saxo tells what is, in essence, a remarkably similar story to Shakespeare's. Amled's father is murdered by his uncle, Fenge, who marries Amled's mother. Fenge claims to have murdered his brother to protect the queen, but Amled learns the truth, feigns insanity to avoid

being killed himself, and persuades the girl sent to expose him as a fraud not to betray him. Fenge then sends another spy, who Amled kills, before finally dispatching Amled to England with two escorts and a letter to the English king asking him to dispose of his troublesome stepson. Amled does the letter switcheroo with the escorts, who are killed instead of him, returns to Jylland (where the royal family lived at that time), gets everyone drunk, and kills the king with his own sword. Unlike Shakespeare, Saxo gave Amled an upbeat ending. He inherits the crown and lives happily ever after.

Saxo was translated and read throughout Europe, and gained new popularity with the advent of printing in 1514. A long lost Amled play by Thomas Kyd was first performed in London in 1589, but it is a later Kyd work, *The Spanish Tragedy*, that is believed to have

Castles & palaces in Sjælland

Kronborg Slot

Kronborg Slot in Helsingør is the most famous castle in Scandinavia and, thanks to Shakespeare (who renamed it Elsinore and set his most famous tragedy, *Hamlet*, within its ramparts; see page 265), perhaps even the world. This mighty Renaissance fortress, guarding the entrance to the Øresund at Helsingør, was built to extract, or, some might say extort, a toll from ships passing between here and the Swedish coast.

The first castle here, Krogen, was built by King Erik of Pomerania (who introduced the toll), during the 1420s, a time when Denmark's sovereignty extended to southern Sweden, but it's likely that some defensive system was in place here much earlier than that. Krogen was improved over the centuries, but a full-scale modernisation took place during Frederik II's reign in the late 16th century, at which time it was renamed Cronenburg or Kronborg. The much enlarged castle now boasted a cavernous ballroom, the largest in Europe.

The current ornately decorated, Scanic sandstone building, with its stunning copper roof and deep, forbidding moat, dates largely from a restoration by Christian IV, after a fire in 1629. Despite Denmark's shaky finances, Christian engaged the services of Hans van Steenwinckel the Younger to rebuild the already lavish castle yet again, financing the work by doubling the Sound Toll.

In 1658-9 Kronborg was looted and occupied by the Swedes (with several of its finest treasures ending up in the Stockholm Museum, a fact that still niggles the Danes), and by 1785 it was no longer a royal residence. Kronborg was used as a military barracks until 1924, after which it was extensively renovated with financial assistance from Carlsberg. The Handels og Søfartsmuseet (Danish Maritime Museum) moved here in 1915 and the royal chambers were opened to the public in 1938.

There's plenty to see at Kronborg today. You might start by walking around the ramparts (the eastern rampart is where Hamlet was supposedly visited by his dead father) for a perspective on the castle's massive scale and the view across the sea to Sweden. You will notice that some of the (new) roofing is copper coloured; the colour change to green takes around 20 years. Visitors enter the castle via the Crownwork Gate to the south-east, before entering the magnificent castle courtyard through the Main Portal, erected in 1576. Before you go through the Main Portal, if you look to your left you will see a small plaque commemorating Shakespeare.

The courtyard was once graced by an Italian Renaissance fountain, but the Swedes stole that (as they did the one at Frederiksborg; see page 267), and melted it down. On the far side is the entrance to the chapel, untouched by the fire in 1629, and lavishly decorated by Christian IV.

Trips Out of Town

inspired Shakespeare. He stole from it Ophelia's madness, the ghost and the visiting actors to help create what would become his longest tragedy, which he began writing in 1599.

The connections between Denmark and England during Shakespeare's time were particularly strong. King James I married the Danish princess Anna in 1589, and Shakespeare (whose company was known as the King's Men, due to their popularity with James), would have heard many stories from returning sailors about the magnificence of Kronborg while carousing in the taverns of south London. What's more, three of his actors had once been a part of the Danish royal court and had even acted at Kronborg. They would probably have had first-hand experience of the so called 'cannon healths', the practice mentioned in the first scene of Hamlet, in which cannons were fired in a toast to the Danish king every time his glass was raised

(given the drinking habits of most Danish kings, it's a wonder the gunpowder lasted).

But did Shakespeare ever visit Denmark? Scholars have been arguing over this for over a century. Those who think he did cite the wealth of detailed description of Danish culture and Kronborg as proof of Shakespeare's first-hand experience, but there is still no concrete evidence.

In his excellent book, *Hamlet's Castle and Shakespeare's Elsinore*, David Hohnen sums up the arguments in favour of a visit from the bard having taken place: Shakespeare does rather overemphasise the cold on the ramparts, and accurately identifies the eastern parapet as the coldest. He also describes the 'morn, in russet mantle clad', a vividly accurate image of the Danish spring dawn. Rosencrantz and Gyldenstierne (Guildenstern) are named after two of Denmark's most powerful aristocrats of the time, while at one point Hamlet describes

Up until this point entrance is free, but there is a fee to see the collections inside the castle. The **Handels og Søfartsmuseet**, through a door on your right as you enter the courtyard, contains a range of seafaring exhibits, from the world's oldest ship's biscuit (dated 1852, and thankfully behind glass) to models, paintings and photographs.

The **Royal Chambers** contain few of the original furnishings, but they have been restored and replenished with art and furniture covering the period from the 16th to the 18th century, during which the royal family often visited. It includes a rich collection of Dutch paintings, ornately decorated ceilings, sumptuous tapestries; and two extraordinary globes dating from 1640. In the 62-metre (203-foot) Great Hall, at one time the largest in northern Europe (the ceiling beams are immense), once hung 40 tapestries depicting 111 of Denmark's kings, but unfortunately they, too, were lost to Sweden and now only seven survive in Nationalmuseet in Copenhagen (see page 62).

Down in the cool, dank, dimly lit and rather spooky subterranean casemates, the main draw is the statue of Denmark's mythical protector, the giant, Holger Dansk. Disappointingly, the present statue of Holger was actually made from cement in 1985, but legend has it that in Denmark's moment of peril Holger will stir to protect his country. Maybe he is biding his time for the federalisation of Europe.

The casemates were once the scene of beheadings, torture and firing squads, as well as being used to store food and house soldiers. During the Anglo-Danish war of 1807-14 prisoners of war were also housed here in appalling conditions.

Helsingør (49 21 30 78/ www.kronborgslot.dk). **Open** *Apr, Oct* 11am-4pm Tue-Sun; closed Mon. *May-Sept* 10.30am-5pm daily. *Nov-Mar* 11am-3pm Tue-Sun; closed Mon. **Admission** 40kr; 15kr-35kr concessions. **Credit** MC.

Frederiksborg Slot

South-west of Kronborg, half an hour north of Copenhagen by train, is the majestic early 17th-century **Frederiksborg Slot** (not to be confused with the lesser Frederiksberg Slot in Copenhagen). This breathtaking Dutch Renaissance red-brick castle, with its ornate copper spires and sandstone façade, stands on three small islands in Slotsø (Castle Lake), in the middle of the town of Hillerød. It is one of the most majestic buildings in northern Europe, and is complimented by elegant baroque gardens, which stretch out on the mainland to the north, and to the west by an English garden with a Renaissance château, dating from 1581, which Frederik II used as his bath house.

Frederik built the first royal castle here (hence the name) in 1560 for use as a summer palace. As he did with most of Sjælland's monuments when he got his ▶

the location of Polonius's body as 'up the stairs and into the lobby', quite possibly meaning the Great Hall. This was the route the actors of the day would have taken to perform for the Danish king. We could go on, as Hohnen does most intriguingly, but whether you are convinced or not, it is tempting to think that Denmark, instead of Spain as is often suggested, could be where Shakespeare spent at least part of his so-called lost years from 1585 to 1592.

Productions of *Hamlet* have been staged at Kronborg since 1816, many by British companies. The first marked the 200th anniversary of Shakespeare's death. Laurence Olivier and his wife Vivien Leigh played here in 1937, but John Gielgud's 1939 Hamlet is generally regarded as the definitive performance (attracting plaudits from Karen Blixen, among others). Since then, Richard Burton, Michael Redgrave, Derek Jacobi,

Kenneth Branagh and, recently, Simon Russell Beale have also given notable Hamlets. The productions usually take place in the castle courtyard during August, and are highly recommended (tickets sell fast; contact BILLETnet 38 88 70 22/www.billetnet.dk).

What to see & do

Danmarks Tekniske Museum

Nordre Strandvej 23, Helsingør (49 22 26 11/ www.tekniskmuseum.dk). **Open** 10am-5pm Tue-Sun; closed Mon. **Admission** 25kr; 10kr-21kr concessions. **No credit cards**.

Karmeliterklostret

Sankt Annagade 38, Helsingør (49 21 17 74/ www.sct.mariae.dk). **Open** (guided tours only) *Mid May-mid Sept* 2pm daily or by appointment. *Mid Sept-mid May* closed. **Admission** 20kr; 10kr concessions. **No credit cards**.

▶ ## Castles & palaces in Sjælland (continued)

hands on them, Christian IV (who was born here) rebuilt the now three-winged palace of Frederiksborg in typically ostentatious style between 1599 and 1620. The palace was the work of Hans van Steenwinckel the Elder and his son (the Younger). Younger Steenwinckel was responsible for the extravagant Dutch marble gallery that faces the inner courtyard as you approach the museum entrance. The courtyard is also graced by the jaw-dropping Neptune Fountain, a 19th-century replica of the original, which like most of the castle's treasures was looted by the Swedes in 1659.

The castle was gutted by fire in 1859, and for a while it looked as though it would remain a ruin. Fortunately JC Jacobsen volunteered to use some of his considerable Carlsberg wealth to restore Frederiksborg and subsequently helped found **Det Nationalhistoriske Museum** (Museum of National History) within 70 or so of its rooms. The museum opened in 1882 and charts Denmark's history through paintings arranged in chronological order. The rooms are also graced with period furniture, though not the original pieces.

Some of the historical paintings here are among the most famous in Denmark, and many were either commissioned by Jacobsen or donated from his collection (he gave 23 paintings by Carl Bloch, for example). They depict the protagonists from Denmark's royal history and the events that surrounded them. Particularly fascinating are the occasional

glimpses of how Copenhagen once was, during, for example, Frederik III's coronation in 1660 (on the right-hand side of the painting you can see how the old Christiansborg Slot appeared) or the bombardment by Nelson. Christian IV is represented in all his glory, from a young boy to the beleaguered monarch he became (only the nose remains the same). Upstairs, on the third floor, meanwhile, is what amounts to Denmark's national portrait gallery, an entertaining array of paintings of famous 20th-century Danes.

One of the decorative highlights of Frederiksborg is its chapel, which, between 1671 and 1840, was used for the coronations of Denmark's absolute monarchs. Since 1693, it has also been the chapel for Danish knights, whose shields hang on the walls; remarkably it's also the local church. The chapel here survived the great fire, and so the interior is pretty much

Helsingør Bymuseet

Sankt Annagade 36, Helsingør (49 21 00 98).
Open noon-4pm daily. **Admission** 10kr; 5kr
concessions; free under-16s. **No credit cards**.

Marienlyst Slot

Marienlyst Allé, Helsingør (49 28 37 91/
www.helsingorkommune.dk). **Open** noon-5pm daily.
Admission 20kr; 10kr concessions.
No credit cards.

Øresundsakvariet

Strandpromenaden 5, Nordhaven, Helsingør
(49 21 37 72/www.oresundakvariet.suite.dk).
Open 10am-5pm daily. **Admission** 20kr;
10kr-20kr concessions. **Credit** MC, V.

Sankt Mariæ Kirke

Sankt Annagade 38, Helsingør (49 21 17 74).
Open *Mid May-mid Sept* 10am-3pm daily.
Mid Sept-mid May 10am-2pm daily.
Admission free.

Where to eat & drink

The **Færgaarden** dining complex, between
the Scandlines ferry terminal and the railway
station, contains Greek (**Samos**, 49 21 39 46),
Mexican (**Gringo's Cantina**, 49 26 14 47) and
Chinese (**Bamboo**, 49 21 22 82) restaurants.

Getting there

Helsingør is a 50-minute train journey from
Copenhagen. Trains run every ten minutes.

Tourist information

Helsingør Tourist Bureau

Havnepladsen 3 (49 21 13 33/www.helsingorturist.dk).
Open *Mid Aug-mid May* 9am-4pm Mon-Fri; 10am-
1pm Sat; closed Sun. *Mid May-mid Aug* phone for
details. **Credit** AmEx, DC, MC, V.

---

as it would have been during Christian's day
(in other words so ornate that you can barely
take it all in). Its altar and pulpit are the work
of the Hamburg goldsmith Jakob Mores, while
the priceless Compenius organ, dating from
1610 and boasting 1,000 pipes, is played
every Thursday between 1.30pm and 2pm.
It is worth timing a visit to hear it.

The 50-metre (164-foot) long **Riddersalen**
(Knight's Hall) is also richly decorated with
Gobelin tapestries (in place of those made by
Karel von Mander in Delft, lost in the fire), a
carved wooden ceiling and a late 19th-century
black marble fireplace from Belgium.

The castle's gardens, with their symmetrical
planting and paths, were laid out by Johan
Krieger during Frederik IV's time after he had
visited similar gardens in France and Italy.
They were restored as part of Copenhagen's
1996 European City of Culture celebrations.

Hillerød (48 26 04 39/
www.frederiksborgmuseet.dk). Train to
Hillerød. **Open** Apr-Oct 10am-5pm daily.
Nov-Mar 11am-3pm daily. **Admission** 45kr;
10kr-40kr concessions. **Credit** MC, V.

Fredensborg Slot

The present-day royal summer house,
Fredensborg Slot (Castle of Peace – named to
commemorate the end of the second Nordic
war in 1720), is a rather more modest affair
than Frederiksborg. This rambling, though
elegant, white-walled, copper-roofed manor
house, eight kilometres (five miles) north
of Hillerød, was built in 1720 for Frederik IV
by the JC Krieger (with four side wings by
Nicolai Eigtved). Fredensborg's understated

Italian baroque charm is no match for the
theatricality of Frederiksborg, but it was this
smaller building that ended the larger castle's
role as the venue for coronations and as a
summer residence for Danish royalty.

Fredensborg Slot's interior is only open to
the public in July, but its location among the
beech forests beside Esrum Sø (Esrum Lake;
Denmark's second largest) ensures the
garden's popularity with visitors year-round.
During the summer you can take a ferry from
a jetty on the lake across to Gribskov Forest
(see page 275), which is an excellent area for
walks. If the Queen is in residence there is a
changing of the guard each day just before
noon; if you're really lucky she may even be
receiving state visitors.

There are 16 kilometres (ten miles) of
paths around the 120 hectares (297 acres)
of informal, romantic gardens (designed by
Nicolai Henri Jardin) at Fredensborg, and they
are open year-round. In an area known as
Normandsland are 69 statues of 'normal'
Danish citizens – farmers, fishermen and the
like – erected by Frederik IV, as well as the
impressive Cascade waterfalls. Fredensborg
is a 10-minute walk, straight down the high
street from Fredensborg station. As is usual
in Denmark, the signposting is diabolical.

Fredensborg (33 40 10 10/www.slotte.dk).
Train to Fredensborg. **Open** *Castle & Chapel,*
Herb Garden & Orangery July 1-5pm daily,
guided tours only. *Gardens* 24 hours daily.
Admission *Castle & Chapel* 30kr; 10kr
concessions. *Herb Garden & Orangery* 30kr;
10kr concessions. **No credit cards.**

The Danish Riviera

Art, nature and frivolity on the affluent coast north of Copenhagen.

The Danish Riviera may sound like a rather optimistic name for the coastline stretching north from Copenhagen to Helsingør, but with its scenic coast road, picturesque fishing harbours (usually full of millionaires' yachts), the country's finest modern art museum, sandy beaches and countless palatial manors and villas, Denmark's Øresund coast more than lives up to its billing. This is one of the country's most desirable residential areas, and the large and expensive properties here attest to its long-held status as an old money enclave. A day or so taking in the sights is particularly recommended for families, though there is something for everyone here.

The coast road, Strandvejen, runs from Copenhagen to Helsingør at the northern tip of the Sjælland coast, often coming within metres of the sea, but it becomes congested during summer. The train service to Helsingør also runs parallel to the water, stopping at most of the towns and villages along the way. As is usual in Denmark, it is quick, efficient and reasonably priced, and there are stations roughly every ten minutes.

As with most modern cities, Copenhagen's boundaries have been somewhat blurred by development and it is hard to know where the suburbs end and the neighbouring towns and villages begin. You could argue that the riviera begins at **Charlottenlund** (*see page 122*), with its pleasant beach and camping area, but a more fitting starting point is probably **Klampenborg**.

Klampenborg is one of the wealthier residential areas within easy reach of Copenhagen, but it also has several draws for visitors, including a pleasant beach, **Bellevue** (*see page 123*), **Bakken** amusement park and a large wild deer park.

Tivoli may be Denmark's most internationally famous amusement park, but Dyrehavsbakken (known as Bakken for short), is equally popular with Danes. Bakken was founded in 1583 and claims to be the oldest amusement park in the world. It is, nevertheless, usually seen as Tivoli's downmarket cousin and does have more of a funfair/beer hall atmosphere. But that doesn't mean there is less enjoyment to be had here. There are 100 or so rides (which tend to be cheaper than Tivoli's), 35 cafés and restaurants,

the famous singing girls and cabaret at Bakkens Hvile, and one of Denmark's most famous revue shows, Cirkkusrevyen. Admission to the park itself is free.

Bakken is located on the edge of a 1,000-hectare (2,470-acre) former royal hunting ground, now a serene and unspoiled deer park, **Jægersborg Dyrehaven**. **Dyrehaven**, as it's better known, dates back to 1231 and is to Copenhageners what Richmond Park is to Londoners. Dyrehaven is closed to traffic; all the better for its large herds of free-roaming deer. In its grounds is the enigmatic former hunting lodge, **Eremitagen**, which has wonderful views to the sea (but is not open to the public). Dyrehaven is one of the best places close to the city to head for good walks and fresh air, though you can also take a ride around it in a horse-drawn carriage (for a steep fee). Horses can also be seen in action at **Klampenborg Galopbane** (*see page 240*), the racing and trotting course to the south of the park.

Between the meticulously clean Bellevue beach and adjacent Klampenborg Station, is **Jacobsen** (*see page 273*), a fine restaurant housed in a building designed by the legendary Danish architect and designer Arne Jacobsen (*see page 38* **Great Danes: Arne Jacobsen**) and featuring many of his most famous furniture designs.

Dyrehaven, Bakken and Bellevue Beach are all within walking distance of Klampenborg Station, 18 minutes by train from Copenhagen Central Station.

Continuing on the train for ten minutes up the coast you arrive at the small, posh harbour village of **Taarbæk**, whose hotel overlooking the yacht basin has a good restaurant. But the next major point of interest along the coast is at the harbour town of **Rungsted**. The harbour itself is attractive and has an excellent restaurant, **Nokken** (*see page 273*), and there are some meagre bathing beaches along the coast here. A short walk inland across Strandvejen brings you to **Rungstedlund**, the former home of the Danish novelist Karen Blixen, now site of **Karen Blixen Museet**.

The internationally acclaimed author (*see page 271* **Great Danes: Karen Blixen**) spent most of her life (apart from the 17 years she spent in Kenya) in Rungstedlund. This

Great Danes Karen Blixen

The incomparable Baroness Karen Blixen is one of the most important figures in 20th-century Danish literature. Working under various pseudonyms, most frequently Isak Dinesen (her maiden name), the aristocratic Blixen wrote dark, complex but compelling short stories, the first collection of which, *Seven Gothic Tales*, was first published in New York in 1934 to great critical acclaim. But it was her private life – a life of tragedy, courage, arrogance and rebellion, made public in her novel *Den Afrikanske Farm* (translated as *Out Of Africa*, and, in 1985, made into a film starring Robert Redford and Meryl Streep) – that cemented the Blixen legend. She received two Nobel nominations, on one occasion losing out to Hemingway's *The Old Man And The Sea*. Upon accepting the award the American author told Blixen she should have won.

Blixen was born in 1885 into a wealthy Sjælland family. Her father committed suicide when she was ten. Karen went on to study painting at the Danish Academy of Art and, later, in Paris and Rome. Aged 28 she married a Swedish second cousin, Baron Bror Blixen Finecke, the twin brother of a former lover. The marriage was one of convenience rather than love – she desired his title, he needed her cash. In 1914 they moved to British East Africa (today known as Kenya), to run his coffee farm, but Bror's womanising eventually led to the end of their marriage. It can't have helped that he gave her syphilis and a legacy of ill health for the rest of her life.

Blixen remained as manager of the farm just outside Nairobi, and found solace in her relationship with an upper class English pilot and game hunter, Denys Finch Hatton. When Hatton died in a plane crash in 1931, a devastated Blixen returned home to the place of her birth in Rungstedlund, north of Copenhagen (originally an inn that had been bought by her father in 1879). Partly out of financial necessity, Blixen began writing, as Hatton had encouraged her to do, about the social class into which she was born.

Blixen's first works in English were only translated into Danish following their initial success in America. Initially, within Denmark Baroness Blixen (as she insisted on being called) was perceived as something of a snob for writing in glowing terms about the aristocracy at a time when they were not particularly in favour, but over the years her celebrity and the Danes' appreciation of her grew. Blixen was photographed by the likes of Cecil Beaton and Peter Beard, befriended Sir John Gielgud and met Arthur Miller and Marilyn Monroe while on a lecture tour of the States.

Seven Gothic Tales, usually considered her masterpiece, was translated into Danish as *Syv fantastiske Fortællinger*. It was followed in 1937 by *Den Afrikanske Farm* (*Out of Africa*) and, in 1942, *Vinter-Eventyr* (*Winter's Tales*). Subsequent works include *The Angelic Avengers* (1946), *Last Tales* (1957) and *Anecdotes of Destiny* (1958). Her writing was characterised by her dry humour and complex storytelling style. She rarely paid much heed to the literary trends of the day.

Blixen's writing influenced many subsequent generations of Danish writers and film makers. Peter Høeg, whose success came in the early '90s with *Miss Smilla's Feeling For Snow*, wrote nine stories, *Night Tales*, in the Blixen style, while in 1987 the Danish film maker Gabriel Axel's adaptation of Blixen's story *Babette's Feast* won an Academy Award for best foreign film.

Before she died, in 1962, Blixen established the Rungstedlund Foundation to take care of the maintenance of the estate, and in 1991 Queen Margrethe opened the **Karen Blixen Museet** on the estate (see page 273). Blixen is buried in the gardens of Rungstedlund, at the foot of Ewald's hill, beneath a large beech tree.

Louisiana Museum For Moderne Kunst

There may be larger modern art collections in the world, but none are located in more blissful surroundings than Louisiana. And though Lousiana's simple, single-storey galleries, ranged, roughly, in a circle among leafy gardens which cascade down to the shore, are no match for the bombastic Tate Modern in London or the Guggenheim in Bilbao, a more peaceful setting for this diverse collection of modern art would be hard to find.

Lousiana began life as a purely Scandinavian art collection. It was founded in 1954 by the industrialist and avid art collector Knud Jensen, but was later expanded with international works thanks to donations from the Ny Carlsberg Foundation. Architects Jørgen Bo and Vilhelm Wohlert added new galleries to the existing 19th-century villa (which already had the name Lousiana after the previous owner's three wives who, bizarrely, where all named Louise), and the resulting, much enlarged complex is characterised by a vaguely Japanese style.

The irregular-shaped, open-plan, whitewashed rooms with their large windows blur the divide between the galleries and the outside sculpture park, giving Lousiana its uniquely tranquil atmosphere. Somehow, the reassuring proximity of beech trees, lawn and sea (with the Swedish coast in the distance), creates a harmony between the buildings and their environment that counterbalances the frequently confrontational, disturbing or impenetrable nature of the works on display. And the light here beside the Øresund is unique.

The first pieces bought by the museum were by Danish artists like Richard Mortensen, Asger Jørn (one of the founders of the abstract COBRA Group; the name was formed from COpenhagen, BRussels and Amsterdam, the home cities of the artists involved) and the constructivist sculptor and graphic artist Robert Jacobsen. The collection soon grew to encompass works by many notable post-war French sculptors like Herbin, Albers, Gabo and Alexander Calder and, from the '50s, Louisiana acquired paintings by Dubuffet, Bacon, Rothko and Reinhardt. Paintings from several of Picasso's periods are among the museum's highlights, while the Pop Art movement of the '60s is also particularly well represented (in fact, the whole museum has something of a flower-power feel), with pieces by, among others, Warhol, Lichtenstein, Oldenburg and Rauschenberg. Lousiana's collection of German art from the '70s is strong. Bringing things right up to date are a few contemporary pieces, including a video installation by British artist Sam Taylor Wood.

The Museum's south wing was added in 1982 and a corridor built connecting it to the old buildings. Along the corridor now hang the colourful geometric paintings of Richard Mortensen. In 1991, a subterranean wing exhibiting graphic art opened.

In the garden you'll find sculptures by Calder, Henry Moore, Joan Míro, Max Ernst and Giacometti, among others (Giacometti also features inside the gallery in a dedicated room that has to rank as one of the highlights of the museum). The gardens are very popular with children, who also benefit from their own indoor area, Bornehuset (the Children's House).

Louisiana holds regular lectures, film screenings and concerts and is famed for its superstar retrospectives (there are usually

simple, early 19th-century house set in 16 hectares (40 acres) of gardens (in which Blixen is buried) also acts as a bird sanctuary. Its north wing has been preserved as if Blixen had just left, with her furniture, paintings and even her distinctive flower arrangements as they were when she lived here. There's a gallery of Blixen's drawings and paintings, and a biographical exhibition, library and small cinema upstairs.

The house was also once the home of another eminent Danish writer, **Johannes Ewald** (1743-81). He lived here in 1773 and wrote several of his lyric poems and heroic tragedies in verse in the same room in which Blixen also chose to write.

Rungstedlund is about ten minutes' walk from the nearest railway station, Rungsted Kyst. Alternatively you can catch a train to Klampenborg and take bus number 388.

Between Rungstedlund and Helsingør are several more small harbours, but the main attraction is the **Louisiana Museum For Moderne Kunst** (Lousiana Museum of Modern Art; *listings page 273*), a ten-minute walk from Humlebæk station.

around six temporary exhibitions a year).
Recent blockbusters have included Monet,
Bacon, Míro and Warhol exhibitions. It has
a large shop selling everything from trendy
garden tools to books and posters, plus a
superb café with a terrace overlooking the
Øresund, graced by one of Calder's
amusing sculptures.

Louisiana Museum For Moderne Kunst
*Gammel Strandvej 13, Humlebæk
(49 19 07 19/www.louisiana.dk).*
Open *10am-5pm Mon, Tue, Thur-Sun;
10am-10pm Wed.* **Admission** *60kr;
20kr-52kr concessions.*
Credit *AmEx, DC, MC, V.*

What to see & do

Bakken
*Dyrehavesbakken, Dyrehavevej 62, Klampenborg (39
63 35 44/www.bakken.dk). Train to Klampenborg.*
Open *Last Thur Mar-last Mon Aug noon-midnight
daily. Last Tue Aug-last Wed Mar closed.*
Admission *free, rides extra (half-price Wed).*
No credit cards.

Karen Blixen Museet
*Rungstedlund, Rungsted Strandvej 111,
Rungsted (45 57 10 57/www.karen-blixen.dk).
Train to Rungsted Kyst.* **Open** *May-Sept* 10am-5pm

Tue-Sun; closed Mon. *Oct-Apr* 1-4pm Wed-Fri;
11am-4pm Sat, Sun; closed Mon, Tue.
Admission 35kr; 30kr concessions.
Credit AmEx, DC, MC, V.

Where to eat

Jacobsen
*Strandvejen 449, Klampenborg (39 63 43 22/
www.restaurantjacobsen.dk).* **Open** noon-3pm, 6-
10pm daily **Main courses** *lunch* 65kr; *dinner* 145kr.
Credit AmEx, DC, MC, V.
Though he never really went out of fashion, the
doyen of Danish design, Arne Jacobsen (*see p38*
Great Danes: Arne Jacobsen), has undergone
something of a revival in recent years, and this stylish restaurant, dedicated to his holistic design
vision and housed in one of his first major commissions – the Bellavista complex, is a direct result
of that renewed interest. Recreated right down to
Jacobsen's frustratingly hard to handle cutlery (as
seen in the film *2001: A Space Odyssey*), this cool
eatery overlooks Bellevue beach, one of the nicest
stretches of coast near to the city, and is a two-
minute walk from Klampenborg station (itself only
18 minutes by train from Copenhagen's Central
Station). It is not particularly recommended for
lunch, since even if the weather is nice, the busy
road in front of the terrace disturbs the peace somewhat. Jacobsen's evening menu, which majors on
inventively prepared seafood, however, is wonderful and definitely helps to broaden the restaurant's
appeal beyond the Jacobsen obsessives who come
simply to experience the thrill of submerging themselves in their hero's vision.

Nokken
*Rungsted Havn 44, Rungsted Kyst (45 57 13 14).
Train to Rungsted Kyst.* **Open** noon-4pm, 4.30-10pm
daily. **Main courses** 195kr-235kr. **Set menus** *lunch*
185kr-245kr; *dinner* 355kr-535kr. **Credit** AmEx, DC,
MC, V.
Beloved of celebrities and eurotrash (Roger Moore
and Posh and Becks have both visited, if that's any
recommendation), this chic harbourside restaurant
is an excellent stopping-off place on a tour along
Denmark's riviera, provided your credit card can
cope. Classy, expensive and ever so snooty, Nokken
has wonderful views over the harbour and its
kitchen dishes up refined Franco-Danish food with
plenty of butter, cognac cream sauces and complex
meat dishes (salted breast of goose with green lentils
turned in foie gras and framboise sauce, for example). Around 30 minutes north of the city.

Getting there

There are trains at least every 20 minutes
heading north along the coast from Central
Station via Nørreport. It takes 18 minutes to
get to Klampenborg, 30 to reach Rungsted
Kyst and 41 minutes to Humlebæk.

Trips Out of Town

North Sjælland

The island's best beaches are little more than an hour away from the capital.

A day or two at the seaside is probably the last thing you'd expect from a visit to Copenhagen, but, if you are prepared to travel an hour or so by train or car, North Sjælland boasts a clean, sandy coastline of immense charm.

This idyllic summer house area is extremely popular with Copenhageners, who migrate here en masse each year from late June to the end of July, but despite this, it remains blessedly free of unsightly development. The Kattegat coast, as it's sometimes known, has retained a beguiling atmosphere redolent of (probably rose-tinted) childhood holidays, with unspoiled stretches of white sand, thatched fishermen's cottages, excellent fresh seafood restaurants and, of course, countless ice-cream vendors.

Here, at the historic fishing towns **Hornbæk**, **Gilleleje** and **Tisvildeleje**, and along the coast in between, are expansive, natural stretches of sand, with shallow, clean water and all the facilities required for a day at the beach (though they are usually kept well out of sight of the beach itself). The beaches are typically fronted by grassy dunes, rugged heathland, ancient coastal forests and the ubiquitous *rosa rugosa*, a wild and pretty pink and red rose that thrives like a weed here.

Because these towns attract Copenhagen's wealthier classes during the summer, you will find several first-rate restaurants and upmarket shops. The period between the end of June and the beginning of August sees circus tents setting up and live music most nights in the cafés and bars, and the super-clean beaches and characteristic thatched, half-timbered summer houses are packed to capacity. As a consequence, even the most humble wooden beach house can command over 600,000kr on the open market. The grandest properties, meanwhile, can fetch many millions more. Despite the area's popularity, the beaches are so spacious that you can usually escape the crowds even if the weather is scorching. There are a host of recreational activities and water sports available here, too: windsurfing is popular, as are deep-sea fishing, jet skiing and sailing.

Hornbæk, like many of the fishing towns along this coast, dates back over 500 years. Hornbæk's harbour is a good place to hire fishing boats and this is also where the annual Sjælland Regatta takes place in June. In the

1870s the town became popular with artists like PS Krøyer and Kristian Zahrtmann who took a shine to the picturesque life of the local fishermen. Hornbæk's Blue Flag beach has the typical white sand that you find all along the north coast and is excellent for children as it shelves gently. There is also wheelchair access.

If you tire of beach life, **Hornbæk Plantage**, a public forest a few kilometres east of the town centre, has several relatively dramatic coastal trails winding through pine forests, endless banks of wild roses and beech trees. Hornbæk has a wide range of accommodation and several good restaurants, mainly located in the town centre. For more information, contact the local tourist information office (49 70 47 47, www.hornbaek.dk).

Dronningmølle (Queen's Mill), the next stop five kilometres (three miles) along the road west towards Gilleleje, also has a very attractive bathing beach, which is usually quieter than those in the larger towns along the coast. (In the case of all of these beaches the distance from the railway station to the beach is walkable.) A further three kilometres (two miles) west of here is **Nakkehoved** and its 18th-century lighthouse. Alternatively, you could take the road south towards Villingerød and turn left at the church to reach **Rudolph Tegners Museum**, the most peculiar and surprising sculpture museum in Denmark (*see page 275* **Great Danes? Rudolph Tegner**).

If you are after a little more life, **Gilleleje**, the largest of the coastal towns, is where you're most likely to find it (though, as with all of these places, it's sleepy in winter). This is a delightful, old-fashioned place, which tends to attract a younger crowd, in contrast to Hornbæk's and Tisvildeleje's more mature visitors.

Gilleleje is the most northerly town in Sjælland and was one of the main escape routes for Danish Jews in 1943 (there is an exhibit on this in Gilleleje Museum; *see also page 21* **Jewish Exodus**). Many of the Jews hid in the roof of Gilleleje Kirke on Hovedgade, which dates from the 16th century and was built from wood washed up on the shore from the frequent shipwrecks of the period.

Gilleleje has a bustling fishing harbour, full of the best seafood takeaways and fishmongers in the country, as well as an alluring smoked fish house, Røgeriet. There's a fish auction here early

Great Danes? Rudolph Tegner

A couple of kilometres inland from the town of Dronningmølle on the north coast of Sjælland lies one of Denmark's most idiosyncratic museums. **Rudolph Tegners Museum** is dedicated to the work of a Danish artist who was either a crazy genius, or the world's worst sculptor, depending on who you believe.

Rudolph Tegner (born 1873) considered himself a great artist. The difference between Tegner and your average arty megalomaniac was that, thanks to his wife Elna's inherited fortune, he had the financial wherewithal to realise his vision. In 1916, Tegner bought a piece of heath beside the coast and, over the next decades, set about preserving his life's work for future generations.

Tegner had had limited success in persuading the rest of Denmark to appreciate his symbolist/art nouveau/Nietzschean-influenced sculptures, and critics were rarely positive. *Berlingske Aften*, the leading evening paper, wrote of one of his pieces: 'The most disheartening thing about Tegner's plaster monstrosity is not... its purely sculptural mediocrity, but the mentality that it expresses. If you have studied the statue long enough and close your eyes, you seem to hear boots tramping in time and bombastic band music, and before your inner eye rise the contours of Haus der Deutschen Kunst in Munich.' In 1940s Denmark this was, understandably, not deemed a good thing. Tegner's home town of Helsingør was also decidedly underwhelmed by his proposal that they found a museum to him, so, like several Scandinavian artists of the time, he realised he would have to do his own PR work.

Today, Tegner's monumental, histrionic works can be seen dotted both among the heather in the 19-hectare (46-acre) sculpture park and inside the museum building. This sinister, virtually windowless, raw concrete bunker, built in 1937, squats among the grazing sheep like the villain's lair from a low-budget Bond movie. It's certainly in stark contrast to the exceptionally beautiful landscape, **Rusland**, that surrounds it, with cornfields stretching down to the sea, dotted with wild flowers and ancient woods.

Visitors enter the museum through an incongruous medieval-style studded wooden door. Within the perilously thin walls is a vast, airy, central hexagonal room, 11 metres (36 feet) high and filled with several of Tegner's epic, if rather basic, plaster sculptures. It is hard to pick out 'highlights', but *Sankt Peder med Nøglen* (St Peter with the Key), is notably dreadful – a monstrously ugly figure with oversized thighs – while *Den Store Mand* (The Great Man), is a colossal figure which looks like the work of an art student who has taken too many drugs, broken into art class, and used up all the plaster.

To be fair, just to keep us on our toes, Tegner did occasionally create something with a genuine grace and beauty, it's just that his bad stuff is so much more entertaining. It is as if Bertel Thorvaldsen's (see page 82 **Great Danes: Bertel Thorvaldsen**) evil twin has been exiled to the countryside (inspired by Thorvaldsen's example, when he died in 1950 Tegner was also buried in his own museum), but whether you find them ghastly, hilarious, or even, at a push, beautiful, we guarantee you won't forget the works of Rudolph Tegner.

Rudolph Tegners Museum

Museumsvej 19, Dronningmølle (49 22 26 11/ www.rudolphtegner.dk). Train to Kildekrog or Dronningmølle. **Open** *Mid Apr-May, Sept, Oct noon-5pm Tue-Sun; closed Mon. June-Aug 9.30am-5pm Tue-Sun; closed Mon. Nov-mid Apr closed.* **Admission** 20kr; 15kr concessions; free under-12s. **No credit cards.**

each morning and a general market, or 'mylder', on Thursdays and Saturdays. Gilleleje also has a decent shopping area. Its 14-kilometre (nine-mile) long beach, although sparklingly clean, with good wheelchair facilities and watched over by lifeguards in summer, is not the most attractive in the area (it is, however, very popular for posing). As with Hornbæk, there are inviting trekking possibilities here in **Gribskov Forest**, a little further south. The area was a favourite stomping ground of Kierkegaard (*see page 112*

Great Danes: Søren Kierkegaard), who is commemorated with an engraved stone a couple of kilometres to the west of town on the coastal trail. A vintage railway from Helsingør also terminates here.

Tisvildeleje is another exceptionally attractive coastal village west of Gilleleje. It is even easier to escape the crowds on the town's long, broad, sandy beach, a short walk downhill from the railway station, past chocolate-box 18th-century fishermen's cottages, most of

Trips Out of Town

Walking in Sjælland

Dyrehaven

The former royal hunting ground is now a popular and extensive deer park with forest paths and open grassland. The main entrance is five minutes from Klampenborg station, ten minutes north of Copenhagen by train.

Gribskov

Beloved of the philosopher Kierkegaard (see page 112 **Great Danes: Søren Kierkegaard**), this massive forest covering 56 square kilometres (22 square miles) beside Esrum Sø in North Sjælland has numerous walking paths (maps are available from local tourist offices). Kierkegaard wrote about the forest in his book *Stages On Life's Way*. He apparently found its network of paths to be an apt allegory for the choices one makes in life and would often take an extremely expensive private carriage here from Copenhagen in order to be alone to wrestle with his tenets.

Esrum Sø

With Frederiksborg and Fredensborg Slots nearby (see page 269), this pretty, placid lake with its surrounding forests (including Gribskov, above) is a popular choice for Copenhageners seeking a day out and is a highly recommended walking destination. It lies 40 minutes north of Copenhagen; the nearest station is Fredensborg.

Tisvilde Hegn

This windswept and enchanting coastal forest in the north of Sjælland features ancient ruins and the spooky Troll's Wood (see below). From Tisvilde station head west to the beach and then inland along any of the well signposted paths (maps are available from the tourist office). The forest lies one and a half hours' train journey from Copenhagen.

---

which are now summer houses. Tisvildeleje is particularly lively in July when the summer houses are full, the local theatre (housed in a railway carriage at the station), puts on its annual revue, and the town's excellent restaurant, **Bio Bistro** – run by one of Denmark's top chefs, Søren Thyboe, and as good as any in Copenhagen – has nightly live music, often courtesy of Denmark's top acts.

If you fancy staying the night in Tisvildeleje, try the excellent **Sankt Helene** holiday complex (Bygmarken 30, 48 70 98 50, www.helene.dk, 325kr single, 650kr double), offering everything from apartments and family rooms to holiday cabins and campsites.

Nearby is one of Denmark's largest forests, **Tisvilde Hegn**, a rugged, public woodland planted 200 years ago to stop coastal erosion, which offers bracing walks (the tourist office has maps). A visit to its **Troldeskoven** (Troll's Wood), characterised by its spooky, wind-twisted trees, is a must, as is the trail that leads to **Asserbo Slotsruin**, the atmospheric remnants of a 12th-century monastery to the south of the forest.

What to see & do

Gilleleje Museum

Pyramiden, Vesterbrogade 56, Gilleleje (48 30 16 31). **Open** *May-Aug* 1-4pm Mon, Wed-Sun; closed Tue. *Sept-Apr* 1-4pm Mon, Wed-Fri; closed Tue, Sat, Sun. **Admission** 25kr; free under-12s. **No credit cards.**

Where to eat

Bio Bistro

Hovedgaden, Tisvilde 38 (48 70 41 91). Train to Hillerød; change for Tisvilde. **Open** *Apr-Aug* 6pm-10pm daily. *Sept-Mar* 6pm-10pm Fri-Sun; closed Mon-Thur. **Main courses** 170kr-210kr. **Set menus** 255kr-345kr. **Credit** AmEx, DC, MC, V. This cosy yet sophisticated restaurant and music venue is exactly what Copenhagen needs. OK, so it's located an hour away in blissful Tisvildeleje, on the north coast of Sjælland, but then, knowing that a gorgeous sandy beach and magical, windswept woodlands lie only minutes away only adds to Bio Bistro's laid-back charm. This spacious, low-ceilinged restaurant has two main lures: its nightly music (some of Denmark's top bands and singers play here during the summer), and the peerless Franco-Danish cuisine, prepared by one of the country's leading chefs, Søren Thyboe. Oh, and the service is as good as any you'll find in the city, but with an added informal charm. No wonder it's a hang out for off-duty royals, politicians and celebs.

Getting there

To reach Gilleleje or Tisvildeleje by train from Central Station, you need to change at Hillerød (40 minutes, then 30 minutes). There's around one train an hour. To get to Hornbæk, change at Helgingør and take the Gilleleje train (50 minutes, then 25 minutes). Dronningmølle is a further seven minutes down the line from Hornbæk. There's one train an hour.

South Sjælland

Rolling rural landscapes, historic towns and some spectacular island cliffs.

The most interesting day trips from Copenhagen lie to the north of the city or across the water to Sweden, but the south of Sjælland has a certain tranquil appeal and an undeniable historical resonance. The area is largely agricultural, with a few medium-sized towns which usually have long and rich stories to tell. The countryside is gently undulating, but becomes more dramatic if you cross to the adjacent island of Møn.

Southern Sjælland has played an important part in Denmark's history, from the Viking period up to the 17th century. The area boasts several Viking sites, and was subsequently the base for the Valdemar dynasty of Danish kings. During the 17th century several of the numerous battles between Denmark and Sweden took place here, most cataclysmically for Denmark in 1658, when the Danish army was unable to halt the progress of the Swedish king Karl X Gustav towards Copenhagen.

There are four small towns in this half of Sjælland: Køge, Ringsted, Næstved and Slagelse. All have fairly well-preserved historic centres, with medieval churches and town squares, half-timbered houses and cobbled streets. Each have a museum, with archaeological nick-nacks, old furniture and the odd ancient grave find. The shops tend to be rather homogenous, and the restaurants are nothing to get excited about either (pizza parlours and cafés in the main).

Køge has a quiet charm, due to the fact that it is one of the best-preserved medieval towns in Denmark. It dates back to at least 1288, but since

The cliffs of **Møn**. See p278.

1400 it has been an important market town and harbour. Køge Bay is known throughout Denmark as the site of one of the country's most famous sea battles. The **Battle of Køge Bay** was fought in 1677 against the Swedish navy who were advancing on Copenhagen. It produced one of Denmark's greatest naval heroes, admiral **Niels Juel**, who orchestrated the defeat of the Swedes as King Christian V watched from the relative safety of the church tower (and not, as the Danish National Anthem would have it, 'by the lofty mast' of his flagship).

Køge has Denmark's oldest town hall still in use, as well as a 15th-century church, **Sankt Nicolai Kirke** (10am-noon Mon-Fri), on Kirkestræde. Nørregade is the town's main shopping street, where you'll also find the town's museum. The main attractions in **Køge Museum** are two large silver coin hoards from the 17th century, one of the oldest half-timbered houses in Denmark (dating from 1500) and the contents of a Mesolithic grave. In the Middle Ages, Torvet, the town square at the end of Nørregade, was the scene of witch trials and executions. The north pier at Køge harbour has several cafés and is a pleasant place to spend an hour or two if the weather is nice.

Ringsted is a crossroads town of 30,000 people, slap-bang in the middle of Sjælland. Before the Viking era it was a major centre of paganism. Its location meant that during the Middle Ages it became an important market town, and up until around the 14th century it was the site of the Landsting, the regional government. There aren't many attractions in Ringsted, other than its 12th-century church, **Sankt Bendts Kirke** (May-mid Sept 10am-noon, 1-5pm daily, mid Sept-Apr 1-3pm daily), built in 1170 by King Valdemar I as a place in which to bury his murdered, and subsequently canonised father, Knud. The church, on the site of a former pagan shrine, was the scene of royal burials for 150 years. Valdemars I, II and III are buried here, along with King Knud and Erik VI. Flat stones in the aisle floor beneath the nave mark their resting places, while the nave itself boasts some superb 14th-century frescos.

Due west from Ringsted is the pretty lakeside town of **Sorø**, the home town of Bishop Absalon (*see page 8*) whose father, Asser Rig, founded a monastery here in the 12th century. Absalon is buried in the monastery church, which also dates from the 12th century, along with five Danish kings and Denmark's most celebrated dramatist **Ludvig Holberg**, who died in 1754. Sorø's monastery was transformed into a school for the children of the aristocracy after the Reformation, and Sorø Akademi (at which Holberg studied) remains one of the country's leading educational establishments.

Further west is **Slagelse**, which has the usual medieval church and town museum, but is better known for the nearby Viking ruins of **Trelleborg**, seven kilometres (four miles) to the west. A thousand years ago Trelleborg was the site of a major Viking ring fortress housing 1,300 men. Little remains apart from some earthen ramparts, but cement blocks mark the outline of the building's foundations, and there is a museum, a shop and a reconstruction of a Viking house here. During the summer numerous events like markets, craft shows and longbow competitions are held within Trelleborg, which all contribute to an enjoyably authentic atmosphere.

The largest settlement in southern Sjælland is the coastal town of **Næstved**, with 45,000 inhabitants. This former Hanseatic trading port is located at the mouth of the Suså river (very popular with canoeists) in a comparatively industrial area of the island. The town's two gothic churches, **Sankt Peders Kirke** (the largest of its kind in Denmark; 10am-noon Tue-Fri) and **Sankt Mortens Kirke** (9-11am daily) are fairly prosaic, but Sankt Peders does have some enchanting 14th-century frescoes.

Næstved Museum is partly housed in Næstved's oldest building, the 14th-century Helligåndshuset (the House of the Holy Ghost). Its chief draw is its collection of Holmegaard glass. The famous **Holmegaards Glasværker** is eight kilometres (five miles) away at Fensmark. Founded in 1825, it is open to the public for tours.

Most tourists see Næstved on their way to the picturesque island of **Møn**, famous in Denmark for its dramatic, 5,000-year-old chalk cliffs, **Møns Klint**, and small independent ceramic producers who make the most of the island's clay soil. Only 12,000 people live on the island, which is 80 kilometres (50 miles) south of Copenhagen (there is a bridge from Sjælland), and there is little public transport, aside from a painfully slow bus service. There are few man-made attractions in Møn, though its medieval churches are renowned for having the best frescoes in the country. **Stege Kirke**, **Keldby Kirke**, **Elmelund Kirke** and **Fanefjord Kirke** are where you'll find them, and a visit is highly recommended.

The island's chief appeal, however, lies in its fiercely protected rural charm, which makes it great for trekking (through virgin forests or along the rugged coast), bird watching, exploring archaeological remains or enjoying the pleasures of its excellent white sand beaches (the beach at Ulvshale is one of the best).

The island's capital is **Stege**, a pretty collection of half-timbered houses and cobbled streets, still surrounded by its medieval ramparts and moat. Its church, **Stege Kirke**, is unusually large for such a sleepy town, and contains some of the island's famous frescos, which were restored in 1892. The town is also home to **Møn Museum**, with various displays charting the island's cultural history.

What to see & do

Holmegaard Glasværker

Glasværkvej 54, Fensmark (55 54 50 00/ www.holmegaardglas.dk). **Open** *Factory mid June-mid Sept* 9.30am-1.30pm Mon-Thur; 9.30am-12.30pm Fri; 11am-2.30pm Sat, Sun. *Mid Sept-mid June* 10am-1.30pm Mon-Thur; 10am-12.30pm Fri; closed Sat, Sun. *Museum & shop* 10am-4pm daily. **Admission** free.

Køge Museum

Nørregade 4, Køge (56 63 42 42). **Open** *Summer* 11am-5pm daily. *Winter* 1-5pm Tue-Fri, Sun; 11am-3pm Sat; closed Mon. **Admission** 20kr; 10kr concessions. **No credit cards.**

Møn Museum

Empiregården, Storegade 75, Stege (55 81 40 67/ www.aabne-samlinger.dk/moens). **Open** *May-Oct* 10am-4pm daily. *Nov-Apr* 10am-4pm Tue-Sun; closed Mon. **Admission** 30kr; 20kr concessions; free under-18s. **No credit cards.**

Museet ved Trelleborg

Trelleborg Allé 4, Hejninge, Slagelse (58 54 95 06). **Open** *Easter-mid Oct* 10am-5pm daily. *Mid Oct-Easter* 1-3pm daily. **Admission** 35kr; 20kr-30kr concessions. **No credit cards.**

Næstved Museum

Rinstedgade 4, Næstved (55 77 08 11/www.naestved-museum.dk). **Open** 10am-4pm Tue-Sun; closed Mon. **Admission** 20kr. **No credit cards.**

Slagelse Museum

Bredgade 11, Slagelse (58 52 83 27/ www.slagelsemuseum.dk). **Open** *Mid June-Sept* 1-5pm Tue-Sun; closed Mon. *Oct-mid June* 1-5pm Sat, Sun; closed Mon-Fri. **Admission** 20kr; free under-14s. **No credit cards.**

Getting there

There are hourly trains from Copenhagen's Central Station to Sorø (45 minutes), which go on to Slagelse (54 minutes). Ringsted is about a 40-minute journey from the capital (three trains an hour), while hourly trains to Næstved take 65 minutes. Køge is 45 minutes from Copenhagen (three trains an hour).

Directory

Directory

Getting Around

Arriving in Copenhagen

By air

In 2000, **Copenhagen Airport** (until recently known as Kastrup) was voted the best in the world by air passengers. In 1999, 17.5 million people passed through the airport, and it received direct flights from 112 cities worldwide.

Flight time from London is about one and a half hours; direct flights from New York (Newark) take as little as seven and a half hours; while the fastest direct flight from North America's west coast is nine and a half hours (from Seattle; coming from LA or San Francisco you'll have to change, and journey time is more like 14 hours). International flights arrive and depart from **Terminals 2** and **3**. (Terminal 1 is for domestic flights only.)

The airport is located ten kilometres (six miles) south-east of Copenhagen on the island of Amager. A new **rail system** links the airport to Central Station and the journey time is just **12 minutes**. The single fare is 18kr. There are six trains from the airport every hour (at 6, 11, 26, 31, 46 and 51 minutes past the hour) from just past 5am every day. The last train leaves a few minutes past midnight. There are also six trains an hour from Central Station out to the airport (on the hour, and at 16, 20, 36, 40 and 56 minutes past the hour), starting at 4.40am on weekdays, and at 5am on Saturdays and Sundays. The last train runs at 40 minutes past midnight. For further

information call **DSB** (Danish State Railways) on 33 14 17 01.

There are plentiful **taxis** at Terminals 1 and 3 (although the convenience and low price of the train link make them redundant for most people); the fare into the centre of the city should be 130kr-140kr. Taxi charges include a tip, so there's no need to add any more.

Local **buses** (9 and 19 to Kongens Nytorv; 96N, the nightbus, to Rådhuspladsen; and 250S to Central Station) run from Terminal 3 every 10 to 20 minutes, but the vast majority of visitors take the train, as the bus fare is only marginally cheaper and the journey longer (about half an hour). For further information on bus services, phone **HT** (Hovedstadsområdets Trafikselskab) on 36 13 14 15 or visit the website at www.ht.dk. There's also a **hotel shuttle bus** (SAS Globetrotter Hotel, 32 87 02 02, 6-10am, 5-10pm daily). A free transit bus runs every five to ten minutes between international and domestic terminals.

AIRPORT FACILITIES

The airport's award-winning facilities include excellent shops and restaurants, banks (most open 6am-10pm daily) in the Transfer Hall and Terminals 2 and 3, as well as cash machines (ATMs) in Terminals 1, 2 and 3. There are lockers in Terminals 1 and 2, left luggage facilities in Terminal 2 (*see page 287*) and car hire desks in Terminals 1 and 3 (*see page 283*). Under the Transit Hall are saunas (95kr for two hours), showers (80kr), solariums (10kr for five

minutes), and even a **Transfer Hotel**, where rooms can be rented for four to 16 hours (from 250kr for a single for four hours). Rooms can be reserved on 32 31 24 55 (5.30am-11pm daily) or by fax on 32 31 31 09.

Copenhagen Airport

Central switchboard 32 31 32 31/ flight info 32 47 47 47/www.cph.dk. Train to Copenhagen Airport. The website lists live information on arrival and departure times. For more specific flight information, call the relevant handling agent:
Novia *32 47 47 47.* For British Airways, Go, Mærsk Air, Premier, Luxair, Iberia, Tarum, Balkan Airlines, Pulkovo, Turkish Airlines.
SAS *32 32 00 00.*
Servisair *32 31 40 76.* For KLM, Air France, Alitalia, Sabena, Swissair, Tab, Muk, Malta.

By rail

DSB (De Danske Statsbaner – Danish State Railways) connects Copenhagen with all of continental Europe's capitals, and, via the Netherlands, the UK. The completion of the **Øresund Fixed Link** (*see page 246*) from Copenhagen to Malmö has greatly speeded up rail journey times to Sweden and Norway. All international trains arrive and depart from **Central Station** (Hovedbanegård), next to Tivoli, in the city centre.

Central Station

Københavns Hovedbanegård (33 14 04 00/www.hovedbanegaarden.dk). **Open** 24hrs daily. **Map** p310 P11. The website is in Danish only.

By road

Highways link Copenhagen with the rest of Europe. The Danish capital is around 300 kilometres (186 miles) from the

German border, and only a half-hour drive over the Øresund Fixed Link to Malmö, Sweden.

Eurolines run express coaches from all over the continent to Copenhagen.

Danish Road Directorate

Niels Juels Gade 13 (33 15 64 44/ Traffic Information Centre 70 10 10 40). **Open** *Traffic Information Centre* 24hrs daily.
Route, roadworks and traffic information for Denmark and Europe.

Eurolines

Eurolines Copenhagen, Reventlowsgade 8 (33 25 12 44/ www.eurolines.com). **Open** 9am-5pm Mon-Fri; 10am-2pm Sat; closed Sun.
Map p310 P11.
Located next to Central Station.

By sea

There are direct ferries between Copenhagen and **Malmö** (35 minutes), **Oslo** (16 hours) and **Swinoujscie** in Poland (10 hours). In addition, there's a ferry route from **Helsingør** (47 kilometres/28 miles north of Copenhagen) to Sweden, from **Esbjerg** (200 kilometres/124 miles west) to the UK, from **Rødby** (150km/93 miles south) to Germany, and from **Frederikshavn** or **Hirtshals** (450 kilometres/280 miles north-west) to Sweden and Norway.
Copenhagen Card (*see page 52*) holders qualify for discounts on Scandlines ferries.

DFDS Seaways

(Copenhagen–Oslo, Esbjerg–Harwich)
Skt Annæ Plads 30 (33 42 30 00). **Open** *Phone enquiries* 8.30am-6pm Mon-Fri; 9am-5pm Sat, Sun. *Personal enquiries* 10am-5pm daily.
Map p312 M17.

Pilen

(Copenhagen–Malmö)
Havnegade 28 (33 32 12 60/www. pilen.dk). **Open** *Winter* 8.30am-9pm Mon-Thur, Sun; 8.30am-1am Fri, Sat.
Summer 8.30am-11pm Mon-Thur, Sun; 8.30am-1am Fri, Sat.
Map p312 N17.

Polferries

(Copenhagen–Swinoujscie)
Nordre Toldbod 12A (33 11 46 45). **Open** 10am-4pm and at times of departure Mon-Fri. **Map** p308 J18.

Scandlines

(Helsingør–Helsingborg)
Stationspladsen 1, 3000 Helsingør (33 15 15 15/fax 49 21 50 86/www. scandlines.dk). Train to Helsingør.
Open 8am-8pm daily.

Scandlines

(Copenhagen–Malmö)
Corner of Havnegade & Nyhavn (33 12 80 88/www.scandlines.dk). **Open** 6am-11pm daily. **Map** p312 N17.

Public transport

Trains & buses

Copenhagen has an extensive, efficient network of local buses (**HT**; Hovedstadsområdets Trafikselskab) and trains (**S-tog**), run by Danish State Railways (**DSB**; *see page 282*). The latter system is made up of

11 different lines, ten of which pass through Central Station. Both use a common fare structure. Trains and buses run from about 5am (6am on Sundays) until around half past midnight, although some buses do run through the night.

HT

Rådhuspladsen (36 13 14 15/ www.ht.dk). **Open** *Phone enquiries* 7am-9.30pm daily. *Personal callers* 9am-7pm Mon-Fri; 9am-3pm Sat; closed Sun. **Map** p310 O12.
Timetables, journey plans, discount cards and lost property information.

Tickets & discount cards

Copenhagen metropolitan area is split into seven zone rings, radiating out from the centre of the city. The **basic ticket** allows travel within two zones and costs **12kr** (6kr for children). As the two central zones include almost every place covered in this guide, it's unlikely that visitors will need to buy anything more than this basic ticket. It also allows transfers between buses and trains, providing that the transfer is made within an hour.

Tickets are stamped with the date, time and departure zone. Two- and three-zone tickets are valid for a period of one hour from the stamped time; four- to six-zone tickets can be used for

The coming of the Metro

At present, trains are really only used to ferry people in to and out of Copenhagen and its suburbs, buses taking care of most other travel within the city. But that will all change when the city's cutting-edge, though thus far beleaguered, mini **Metro** system opens, supposedly in 2002. The Metro is an ambitious two-line rail link which, when completed, will run for 21 kilometres (13 miles; half above and half below ground) from Vanlose to the west of the city, through stations in Frederiksberg, Kongens Nytorv and Christianshavn (plus several others en

route), before dividing to head for two destinations on Amager: the airport and Ørestad, at the Danish end of the new link to Sweden. Trains will run every 90 seconds around the clock. Whether the city actually needs yet another public transport service is debatable; after all, there are only 1.5 million people in the whole of Greater Copenhagen area and they already have the buses and local trains (S-tog) to efficiently whisk them in and out of town. But perhaps Copenhagen won't quite feel like it is a grown-up capital until it has its own Metro.

Directory

On your bikes

The whole of Scandinavia is, of course, famed for its use of the bicycle as everyday transport, and Danes cycle, on average, 600 kilometres (375 miles) per year. But, if anything, Copenhageners take things a step further. Literally everyone, regardless of income or social status, cycles in Copenhagen. What's more, Copenhageners take their cycling deadly seriously and woe betide anyone who, during rush hour, ventures out on the city's many kilometres of cycle paths with a faint heart. Copenhagen's two-wheeled commuters take no prisoners and there are rules that may not be immediately apparent to foreigners. For instance, bus passengers (either embarking or disembarking) at bus stops have right of way and all cyclists must stop and wait until the bus doors have closed. Left-hand turns on main roads are not permitted for cyclists, you must dismount and cross the road (with the green man, of course) as a pedestrian would. As a rule you should ride on the right-hand side of the cycle path; if someone rings

their bell behind you (never more than once, that is considered impolite), it is to indicate that you should move over and let them pass on the left. When you want to stop, raise your right hand (which usually looks like a rather fey salute). None of this seems to apply to cycle couriers, however. They do precisely as they please.

Between April and September the city operates a public bike rental scheme called **Bycykler** (City Bikes), where, as with shopping trolleys, you put a 20kr piece in the slot to borrow a bike from one of the 125 bike deposits around town. The sponsored, gearless bikes are only good for short journeys, however, and by midsummer most of the 2,500 have disappeared or lie in ruins. A better bet is to rent a bike from one of the city's many bike shops (see page 283). This usually costs from 50kr per day (it becomes cheaper the longer you rent) for a simple three-speeder. Bicycle theft is an accepted part of everyday life in Copenhagen, so always lock yours.

---

one and a half hours; all-zone tickets are valid for two hours.

Tickets are on sale at railway station ticket offices, from machines at stations and from bus drivers. Coloured zone maps can be found at bus stops and in rail stations.

CHILDREN

Two children aged under 10 can travel for free when accompanied by an adult. Children aged 10 to 15 pay the child fare or can use a child's discount card. Two 10 to 15-year-olds can travel on one adult ticket or on one clip of an adult's discount card.

DISCOUNT CARDS

Discount **clip cards** ('klippekort') are available for **ten journeys** within two, three, four, five, six or all zones (two-zone cards cost **80kr**; 40kr children). When you start your journey you must punch your card in the yellow machine on the bus or in the station. One

clip covers you for travel within the zones printed on the card. If you want to travel beyond those zones, then several simultaneous clips are needed (eg if you have a two-zone card, two clips allow you to travel within three or four zones, three clips allow you to travel within five or six zones, and so on). Cards can be bought from stations, most ticket machines and HT ticket offices.

24-HOUR TICKET

This ticket allows unlimited travel for 24 hours on Copenhagen's buses and trains. It costs **70kr** (35kr children), and should be clipped in the yellow machines in buses and stations at the start of the journey. Two children under ten can travel free with an adult holding a 24-hour ticket. It can be bought from manned rail stations and HT offices.

COPENHAGEN CARD

As well as free admission to more than 60 museums and

sights, the **Copenhagen Card** offers unlimited travel by bus and train within Greater Copenhagen. Cards are available for 24, 48 or 72 hours. For prices, *see page 52*. The card can be bought from HT ticket offices in Rådhuspladsen and Toftegårds Plads, main stations, most tourist offices and from many hotels.

National rail system

DSB (Danish State Railways) has a journey planner (in English) on its website for rail journeys within Denmark.

DSB

Central Station (domestic journeys 70 13 14 15/international 70 13 14 16/S-tog 33 14 17 01/www.dsb.dk). **Open** 7am-10pm daily; S-tog 6.30am-11pm daily. **Map** p310 P11.

Taxis

Taxis can be flagged down anywhere in Copenhagen. If the yellow 'Taxa' light on the roof of the car is on, the taxi is available for hire. You usually don't have to wait long for a cab (although high licence fees have led to a drop in taxi numbers in recent years), but they are expensive. The basic fare is 22kr plus 7.7kr per kilometre (rising to 9.6kr at night-time and weekends). Though not exactly friendly, Copenhagen's taxi drivers are generally efficient and reliable. Fares include a service charge, so don't tip unless you have received particularly good service; most cabs accept credit cards (though you are supposed to tell the driver at the beginning of the journey if you intend to pay with a card).

Hovedstadens Taxi 38 77 77 77.
Københavns Taxa 35 35 35 35.
Taxa Motor 38 10 10 10.

Cycling

See page 282 **On your bikes.**

Bike hire

Danwheel Cykeludlejning
Colbjørnsensgade 3, Vesterbro (33 21 22 27). **Open** 9am-6pm Mon-Fri; 9am-2pm Sat, Sun. **Rates** 35kr/day, 200kr deposit. **No credit cards**. **Map** p310 P10.

Københavns Cyklebørs
Gothersgade 157 (33 14 07 17). **Open** 8.30am-5.30pm Mon-Fri; 10am-1.30pm Sat; closed Sun. **Rates** 40kr/day, 200kr deposit. **Credit** MC, V. **Map** p307 L14.

Københavns Cykler
Reventlowsgade 11, Central Station (33 33 86 13). **Open** 8am-6pm Mon-Fri; 9am-1pm Sat, Sun. **Rates** 50kr/day, 300kr deposit. **Credit** MC, V. **Map** p310 P11.

Loke
HC Ørstedsvej 45, Frederiksberg (35 37 15 60). Bus 2, 3, 11. **Open** 9am-5.30pm Mon-Thur; 9am-6pm Fri; 10am-2pm Sat; closed Sun. **Rates** 40kr/day, 500kr deposit. **No credit cards**. **Map** p111 N7. **Branches**: Ranzausgade 8B, Nørrebro (35 37 15 71); Griffenfeldsgade 45A, Nørrebro (35 37 15 89); Nørrebrogade 12, Nørrebro (35 37 15 90).

MP Cykler
Hostrupsvej 3, Frederiksberg (35 36 37 16). Bus 18. **Open** 8am-6pm Mon-Fri; 9am-2pm Sat; closed Sun. **Rates** 35kr/day, must be able to confirm identity with picture. **No credit cards**.

Østerport Cykler
Oslo Plads 9, Østerbro, next to Østerport Station (33 33 85 13). **Open** 8am-6pm Mon-Fri; 9am-1pm Sat; closed Sun. **Rates** 50kr/day, 300kr deposit. **Credit** MC, V. **Map** p307 H15.

Organisations

Dansk Cyklist Forbund
Rømersgade 7 (33 32 31 21/ www.dcf.dk). **Open** *May-July* 10am-5.30pm Mon-Fri; 10am-2pm Sat; closed Sun. *Aug-Apr* noon-5.30pm Mon-Fri; 10am-2pm Sat; closed Sun. **Map** p306 L12.
Order cycling maps, or check out the informative website. The organisation also runs cycling tours.

Driving

Don't. The Danes, or rather their government, hate private cars and do everything in their power to discourage their use. Parking and petrol are very expensive, the cost of buying a new car is several times that in most countries, and car hire is also much more pricey. Bridge tolls for motorists to Fyn and Sweden are extortionate, regardless of the number of passengers in the vehicle.

The Danes drive on the right. When turning right, drivers give way to cyclists coming up on the inside and to pedestrians. You must drive with dipped headlights during the day.

You should also be aware that, outside Copenhagen, Danish road signs are about as reliable as a tabloid horoscope.

You must pay for on-street parking in the city 8am-8pm Mon-Fri, 8am-2pm Sat.

Car rental

Avis
Kampmannsgade 1 (33 15 22 99). **Open** 7am-7pm Mon-Fri; 7am-5pm Sat, Sun. **Map** p310 N10.

Terminal 3, Copenhagen Airport (32 51 22 99). **Open** 7am-10pm daily. **Credit** AmEx, DC, MC, V. **Rates** 700kr-800kr/day; 4,000kr-4,500kr/week.

Budget Rent a Car
Helgolandsgade 2 (33 55 70 00). **Open** 8am-6pm Mon-Fri; 8am-1pm Sat, Sun. **Map** p310 Q10.
Terminal 3, Copenhagen Airport (32 52 39 00). **Open** 7am-10pm daily. **Credit** AmEx, DC, MC, V. **Rates** 620kr/day; 2,850kr/week.

EuropCar/ Pitztner Auto
Gammel Kongevej (33 55 99 00). Bus 1, 14. **Open** 7.30am-7pm Mon-Fri; 8am-4pm Sat; 8am-7pm Sun. **Map** p111 P8.
Terminal 3, Copenhagen Airport (32 50 30 90). **Open** 7am-10pm daily. **Credit** AmEx, DC, MC, V. **Rates** 950kr-1,100kr/day; 3,300kr/week.

Hertz
Ved Vesterport 3 (33 17 90 20). **Open** *May-Oct* 7am-7pm Mon-Thur; 7am-8pm Fri; 7am-5pm Sat; 8am-7pm Sun. *Nov-Apr* 7am-6pm Mon-Thur; 7am-7pm Fri; 7am-5pm Sat; 8am-5pm Sun. **Map** p310 O10.
Terminal 3, Copenhagen Airport (32 50 93 00). **Open** 7am-10pm daily. **Credit** AmEx, DC, MC, V. **Rates** 893kr/day; 3,049kr/week.

Mudan Car Rent
Banegårdspladsen 1 (33 11 21 17). **Open** 8am-6pm Mon-Fri; 9am-4pm Sat, Sun. **Map** p310 P11.
Terminal 3, Copenhagen Airport (32 51 15 51). **Open** 7am-10pm daily. **Credit** AmEx, DC, MC, V. **Rates** 605kr/day; 2,541kr/week.

Breakdown services

Falck Redningskorps
Emergency 70 10 20 30. **Open** 24hrs. **Rates** *Non-members* approximately 586kr/hour Mon-Fri; 1,172kr/hour Sat, Sun.

24-hour petrol stations

Q8
Nørre Allé/Jagtvej, Østerbro (35 37 10 47). **Map** p121 C10. *Enghavevej 76, Vesterbro (33 22 11 74).* **Map** p111 S7. *Nyropsgade 42, Vesterbro (33 14 17 07).* **Map** p310 O10.

Statoil
Vendersgade, Israels Plads (33 11 89 55). **Map** p306 L12. *Strandboulevarden 91, Østerbro (33 42 02 22).* **Map** p121 A14.

Directory

Resources A-Z

Business services

At the airport

There's an excellent business centre on the fourth floor of Terminal 3 at Copenhagen Airport (32 48 30 00/fax 32 48 30 01/cph.business@ssp.dk).

Couriers

ASAP-kurérservice København

Egensevej 25, Kastrup (32 50 56 30). **Open** 24hrs. **Prices** phone for details. Express delivery within 30 minutes in Copenhagen; deliveries in Denmark and worldwide. Car rental with or without chauffeur.

De Grønne Bude

Blågårdsgade 22, Nørrebro (35 39 35 39). **Open** 24hrs. **Prices** from 34kr in the city centre.
Most deliveries are made in Copenhagen by couriers on bikes, but the company also covers the rest of Denmark and the world.

Equipment hire

Business line

Store Kongensgade 45 (33 32 52 29). **Open** 9am-5.30pm Mon-Fri; 9am-1pm Sat; closed Sun. **Credit** MC, V.
Rents out and installs telephones, switchboards, and so on.

COMTECH

Bådehavnsgade 12 (36 46 10 10). Bus 3, 10, 18, 100S to Mozarts Plads, then 10-minute walk. **Open** 8.30am-4.30pm Mon-Fri; closed Sat, Sun. **No credit cards.** Rents out audio-visual equipment for conferences and outdoor events, eg video/data projectors, microphones and sound systems.

Photocopying/ printing

Vester Kopi

Vesterbrogade 69, Vesterbro (33 27 88 33/www.vesterkopi.dk). **Open** 8.30am-5.30pm Mon-Fri; closed Sat, Sun. **Map** p111 P9.
Nørregade 7 (33 14 58 33/www.vesterkopi.dk). **Open** 8.30am-7pm Mon-Thur; 8.30am-5.30pm Fri;

10am-1pm Sat; closed Sun. **Map** p310 M12.
Gothersgade 12 (33 32 58 33/www.vesterkopi.dk). **Open** 8.30am-5.30pm Mon-Fri; closed Sat, Sun. **Map** p311 M15.
Credit MC, V.
A comprehensive range of copying and printing services.

Secretarial

Manpower

Nørre Voldgade 19 (33 69 80 00/www.manpower.dk). **Open** 8am-5.30pm Mon-Fri; closed Sat, Sun. **No credit cards. Map** p310 M12.
Matches clients with secretaries who speak two or more languages. Rates vary according to requirements.

Translation

Check also the yellow pages under 'Oversættelse'.

Berlitz

Vimmelskaftet 42A, Strøget (70 25 35 60/www.berlitzit.com). **Open** 8am-5pm Mon-Fri; closed Sat, Sun. **Credit** MC, V. **Map** p311 N13.
A global company that offers translators and interpreters in most languages. Prices vary according to requirements. For online translations check out the website.

Tolkesekretariatet

Falkoner Allé 7, Frederiksberg (38 86 31 86). **Open** 9.30am-5pm Mon-Fri. **Credit** MC, V. **Map** p110 N5.
Simultaneous and consecutive interpretations. Bookings should be made well in advance. Prices are from 4,000kr per day for an interpreter.

Customs

The following can be imported into Denmark without incurring customs duty by non-Danish residents arriving from an EU country with duty-paid goods purchased in an EU country:

- 1.5 litres of spirits or 20 litres of sparkling wine (under 22 per cent) or 90 litres of table wine;
- 300 cigarettes or 150 cigarillos or 75 cigars or 400 grammes of tobacco;
- other commodities, including beer: no limit.

Residents of non-EU countries entering from outside the EU with goods purchased in non-EU countries can bring in to Denmark:

- 1 litre of spirits or 2 litres of sparkling wine (maximum 22 per cent);
- 2 litres of table wine;
- 200 cigarettes or 100 cigarillos or 50 cigars or 250 grammes of tobacco;
- 500 grammes of coffee or 200 grammes of coffee extracts;
- 100 grammes of tea or 40 grammes of tea extracts;
- 50 grammes of perfume;
- 250 millilitres of eau de toilette;
- other articles, including beer: 1,350kr (750kr if purchased on plane/ferry).

Only those aged 17 or over can use the alcohol and tobacco allowances; coffee and coffee extracts allowances are valid only for those aged 15 or over. It is forbidden to import fresh foods into Denmark unless vacuum packed.

Although duty-free goods within the EU were abolished in 1999, and there is now no legal limit on the quantities of alcohol and tobacco travellers may import into most EU countries (provided they are for personal use), Denmark, Finland and Sweden will continue to impose limits for the foreseeable future.

For customs enquiries, call 32 88 73 00.

Disabled visitors

Facilities for disabled people in Copenhagen are generally excellent relative to other European capitals, as you'd expect in a country where equality of opportunity is taken so seriously. *Access in Denmark – A Travel Guide for the Disabled* is available from the **Danish Tourist Board**

Seeing red

After a short time walking in Copenhagen you will notice the Danes' strictly regimented pedestrian crossing behaviour. Under no circumstances can the average Dane be induced to cross unless the green man is illuminated. Thus, crowds of Danes waiting obediently by the roadside for the green man to show (regardless of the fact that there might not be any vehicles for miles in either direction), is the norm. If you do see anyone crossing on a red, they are either foreigners, or Danes who have had their heads turned by a recent trip abroad. Whatever, people who cross on a red are considered smart-arses and may even experience the odd 'tut'. Our advice? Relax and follow the herd.

in London at 55 Sloane Street, SW1X 9SY (020 7259 5959). In addition, much Danish tourist literature, including the Wonderful Copenhagen website (www.woco.dk), lists places that are wheelchair-accessible and lists useful information on specific facilities for the disabled.

Two Danish organisations may be able to offer help to disabled visitors:

Dansk Handicap Forbund

Kollectivhuset, Hans Knudsens Plads 1A, 2100 Copenhagen Ø (39 29 35 55).
Phone enquiries 8.30am-3.45pm Mon-Thur; 8.30am-1.30pm Fri; closed Sat, Sun.
Staff members speak English and may be able to help tourists. However, members of the organisation have priority.

Videnscenter for Bevægelseshandicap

Egebæksvej 26, 8270 Højbjerg (86 27 05 22/fax 86 27 05 36/ www.vfb.dk).
The Danish Information Centre for Physical Disability collects, develops, adapts and disseminates information about subjects relating to physical disability in Denmark.

Electricity

Denmark, in common with most of Europe, has 220-volt AC, 50Hz current and uses two-pin continental plugs. Visitors from the UK will need to buy an adaptor for their appliances, while North Americans won't be able to use their 110/125V appliances without a transformer.

Embassies & consulates

American Embassy

Dag Hammarskjöld Allé 24, 2100 Copenhagen Ø (35 55 31 44/ www.usaembassy.dk). **Open** *Phone enquiries* 2-4pm Mon-Fri; closed Sat, Sun. *Personal callers* 8.30am-11.30am Mon, Tue, Thur, Fri; closed Wed, Sat, Sun. **Map** p307 G15.

Australian Honorary Consulate

Strandboulevarden 122, 2100 Copenhagen Ø (39 29 20 70). Bus 9, 19 (from Østerport Station), 40 (from Nordhavn Station). **Open** 8.30am-4.30pm Mon-Thur; 8.30am-3.45pm Fri; closed Sat, Sun. **Map** p121 D16.

British Embassy

Kastelsvej 36-40, 2100 Copenhagen Ø (35 44 52 00/ www.britishembassy.dk). Train to Østerport Station, then 10min walk/1, 6, 650S bus, then 5min walk. **Open** 9am-5pm Mon-Fri; closed Sat, Sun. *Visa dept* 9am-12.30pm Mon-Fri; closed Sat, Sun. **Map** p121 F15.

Canadian Embassy

Kristen Bernikowsgade 1, 1105 Copenhagen K (33 48 32 00/ www.canada.dk). **Open** 8.30am-4.30pm Mon-Fri; closed Sat, Sun. **Map** p311 M15.

Irish Embassy

Østbanegade 21, 2100 Copenhagen Ø (35 42 32 33). Bus 9, 19. **Open** 10am-12.30pm, 2.30-4.30pm Mon-Fri; closed Sat, Sun. **Map** p308 G16.

Emergencies

To contact the police, ambulance or fire service in an emergency call **112** (free of charge). For central police stations, *see page 289*.

Health

All temporary foreign visitors to Denmark are entitled to free medical and hospital treatment if they are taken ill or have an accident.

Accident & emergency

The following central hospitals have 24-hour emergency departments.

Amager Hospital

Italiensvej 1, Amager (32 34 32 34). Bus 100S.
Emergency department: Kastrupvej 63. Bus 9.

Bispebjerg Hospital

Bispebjerg Bakke 23, Bispebjerg (35 31 35 31). Train to Bispebjerg/ 10 bus.

Frederiksberg Hospital

Nordre Fasanvej 57, Frederiksberg (38 34 77 11). Bus 2, 11, 29, 39, 100.

Alternative medicine

Alternative medicine is big in Denmark. A third of Danes have personal experience of alternative treatments and 63 per cent believe that it is important to develop alternative solutions as a supplement to traditional medical treatments. Among the most common such treatments in Denmark are reflexology, acupuncture, massage and homeopathy.

The yellow pages lists plenty of addresses under

'Alternativ behandling'. For personal recommendations concerning alternative treatment call:

Alternativ-nøglen

45 80 70 77. **Phone enquiries** 9am-noon Mon, Tue, Thur; closed Wed, Fri-Sun.
This organisation's database covers most of the alternative medical market in Denmark.

Center for Klassisk Homøopatikøbenhavn

Grundtvigsvej 25A, Frederiksberg (70 26 34 00/10/20/30). Bus 1, 14.
Open phone for details.
The homeopathic practitioners speak English, German, Dutch and French.

Danish Reflexologists Association

Christian Winthersvej, Kolding (75 50 12 50/www.fdz.dk).
Phone enquiries 8am-1pm Mon-Wed, Fri; 8am-1pm, 4-8pmThur; closed Sat, Sun.
Contact this organisation for information about local reflexologists.

Contraception

Condoms are widely available and are sold in most supermarkets and pharmacies as well as from vending machines in bars and on the street. Birth control pills can be obtained from pharmacies, but require a doctor's prescription.

Dentists

Tourist offices (*see page 292*) can refer foreign visitors to local dentists.

Dental Emergency Service

Oslo Plads 14 (35 38 02 51).
Open 8-9.30pm Mon-Fri; 10am-noon Sat, Sun. **Map** p307 H15.
Personal enquiries only. Treatment must be paid for in cash.

Doctors

Lægevagten

33 93 63 00. **Price** from 250kr per visit. EU citizens are not charged.
Call the above number if you need to see a doctor between 8am and 4pm. Between 4pm and 8am, phone 38 88 60 41.

Insurance

Citizens of EU countries are entitled to free treatment and essential medication. The UK has a reciprocal health agreement with Denmark which means that, in addition to free emergency treatment, UK citizens can usually obtain free medical treatment from a doctor, and hospital treatment if referred by a doctor. Presentation of a UK passport is usually all that is required (form E111 is not strictly necessary). Citizens of non-EU countries should ensure they have adequate health insurance.

Pharmacies

There is no shortage of pharmacies in Copenhagen; look for the 'apotek' sign.

City Helse

Vendersgade 6 (33 14 08 92).
Open 9.30am-5.30pm Mon-Fri; 9.30am-2pm Sat; closed Sun.
No credit cards. Map p306 L12.
Wide selection of health food and natural medicines.

Steno Apotek

Vesterbrogade 6, opposite Central Station (33 14 82 66). **Open** 24hrs daily. **No credit cards.**
Map p310 P11.

Internet

Internet service providers

The main Danish internet service providers are:

Cybercity

Esplanaden 6-8 (33 33 94 96/ www.cybercity.dk). **Phone enquiries** 9am-5pm Mon-Fri; closed Sat, Sun.

TeleDanmark Internet

80 80 80 35/www.opasia.dk.
Phone enquiries 8.30am-10pm Mon-Fri; noon-8pm Sat, Sun.

Worldonline Denmark

Peter Bangsvej 26, Frederiksberg (38 14 70 07/www.worldonline.dk).
Phone enquiries 9am-5pm Mon-Fri; closed Sat, Sun.

Cybercafés

The following cybercafés all provide web access. Check out www.cybercafes.com.

B1

Bragesgade 1, Nørrebro (35 82 25 17/www.aok.dk). Bus 4E, 5, 16, 350S. **Open** 2pm-3am Mon-Thur, Sun; 2pm-7am Fri, Sat. **Terminals** 28. **Prices** 20kr-25kr per hr.
No credit cards.

Babel

Esromgade 15, opg 3, entrance from Nørrebrogade (www.babel.dk).
Open 2-11pm Mon-Sat; closed Sun. **Terminals** 9. **Prices** 30kr per hr; 150kr per 5hrs; 200kr per 10hrs. **No credit cards.**

Brainstorm

Vesterfælledvej 59, Vesterbro (33 24 37 34/www.brainstorm.dk).
Train to Enghave. **Open** 1pm-midnight Mon-Fri; 11am-midnight Sat, Sun. **Prices** before 7.30pm 27kr per hr; after 7.30pm 22kr per hr. **No credit cards.**
Map p111 S6.

Cyber Space Net Café

Jagtvej 55, Nørrebro (35 83 11 45/www.cyb-space.com).
Bus 18. **Open** noon-6pm daily.
Terminals 25. **Prices** from 10-100kr per hr. **No credit cards.**
Map p119 H7.

DropZone

Frederiksborggade 41 (33 93 68 88).
Open 2pm-midnight Mon-Thur, Sun; 2pm-8am Fri, Sat. **Terminals** 14.
Prices 20kr-25kr per hr. **No credit cards. Map** p306 L12.

E-me

Vimmelskaftet 49, Strøget (33 33 08 05/www.e-me.dk). **Open** 10am-5pm Mon-Fri. **Terminals** 4-6.
Price varies; phone for details.
No credit cards. Map p311 N13.

Gamestation

Vesterbrogade 115, Vesterbro (33 25 97 96/www.gamestation.dk).
Bus 6, 550S. **Open** noon-6pm Mon-Thur, Sun; noon-6pm, midnight-8am Fri, Sat. **Terminals** 29. **Prices** phone for details. **No credit cards.**
Map p111 Q7.
Branch Strandboulevarden 151 (35 43 97 96).

Nethulen

Istedgade 114, Vesterbro (33 24 04 07/www.nethulen.dk). Bus 16.
Open 9.30am-11pm Mon-Fri; 4-11pm Sat, Sun. **Terminals** 11. **Prices** 15kr-20kr per hr. **No credit cards.**
Map p111 R9.

NetWeb – Internetcafé

Nørregade 26 (33 14 50 60).
Open 1-10pm Mon-Sat; closed
Sun. **Terminals** 12. **Prices** 20kr
per 30mins. **No credit cards**.
Map p310 M12.

Take Two Internetcafé

*Åboulevarden 80, Nørrebro (35 37 53
35/www.aok.dk/E/V/CPHDK/0004/
41/83). Bus 67, 68, 69, 250S.* **Open**
noon-6am daily. **Terminals** 40.
Prices 15kr per hr. **No credit cards**.
Map p119 L8.

Language

See page 294.

Language classes

AOF sprogcentret København

*Gadelandet 18, 2700 Brønshøj (33
69 85 00).* **Phone enquiries** 10am-
4pm Mon-Fri; closed Sat, Sun.
Offers courses at all levels, including
intensive courses in Danish.

Berlitz

*Vimmelskaftet 42A, Strøget
(70 21 50 10/www.berlitz.com).*
Open 8am-9pm Mon-Fri;
closed Sat, Sun.
Courses taught by native teachers;
most are tailored to individual needs.

Left luggage

Airport

There are lockers between
Terminals 1 and 2 (across
from the post office and Den
Danske Bank; 20kr for 24
hours; 72 hours maximum),
and left luggage facilities at
the eastern end of Terminal
2, next to the Mini Market
(32 47 47 43; 6am-10pm daily;
30kr per item per day).

Rail station

There are lockers by the
Reventlowsgade entrance at
Central Station. Prices are 25kr
or 35kr for 24 hours, depending
on the size of the locker. Prices
for personally supervised
storage (5.30am-1am Mon-Sat;
6am-1am Sun) depend on the
quantity and size of the items
and vary from 30kr to 40kr.

Lost property

The main Copenhagen lost
property office is:

Copenhagen Police

*Slotsherrensvej 113, Vanløse (38 74
88 22). Train to Islev.* **Open** 9am-
5.30pm Mon-Thur; 9am-2pm Fri;
closed Sat, Sun.

Airport

If you lose luggage or other
possessions on a plane, contact
the relevant airline or:

Copenhagen Air Services

Copenhagen Airport (32 47 47 25).
Open 8am-8pm daily.

Buses/trains

If you lose something on a bus,
call HT general information (36
13 14 15; 7am-9.30pm daily); if
you lose it on a train, phone the
relevant terminus or the central
S-tog information office (36 14
17 01; 7am-11pm daily).

Taxis

Call the taxi company. After a
couple of days items will be
transferred to the central lost
property office (*see above*).

Money

The Danish **krone** (crown) is
divided into 100 **øre**. There are
coins in denominations of 25
øre, 50 øre (both copper), one
krone, two kroner, five kroner
(silver, with a hole), ten kroner
and 20 kroner (brass). Notes
come in 50, 100, 200, 500 and
1,000 kroner denominations. In
this Guide the abbreviation 'kr'
is used. At the time of writing,
£1 = 12kr; US$1 = 8.7kr.
There's no limit on the amount
of foreign or Danish currency
you can bring into Denmark.

ATMs/cash machines

The majority of Danish banks
have ATMs, which offer a
convenient way of withdrawing

Danish kroner on a credit or
debit card. Most major cards are
accepted (although be sure to
have established a PIN number).

Banks & bureaux de change

Banks tend to open from
9.30am to 4pm on weekdays,
with late opening until 6pm on
Thursday. Some have longer
hours and open on Saturdays.
Most will change foreign
currency and travellers'
cheques, as will the plentiful
bureaux de change. There are
also a number of machines
scattered throughout the city
that will exchange foreign
currency for kroner.

Lost/stolen credit cards

Emergency numbers:
American Express *33 11 25 00*
(8am-5pm); *80 01 00 21* (5pm-8am).
Diners *36 73 73 73* (24hrs).
Mastercard/Eurocard *80 01
60 98* (24hrs).
Visa *80 01 85 88* (24hrs).

For other credit cards, call
the 24-hour **Danish PBS
Hotline** (44 89 25 00).

Money transfers

Usually, **Den Danske Bank**
can make money transfers
within 12 hours. Ask for a so-
called 'swiff address' and a
registration number which
you pass on to the local bank
in your home country. Then
contact your local bank
concerning the amount of
money you wish to transfer.
Transactions normally cost
100-200kr. Den Danske Bank
has several branches, including:

Den Danske Bank

Central Station (33 12 04 11).
Open 8am-8pm Mon-Sat;
10am-8pm Sun. **Map** p310 P11.
*Amagertorv 2, Strøget (33 74
29 00).* **Open** 9.30am-4pm Mon-
Wed, Fri; 9.30am-6pm Thur;
closed Sat, Sun.
Map p311 N14.

Newspapers & magazines

Most of the big national newspapers in Denmark started out as pamphlets for various political parties. Today, however, these papers, keen to target a wider readership, cover domestic and foreign affairs, culture, business, technology and lifestyle as well as offering detailed investigations into party policy. Of course, Denmark also has its tabloid papers, but compared to other countries they are generally less sensational.

Aktuelt

Formerly the official publication of the Social Democratic Party, *Aktuelt* has increasingly tried to find its own, more critical and direct profile, despite still being owned by the party. Strong on education, environmental affairs, labour and social welfare.

Berlingske Tidende

A liberal newspaper that aims to promote trusty old social values such as honesty and morality. Its decent quality articles and attractive layout are centred around business and culture.

Børsen

Essentially a business publication, *Børsen* keeps tabs on the latest stock market developments, economic predictions and the major players in Danish finance.

BT

A tabloid paper that lags a little way behind *Ekstrabladet* in the sleaze and celebrity stakes, and so places an emphasis on football and other sports.

Ekstrabladet

The most controversial of the Danish tabloids, *Ekstrabladet* relies heavily on celebrity sleaze, opinionated editorials and endless campaigning. It also features a nude model every day on page 9 and suffers from very low credibility.

Information

Information was founded as 'the newspaper of the Danish Resistance' on the night of Denmark's liberation at the end of World War II. Today, the paper has no significant political leaning, its objective being to give its readers important background information on current affairs. The layout is traditional (some might say bland) but its articles are often interesting and well written.

Jyllandsposten

Though apparently the most royal and conservative of the national papers, *Jyllandsposten* also features the best foreign correspondents and the broadest international coverage. Independent of institutional or political affiliations, it has the fastest growing readership in Denmark.

Kristeligt Dagblad

A Christian publication that focuses on questions concerning ethics, belief and religion. *Kristeligt Dagblad* features articles about the Pope and the religious establishment, but also prints interesting features on charity and aid work.

Politiken

Once the paper of the Social-Liberal Party, *Politiken* now focuses, above all, on cultural matters. Often accused of being too Copenhagen-orientated, *Politiken* remains a great paper for those who actually live in the capital.

Weekendavisen

A weekly publication that offers a round-up of news from the previous seven days. *Weekendavisen* aims to offer insight into cultural, political and ethical matters in Denmark and the rest of the world. Most of its journalists are specialists in their fields, which shows in the quality of the articles.

English-language press

Most of the major newspapers from Britain and the US are available in Copenhagen from kiosks around the city (including Kongens Nytorv, Jorchs Passage, Central Station, Rådhuspladsen and the Illum and Magasin du Nord department stores). You'll also find up to 120 English-language fashion and lifestyle magazines. For more information call **Dansk Bladdistribution** (32 54 34 44).

Copenhagen Post

www.cphpost.dk
A weekly magazine with Danish news in English. Short and informative. The *In & Out* supplement picks out the best of the current eating, drinking, entertainment and sightseeing options.

Copenhagen Living

www.cphliving.dk
A lushly glossy and sharply designed magazine covering design, food, architecture, fashion, shopping and leisure in Denmark. It's published twice a year.

Radio

Copenhagen's biggest radio stations are all owned by **Danmarks Radio** (the Danish Broadcasting Corporation). DR has a fine tradition of high quality programming, but it's also possible to pick up foreign radio stations, mainly from Sweden and Germany. Radio news in English is broadcast on weekdays at 8.40am, 11am, 5.10pm and 10pm on Radio Denmark International (1062 Mhz), which also offers a telephone news service (70 26 80 80) and website (www.dr.dk/news).

P1

90.8 Mhz
Typical broadcasts include radio plays, current affairs magazines, documentaries and news. Broadcasts from 6am to midnight.

P2 & P4/Københavns Radio

96.5 Mhz
Broadcasting through the night (6.50pm-6.10am), P2 is predominantly a classical music station, but also plays jazz from time to time. The same frequency is occupied by P4/Købenshavns Radio during the day (6.10am-6.30pm), which features pop music (including the Danish pop charts), listeners' requests, phone-ins, local news and traffic reports.

P3

93.9 Mhz
Targeted mainly at Danish youth, this station features young comedians and DJs who play pop and chart music during the day, with programmes offering more alternative content at night. Broadcasts 24 hours.

POPFM

104.4 Mhz
Owned by The Voice; plays pop 24 hours a day.

The Voice

104.9 Mhz
A 24-hour chart/dance music station, The Voice is the only commercial

station with more than a million listeners a week. It's very popular with younger people. Some of the station's DJs also play at Copenhagen's nightclubs.

Television

Founded as a public service organisation and funded by individual licence fees, Danmarks Radio still dominates the television scene (it actually enjoyed a monopoly on radio and TV broadcasting until 1986). However, over recent years, the old stations (DR1 and DR2) have been steadily losing ground to younger, more challenging, commercial broadcasting companies that are not subject to any public service obligations.

DR1
The first television channel in Denmark, DR1's strengths include news and current affairs, documentaries and children's and youth programming. However, its more frivolous quizzes and talkshows also prove popular.

DR2
The little sister to DR1, and a more alternative channel. Regular evenings of themed programming (including documentaries, interviews and movies) have previously featured subjects as diverse as the life of Picasso, the small islands of Denmark and the Rolling Stones.

TV2
Despite introducing morning television and *Wheel of Fortune* to the Danes, TV2 largely resembles DR1, principally because TV2 is also a licence-financed station, with similar public service obligations.

TV3/TV3+
Targeting young people and families with kids, TV3 is a commercial station that aims to provide quality light entertainment, with Danish soap operas and docu-soaps among the most popular programmes. Its sister channel TV3+ is the leading station for sport.

TVDanmark 1/ TVDanmark 2
Despite the name, most of the programmes on TVDanmark are American sitcoms and soap operas, though it occasionally broadcasts Danish docu-soaps.

Opening hours

The majority of shops in Copenhagen open from 9am to 7pm on weekdays and from 9am to 2pm or 5pm on Saturday, with only bakers, florists and souvenir shops open on Sunday. Banks tend to open from 9.30am to 4pm on weekdays, with late opening until 6pm on Thursday (only a few open on Saturday). Office hours are usually 9am to 4pm from Monday to Friday.

Police & security

Though there is occasional violent crime in Copenhagen, incidents are comparatively rare, and are virtually unheard of in the city centre, even after dark. In fact, there are very few quarters of the city (parts of Vesterbro and Nørrebro, perhaps) that are even remotely intimidating, day or night. Some of the suburbs such as Ishøj or Brondby Strand, however, are a different matter, and should be approached more cautiously after dark. In the unlikely event that you are a victim of crime, contact the Danish Police immediately. In emergencies, call **112** (free of charge).

Police headquarters
Polititorvet (33 14 14 48).
Open 24hrs. **Map** p310 Q13.
Open 24 hours, the Police HQ can direct you to your nearest station. These include Central Station (33 15 38 01; map p310 P11); Halmtorvet 20, Vesterbro (33 25 14 48; map p310 Q10); Store Kongensgade 100 (33 93 14 48; map p308 K16).

Postal services

Most post offices open from either 9am to 5.30pm or 10am to 5pm Monday to Friday, and from 9am or 10am until noon on Saturday. Telegrams can be sent from any post office, and faxes from the larger branches. Copenhagen's largest post offices are listed below.

Main Post Office
Tietgensgade 35-39, Vesterbro (33 41 56 00). **Open** 11am-6pm Mon-Fri; 10am-1pm Sat. **Map** p311 P13.

Central Station Post Office
Central Station (33 41 56 00).
Open 8am-9pm Mon-Fri; 9am-4pm Sat; 10am-4pm Sun. **Map** p310 P11.

Postal rates

In addition to the rates below, express delivery services are also available. Contact any post office for details. Letters up to 20 grammes cost 4kr to Denmark, 4.50kr to Europe and 5.50kr to other countries; letters up to 50 grammes cost 5.25kr to Denmark, 6.50kr to the rest of Scandinavia, 9.75kr to the rest of Europe and 12.25kr to other countries; letters up to 100 grammes cost 5.75kr to Denmark, 8kr to the rest of Scandinavia, 13kr to the rest of Europe and 18kr to other countries.

Poste restante

Mail can be received care of Poste Restante and collected from any post office in Denmark; it will normally only be kept for two weeks. If Poste Restante mail isn't addressed to a specific post office, it will be sent to the main post office in Vesterbro (*see above*).

Express delivery services

Budstikken is a private courier company approved by the public mail services. Call 33 26 90 00 (24 hours) for information.

Public holidays

The following are public holidays in Denmark:
New Year's Day (Nytårsdag; 1 Jan);
Maundy Thursday (Skærtorsdag; 1 Mar 2001; 14 Feb 2002);
Good Friday (Langfredag; 13 Apr 2001; 29 Mar 2002);

Directory

Easter Monday (2.påskedag;
16 Apr 2001; 1 Apr 2002);
Day of Prayer (Stor Bededag;
11 May 2001; 26 Apr 2002);
Ascension Day (Kristi
Himmelfartsdag; 24 May 2001;
9 May 2002);
Whit Monday (2.pinsedag;
4 June 2001; 20 May 2002);
Constitution Day (Grundlovsdag;
5 June; from noon);
Christmas (Jule; 24-26 Dec).

Most businesses and banks
close on public holidays. School
summer holidays in Denmark
run from about the third week
in June to the second in August,
and schools also take a week
off in February, in mid October
and over Christmas and New
Year. Many Danes take their
main summer holidays in the
first three weeks of July.

Public toilets

There is no shortage of public
toilets in Copenhagen; most are
clean and free to use.

Religion

There are close ties between
Church and State in Denmark
and the Constitution declares
the **Evangelical Lutheran
Church** to be the national
church. The **Danish
Folkekirken** (the People's
Church) is funded by church
members through 'Church
Tax', but in spite of the fact
that most Danes (87 per cent)
are members, only a few would
call themselves religious.
Many churches are empty on
Sundays, and are mainly used
at Christmas, Easter, or for
private arrangements such as
weddings. The second largest
religious community in
Denmark is Muslim, the
third Roman Catholic. The
following churches hold
services in English.

American Church

*US Embassy, Dag Hammarskjöld
Allé 24, Østerbro (35 55 31 44).*
Services phone for details.
Map p307 G14.
Protestant and interdenominational.

Great Synagogue

Krystalgade 12 (33 12 88 68).
Services 6.45am Mon, Thur; 7am
Tue, Wed, Fri; 9am Sat; 8am Sun.
Map p311 M13.

International Church of Copenhagen

*Vartov Church, Farvergade 27
(39 62 47 85).* **Services** 11.30am
Sun. **Map** p311 O13.
Affiliated with the American
Lutheran Church.

St Alban's Church

*Churchill Parken, Langelinie (39 62
77 36).* **Services** *Holy Communion*
10.30am, 6.30pm Wed; 9am, 10.30am
Sun. **Map** p308 J18.

Sakrementskirken

*Nørrebrogade 27, Nørrebro
(44 94 76 78). Bus 5, 16, 4E, 350S.*
Services 5pm Wed; 6pm Sun.
Map p306 J10.
Roman Catholic.

Sankt Annæ Kirke

*Hans Bogbinders Allé 2, Amager
(32 58 21 02). Bus 2, 11, 28, 250S,
350S, 73E.* **Services** 5pm Sat, Sun.
Roman Catholic.

Smoking

The number of smokers in
Denmark is decreasing, but
34 per cent of Danes still can't
live without their cigarettes,
and the percentage of female
smokers remains among the
highest in Europe. The
attitude to smoking is
generally quite liberal, and
smoking is permitted in
most cafés and restaurants,
although it's not usually
allowed in public buildings,
schools and on public
transport. But wherever you
are it's always a good idea to
check for no-smoking signs
before you light up.

Students

Danish institutions for higher
education have a friendly
and open-minded policy
towards international students.
Exchange programmes
provide links between
Danish universities and their
international counterparts and
in recent years exchanges have

increasingly been developed
through programmes such
as SOCRATES/ERASMUS,
LINGUA and TEMPUS, which
are all supported by the
European Union.

Some of the institutions
also have summer schools,
and the largest universities
and colleges have their own
international offices. For more
information on courses, contact
the individual institutions.

Universities/colleges

Copenhagen's universities
and colleges offer a variety
of qualifications over a broad
spectrum of subjects. The
University of Copenhagen
(35 32 26 26/www.ku.dk) is the
city's flagship establishment.
Founded in 1479, it is
Denmark's oldest educational
institution, and, with 35,000
students, it's also the largest.
The city has two business
schools, **Copenhagen
Business School** (38 15 38
15/www.handelshoejskolen.dk)
and **Niels Brock College**
(31 41 94 00/www.brock.dk)
that combine expert tutoring
with strong ties to the
Danish business community.
**Det Kongelige Danske
Kunstakademi** (33 74 45
00/www.kunstakademiet.dk),
the Royal Academy of Fine
Arts, offers a variety of fine art
courses and tutoring, as well
as incorporating the **School
of Architecture** (32 68
60 00/www.karch.dk), the
Danish Film School (32
68 64 00/www.filmskolen.dk),
the **National Drama School**
(32 83 61 00/www.teaterskolen.
dk) and the **Rhythmic
Music Conservatory** (32
68 67 00/www.rmc.dk).
**Det Kongelige Danske
Musikkonservatorium**
(33 69 22 69/www.dkdm.dk),
the Royal Danish Music
Conservatory, is located next
to the Glyptotek and places
an emphasis on classical
music training.

International offices

Copenhagen Business School
International Office, Dalgas Have 15, 2000 Frederiksberg (38 15 30 06). Bus 1, 14. **Open** 10am-noon, 1-3pm daily.

Roskilde Universitetscenter
International Office, Bygning 01, Postbox 260, 4000 Roskilde (46 74 20 06). **Open** 9am-12.30pm Mon, Wed, Fri, 12.30-3.45pm Tue; closed Thur, Sat, Sun.
The international office has the overall responsibility for international activities at Roskilde University. These include co-operative programmes like ERASMUS.

University of Copenhagen
International Office, Fiolstræde 24, 1, 1010 København K (35 32 26 26/www.ku.dk/sa/inter). **Open** 10am-3pm Mon-Fri; closed Sat, Sun. **Map** p311 M13.
Offers advice to exchange students at the University of Copenhagen on practical as well as academic matters, including admission, course registration, exam transcripts, housing, mentor contacts and contacts with other universities.

Other organisations

AFS Interkultur (American Field Service)
Nordre Fasanvej 111, 2000 Frederiksberg (38 34 33 00/www.afs.dk). Bus 39, 100S, 171E. **Open** 10am-4pm Mon-Fri.
AFS is an international, voluntary organisation that provides educational exchange programmes for people between 15 and 30 years of age.

STS High School and Au Pair
Klosterstræde 13 (33 36 67 67/www.sts.dk). **Open** 9am-5pm Mon-Thur; 9am-3pm Fri. **Map** p311 N13.
STS provides personal and/or academic education at high schools, language schools or for au pairs. You have to be between ten and 26 years of age, depending on which programme you want to follow.

Libraries

Hovedbiblioteket
Krystalgade 15 (33 73 60 60/www.kkb.bib.dk). **Open** 10am-7pm Mon-Fri; 10am-2pm Sat. **Map** p311 M13.

The central library has international newspapers and magazines in English, phone and fax facilities and colour photocopying.

Det Kongelige Bibliotek
Christians Brygge 8 (33 47 47 47/www.kb.dk). **Open** *Information & lending department Sept-May* 10am-7pm Mon-Fri; 10am-2pm Sat; closed Sun. *June-Aug* 10am-5pm Mon-Fri; 10am-2pm Sat; closed Sun. *General Reading Rooms Sept-May* 10am-5pm Mon, Tue, Thur, Fri; noon-7pm Wed; closed Sat, Sun. *Sept-Dec* 10am-4pm Mon, Tue, Thur, Fri; noon-4pm Wed; closed Sat, Sun. *Newspapers & periodicals Sept-May* 10am-4pm Mon, Tue, Thur, Fri; 10am-7pm Wed; closed Sat, Sun. *June-Aug* 10am-4pm Mon, Tue, Thur, Fri; closed Wed, Sat, Sun. *Research Reading Room Sept-May* 10am-9pm Mon-Fri; 10am-7pm Sat; closed Sun. *June-Aug* 10am-7pm Mon-Fri; 10am-4pm Sat; closed Sun. *Exhibitions* 10am-7pm Mon-Fri; closed Sat, Sun. **Admission** free. **Map** p311 P15.
The Royal Library on Slotsholmen is Denmark's national library, but the building (including the stunning 'Black Diamond' extension; *see p86*) also serves as a general research centre, a cultural centre and a meeting place (within the building is the chic **Søren K** restaurant; *see p140*).

Telephones

Like most public services in Denmark, the phone system is efficient and simple to use. Danish phone numbers have eight digits and there are no area codes.

International dialling codes

The international dialling code for Denmark is 45. Thus, to dial Copenhagen from outside Denmark, dial 00 45 and then the eight-digit number.

To call abroad from Denmark, dial 00 followed by the country access code, the area code (minus the initial 0, if there is one), and then the local number. The international code for the UK is 44; 1 for the US/Canada; 353 for Ireland; 61 for Australia.

Mobile phones

Denmark is part of the worldwide GSM network, so compatible mobile phones should work without any problems. If your phone is not GSM compatible you will have to contact your own service provider before you leave for Denmark. The following are Denmark's main service providers (all lines are open 24 hours and calls are free):
Mobilix *80 40 40 40.*
Sonofon *80 29 29 29.*
TeleDanmark *80 80 80 20.*
Telia *80 10 10 80.*

Operator services

For directory enquiries, call 118 (domestic) or 113 (international). For operator assistance, call 141 (free of charge) or 80 60 40 10. You will be charged if the operator connects you.

Public phones

You'll find both card- and coin-operated phones in Denmark. Cards ('telekort') come in denominations of 30, 50 and 100kr and can be used for both local and international calls; they are available from kiosks and post offices. Coin phones will accept 1, 5, 10 and 20kr pieces for local or international calls.

Telegrams

The easiest way to send telegrams is over the phone; dial 122 or 80 60 40 10. To send a three-line telegram within Denmark costs 160kr, or 320kr if you want to send one abroad. You can also send telegrams from post offices.

Time & dates

Denmark observes Central European Time, usually one hour ahead of Greenwich Mean Time, and six hours

Directory

ahead of Eastern Standard Time. Clocks are moved a further hour forward between the last Sunday in March and the last Sunday in October. Thus in summer, Copenhagen will be two hours ahead of London and seven hours ahead of New York. Danes use the 24-hour clock.

When writing dates, Danes follow the day with the month, so 7 January 2002 will be written 7/1/02.

Tipping

Service is normally included on restaurant, hotel and taxi bills, so any further tips should only be given for unusually good service. It's not uncommon, however, to round up a bill.

Tourist information

In addition to the resources available at the tourist offices below, the website **www.aok.dk** is an indispensable source of information on festivals, arts and entertainment in Copenhagen, plus listings of where to eat and drink. There's also a link to the *Copenhagen Post* (*see page 288*), an English-Danish dictionary, and even a talking phrase book. For other useful websites, *see page 295*.

Danish Tourist Board
Vesterbrogade 6D, 1606 Copenhagen V (www.visitdenmark.com).
If you plan to travel beyond the capital, this is the place to come for all the necessary information. The website is very useful for both practical advice and news about forth-coming attractions. The DTB don't encourage personal callers.

Use It
Rådhusstræde 13, 1466 Copenhagen (33 73 06 20/fax 33 73 06 49/ www.useit.dk). **Open** *Mid Sept-mid June* 11am-4pm Mon-Wed, Fri; 11am-6pm Thur; 11am-2pm Sat; closed Sun. *Mid June-mid Sept* 9am-7pm daily. **Map** p311 O13.

Aimed primarily at youthful visitors to the city, this excellent resource centre can supply not just printed info, but can also book rooms, hold mail and store luggage. The website is also well worth a look.

Wonderful Copenhagen Tourist Information Bureau
Bernstorffsgade 1, 1577 Copenhagen (33 11 13 25/70 22 24 52/ www.woco.dk). Open *1 May-1 Sept* 9am-8pm daily. *2 Sept-30 Apr* 9am-4.30pm Mon-Fri; 9am-1.30pm Sat; closed Sun. **Map** p310 P11.
The official Copenhagen tourist office has a wealth of information on the city's attractions and offers a free accommodation booking service.

VAT refund

VAT (MOMS) on goods in Denmark is levied at 20 per cent. Non-EU residents are entitled to claim back 14 to 19 per cent of the total price of any item bought in the country (providing that the purchase exceeds 300kr, and that Denmark is their final EU destination before returning home). Visitors should ask shops to issue a **Global Refund Cheque** for each purchase. These should then be stamped by customs (in Copenhagen Airport's Terminal 3) before you check in your luggage, and then handed in at the **Global Refund** desk in the Transit Hall (6.30am-10pm daily). For further information, contact Global Refund Danmark (32 52 55 66/fax 32 52 55 61/ www.globalrefund.com).

Visas/passports

Citizens of EU countries (outside Scandinavia) require a national ID card or passport valid for the duration of their stay in order to enter Denmark for tourist visits of up to three months. US citizens require a passport valid only for the duration of their stay, but citizens of Canada, Australia and New Zealand require passports valid for two

months beyond the last day of visit. South African citizens need to apply for a tourist visa prior to travel.

Weights & measures

Denmark uses the metric system. Decimal points are indicated by commas, while thousands are defined by full stops. In this Guide we have listed all measurements in both metric and imperial.

When to go

Considering it's northerly location, the climate in Denmark isn't particularly severe. However, **winters** are cold and some tourist attractions are closed. **Spring** kicks off in late April, but can take a while to warm up. May and June are usually fresh and bright, with warm temperatures and not too many tourists. **Summer** peak season is in July and August, when Copenhagen's street life is at its most vibrant and enjoyable – there are plenty of festivals and open-air events – and lots of visitors. (Although, be warned that some restaurants are closed in July.) By mid August the Danish school year has started, and from then into September and early **Autumn** is a particularly good time to visit, with fewer tourists and kids, but still plenty to see and do and (hopefully) mild weather.

Women

Denmark is a country famously committed to equal opportunities for all citizens, and a lot of effort has been made to achieve equal rights for women. The State's generous childcare programmes, and welfare for the elderly and disabled, have

After you…

Probably more vexing for American and British tourists than worries about the virtually non-existent risk of crime in Copenhagen is the question of everyday manners. Ordinarily, Copenhageners are the most friendly of people. They are usually delighted to assist tourists, or just shoot the breeze, and have a remarkable ability to appear (or perhaps they really are) genuinely interested in strangers. They appreciate you coming to their capital and will exhibit uncontained joy if you can give examples of why you like it so much.

But, when it comes to common courtesies, like opening doors, moving aside to let someone through, or, worst of all, queueing (despite their ordered façade, the Danes are shameless queue-jumpers, so bus stops are essentially chaotic free-for-alls), they revert to Viking type. Open the door to Illum department store to allow a Copenhagener to walk through in front of you and not only will you be ignored, you'll need Moses to part the waves of opportunists who will march straight through without so much as a nod of thanks. Unless you have your wits about you, you will be shoulder-barged on buses, lose your place in queues, or die of frustration waiting for a thank you. Most tellingly of all, 'please' is a word that simply does not exist in the Danish language.

helped women achieve a strong position in the job market. Danish women, as a rule, are assured, independent and entirely comfortable with their equal status with males in Danish society. However, this development also has its down sides – you'll not find many Danish men who will hold the door open for a woman… (*see above* **After you…**).

Women visitors to Denmark are very unlikely to encounter any harrassment problems. Copenhagen is one of the world's safest cities, even after dark, although, of course, it makes sense to take the usual precautions.

Kvindehuset

Christians Brygge 3 (33 14 28 04). **Open** noon-5.30pm Mon-Fri; closed Sat, Sun. **Map** p311 P15. A cultural centre for women. Recycling of clothes, lesbian films, a choir, an artists group, folk dances, social events and debates are held regularly.

KVINFO

Christians Brygge 3 (33 13 50 88/ www.kvinfo.dk). **Open** *Sept-June* 10am-6pm Mon-Thur; closed Fri-Sun. *July-Aug* 1-5pm Mon-Thur; closed Fri-Sun. **Map** p311 P15. The Danish Centre for Information on Women and Gender has a wealth of resources relating to women's issues, including a library and information centre for gender studies.

Working in Copenhagen

As most people in Denmark speak English, and many companies use English as a working language, it is not too hard to find a job in Denmark. The current unemployment rate is very low.

EURES is a database of job vacancies throughout the EU and contains useful information about working conditions throughout Europe. It can be consulted at job centres in most European countries.

Det Danske Kulturinstitut

Kultorvet 2, 1175 Copenhagen K (33 13 54 48). The Institute publishes a range of literature about the country and arranges job exchange programmes for a number of professions.

Work permits

All EU citizens can obtain a work permit in Denmark; non-EU citizens must apply for a work permit abroad and hand in the application to a Danish embassy or consular representation. The rules for obtaining work permits vary for different jobs; contact Danish Immigration Service:

Udlændingestyrelsen

Ryesgade 53, 2100 Copenhagen Ø (35 36 66 00/fax 35 36 19 16/ www.udlst.dk). **Open** 8.30am-noon Mon-Wed, Fri; 8.30am-noon, 3.30-5.30pm Thur; closed Sat, Sun.

Useful addresses

The **EU** has a website (http://citizens.eu.int) and helpline (80 01 02 01) providing general information on your rights and useful telephone numbers and addresses in your home country. It also holds specific information on the rules for recognition of diplomas, your rights on access to employment, rights of residence and social security, the national education system and a route map for job applicants in the EU.

For general information about the Danish tax system, take a look at the **Skatteministeriet** (Danish Ministry of Taxation) website (www.skat.dk) or contact **Told-og Skattestyrelsen** (Customs and tax administration) with more specific questions.

Told-og Skattestyrelsen

Østbanegade 123, 2100 Copenhagen Ø (35 29 73 00/fax 35 43 47 20). **Phone enquiries** 8.30am-4pm Mon-Thur; 8.30am-3.30pm Fri; closed Sat, Sun.

Directory

The Language

Danish can be a deceptive language. Although its written form is not impenetrable to those with a little knowledge of Germanic languages, spoken Danish is packed with idiosyncratic quirks (such as frequent glottal stops and the swallowing of parts of words) that make pronunciation a minefield for the uninitiated. Add to this the fact that so many Danes have excellent English and it's tempting for visitors not to bother to try to learn any Danish. As with most countries, though, an attempt to learn a few basics is always appreciated.

Here's a brief guide to pronunciation and some useful basics. Note that, in Danish, the definite article 'the' (-et or -en) is often added to the end of the relevant noun. Thus, 'Nationalmuseet' translates as 'the National Museum. Also, there is no possessive apostrophe in Danish (eg Thorvaldsens Museum).

Vowels

a	as in 'rather' or as in 'pat'
å, u(n)	as in 'or'
e(g), e(j)	as in 'shy'
e, æ	as in 'set'
i	as in 'be'
ø	a short 'er' sound
o	as in 'rot' or as in 'do'
o(v)	a short 'ow', as in 'cow'
u	as in 'bull' or as in 'do'
y	a long, hybrid of 'ee' and 'oo'

Consonants

sj	as in 'shot'
ch	as in 'shot'
c	as in 'send', but as in 'key' before a, o, u and consonants
(o)d	as the 'th' in 'those'
j	as the 'y' in 'year'
g	as in 'got', when before vowels
h	as in 'heart'
k	as in 'key'
b	as in 'bag'
r	a short guttural 'r' (less guttural after a vowel)
w	a 'v' sound

Useful words/phrases

yes	ja, jo ('ya', 'yo')
no	nej ('ny')
please	vær så god ('verser-go') vær så venlig (verser venlee')
thank you	tak ('tack')
hello (formal)	goddag ('godday')
hello (informal)	hej ('hi')
I understand	jeg forstår ('yie for-stor')
I don't understand	jeg forstår ikke ('yie for-stor icker')
do you speak English?	taler du engelsk ('tarler doo engelsk')?
excuse me (sorry)	undskyld ('unsgull')
go away!	forsvind! ('for-svin')

indgang	entrance
udgang	exit
åben	open
lukket	closed
toiletter	toilets (herrer: men; damer: women)
today	i dag
tonight	i aften/i nat
tomorrow	i morgen
yesterday	i går
Monday	mandag
Tuesday	tirsdag
Wednesday	onsdag
Thursday	torsdag
Friday	fredag
Saturday	lørdag
Sunday	søndag
January	januar
February	februar
March	marts
April	april
May	maj
June	juni
July	juli
August	august
September	september
October	oktober
November	november
December	december

0	nul
1	en
2	to
3	tre
4	fire
5	fem
6	seks
7	syv
8	otte
9	ni
10	ti
20	tyve
30	tredive
40	fyrre
50	halvtreds
60	tres
70	halvfjerds
80	firs
90	halvfems
100	hundrede
1,000	tusind
1,000,000	million

Food & drink glossary

æble	apple
æg	egg
ærter	peas
appelsin	orange
banan	banana
brød	bread
bønner	beans
champignon	mushroom
chokolade	chocolate
citron	lemon
dampet	steamed
eddike	vinegar
fadøl	draught beer
fisk	fish
fløde	cream
forel	trout
frisk	fresh
frugt	fruit
grilleret	grilled
gryderet	stew
grøn bønne	green bean
grøntsager	vegetables
gulerødder	carrots
hvidløg	garlic
is	ice-cream/ice
jordbær	strawberry
kaffe	coffee
kage	cake
kål	cabbage
kartoffel	potato
kød	meat
kogt	boiled
kold	cold
kylling	chicken
laks	salmon
lamme	lamb
løg	onion
marineret	marinated
mælk	milk
nødder	nuts
oksekød	beef
øl	beer
olie	oil
ost	cheese
ovnstegt	roasted
peber	pepper
pocheret	poached
pommes frites	fries/chips
pølse	hot dog
ris	rice
røget	smoked
rå	raw
senap	mustard
sild	herring
skinke	ham
smør	butter
stegt	fried
suker	sugar
supper	soup
svinekød	pork
te	tea
torsk	cod
vand	water
varm	warm, hot

Further Reference

Books

Non-fiction

JR Christianson *On Tycho's Island: Tycho Brahe and His Assistants, 1570-1601.*
Biography of the famous astronomer.

Helen Dyrbye, Steven Harris, Thomas Golzen *Xenophobe's Guide to the Danes.*
Irreverent, spot-on dissection of Denmark and the Danes.

Vivian Greene-Gantzburg *Biography of 19th-century Danish Literary Impressionist Herman Bang (1857-1912).*
A detailed biog of Danish novelist and avant-courier of European impressionism, Herman Bang.

Carsten Holbraad *Danish Neutrality.*
Analytical account of Danish foreign policy from 1720 to 1990 that examines a succession of different versions of the nation's neutrality.

Stig Hornshøj-Møller *A Short History of Denmark.*
Authoritative summary of the country's past from the Stone Age to the present day.

Jorgen Steen Jensen, John Lund, Bundgaard Rasmussen (eds) *Christian VIII and the National Museum.*
An examination of the contribution made by King Christian VIII (1839-48) to the foundation of the National Museum in Copenhagen.

Gwyn Jones *A History of the Vikings*
An authoritative and readable account of Vikings and their world.

Thorkild Kjærgaard *The Danish Revolution, 1500-1800: An Ecohistorical Interpretation.*
A study of how over-population, extensive military armament and exploitation of natural resources led to an ecological crisis in 18th-century Denmark.

Ellen Levine *Darkness over Denmark: The Danish Resistance and the Rescue of the Jews.*
The story of the exodus of Danish Jews to Sweden during the war.

Lansing D McLoskey *Twentieth Century Danish Music.*
An overview of influential figures and stylistic developments in 20th-century Danish music.

Kasper Monrad, Philip Conisbee, Bjarne Jornaes *The Golden Age of Danish Painting.*
The works of 17 painters from the first half of the 19th century.

Herbert Pundik *In Denmark It Could Not Happen: The Flight of the Jews to Sweden in 1943.*
Another account of the war-time escape of the Jews in Denmark.

Peter Sawyer (ed) *The Oxford Illustrated History of the Vikings*
An enjoyable, lavishly illustrated journey through Viking history.

Bridgette Soland *Becoming Modern*
A detailed examination of how notions of femininity and womanhood were reshaped in Denmark after World War I.

Ray Spangenburg, Diane K. Moser, Diane Moser *Niels Bohr: Gentle Genius of Denmark (Makers of Modern Science).*
Analysis of the great Danish nuclear physicist.

Paul Strathern *Kierkegaard in 90 Minutes (Philosophers in 90 Minutes).*
An attempt to make sense of the thoughts of the founding father of existentialism.

Alastair H Thomas, Stewart P Oakley *Historical Dictionary of Denmark.*
An invaluable reference book charting Denmark's cultural history from its earliest archaeological remains to the modern, design-obsessed nation.

Victor E Thoren *The Lord of Uraniborg.*
Detailed and informative biography of 16th-century astronomer Tycho Brahe.

Christopher Woodward *The Buildings of Europe: Copenhagen.*
This informative guide details all of Copenhagen's significant buildings. Photographs, dates, architects and locations are provided.

Fiction

See also p296 **20th-century Danish Writers**.

Hans Christian Andersen *The Complete Fairy Tales.*
More than 150 of the great Dane's best-loved fairy tales.

David Hare *Copenhagen.*
Play based on the visit of the great German physicist Werner Heisenberg to his erstwhile mentor and friend Niels Bohr in Copenhagen in 1941.

Virginia Haviland (ed) *Favorite Fairy Tales Told in Denmark.*
An extensive collection of traditional Danish fairy tales.

Jacqueline Simpson (ed) *Danish Legends.*
This collection comprises over 160 Danish folktales and legends.

William Shakespeare *Hamlet.*
The bard's Danish blockbuster.

Willy Sorensen *Harmless Tales.*
In these tales, bizarre and surreal episodes continually disrupt the frenetic attempts of the author's characters to live in an ordered and predictable world.

Rose Tremain *Music And Silence.*
Beautifully written fictional account of the latter years of Christian IV.

Film

See page 196.

Music

See pages 224 and 228.

Websites

AOK.dk
www.aok.dk/Copenhagen/Visiting_Copenhagen
Extensive details of the major museums, galleries and sights (with information on current exhibitions), shops, tours, etc, plus a search engine. The English is faltering.

Copenhagen Mushroom Site
www.cheathouse.com/cmc/
Weird and wonderful – and we're not talking morels or shiitake. Only in Danish though.

Copenhagen News
www.copenhagennews.com
Portal to news about Copenhagen and Denmark appearing in the world's media.

Copenhagen NOW
http://copenhagen.now.dk
Comprehensive listings of hotels, restaurants, bars, theatres, live music and attractions in and around the city. No editorial comment though.

Copenhagen Post
www.cphpost.dk
Weekly news in English from the Danish capital. The *In & Out* guide provides a selection of the best restaurants, cafés, bars, clubs and concerts, and a day-by-day guide to what's on in the city.

Crafts.dk
www.crafts.dk
Well-designed site offering a wealth of information about modern crafts and design in Denmark.

DSB (Danish State Railways)
www.dsb.dk
Journey planner for train journeys within Denmark (in English). Rest of site is in Danish.

Directory

Danish Tourist Board
www.dt.dk
The national tourist board's website
offers a good general guide to
Denmark and Copenhagen, with
useful information on accommodation
(with direct links to hotel websites),
restaurants, transport, attractions
and activities.

Find a Grave
www.findagrave.com/country/27.html
Find where the famous are buried in
Copenhagen's graveyards. .

HT
www.ht.dk/turist/engelsk.htm
Detailed information from the city's
bus authority on getting around
Copenhagen by bus and train.

Jazz in Copenhagen
www.mic.dk/jazz/index.htm
An excellent resource for jazz lovers.
Includes a rundown of Copenhagen's
distinguished jazz history, profiles
of, and interviews with, the top
Danish jazz musicians, info on the
Copenhagen Jazz Festival and details
of the city's jazz venues and prices.

20th-century Danish writers

Karen Blixen (1885-1962)

See page 271.

Tom Kristensen (1893-1974)

Though popular in Germany and Spain,
Kristensen has never been introduced to
the English-speaking world, which is a pity
considering the profound success of his
autobiographical *Hærværk* (*Vandalism*), about
a journalist drinking himself to death. Feeling
he had nothing to live for, he sunk deeper
and deeper into depression, before suddenly
making an about face, and spending his last
years leading the life of a saint.

Aksel Sandemose (1899-1965)

Loved by the Danish public, despite having
turned his back on Denmark, Sandemose
moved to Norway in 1930 to get away from
the Danes, who he felt were like a flock of
lemmings. His famous *Janteloven* (*The Law
of Jante*) was a fictitious legal precedent
used in several of his books to describe the
way Danes stab each other in the back,
and reward success with alienation (see
also page 15). Sandemose wrote many
masterpieces, most of which are available
in English, but *The Werewolf* (*Varulven*) and
A Fugitive Crosses His Tracks (*En Flygtning
Krydser Sit Spor*) are among his best.

Martin A Hansen (1909-55)

Several of Hansen's books are available in
English, including his masterpiece of small-
town life *The Liar* (*Løgneren*). Hansen's
depictions of intimate power struggles,
combined with his ironic distance, make
him seem quite critical, if not cynical, but,
if the truth be known, Hansen loved his
subjects dearly.

Halfdan Rasmussen (1915-)

Incredibly Danish, incredibly funny, this prolific
multi-talent is known for his beautiful use of
the Danish language – which is probably the
reason he's never been translated to English.
One of his good friends, the late crime

novelist and public spectacle Dan Turrèll (see
page 297), teamed up with him for a book
that is a must for any cult Copenhagener.

Tove Ditlevsen (1917-76)

Perhaps the best-loved author in modern
Danish history. Ditlevsen was a tragic figure,
and eventually took her own life in 1976.
From her debut in 1939 she wrote social
realist depictions of life among the extreme
poor in Copenhagen's Vesterbro district. One
of her major works, *Early Spring* (*Det Tidlige
Forår*), is available in English.

Martha Christensen (1926-95)

Christensen has been well received both in
Denmark and abroad after the huge success
of the film version of her book *Dansen Med
Regitze* (filmed as *Memories of a Marriage*),
with the queen of Danish film and theatre
Gitte Nørby in the lead. Until then, the prolific
Christensen had gone relatively unnoticed.

Klaus Rifbjerg (1931-)

Often credited with revitalising the Danish
language with his incredibly beautiful poetry,
Rifbjerg is mostly a poet and critic, and is
nationally respected. Fear of the unknown
is a recurring theme in his work, as are
the colours and sounds of Spain, where
he spends much of his time. His most
recent book available in English is *War*
(*Krigen*, 1995).

Poul Borum (1934-96)

To his dying day an *enfant terrible*, Borum
founded the Author School in Copenhagen
and was instrumental in redefining critical
journalism and editorial in his later years.
Despite his freakish punk rock clothes and
piercings, Borum commanded respect for his
prolific writings, and the quality of teaching he
afforded his students at the Author School.

Inger Christensen (1935-)

Of all Danish 20th-century poets, Inger
Christensen and Henrik Nordbrandt are
considered the most important. The heaviest

Directory

Use It
www.useit.dk
This excellent government-funded organisation offers a wealth of free information for young, budget concious visitors to Copenhagen. The website was being redesigned as this Guide went to press but promises to be a valuable resource.

Where 2 Go
www.where2go.dk
The Where 2 Go site includes an excellent interactive map of Copenhagen that features remarkably smooth scrolling and zoom facilities. The level of content (bars, cafés, shops, restaurants, etc) is relatively low, but this is one to watch.

Wonderful Copenhagen
www.woco.dk/www.visitdenmark.com
The official website of the city's tourist authority offers detailed information about the city's hotels, restaurants, bars, theatres theme parks and museums. The exhaustive guide to sights and attractions is particularly useful.

intellectuals prefer Christensen, no doubt because of her incredibly artistic use of the Danish language, especially evident in *Azorno*, which is based on the logic of a Chinese box. Her popularity in Germany is enormous for a Danish poet, and two of her novels have recently been translated into English: *Alphabet* (*Alfabet*, 2000) and *The Painted Room* (*Det Malede Værelse*, 2000).

Henrik Stangerup (1937-98)
Brother of popular fiction novelist Helle Stangerup (close friend of Queen Margrethe), Henrik Stangerup and his sister are said to have a less than amicable relationship. In fact, familial instability is a recurring theme in his books. He's well known for his film scripts, and his novels are very popular. *The Road to Lagoa Santa* (*Vejen til Lagoa Santa*) and *Mother: A Son's Remembrance* (*Mor*) are two of his translated works.

Suzanne Brøgger (1944-)
Debuting in 1973, Brøgger has become one of the most important contemporary novelists and playwrights in Denmark. Her work re-evaluates feminism, tending to focus on the shared predicament of all women when it comes time to foot the bill for the struggle. *The Jade Cat* (*Jadekatten*), about the rise and fall of a Jewish Danish family, along the lines of Orson Welles' *Magnificent Ambersons*, is considered her best. *A Fighting Pig's Too Tough To Eat* (*En gris som har været oppe at slås kan man ikke stege*) is one of her few works translated to English.

Ib Michael (1945-)
Ib Michael is the only Danish author who can claim to write in the style of magical realism. His many journeys through Latin America and Asia have inspired him, and their mystical and magical worlds are evident in all of his work. He's won just about every prize an author can win in Denmark, and his newest novel *Prince* (*Prins*, 1999) is his first to be translated into English.

Henrik Nordbrandt (1945-)
Winner of the Nordic Council's literature prize, among others, Nordbrandt is loved and respected in Denmark for his poetry. Having lived in self-imposed exile in various Mediterranean countries for most of his life, it is no wonder that he is often characterised as a stateless poet. He has produced 20 poetry collections, several books of essays, a few children's books, a Turkish diary and a cookbook. Two of his collections, *Selected Poems* (1982) and *Armenia* (1982) are available in English.

Dan Turèll (1946-93)
One of the very best-known and loved authors in Denmark. Turèll's decadent habits eventually caught up with him, as he recklessly lived himself to an early death at the age of 47. Seldom has there been an author that could describe social realistic Copenhagen like Turèll. Appropriately, he's even had a bar named after him (see page 147).

Peter Høeg (1957-)
The former ballet dancer is the author of five bestsellers, all translated into English. Among them, *Miss Smilla's Feeling for Snow* (*Frøken Smilla's Fornemmelse for Sne*) is probably the most famous, although probably his most critically acclaimed work is *The Naked Ape* (*Den Nøgne Abe*). Høeg's international success has been instrumental in focusing attention on contemporary Danish literature.

Michæl Strunge (1958-86)
Translated into five languages, this controversial poet was the voice of a generation, and one of the prime movers of poetry's rebirth in hip late '70s/early '80s Copenhagen. At the time of his suicide, Strunge had developed a following that spanned the nation, appealing to the disenfranchised and downtrodden with his soulful yet harsh prose.

Directory

Advertisers' Index

Please refer to the relevant pages for addresses and telephone numbers.

Index

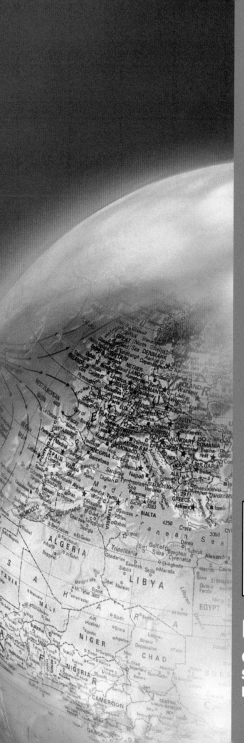

Place of Interest and/or Entertainment	
Railway Station	
Park	
College/Hospital	
Pedestrian Streets	
Area Name . . . . AMAGER	

Maps

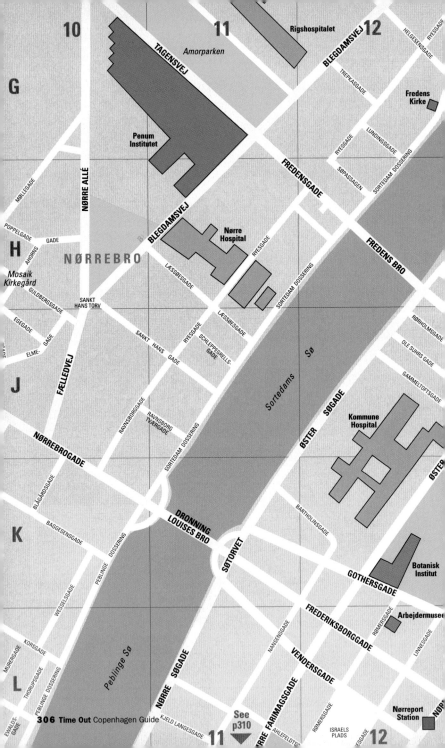

Rigshospitalet

HELGESENSGADE

RYESGADE

TAGENSVEJ

Amorparken

G

BLEGDAMSVEJ

TREPKASSADE

Fredens
Kirke

Penum
Institutet

FREDENSGADE

RYESGADE

LUNDINGSGADE

SØPASSAGEN

SORTEDAM DOSSERING

NØRRE ALLÉ

GADE

MØLLEGADE

POPPELGADE

H

BLEGDAMSVEJ

Nørre
Hospital

FREDENS BRO

NØRREBRO

AHORNS

LÆSSØESGADE

RYESGADE

SORTEDAM DOSSERING

Mosaik
Kirkegård

GULDBERGSGADE

SANKT
HANS TORV

RØRHOLMSGADE

EGEGADE

LÆSSØESGADE

ELME-

GADE

SANKT HANS GADE

RYESGADE

SCHLEPPEGRELLS-
GADE

Sortedams Sø

OLE SUHRS GADE

GAMMELTOFTSGADE

J

FÆLLEDVEJ

RAVNSBORGGADE

RAVNSBORG
TVÆRGADE

SORTEDAM DOSSERING

ØSTER SØGADE

Kommune
Hospital

ØSTER

NØRREBROGADE

BLÅGÅRDSGADE

BAGGESENSGADE

K

PEBLINGE DOSSERING

DRONNING
LOUISES BRO

BARTHOLINSGADE

WESSELSGADE

SØTORVET

GOTHERSGADE

Botanisk
Institut

FREDERIKSBORGGADE

Arbejdermuseer

RØMERSGADE

LINNESGADE

NANSENSGADE

VENDERSGADE

L

MURERGADE

KORSGADE

THORUPSGADE

PEBLINGE DOSSERING

Peblinge Sø

NØRRE SØGADE

NØRRE FARIMAGSGADE

RØMERSGADE

Nørreport
Station

NØR

EWALDS-
GADE

KJELD LANGESGADE

▼

See
p310

AHLEFELDTS

ISRAELS
PLADS

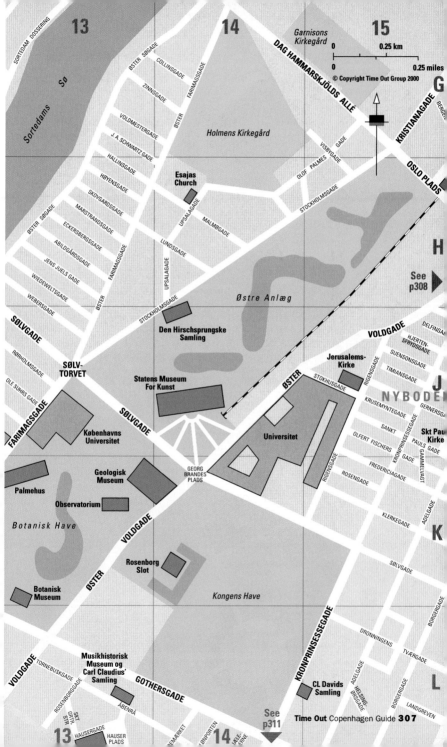

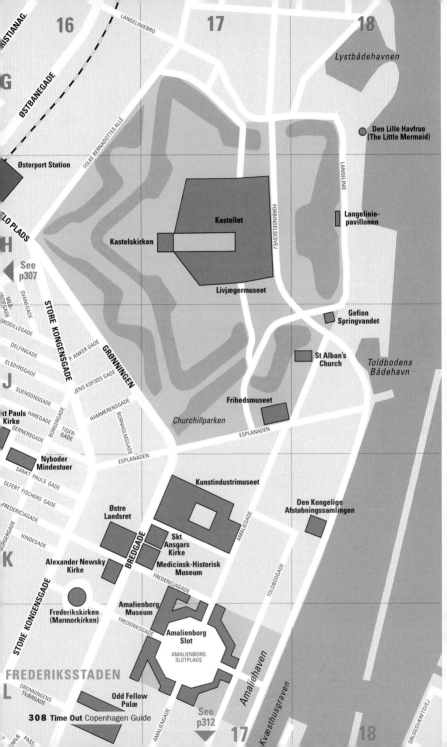

Lystbådehavnen

ØSTBANEGADE

CHRISTIANAG.

G

LANGELINIEBRO

FOLKE BERNADOTTES ALLÉ

Den Lille Havfrue
(The Little Mermaid)

Østerport Station

LANGELINIE

LO PLADS

Kastellet

Langelinie-
pavillonen

H

FORBINDELSESVEJ

Kastelskirken

See
p307

STORE KONGENSGADE

SVANEGADE

SKODILLEGADE

WILD
ANDG.

Livjægermuseet

Gefion
Springvandet

GRØNNINGEN

DELFINGADE

P. ANKER GADE

ELSDYRSGADE

St Alban's
Church

*Toldbodens
Bådehavn*

J

SUENSONSGADE

JENS KOFODS GADE

HAMMERENSGADE

BORNHOLMSGADE

Frihedsmuseet

t Pauls
Kirke

HAREGADE

BORGERGADE

GERNERSGADE

TIGER-
GADE

Churchillparken

ESPLANADEN

SANKT PAULS GADE

Nyboder
Mindestuer

ESPLANADEN

Kunstindustrimuseet

OLFERT FISCHERS GADE

FREDERICIAGADE

Østre
Landsret

BREDGADE

Den Kongelige
Afstøbningssamlingen

BORGERGADE

HINDEGADE

Skt
Ansgars
Kirke

AMALIEGADE

K

Alexander Newsky
Kirke

Medicinsk-Historisk
Museum

FREDERICIAGADE

TOLDBODGADE

STORE KONGENSGADE

Frederikskirken
(Marmorkirken)

Amalienborg
Museum

FREDERIKSGADE

Amalienborg
Slot

AMALIENBORG
SLOTPLADS

Amaliehaven

FREDERIKSSTADEN

L

DRONNINGENS
TVÆRGADE

Odd Fellow
Palæ

308 Time Out Copenhagen Guide

AMALIEGADE

See
p312

Kvæsthusgraven

ORLOGSVÆRFTSVEJ

PASS

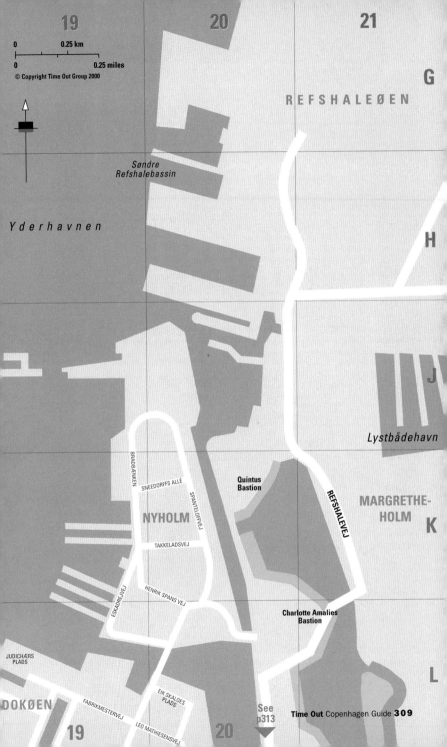

G

REFSHALEØEN

0   0.25 km
0   0.25 miles
© Copyright Time Out Group 2000

*Søndre
Refshalebassin*

H

Yderhavnen

J

Lystbådehavn

BRADBÆNKEN

SNEEDORFFS ALLÉ

SPANTELOFTVEJ

Quintus
Bastion

REFSHALEVEJ

MARGRETHE-
HOLM

K

NYHOLM

TAKKELADSVEJ

ESKADREVEJ

HENRIK SPANS VEJ

Charlotte Amalies
Bastion

L

JUDICHÆRS
PLADS

DOKØEN

FABRIKMESTERVEJ

EIK SKALØES
PLADS

LEO MATHIESENSVEJ

See
p313

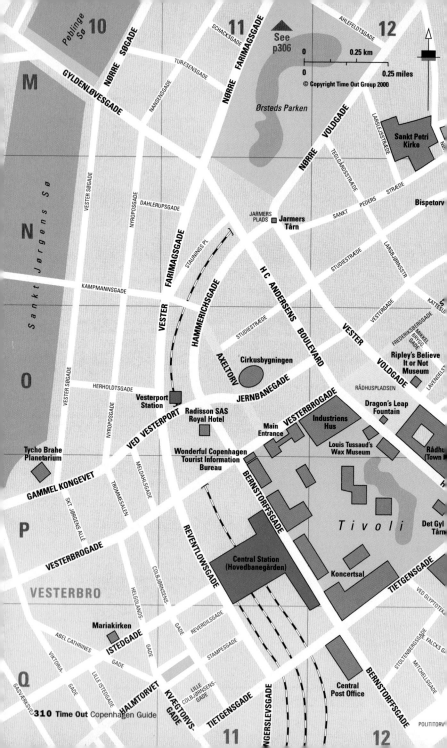

Peblinge Sø

10

11

SCHACKSGADE

FARIMAGSGADE

NØRRE FARIMAGSGADE

AHLEFELDTSGADE

12

See p306

0   0.25 km

0   0.25 miles

© Copyright Time Out Group 2000

M

GYLDENLØVESGADE

NØRRE SØGADE

TURESENSGADE

NANSENSGADE

Ørsteds Parken

NØRRE VOLDGADE

LARSLEJSSTRÆDE

Sankt Petri Kirke

VESTER SØGADE

NYROPSGADE

DAHLERUPSGADE

JARMERS PLADS

Jarmers Tårn

SANKT PEDERS STRÆDE

TEGLGÅRDSSTRÆDE

Bispetorv

N

Sankt Jørgens Sø

FARIMAGSGADE

STAUNINGS PL.

KAMPMANNSGADE

HAMMERICHSGADE

H C ANDERSENS BOULEVARD

STUDIESTRÆDE

LARSBJØRNSSTR

LARSBJØRNSSTR

VESTERGADE

KATTESU

O

VESTER SØGADE

HERHOLDTSGADE

NYROPSGADE

VESTER

AXELTORV

Cirkusbygningen

JERNBANEGADE

VESTER VOLDGADE

RÅDHUSPLADSEN

FREDERIKSBERGGADE

MIKKEL BRYGG. GADE

LAVENDELST

Ripley's Believe It or Not Museum

Vesterport Station

Radisson SAS Royal Hotel

VED VESTERPORT

Main Entrance

VESTERBROGADE

Dragon's Leap Fountain

Industriens Hus

Rådhu (Town H

Tycho Brahe Planetarium

GAMMEL KONGEVET

MELDAHLSGADE

Wonderful Copenhagen Tourist Information Bureau

BERNSTORFFSGADE

Louis Tussaud's Wax Museum

Råd (Town

P

VESTER SØGADE

TROMMESALEN

SKT. JØRGENS ALLÉ

VESTERBROGADE

REVENTLOWSGADE

COLBJØRNSENS GADE

Central Station (Hovedbanegården)

T i v o l i

Det Gyl Tårn

Koncertsal

TIETGENSGADE

VED GLYPTOTE

VESTERBRO

Mariakirken

ABEL CATHRINES GADE

ISTEDGADE

REVERDILSGADE

STAMPESGADE

STOLTENBERGSGADE

FALCKS G.

MITCHELLSGADE

BERNSTORFFSGADE

Q

VIKTORIA GADE

GASVÆRKSVEJ

LILLE ISTEDGADE

HALMTORVET

KVÆGTORVS- GADE

LILLE COLBJØRNSENS- GADE

TIETGENSGADE

INGERSLEVSGADE

Central Post Office

BERNSTORFFSGADE

POLITITORV

11

12

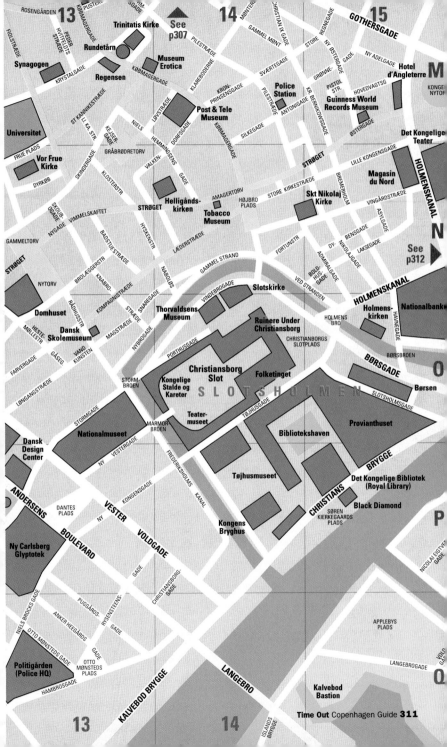

PHILIP DE LANGES ALLÉ

SAMSØES ALLÉ

PER KNUTZONS VEJ

KANONBADVEJ

DANNESKJOLD

OTHEODOR CHR. PLADS

FREDERIKSHOLM

HOLMEN

GALIONSVEJ

REFSHALEVEJ

Carls
Bastion

BOHLENDACHVEJ

SØARTILLERIVEJ

HALVTOLV

ARSENALØEN

ARSENALVEJ

Vilhelms
Bastion

REFSHALEVEJ

LANGGADEN

KLØVERMARKSVEJ

Sofie Hedevigs
Bastion

IANIA

Ulriks
Bastion

KLØVERMARKSVEJ

AMAGER

0   0.25 km

0   0.25 miles

© Copyright Time Out Group 2000

19

20

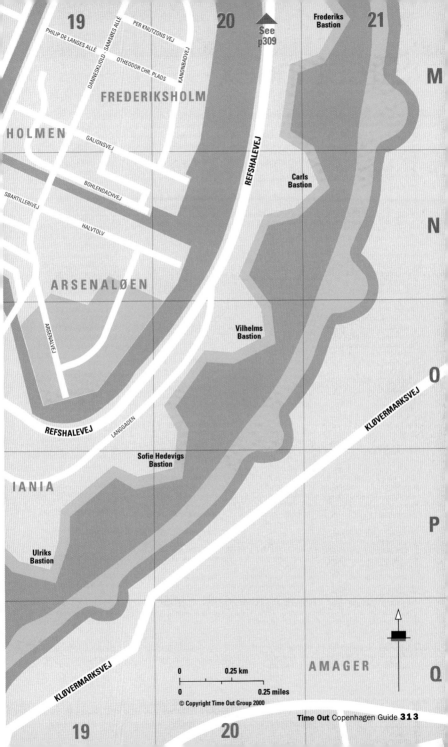

Street Index

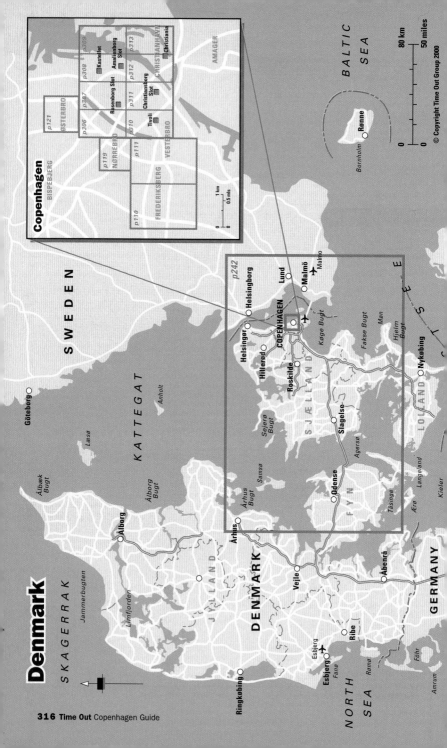

Denmark

Copenhagen

p121 ØSTERBRO
p306 p307 p308 p309
Rosenborg Slot ■Kastellet
■Amalienborg Slot
p119 NØRREBRO p310 p311 p312 p313
BISPEBJERG ■Christianshavn Slot ■Christianie
p111 ■Tivoli CHRISTIANHAVN
VESTERBRO AMAGER
FREDERIKSBERG
p110

0 0.5 mls
0 1 km

SWEDEN

Göteborg

SKAGERRAK

Jammerbugten

Ålbæk
Bugt

Limfjorden

Ålborg
Bugt

KATTEGAT

Læsø

Anholt

Sejerø
Bugt

Samsø

Agersø

Helsingborg

Lund
Malmö
Malmö

p242

Helsingør
Hilerød
COPENHAGEN
Roskilde

SJÆLLAND

Slagelse

Køge Bugt

Fakse Bugt

Møn

Hjelm
Bugt

Ringkøbing

NORTH
SEA

Esbjerg
Fanø

Ribe

Rømø
Amrum
Föhr

Ringkøbing

JYLLAND

DENMARK

Århus
Bugt

Århus

Vejle

Åbenrå

FYN

Odense

Ærø
Tåsinge
Langeland
Kieler

LOLLAND

Nykøbing

BALTIC
SEA

Bornholm
Rønne

GERMANY

80 km
50 miles

© Copyright Time Out Group 2000

316 Time Out Copenhagen Guide